Contents

Rhodesian Air Force Operations 2
Copyright © 2014 by Preller Geldenhuys 2
Introduction by Group Captain Tol Janeke, DMM 3
1 The Beginning: Digital Edition 4
   Operations – Alphabetical Listing 7
   Early History 12
2 Operations – 1959 to 1967 18
3 Nickel and Cauldron 28
4 Hurricane 85
   No 5 Squadron – 'A' Flight Commander 91
   FAF 2 - Kariba 130
5 Operation Thrasher: February 1976 136
   Operation Repulse: FAF 7 - Buffalo Range: 16 March 1976 141
6 Mahogany Bomber 184
7 Operations 1979 231
   Rhodesian Air Force Aircraft Shot Down or Crashed 286
   Air Strike Log 291
8 Air Strike maps 329
Roll Of Honour 338
Index 341

Introduction by Group Captain Tol Janeke, DMM

    Prop has dedicated this book to his wife Rina and everyone mentioned in its pages. But it certainly covers a far greater readership than mentioned in his dedication. He has painstakingly and methodically recorded the history, not only of the airmen who were privileged to fly the aircraft involved in the air strikes, but so many others. All the wonderful support given by men and women within the Air Force and by the sister Services. And then there were the civilians who gave of their precious time to become members of the Volunteer Reserve and the Police Reserve Air Wing.

    Their names too you will find in these pages, meticulously recorded and indexed for the generations still to come. Here are the names of soldiers, policemen and internal affairs, men and women who added to the often unheralded courage behind the exciting story of these air strikes. The troops on the ground and those that flew in our aircraft with us, some of whom hated leaving their own familiar environment on the ground and in the bush.

Whilst the recording of all these air strikes in itself is a fascinating story, none of the almost clinical efficiency of this small Force could have happened if it were not for the many years of training and development that preceded the conflict. Certainly based upon the methods and structure of the pre-war Royal Air Force, the solid foundations of the Rhodesian Air Force were set in the Second World War.

A spirit of comradeship and loyalty developed within this, by world standards, tiny unit, which drew the admiration of even the dissenters of Rhodesia. For those of us who were part of this Air Force there was a special feeling of belonging. A pride that was quite extraordinary that in turn developed magnificent morale and the will to succeed. For most of the participants mentioned in this book the culmination of the war has lead to very different lives in Civvy Street. Many have become successful in their second careers, but very few indeed have again experienced the wonderful comradeship, passion and dedication they experienced in the Air Force.

To those historians and collectors of militaria, this book is one that fills in much detail. It shows how operations in Rhodesia started slowly and built up to a situation where virtually the entire country became involved. The mass of little numbered dots on the maps shows the position of widespread strikes in all the operational areas. To the very end the Air Force kept up its valiant task of securing the airspace for our troops, the BSAP, the farmers and industry. This in addition to the direct support for those missions across the borders.

By retaining centralised command it was possible to provide air fire power into all corners of the country. Often a single aircraft and its crew were carrying out strikes in three different areas of the country in a single day. And this from an Air Force that should have, in the words of our detractors, "ceased to exist" many years before the end of the war.

I am often asked whether I regret my involvement in the Rhodesian conflict. To this I can honestly say an emphatic no. At the time the Southern tip of Africa was undergoing massive political change. In its own way the long drawn out battle gave the Southern African countries time to mature and to reflect. Time for the erstwhile colonies of Europe to reconsider the wisdom of the hurried abandonment of their responsibilities to their erstwhile territories.

South Africa was given the time to recognise the futility of its policies and to recognise the need for a negotiated change. Also it showed the communist countries that their philosophies would not prevail in Southern Africa. The more pertinent question should be 'what would Southern Africa look like now if Rhodesians had abandoned their duties and the Air force had not played its crucial role in the war'? To have been part of these historic times was in itself reward enough. To have contributed in a small way to them made the reward even greater.

Prop has acknowledged that even this record is not complete. There are bound to be errors where records have been destroyed or are not accessible. It is important therefore that these gaps be filled in and corrections made while many of those who took part in the air strikes are still alive and have personal records reflecting the history. It is a history which deserves to be recorded. This book will keep alive the memory of an outstanding Air Force fighting for a special country and its extraordinary people.

F.D Janeke
Westville, Durban, May 2007

1 The Beginning: Digital Edition

The first edition was launched in July 2007, at the Virginia Air Show. The response and demand has been very encouraging and a reprint was done – after a special appeal to delete a small section about spilling the beans how the 'Rhodesian Security Force' (RSF) historical records came to be in the United Kingdom. This request was acceded to, despite the information being readily available in the public domain.

The updated edition contained a few more Operations and Air Strikes, more maps, a couple of firsthand accounts, many corrections and a few book reviews which have been re-produced

Rhodesian Air Force Operations

'Prop' Preller Geldenhuys
For Rina – and everyone mentioned

Copyright © 2014 by Preller Geldenhuys

The rights of the author of the Work have been asserted by him. ©Copyright in the text rests with the author, Preller Geldenhuys

All rights reserved. No part of this publication may be reproduced, stored in a retrieval system, or transmitted, in any form or by any means, without the prior written permission of the publisher or the author, nor be otherwise circulated in any form of binding or cover other than that in which it is published and without a similar condition being imposed on the subsequent purchaser.

First published 2007 Just Done Productions Publishing
This edition Peysoft Publishing
Other books by the author:
  Nickel Cross - biography
  Operation Miracle: A Tribute to three bold Airmen
  Rhodesian War Casualties
  Geldenhuys Genealogy: 12 generations
  The Anglo-Boer War diaries of Jan Geldenhuys
  Rhodesia - Zimbabwe Roll of Honour (epub)
PDF ISBN: 978-0-9941154-1-6

EPUB ISBN: 978-0-9941154-0-9

Paeroa
2014

on the back cover. This led to more Army colleagues asking me to change or delete 'political sensitive' revelations – which I have now again agreed to. However, the deletions were more than adequately off-set with further Operations and Air Strike inputs, so much so that splitting the book into two volumes again made this a more viable proposition.

I am grateful to everyone who made a contribution to this more up-to-date and improved edition, and especially those who gave me copyright permission to re-use their drawings, maps, air strikes and stories.

This digital edition was prompted by seeing my book already available as a Nook book (Barnes and Noble) but not benefiting me with revenue payments. This has resulted in me now promoting this e-book formatted edition from New Zealand.

The facts expressed herein, the inferences drawn from them, as well as any errors and omissions, are my own.

"Prop" Preller Geldenhuys
Paeroa, New Zealand
September 2014.

This Certificate
serves to record that
Pey Geldenhuys
contributed financially toward the
production of this authoritative history of

RHODESIA
1948–1980

Ours is a unique tradition, and this history should find a place in the heart and home of every true Rhodesian. If the memory of these things perishes, and the bright example grows dull and tarnished, we will have failed to pass on this proud heritage to later generations. I am deeply indebted to everyone who stood by Rhodesia in the years that we strove to preserve, at whatever cost, our national liberty and individual freedom.

Ian Douglas Smith

Copy No 11

To Prop & Pey Geldenhuys
My best wishes
I. Douglas Smith

Treasured correspondence with the Prime Minister of Rhodesia, the Honourable Ian Douglas Smith (who declared the historical Unilateral Declaration of Independence)

Operations – Alphabetical Listing

Op Abduction - June to July 1978
Op Acrobat - 12 February 1978
Op Agila - 20 to 27 December 1979
Op Alcora - 6 June 1973 to 19 August 1973
Op Altar - 1982 to 1983
Op Amnesty - 14 June 1979
Op Anvil - 25 November 1981
Op Apollo - 29 November 1970
Ex Armchair - 18 to 23 April 1966
Op Armchair - 19 to 24 September 1966
Ex Army FAC - 1 June 1964 to 17 June 1966
Op Askoek - 8 August 1968
Op Aspect [Bastille] - 13 April 1979
Ex Aurora - 18 to 22 April 1966
Op Aztec - 28 May to 2 June 1977
Project Barnacle - July 1982
Op Bastille - 12 to 13 April 1979
Op Bene – Tete - 25 to 30 July 1968
Op Big Bang - 9 August to 1 October 1974
Op Big Push - August 1970
Op Birch - 8 to 28 January 1970
Ex Birds Nest - 2 to 6 June 1971
Op Biscuit - 9 September 1974
Ex Black Jack - 4 to 9 June 1972
Op Blanket - 10 to 30 August 1974
Op Blanket II - 23 to 31 July 1979
Op Bluebell - 16 January to 19 February 1977
Op Bluebolt - 29 to 31 July 1975
Op Bondage - 12 May 1979
Op Bonfire - 23 December 1967
Op Bootlace - 2 to 9 September 1979
Op Bos (BOS 2947) - February to March 1969
Op Bouncer - August to September 1979
Op Bowler - September 1979
Op Boxer - 20 August to 18 September 1979
Ex Brass Ring - 21 to 22 February 1967
Op Breampool - 1 to 2 November 1965
Op Breeze - 29 December 1967
Op Brisket - 29 June to 27 September 1977
Op Bristol - 1982 to 1983
Ex Broken Arrow - 18 to 24 March 1965
Ex Brown Water - February 1963
Op Bulldog - 23 July to 22 August 1979
Op Bumper - 12 October to December 1979
Op Cantata - 17 July to 12 August 1966
Op Capsule - 8 to 12 December 1979
Op Cardigan - 10 April - 4 June 1968
Op Carlota - 1975
Op Carpet - 26 June 1979
Op Cauldron - 18 March to 8 April 1968
Ex Cauliflower - June 1973
Op Chamber - 4 June 1979
Op Cheese - 3 to 12 October 1979

Ex Chessman - 20 July to 14 September 1972
Op Chestnut - 20 February 1970
Op Chicory - 1 July 1979
Op Chinaman - September to November 1967
Op Christmas Cracker - December 1978
Ex Cobra - 19 to 20 November 1966
Op Condor - 11 to 12 November 1971
Op Coolith - 25 to 26 August 1987
Op Coondog - 1 to 3 May 1964
Op Cosmic - 7 April 1968
Op Cowboy - 2 to 6 March 1977
Op Crater - 30 October to 15 November 1972
Ex Crocodile Fever - 22 May 1967
Op Crusader - November 1941
Op Cucumber - 6 to 9 July 1979
Op Dabchick - 6 February 1979
Op Daffodil - 10 to 21 November 1967
Op Damper - 12 September to 26 December 1979
Op Detachment - May 1976
Op Detonate - See Op Splinter
Op Dice - 16 to 20 November 1979
Op Dingo - 23 to 26 November 1977
Op Dinky - 12 to 13 April 1979
Op Dirk - July to August 1975
Op Disco Scene - September 1979
Op Dragon - 21 September to 13 October 1977
Op Driver - 22 to 29 May 1977
Op Ecstasy - 17 May 1979
Op Elbow - 1 January to 12 June 1978
Op Eland - 8 to 12 August 1976
Op Enclosure - September 1979
Op Ermine - 25 September 1967
Ex Evaluation - [PTS] 11 February to 11 March 1960
Op Excess - 28 July to August 1968
Op Exodus - May 1945
Ex Fabric - 20 to 21 May 1967
Op Fiddle - 6 to 11 July 1979
Op Flock - 1970 to 1971
Op Flotilla - 16 April to May 1968
Op Free-fall Jump - 19 January 1973
Op Gaiter - 11 January to 22 March 1979
Op Gatling - 18 to 19 October 1978
Op Gericke - 15 November 81
Op Glamour - 17 May 1967
Op Glove - May 1968
Op Gordion Knot - May 1971
Op Grampus - 30 July 1966
Op Granite - 10 April 1970
Op Grapple - August 1977
Op Gravel - July to August 1968
Op Greenhills - 30 November to 2 December 1965
Op Greentrees - 9 November 1965
Op Griffin - 18 to 19 July 1968
Op Grinder - 18 to 24 October 1977
Op Grovel - 23 February 1979

Op Hectic - December 1979 to February 1980
Op Hedgehog - 4 May to 2 June 1964
Op Hemp - 11 and 13 December 1972
Op Heup - 3 April 1973 to 1975
Op Hooper - SAAF – see Op Modular
Op Hotdog - 8 December 1978
Op Hottentot - 28 February to 26 March 1969 to 17 July 1971
Op Hurricane - December 1972 to 21 December 1979
Op Husk - 13 June 1967
Op Hustler - 7 March 1977
Op Hydra - August 1943
Op Ignition - November 1976
Op Ingrid - 31 May 1979
Op Inhibit - 17 to 25 December 1978
Op Inhibit II - 8 February to 18 June 1979
Op Inspan - 13 to 31 July 1979
Op Instant - 7 April 1979
Ex Irish Stew - 28 October to 2 November 1969
Op Isotope - June 1967
Op Isotope II - 5 to 9 August 1967
Op Jacaranda - 30 September 78 and 1971
Op Jacket - 2 November 1978
Op Jezebel - 31 October 1967
Op Junction - 13 June to 4 August 1972
Ex King Kabanga - 23 to 26 August 1971
Op Knuckle - 26 August to 11 November 1968
Op Kodak - January to March 1977
Ex Liberator - 11 to 12 March 1967
Op Lion Cub - 16 September 1949
Op Liquid - April 1979
Op Lobster - 31 August to 3 September 1971
Ex Longdrag - 23 August to 1 September 1965
Op Long John - 25 June 1976
Ex Luanda, Angola - 17 to 18 September 1973
Op Luso, Angola - 26 February 1979
Op Mackerel - 16 October 1962
Op Manacle - October to 8 November 1979
Ex Mannix - October to November 1968
Op Mansion - 20 July 1968
Op Manyatela - 30 December 1976 to 17 January 1977
Op Marble - 6 June 1974
Op Mardon - 30 October to 2 November 1976
Op Market Garden -   November 1974
Op Mascot - 10 July to 1 August 1978
Op Mayibuye - February to July 1963
Op Melon - 26 October 1977 to 11 April 1978
Op Meltone - 23 November 1967
Op Merger - 1980 - 1987
Op Metric - 30 July 1978
Op Mica - 9 to 11 September 1974
Op Midford - 20 December 1979 to 16 March 1980
Op Mila - 1983
Op Milk Float - February 1979
Op Mineral - 9 June 1979
Op Miracle - 21 September to 6 October 1979

Op Mixer - 31 July 1981
Op Modular - SAAF, see Packer
Op Motel - 23 August 1979
Op Mulligan -16 June 1979
Op Murex - 2 November 1979
Op Mustard - 13 to 15 June 1979
Op Mute - 1982 to 1984
Op Natal - 7 December 1968
Op Neutron - 15 February to March 1979
Op Neutron II - 12 September 1979
Op Newton - 18 to 25 June 1975
Op Nickel - 12 August to 8 September 1967
Op Nimbus - 21 April to 7 May 1972
Op Noah - 1955 to 1961
Op Norah - 12 September 1979
Op Knuckle - 26 August to 11 November 1968
Op Octopus - June to October 1982
Op Onyx - July to August 1973
Op Oppress - 29 April 1979
Op Overload - 1973 to 1974
Op Overtone - 15 to 24 October 1967
Ex Oxtail - 23 to 29 November 1970
Op Oyster - 1968
Op Packer - SAAF, see Beaver
Op Pagoda - 22 to 24 June 1966
Op Paladin - 13 to 19 May 1979
Op Paladin II - 10 to 11 October 1979
Op Panga - 17 April 1971
Op Pannier - 27 February 1978
Op Pantechnicon - 26 May 1967
Ex Panther - 24 to 26 July 1965
Op Parker - SS Scapegoat
Op Partisan - 29 October to 5 November 1977
Ex Pea Soup - August 1969
Op Peptic - 27 June to 29 July 1977
Op Petal - March - April 1979
Op Peyboy - 22 December 1970
Op Phoenix - 16 to 30 October 1964
Op Placid - 21 to 24 August 1979
Op Pluto - 4 to 13 March 1970
Op Polar - 4 June to 2 September 1974
Op Polo - 1967 to August 1976
Ex PRAW - 4 to 11 June 65 & 26 - 28 March 1971
Op Prawn - August 1976
Ex Promptforce - 10 to 11 May 1967
Op Purple - 13 June to 13 July 1979
Op Pygmy - November to December 1978
Op Pyramid - 1 to 10 September 1967
Op Quartz - February to March 1980
Op Racket - 11 to 12 April 1979
Op Ranger - August 1977
Op Reindeer - 1978 (SA assault)
Op Reptile - 1 November 1966
Op Repulse - 1 May 1976 (Mar 76?)
Op Rhino - 14 September 1970

Op Robinson - October 1942
Op Robust - 2 to 8 November 1967
Op Sable - 8 May to 11 November 1972
Op Sabre - September 1961
Salops - August 1977
Op Sand - 1971 - 1978
Op Sculpture - 12 October to 1 December 1966
Op Sea Sheikh - 1961
Op Seed - 1982 – 1983
Op Shovel - 15 December 1978
Op Show Plane - August 1957
Op Sinoia - 28 to 29 April 1966
Op Slipshod - 14 to 15 November 1964
Op Small Bang - February 1976
Op Snoopy - 20 to 29 September 1978
Op Spider - February 1959
Op Spiderweb - March 1968
Op Splinter - 1 May 1978
Op Sponge - 22 August 1979
Op Starjump - 2 March 1977
Op Steeple - 9 to 20 January 1979
Op Stripper - 2 to 9 March 1977
Op Sunrise - 29 February 1959
Op Swordstick I - 29 September to 30 October 1972
Op Swordstick II - 29 to 30 October 1972
Op Tangent - August 1976
Op Tarpaulin - November 1968 to 1971
Op Teak - 29 January 1970
Op Tempest I & II - 1 September to 16 December 1972
Op Tepid - 18 to 20 October 1979
Op Terminate - 19 September to 21 October 1977
Op Terminate II - 15 March to 15 August 1978
Op Thrasher - February 1976
Op Tombola - WW 2 - 1945
Op Traveller - April to May 1976
Ex Treble Chance - April 1960 – see Evaluation
Op Tripper - 7 December 68 - See Op Natal
Op Turkey - February 1975
Op Turmoil - 26 February to 10 March 1978
Op Underdog - January 1976
Op Uric - 1 to 20 September 1979
Ex Vanguard - 31 July 1974
Op Vanity - 26 February 1979
Op Vermin - 21 to 30 September 1966
Op Virgo - January to July 1977
Op Virile - November to 19 December 1977
Op Vodka - November to 22 December 1978
Ex VR-Preston - 18 June 1966
Op Winter - February 1980
Op Wizard [UDI] - 10 to 19 November 1965
Op Wrestler - 2 March 1977
Op Yodel - September 196

Early History

The study of Air Force History is an essential aspect of pilot training. Because it has been so well documented in several very good publications like *A Pride of Eagles*, Ozzie Penton's *Half a Century in Uniform* and Winston Brent's *Sanction Busters*; I have elected to mention only some of the significant operations and the odd research findings recorded in my earlier book *Nickel Cross*.

The proud Rhodesian military tradition was second to none in the British Empire. Sixty four percent of the country's available manpower served in the First World War. It contributed money (nearly £250 000), machines and men to the 1914-1918 Allied war effort. More than 6,000 white Rhodesians - out of a total European population of less than 24,000 - went to the fighting fronts in Europe, East Africa and South West Africa. This represented two thirds of all European men between the ages of fifteen and forty-four. Rhodesians served in eighty Imperial regiments ranging from the Black Watch (all twelve who joined this unit were killed) to the Tank Corps, RAF and Royal Navy. This, in addition to those who joined the 1st and 2nd Rhodesia Regiments (another 2,000 men), the BSAP, the Union of South Africa forces and the 400-man Rhodesia Platoons of the King's Royal Rifle Corps. In addition, some 2,800 men of African and mixed race also went to war. The price paid - nine hundred Rhodesians killed (of whom 732 were European), and a total of 527 decorations, ranging from Britain's Victoria Cross to Russia's Order of St Vladimir and France's Croix de Guerre.

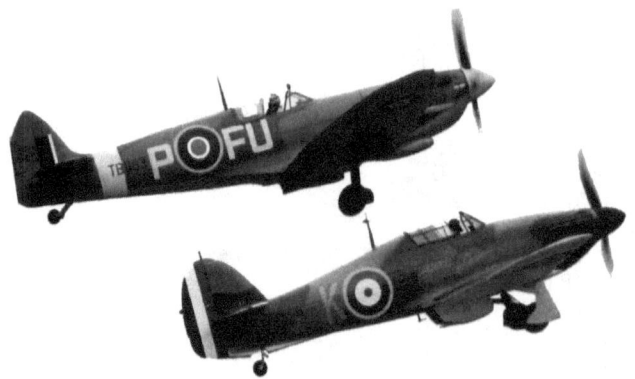

Spitfire and a Hurricane

In World War II, Rhodesians once again voluntarily came to Britain's aid, and supplied more troops per capita to the British War effort than any other country in the Empire. Some 6,650 white and 1,730 black Rhodesians served outside Rhodesia, and more than a quarter of them served in the Royal Air Force. The squadrons performed splendidly. Three squadrons were entitled to the designation 'Rhodesia'. Ian Douglas Smith, destined to become the country's most famous Prime Minister, flew for the RAF. He was a fighter pilot with No 237 (Rhodesia) Squadron, equipped with Hurricanes and Spitfires and, after a long run of successes, one of which put him into hospital, he rejoined his squadron to lead a strafing sortie to the Po Valley attacking locomotives and fuel tanks. As he pulled out of his second dive, his Spitfire was hit and he was forced to bail out. He joined the partisans and became a member of a company high command and inner war council.

The Rhodesian Squadrons build up a proud tradition on many fronts. Some of the noteworthy early operations include the following: -

- Op *Crusader* – No 237 Squadron helped lift the siege of Tobruk (Libya) in November 1941.
- Op *Robinson* – No 44 Squadron attack on the Schneider Armament Works at Le Creusot, France, in October 1942.
- Op *Hydra* – No 44 Squadron attack on the rocket factory at Peenemünde in August 1943.

- Op *Exodus* – Evacuation of Allied prisoners of war, at the cessation of hostilities with Germany, by No 44 Squadron during May 1945.
- Op *Tombola* – 1945, by the British Special Air Service, warrants mention in that it was the forerunner of our own 22 Squadron Special Air Service (Malaya) Scouts.

Some 2409 Rhodesians, a number which was out of all proportion to the country's manpower resources, served with the RAF and SRAF during World War II; of the 977 Officers and 1,432 Other ranks, a total of 498 were killed in action: and 97 wounded. They were distributed over all Commands and in every theatre. They earned 146 decorations, including nine DSOs, 106 DFCs, eight AFCs, 22 DFMs and one CGM. World War II ended on 15th August 1945. In the Korean War, 1951-1953, one hundred Rhodesians served in the Far East Volunteer Unit in Malaya.

After the war the SRAF and squadrons were to all intents and purposes disbanded, but not for long. In 1947 a dedicated group of flying men formed the nucleus of a small communications flight. From the humble beginnings of the Southern Rhodesia Staff Corps the Rhodesian Air Force developed into the modern day force many came to know and respect. The table below, showing aircraft acquisitions, points to a fascinating story - history.

Air Force Aircraft Acquisitions
Nov 1935:
- 6x De Havilland Tiger Moth DH82A for the Air Unit TF RR (Rhod Regt Territorial)
- 7x Avro Anson
- 1x De Havilland Leopard Moth
- 2x De Havilland Rapide

Nov 1947:
- 6xDe Havilland Tiger Moth (rebuilt) for Southern Rhodesia Air Force

1948:
- 1x Douglas Dakota, ex SAAF, for SRAF

June 1949:
- 2x North American Harvard Mk IIa (ex Rhod Air Training Group)
- 6x North American Harvard Mk IIa (ex RATG) for OCU
- 12x North American Harvard Mk IIa (ex SAAF) for AFS
- 3x Avro Anson Mk9
- 1x Auster J/1
- 2x Auster J/5

Mar 1951: 22x Supermarine Spitfire F22
Dec 1953:
- 4x De Havilland Vampire FB9 for OCU - Operational Conversion Unit
- 2x Hunting Percival Pembroke for Transport Flight
- 12x Hunting Percival Provost TMk52 for No 4 Squadron
- 4x Hunting Percival Provost TMk52 for No 4 Squadron
- 7x Douglas C-47B Mk4 Dakota for No 3 Squadron

Apr 1954:
- 16x De Havilland Vampire FB9 for No 1 Squadron
- 16x De Havilland Vampire TII for No 2 Squadron

1959:
- 15x English Electric Canberra B2 for No's 5 & 6 Squadrons
- 1x Canadair C-4 for No 3 Squadron
- 1962: 5x Aerospatiale Alouette III for No 7 Squadron
- 1963: 12x Hawker Siddeley Hunter FGA9 for No 1 Squadron

Aug 1963:
- 8x Aerospatiale Alouette III for No 7 Squadron
- 11x Aermacchi-Lockheed AL60 "Trojan" for No 4 Squadron
- 6x Britten-Norman Islander BN2A for No 3 Squadron

1976:

- 18x Reims- F.337 "Lynx" for No 4 Squadron
- 1x Cessna 410A for No 3 Squadron
- 17x SIAI-Marchetti SF260Mx "Genet" for No 6 Squadron
- 14x SIAI-Marchetti SF260W "Genet"
- 1x Beechcraft Baron for No 3 Squadron

1978:
- 12x Agusta-Bell AB205A "Cheetah" for No 8 Squadron
- 2x Agusta-Bell 412 for No 7 Squadron
- 1x Hawker Hunter T8 for No 1 Squadron

Jul 1982:
- British Aerospace Hawk Mk60 for No 2 Squadron1

Air Force History - Units, Squadron Commanders, Officer Commanding Flying Wings (OCFW's) and Volunteer Reserve Squadrons are listed hereunder. Regrettably, the listing is incomplete – as no source could be found from which the information sought could be extracted. What follows is what the writer was able to piece together – prior to going to print. It is hoped that this record will prompt interested readers to contact the writer in order to compile an accurate History of the Rhodesian Air Force.

Units
    Southern Rhodesia Air Unit   SRAU - Nov 1935
    Southern Rhodesia Air Force - SRAF - 19 Sept 1939
    SRAF absorbed into RAF - April 1940
    Rhodesian Air Training Group - RATG - World War II
    Southern Rhodesia Air Force - SRAF - 28 Nov 1947
    Royal Rhodesian Air Force   RRAF - 15 Oct 1954
    Rhodesian Air Force   - RhodAF - March 1970
    Air Force of Zimbabwe - AFZ - April 1981.

Commanders Of The Air Force
    Major Dirk Cloete: 1936 - 1938
    Lt Col CW Charles Meredith: 1939 - 1946
    Lt Col Keith Taute: 1947 – 1949
    Lt Col/AVM EWS Ted Jacklin: 949 - Jun 1961
    AVM AM Raff Bentley: 1961 - Apr 1965
    AVM Harold Hawkins: 1965 - 1969
    Air Marshal AOG (Archie) Wilson: 1969 - Apr 1973
    Air Marshal MJ (Mick) McLaren: 1973 – 1977
    Air Marshal FW Frank Mussell: 1977 - 1981
    Air Marshal Norman Walsh: 1981 – 1984
    AFZ Air Marshal Daudpota: 1984 - 1985 (Pakistani)
    Air Marshal Josiah Tungamirai: 1986 - 1988
    Air Marshal Perence Shiri: 1988

Squadrons
    No 1 Sqn - Spitfire, Vampire FB9, Hunter FGA9
    No 2 Sqn - Vampire T11, Provost, Genet, Hawk
    No 3 Sqn - Anson, Dakota, Pembroke, Canadair, Islander, Cessna 410 and Baron
    No 4 Sqn - Provost, Trojan, Lynx
    No 5 Sqn - Canberra
    No 6 Sqn - Canberra, Vampire T11, Genet
    No 7 Sqn - Alouette II and III
    No 8 Sqn - Bell 205 Cheetah

Station Commanders – Thornhill
    Wg Cdr Archie Wilson: Jun 1957 to Jun 1959
    Gp Capt Johnny Deall: Jun 1959 to May 1961
    Gp Capt John Moss: Jun 1961 to Nov 1961
    Gp Capt Jock Barber: Nov 1961 to Dec 1963

Gp Capt Doug Whyte: Dec 1963 to Jun 1966
Gp Capt Charles Paxton: Jun 1966 to Jan 1968
Gp Capt Frank Mussell: Jan 1968 to Apr 1970
Gp Capt Dickie Bradshaw: Apr 1970 to Feb 1972
Gp Capt Kas Edwards: Feb 1972 to Jan 1975
Gp Capt Porky MacLaughlin: Jan 1975 to Mar 1977
Gp Capt Tol Janeke: Apr 1977 to 1978
Gp Capt Len Pink: 1978 to 1979
Gp Capt Harold Griffiths: ?May 1980
Gp Capt Dag Jones: ?Jul 1981

Wing Commanders – OCFW
Flt Lt/Sqn Ldr Dickie Bradshaw: Oct 1955 to May 1960
Sqn Ldr Sandy Mutch: Jun 1960 to Dec 1960
Sqn Ldr Frank Mussell : Jan to Jul 1961
Sqn Ldr Dickie Bradshaw: Jan 1961 to Oct 1961
Wg Cdr Charles Paxton: Nov 1961 to May 1963
Wg Cdr Dad Cunnison : Jun 1963 to Nov 1963
Wg Cdr Sandy Mutch: Dec 1963 to Jun 1965
Wg Cdr Mick McLaren: Jun 1965 to Sep 1967
Wg Cdr Chris Dams: Oct 1967 to Oct 1968
Sqn Ldr Ted Brent (A/OCFW): Nov 1968 to Dec 1969
Wg Cdr Porky MacLaughlin: Feb 1969 to Feb 1971
Wg Cdr Keith Kemsley: Feb 1971 to Nov 1973
Wg Cdr Tol Janeke: Jul 1973 to Feb 1975
Wg Cdr Keith Corrans: Apr 1975 to Dec 1976
Wg Cdr Eddy Wilkinson: Jan 1977 to Aug 1977
Sqn Ldr Rich Brand (A/OCFW?): 1977?
Wg Cdr Hugh Slatter: Aug 1977-
Wg Cdr Harold Griffiths: Jan 1979
Sqn Ldr Vic Wightman: Aug 1979
Wg Cdr Harold Griffiths: Sep 1979 to Apr 1980
Wg Cdr Dag Jones: May 1980

OCFW – New Sarum
Wg Cdr Oz Penton - to 1968
Wg Cdr John Rogers - to Nov 1969
Wg Cdr Norman Walsh - Dec 1969 to1970
Wg Cdr John Mussell - 1970 to Jun 1972
Wg Cdr Bill Jelley - Jul 1972 to May 1975
Sqn Ldr Randy du Rand - May 1975 to
Wg Cdr Wally Hinricks - Jul 1975

Squadron Commanders
OC Training Squadron
Flt Lt Robbie Blair - May 1955 to Aug 1955
No 1 Squadron
Sqn Ldr Dickie Bradshaw - Jan 1956 to Dec 1956
Flt Lt/Sqn Ldr Sandy Mutch - Dec 1956 to Jun 1957
Sqn Ldr Charles Paxton - Jul 1957 to Mar 1959
Sqn Ldr Dickie Bradshaw - Sep 1958
Flt Lt Colin Graves - Dec 1958 to May 1959
Sqn Ldr Sandy Mutch - May 1959 to May 1961
Flt Lt Bob Woodward - Jan 1960 to Apr 1960
Sqn Ldr Sandy Mutch - May 1960 to May 1961
Sqn Ldr John Mussell - May 1961 to Dec 1962
Sqn Ldr Mike Saunders - Jan 1963 to Apr 1964
Sqn Ldr Norman Walsh - May 1964 to Apr 1966

Sqn Ldr Chris Dams - May 1966 to Sep 1967
Sqn Ldr Ted Brent - Oct 1967 to Mar 1969
Sqn Ldr Roy Morris - Apr 1969 to Sep 1971
Sqn Ldr Randy du Rand - Oct 1971 to Jun 1972
Flt Lt Dag Jones - Jul 1972 to Nov 1972
Sqn Ldr Rob Gaunt - Dec 1972 to Dec 1975
Sqn Ldr Rich Brand - Jan 1976 to May 1978
Sqn Ldr Vic Wightman - Jun 1978 to Jul 1980

No 1 Squadron (Special Duties)
Sqn Ldr Keith Corrans - 15-31 Jan 1972
(Mirage squadron at Waterkloof)

No 2 Squadron
Sqn Ldr Charles Paxton - Jan 1956 to Jul 1957
Flt Lt Colin Graves - May 1956 to Aug 1956
Flg Offr John Mussell - Jun 1956
Sqn Ldr Dickie Bradshaw - Jul 1958 to Aug 1958
Flt Lt Ozzie Penton - Sep 1958 to Dec 1958
Flt Lt Bob Woodward - Mar 1960 to Dec 1962
Sqn Ldr Mick McLaren - Jan 1963 to Dec 1963
Sqn Ldr Chris Dams - Jan 1964 to Nov 1964
Sqn Ldr Keith Kemsley - Nov 1964 to Jun 1967
Sqn Ldr Bill Jelley - Jul 1967 to Apr 1969
Flt Lt Varky Varkevisser - Mar 1970 to Apr 1970
Sqn Ldr Tol Janeke - May 1970 to Nov 1971
Sqn Ldr Harold Griffiths - Dec 1971 to Jun 1973
Sqn Ldr Hugh Slatter - Oct 1973 to 1973
Sqn Ldr Chris Dixon - Jun 1975 to Jun 1976
Flt Lt Varky Varkevisser - Apr 1977 to May 1977
Sqn Ldr Rich Brand - Aug 1977
Sqn Ldr Steve Kesby - Sep 1977 to Jun 1979
Sqn Ldr John Blythe-Wood - Jun 1979 to 1980

No 3 Squadron
Sqn Ldr Ted Cunnison
Sqn Ldr Harry Coleman - Jul 1958 to Sep 1958
Sqn Ldr Mike Gedye - Sep 1968 to Feb 1972
Sqn Ldr George Alexander - Mar 1972 to Oct 1978
Sqn Ldr Peter Barnett - Nov 1976 to Jan 1977
Sqn Ldr Bill Smith - Feb 1977 to
Sqn Ldr George Alexander
Sqn Ldr Tudor Thomas -1980

No 4 Squadron
Sqn Ldr Doug Whyte - May 1956 to Dec 1956
Flt Lt Kas Edwards - Oct 1958 to Jun 1959
Sqn Ldr Bill Dawson - Jul 1959 to May 1961
Sqn Ldr Ozzie Penton - Jun 1961 to Dec 1963
Sqn Ldr John Mussell - Jan 1964 to Sep 1964
Sqn Ldr Kas Edwards - Oct 1964 to Nov 1966
Sqn Ldr Bill Jelley - Dec 1966 to Jul 1967
Flt Lt Varky Varkevisser - Jun 1967 to Jul 1967
Sqn Ldr Peter Cooke - Aug 1967 to Jul 1968
Flt Lt Peter Knobel - Jul 1968 to Aug 1968
Sqn Ldr Peter McClurg - 1972?
Sqn Ldr Peter Petter-Bowyer -Jan 1973 to Nov 1974
Sqn Ldr Cyril White - Dec 1974 to Apr 1975
Sqn Ldr Dag Jones - 1976 to Oct 1978

Sqn Ldr John Bennie - Nov 1978 to 1980

No 5 Squadron
Sqn Ldr Charles Paxton - Jul 1959 to Sep 1960
Sqn Ldr Ozzie Penton - Oct 1960 to Jun 1961
Sqn Ldr Mick McLaren - Jul 1961 to Apr 1962
Sqn Ldr Frank Mussell - Apr 1962 to Jun 1962
Sqn Ldr Keith Kemsley - Jun 1962 to Dec 1963
Sqn Ldr Porky MacLaughlin - Dec 1963 to Apr 1966
Sqn Ldr Ian Donaldson - May 1966 to Nov 1967
Sqn Ldr Desmond Rogers - Dec 1967 to Aug 1968
Sqn Ldr Peter Knobel - Sep 1968 to Nov 1970
Sqn Ldr Ted Stevenson - Dec 1970 to Nov 1971
Sqn Ldr Tol Janeke - Dec 1971 to Sep 1973
Sqn Ldr Randy du Rand - Oct 1973 to 1976
Sqn Ldr Chris Dixon - 1976 to Feb 1979
Sqn Ldr Ted Brent - Mar 1979 to 1981

No 6 Squadron
Sqn Ldr Dickie Bradshaw - May 1959 to Mar 1960
Sqn Ldr Chris Dams - May 1962 to Nov 1963
Sqn Ldr Eddie Wilkinson - Jul 1971 to Jul 1972
Sqn Ldr John Barnes
Sqn Ldr Hugh Slatter - 1975
Sqn Ldr George Wrigley
Sqn Ldr Rob McGregor
Sqn Ldr Dave Thorne -1976
Sqn Ldr Steve Baldwin

No 7 Squadron
Sqn Ldr Bill Dowden - May 1962 to Dec 1963
Sqn Ldr Ozzie Penton - Jan 1964 to Dec 1965
Sqn Ldr Desmond Rogers - Jan 1966 to Dec 1967
Sqn Ldr Norman Walsh - Jan 1968 to Dec 1969
Sqn Ldr Gordon Nettleton - Jan 1970t o Jul 1970
Sqn Ldr Mick Grier - Feb 1972 to Mar 1973
Sqn Ldr Eddie Wilkinson - Mar 1973 to Jun 1975
Sqn Ldr Harold Griffiths - Jul 1975 to Jan 1978
Sqn Ldr Graham Cronshaw - Feb 1978 to Nov 1978
Sqn Ldr Ed Potterton - Dec 1978 to Apr 1980

No 8 Squadron
Sqn Ldr Ted Lunt - Aug 1978 to Apr 1980

Volunteer Reserve Squadrons
No 1 (BYO) Bulawayo VR Sqn
No 2 (GLO) Gwelo VR Sqn
No 3 (SBY) Salisbury VR Sqn
No 4 (UMT) Umtali VR Sqn
No 5 (AM) Air Movements VR Sqn
No 6 (CHI) Chipinga Flt
No 7 (LVD) Lowveld VR Sqn
No 8 (FLD) Field VR Sqn

2 Operations – 1959 to 1967

Operation Spider: February 1959

Op *Spider* was a BSAP counter-insurgency operation in February 1959 that had rounded up 500 leading nationalists, and was the biggest operation of its kind to date. Joshua Nkomo escaped the net because he was out of the country at that time. This pre-emptive action prevented Nkomo's 'Youth' from causing mayhem 'to create a crisis in Southern Rhodesia' - to coincide with Nkomo's allegations at the United Nations that "Rhodesia was in crisis". The mid-1960s were momentous and historical years. It concerned stories of men and nations caught up in the turmoil of war - be they heroes or villains, and sometimes both.

Operation Sunrise: 29 February 1959

Op Sunrise was the Whitehead Government banning of the African National Congress, and rounding up of the so-called liberation struggle leaders by BSAP contingents backed up by Army units. Op Sunrise was synonymous with Op Spider. The National Democratic Party replaced the banned ANC, and by December 1961 the NDP was outlawed – to be replaced by the Zimbabwe African Peoples Union. ZAPU was banned in October 1962 – and replaced by the PCC – Peoples Caretaker Council.

Operation Sabre: 13 to 22 September 1961

The Rhodesian Federal Security forces mounted Operation *Sabre* to handle the flood of refugees into Northern Rhodesia during the Congo Emergency of 1960/61. A Canberra was detached to Ndola on 13th September 1961, and on the 22nd the Squadron was called upon to carry out a photographic survey of a tragic crash site. Using the F 49 camera of Canberra RRAF 170, the crews filmed high and low-level shots of the wreckage of the Douglas DC-6B which carried UN Secretary General Dag Hammarskjold to his doom.

Operation Mayibuye: May to July 1963

Operation (Africa) *Mayibuye* (operation for its return to the masses) was formulated by the South African Communist's Central Committee and the Umkhonto we Sizwe (MK) High Command in May 1963. It was a plan to overthrow white-ruled South Africa. Details of the operation were revealed when the Rhodesians arrested eight Ethiopian-trained MK cadres that were in transit to South Africa. Four years later, Umkhonto we Sizwe (spear of the nation) terrorists would clash with Rhodesian Security Forces during Operation *Nickel* in the Wankie area.

The Federation of Rhodesia and Nyasaland came into being on 7th November 1953, and ended on 31st December 1963.

Operations Coondog & Hedgehog: May 1964

No 4 Squadron Provost pilots flew border reconnaissance sorties on "Operation *Coondog*" missions at Bumi Hills. On the Monday morning, 1st May, I got off to an early start and departed Thornhill for Salisbury for Operation *Hedgehog*. The air task detailed a reconnaissance of the north-east Portuguese / Moçambique border with SAS Lieutenant Brian Robinson. Our mission was a recce in the Kariba area. On 13th May, I flew a recce of the Gokwe area with Army Captain Ellis.

On 1st June, two sorties were flown with RAR Captain Geoff Atkinson on an Army FAC Course. Next was SAAF pilot Lieutenant Labuschagne who had come up from South Africa on the Rhodesian FAC Course. Rhodesian inter-service was good, thanks to No's 4 and 7 Squadrons' close army co-operation. The South Africans gained valuable front line experience. Operation *Hedgehog* entailed uplifting Major Johnson from Kumalo for a recce in the Kariba area, landing Wankie to refuel and then on to Bulawayo, recovering at night to Thornhill. The next day Army RAR Captain Peter Hosking was flown on a lengthy reconnaissance of the Mfungabusi Plateau.

An Ill Wind Blows

Dissatisfied members of the ZAPU factions formed ZANU - Zimbabwe African National Union - on 8th August 1963. In the same year, ZANU's Emmerson M'nangagwa led the first squad of recruits of its military wing (ZANLA) to China for guerrilla training. From March to June 1964, 150 ZAPU and ZANU leaders were detained. In August the government banned the parties. Joshua Nkomo was sent to a detention centre at Gonakudzingwa, at Boli in south eastern Rhodesia. Robert Mugabe was imprisoned in Salisbury, then moved to Wha Wha outside Gwelo, then transferred to Sikombela jail, Que Que. The detainees were moved time and again from one centre to another in order to prevent the formation of nationalist "blocs". This action also contributed to open warfare between ZANU and ZAPU. If anything, this rift kept widening - and led to much killing of opposing parties. Supporters of both parties fought frequently and violently. Houses were burned; some that barricaded themselves inside died in the blazes. Mob rule had taken over in the low-income areas of Salisbury and also in some of the Tribal Trust Lands. The inter-party warfare played into the hands of Ian Smith's government, reinforcing their argument that the Africans were simply not ready, capable or worthy of running the country.

On the 4th July 1964 Petrus Oberholtzer was ambushed and killed by terrorists at a roadblock near Melsetter on the eastern border. Oberholtzer was the Rhodesian Front branch chairman and was the first white farmer to die in an act of war by the terrorist gang that became known as the "Crocodile Gang", led by a member of the ZANLA high command, Ndangana. Oberholtzer had been stabbed to death when he stopped his car at the crude roadblock. Ndangana escaped and became the commander of the first intake of trainees at the Tanzanian Itumbi camp that opened in 1965. The Itumbi camp became well known later on during the Bush War. The ill winds of change would soon become winds of destruction – to coin my flying instructor Peter Petter-Bowyer's finding.

The OCC - Operations Co-ordinating Committee was formed in 1964. The members were Air Vice-Marshal Bentley, Commissioner of Police Barfoot and Director CIO Flower. Major-General Putterill replaced Major General 'Jock' Anderson, and Air-Vice-Marshal Harold Hawkins replaced Bentley.

Operation Phoenix: October 1964

Britain had stated unequivocally that it was not going to grant independence to Rhodesia as its franchise was more restrictive than any other British territory to which independence had been granted. British Premier Sir Alec Douglas-Home told Rhodesian Prime Minster Ian Smith that if he wanted independence under the 1961 Constitution, which widened the franchise to allow Blacks into Parliament for the first time, then he must show that this was acceptable to the people as a whole. A referendum was duly held, and the white electorate voted ten to one in favour of independence. The 'indaba' - a meeting - was held, and consisted of six hundred and twenty-two African chiefs and headmen. Since Smith was very wary of the intimidation which was rife amongst the blacks, the Army and Air Force were mobilised and deployed to the six hundred and twenty-two locations, while all the chiefs and headmen in the country were summoned to state their opinions. Thus Operation *Phoenix* was mounted, with the purpose of flying over all the Army units and all the chiefs and headmen's kraals in Matabeleland to ensure that all was well.

The No 4 Squadron detachment to Bulawayo consisted of Barry Matthews and me flying two Provost Aircraft, accompanied by Wing Commander Mutch. We based with 1 Brigade, Brady Barracks. The Matabeleland North reconnaissance route was to Bubi, Nkai, Lupani and return to Brady. On the 18th I flew the northern circuit with one of the No 101 (Bulawayo) Volunteer Squadron crew, Pilot Officer Hobbs, and also with VR Flying Officer Ruby. The 18th was a mammoth morning 4-hour 25-minute sortie with Barry, followed by a three-hour trip to Bulalima Mangwe in the afternoon. This pattern of flying would repeat itself until the end of the month. We often landed at Tjolotjo, Nkai and Lupani. *Phoenix* ended on 30th October 1964.

As with the Salisbury Indaba of 1964, the Chiefs and headmen supported Ian Smith / Alec Douglas-Home's call for independence, but by then Britain had a new Prime Minister. Harold Wilson and his Labour Party were determined to complete the colonisation process of central Africa through majority rule in Rhodesia, and refused to accept the meeting with the chiefs as a valid indication of black opinion. Britain was not going to grant independence until majority rule was guaranteed – NIBMAR.

Operation Slipshod: 14 to 15 November 1964

Operation *Slipshod* was a two-day op from Kutanga, to carry out reconnaissance sorties to the south of Gwelo in conjunction with the Army School of Infantry. Then on 10th December 1964 I had two interesting sorties with Brownjob Captain Geoff Atkinson. The first was dropping supplies to Army call-signs, and the second was an hour's search for escaped convicts.

Operation Broken Arrow: 18 To 24 March 1965

This was an air-support of Army and Police forces in the Tjolotjo and Nyamandlovu area north of Bulawayo – which will be remembered for the tragic death of Pilot Officer Barry Matthews and Chief Technician Sandy Trenoweth, during a low-level barrel-roll tail chase manoeuvre.

Exercise Panther: 24 to 26 July 1965

This was an Air Force two-day weekend exercise for about 150 Air Force regulars and 200 VRs and some Territorial Forces at six advance and three main air bases throughout the country.

Exercise Longdrag: 23 August to 1 September 1965

On 23rd August I departed Thornhill for Karoi, in Provost 308, on an Army exercise in the northwest of the country. Chris Weinmann accompanied me. The next day we flew on a local reconnaissance mission along the Sanyati Gorge and Umniati River that runs into the Lake. Our first sortie of the 26th is recorded as "Battle of the Angwa River" – for reason which now escapes me. Then later that day, I carried out an "umpire flight" to evaluate troop deployments by Army Major Conn. The next three day's flying missions were rather uneventful - Chris and I flew another reconnaissance sortie to the Kariba area, followed a day later by a recce along the Kariba power line. Then on the 29th, we carried out a recce of the Tengwe River area, where the fledgling town was being established.

Then the most eventful flight of Exercise *Longdrag* followed. I was tasked to fly Major Conn down the Umniati River to Lake Kariba. We duly took off from Karoi in a Provost and set course for the Sanyati Gorge. No sooner had we got airborne than one of the nine cylinder heads of the Leonides engine 'blew its top', spewing engine oil all over the windscreen. Fortunately one of the 'top' cylinders failed and not a bottom one. A successful partial engine failure forced landing was carried out back on Karoi airstrip.

Operation Reptile: 1966

The first pseudo-terrorist groups (own forces posing as the enemy) were formed in 1966. Prior to this, The Special Branch had infiltrated agents into the nationalist operational movements. It took the likes of SAS Captain Brian Robinson to establish the School of Infantry Tracking Wing at Kariba, and Air Force Flying Officer Basil Moss during Operation *Reptile*, to develop exercises at operating pseudo gangs along the lines used during the Mau Mau uprising in Kenya. Skills were honed and as the number of "turned" terrorists grew, the pseudo operator concept was resurrected and several years later, from these groups, evolved the Selous Scouts. COIN OP techniques were perfected in Rhodesia. Most of the tactics the Rhodesians evolved were masterly in concept and determined in execution, with the Rhodesian Air Force at the cutting edge of most operations.

Operation Breampool: 1 to 2 November 1965

Operation *Breampool* was a short but intensive Army affair in the Zambezi Valley at Chirundu. I flew five missions on day one. The first was with Brownjob Captain McConnell for a reconnaissance along the road from Chirundu to Makuti and return. The second sortie was identical, except this time it was with a Captain Stokes. The next two sorties were flown with

Captain Rich. We flew to, and landed at Kariba. From Kariba we flew up to Makuti and then also recce'd the road down to Chirundu.

Exercise *Greentrees* was a short one-day School of Infantry exercise in the mountainous area of Selukwe, for reconnaissance missions and cordon *sanitaire* manoeuvres.

Operation Wizard: UDI - 11th November 1965

The day before UDI, I was deployed to Kariba in Provost 308, which was armed with 1300 rounds of ·303. Peter Piggot supported the Kariba detachment in an Alouette III helicopter. Canberra navigator Polly Postance was deployed as the Operations Officer and Monty Maughan was the Technician. No 4 Squadron deployed two Provost Aircraft to the northern border areas, while I went to Kariba and in essence established Forward Air Field 2 - or FAF 2. The other Provost was sent to Wankie where FAF 1 was established.

On arrival the Blues set up camp while the Army unit - the RLI (Rhodesian Light Infantry) - started digging slit trenches all over the place. They had parked their Land Rovers at 100 metre intervals on the runway in order to prevent any airborne assault on Kariba Township. Rhodesian Intelligence was anticipating Royal Air Force Javelin aircraft, and we needed to be prepared for any eventuality. Old Bloodhound Armoured Cars were taken out of mothballs and, accompanied by the odd Ferret Scout Cars, also set off for Kariba in support of airfield defence - in those days Airfield Defence was an Army responsibility. However, the Panhard engines of the Bloodhounds found it heavy going, and several needed towing into the airstrip.

On 11th November 1965 (Armistice Day), I was manning the Operations Room at Kariba at midday when Prime Minister Ian Douglas Smith proclaimed UDI:

In order to show the flag, I took off on the 13th for a thirty-minute armed reconnaissance sortie of the Zambian border, being careful not to violate their airspace. Zambian troops had also been deployed at various points, but they dared not be seen as the aggressors with the Rhodesian defiance. They set up an O.P. - Observation Post - across the dam wall, and the two opposing sides continued a vigil of spying each other out with their binoculars. All forms of troop movements would be transmitted back to their respective command centres. Harold Wilson immediately dispatched Royal Air Force Javelin jet fighter bombers to Zambia, and they needed Salisbury air traffic controllers to kindly guide them in. Officially, they had been sent in to defend Zambia's airspace but, according to authoritative journalist Chapman Pincher, their purpose was simply to occupy the airfields to prevent the Russians from doing so. In fact, such was the value of the 'kith and kin' factor, that the Royal Air Force officers later toasted Ian Smith's health during their New Year's Eve celebrations in their Lusaka Mess. They even visited Salisbury during their time off and had a few beers with the Rhodesian Air Force pilots. It was also reliably heard that they used to meet the Hunters over the Zambezi and fly formation down the river until they both peeled away to land at their respective bases. My sortie on the 13th did not elicit any response from the RAF Javelin Squadron. Then, a rather prolonged cat and mouse game started which lasted just under a week, with very little air activity. Finally, on 19th November 1965, I returned to Thornhill with trusty Provost 308. Operation *Wizard* was rather a damp squib from a flying perspective.

UDI will be remembered as an event of historical significance. I venture to predict that future generations will fail to appreciate what it was all about. It is thus worth repeating, in Ian Douglas Smith's own words, that the Rhodesians rebelled against the British Empire because "UDI had been brought about by one single factor: the British government's failure to honour the agreement made with us at the Victoria Falls conference in 1963." With the break-up of the Federation of Rhodesia and Nyasaland, the British betrayed the Rhodesians by granting independence to Zambia and Malawi, while withholding independence from Southern Rhodesia.

No 4 Squadron, Royal Rhodesian Air Force – December 1965
Hugh Slatter, Chris Weinmann, Bill Buckle, John Bennie, Mark McLean, Harold Griffiths, Prop Geldenhuys, Pat Meddows-Taylor, Bill Jelley, Sqn Ldr KAS Edwards, Nobby Nightingale, Rob Tasker and Varky Varkevisser

Operation Noah

No mention of Kariba will be complete without the mention of Operation *Noah* - the operation that rescued most of the wild animals when construction of the dam wall began in 1955 and the lake started filling up. Lake Kariba is 280 kilometres long and raised the dry weather height of the river by more than a hundred metres - covering an area of some 5 200 square kilometres. Operation *Noah* had been a fantastically successful exercise, rescuing thousands of wild animals, something unique and which had never previously been done in the world.

Exercise Greenhills: 1 to 2 December 1965

This short two-day exercise was another Army Co-operation liaison mission for the School of Infantry. I flew a total of three sorties. The first was a reconnaissance exercise with Pilot Officer Bill Buckle. The next was with Brownjob Sergeant Major Devine (I recall he served his country well during the subsequent Bush War), carrying out air supply drops to the troopies on the ground. The last sortie was flown with a Sergeant Tatton - but this was not so pleasant for the ground troops because we dropped a total of twenty tear-smoke canisters. Being on the receiving end brings a tear to the eye - involuntarily.

Exercise Armchair (Binga): 18 to 23 April 1966

Exercise *Armchair* was a short Army Co-operation exercise in the Binga area. The Rhodesian Security Forces wanted their presence along the Zambian border known - and also gave prying eyes evidence that military activity was being supported by air power. Border reconnaissance flights westward to Deka and Bumi Hills to the east, were carried out. On 23rd April I carried out a Zambian Border reconnaissance with a Major Howden. I trust the Zambian prying eyes were taking note of all our air activity. The Brownjob sweated profusely in the cockpit, and I was able to provide a little relief by opening the canopy. Our two and a half-hour sortie was somewhat shorter than the one I had flown with Conex (Conservation and Extension)

Mr Spiret. I guess the reason was Spiret was permanently based at Binga and had a genuine interest in the conservation activities, whereas the Brownjob was more at home on the ground. Nevertheless, this type of co-operation certainly helped to foster the exceptionally good relations that were so essential during the course of the Bush War.

Shortly thereafter, we received the news that seven terrorists had been killed in the "Battle of Sinoia".

Operation Sinoia: 29 April 1966

Herbert Chitepo, based in Lusaka, organised an army of guerrillas to "wage war". He was tasked to assume overall responsibility for ZANU's affairs while the leadership remained in Rhodesian detention. During April 1965, twenty-one ZANU infiltrated Rhodesia from Zambia then split up into three sections. One group headed for Umtali in an abortive bid to blow up the Beira - Umtali oil pipeline and kill white farmers, and a second group headed for Fort Victoria. Both groups were rounded up. A third group of 14 ZANU terrorists was ordered by Chitepo to destroy electrical power pylons at Sinoia. One hundred and twenty police and reservists, supported by the Air Force, chased the third group, in the biggest counter-terrorist operation the country had seen to-date. The terrorists infiltrated 250 kilometres (155 miles) into Rhodesia, and reached Sinoia some 120 kilometres (70 miles) from Salisbury.

An informer, working for the Rhodesian Special Branch, had infiltrated the gang and managed to slip away from his comrades to tip off the police - the net tightened, a fierce battle ensued - and seven insurgents, some trained at the Nanking Military College near Peking, were killed. The battle had been nothing more than a fiasco for the terrorists, but it had been the deepest penetration into Rhodesia to date. ZANU subsequently gave the excuse that their "freedom fighters" were in fact ill equipped, poorly trained and badly led (as quoted from Mugabe's biography by David Smith). This event, however, would in future be marked as the first day of Zimbabwe's "war of liberation", their Chimurenga Day.

My flying instructor, Squadron Leader Peter Petter-Bowyer acquitted himself well - he was the leader of four helicopters providing the vertical support, which contributed immeasurably towards the final outcome. This effectively, was one of the first joint operations with the BSA Police against terrorists. In those early days, the helicopters weren't yet armed, and despite the unarmed aircraft coming under ground fire, P-B remained in close proximity to the terrorist position, and thereby provided a highly effective airborne control post for the Police Force.

Two noteworthy formation sorties were flown on 29th April and 12th May 1966. On the 29th I was tasked to fly number six in a formation of Provost Aircraft. I was then selected to lead a box of four aircraft and was given a couple of pansy formation practices, and 'promoted' to number nine position. On 12th May we managed to get eleven Provosts airborne, with me as the number 9. Now that is no joke, as any piston engined pilot will tell you, flying an echelon formation with such a large formation is quite a challenge - and hairy at times. Some of the pilots who flew in these large formations included Varky Varkevisser, Pat Meddows-Taylor, Rob Tasker, Chris Weinmann, Steve Kesby, Bill Buckle, John Bennie, Mark McLean, possibly KAS Edwards and A N Other.

Exercise Aurora: 18 to 22 May 1966

Exercise *Aurora* was a Volunteer Reserve exercise for No 101 Bulawayo Squadron at the Army Camp at Llewellin Barracks in Bulawayo. On 18th May, Rob Tasker and I flew from Thornhill down to Bulawayo. We got settled in and attended the briefings on the Exercise *Aurora* sorties that lay ahead. The next day I flew a short reconnaissance sortie to exercise our volunteer reservists in operations room procedures and command and control exercises. On the 20th I carried out another reconnaissance sortie with Rob Tasker.

VR Flight Lieutenant Derrick Purnell joined me on 22nd May. We flew for two hours and fired 100 x ·303 from our wing mounted Browning machine guns. Derrick was a World War II pilot and I'd bet he enjoyed the airstrike experience - smelling the wafts of cordite that tend to enter the cockpit of the Provost. He also relished the opportunity of getting his hands onto the control column and doing a bit of real flying again. Later that afternoon Rob Tasker and I flew back to Thornhill at the conclusion of exercising our Reservists. I believe they enjoyed the get-togethers as much as we Regulars did.

Operation Pagoda: June 1966

For many people the real war began when the Viljoens were the first Rhodesians to die at the hands of communist-trained and armed terrorists (CTs). Johannes Hendrik and Barbara Viljoen lived on a remote farm twenty-five kilometres (15 miles) from Hartley, and were murdered when they answered a knock on their front door. Johannes was shot at point blank range as he slammed the door shut; a bullet that passed through the door also killed his wife as she came to her husband's rescue. "Then Mummy and Daddy lay down and went to sleep on the floor," their young son told police.

Within days of the Viljoen murders the Security Forces had killed 14 of the terrorists. ZANU tried to glorify the terrorist failure to destroy the power pylons, by calling it the "Battle of Sinoia". ZANU's war council (called the *Dare re Chimurenga*) planned these offensive actions. They tried to make publicity mileage from their so-called battle. But their only successes were the very soft targets (Petrus Oberholtzer - murdered). They seldom targeted military targets. The Viljoen's were avenged with the death of the war monger Herbert Chitepo when he became a victim of his own making – planting mines to kill the defenceless. He, who lives by the sword, shall die by the sword. In February 1967 a captured terrorist Edmund Nyandoro went on trial for the Viljoen murders. He was convicted and sentenced to death.

It was also at the end of August 1966 that the British announced that their RAF Javelin Squadron and British troops in Zambia were returning home. They were given a grand farewell party by the Rhodesians at Victoria Falls.

Operation Yodel: September 1966

Operation *Yodel* was the second internal security counter-insurgency operation, after Operation *Pagoda*. The Security Forces, mainly the BSAP supported by elements of the Army, made short shrift of the invaders, with the survivors hot-footing it back to Zambia. The border reconnaissance sorties flown during Exercise *Armchair* complemented Operation *Yodel* in that an air presence had been shown to spying eyes in Zambia, and secondly, the Brownjobs that flew had been given valuable air experience. Operation *Vermin* followed two months later.

Exercise Armchair – Wankie: 19 to 24 September 1966

Flight Sergeant Ken Spoor and I, with Pilot Officer Bill Buckle and A C Brislin in the second Provost positioned Wankie on 19th September. The next day, *Armchair* got off to a flying start with a morning reconnaissance of the Zambian and Bechuanaland/Botswana border with Brownjob Lieutenant Boyd-Sutherland. After landing we received a report of an armed African male and the Air Force was requested to help with an air search. We were only too happy to oblige, and so it was decided that we would send up only one Provost, but that Bill Buckle would come with me in order to have another pair of eyes to scan the thick scrub that is so prevalent in the Wankie area. The air activity kept the fugitive's head down and the ground forces were able to affect an arrest. It was a good sortie for Bill and me.

The next day I flew with a second Brownjob - Sergeant-Major MacMaster. Our mission was a reconnaissance along Lake Kariba. The recce on the 22nd was an earlier repeat – also along the Bechuanaland and Zambian border. Then on 23rd September I flew with Bill's technician, Aircraftsman Brislin eastwards for a Lake Kariba recce, landing at Binga. After our normal end of detachment thrash, Ken Spoor and I headed back to Thornhill on the 24th September 1966, and so ended Exercise *Armchair*.

Operation Sculpture: 12th October 1966

Operation *Sculpture* was an abortive exclusively Special Air Service squadron affair intended to destroy the ZANU Headquarters in Lusaka, involving Lieutenant Brian Robinson. The deaths of SAS operators Warrant Officer II Bob Bouch and Colour Sergeants Mick Cahill and George Wright (together with seconded BSAP Chief Superintendent John Wickenden on 12th October 1966) who also intended blowing up the ZANU Headquarters in the Zambian capital, was tragic. A couple of months later, a Cessna 206 flew in Lieutenant Brian Robinson and his two SAS operators. When the would-be saboteurs reached their target they were thwarted in their efforts to carry out their mission as fierce inter-faction fighting was taking place at the headquarters, and they had to abandon their task as time was running out on them. They had been given three hours in which to complete their assignment and with no sign of the faction fighting abating, they had to make their way back to Lusaka's international airport where they boarded their Rhodesian aircraft for Kariba and a disappointing debrief. At least one essential lesson was learned from this operation and that was namely that HF (High Frequency) communications were absolutely vital to the success of clandestine missions.

Both the preceding counter-insurgency Operation *Yodel*, and Operation *Vermin* that followed during November 1966, were quickly brought to a successful conclusion. Little did the penny drop for the infiltrators that the Rhodesians had the capacity to wrap up, and account for most if not all the terrorists, that dared to 'tango' with the Security Forces. Their squabbling no doubt caused the lull of some seven months between Operations *Vermin* and *Isotope*.

Exercise Cobra – Wedza: 19 to 20 November 1966

No 4 Squadron participated in a weekend camp for the Volunteer Reserve code-named *Cobra*. I was detailed to deploy to Wedza, with my technician Flight Sergeant Ken Spoor. The VRs could only exercise during weekends and we regulars could only respect and fully support these part-time airmen who so willingly gave of their valuable time and effort. As was customary, we pulled out all the stops. Wedza is a small township about 50 kilometres south of Marandellas and is the administrative and trading centre for a tobacco and mixed farming area to the north, and the Wedza TTL to the south.

The Wedza Mountains lie just to the south of the airstrip and the village. The highest point is Dangamvuri, or as it is more commonly called, Wedza Mountain, which rises to 1,800 metres above sea level. Having visited the place, Wedza Mountain became an easy landmark to recognise for many years to come. No 4 Squadron criss-crossed the country so frequently that the Squadron pilots came to know Rhodesia like the back of their hands. Anyway, on 20th November 1966, Volunteer Reservist Flying Officer Brian Patton came along for the ride of his lifetime. Ken Spoor had armed up our Provost with live fragmentation bombs and had cocked our two wing mounted Browning Machine guns, for the Weapons Demonstration, which was the main feature of Exercise *Cobra*.

With the start of the summer rainy season, storm clouds were brewing. Despite a lowering cloud base, we were able to drop our eight frag bombs for the benefit of all the spectators. We then fired off two hundred rounds from our front guns. Brian was pre-warned to brace himself for the six 'g' during the high dive recovery, and he coped with the manoeuvres like a true veteran. I had witnessed a "roll cloud" the preceding afternoon when the airstrip had been lashed momentarily by strong shear winds. This type of wind-shear has accounted for many fatal aircraft crashes through pilots taking off immediately before a thunderstorm. I remember the mass of black cloud passing over Wedza like one massive steamroller, only a couple of hundred feet above the runway. The strange phenomenon generated much debate amongst the aircrews. Later that day, after a good detachment wash-up (debrief), Ken Spoor and I returned to Thornhill.

Operation Vermin: November 1966

Operation *Vermin* followed shortly after Operations *Yodel* and *Sculpture*. I guess the nationalists' objective was to make a political statement coinciding with the looming HMS Tiger talks between Rhodesian premier Ian Smith and the British Prime Minister Harold Wilson. A secondary aim was possibly to demonstrate that the terrorists were still in business following the SAS raid into Zambia. But, once again, the terrorists were soundly beaten at their own game. They soon realised that in order to survive, they needed to avoid confrontation with the Rhodesian Security Forces, and opted to concentrate on soft targets like isolated farm homesteads and outlying police posts. They also had a long way to go to intimidate and infiltrate innocent black kraals and villages.

Following the dismal failure in realising any of their objectives, a lull in counter insurgency operations followed until June 1967 when Operation *Isotope* was launched. On the constitutional front, the first formal moves to settle were being made on the Royal Navy cruiser *HMS Tiger*. Ian Smith flew to Gibraltar on Friday morning 2nd December 1966 - and was asked to sign Rhodesia's own death warrant.

Exercise Liberator: 10 to 12 March 1967

On 11th March 1967 I departed Kutanga for Rusape with Corporal van der Merwe, to participate in the on-going plan to exercise our Volunteer Reservists with field deployment exercises. The Salisbury and Umtali VR Squadrons participated. They were required to set up the camp, establish the field kitchen, requisition supplies and set up the forward airfield operations room/tent. That same afternoon I was air tasked to carry out a reconnaissance of the eastern border with Moçambique. Flying Officer Brian Patton came along for the ride to the Inyanga area, around Troutbeck and the spectacular Inyangani Mountain.

Inyangani Mountain is in fact the highest mountain in Rhodesia, rising up to 2594,8 metres at the southern end of the mountain range. Troutbeck village was the brainchild of Major Herbert McIlwaine who conceived the idea of a holiday resort where trout fishing was established. My second sortie of the day was again with Brian Patton, and we carried out a rather short fifty-minute reconnaissance of the Umtali area - sufficiently long enough for the VR to exercise our command and control technique. A 'wash-up' (or debrief) of Exercise *Liberator* followed for the benefit of our Reservists. And so, after lunch on 12th March 1967, my technician Corporal van der Merwe and I departed Rusape in our Provost and headed back to Thornhill.

Exercise Crocodile Fever: 22 April 1967

This exercise was but a one-day affair whose highlight was a dawn strike with deployment to Gokwe. Gokwe is situated some 120 kilometres northwest of Que Que. We spent the afternoon planning a take-off around four the following morning, conducting an airstrike as soon as it became light enough to recognise ground features, then dispersing to a satellite airfield. Early on 22nd April 1967 Pilot Officer Derrick Rainey and I got airborne from Thornhill, flew on a fifty-minute night cross-country, carried out our dawn strike as planned and landed at Gokwe ten minutes later. We did not have any refuelling facilities at Gokwe and still needed to do a reconnaissance mission with our remaining fuel. Gokwe in the 1960s was a small village, with the airfield situated on top of the Mafungabusi plateau. Population was around 50 Europeans and about 540 Africans. The country to the south is fairly heavily wooded, and reserved for forestry. To the north the land was farmed largely at a subsistence level with the emphasis on cattle ranching.

After a leg-stretch and a smoke break, Derrick and I got airborne again and flew our two hour exercise *Crocodile Fever* reconnaissance, landing back at Thornhill, to prepare for a live weapons demonstration.

Exercise Promptforce: May 1967

This was a squadron competition exercise in the Que Que area on 10th May 1967. It also entailed dropping 1 x 20lb high dive and 3 x 20lb medium glide bombing competitions.

Exercise Fabric: 17 to 21 May 1967

Exercise *Fabric* took place at Llewellin and Bulawayo. On 17th May 1967 Tudor Thomas and I dispersed to Kenilworth, a small airstrip south-west of Gwelo. From there, we got airborne again for a simulated attack on Bulawayo. We landed at the main Bulawayo airfield, for a night stop. The next morning we returned to Thornhill. Then on 20th May I positioned Llewellin Barracks with Corporal Trevor Booth. There was a changeover of squadron technicians, and later in the day I took off with Sergeant Doop du Plessis on a simulated-armed reconnaissance of the Shangani area. The following day I flew with Corporal Lafferty on a rather interesting mission. Our task was to catch Thornhill unawares and carry out simulated attack on Vampires. I might add that we were also on the receiving end when the Vampires carried out surprise attacks at our airfield. I remember diving for cover under the chassis of our water bowser - but heard the scream of the jet engine overhead before I reached the safety of the water trailer. Exercise *Fabric* ended on 21st May, with me returning to Thornhill with Trevor Booth after lunch.

Operation Pantechnicon: 26 May 1967

This was a SAS and SB COIN operation to eliminate a ZANU group hidden in a truck, in the Chirundu – Makuti area. Conway earned the Bronze Cross for his bravery. Coventry was wounded in the thigh.

Operations Isotope and Husk: June 1967

Operations *Isotope* and *Husk*, both taking place during June 1967, were also of those short duration counter-insurgency affairs where the most efficient Security Forces accounted for all of the infiltrating terrorists from Zambia.

August 1967 was rather special in my life, and warrants a detailed report because it signalled using air power in anger. It was one thing carrying out simulated strikes, or firing live weaponry at pre-positioned ground targets. It was a totally different matter shooting at terrorists. The curtain went up on Operation *Nickel* - and came down on all the exercises that prepared the Rhodesian Air Force to play its full part in the impending Bush War.

Operation Isotope 2: 5 to 9 August 1967 - Kariba, Wankie

August 1967 started off with Army Co-operation tasks, with introducing Captains Trevor Desfontein and Coetzee to FAC - Forward Air Control simulated strikes. The Brownjobs were on a School of Infantry COIN course and part of their training was to acquire the necessary skills to direct striking aircraft onto ground targets. No sooner had I landed with Coetzee than I was instructed to pack my bags for a scramble to Kariba where units of No 2 Indep. (A territorial force battalion, based on Kariba Heights ever since UDI), had made contact with a group of terrorists that had infiltrated across the Zambezi below the Kariba Gorge. Provost 312 was armed up and waiting for me.

That same afternoon, 5th August, I got airborne with Pilot Officer Ken Law for Makuti and made radio-contact with the ground forces for a general patrol of the area. An Air Force ground party had meanwhile set off to await our arrival at Kariba to set up the forward airfield - FAF 2. Having landed at Makuti, we were briefed on the Army plans for the following day, and then took off from Makuti for Kariba for a night-stop, to await further instructions. There had been a Zambezi crossing at Chirundu of ZAPU terrorists on the night of 31st July / 1st August and tracks were now about five days old, crossing the escarpment. The Operation was codename *Isotope II*. The next day, the 6th, Ken Law and I had a rewarding armed reconnaissance sortie of over two and half-hours. Army units had captured three gooks - 3 BTs - barbarian terrorists, as was normal reference at that point of time. It did not take long for the Special Branch fellows to do their thing - with the result that the BTs days were numbered. On the 7th Flying Officer Terry Jones joined me on a three hour ten minute armed recce sortie during which one BT was killed in a contact with ground forces. The tactical intelligence extracted from the earlier captures was starting to produce the desired results. The next day I got airborne for my third armed reconnaissance sortie, with Senior Technician James. We hit the jackpot. No fewer than ten BT were in the bag. After this 3 hour 10 minute sortie, my passenger and I landed back at Kariba. Having accounted for 14 terrorists in three days seemed par for the course, and with Security Force morale sky high we duly celebrated our success in the Forces pub. As we were convinced that this group was no longer a threat to internal security, I flew back to Thornhill on the 9th with Chief Technician Derrick Utton, having handed the FAF over to Pilot Officer Tudor Thomas.

A further three BT's were captured shortly thereafter. It transpired that by 9th August, eighteen had been accounted for (one killed and 17 captured). Twenty-one had crossed, intending to operate in the Sipolilo area. But the Security Forces had horribly upset their plans. Two gooks were later captured in the Midlands and the remaining survivor got out of the country (he lived to fight another day – on Operation *Excess* a year later – only to be killed. But that is another story).

A unique painting of a Hunting Percival Provost T Mk 52 Aircraft, by Roland Pletts, as supplied by John "Mac Kutanga" McKenzie

3 Nickel and Cauldron

Operation Nickel

On 12th August 1967, together with "Vulch" (short for the vulture tattoo that Richard Beaver sported), I got airborne in Provost 308 and set off for Wankie and the start of Operation *Nickel*. A ZAPU terrorist had been captured two days earlier, on the Lukosi railway bridge directly south of Wankie Town. Lieutenant Anthony Grace of 2RR then was led by the capture to the crossing place across the Zambezi.

The second Provost crew to accompany us was Flying Officer Chris Weinmann and Acting Pilot Officer Brian Penton. No sooner had we landed at Wankie than I was scrambled on an armed reconnaissance mission to the east of the coal-mining town. The First Battalion of the Rhodesian African Rifles had already deployed their ground forces, and was hot on the tracks that revealed a 'small' group of five BTs - Barbarian Terrorists. 1 RAR captured one of them who squealed under interrogation that his group was heading in a southerly direction. Information gleaned, but initially underrated, was that high-powered ANC terrorists were en route to South Africa. Detective Inspector Phillips, the police intelligence fundi, was dispatched to join the Army units on the ground. BSAP Section Officer Barry Tiffin was meanwhile following spoor through thick bush near Inyantue siding. A railways repair team had spotted some of the BT's at Inyantue Bridge where they had found water for the first time in days.

The ANC (SA), formed in 1912, was outlawed in 1960 and opted for the armed struggle in 1961. Their military wing, Umkhonto we Sizwe (Spear of the Nation), operated from bases in the latterly so-called Front Line States. Operation *Nickel* witnessed the first major incursion through Rhodesia - entering via Deka on the Zambezi River, chased through the Wankie Game Reserve, and exiting into Bechuanaland (now Botswana) west of Tjolotjo.

Battle of Inyantue

Two Provosts of No 4 Squadron (Chris Weinmann and I) and one Alouette III from No 7 Squadron (Murray Hofmeyr) had by now assembled at Wankie airfield, also named Forward Airfield One - or FAF 1 for short. Rich Beaver and I had already logged our first operational armed recce sortie around Deka and along the Inyantue River due east of Wankie. We were aware of the terrorist tactic of walking on high points at night, and lying up by day.

August 13th was an unlucky day for the security forces during the "Battle of Inyantue". I got airborne during the morning to provide top cover for BSAP Barry Tiffin and the 1 RAR troops following spoor. The ground forces made contact with a group of terrorists, still believed small in number, who were in a strong defensive position about 30 metres from the trackers. In fact, at this stage, only five sets of tracks, with the figure 8 boot print, was being tracked by the Army trackers.

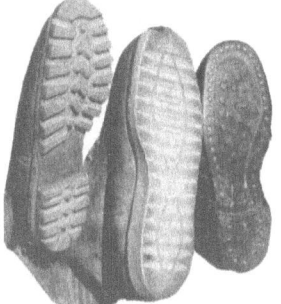

Suddenly, all hell broke loose and Rich Beaver and I found ourselves in the thick of a firefight between Rhodesian African Rifles troops and the terrorists in the dry river bed of the Inyantue River. Tiffin and his men were also pinned down. Fire was exchanged and reinforcements called in. We were itching to contribute with our 2 x ·303 front guns, but the safety distance was not sufficient. In those early days, a safety distance of between 100 to 300 yards was needed in order to discharge air to ground weapons from attacking aircraft. Helicopter crews Mick Grier and Bob Whyte came to the assistance of the ground forces, dropping off Inspector Fred Phillips and other reinforcements. Under heavy fire from the ground, Bob attacked the terrorist position. Despite continual fire from the helicopter the insurgents kept up the attack. During our 2 hour 40 minute top cover sortie, three terrorists were killed. As was our tactics, I would radio the FAF to request relief by Chris Weinmann in the second Provost, before I could return to the FAF to refuel. During a contact, we would fly about 1000 feet above ground level, in order to attack at an optimum 20°-dive angle. But because high engine settings were used, the Provost's endurance would be significantly reduced. Anyway I remained at the scene until Chris took over from me.

By now it had been decided that the ground party should move to a more secure position to provide the necessary safety distance for the fixed wing airstrikes. During this manoeuvre the security forces sustained casualties. Section Officer Tiffin crawled to join the reinforcement group and was seriously wounded in the thigh. Private Simon Chikafu of the RAR emptied his 20-round magazine into the enemy position and then crawled forward to the wounded policeman, dragging him to cover and then carrying him to the waiting helicopter.

I had no sooner landed, than the helicopter was airborne to bring in the dead terrorists. My aircraft was rapidly turned round (i.e. refuelled, re-armed when necessary, and made ready for immediate take-off). When Hofmeyr returned with the three 'floppies' (BTs), I was there to meet it. I can still vividly recall grabbing one gook by his belt to haul the limp body out of the chopper. He was still warm to the touch and rigor mortis was still some way off. Anyway, as I dragged the body out, the belt broke under his dead weight resulting in his head striking the helicopter step with such a thud that I am convinced to this day, that that was in fact the moment of death for this particular 'floppy' - he truly went 'flop'. His arm and torso had obvious signs of automatic gunshot wounds. Another gook probably didn't know what hit him - he had been shot in the head so badly that his skull was split wide open, with grey matter all over the place. I can't recall the third floppy - possibly because my stomach could not take too much of this gory sight. I do remember that all the terrorists wore several sets of clothing, and the good quality denim trousers in particular were always a treasured prize for the victors. Anyway, it was not long for my turn to be back at the scene.

I was scrambled again just before last light. We had been airborne only ten minutes before night fell. Another one hour forty minutes of night flying lay ahead for Rich Beaver and me. We had heard the news that two 1 RAR soldiers had been killed in action - Acting Corporal Davison and Private Karoni. Although tracks of only five sets of spoor had been followed, we learnt that the terrorists now in fact numbered about 23, because they had been marching in each other's footsteps. The battle was not going to be over as soon as we had expected. A tough fight was still in the offing. Anyway, there was no chance of getting the dead soldiers out during the night and the remaining troops were required to take up ambush positions in order to prevent a breakout. The gooks would have had pre-planned rendezvous points in the event of contact with the Security Forces, or whenever they split up. Ambush positions would have been set up on all the most likely escape routes. Rich and I had done what we could and landed sometime around eight at night, exhausted by now.

Not having much of an appetite for supper at this late hour, we headed for the pub instead, to drown our sorrows. We were still drinking in the pub when we got the news that Police inspector Fred Phillips had been shot and was badly wounded. Volunteers were called to get airborne in the dead of night. Now, it is not so good when a pilot has got a couple of beers under his belt. One's judgement goes for a ball of chalk. After much deliberation, it was decided that the two most experienced pilots should risk the single line flare take-off and landing - and Flying Officer Chris Weinmann and myself took off in the darkness on that fateful sortie for mainly "telstar" duties. Telstar meant acting as an airborne radio relay station between the troops on the ground and the command post. Despite being under the weather, and with swollen bladders, we were to remain airborne for two hours and twenty minutes. The single line flare night take-off was 'hairy' to say the least.

The actual hero of the events of that night was a Sergeant Major Korb. We learnt that there were in fact four Security Force casualties, the worst being Phillips who had been shot in the head. Fred Phillips was still alive, but only just and needed urgent medical attention. There was no way that a helicopter could get airborne - there was no horizon and it was pitch black – "like a witch's tit" - as the air force saying goes. Even I had difficulty, in my inebriated state; to differentiate between the few stars that were visible and the sparse homestead lights. The hills between Inyantue and Wankie Colliery tended to blanket out the only built-up and lit-up area. We could not climb too high, because of the extreme cold at altitude. The cold did help us to sober up promptly, but did not help the beer filled bladders much. Korb reported that any ground movement solicited a hail of gunfire - and they had no option but to keep their heads down. Anyone trying to get to the wounded would have his head blown off. Korb was instructed to leopard crawl up to the wounded and attempt to get them, particularly Phillips, down to the railway siding where a railway cart would be sent to evacuate them. Korb succeeded and when the rail rescue vehicle arrived, Chris and I landed, or a better description, perhaps 'arrived' back at base - by now well after midnight. I was advised to get some shut-eye, because an airstrike was called for at first light.

Unbeknown to me at the time, respected Peter Hosking had become separated from his RAR call-sign, who fled the scene (with their only radio), when the "fertiliser hit the fan" so to speak. Peter had been shot in the leg, with his femur being shattered. I can't recall whether his troops abandoned him when he was shot, or whether he sustained his injury subsequent to his stick deserting him. Anyway, Peter found himself all alone – and had to crawl away from the killing ground to ensure his survival, fortunately the night being pitch black. He managed to find a safe gully to make good his escape, but was then faced with a more serious dilemma from loss of blood from his gunshot wound. Without any radio communications to let anyone know of his predicament and precarious situation, he had visions of bleeding to death. But all is well that ends well, for elements of his stick had reached safety and reported Peter missing. A search party was organised and Peter was rescued after being found in the gully.

Meanwhile, back at the FAF, I awoke to a historical event for No 4 Squadron, Royal Rhodesian Air Force.

Air Strike Report No 03; Date 14/08/1967

Aircrews:
- Prop Geldenhuys with Richard Beaver
- Murray Hofmeyr

Target: MK 650505 Inyantue Ridge, Wankie area; Aircraft Provost 309 and Alouette III
Weapons: 230x.303 Browning
Result: Two BT killed, possibly from the night before.

On 14th August 1967, at the Battle of Inyantue, Flying Officer Prop Geldenhuys with Acting Pilot Officer Richard Beaver, in Provost No 309, put in the first Airstrike of Operation *Nickel*. We fired a total of two hundred and thirty rounds of ·303 from our two Browning machine guns. 1 RAR had pulled out their ambush parties to a safe distance and we would then spray the hilltop and riverine area with our front guns. Even Richard was given the unique opportunity to squeeze the trigger before his formal OCU gunnery training. However, the experience gained was worth more than many hours of academic instruction. After numerous attacks, we remained airborne for over 2¼ hours while the ground sweep took place. Two further terrorists had been killed. Nobody laid claims - it could have been the gunfights the night before, or even the airstrikes. One of the noticeable terrorists was the commissar of the Lupane Detachment, James Masimini. In any event, the surviving gooks were gone.

It should be noted that in the early stages of the bush war, firing from fixed wing aircraft required approval at the highest level. Ken Flower, Rhodesia's CIO, is on record saying that Air Vice-Marshal Harold Hawkins had assured the OCC (Operations Co-ordinating Committee) that the Air Force would apply the 'principle of minimum force'. The Air Vice-Marshal gave the assurance after the Battle of Sinoia: - "that he would not, in future, permit his aircraft to be used in a killing role where the alternative use of ground forces could be equally effective and result in less loss of life; (and he ruled out bombing or strafing of civilians from the air)". I was thus very privileged to have fired those two hundred and thirty rounds on that notorious 14th August.

The hunt was soon on. The terrorists had flown the coop and headed in a southerly direction, as if by straight-line compass bearing. I took off again late afternoon on the 15th, still in Provost 309, but this time with Varky Varkevisser. We flew 2 hours 40, of which 1.10 was logged as night flying. My logbook records "1 BT captured". The following day, the 16th was a rare day of rest, and to catch up on some much needed sleep. I remember noting how tired and drawn Helicopter pilot Hoffy (Murray Hofmeyr) was looking - unshaven and bedraggled. The helicopters were being extensively used in leapfrogging tactics, with the purpose of laying ambushes ahead of fresh tracks. In those early days, it was normal for the tracker to be ahead of the follow up troops so that the troops would not mistakenly obliterate any spoor. The troops would follow in a semi single file formation, and would be called forward whenever the tracker assessed the gooks as being very close. The trackers were expert at judging age and what sort of loads being carried - just by footprint telltale signs. Police tracker dogs were also used during joint operations. In fact, the police also suffered tracker dog casualties during this particular operation.

The Intelligence jigsaw puzzle was gradually taking shape. A large force of 94 terrorists had crossed the Zambezi River on the night of 31st July - 1st August, using rubber boats. They made their way into the sparsely populated area and had been in the country for ten days before the first capture on 10th August, on the Lukosi Bridge. This group was composed of members of the SAANC and Joshua Nkomo's ZAPU. The operation was under the control of John Dube (ZAPU) and George Driver, a Coloured (SAANC). Their Chief of Staff was Leonard Mandla (Danger) Nkosi who had spent a year in Moscow at a Military Academy. The aim of the 52 SAANC members was to penetrate through Rhodesia and Botswana and infiltrate into the Republic of South Africa.

Having crossed the river successfully with their supplies the men made their way to the Wankie-Dett area, where several camps were constructed, containing dugouts, weapons pits and observation posts. The first contact between this group and the Security Forces came on 1st August when one member was apprehended, whilst found walking down a road in the Wankie National Park near Shapi Pans. The piecing together of the puzzle set in motion this full-scale anti-terrorist operation code-named '*Nickel*' in which the Air Force was heavily involved. The Air Force initially dropped leaflets and carried out armed reconnaissance sorties in the Zambezi Valley. The leaflets, which were in English and ChiShona, called on the infiltrators to give themselves up. Also printed on the back of the leaflets were photographs of two terrorists who had recently surrendered. The infiltrators had meanwhile moved towards the Bulawayo/Victoria Falls Road where Game Scouts searching for poachers (the Shapi Pan incident) discovered their tracks.

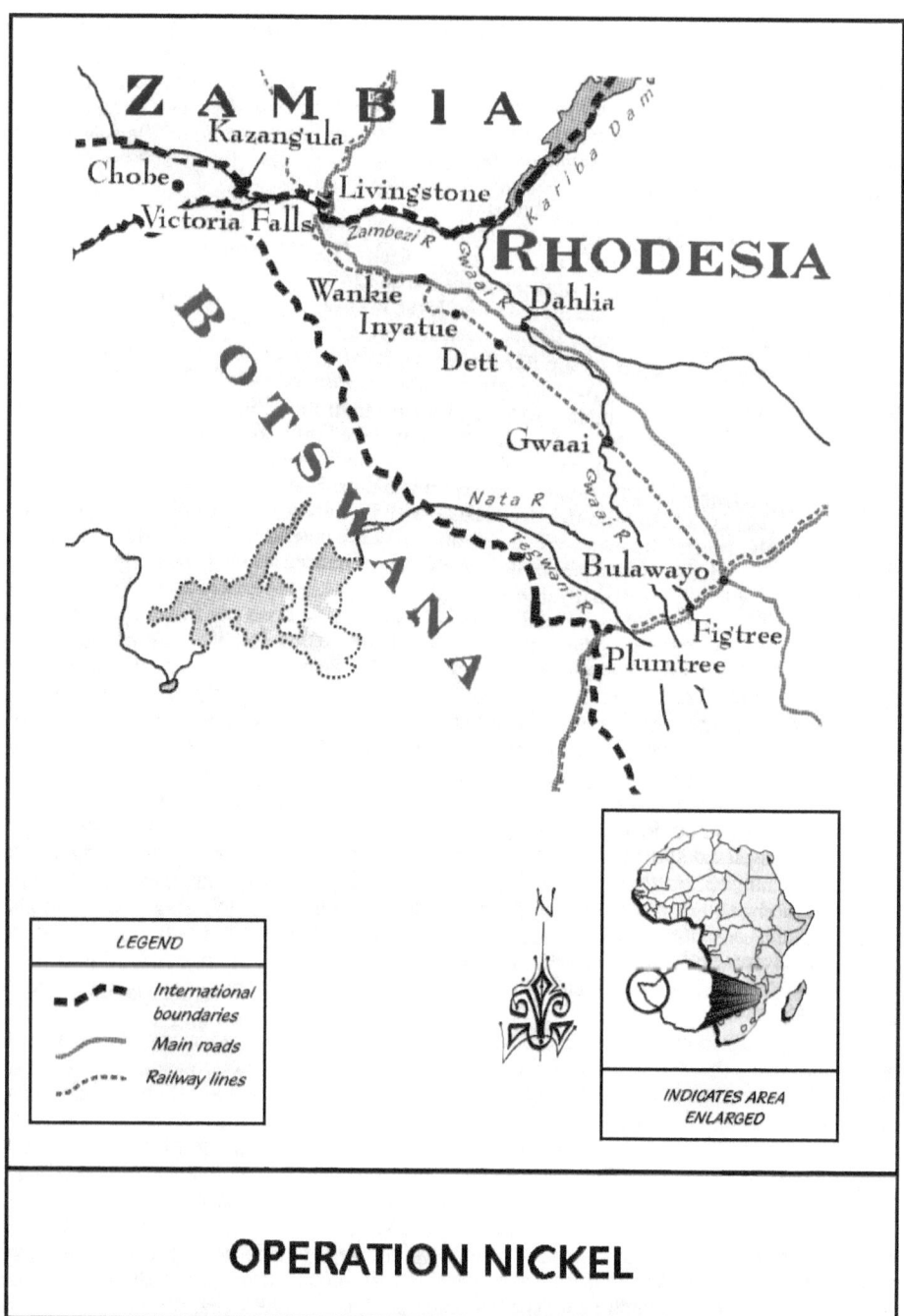

OPERATION NICKEL

The map of the operational area is reproduced by kind permission of the publisher of *A Pride of Eagles,* by Beryl Salt.

On 17th August, I took command of Provost No 308 and Rich Beaver and I took to the air again, for two very lengthy sorties, totalling seven hours flying time. One BT was killed during the first four-hour sortie, and the second three-hour sortie was mainly for Telstar (relay station) purposes in addition to armed reconnaissance. By now the terrorists had entered the Wankie Game Reserve, still maintaining their southerly course. Helicopter leap-frogging tactics facilitated the 1 RAR gaining tremendous ground in hot pursuit of the terrorists. In fact, Lieutenant Ian Wardle's tracking stick was able to cover 85 kilometres in just 48 hours. On the 18th Acting Pilot Officer Brian Penton joined me for two highly successful armed recce sorties - the first netting eight BTs killed and the second six BTs captured. During the first contact a large bush fire was started in the Angwa Vlei - where five of the first eight were burnt to death. The veld fire raged for some time and destroyed large tracts of grazing for the park animals. The troops were also 'bushed' after this highly successful engagement, and I can recall the helicopters flying in several 44-gallon drums of water to quench their thirst. The gooks must also have suffered severely from thirst due to both the firefight and the veld fire - but they did not have the benefit of vertical air support. At the subsequent debrief, the 1 RAR Lieutenant Ian Wardle reported that a terrorist carrying a backpack full of ammunition had been hit, which caused the explosion in the terrorist 'hide' and which was the actual cause of the fire. His body was so badly burnt and shrivelled up that his features were hardly recognisable. It must have been a gruesome but quick death for the poor fellow.

It was during our second sortie of the day that the six gooks of this group were captured. One terrorist managed to escape this contact - only to be killed the following day. Ian Wardle accounted for the captures – the first four surrendered after Ian and his men found themselves in the centre of a well-concealed terrorist position. One of the captured terrorists squealed, revealing where the others were nearby. In this particular action, six terrorists were killed and an additional two captured.

The Battle of Inyantue was a success for the SF, despite the loss of two soldiers killed and four casualties, including policemen Phillips and Tiffin. We bagged 14 terrorists killed and eight captured - a total of 22 terrorists. The bulk was accounted for during the 'battle' and follow up operations. However, Operation *Nickel* was nowhere near over. We would in fact relocate camp two more times. The intelligence picture was clearing all the time, with the Special Branch extracting all sorts of terrorist plans from the prisoners. It was meanwhile established that on Wednesday 14th August George Driver, the Coloured leader of the 52 strong SAANC group, had stolen (hijacked) a car in Dett, wounding a Security guard. He drove towards Bulawayo, evading several roadblocks on the way. His aim obviously was to make his way through Bulawayo to the South African border.

Main Camp – Wankie National Park

By Friday 16th George Driver had reached Figtree, south of Bulawayo, where he took a farmer's wife and her six-year-old son hostage, but the woman and child managed to escape with the help of their gardener. Security Forces were called in, the house surrounded and Driver was killed. Rumour initially had it that Joe Modise was amongst the SA ANC terrorists en route for South Africa – but it transpired that he, together with Oliver Tambo did not actually cross the Zambezi, but saw the groups off at the Batonka Gorge crossing – some 35 kilometres downstream from Victoria Falls. Joe Modise was destined to become Nelson Mandela's first black Minister of Defence, but he retired late 1999. His son Tim became a regular interviewer on SABC.

On 19th August 1967, I got off to an early start, with Richard Beaver, to follow along the terrorist's line of flight, and landing at Wankie Main Camp after another mammoth 4 hour armed reconnaissance sortie. After lunch, I teamed up with Brian Penton for a 3 hour 10 minute sortie, during which one terrorist was killed. The total 7 hours 10 minutes made it a really tiring day, not leaving much energy to enjoy the comforts of the Game Park facilities. I quietly supped my evening chibuli (beer) lying on my fartsack in the hastily erected tents on the airfield. I need to mention our magnificent caterers, who always had for us a steaming mug of coffee between sorties - and one could catch a meal any time of the day. We spared a thought for the follow up troops who did not have the home comforts that we Bluejobs enjoyed - and even less so the terrorists who were by now on a beeline flight for the Bechuanaland border. The next day I took Senior Technician Jim Ritchie with me on an armed recce Telstar mission of three hours duration. The following day, 21st, Vulch joined me for two sorties, of nearly six hours duration. The

Bechuanaland Police had made one BT capture, and Telstar was required to relay messages from the ground troops to base headquarters. It seemed that although the incursion group had been dispersed by all the air activity, they were still capable of putting up fierce resistance. Both sides were gaining valuable IS Ops experience.

The abbreviated term for Communist Terrorist (or Communist trained guerrillas - for the liberated), CTs had its origin during this latter part of Op Nickel. Communism was anathema to most Rhodesians, and perhaps even more so to the South Africans. The ANC National Executive member Joe Slovo propagated the doctrines of Marxism-Leninism. As head of the South African Communist Party, as well as an ANC bedfellow, he was iniquitous in his modus operandi towards the unsophisticated local population. Communism, even today, although part of the present ANC government, remains anathema to a sizeable pro-west, capitalist portion of South Africa, and that this sector is responsible for much of the GDP of the country. It was the ANC presence that prompted John Vorster to dispatch South African Police - SAP - to stem the tide of communism. We started using the terms CTs to impress urgency on South African support, and tended to use BTs to propagate barbaric slaughter of missionaries and innocent civilians.

One tactic which the terrorists employed warrants elaboration. Whenever they would rest up, or bed down for some shut-eye, they would go in single file and then follow a 'shepherds crook' path, backtracking in the opposite direction, and quite close to their 'obvious' track. They would then dig shallow hides, leave one lookout to keep guard and also to sound the alarm whenever the Security Forces were close on their heels. They would then arrange their defence and next rendezvous point. It was a perfect ambush tactic - and heaven help the poor tracker who would be in the direct line of fire when the ambush was sprung. With all the Security Force following behind the tracker, they would be all lined up like a long line of skittles, waiting to be mowed down when the first volley rang out. The tracker would invariably be the main terrorist target, and would be the first one to fall, because the terrorists realised that that would slow down pursuit. It was easier to replace troopies than to replace good trackers.

To counter this weakness, the RAR first adopted an arrow head type formation, with the wings affording a greater measure of protection to the tracker. Only limited success was achieved. This formation was then modified to a gull-wing, where the flanks were ahead of the tracker, but sufficiently far ahead, without distracting the tracker. A tracker had his head down all the time, with eyes focused on the telltale signs - whereas the troopies could focus ahead on all likely ambush positions.

On 22nd August we had a real ding-dong running battle. What a day the 22nd was. Rich Beaver and I got airborne early and proceeded with our armed recce in support of the RAR. By now, Lieutenant Ken Pierson deployed stop groups along the Nata (also called the Manzamnyama) River. Our airborne presence meant that the gooks could not cover a lot of ground, lest they be spotted. Every time we were close to them, they would go to ground and allow the Army call-signs to catch up to them. The stop groups were also intended to block their escape routes. Whilst we were circling Lieutenant Nic Smith's call-sign, all hell broke loose. A fierce firefight ensued. Every time we flew over the enemy, we were subjected to a hail of lead passing our way - and this distraction would reveal their concealed positions to Nic Smith. After a short while the radio went dead - but Warrant Officer Timitiya came on the air to say that the Lieutenant had been hit. The din of rifle fire was so loud that he had difficulty in hearing our transmissions. When he pressed the transmit button (to speak to us), we could actually hear the rifle fire in our earphones. He asked us to "wait one" but shortly thereafter all contact was lost with Timitiya. It was during this lull in the battle that an AK 47 slug hit Provost 308.

I was circling the gook fortification when my port wing opened up right before my eyes. The bullet then struck my side of the canopy, just behind my head, and rattled itself to a standstill inside the cockpit - fortunately without striking either my pupil pilot or myself. On being hit, I banked sharply to starboard. Beaver meanwhile thought that I had been shot and was trying to wrest control during my violent air manoeuvres. I, simultaneously, thought that he had been hit. When we both realised we were okay; we regained our senses and then directed our attention to checking out the aircraft for any other obvious signs of damage. I might add that when one is on the receiving end of ground to air fire, it sounds exactly like the noise of sticking your finger into a fast rotating fan. The tat-tat-rat-a-tat-tat sound of automatic gunfire can be very unnerving. By now our radios had gone dead and we had lost all contact with Nic Smith. As we were nearing the end of our endurance, we called for Chris Weinmann to relieve us in order to have the aircraft checked out. My concern was that our fuel tank in the port wing had been holed. As the relief Provost passed us, we gave them the contact grid-reference and Dimities' call-sign. Five BTs/CTs were killed in this contact with the RAR.

In the interim, heavy air power was called for. It was round about this time that a major jet airstrike was called for against a base camp with 50 terrorists, along the Tegwani River. Canberras from No 5 Squadron, New Sarum, and a pair of Hunters from No 1 Squadron, Thornhill, were instructed to keep a wide berth from our own troop positions. Safety distances were increased to 1000 metres for the Canberras, led by Nobby Nightingale / Berni Vaughan and Rikki Culpan / Polly Postance to drop their 96 fragmentation bombs, and the Hunters to fire their 30mm cannon. However, the gooks had moved more slowly than had been expected and so the airstrike was not successful. At least the sub-sonic noise of the Hunters alone would have frightened the daylights out of the gooks.

On landing, our techs checked out my aircraft, confirmed no vital organs damaged, and applied several strips of masking tape over the bullet holes as a temporary measure. Once refuelled, I set off again and proceeded to the contact scene. By now it was late afternoon. We were saddened to hear that both Lieutenant Nic Smith and Warrant Officer Class II Timitiya had been killed. We made radio contact with Lieutenant Ken Pierson who was in charge of the stop groups and had all his units strung out along the Nata River to ambush the fleeing gooks. Claymore mines were placed at likely river crossing points and his units were spread out at about 100-yard intervals. We remained in the area as long as we could, to relay messages between all the army units. Our last contact with Ken, whom I knew personally, was asking him to give the gooks stick, to avenge the earlier loss of our two well-respected Army colleagues Smith and Timitia. We logged two and a half-hours, of which 1 hour 30 minutes was night/actual instrument flying. I did not realise it at that time, but my conversation with Ken would be the last. I was more concerned with another late night landing back at base - finding Main Camp without the benefits of the glow that a built up area gives a pilot.

However, during the early hours of the morning, at 01h30 comms were established between the stop groups and the Army Sunray Major (the most senior Army officer in charge). An urgent casevac request was received at the FAF. My fellow 16 PTC course member Chris Dixon was tasked with this duty which entailed making a night flight of about 40 miles over the inhospitable country. Chris handled the hazard of landing and taking off in a small badly lit landing zone and carried out the evacuation successfully, delivering two casualties to hospital.

By now, PRAW pilot Peter Scales from Bulawayo had joined us. He was to be employed in Army co-operation, Telstar and casevac roles.

Early next morning, on 23rd August, I took off before dawn, with Pilot Officer Derrick Rainey. We flew ten minutes in darkness, in order to arrive over the Nata River at first light. It was then that we heard the dreadful news - Ken Pierson had been shot the night before. Our total flight time for this operational mission was a lengthy three hours fifty minutes - maximum endurance for this type of flying. It was primarily to piece together the events leading up to the loss of two commissioned officers and a Warrant Officer - a loss the highly successful RAR could ill afford. It was established that Timitiya had been shot in the head, when it became exposed between the forks of a tree. This was whilst transmitting on the army field radio which he had taken off his dead lieutenant Nic Smith. Ken Pierson had then also been shot, apparently by one of his own ambush units, while responding to a flanking manoeuvre by the gooks trying to break through the ambush line. When the firing had broken out in the dead of night, Ken went crashing through the dense scrub and had been mistaken for a terrorist. Terrorist casualties were one BT captured and the gang leader wounded/captured. Derrick Rainey assisted me in relaying the news to Sunray Major - the Brigade Major at Battalion field headquarters. The early morning start had been both tiring and demoralising. Little did I realise that another three sorties lay ahead that day - with another night landing at a strange airfield.

No sooner had I landed, than I was required to get airborne again, this time in Provost 304 (in order to effect more permanent repairs to my holed faithful 308). My co-pilot for this rather short Telstar mission was the other OCU student, Acting Pilot Officer Brian Penton. It started to appear that I was doing all the flying, and with the other squadron pilots coming along with me for the ride. In all honesty, in retrospect I doubt it - because all this bush experience would stand everybody in good stead for the years ahead. Anyway, nothing much came from this sortie, except perhaps an assurance to the ground forces of continued air support, and an opportunity to regroup after the hectic events of the preceding 48 hours. We did what we had to do and landed after a rather brief hour forty minutes. By late afternoon, we were scrambled to Tjolotjo, in order to be closer to the action.

Tjolotjo

I remember well how Police Reserve Air Wing pilot Peter Scales and I had a bet as to who would get to Tjolotjo first, and also before nightfall. Scales was airborne before I even started the Leonides engine. However, with Rich beside me, I pointed out the advantage of height or speed for air-to-air manoeuvres. I adopted a powered climb to gain height and then settled into a high-speed shallow dive to catch up with Scales who was making a tree-hopping beeline towards our next forward airfield. We had no sooner overtaken the PRAW aircraft, when Rich Beaver pointed out that his front gun cover was held closed by only one Dzus fastener. The gun cover was hinged at the back and whereas it was normally fastened by a series of screws around the sides and leading edge. With only one screw holding the flap closed, we would have great difficulty in maintaining straight and level flight. The aircraft would go into a spiral dive should the loose gun cover fly open - especially at high speed - which we were doing when we passed Peter Scales. I had no option to pull out of the race, convert speed to a safe height, throttle back and crawl along at near stalling speed. In our haste to get airborne, we had literally 'kicked the tyres and lit the fires', not waiting for the armourer to properly cock our guns and button up the gun covers. The end result was that we were the last to arrive, limping in ten minutes after nightfall. Not only was that was a close shave, but a lost bet as well.

We were in the process of settling into our new surroundings when the call came that there was another contact with the gooks. I again volunteered to do his duty and prepared for another late night take-off. Derrick Rainey volunteered to come along for this Telstar sortie. When we got to the contact area we learned that Corporal Cosmas from 1 RAR had been shot and killed and that Patrol Officer S Thomas had also been killed in action. Patrol Officer Thomas was from the British South African Police Dog Unit. August 23rd had been a long day, four sorties, nearly eight hours flying, airborne before dawn, new airfield, two night landings, two Security Force dead and only one gook leader captured/wounded.

On August 24th, I was given a break with only one late afternoon/night armed recce/telstar mission, with Brian Penton, and favoured Old Faithful - Provost 308. 308 was then flown back to Thornhill the next day for major servicing and repair. It had served the war effort well. I still had more work to do. On the 26th I flew with my preferred student pilot Rich Beaver and the next day with Brian, on armed reconnaissance and Telstar sorties. This pattern of alternating the students continued for the next three days. On the 28th and the 30th, a total of seven gooks were accounted for. Feedback was received that the gooks were taking Sangoma Muti that made them immune to SF weaponry. On 30th August I flew two sorties with Richard, and the Security Forces, with our assistance, bagged four BT killed and one captured.

Later that afternoon the terrorists were waiting in ambush and at 17h15 they attacked, pinning the security forces down. The fight that developed against 1 RAR was carried out at extremely close quarters, and lasted more than an hour before the gooks withdrew. During this contact movement of the ground forces in the area was directed by No 7 Squadron helicopter, piloted by Mick Grier. The gunner directed his fire onto the gooks strong defensive position, about 30 metres away. The helicopter came under determined fire from the ground.

On 1st and 2nd September 1967, I then flew with Flight Lieutenant Sos Nederlof and Flying Officer Harold Griffiths - one BT was captured on the second sortie.

My second sortie on the 2nd, with Rich Beaver, accounted for another six terrorists captured. On 4th September, three were killed. I did not fly on the 5th. The armed reconnaissance sorties on the last two days were flown solo. On the 6th, a soldier of 1 RAR was killed. His death was avenged the next day, however, when a further 14 terrorists were accounted for.

**The Nickel Cross
Medal Presentation**

That night, the Bluejobs celebrated with their Brownjob and Bailiff (BSAP) counterparts. Inter-Service co-operation and respect for one another was greatly enhanced. We had all of us, worked together as a team. Our air superiority was valued by the ground forces, especially the vital role of Telstar radio relay when the sticks in remote areas were able to get the most up-to-date intelligence, and the command centres were kept informed of situation reports on the ground.

Only one of the original group of 94 terrorists managed to reach South Africa, and he was caught later. Those taken prisoner were in bad shape. The official report said, "The incessant harrying by the Security Forces had forced them to abandon some of their equipment. They had been suffering from lack of food and water. They were completely disillusioned about the situation in Rhodesia, having been led to believe that they would not meet strong opposition. Another surprise for them was the fact that local tribesmen refused to help them". It was later, much later, established that an escapee named Graham Mashiko had claimed that he was part of the ANC "Wankie Regiment" who was present at the Tanzanian Morogoro conference. Mashiko tabled an agenda item stating that the ANC MK terrorists had become disenchanted fighting their way through Rhodesia to get to South Africa. Socialist Alfred Nzo was elected as the Secretary General at the Morogoro Conference (he was destined to become Nelson Mandela's Minister of Foreign Affairs). Nzo had solicited Soviet aid. Russia also supported ZAPU and their armed wing ZIPRA. The ANC/MK's strategy to "fight Ian Smith's soldiers" en route to SA disillusioned the terrorists because they did not expect the Rhodesians to be so swift in mopping up Operation *Nickel*. At Nzo's funeral in January 2000, Mashiko appeared on SATV and stated that he, with the likes of a Chris Hani and Leonard Nkosi, were known as the "Wankie Cadres" that accompanied the ZAPU/ZIPRA infiltration. John Dube was one of the 'main manne'. Mjojo Mxwaku commanded the Luthuli Detachment (that included Thula Bopela and Daluxolo Luthuli – see their war story *Umkhonto we Sizwe)*. According to the latter, the entire Lupane Detachment was wiped out at the

Battle of Inyantue.

Operation *Nickel* had accounted for no fewer than 67 terrorists. Casualties were: -
33 terrorists killed (12 ZAPU and 20 SAANC)
34 terrorists captured
8 security force members killed
About 12 SF wounded

Captured Terrorist Weapons

Remembering that the Makuti Operation *Isotope* had also bagged 14 gooks, the total stood at 81 terrorists for the loss of eight Security Force - a ratio of ten gooks for every security force member killed. As a result of the Security Force casualties, the captured terrorists were tried for murder and for carrying weapons of war, which under the Law and Order (Maintenance) Act carried the death penalty. Seven of the prisoners were convicted on both counts and sentenced to be hanged. (Input is acknowledged from Beryl Salt's *"A Pride of Eagles"* with thanks to my Boss at that time - Peter D Cooke).

Major Terry Hammond, on behalf of the ground forces, made a surprise presentation to me of the Nickel Cross, expertly made by the Army Engineers, from a "condensed milk blikkie". A ribbon of sorts was fashioned from a colourful piece of cloth and the 'medal' duly presented to me at a fairly sombre gathering of really good combatants. I was honoured, and certainly humbled, by this token of appreciation.

It is this event which convinced me that the title of this story is in no small measure dedicated to those who sacrificed their lives for their country. For me, the real heroes of this operation had been Warrant Officers Timitiya and Korb, and police Inspector Phillips. I also regret losing good friends in Ken Pierson and Nic Smith.

Lieutenant Ian Wardle had returned to 1 RAR base after his phenomenal follow up operation through the Wankie National Park; he was awarded the Bronze Cross of Rhodesia for his gallantry. Ian subsequently joined the SAS in 1969; and eventually left the Rhodesian Army to fight in the Middle East. Although I treasure my award of the unique "Nickel Cross" by 1 RAR, I was disappointed that recognition for the deeds of Sergeant Major Korb and Warrant Officer Timitiya were not given due appreciation.

On 8th September 1967, I took off from Tjolotjo, made a wide circular turn, dived down on the spectators for a low level pass, followed by a victory roll salute and headed for Thornhill. Sometime later, I believe it was on the 24th, I learned Private Nyika of 1 RAR lost his life as a result of gunshot wounds.

In retrospect, ZIPRA made a political blunder when they infiltrated with the South African ANC (African National Congress), because Pretoria dispatched 2 000 'riot policemen' and SAAF helicopters (in the guise of non-existent SAP helicopters) to strengthen Rhodesia's security. They became more involved from the following year and were to stay patrolling the Valley until 1975. An extract from Ken Flower's *"Serving Secretly"* mentions that the Rhodesian military commanders initially declined General van den Bergh's (Head of BOSS - Bureau of State Security) offer of a detachment of South African 'Riot Police' as unnecessary. He goes on, and I quote: -

"South African aid, whether 'police' or 'military' proved a mixed blessing, politically and militarily. On the political front it gave Vorster the advantage because his offer had been unsolicited, and he later used this advantage when twisting Smith's arm over settlement by threatening to withdraw South African contingents after they had become part of Rhodesia's joint defence system. On the military front, *the South African units were a liability initially*. The riot police had received their training in an urban context and were thus totally inexperienced in the hazards of bush warfare; the Rhodesian Forces had to operate as 'long stop' to the South Africans in order to plug a gap in the overall defences. This was necessary despite the efforts of the South Africans' outstanding Commander, Major-General Pat Dillon who, with his own vast experience in Africa, realised only too well that it would take some time to get his men trained and experienced in counter-insurgency. Ultimately, the involvement of South African units in Rhodesia's war was of no more use to South Africa than Rhodesia in that South Africa *used* Rhodesia as a training ground, withdrawing units as they became trained and replacing them with untrained ones."

In Peter Stiff's The Silent War, he also referred to Operation *Nickel* as "this major action". He commented on liaisons between General van den Bergh and Ken Flower, and the South African Defence Force's fury that Van den Bergh had used his influence to get Vorster to send 'riot police' instead of soldiers to Rhodesia to patrol the border with hostile Zambia.

Volunteer Reservist, Corporal Ian Dixon was one of six Salisbury based 106 (Air Movements) Squadron members who were called up in support of Operation *Nickel*. He related an interesting side of 'air movements' loading up to nine Dakotas a day at Tjolotjo. The poor fellow was berated for his apparent disregard for 'rank' by an Army Lieutenant whilst loading one particular Dakota. His side of the story, quoted verbatim, reads as follows: -

"To be a member of the Volunteer Reserve meant membership of a very select club. It took me from Operation *Nickel* in 1967, to hob nobbing with the British in 1980. In retrospect it was an epoch of high drama, with many personal highlights, here are a few of them. In August 1967 elements of 106 flew to Nyamandhlovu (writers note – I believe he meant Tjolotjo) to set up a forward airfield, where they could hump and heave (which was their wont). At that time, the Rhodesian Army were heavily engaged in chasing a large group of terrs, made up of equal numbers of ZAPU, and ANC cadres, totalling 80 men around Western Matabeleland.

"Anyway, it was against this dramatic background that six worthies from 106 struggled to contribute their own pennyworth. It was hot as the hobs, and we were turning around nine Dakotas a day, which meant the daily humping, and heaving, of 54 tons of dead weight. Though none of us were in our prime, we did it. Being a very democratic bunch, and personal friends, rank did not rate high in our reckoning (except when the regulars were around). We devised our own loading schemes, which were why an SAC could be in charge of a loading detail consisting of a Pilot Officer, WO II, Flight Sergeant, and a Corporal. In other words, everyone had a chance to be "in charge".

"On the day of which I write I was supervising the loading. Sporting the dizzy rank of Corporal, my "gang" consisted of a Pilot Officer, a WOII, a Flight Sergeant and an SAC. I was giving them stick, as we were racing against the clock (as usual). Because he was not pulling his weight, I told the Pilot Officer. "Pull your bloody finger out, this isn't a Granny's tea party. Get the lead out, you bloody spastic." I looked up to see a young Army lieutenant standing in the doorway and said to him, "Can I help you, Sir?" He replied, "Yes, Corporal, can we talk outside?" Yelling at the gang to hurry up, I told them I would expect everything aboard to be properly lashed when I returned. Wiping the sweat from my brow, I walked up to the Army standing under the wing, saying "Sir?"

"His response was unexpected. I was called to "Attention" and responded instinctively. The Army then stuck its face into mine, saying, "What the bloody hell do you think you are doing Corporal?". My reply was, "Why loading the aircraft, Sir .", which seemed to incense him more. It was then that daylight dawned, as he started to berate me. "How dare you speak to an officer without respect. You will not do so in the presence of my soldiers. It undermines good conduct. I am going to put you on a charge." I had clearly outraged his sense of discipline.

"Unfortunately, I was tongue-tied which only made the Army more vocal. He was turning very red, and going mad bawling me out. The uproar attracted the attention of my loading gang, who were intrigued by my dressing down. When the Army had run out of breath, the Pilot Officer in my gang addressed him, saying, "Lieutenant, leave my bloody Corporal alone. He knows what he is doing, which is probably, more than anyone can say about you. Leave us now and go and clean your boots, or whatever it is that the Army does."

"The Lieutenant was thunderstruck. Turning about, he walked away shouting, at the top of his voice, "Bloody Air Force. Bloody Air Force. What a bloody Circus." - Such then, Sir, were the men of 106."

Another infiltration occurred in northern Matabeleland around September 21st to 30th – but this gang was rounded up within a matter of days. The terrorist presence was discovered when a herdsman, searching for his lost cattle, sighted a terrorist digging a hole miles from the nearest habitation. The herdsman reported his find to the village elders, who in turn notified the police. By now the hole had been covered up, and whilst the locals were waiting for the police to arrive, automatic gunfire rang out and the poor kraalhead was fatally wounded. When the police arrived on the scene they found a note pinned to the body, threatening death to tribesmen who became police informers. The note and a number of expended cartridges of Russian origin confirmed that a gang of three terrorists had committed the cold-blooded murder. Units of the Air Force, Army and Police were brought in.

On 22nd September the trackers were on the spoor of the three retreating terrorists. The tracks initially moved in a westerly direction, then swung in an arc of some fifteen miles, and then took a southerly direction – indicating that the fugitives were taking steps to cover their tracks. After a day and a half on the trail, the trackers were 24 hours behind, and by now a fourth terrorist had joined the group. A little further on, a further two tracks now joined the four. Then on 24th September, after excellent tracking over thirty miles, the tracks were lost. The Air Force had continually supplied and supported the follow-up troops during the whole tracking task. Then on 25th September a tribesman came forward to admit that he had visited the terrorists' camp on the same afternoon, and led the police patrol to the site. The camp consisted of seven holes in the ground. All but two of them had been filled in. The holes were extremely well camouflaged. One was a round hole about 2ft 6ins deep with a diameter of some 6 feet, and the other was rectangular, two feet deep and about six feet long. Both were covered with branches and thatch – and such was the degree of concealment that one of the holes was discovered before the informant's indication, when one of the police details actually standing on the roof remarked that the ground beneath him was more resistant than the surrounding soil. The only equipment left at the camp was a few cooking pots.

The local who had led the Security Forces to the camp indicated that a gang of six terrorists had been active in the area. They had initiated a programme of indoctrination of the local people, had extracted food and supplies from them, and had made efforts to increase the size of the gang with local recruits.

On the same afternoon, 25th September, information was received of the possibility that two of the gang were in the vicinity of a kraal some fifty miles from the original area. A CID team, with Army support, responded – but found the kraal deserted. However, within minutes of the team's arrival two terrorists walked into the kraal, one of them carrying a PPSH sub-machine gun. On being challenged, the armed terrorist surrendered immediately, but the other made off in a desperate bid for freedom. He was wounded low in the body. When searched, he was found to have a primed grenade in his pocket. His companion was likewise found to be carrying two grenades and two magazines of ammunition for his weapon; an SKS Siminov carbine was retrieved from the bush. Two more grenades were found in the same place. Following the capture of these two terrorists and with information gathered from local tribesmen, some pattern of the gang's activities emerged.

The group had originally numbered eight men who had been trained in Algeria, had infiltrated from Zambia and had been in Rhodesia for some time. Their mission had been to carry out a recruiting and training programme among the locals before moving on to bigger things. The original leader of the gang and another terrorist had been arrested after the latter accidentally shot himself through the shoulder and they had travelled to Bulawayo in search of help. The other was arrested in Salisbury. Another member of the remaining six had assumed the leadership, and two locals had been recruited to restore the gang to its original strength of eight. The two newcomers had been armed with the weapons left behind by the two who had been captured. The two terrorists arrested entering the kraal at dawn were original members who had been operating apart from the remainder. This accounted for the distance between the two spheres of activity.

The new leader of the gang had decided that the group should be further split into two groups of three. Each trio consisted of two founder members with a new recruit. It was deduced that it was the leader's team which had been responsible for the murder of the kraalhead following the herdsman's report that he had seen an African (the leader, as it transpired) digging the hole. This was the first stage in the construction of another terrorist underground camp – and weapons cache. The amount of information obtained by the arrest of the two terrorists was considerable due to the fact that, after the murder, the gang leader had picked up the other three members of the splinter group and had then trekked with them to the kraal where he had explained the latest developments to the remaining two. He had warned them to lie low where they were but also gave them some indications of his own future plans.

His idea was that the other six should travel south far beyond the present area of suspicion where they would attack an isolated farm to obtain food and money. As the Security Forces switched to the area of the proposed attack and were withdrawn from the gang's original base area, the group would backtrack to their former well-prepared and well-equipped hunting ground. There they would lie up, until the heat was off. The fact that the terrorist leader had covered some ninety miles in the three days following the murder in order to warn the detached pair, had picked up the other section of the gang in his travels and had also successfully covered the tracks of the party, gave an indication of the calibre of this cadre.

This then was the position on the morning of 26th September 1967. Then on the following day, a large cache of equipment was found in the vicinity of the murder. In a large tin, sunk in concrete, were found considerable amounts of ammunition, seven blocks of TNT and a quantity of subversive literature. The early hours of 28th September brought another breakthrough. The father of one of the local recruits reported that his son had deserted the gang and had returned to his kraal. He was arrested just after dawn in possession of an SKS carbine and ammunition. It was significant that this man made no attempt to evade arrest. He indicated the spot at which he had left his companion, a founder member, when he entered the kraal in search of food. At this spot was found another SKS rifle, two grenades and ammunition. Unbeknown to the Security Forces, the founder member witnessed the recovery of his weapon – he remained in hiding overnight and surrendered to a passing police vehicle.

The score by now was four down and four to go. The outstanding members of the gang were its leader, two of the original group, and the remaining local recruit.

The local recruit was arrested in circumstances similar to those resulting in the capture of the first recruit – he simply walked into his father's kraal, and into the arms of the law. His SKS was quickly located. The capture was tired and hungry.

It was obvious by now that the remaining trio were desperate for food. With this in mind, all points at which the fugitives might seek food were ambushed. During the night of 29th/30th September, the leader walked into an ambush around one of the kraals, while his mates remained hidden. But the net was closing and the outstanding terrorists were rounded up by midday the following morning. In the interim, the terrorist leader pointed out a remaining cache consisting of a 44-gallon drum containing ammunition, explosives and an assortment of other equipment. An added bonus was the recovery of the leader's PPSH sub-machine gun. The hunt was over. All members of this gang and their weapons were accounted for – four PPSH sub-machine guns, five SKS carbines, fourteen grenades, hundreds of rounds of ammunition and explosives. There remained only the formalities of the murder investigation to be completed.

The notebook from which pages had been torn to provide warnings found on the kraal head's body was recovered in the possession of one of the terrorists, the stubs were matched with the notes and a handwriting comparison positively proved his complicity. The murder weapon was identified by ballistics examination and it was found that the same weapon had fired all the shots at the scene of the murder.

The final chapter was enacted in the Bulawayo High Court where three of the gang were sentenced to death. The remainder of the gang received long terms of imprisonment for being accessories after the fact to murder and for possession of offensive weapons and material. In an earlier hearing, seventeen tribesmen who had given assistance and received training from the gang were convicted and imprisoned.

At the conclusion of the case, the Judge commended the Security Forces generally and the investigating team for the high standard of conduct of the operation. It had been a successful operation, exemplifying the finest standard of command, control and close co-operation between the Police, Army and Air Force – throughout all levels of personnel.

Operation Chinaman: September to November 1967

Operation *Nickel* promptly brought the South African Police assistance to the aid of the Rhodesians. Cessna 185 aircraft and crews, together with a couple of Alouette helicopters, ably supported the SAP. The operation was named *Chinaman*, and it initially comprised elements from 42 Army Air Reconnaissance Squadron, Potchefstroom. Seven Cessna's and their crews assembled in Pretoria on 1st September 1967, where the crews were sworn in as members of the SAP and briefed about their duties in Rhodesia; which entailed performing early morning and late evening visual reconnaissance flights along the Botswana and Zambian borders.

They left Swartkop for Gwelo on 6th September, but flew into low cloud and rain en route and were forced to divert into West Nicholson to wait until the weather improved. Once they arrived at Thornhill, with ATC radar guidance, they were issued with Rhodesian kit and briefed on RRAF operational procedures. The Cessna's were code-named *Kiewiets* by the Rhodesians, to facilitate easy ground-to-air communications and telstar identification. The seven pilots were Major Fred Potgieter, Captain Karel van Heerden , and Lieutenants Tony Geldenhuys, Kon van Heyningen, Burrie Barnard, Jas Crous and Ryno du Toit. They stayed at Thornhill until the 9th when they were deployed to the forward areas.

Operations Pyramid, Ermine and Overtone: 10 September to 24 October 1967

Operation *Pyramid* officially commenced on 1st September 1967, and lasted to 10th. Two of the Cessna's of Operation *Chinaman* left Thornhill on the 9th and were deployed to the FAF1 Wankie area – to service the SAP Camp established at Sprayview, Victoria Falls. Major Fred Potgieter did not remain long in Rhodesia – he only went along to see that everything went smoothly, as well as to ferry one of the Cessna's as a reserve aircraft – and returned to South Africa.

Operation *Ermine*, which took over from Pyramid, lasted up to 25th September 1967, was supplemented by a third Kiewiet, when several smaller groups of terrorists tried to infiltrate into Rhodesia (but without success). Reconnaissance sorties were flown in the Wankie area, mainly in support of SA Police and Rhodesian Army patrols along the Zambia border.

Operation *Overtone* lasted from 15th to 24th October – again in the Wankie area. Two Kiewiets were allocated for aerial reconnaissance.

Operation Jezebel – Kariba: 31 October 1967

One of the Kiewiets ex Ops *Pyramid / Ermine* was deployed from the Wankie area to the FAF 2 Kariba area for Operation *Jezebel* that lasted to 31st October 1967.

Operations Robust, Daffodil and Meltone: 2 to 23 November 1967

These three SAP operations all occurred in the Kariba area, Robust and Daffodil with the Jezebel Kiewiet, from 2nd to 8th and 10th to 21st November, respectively. Meltone differed only in that it was supported by the addition of another two Cessna's from the Wankie area – in the fight against terrorists. The South African operations are indicative of the sterling work carried out by these unsung heroes who came to our aid when the rest of the world was increasingly applying pressure by way of sanctions on a small country who dared challenge big bully Britain.

In his excellent pictorial research work *"Rhodesian Air Force – The Sanction Busters"*, with foreword by Air Vice-Marshal Chris Dams, author Winston Brent has gone to fascinating lengths to expose the intrigue of the work done by those who "busted" sanctions.

Operation Bonfire: 23 November 1967

This was an internal COIN operation by SAS and RLI against a group of nine ZANU insurgents, targeted over a wide area stretching from Mana Pools, Mtoko and Inyanga. The whole group was eliminated. Prior to this, on 24th May, the SAP had found terrorist equipment stashed on the Rhodesian bank of the Zambezi River, opposite Lusitu Boma in Zambia, about 8 km south of Chirundu. This subsequently resulted in a SAS contact with ZAPU at grid ref PN 993156 on 19th November 1967.

Operation Cauldron: 18 to 31 March 1968

On 18th March 1968 I was tasked to fly to Salisbury for an airstrike briefing on Operation *Cauldron* which had been mounted to counter a large insurgent infiltration across the Zambezi River. "A" Troop of the RLI and a platoon of the RAR had made contact at close range with a large and well armed terrorist gang numbering over sixty men. My Vampire aircraft was armed with 60lb squashhead rockets and 20mm HEI shells.

The Vampire strike was due to follow the Canberras', but because of a delayed Canberra departure the Vampire air strike went in ahead of them. Flight Lieutenant Mark McLean marked the target with white phosphorus grenades but foolishly flew his Alouette right over the target. In three attacks I fired off 3 x 60lb three-inch rockets together with 151 x 20mm HEI, thanks to the excellent FAC target marking. Squadron Leader Bill Jelley who was flying the second Vampire was also able to conduct a successful air strike. We then returned to base to re-arm and develop the air-to-ground cine film.

In the interim, our Canberras unwittingly dropped a bomb box load of 96 x 20lb fragmentation bombs on the RLI men of Army Captain Chris (Dumpie) Pearce who had manoeuvred themselves around a river bed in order to catch part of the action. As a result thereof, the remainder of the airstrike was called off because bomb shrapnel wounded several ground troops. Not so fortunate were RLI Trooper E Ridge and 1 RAR Corporal Erisha who were killed in action from gunshot wounds during a contact.

I will always remember that the Vampires were spot on target. Both Boss Jelley and I had fired at exactly the same spot - when we viewed the films which our gyro-gunsight cameras had taken the identical large baobab tree featured in the top right hand corners of the film frames. In fact, the two separate films shot from the different aircraft were "as near as dammit" identical. The actual target was heavily wooded, mainly with Mopani trees, which gave excellent cover to the terrorists. However, after the first couple of squash-head rockets had been right on target, and the subsequent spraying by high explosive incendiary cannon, the bush was reduced to a wasteland. I guess the CT's must have been somewhat demoralised by all the devastating air-power being thrown at them.

The next day, on 19th March, the Rhodesian Herald ran the "*Air Force In Zambezi Action*" headline. The Communiqué stated, "One member of the security forces has been killed and two wounded. There have been other "minor injuries". No official details have been released about the number of terrorists who crossed into Rhodesia or when and where they exchanged fire with the security forces. Two communiqués were issued yesterday by security forces headquarters through the Information Department, the first at midday, and the second at 10 p.m. From the second it became clear that the security forces had, with co-operation from the RRAF, successfully maintained contact with the terrorists. The midday communiqué read: "There has been an infiltration of terrorists from Zambia and security forces are now in contact with them. Early reports indicate that so far nine terrorists have been killed, one wounded and others captured. One member of the security forces has been killed and two wounded. The next-of-kin have been informed. Security forces are pursuing the remainder of the terrorists."

Then shortly after 10 p.m. last night it was announced that: - 'Since the last communiqué was issued today the security forces have continued in pursuit of the terrorists. Two more terrorists have been killed. Our security forces suffered only minor injuries. It has now confirmed that a total of eleven terrorists have been killed and additional terrorists have been captured. During the course of the day air strikes were mounted on the terrorists by the Royal Rhodesian Air Force in conjunction with ground forces."

"The names of the security men killed and wounded have not been announced. The first details the Rhodesian public received came from the Rhodesian Broadcasting Corporation, which relayed the South African Broadcasting Corporation's news at 8 a.m. yesterday. During fighting in Matabeleland in August and "mopping up" operations the following month, 31 terrorists were reported killed. Losses to the security forces were given as seven – two Europeans and five Africans. At the beginning of January, one terrorist was shot and an unspecified number captured by patrols in the Zambezi Valley. The security forces suffered no casualties.

From Luanda the Herald Africa News Service reports that that in the Lumai area, opposite the Zambian border, terrorists recently attacked a number of Angolan villages and killed 15 people and took one prisoner.

In the Zala area, to the north, two farm workers were killed, 10 wounded and 40 missing after terrorist attacks in the area. The Portuguese security forces have destroyed seven terrorist camps in the Bembe area in north-eastern Angola and have captured a number of canoes and boats carrying explosives and weapons.

The August action referred to was Operation *Nickel*. The next day, 20th March, the Rhodesian Herald ran an article on the RLI troopie who was killed – 19-year-old Eric Ridge – a nephew of the Secretary for Defence E Trollip, and an ex Plumtree schoolboy. The paper also ran another article, titled: - "*Second soldier is killed - Now 14 Terrorists Dead*"

"A second Rhodesian soldier has been killed in action and three more terrorist infiltrators, Security Forces headquarters announced in Salisbury last night. The soldier was named as Corporal Elishe of the Rhodesian African Rifles. The total of reported terrorist casualties is now 14 dead and one wounded. On Monday an unspecified number was said to have been captured. The communiqué said Rhodesian troops continued in pursuit of the terrorists yesterday. More terrorists had been captured and a quantity of arms, ammunition and equipment of Communist origin seized. Local Africans had helped capture some of the infiltrators. It was reported that members of the banned African National Congress of South Africa were included in the terrorist group, it added. Operations were continuing."

"The name of the first soldier killed was released yesterday by Security Forces Headquarters through the Ministry of Information as Trooper Eric Noel Francis Ridge of the Rhodesian Light Infantry. Two have been wounded and others received minor injuries. It is the second time that the Rhodesian Air Force has made air strikes in the anti-terrorist campaign. The first reported occasion was when RRAF planes strafed a gang in western Matabeleland in August, the last confirmed major clash with infiltrators.

The Herald London Bureau reports Patrick Keatley, Commonwealth correspondent of the Guardian, as writing that the latest guerrilla operation launched against Rhodesia from Zambian territory has been timed to coincide with the Special meeting of the United Nations Security Council.

The Commonwealth staff of the Times reporting on the crossing of infiltrators into Rhodesia from Zambia, said it was an indication that President Kaunda had relaxed the control on the border. It was not widely realised, the report said, that the President had been trying to minimise such infiltration. He had, however, been hampered by limited manpower, the length of the frontier and local sympathy."

On March 22nd and 23rd I flew a further two armed top cover sorties in support of the follow up ground troops. For days after the airstrike the Army call-signs located dead bodies - several terrorists who had bled to death, drowned in the rivers or become too much of a burden for the fleeing gang. In the running battle with the 125 terrorists that had infiltrated the country, sixty-nine were killed, and fifty were captured. Deputy Minister of Information Pieter (P K) van der Byl who had been choppered into the airstrike site reported to the media, that ". . there is blood everywhere". Fortunately, the Air Force did not make a big deal of an otherwise perfect airstrike.

The report in the Rhodesian Herald on 23rd March quoted PK, and was headlined - *"Air Strike Impresses Van Der Byl on Visit"*.

"The Deputy Minister of Information, Mr P K van der Byl, in a television interview in Salisbury yesterday described the scene of an air strike he visited in the Zambezi Valley on Thursday. He said he was most impressed. The success of the air strike was not apparent at the time it was made, but the area was limited in extent and explosions had taken place "right in the target area". "It was somewhat disappointing in that numerous corpses were not found," but there was clear evidence that a large number of terrorists – possibly six or seven – had been killed. "There was a tremendous amount of blood lying about – it was splattered all over the place and in some cases it was up to a height of 17 or 18 feet over a fairly extensive area." He was certain the terrorists had carried the dead with them when they withdrew. "There is no doubt that the strike was a success from every point of view." The terrorists were discovered when tracks were spotted by a man from the Game Department. He followed the tracks, saw the terrorists and reported to the Security Forces.

Mr. van der Byl said men from the Game Department were not used as a matter of course but had played extremely valuable supporting roles. He thought criticism of Government releases on terrorist activities in Rhodesia had been "entirely unwarranted". "The major consideration must be the welfare and the protection of the Security Forces. Simply to satisfy the natural curiosity of the public, we will not divulge information, which is going to be picked up by Lusaka and used by organisations, which are running these terrorist outfits to the detriment of our troops.

"I think the information coming forth is as good as it can be." – Iana.

Squadron Commander Bill Jelley had the foresight to keep all the news clippings, and these, together with other first-hand personal experiences, assisted in piecing the Operation *Cauldron* jigsaw puzzle together. The main Rhodesian Herald headline on 23rd March read as follows: - *"Bravery, Endurance, At 'Front'* - First-hand report from the forward areas - *"Our Troops Are Fit and Confident"*

"Behind the laconic communiqués listing the 18 terrorists killed and our own mercifully small number of casualties since the present engagement in the Zambezi Valley began, lies a story of bravery, endurance and co-operation between all branches of the Defence Forces for which Rhodesians have been waiting and of which they can be proud. I was able yesterday to visit one of the forward areas, talk freely with the men operating there and visit the scene of one of the major clashes. – By a Staff Reporter.

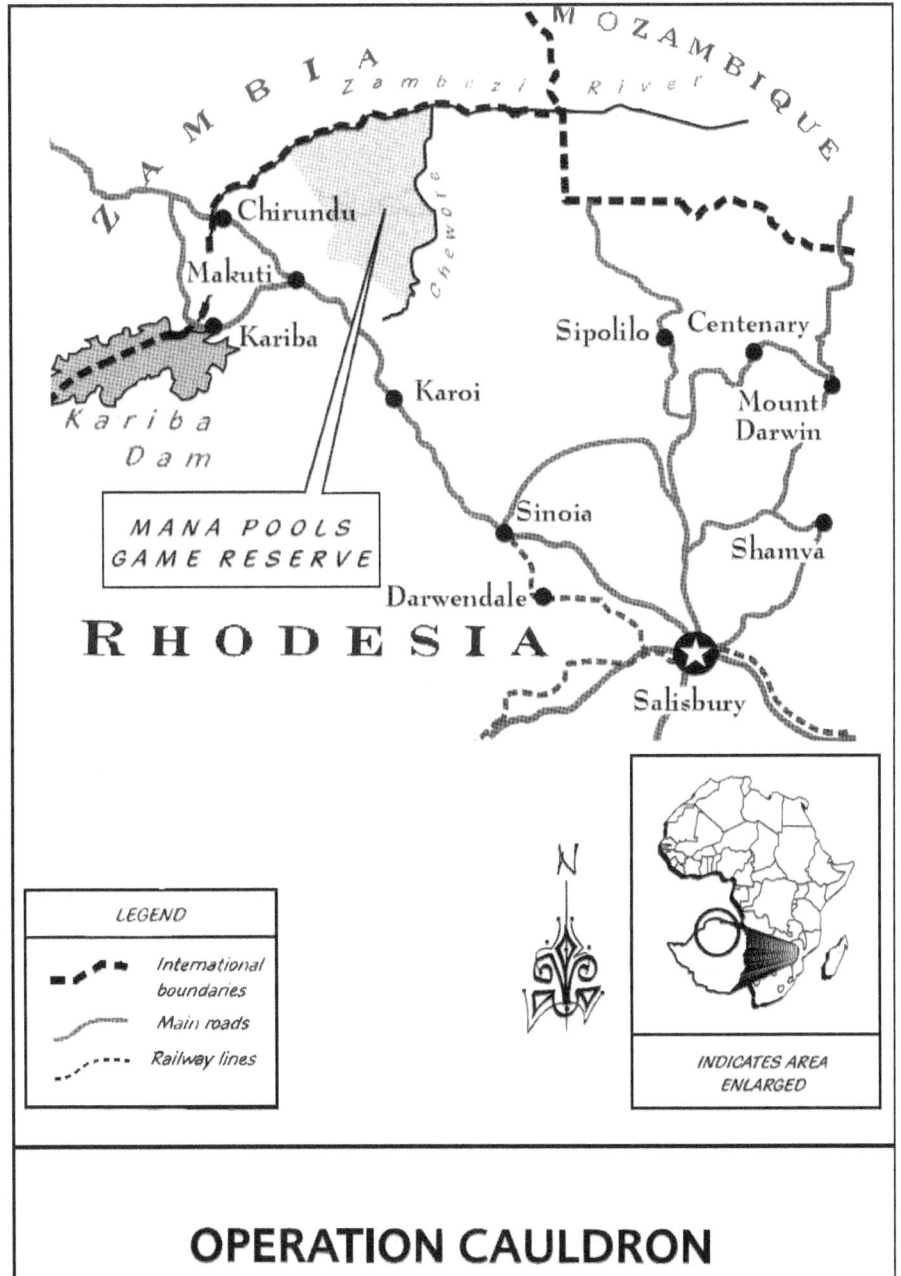

OPERATION CAULDRON

*Acknowledgement is gratefully made to Maryna Swarts,
Publisher/Editor of Covos Day Books, for permission granted to use
the Operation Cauldron map*

"The trip was organised by the Joint Operations Command and the Information Ministry. If some details are glossed over it is for the obvious reasons that information should not be published while the enemy is still guessing what we know and what we do not. By plane and jeep I was taken first to the advance Joint HQ and then by helicopter to some of the forward troops. They are fit, tails well up, and are supremely confident that they will catch and break up any other gangs that may venture into their "home paddock". The first clash of the present series appears to have been the most violent. A detachment of the Joint Services bumped into the gang they had been tracking through some of the most wicked patrolling country imaginable. The enemy was well established in a good defensive position, on top of a cliff, with open ground before them on the only practical line of approach, and gave as good as he got. The troops – mainly BSAP and RLI – called in the RRAF, who blasted the positions and after a further infantry attack dislodged the enemy. The remnants of that group are now being harried in the blocked areas. From all accounts those remnants are split up, becoming short on food and long on demoralisation. But the troops are having it impressed on them that even those remnants can be dangerous; theirs now is a definite "search and destroy" mission. The camp where this first action took place was one occupied by the gang after its crossing over the Zambezi from Zambia. It covered a couple of acres – the "quartermaster's stores", various bivvy areas, arms dumps and so on well spread out under the trees and bushes.

"The camp area has changed its character since that first fierce fight. Torn and bloodstained trees and bomb craters bear evidence to the accuracy and power of the RRAF. Back at Operational HQ are stores of arms, ammunition – many thousands of rounds – and equipment captured in this part of the Valley. Among the exhibits being kept for a Court's later notice are Chinese copies of Russian automatics and other arms; a weapon I was assured was a "bamboo bazooka" with its (non-bamboo) projectile; Russian TNT; Czech grenades; American incendiaries; piles of ammunition for the automatics; and a heap of "victory medals". Samples of captured rations showed a reasonable quartermaster staff. Rhodesian tinned foods and South African tinned fish – available in Zambia – were prominent. Captured ration books showed that the camp distribution of the packed rations and any game shot (rhinos were accounted for) was done regularly and methodically.

The terrorists carried good medical equipment, with modern drugs and dressings, including snakebite kits. Their transistor radios enabled them to keep in touch with world events and to milk broadcasts of useful information. This information was noted in a group "war diary". Also at Operational HQ was a prisoners' cage. The number of prisoners is a closely guarded secret – "keep the enemy guessing" – but I was assured on all hands that the casualty lists of enemy and Rhodesians are honest and above board. One of the prisoners, incidentally, was having a wound dressed by a medical orderly. So much for tales of barbaric treatment of our prisoners. Others were drinking soft drinks.

In the mortuary lay three bodies on which routine post-mortem examinations were about to be performed. Local opinion is that more bodies will soon arrive at the mortuary. Police dogs are now being used to seek bodies in the bush, and also to find any walking wounded. So the campaign goes on. Patrol, contact if you're lucky, kill or capture. The men are on top of their job, though the terrain would soon exhaust any but superbly fit and well-led troops. The patrols go out self-sufficient for a given number of days. (A more concentrated patrol reaction pack might be an advantage; a tired man cannot cope with the bulk that goes down easily in camp.) If a patrol bumps into the enemy it can readily be supplied from the air. Not only does the platoon soldier patrol. Drivers and others are eager not to be left permanently at HQ, and have been promised their chance to flush a terrorist. There is no hiding everyone's eagerness to be in and at 'em.

As you read this, young Rhodesians will be off into the bush. Tall trees growing close together, undergrowth and grass all hamper movement and visibility. Every tree or rock may hide a terrorist. Tsetse and mopani bees are a constant irritant. Only water is plentiful – a blessing which also widens the area in which the enemy must be sought. But if there are any enemy left in their area the men there – Air Force, Army and Police, with tracker dogs – will find them, despite the excellent cover from air as well as ground observation. Only the occasional buck and other game is available for the terrorist on the run, and they are thought to be becoming a bit chary at possibly giving away their positions by shooting for the pot. People are even scarcer than food, and those in and around the area are on our side. All ranks realise the importance of keeping them that way.

However, we subsequently learned that Professor Thompson from the BSAP forensic science laboratory analysed some of the apparent blood on the underside of leaves of the trees as mopani sap. The fact of the matter was that the terrorists took a proper 'stonking'. Although I flew only the three operational sorties (a total of five and a quarter hours air time), squadron morale was sky high.

Other "1" RLI killed in action casualties were Trooper C Wessels and Recruit R Brink on 26th March 1968. In addition Trooper M. Mullin of the SAS was killed on the same day in a gunshot accident. Two weeks later on 10th April Trooper M. Thornley of the RLI was killed in action as a result of gunshot wounds in a contact with the terrorists. The official losses totalled six Security Force personnel, for over one hundred terrorists killed.

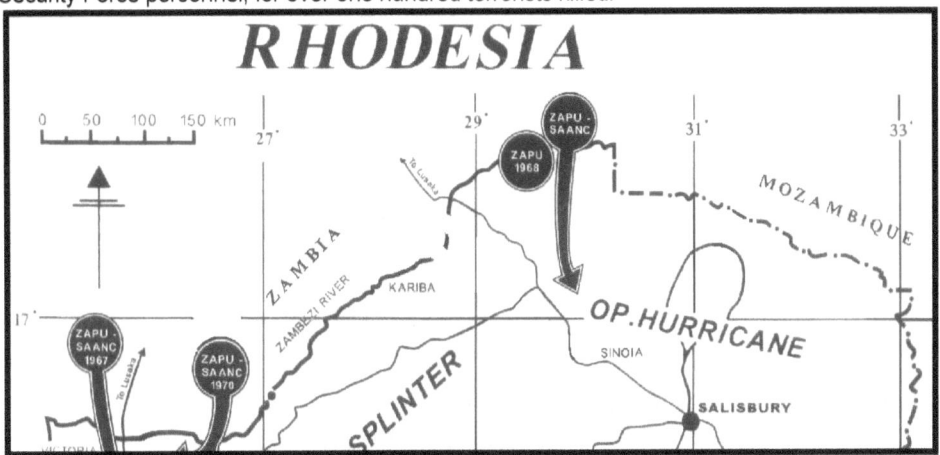

It transpired that the insurgents were trying out new tactics of using a supply line across the Zambezi River and forming a chain of well-stocked bases across the inhospitable valley floor during the rainy season. This was their biggest incursion to date, with the terrorists taking their time, planning carefully, moving by night, and confining themselves to the tribal areas where they could evade contact with white people. The route that they had chosen was in the remote Chewore area, where they had hoped to escape detection until they could climb the escarpment area. They intended to find refuge among tribesmen who would be better disposed to their cause than the people of the Valley, the nomadic Vadoma, who were feared (wrongly) as cannibals. Not only were their intimidatory tactics against the tribesmen merciless and effective, but they were also putting into effect their Marxist-Leninist psychological tactics, in which they had been well drilled. They were telling the locals that their plan was to take away all the good things from the white people and hand them over to the blacks. Simple people, who inhabit remote areas and have no comprehension of what is going on in the world around them, are easy targets for such tactics.

The terrorists established their main camp some eighty kilometres inside the country above the escarpment overlooking the Zambezi valley, in mountainous, well-wooded country, with much grass for additional cover. They established a number of underground dugouts, in which they lived and kept the equipment and arms that they were storing for attacks against the commercial farming areas lying further south. In spite of all their precautions, however, they should have realised that it was only a matter of time before they would be discovered.

But the temptation to supplement their rations by shooting for the pot after three months of portage led to their discovery by a perceptive Game Ranger who noticed a change in the pattern of animal movements. Upon investigation, the National Parks fellows found human tracks where none would have been expected. From his description of the unusual boot-print on the ground, it was soon identified as being of Chinese origin. This triggered the Security Forces to mount Operation *Cauldron*. Although the terrorists were well dug in and put up some resistance, they were rooted out. They had built up a considerable amount of equipment, arms, clothing and food, of both Russian and Chinese origin.

Despite our losses, Operation *Cauldron* was rated highly successful because it revealed new sophisticated Vietnam communist type planned tactics employed by well-trained insurgents. Their extensive arms caches and staging posts stretching from the Zambezi in a dead straight southerly route were indeed well planned. Back in Gwelo the School of Infantry named one of its most modern army training lecture halls 'Cauldron'. Also, in spite of denials from the British, Salisbury was satisfied as to the accuracy of the report from Lusaka that their High Commission had been aiding and abetting the terrorist cause with travel documents and finance.

The beauty of flying jets was that operational sorties were a case of 'strike - recover to base'. Unlike the chaps on Provosts and Alouette helicopters - they would deploy with the ground troops for weeks on end. I had the best of both worlds in that I flew Provosts on Operation *Nickel* and Vampires on Operation *Cauldron*. It was because these two operations were so effective that terrorist infiltrations took a nosedive after 1968. Operations Cardigan, Griffin and Mansion followed in quick succession and were of shorter duration.

On 10th April 1968, BSAP Field Reservist James Barker displayed brave and gallant conduct whilst part of a combined Security Force patrol engaged in anti-terrorist operations. They were ambushed and during the ensuing contact, an Army machine-gunner was severely wounded. Because of bursts of enemy fire, James was not able to recover the machinegun but did manage to extricate the wounded Brownjob gunner to safety. Whilst withdrawing, another policeman, Benjamin Marshall, was seriously wounded by a gunshot wound to the head, and James was also able to get the Police section officer to safety as well. The PATU guys certainly played their full part – whether on their own or as part of combined operations.

Operation Spiderweb: March 1968

Operation Cardigan: 28 May to 4 June 1968

For me, Operation *Cardigan* lasted from 28th May to 4th June 1968. I boarded a Dakota from No 3 Squadron for a ground tour of duty at Forward Airfield 1, Wankie. It was not all work and no play, because I was fortunate enough to fly with South African Air Force Captain Breedt in a Cessna 182 on 1st June. The SAAF Kiewiets were deployed in Rhodesia to primarily support the South African Police units engaged in border control duties. My sortie with Captain Breedt was a short twenty-minute circuit and landings, and I welcomed the invitation to get my bum in the air. The Kiewiet pilot had been idle for a couple of days and wanted to do a few circuits, remaining close to the airfield in case an operational sortie came up. I did not relish these ground stints, but accepted the fact that the Air Force knew best — they would send the General Duties Pilots to areas where their skills could be put to best use. After my field deployment, I did not have long to wait to do what I knew best - to utilise the Vampire for ground attack. I carried out an airstrike the day after I left Wankie.

On 5th June my first sortie was a dawn FRA - first run attack, firing 50 x 20-mm HEI training flight. Three weapons sorties were flown on that day - the last being 4 x 60lb rockets where I scored a one yard average - not too bad, I thought.

In an unrelated operation, the SAS was tasked with the demolition of the Luangwa Bridge, in Zambia, which they accomplished on 9th June 1968.

Operation Griffin: 18 and 19 July 1968

A large group of terrorists totalling over ninety men was sent simultaneously to cross the Zambezi as far apart as could be managed, presumably to test the Rhodesian defences over a wide front. Before crossing the Zambezi, the group was split into four separate groups, three mixed ZAPU/ZANLA groups and one South African ANC group. The four groups crossed the Zambezi separately near the Gwaai/Zambezi river junction, the Zambezi/Kariba Lake entrance, between Kariba Dam and Chirundu, and the Chewore junction area. Within hours after the incursion occurred, the Rhodesian and SAP units engaged all four groups.

As normal, No's 4 and 7 Squadrons were the first to be deployed. OC 7 Squadron Norman Walsh was deployed to Kariba where RLI 2nd Lieutenant Jerry Strong made contact with a large, heavily armed group of thirty terrorists in a ravine of the Chimva River. Squadron Leader Norman Walsh was deploying stop groups in the surrounding mountainous country, positioning reinforcements for the troops engaged in the contact. Jerry Strong's RLI troop was pinned down in a deep gorge, and despite the heavy machine-gun and RPG bazooka fire from the terrorists, Norman Walsh was able to withdraw the troop to a more favourable position. His helicopter sustained hits whilst evacuating a wounded soldier from the contact area, but was still able to carry out accurate target marking for the Provost pilots to conduct their airstrikes.

Flight Lieutenant Tony Smit, together with a second Provost aircraft, flown by Air Lieutenant Ken Law, was also sent to Kariba. On 18th July 1968, the Rhodesian Security Forces made contact with a group of terrorists in the Zambezi Valley, and Tony Smit and Ken Law were soon overhead to provide air cover while the ground troops were pinned down by some effective fire from the terrorists. Tony and Ken were called in to make Provost airstrikes, which they were able to do with pinpoint accuracy, bearing in mind that they had no option but to drop their frantan bombs over the heads of our own troops. This action led to casualties among the enemy without causing loss among our own forces.

Air Strike No 05; Date 18/07/1968
Aircrews:
- Norman Walsh with Tinker Smithdorff
- Pete Nicholls with TJ van den Berg
- Tony Smit
- Ken Law

Target: Chimwa river ravine, Kariba; Aircraft 2xAlouette + 2x Provost
Weapons: MAG and Frantan
Result Both helicopters hit by ground fire. Const Danie du Toit, first SA policeman killed in action.

Air Strike No 06; Date 18/07/1968
Aircrews:
- Norman Walsh with Tinker Smithdorff
- Mick Grier with Butch Graydon
- Bill Jelley
- Keith Corrans
- Prop Geldenhuys
- Rich Brand

Target: Contact with 30Terrs, Zambezi – Kariba; Aircraft 2xAlouette + 4xVampire
Result: Insufficient safety distance between FLOT – forward line of own troops – and the target, to permit jet strikes. First pair of Vampires diverted to New Sarum.

Squadron Leader Bill Jelley and Flight Lieutenant Keith Corrans also took part in Operation *Griffin*. Bill recalls: "Keith and I were on standby and at about 14h00 we were called out to respond to a contact in the hills near Kariba town. The two aircraft were armed with RP (rocket projectiles) and 20 mm cannon as normal. We arrived in the area and established comms with Norman Walsh in the Alouette. He gave us verbal directions, target and front line own troops etc. The reference point was a yellow bush clearly visible from the air. I was not happy, as own troops were too close and short of the target along the line of attack. It was agreed that we would initiate an attack and only fire if the picture appeared better during the dive. It was not, so we waved off."

"Our diversion was New Sarum as there were no Vampire starting facilities at Kariba. I remember clearly the "Bingo" (minimum permissible) fuel was 1350lbs, which we had as we climbed out. A problem became apparent as we were abeam of Karoi; fuel was lower than anticipated and marginal to reach destination. We realised that with the stores still on board and therefore a lower speed, the "bingo" figure should have been greater. We cruise climbed, requested a priority landing due fuel shortage and planned for a flame out approach which fortunately wasn't necessary. A normal landing was made with both aircraft fuel gauges reading zero and insufficient for a go around. A very uncomfortable situation indeed. Needless to say SOP'S (standard operating procedures) were changed. I also recall that you (the writer) and

Rich Brand joined us at New Sarum that night; we were stood down the next morning and returned to Thornhill later that day. This was not one of my better days!"

Meanwhile, Squadron Leader Mick Grier and Flight Lieutenant Pete Nicholls, flying two Alouette helicopters, carried out hazardous casevacs, at 22h00, from a deep ravine. It was a very dark night and both pilots had to uplift the casualties from a small landing zone on a steep slope. The helicopter technicians involved in these operations were Sergeants Butch Graydon and Tinker Smithdorff. SAP Constable Danie du Toit had been shot through the head and killed instantly. SAP Platoon Commander Captain NJ Henning, Lieutenant JH Voster and Constable van Greunen were wounded. Although the SAP had now been in the Zambezi Valley since Operation *Nickel* in September 1967, this operation was to be their first major operation against terrorists – and Danie du Toit was thus the first SA Policeman killed in action.

I was detailed to fly to Salisbury, with armed Vampires, for standby duties in the event that additional jet airstrikes would be needed. Rich Brand and I joined Bill Jelley and Keith Corrans at New Sarum. Bill and Keith had been tasked for an airstrike, but unfortunately the Browns were inside permissible safety distances. I flew armourer Senior Technician Rodney Brodryk from Gwelo up to Salisbury in a Vampire. In view of Tony's Provost airstrike during the course of the 18th, I was deployed to Salisbury to be closer to the action, because of the limited range and endurance of the Vampire when armed.

Operation *Griffin* was virtually over before it had begun, mainly due to early detection and quick reaction. It will be recalled that the tactic to leapfrog was first successfully employed by Ian Wardle of the RAR during Operation *Nickel*.

In the ensuing widespread engagements, thirty-nine terrorists were killed and forty-one captured. The middle group of twenty-eight who crossed between Kariba and Chirundu was chased by fast-moving Security Force tracker units who hung on to the terrorists' trail over the most difficult terrain. The SF were able to gauge the gook speed and direction so accurately that other units could leapfrog ahead to lay a series of ambushes; of this terrorist group, twenty-four were killed, three were captured and one managed to escape. Although my mathematics may well be suspect (as pointed out by historian Professor Richard Wood), Herman Bosman in "*Eye in the Sky*" reported that of the total 91 that crossed, 80 were killed and 11 taken prisoner.

I returned to Thornhill the next day July 19th with Vampire 2400 for Operation *Mansion*. Bill Jelley, Keith Corrans and Rich Brand also recovered to Thornhill.

Operation Mansion: 20 July 1968

Operation *Mansion* started the next day with a successful Vampire airstrike in Devils Gorge with 4 by 60lb squashhead rockets and 280 rounds 20mm HEI cannon, landing at Bulawayo to refuel and return to Thornhill, in Vampire R 4024. The airstrike was carried out in the Zambezi Valley, upstream from Lake Kariba at Devil Gorge. Although the river crossing was dangerous for the ZAPU terrorists, this group believed that they were safe due to the high-rock gully of Devils Gorge and would not be found by the security forces.

The group of terrorists was fairly well protected by the rocky outcrop but they were in fact trapped. Those who tried to get over the top of the Gorge were shot by the troops, while others sought shelter in the granite gully. Although they had taken cover behind granite boulders, the cover was not good enough to withstand the devastating effects of the rocket and cannon airstrike. The two CT casualties pictured below, albeit shown in rather gory fashion, were but scant revenge for the many airmen who lost their lives during the Bush War – my Roll of Honour, at the back of the book, bears testimony to that.

A lot of the early successes can be attributed to very good ground intelligence. As already mentioned, the first pseudo-terrorist group formed in 1966 included "turned" terrorists. The original 'pseudos' worked, fought and died alone. If there were any citations (and this was rare, even posthumously), they were one-line entries that gave little intelligence away: 'For brave and gallant conduct above and beyond the call of duty'. Sometimes a slight elaboration was permissible, at the risk of raising an eyebrow: 'Killed in the operational area whilst undertaking assignments which demanded of him brave and gallant conduct beyond the normal call of duty'. For over six years after their formation, the activities of the 'pseudos' remained unknown to the nationalists and throughout this period they were therefore extremely effective.

Small groups of six to ten guerrillas disappeared time and again without trace. A lull in the terrorist war ensured. The 'pseudos' were the forerunners of the Selous Scouts, and their hell bent for glory approach somewhat compromised the early successes enjoyed by the Security Forces.

Isops (Internal Security Operations), were meanwhile, relatively successful. The years 1967 and 1968 were a low point in nationalist activity in Rhodesia – the nationalists failed to make any headway. More terrorist groups were infiltrated into Rhodesia from Zambia and Tanzania - but with little result for the liberation movements. Although the Sinoia battle of April 1965 had heartened the nationalists, they faced failure after failure. Their excuse was that they were inadequately armed and trained. While the Security Forces had strengthened, the straightforward military problems that the terrorist forces faced had increased.

Two Terrorists – who would terrorise no more. The reality was, kill or be killed.

It became increasingly difficult for the terrorists to infiltrate undetected. While dissidents fled to Zambia and Tanzania, village people became more docile and compliant, refusing to involve themselves in any activity that would bring themselves to the attention of the Security Forces. Incidentally, the terrorists had three designated operational zones: -

- BBZ zone, for Botswana Zimbabwe, – i.e. Wankie / Bulawayo area
- ZZ zone, for Zambia Zimbabwe, – i.e. Kariba, inland and including the Lake area
- MMZ zone, for Moçambique Zimbabwe, – i.e. Sipolilo, Centenary, Mount Darwin and Mtoko areas.

In hindsight, Ian Smith commanded a strong hand during the 1966 *Tiger* talks as well as the October 1968 talks on board HMS *Fearless*. It was during October that the assassination plot backfired. Sithole tried to smuggle letters out of Salisbury jail, instructing contacts in Highfields to carry out his orders to assassinate Prime Minister Ian Smith and Rhodesian Front ministers Desmond Lardner-Burke and Jack Howman. Sithole had confided in Maurice Nyagumbo who was intrigued by the assassination idea. Sithole was caught in the act of throwing instructions encased in oranges over the prison wall to members of his ZANU party who, by pre-arrangement, assembled as visitors waiting for the gates to be opened. Members of the Special Branch lounging around confiscated the oranges. The fruit had been cut out and expertly stuffed with instructions on how Prime Minister Ian Smith was to be assassinated.

On 7th November 1968, British Minister for State without Portfolio, George Thomson, flew into New Sarum Air Force base for a 90-minute talk with Mugabe, Takawira and Sithole - to brief them on what emerged from the *Fearless* talks.

Operation Excess: August 1968

Operation *Excess*, to many Intelligence Officers, was considered to be that phase in the Rhodesian Bush War, which signified the last consequential action in Mashonaland in 1968. The lone escapee from Op *Isotope* the year before returned on Op *Excess*, only to meet his doom. The phase started from 1964, after Zambian independence when terrorists began to infiltrate across the Zambezi River. Operations against terrorist incursions were invariably of very short duration, with successful wrap-ups accounting for all the terrorists that dared to venture into the country.

The next phase commenced with the lull until the attack on the Altena Farm at the end of 1972. The last phase was the decisive phase, with widespread and rapid escalation of hostilities – and including several international attempts to achieve a negotiated settlement. It ended with the cease-fire agreement signed on 21st December 1979.

Operation Knuckle: 26 August to 11 September 1968

No 2 Squadron Detachment to Bulawayo commenced on 26th August. The objective was to test the operational preparedness of his Squadron to operate away from the home comforts of Air Force Base Thornhill. I duly flew to Bulawayo on that noteworthy day with Chief Technician D Whyte for the start of 'Operation' *Knuckle*.

The detachment routines also permitted me to enjoy solo flying, such as in low-level interceptions, as well as firing 60 x 20mm cannon and 2 x 60lb RP FRAs.

On 4th September, I flew a forty-five minute low-level Vampire intercept with Boss Jelley. Intercepts were normally flown with clean aircraft i.e. without the drop tanks fitted. The high-speed low-level profile also significantly reduced endurance, and so these types of exercises normally did not take long. The next day, the 6th, was my turn to "instruct the Boss". According to my logbook entry the reason for this was my appointment as Squadron PAI (Pilot Attack Instructor), and the duty was appropriately cine-weave - this was an exercise in steady tracking - trying to keep the pipper on the target aircraft during mild evasive manoeuvres. Filming the sortie permitted accurate evaluation of air-to-air tracking performance. Then on the very next day, we again flew together, this time on gunnery; firing 60 x 20mm Hispano cannons on first run attacks.

Operation Knuckle line-up of eight Vampire Jets – at Bulawayo Airport

The 8th September was another memorable day. The squadron fielded eight Vampires, led by Boss Jel (for Jelley – as he was affectionately referred to), and with me as the No 5, we flew various flypast formations over the City of Bulawayo. A ground photographer captured our performances on film and I treasure one or two photos of these formations in my album. A repeat farewell of eight Vampires was also flown on the day of our return to Thornhill on 11th September 1968.

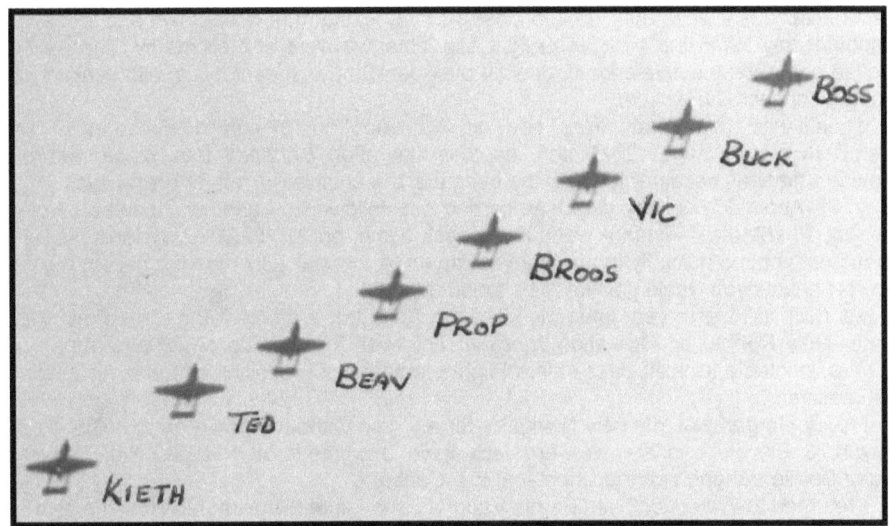

Echelon Formation – Bill Jelley, Bill Buckle, Vic Cook, Bruce Smith, Prop Geldenhuys, Rich Beaver, Ted Lunt and Keith Corrans

On the same day (9th October), Prime Minister Ian Smith took off from Salisbury, with Jack Howman and Des Lardner-Burke for Gibraltar for renewed settlement efforts on board *HMS Fearless*. These, like *Tiger*, would end in failure because of unrealistic British demands and their obsession with NIBMAR - No Independence before African Majority Rule.

Mixed Types

With Bill Jelley as OC 2 Squadron, we experienced a shortage of Vampire aircraft and were supplemented by the addition of piston engined Provosts. This made for interesting, as well as a greater variety of, flying requirements. As a pilot attack instructor, for me it meant remaining proficient on both types - on jets as well as piston-engined aircraft. The Force needed to train pilots on operational conversions meaning that I had the unique opportunity to fly with a large cross section of qualified pilots as well as raw students. An instructor's reward is the satisfaction of following the fruits of his labours, and to note the career advancements of some of his students.

Flying mixed types prompted me to review my flying log, and to list alphabetically, those pilots who I trust, had benefited from the skills that the Air Force had bestowed upon me. The student that impressed me most was undoubtedly Chris Wentworth. He had near natural flying ability - his rolling manoeuvres, in particular, been better than I was able to execute. It is also perhaps coincidental that my path crossed Richard Beaver's with pleasant regularity.

Waterkloof - SAAF Base

Two Rhodesian Vampires arrived at Waterkloof from Thornhill. After they had completed their turn-round, refuel etc, they started up and taxied out for a stream take-off - just like the routine I had performed a month earlier. I boarded a strange unnumbered South African Vampire, started up in an out of sight hangar and taxied out to 'secretly' latch onto one of the Rhodesian aircraft. They carried out their normal stream take-off - but meanwhile, there were two additional foreign aircraft that remained latched on for close formation take-off. You guessed it. Jan Smuts Radar had witnessed two Vampires approach and land, - then saw two blips depart - whereas there was in fact now a total of *four* Vampires, with yours truly maintaining a tight close formation. More about the drama later on (like failing pressurisation, bloated tropical fish, radios that didn't work, night landings at Thornhill, night flight to New Sarum where the silver Vampires were turned, like chameleons, into camouflaged aircraft).

My next trip to Waterkloof was made in Hunters, on 21st and 22nd September 1970. What made this flight interesting was that I was now able to adopt Mirage type techniques against the

Sabre interceptions - when they got too close I simply stuffed the nose down and 'ran away to fight another day'. With the Mirages I might add, alas, we were at their mercy. The Air Traffic Controlled approach into Waterkloof, directly over Jan Smuts, meant flying with blinkers on, in view of the congested airspace.

Then it was back to Vampires. I flew into Waterkloof on 10th and 11th February 1971 for a night-stop. A month later, 12th March, another Operation *Hottentot* took place, where two Rhodesian Vampires became "four" for the benefit of the uninitiated, not for prying eyes.

Then on 7th April 1971, a day stop was carried out, followed by another Operation *Hottentot* mission on 15-16th July. Within a week I was back again, on 21st to 22nd July for a proper jolly which did not entail a quick fly in and then out again. A 'normal' jolly meant a decent night-stop and to visit haunts you would not like to be found dead in!

My next visit was a year later, on 13th June 1972, but this time flying Canberras, with my navigator Mike Ronne, on Operation *Junction*. This was followed up on 3rd November in the same year, primarily to uplift passengers Flight Lieutenant Bruce Collocott and Air Lieutenant Ken Burmeister.

Paddy Morgan was my new Navigator for my next Canberra sortie on the night-stop 3rd-4th May 1973. Eleven days later we were back again, this time to drop off pilot Rich Beaver and navigator Bernie Vaughan for the Doppler fit to a Canberra.

I returned to Waterkloof with Bernie Vaughan and Flight Sergeant Mo Houston on 18/19th June 1973 for Doppler trials.

Operation Hottentot: 28 February 1969 to 16 July 1971

Operation *Hottentot* was an exercise of which I was particularly proud. This was a classic and historically significant case of Rhodesian Sanctions Busting. As a landlocked country, with the whole world crying foul following UDI, and being wholeheartedly in sympathy with Prime Minister Ian Douglas Smith's *Great Betrayal* by the western industrialised nations, I can still sleep peacefully at night. Given the opportunity, I would do it again - my conscience is clear, and my loyalty unquestionable.

No 2 Squadron Staff Pilots – March 1969 – Bill Sykes, Vic Cook, Bill Buckle, Bruce Smith, Squadron Leader Tol Janeke, Rich Brand, Prop Geldenhuys and Rich Beaver

At that time, it was just one of many previous re-equipping initiatives that baffled people more clever than I. Squadron Leader Peter Cooke had taken delivery of sanction busting Trojans in 1967 (while I was full time on Operation *Nickel*), then followed the Vampires, Lynxes and Genets. I was involved in the jet acquisition – South African Air Force mothballed Vampires that served Rhodesia well in the Bush War. I don't know how many people were in the know at that time, but I guess pretty few. Even the flights into Rhodesia were so timed that arrivals would be at night, to further minimise compromise. Junior members of the Squadron belonged to the mushroom club - they were kept in the dark and fed on sh_t, as the saying goes.

The *modus operandi* in the initial stages was for the two ferry pilots to be flown down south in a civilian airliner - either South African Airways or Air Rhodesia. Customs formalities in South Africa would be curtailed via diplomatic immunity, and one would be whisked away in a waiting staff car off the Jan Smuts apron. On 28th February 1969 I flew a practice run to Waterkloof, followed a month later by the real McCoy. So on 27th March 1969 I flew down to Jan Smuts on SAA in civilian dress. The Rhodesian Attaché in an official diplomatic car, Wing Commander Bill Smith, met me. I was chauffeured around Pretoria, escorted to the Uniewinkels to buy tropical fish in a plastic bag, and deposited at Waterkloof for our Smersh dusk take-off for Thornhill and New Sarum in a 'no name brand' Vampire. I was briefed in the OC Flying Wing Waterkloof's office and then taken to view a gleaming silver Vampire tucked away in an obscure hangar. Although I make the observation that the mothballed jets were 'gleaming' silver, to emphasise the contrast to the camouflaged Rhodesian equivalents, they were as the name implies, mothballed and hardly airworthy. Although ground runs had been carried out by our South African counterparts, it is highly questionable whether any air testing had been carried out. In fact, I doubt whether the SAAF had any current Vampire pilots at that time. It was only when one got airborne that one learnt the hard way whether the pressurisation, instrumentation and flying characteristics functioned as they should. On my very first *Hottentot* flight, I nearly had to scrape tropical fish off the canopy - because of poorly functioning pressurisation at altitude - my bag of live fish had puffed up to nearly double its size. (I had been permitted a quick pit-stop at the Uniewinkels in Pretoria's Church Street, to stock up my home aquarium with hard-to-come-by specimens).

While I had flown into South Africa by civilian airline, a pair of Rhodesian Vampires had meanwhile carried out a routine navigational training exercise, which in the normal course of events would hardly raise any eyebrows. The Rhodesian Vampires would park off out of sight of the hangar housing the South African Vampires. Before start-up, radio contact would be established between the two pairs, watches synchronised, and at the prearranged time, "press tits". Not the female type, but the re-light button on the end of the HP Cock to initiate the jet starting sequence. The South African aircraft would actually start up while still in the aircraft hangar, taxi out and only join up with the Rhodesian pair as they prepared for take-off. The normal take off from Waterkloof meant passing quite close to the Union Buildings. As such it was standard operating practice to avoid the built-up areas by banking as soon as possible, and commencing the climb to minimise the jet noise of take-off. In our case, we had to turn steeper, remain on a shallow climb to reach climbing speed sooner. We would then power climb so as to make spotting on Jan Smut's radar more difficult - in differentiating just two blips for two aircraft, whereas the two blips in fact represented two pairs of Vampires (now total four aircraft). Close formation would be maintained until over the Rhodesian border - and out of South African radar range. The four aircraft could then relax in a loose battle formation, in order to check out the aircraft operating systems properly.

Flight plan timing would be such that Thornhill would be approached at dusk when colour differentiation between the South African silver aircraft and the camouflaged Rhodesian Vampire impossible. Thornhill ATC would advise Salisbury that two Vampires are continuing up to New Sarum, where we would then land and taxi to ASF - Aircraft Servicing Flight, for over-night transformation into Rhodesian Vampires - colour scheme and all. Two aircraft departed the country, four returned. What do you know - we had made babies without joining the Mile High Club.

Operation *Hottentot* missions were thus carried out on 28th February and 26th March 1969, and then again two years later on 12th March and 16th July 1971. Rhodesian Air Attaché Wing Commander Bill Smith would meet us - in his posh black diplomatic limousine. The Wing Co kindly permitted me to use his limousine (with flags flying) to visit my father who was stationed at 10 Air Depot, Voortrekkerhoogte. On approaching the security guardroom, the boom would be raised with no questions asked. There was absolutely no need to park off the diplomatic immunity car - I was able to drive right up to my father's office. I could not fail to notice all the curious onlookers and imagined them thinking "Who is this VIP hobnobbing with Geldenhuys?"

The tropical fish tale warrants further explanation. I had become an avid collector, and grasped every opportunity to add to my collection. South Africa offered a much wider variety than what was available locally. Tropical fish are commonly transported in plastic bags half filled with water, and the other half filled with air. I underestimated the fact that there would be only partial pressurisation in the Vampire at altitude. Flying close formation to cruise altitude did not permit me keep an eye on the fish as well. Imagine my surprise when my fish bag had ballooned to enormous proportions. I punctured the plastic bag before it exploded tropical fish all over the cockpit, but then did not reckon on a rather flat, shrivelled up plastic bag upon de-pressurisation. My tortured fish struggled to survive the flight - and resembled dehydrated specimens fighting for their lives in an oversized elongated used French letter.

No 2 Squadron – August 1969 – Staff Instructors with OCU Students
Roger Watt, Dick Paxton, Giles Porter, Trevor Baynham, Roy Hulley(†), Brian Murdoch(†),
Spook Geraty, Rob Dayton and John Blythe-Wood
Mike Mulligan, Bruce Smith, Sqn Ldr Tol Janeke, Rich Brand and Prop Geldenhuys

My last *Hottentot* trip was with Squadron Leader Eddie Wilkinson. We had flown up to New Sarum, together, on the 15th, night-stopped, then flew down by civil air the next day. On 16th July I flew solo Waterkloof straight back to Salisbury (obviously in formation), and returned to Thornhill, with Eddy, the next day. This equated to a three-day, two-night jolly. Although Operation *Hottentot* was only a mere four-sortie exercise for me, its impact contributed significantly to the Sanctions Busting objectives, aircraft acquisitions and prosecuting the Bush War effort.

Squadron Leader Porky MacLaughlin took over from Wing Commander Chris Dams as Officer Commanding Flying Wing, Thornhill, during November 1968. Squadron Leader Tol Janeke took over from Bill Jelley as OC 2 Squadron at the end of March 1969.

Exercise Irish Stew: 28 October to 2 November 1969

Air Staff at Air Headquarters had planned an all-out Forcex (Air Force Exercise) that tested all aspect of operations, with some miraculous as well as disastrous results. The first day entailed mass dispersal to all over the place. I got airborne early on 28th October, armed with 2 x 60lb rockets, and flew to South Africa for air-to-ground attacks on Roedewal air weapons range north of Pietersburg, and then continued on to Moçambique for refuel at Lourenço Marques. Take-off from LM was scheduled for late in the afternoon with a night landing at Vic Falls, an impossible distance in a Vampire. The planning error at Air HQ had come about as a result of the fuel consumption figures given to HQ by the squadron prior to the exercise. The squadron had given the figures for takeoff from the altitude at Thornhill, whereas the actual figures should have been from sea level, at LM. The fuel consumption for a climb out from sea level is vastly different from that of 5,000 feet.

Bill Sykes who was one of the pilots with us at LM states:

"I was the last of the six aircraft to take off from LM that evening, and so was commandeered by the Boss, Tol Janeke to help take the rocket rails off his aircraft, in order to reduce the drag to a minimum and thus enable him to have a better chance of getting to Vic Falls. The Vampires were supposed to leave at 10 minute intervals, but having seen the Boss off, I still had to do my pre-flight, and strap in without any assistance from the other pilots who were long gone. As a result I got airborne very late and it was getting dark even before I was abeam Pietersburg. A dark bank of cloud loomed ahead near the border and the decision was made there and then to land at Thornhill, or if the going became too rough, divert to Bulawayo. The other alternative was to stay below the cloud and head straight for Thornhill.

My Vampire was one of those Op *Hottentot* ones that had not been fully reconditioned and was not really suitable for night flying. In fact, as the sortie progressed it was found that the radio was weak, the Radio compass did not work and the cockpit lighting was almost non-existent – hardly the ideal situation for a night letdown in bad weather into Thornhill.

Because of the poor cockpit lighting I decided to go below cloud and maintain a visual reference as long as possible with the ground. But the cloud base got lower and lower until I was flying at Flight Level 150 (15,000ft). It didn't take much to realise that at that altitude the fuel would not get me home, so I elected to climb up again. The weather worsened and lightning began flashing all around. A call to Thornhill Approach at a range of about 80 miles got no answer. In fact the next ten minutes seemed like a whole day – there was total silence on the air and the very real probability of a Martin Baker letdown (by parachute) loomed large. It would be a case of keep flying northwards until the fuel ran out.

Spending a night in the cloud and rain with two broken ankles (the Vamp has a small parachute) and little hope of being found for the next 12 hours certainly solidified my resolve to stay with the aircraft. Then, as all hope was beginning to fade came the distant voice of Blake Few at strength one. "Go ahead I can read you." Never have I heard such a sweet sound. The storm was at its highest, the turbulence was intense and great tree trunks of lightning flashed past the cockpit.

Blake's calm professional voice led me to overhead and then down onto the centreline and glide path for runway 13. The visibility was zero, but the Air Force training now took over completely – there was only one chance. There was not enough fuel to overshoot and have another try, so it was land first time or eject. Down through break-off altitude of two hundred feet and still no runway lights visual. Then, as Blake said "You are on the centreline, you are on the glide path, the runway is directly ahead – you have half a mile to run," the runway lights appeared as a huge blur through the driving rain. Aiming at the beginning of the blur the aircraft thumped onto the tarmac and the runway lights flicked past one by one. The Vamp was safely down.

High praise must go to Blake for handling a real emergency in the calm and collected manner that we had come to expect of our controllers and a situation in which the pilots gain tremendous confidence.

This was not the end of the evening's entertainment as two of our Vampires had not appeared at Thornhill yet and we heard that they had wisely diverted to Bulawayo, short of fuel too. The two had somehow met up over Bulawayo, and as only one of them had a working Radio compass, the other had to do a formation landing in the dark. Their first attempt at landing proved disastrous as they were not lined up properly on their letdown (no GCA talk down at Bulawayo), and as they overshot the leader nearly wiped out the number two against the Control Tower. The second attempt was better and both landed successfully.

Meanwhile back at Thornhill, Ted Lunt was coming down the glide path in his Hunter. It was still raining heavily and those who have flown a Hunter will know that the visibility in rain is zero. At least the Vamp has a D/V panel that gives the pilot a bit of a chance. Ted overshot on his first attempt and the pilots of No 2 Squadron went out in the rain to listen for the ejection seat 'bang'. Nothing – then two minutes later the shark like form appeared out of the storm, only to overshoot again. Surely he would not have enough fuel for another try. Still no noise. Then another two minutes, and as he was overshooting for the third time he suddenly saw the lights, stuffed the nose down and threw the Hunter onto the runway just short of the halfway mark. The aircraft was so light that it managed to stop before the end of the runway. The technicians, after refuelling said that there could only have been fumes left in the tanks.

With all these incidents, someone on the squadron remarked that we were doubtless going to lose an aircraft during the Forcex if the weather continued. And this was only the first day....."

The next morning we flew on to Victoria Falls - I was formating on the lead Vampire piloted by Bruce Smith when we ran into some really foul weather. We entered 8/8th cloud and shortly thereafter experienced severe icing. A form of 'impact ice', super-cooled rain droplets that turn into ice as soon as they strike all leading edges, built up rapidly on both Bruce's and my Vampires. As the quantity of ice builds up, large chunks break off and can actually damage the tail-planes. I had no option but to maintain close formation in the cloud, which at stages was becoming very dark indeed. We tried climbing out of the freezing level but could not get out of the cloud. Bruce then wisely decided on a gentle glide to below the freezing level, lest one of us were faced with an engine flame out. When we arrived at the Victoria Falls airfield, it was raining cats and dogs, but both of us managed safe landings without any further mishaps.

Barrier Engagement – by Mike Mulligan
(Note: Not actually related to Ex. Irish Stew)

A Hunter flown by Squadron Leader Roy Morris was not as fortunate - he aquaplaned on landing and skidded off the runway.

Canberra R 5212 crew of Pilot Officer Jim Stagman and Flying Officer Dave (Polly) Postance (Polly of UDI / Operation *Wizard* / Bonedome fame) were even less fortunate. Jim's recollection follows:

"We were tasked to carry out a 'hi-lo-hi' navex which involved bombing and photo at Kutanga Range. We took off from Victoria Falls and flight planned to return there. Two aircraft were tasked with Pilot Officer B G Graaff and Flying Officer Robertson flying the other Canberra as formation leader. Everything went as planned until we were climbing out of Kutanga to return to Vic Falls. The weather was very cloudy, typically early rainy season with the ITCZ (Inter-Tropical Convergence Zone) across Rhodesia. We were climbing in close formation. Throughout the flight there had been a problem with canopy and DV (direct vision) panel misting, so the navigator was sitting on the Rumbold seat next to me wiping the canopy clear so that I could keep the lead aircraft in sight.

"At just over 40,000ft, we flew into an embedded cumuli nimbus. There was a lot of turbulence, rain and lightning. As we were operating near the rpm limits, both engines flamed out and we immediately lost the leader. We glided down into the cumulus with its associated lightning, turbulence and rain, turning towards Salisbury and to get out of the cloud. By 20,000ft we had re-lit both engines. We thought that the aircraft had been struck by lightning but it appeared that no damage had been done and as we had sufficient fuel etc., decided to resume course to Vic Falls. We were still in cloud but had no navigational aids except the ADF, which was out of range. We started a DR nav plot from the position of the flame out given to us by the lead navigator. When we did not pick up Vic Falls on the ADF at the expected time, we decided to descend below the cloud, find our position and map read to the destination. We had to descend to about 3,000ft to get below the cloud where it was fairly dark in the late afternoon. We were unable to pinpoint our location and by now had insufficient fuel to divert anywhere.

'We realised that the ADF had been put out by a lightning strike. We were in VHF contact the whole time with the Operations directors at Victoria Falls airfield. We described the visible ground features and the general opinion was that we must have deviated north into Zambia. We were told to fly south to pick up the Zambezi River. This we did until we ran out of fuel. We later ascertained that we had been 15-20 miles south of Vic Falls. An issue was later made of the fact that we had not carried out a square search. The reason for this was that we had been advised not to, for fear of the expected repercussions (political and personal) if we had been caught in Zambia. When we ran out of fuel the navigator ejected and I turned, gliding again to eject close to him. We landed within a mile of each other. I landed in the dark and broke my ankle. The navigator spent the night in a tree - a decision prompted by the roaring of lions and other night sounds. I managed to make a tent out of my dinghy and spent the night where I had landed.

"I heard a passing search aircraft, fired flares and was picked up by a helicopter at about 02h00. I directed the helicopter to the area where the navigator had landed; we searched for him for a short while and then decided to continue the search at daybreak. The navigator meanwhile was 100 yards away when we left the area. He was picked up the following morning.

"After the wreckage was examined by the RhodAF investigating team, it was blown up; salvage operations would have been too costly."

Jim faced a court-martial, one of the charges being "Losing a Canberra". "I did not lose it," he said, "I'll show you exactly where it is."

Exercise *Irish Stew* ended with my return to Thornhill from Victoria Falls on 2nd November.

Exercise Mannix

Mannix was a Police ATOPS (anti-terrorist operations) exercise close to Umtali and supported by three Alouettes and PRAW aircraft. Two of the three helicopter pilots were Norman Walsh and Peter Petter-Bowyer. During this mountainous eastern district war games exercise, PB and Boss Norman carried out a Casevac of a severely injured Gona re Zhou game ranger who had been gored by an angry cow elephant at Buffalo Bend on the Nuanetsi River.

Operation Natal (Tripper): 7 December 1968

Four helicopters, under the command of Wing Commander KAS Edwards, deployed into Moçambique to assist the Portuguese to combat FRELIMO, with the aim to render them incapable of providing ZANU or ZAPU safe passage to Rhodesia through Tete. The detachment, based at a hamlet called Bene, lasted initially for ten days. The crews included Peter Petter-Bowyer, Randy du Rand, Mark McLean, Tudor Thomas and with Alouette technicians Tinker Smithdorff, Butch Graydon, Bob St. Quentin and TJ van den Berg.

Operation Granite: 10 April 1970

Operation *Granite* was of short duration, involving No 4 Squadron chasing a group of seven terrorists. The operation was launched when two terrs were identified as such at a local store in the Matopos area, south of Bulawayo. Part of their arms cache was found hidden in a cave, and shortly thereafter the local tribesmen arrested a third member of the gang. However, this man managed to escape before the arrival of the security forces, and he most likely "threw pearls of wisdom" to his fellow gangsters. I was not involved in this Op, but my 16 PTC colleague Graham Cronshaw provided the necessary recces and telstar air support. A further two terrorists were reported captured by the Botswana Police. The operation was duly wound up when it was determined that the remnants of the gang had crossed the border to seek safe refuge.

Operations Birch, Teak and Chestnut

Within two weeks of going solo on Hunters, I had a nice lengthy two hour Border Reconnaissance sortie on Operation *Birch*. Flying at seven miles a minute, it was amazing what distance could be covered in the two hours. Twenty-two terrorists crossed the Zambezi on 8th January 1970, at a point west of the Chewore river. Tracks were picked up on the escarpment near the Hunyani river and contact was made with the group on the 16th. The terrs split up into four groups and were hounded on the ground by air support from the Internal Security squadrons, No's 4 and 7 (leap frogging, top cover and telstar).

A further contact ensued on 18th January, accounting for seven terrs killed and 14 captured. Fellow 16 PTC course colleague Graham Cronshaw acquitted himself well – while piloting a Trojan, with my ex pupil Chris Wentworth, he carried out the airstrike with matra rockets in the Hunyani River contact. They were supported by a 7 Squadron Alouette helicopter, firing their MAG machine gun. The sole escapee from this group must have been terribly demoralised.

The awesome Hawker Hunter armaments

I then flew similar Hunter recce sorties on Operation *Teak* on 28th and 29th January. In this case, the SAP camp at Sprayview and the Victoria Falls Airport came under attack. The terrs had infiltrated near the Gwaai river, where a police patrol boat had been fired on. Tracks were followed to Kamativi, where they were lost due to effective anti-tracking measures. Then the SAP camp at Chisuma came under a gook hit-and-run attack, which wounded four policemen. However, five terrs were killed, six were captured and the balance of nine made good their exit via Botswana. I did not fire any weapons, but did contribute with my two Hunter sorties. Dakotas from

No 3 Squadron were also engaged in effective sky-shout missions – which were confirmed when the captured terrorists were interrogated.

Showing the flag, especially for our Zambian adversaries' benefit, entailed fairly frequent border reconnaissance missions. To name a couple, these 'hi-lo-hi' sorties were flown on 16th February, and 9th, 14th April, and 11th and 25th June, 1st July, 14th September and 27th November.

Operation Chestnut: 20 February 1970

Operation *Chestnut* started on my birthday – 20th February 1970. I was not involved, but Air Lieutenant Ed Paintin represented No 4 Squadron. The presence of seven ZIPRA terrorists came to light when one terrorist was caught at the Dett siding in the Wankie area. No 4 Squadron established a temporary mini-FAF at Dahlia, and Ed Paintin carried out armed recces and leaflet drops, while Army patrols were carried out to the south-west of Dahlia. Nothing significant materialised from this small group, which was thought to have made sex their departure back to Zambia. ZIPRA was known to favour the Gwaai area.

The Diamond Nine Pilots – Ed Potterton, Rob McGregor, Rich Brand, Dag Jones, Sqn Ldr Roy Morris, Nobby Nightingale, Steve Kesby; crouching: Prop Geldenhuys and Rikki Culpan

Operation Pluto: 4 to 13 March 1970

Operation *Pluto* started on the night of 4th March 1970 after a group of terrorists attacked the Kariba Airport transmitter site, when RPG rockets were fired into the roof of the building. Little damage was done as the projectiles were not fused. The tracks were followed for several days until they were lost. When no further trace of the terrorists was found, the operation was brought to a close on 13th March 1970.

As one operation wound up, with most or all of the terrorists accounted for, another opened. The terrorists streamed over the Zambezi River from Zambia, striking inland for the cities and farming regions. The Zambezi Valley became the battleground that was not always neutral. For the Rhodesian Light Infantry, Rhodesian African Rifles, Special Air Service, Police and National Parks personnel and TF soldiers taking the field in the burgeoning conflict, it would prove to be only a curtain-raiser, albeit a long and bloody one, for the main event which was yet to come (Operations *Tempest* and *Hurricane*). While the IS – Internal Security squadrons were more intimately involved, the jet squadrons would be destined to play a more active role as time progressed. It is a military fact that the Rhodesian Air Force was a cardinal factor in the counter-insurgency bush war.

In November of 1969, ZANU met with FRELIMO in Lusaka to ask for access to Rhodesia through Tete - ZANLA was reassessing their military strategy to set up staging camps for their forces. FRELIMO had meanwhile crossed the Zambezi in Tete, and in 1970 ZANLA terrorists Urimbo, Chauke, Mpofu and Shumba joined FRELIMO in Tete. Chauke and Amon Zindoga were destined to cross into Rhodesia, near Mukumbura, from Tete in December 1971.

The mention of *Frolozi* is perhaps opportune at this juncture. The Front for the Liberation of Zimbabwe – Frolizi – was formed on 1st October 1971 by militant members of ZANU and ZAPU. Its objective was twofold: its primary aim was a unifying effort to appease Kaunda's frustration regarding power struggles and internal squabbles amongst the two parties. The second objective was a "political-military instrument dedicated to revolutionary action against capitalist imperialists and the colonial settlers in Zimbabwe." Suffice it to say that it was doomed to failure, mainly because of the continuing politics of inter-party rivalry.

A brief mention of sanctions busting is here warranted: the where's and how's of laying one's hands on scarce Hunter spares were fascinating and ingenious. Some aircraft spares were brought in from Oman, often in the original crates marked with the names of British suppliers. Four spare engines for the Hunters were found in Oman; two of them came from the island of Masirah, which was previously the main Royal Air Force base in the region, and two from Salalah on the mainland. Six other Hunter engines were recovered from aircraft abandoned by the RAF on a desert airstrip in the state of Shariah in the Arabian Gulf. A party of Rhodesians flew in a DC 8 F to Sharjah, in a well-organised secret operation. They offloaded a consignment of Castle beer and Willard's potato crisps, went into the desert and stripped the engines, which proved invaluable additions to the Hunters.

March 1970 was also a historically important date for the RRAF – the word 'Royal' was dropped from the title to form the title 'Rhodesian Air Force'. The following month a new flag and aircraft marking were introduced. This occurred during my time in Air Force Intelligence, and I also participated in the numerous flypasts that the Hunters were called upon to do. Also, with the change in insignia, "my" Hunter was one of the first aircraft to sport the 'Lion with Tusk' emblem, as well as the new camouflage colour scheme. Note in the Diamond Nine formation, my aircraft in the centre is somewhat darker than the other eight Hunters.

The 1st July was a tragic day for the Air Force – we lost our first helicopter crew. Squadron Leader Gordon Nettleton and Flight Lieutenant Mike Hill were killed near New Sarum while carrying out Instrument flying. The cause was never established, but the Board of Inquiry did attribute the accident to flicker vertigo.

Operation Big Push: August 1970

No 1 Squadron was not involved with Operation *Big Push*. Members of No 3 Squadron were deployed for eight days during August 1970, to Meuda in Moçambique, to carry out sky-shout missions. It was a rather minor operation as far as the Rhodesians were concerned, but considered a major exercise by the Portuguese – to have our enthusiasm versus the general lethargy so evident from them. Our crews enjoyed their generous supply of liquid refreshment, though!

During my stint on the Squadron, ceremonial flypasts played an important role for the Squadron. I was fortunate to keep a couple of photographs of the various flypasts – and have now found a suitable "home" for them in this book and *Nickel Cross*.

The Independence Flypast in particular warrants elaboration, because at no time in the past, or in the future, did the Air Force have so many aircraft in the same piece of sky as they did on this occasion. I was pleased with my performance, and felt extremely proud, just being a participant in this historical event. The flypast consisted of flying seven formations of aircraft flying down the main street in Salisbury, passing over the saluting dais at 45-second intervals. Air speeds varied from a very slow 137 kph for the helicopters and our fast 670 kph in the Hunters. It was no mean feat putting 60 aircraft up for this memorable flypast. It consisted of seven Alouette helicopters, followed by nine Trojans, ten Provosts, six Dakotas, seven Canberras, twelve Vampires and our nine Hunters bringing up the rear. During my whole Air Force career I don't recall us ever repeating this sterling effort. The *Rhodesia Herald* publicised this event with a feature that jokingly suggested that an unholy pile up needed to be averted somewhere over Glamis Stadium, because that was were the faster Hunters would be breathing up the exhaust pipes of all the other slower aircraft ahead of them.

Boss Roy did us proud. Our timings over Cecil John Rhodes's Statue in Jameson Avenue were perfect. This awesome display of the Rhodesian Air Force's capability certainly sent a very clear message across the globe – particularly to the belligerent so-called Black Front Line States. Not bad position holding, even if I say so myself. I also had the privilege of leading a Diamond Nine formation around the country – but then that would be expected from a Flight Commander on No 1 Squadron.

But not all the flypasts ended successfully. It was during my time on the Squadron that we suffered the huge loss of a valuable Hawker Hunter during timing runs carried out at Bulawayo.

Rob Dayton, Rikki Culpan, Ed Potterton, Al Bruce, Nobby Nightingale
Dag Jones, Minister of Defence Jack Howman, Squadron Leader Roy Morris, Air Force
Commander Air Vice-Marshal Archie Wilson and Prop Geldenhuys

Exercise Oxtail, Capex

Exercise *Oxtail* was one of those squadron operational preparedness tests as planned by Strike 1 at Air Headquarters. It lasted from 23rd to 29th November 1970, with a detachment to New Sarum. Take-off was from Thornhill, firing 1 x 60lb rocket at Bumi Hills Range and landing Victoria Falls for turn-round and refuel. A timing exercise followed, with a landing at Salisbury.

The first sortie on the 24th was an intercept of Canberras, then a 60 x 30mm HEI cannon firing mission at Kutanga Range. The second sortie of the day was another HEI cannon, plus two rocket firing missions on a bush target at Nyamasoto.

On 25th and 26th I flew a visual reconnaissance sortie and a ciné simulated airstrike. The 27th was a lot more interesting - my log records a 'Zambian border violation and a VIP demonstration of live cannon and rocket ground attack'.

Exercise *Oxtail* ended on 29th November 1970 with my return to Thornhill base. The sortie on the last day of the month was an enjoyable Battle formation with DFC - day fighter combat. This entailed exercising finger four formations – extended line abreast at medium or high level, moving to a more line astern formation for weaving at low level. Aerial combat was always a relaxing break when compared to ground attack sorties.

Between the 31st October and 1st November 1970 the SAS carried out recce's in Zambia, searching for an arms cache, in the vicinity of the ZIPRA Eastern Sector Reconnaissance Camp (See also Operation *Big Bang* – October 1974).

Operations Apollo and Jacaranda: November 1970

Operation *Apollo* took place south and south-west of Cabora Bassa gorge. Elements of No's 4 and 7 Squadrons deployed to Chicoa in the Tete province of Moçambique on 29th November, to assist the Portuguese in COIN-Ops. ZANLA, with assistance from FRELIMO, were establishing bases south of the Zambezi. The Rhodesians soon realised that the Portuguese had no stomach for risking their lives in a lost cause, and it was thus in our own interests to stem the tide of southern ZANLA movement. Wing Commander Ozzie Penton was in charge of the Air Force contingent, and used No 3 Squadron to good effect with sky-shout and air re-supply. In 1971, Operation *Jacaranda* took over where *Apollo* left off, and involved the Dakotas of No 3 Squadron. I was not personally involved with these operations. "It is indeed astonishing that nine of the original twelve (Hunters) delivered before UDI were still flying at the end of the war," said Dudley Cowderoy and Roy Nesbit, in their book *War in the Air. Rhodesian Air Force 1935 – 1980*.

Operation Gordion Knot: May 1971

Operation *Gordion Knot* was a Portuguese failed offensive launched in May 1971 by General Kaulza de Arriaga to seal off the Moçambique and Tanzanian border to curtail FRELIMO movement. FRELIMO had been infiltrating Moçambique across the Rovuma River since 1964, and the Portuguese General committed 50,000 troops to achieve his objectives.

However, FRELIMO cunningly retaliated by increasing terrorist activity in the army's rear, and failed to capture Porto Amelia (whose garrison had been dispatched to join the northern attack) by only a narrow margin. FRELIMO also stepped up attacks south of the Cabora Bassa hydro-electric scheme adjacent to the Rhodesian border. The Portuguese did, however, manage to force FRELIMO back into Tanzania from Moçambique's northern border area, which they had previously claimed as occupied territory. On 17th September 1971, the *Rhodesian*

Herald commented: "It becomes apparent that the terrorist activity in Tete, neighbouring Cabora Bassa region, represents a greater danger than official communiqués have disclosed."

Rhodesia's CIO Chief, Ken Flower, was dispatched to Portugal by Prime Minister Ian Douglas Smith to persuade President Caetano that his 'peripatetic, posturing generals in Moçambique would lose the war for him unless more reliance was placed on the indigenous population and the police were afforded more appropriate responsibility'. Ken Flower was obliged to criticise General Kalza de Arriaga's conduct of the war. When taking leave of the President, Flower asked him to treat the Rhodesian criticism confidentially.

Dr. Caetano summoned his army chief, General Costa Gomes, and instructed him to recall de Arriaga because 'the Rhodesians and Mr Ken Flower in particular, thought he was a "bum General".' Flower, feeling depressed after leaving the President, sought the company of a lady of the night – and was surprised to learn that people on the street were overwhelmingly against Portugal's continued involvement in Africa. Ken Flower briefed the Rhodesian Cabinet on his return.

Ian Smith, concerned with the deteriorating situation in Moçambique, met with the Portuguese Prime Minister on 14th and 15th October 1972. There were no official announcements on the results of the talks, but Marcello Caetano said in a broadcast (in response to BBC news story suggesting Rhodesian anxiety): 'Our timorous neighbours (the Rhodesians) were more concerned over the situation in Moçambique than the Portuguese themselves who are well used to such state of affairs and perfectly capable of coping with it.'

Although long officially denied, the Rhodesian Air Force, the SAS, the RLI and the Rhodesian African Rifles had commenced operating in the Tete Province of Moçambique in support of the Portuguese in 1970. It was in Rhodesia's interest to keep FRELIMO insurgents away from our north-eastern border.

If we did not do it, nobody else would – for the Portuguese had virtually abandoned the countryside and were concentrating their forces in the towns and *aldeamentos* – protected villages. A major problem for the Portuguese military was that the brunt of the war was being borne by National Servicemen drawn from the peasant class, and they had a marked disinclination to expend their lives for a piece of African real estate they hated.

In January 1972, the Rhodesians stepped up operations in Moçambique. A Tactical Headquarters was established in the Makonde aldeamento, south of the Zambezi River. The Rhodesian African Rifles patrolled the sector from the Zambezi River to Rhodesia's northern border, while the SAS worked the mountain area to the north.

Two years later, in January 1974, the South African Recces got permission from SAS Commanding Officer Major Brian Robinson to send a stick of four men headed by Sergeant Major FC van Zyl, in Rhodesian camouflage, to join the SAS. The Recce 2-i/c, Major Nick Visser, went along as liaison officer. A Rhodesian Air Force Dakota flew them to the SAS Tactical Headquarters at Mozangadzi Mission – north of the Zambezi River and west of Tete. Although I have jumped the gun somewhat, it is relevant to sketch the background to "Mahombe Konde" (Macombe) – and the Canberra airstrikes that would take place in the Zambezi area, and Tete Province in particular. I was flying Canberras at that time, and the South Africans called for several airstrikes.

Strike From Above – No 2 Squadron

I was posted back to No 2 Squadron on 1st January 1971. Flight Lieutenant 'Varky' Varkevisser, pending Squadron Leader Tol Janeke assuming command in March, commanded the squadron. On the fourth, Air Lieutenant Mike Mulligan gave me a thirty-minute refamiliarisation on the Vampire. I flew one instrument flying sortie with the Boss on the 7th, and the next day he gave me my Green Rating test. A couple of sorties with Air Sub-Lieutenant Alf Wild followed, and then on the 19th Chris Dixon reintroduced me to the Vampires excellent cannon-firing attributes. By mid-month, my IRE and PAI categories had been reinstated and I then rated Air Lieutenant Chris Weinmann on his formal Operational Conversion Unit course. I was also allocated Air Lieutenant Chris Wentworth for his OCU.

On 8th February 1971, Bill Jelley took me up in Provost 3609 for a refamiliarisation sortie that lasted an hour and fifteen minutes. I had not flown a Provost since September 1969. This was the last time that Bill and I flew together in single engined aircraft (our next sortie would be July/August 1974). But I was considered sufficiently proficient to do a general solo the same day. In fact so much so that immediately after my return from South African Air Force Base Waterkloof, I recommenced my PAI responsibilities by instructing Air Sub-Lieutenant Brian Murdoch on 4 x 20lb Fragmentation High Dive-bombing. On the 15th I flew to Kutanga in Provost 3605 for Range Safety Officer duties. On 16th and 17th February I rated Chris Dixon and John Carhart 'Green' instrument rated on Vampires. I was now back in the groove flying both Vampires and Provosts alternating. This certainly made for diverse and interesting flying.

The first two weeks of March 1971 were essentially OCU instruction for Mark McLean, Chris Wentworth and Chris Weinmann on Vampires. Then on the 12th it was a quick sortie to Waterkloof to bring back a pair of South African Vampires on Operation *Hottentot*, with an after-dark landing at Thornhill. The next day Alf Wild flew with me in a Provost on a 300 x ·303 front gun, with 8 x 20lb fragmentation bomb demonstration.

A Kutanga Weapons Detachment on Provosts was carried out from 15th to 19th March for Air Sub-Lieutenants Dick Paxton, Alf Wild and Brian Murdoch. Several gunnery, bombing and one frantan sortie was also flown solo for weapons categorisation purposes. The detachment ended with a simulated dawn strike on Thornhill air base.

Praw Exercise: 26 to 28 March 1971

This Police Reserve Air Wing exercise was carried out on Provosts, me flying with Air Sub-Lieutenant Alf Wild. Our first sortie was a cross-country navigational exercise, landing at Lusulu. After a turn-round, we flew on to FAF 1 Wankie for a night-stop. On the 27th we carried out two border reconnaissance sorties along the Zambezi River, over-flying the various SAP camps for morale support. After another night-stop at the FAF, we flew to Libuti where we landed, and then continued on to Thornhill on the completion of the PRAW exercise.

The month ended with two Vampire sorties, the latter a refamiliarisation for Squadron Leader Tol Janeke, who had been posted on to the Squadron. Flying over 38 hours for the month was way above average – and a pleasant change from the maximum of 29 whilst on Hunters. On 6th April 1971 I flew down to Waterkloof Air Force base with Air Sub-Lieutenant Barry Heard. It was a day stop. I believe it was another Operation *Hottentot* sortie, despite there being no mention thereof in my logbook. I think it was a decoy mission, because my log states "Air test – Operation *Hottentot* "on 26th April (after our technicians had time to carry out the various modifications of the South African Vampires to bring them up to our somewhat high standards of acceptability).

I then had a two-week gap – from 8th to 20th April 1971, which could have been an Officers Administration Course, Army Coin Course, or even a spot of leave. Anyway, once back on No 2 Squadron, Squadron Leader Tol Janeke and I flew a general sortie in a Provost. Then it was back to Vampires, dropping 4 x 20lb smoke bombs using frantan bombing profile. Dropping the small smoke bombs was obviously a lot more economical for the Vampire than dropping the 50 gallon specially developed napalm bomb. On 26th April I flew with Danny Svoboda up to new Sarum to do the Operation *Hottentot* Vampire Air test, and returned to Thornhill flying another Provost – which I think Danny had air tested, while I was doing the Vampire Air test.

On 27th April 1971, I flew a night cross-country in a Vampire with Air Lieutenant Brian Murdoch. The next day I instructed Air Lieutenant Chris Weinmann on jet interceptions. Later in the day I flew with Flight Lieutenant John Barnes on a Vampire engine change air test. My sorties at the end of the month were significant for two reasons. I flew to Salisbury with Chris Weinmann on a DFC instructional sortie – this being my last sortie with Chris (he was killed in action in Moçambique exactly three years later). It will also be recalled that Chris Weinmann and I were the first two Provost pilots who deployed to Wankie for Operation *Nickel*.

No 2 Squadron 1971
Dick Paxton, Chris Wentworth, Danny Svoboda, Spook Geraty, Brian Murdoch, Alf Wild
Prop Geldenhuys, Varky Varkevisser, Sqn Ldr Tol Janeke, Chris Dixon and John Carhart

The other reason why 30th April 1971 was significant is that my return flight from Salisbury was in one of those Operation *Hottentot* Vampires, number R 4221, with Technical Officer Squadron Leader Jimmy Boyd. We experienced total electrical failure. Chris Weinmann was flying the second Vampire back, while as the senior pilot it was my duty to fly the South African acquired aircraft. I would think Jimmy Boyd, being an engineer, didn't feel so confident flying in an aircraft that had no electrics whatsoever. But the emergency was no real big deal. The hydraulics worked to get the undercarriage down, but because I had no "three greens" instrumentation in the cockpit, I still needed to do a slow, low pass over the Control Tower to confirm that my wheels were down for the emergency landing. I imagine the engineer 'blasted' the New Sarum technicians for putting one of their kind in a Vampire with 'no electrics.' I didn't find out what caused the failure – possibly just a blown fuse from an aircraft that had been mothballed for many months.

In May 1971 I made a rather hasty decision that I subsequently regretted. My fellow course colleague Chris Dixon was appointed Flight Commander on No 2 Squadron. He offered me to take over all the operational conversion training. Foolishly, I declined. I opted to focus on Specialist Weapons Instruction, but not OCUs. I was enjoying the good weapons results I was getting, and I felt I could develop further by being challenged with instructing more experienced pilots, rather than training raw recruits in the rudiments of air weaponry. I realised later that my future career prospects were negatively influenced by my declining to take over all OCU training. I thought Chris was shirking his responsibility, whereas in effect he was quite rightly delegating authority to best effect. Also, at that time, I was chewing a lot of Rennies for a duodenal ulcer, and I thought that the extra worries would just add to my woes. Being the conscientious type, I was really enjoying my flying, with not a care in the world. My time on No 1 Squadron as the Flight Commander had taken its toll. To make matters worse, it came to the ears of Boss Tol Janeke.

May 1971 was like most other months – with a great variety of flying the piston-engined Provost and the jet-engined Vampire. The month commenced with three instructional standardisation sorties for Air Lieutenants John Carhart, Brian Murdoch and Chris Wentworth. I then had a trip, in a Provost, to Salisbury and return. On 10th May the Specialist Weapons Course commenced, my students being Air Lieutenants John Carhart, Brian Murdoch, Ed Potterton and Bill Sykes. The SWC exercises included Battle Formation flying, 20mm gunnery, as well as going out to the Kutanga Weapons Range in a Provost as Range Safety Officer – also to provide advice and guidance for the students. I also flew 12-gallon frantan trials with Alf Wild, did aircraft flight-tests and flew solo first run attacks for categorisation purposes.

There were also the interesting rehearsals and the actual "Freedom of Entry – Salisbury City" Flypasts. I flew to Salisbury with Dick Paxton, changed over with Varky Varkevisser for the flypast timings, and then returned with Dick for night formation flying. We rehearsed on the 18th, 23rd 24th and carried out the actual flypast on 25th May 1971. I was number five in a formation of eight Provosts – in other words, I flew the lead in the second box of four Provosts. I hope to trace the official photograph of this historical event one day.

Operation Panga: 17 April 1971

This was an Air Force supported SAS external operation. A 10-man SAS force attacked a ZAPU terrorist camp on the Mushenshi River in Zambia, on 17th April 1971. One terrorist was killed and one wounded. Equipment and intelligence was recovered in this raid.

Exercise Birds Nest: 2 to 6 June 1971

Exercise *Birds Nest* took place in the Chiredzi and Kariba areas, and was a Forcex designed to test the operational effectiveness of the Air Force in discharging its duties to the Rhodesian tax payer. On 2nd June 1971 I got airborne in an armed Provost, routed via Kutanga Range, fired fifty rounds front gun and dropped two 20lb smoke bombs on frantan profile, and then proceeded to Kariba for the start of the Forcex.

It was during Forcex Birds Nest that an Army call-sign had got themselves lost and I was tasked to fly with South African policeman Lieutenant Koning to locate the missing soldiers in the Zambezi Valley. We took off just before dusk, and landed an hour later, having located them.

On 4th June Air Sub-Lieutenant Barry Heard flew with me on a low-level navex, firing 60 x ·303 rounds and dropping 2 x 12gallon napalm bombs on Manyumi weapons Range. The next day I carried out a search and rescue mission for two paratroopers who had been dropped by Dakota inland of Lake Kariba in mountainous terrain. Helicopters were dispatched to uplift the paratroopers. Exercise *Birds Nest* ended with a live weapons demonstration for Bulawayo Army units at Kutanga Range – with me dropping 6 x 20lb fragmentation bombs on high-dive bombing, and landing back at Thornhill.

Geoff Fenn of 107 (VR) Squadron looked after the Air Force detachment to Chiredzi. Some of the names that came to mind included Roger Andrews (who was later killed with Willy Wilson), Reg Blumeris, Sid Brown, Nelson Collins, Emmo Emmerson, Norman Farrell, Bill le Roux, Alec Scott, Scottie Valerie and Trevor Vine. I had flown with most of them, if not all, during my service career.

I then had a week's break, and resumed my Specialist Weapons training on Vampires for Air Lieutenant Brian Murdoch on 14th June 1971, and SWC instruction for Bill Sykes for the remainder of the week.

The third week of June took up air testing of Vampires at Thornhill and New Sarum. I flew a rudder trim check with Chris Wentworth at Thornhill, then went up to Salisbury with Chris Dixon and did four airtest sorties over two days. My trip back to Thornhill was with Air Lieutenant Al Bruce – another fellow course member of No 16 PTC, with whom I had been serving on Hunters when he had ejected near Bulawayo airport. The month ended with a couple of Vampire conversion instructional sorties for Air Lieutenant Jim Stagman. July 1971, like most other recent months on No 2 Squadron, provided pilot satisfaction with a large variety of challenging flying tasks. The Specialist Weapons Course continued with weapons firing and progressed to aerial day fighter combat instruction. Students instructed on a variety of exercises included Jim Stagman, Brian Murdoch, Bill Sykes, John Carhart, Ed Potterton and Danny Svoboda. The highlights of the month were another Operation *Hottentot* mission, an Army Coin Course weapons demonstration and laying on a static Provost weapons display for a Coin

Course in Salisbury. I also flew a variety of sorties with Squadron Leader Eddie Wilkinson, Spook Geraty, Air Sub-Lieutenant Gardener and Sergeant Westbrook – in either Vampires or Provosts.

The sortie with Squadron Leader Eddie Wilkinson is noteworthy in that it involved one of those secret Vampire acquisitions sorties, at that time, from South Africa. I flew Eddie from Thornhill to Salisbury on 15th July 1971. At New Sarum Air Force Base, I was taken across to the civilian airport side, boarded South African Airways flight to Jan Smuts airport, night-stopped, and flew a SAAF mothballed Vampire from Waterkloof to Salisbury. The Rhodesian Vampires landed at Thornhill, while the pair of South African Vampires continued on to New Sarum, landing after dark, in order that the silver painted aircraft would not be easily spotted by prying eyes. After another night-stop, I flew Eddie Wilkinson back to Thornhill on 17th July 1971. Barry Heard and I also had a night-stop jolly to Waterkloof, routing via the Natal town of Vrede, on 20th July 1971.

The Coin Course demonstrations included firing 200 x ·303 rounds front gun and dropping 2 x 12gal frantans. The Provost had one Browning mounted in each wing, and to carry out an airstrike with both guns blazing away resulted in the whiff of cordite filtering into the cockpit. The smells and sights of a Provost still excite me to this day.

I added quite a few more OCU students to my list – these were the new pilots that had been awarded their Wings during July. My new students included Air Sub-Lieutenants Greg Todd, Tony Oakley, Steve Murray, Mike Litson, Steve Baldwin and Pete Simmonds. Pete Simmonds, or Simmo as he was referred to, tells a very interesting story when he was shot in both legs while flying a Provost – his tale to be recounted later. On 12th August 1971, I tested and passed Air Sub-Lieutenant Barry Heard for his White Instrument rating on Vampires. Ten days later he was killed in an auto accident. What a waste. Barry had just completed his OCU phase, and was now a fully-fledged DF/GA – Day Fighter/Ground Attack pilot.

Vampire TII's – in RRAF markings – with kind permission of Bill Jelley

Exercise King Kabanga: 23 to 26 August 1971

Exercise *King Kabanga* was an Army Armoured Car Regiment co-operation exercise to demonstrate the effectiveness of air power in combined operations. The Army was also exposed to how the Air Force can disrupt and cause confusion to the enemy when caught unawares. My first sortie was flying a Vampire on 23rd August 1971, to carry out simulated airstrike on a convoy of Eland 90mm cannon vehicles, en route to Kutanga Range. The convoy knew that we would be attacking them, but did not know when or where. I was flying in a formation pair, and we achieved the element of surprise by jumping the Army convoy when they least expected it – sending vehicles careering all over the place. I could just imagine the fear and instinctive reactions of those poor Brownjobs as our Vampires screamed over the convoy – purposely remaining low after carrying out our strafing runs. The troops baled out from their troop carriers and support vehicles to seek cover in the culverts, drains and whatever little anthill cover they could find. Before the last fleeing fellow got himself behind a shelter, we were doing victory rolls over the resultant shambles on the ground, and were on our way back to base.

On 24th August I flew a routine 4 x 60lb first run attack airstrike at Kutanga Range. Then two days later, I carried out a live airstrike on Exercise *King Kabanga*. This time, still with Vampires, I dropped four-20lb fragmentation bombs on shallow glide attacks, and also fired 46 x 20mm high explosive incendiary cannon.

As was normal for John McKenzie, he royally accommodated the Brownjobs at the Range, as well as attending to their every need to make the airstrike targets as realistic as possible.

On 27th August I flew with Air Sub-Lieutenant Mike Litson, firing 4 x 60lb rockets. On August 30th, I flew a routine OCU instructional sortie with Air Lieutenant Jim Stagman (of Canberra ejection fame), on low level battle formation.

The other significant event in August was bidding farewell to Wing Commander Porky MacLaughlin as Officer Commanding Flying Wing, Thornhill, and welcoming the new OCFW in Keith Kemsley. Porky Mac had been OCFW since November 1968, when Squadron Leader Bill Jelley was OC 2 Squadron. Porky, always soft spoken, had been a first class Officer and Gentleman. His promotion to Group Captain was welcomed by many. The other noteworthy event in August was the start of Operation *Lobster*.

Operation Lobster: 31 August to 3 September 1971

Operation *Lobster* was a contact with FRELIMO terrorists in the far north-eastern corner of Rhodesia. I was at home when Squadron Leader Tol Janeke called me to pack my bush kit and fly an armed Provost to Rushinga, where an Army call-sign had a fleeting contact with an unknown number of terrorists. In view of the short notice, the Boss Tol assured me that he would send a relief at the earliest opportunity.

When I got to the Squadron, our technicians already had the Provost armed up with frantan and ·303 Browning front guns. It was already fairly late in the afternoon on Tuesday 31st August 1971. As soon as Sergeant Andrews arrived with his kit, we took off from Thornhill in Provost R 3163 and flew the one hour fifty minute sortie to Rushinga. The sun had set an hour earlier, and I did not relish landing with runway flares – my previous night flying sortie on Provosts had been three months ago. Anyway, I was fortunate in that the moon was up, which also explained why FRELIMO had carried out their infiltration into Rhodesia. Rushinga airstrip was also not the easiest to land on, especially at night, because of its very stony surface and marked camber. Anyway, we made it, without any serious mishap. I did sense, though, that my squadron technician gave a sigh of relief when we came to a stop.

Nothing came up for the next two days. I was just about to whinge about the 'hurry up and wait' frustration when a plumb airtask arose. The helicopter guys had been leapfrog trooping and reported that the trackers were now hot on the spoor of a gang making a beeline for the Tete Province in Moçambique. I was asked to get airborne and provide top cover just in case the follow-up call-sign should run into an ambush. Secondly, the No 7 Squadron helicopter pilot would also feel more comfortable with air power being close at hand. I duly got airborne for armed aerial reconnaissance after breakfast on that Friday morning 3rd September 1971.

It became apparent that my aerial presence had slowed the gooks down. When a stopper group didn't pick up any tracks on their cross-graining patrols, the net started to close in on "Freddie". Very shortly thereafter, a fleeting contact took place and one FRELIMO was killed – this being my first battle that recorded an actual FRELIMO terrorist killed. The gooks bombshelled and it became an unproductive exercise to dispatch sticks in different directions. A further stopper group was leap-frogged along their line of flight and I needed to return to Rushinga to refuel – having provided armed top cover for over three hours. The contact with FRELIMO so close to our border was indeed a very significant occurrence. It transpired that ZANLA was being trained at Itubi until late 1971, by which time a new base had also opened up at Mgagao in Tanzania.

When I landed, I was surprised to find that my relief had flown up from Thornhill. I can't recall who it was, but he wasted no time in helping my technician Sergeant Andrews to hand pump Avgas into my Provost. The recent contact just added to my frustration – just as things were showing signs of hotting up, here I was about to return to base. I felt relieved that this operation had not turned out to be another "*lemon*" and that I had at least done my bit, despite sitting for two days twiddling my thumbs. I had enough time to grab a quick bite to eat, and see my relief off to take over the armed cover role needed to support for the ground forces. I hastily packed my bags, bade farewell to my technician and set off in the ferry Provost R 6300 back to Thornhill, arriving before sunset. Logging five hours flying for the day was reminiscent of my Operation *Nickel* days.

Operation Condor: 11 to 12 November 1971

On 11th November 1971, it was time for me to fly Provosts again. My old Vampire instructor, Flight Lieutenant Rob Tasker and I flew to Salisbury in Provost R 3161 to position for Operation *Condor*. I can't recall exactly the details of this operation, but I suspect it may have been an Air Force contribution towards contingency plans for any civil unrest related to the 1965 UDI. However, having been given a Codeword, it was more likely a case of Air Force preparedness just in case air effort was needed in the event of a punch-up with misbehaving Nationalists, or with a group of terrorists. I really didn't mind, because I really enjoyed flying the piston-engined Provost. As it turned out, my return flight to Thornhill in the same Provost, on 12th November 1971, would turn out to be the last time I 'captained' a Provost. It was my 1601th-hour on type. I did however fly in a Provost some four years later, for my knowledge and experience on the Board of Inquiry into the fatal crash of Air Sub Lieutenant Ray Boulter.

On 16th November 1971, I tested Air Lieutenant Roy Hulley for his White Instrument rating on the Vampire. Two days later I carried out a Green rating test for Air Lieutenant Brian Murdoch. He was killed on active service whilst on a casevac mission at Mushumbi Pools in December 1974. On 23rd November 1971, I instructed Roy Hulley in air to ground gunnery and rocket firing – we fired off 47 x 20mm ball cannon and 4 x 60lb rockets. The next day I upgraded Roy Hulley's instrument rating from White to Green. Roy was killed five years later, at Kutanga Range, whilst doing 20mm gunnery in a Vampire. The sortie with Roy Hulley on 24th November 1971 was my last on No 2 Squadron. Squadron Commander Tol Janeke gave me a decent farewell party – knowing that he would be joining me on Canberras. He assessed me as an "Above Average" Provost pilot, with the comment "An experienced and conscientious Provost operator". My assessment on Vampires read "High Average, Weapons results Above Average".

No 5 Squadron: Find and Destroy

I was posted to No 5 Canberra Squadron on Monday 27th November 1971. New Sarum would become home for the next three years. Squadron Leader Tol Janeke, my commander on No 2 Squadron, was also posted at the same time to assume command of the Canberra Squadron.

No 5 Squadron enjoyed a fine reputation and a bit of its past history is essential. The squadron was formed in 1959 with the arrival of the Canberras. Eighteen aircraft were ordered in late 1957, 15 B 2's and three T 4's. The B 2's were immediately available, in storage at 15 Maintenance Unit (MU) at Wroughton, Wiltshire in England. These needed to be brought out of storage, serviced, modified for Rhodesian requirements and made ready for ferrying. For the T 4 order, it was necessary to convert three B 2's. The 18 aircraft cost £50,000 each, with six spare Rolls-Royce Avon MK1 engines at £16,000 each. £30,000 of spares and ground support equipment, modifications, conversion of the three B 2's to T 4's, crew training, brought the total cost to a little over £2,000.000. The Canberras were flown out in four ferries, of four aircraft - on 9th March, 7th April, 4th May and 1st June 1959.

No 5 Squadron was allocated Canberras 160, 162, 164, 167, 170, 172 and 173. No 6 Squadron was allocated Canberras 159, 161, 163, 165, 166, 168, 169 and 171.

Cyprus Detachments

In 1959, the Royal Rhodesian Air Force acquired a wider responsibility as part of the Royal Air Force's potential in the Middle East. The RRAF helped the British to cover such hot spots as Aden, Kuwait and Cyprus, with their Vampires and Canberra bombers. The Canberras participated in several Cyprus Detachments - October 1959, February 1960, July 1960, with the last being in July 1963. Squadron Leader Charles Paxton commanded No 5 Squadron for the first three detachments. I was at Thornhill to witness the last departure. Wives and children were permitted to enter the Security area to bid farewell to their loved ones. It was a carnival occasion as the aircrews started their engines, taxied out and took off for Cyprus.

Our Squadrons fared pretty well, when compared to their British counterparts. Our high serviceability rates and the amount of flying that our chaps did baffled the Royal Air Force aircrews. The experience in operating our Squadrons in harsh desert conditions exercised all aspects of our operational effectiveness.

Alec Roughead and Loss of Canberra R2510

About ten days before I joined No 5 Squadron, Flight Lieutenant Alec Roughead, and his navigator, Air Lieutenant Guy Robertson, were killed in Canberra R 2510. Alec and I had flown together many times, and he had ingeniously 'blown' me up with cordite stuffed into squash balls on quite a few occasions.

Mike Hamence, who co-authored *"Canberra – in Southern Africa Service"* researched and recorded this tragic aircraft accident thus: -

"On 16th November 1971, Flight Lieutenant Alec Roughead with Air Lieutenant Guy Robertson was tasked to fly Canberra R 2510 on a routine 'hi-lo-hi' cross-country training exercise from New Sarum Air Base to the RhodAF bombing range at Kutanga near the small mining town of Que Que, 80 miles to the south-west of Salisbury.

"The weather was typical for the start of the rainy season over the Central African plateau – dense cloud cover with poor visibility in low-level mist and drizzle. The take-off on runway 06 at about 08h00 was seen to be normal. Later transcripts of radar plots and ATC communication with the pilot showed that he had made a normal procedural turn to the south-west after take-off but then had made two sharp reversals of heading after being asked to change course by the approach controller. It also appears that he sounded annoyed when he acknowledged this request.

"He did not answer any further ATC messages and an emergency was declared when the track of the aircraft disappeared from the radar screen. It was some time before the airport fire service found the wreckage of Canberra R 2510. The bodies of the crew were still strapped in the ejection seats in the remains of the front fuselage. The RhodAF investigating team found later that there had been a sudden, catastrophic break-up of the aircraft in mid-air and the crew had had no chance to eject. What caused the aircraft to break up was never proved beyond doubt. The evidence implied that a mainplane had broken off at the main attachments to the fuselage. The aftermath of this accident was to have a profound effect on Canberra operations for the next ten years.

"The question of Canberra structural safety was to be a cause of much acrimony between the Rhodesian Air Force's Air and Technical Staffs."

No 5 Squadron – December 1971
(Front row) Paddy Morgan, Prop Geldenhuys, Bill Stevens, Wedge Brown, Rich Brand, Sqn Ldr Tol Janeke, Glob Pasea, Father Dakyns, John Bennie, Rich Airey and Rich Beaver

It was with this immediate background, that I joined No 5 Squadron to fly Canberras. Failure of "frame 21" was a risk that many pilots were very wary of – myself included. It was logically concluded that a lot of the structural damage had been a result of the ground rocketing that the Canberras had done previously. One of the first changes made was that pilots were not to exceed 4G turns while applying aileron – or in other words, not to try and fly a bomber like a fighter aircraft.

Canberra B 2 – Royal Rhodesian Air Force

Canberra T 4 & B 2

My first sortie in a Canberra was flown on 15th December 1971. My instructor was Flight Lieutenant "Father" Pete Dakyns, with navigator Air Lieutenant Mike Ronne. The sortie, in the T 4 R 2175 was an OCU conversion, familiarisation with a SLD - standard letdown and NDB. Two days later we flew my second dual sortie, Exercise 2, which included circuits and landings as well.

Then on 21st December 1971 I had a rather special sortie in a Vampire. Because I was still current on the Vampire, and to save having to send for a No 2 Squadron pilot all the way up from Thornhill just to do an airtest, I was asked if I would mind carrying out the necessary airtest and a high speed run. What a question. Wing Commander John Mussell came along for the ride, and to help fill in the airtest report. We flew around for an hour and I really enjoyed pushing Vampire T 11 no 4126 to its maximum speed of Mach 0.84. This is the speed at which the effects of compressibility results in the Vampire starting to 'porpoise' - a yawing cum pitching motion as the shock-wave moves fore and aft over the wings. I had previously flown this particular Vampire on 2nd November with Air Lieutenant Ed Potterton. At that time we had cut our sortie short because of jet pipe temperature failure. I can't remember whether it was this snag that had required the Vampire to be serviced at the Aircraft Servicing Flight, New Sarum.

The 24th December 1971 was another milestone in my Air Force career. It was an early Christmas present to go solo on both the Canberra T 4 and B 2. Father Dakyns had given me four sorties, which included asymmetric flying and the solo check. Immediately after my T 4 sortie, he came along on the B2, sitting on the rumble seat. I then took Canberra B 2 number R 2514 up for a forty-five minute sortie with Mike Ronne. There wasn't much to do for my navigator, except perhaps to check on me to lower the undercarriage and make snide remarks about my landings. The control surfaces on the Canberra operate on torque tubes, which result in a slight delay between the pilot making a control column change and the aircraft responding. It took a while to get used to this delayed action - unlike the Hawker Hunter with its very sensitive and responsive behaviour. A nice feature was the twin Rolls-Royce Avon 101 engines - flight on one engine was possible, providing the aircraft inertia was more than 85 knots. Each engine develops 3 000-kg static trust at sea level. I'd flown four sorties on the Christmas Eve and I was content to add another two types to the number of aircraft I had now flown solo. I was very happy with my Christmas presents.

I ended 1971 with a couple of navexs with Mike Ronne and Flight Lieutenant Phil Schooling. On Old Year's Eve, Father Dakyns gave me an asymmetric solo check. This was but a start to a very rewarding flying tour with Rhodesia's main deterrent squadron. I looked forward to my contribution in performing the diverse roles of the Canberra – tactical and strategic bombing, photo-reconnaissance and high-speed courier.

1972 started off with a continuation of my Canberra OCU Conversion. These included being instrument rated, navexs, day and night bombing and general conversion exercises. Armament configurations included 450, 225 or 112-kg bombs, fragmentation bombs and flares carried in the bomb bay. My Canberra Operational Conversion Unit phase was completed on 9th February 1972. Father Dakyns rated me "high average". As a reward, my first jolly, to Cape Town with bombing on the Hopefields Range, came around on 10th and 11th February.

Operation Nimbus: 21 April 1972

Op Nimbus was a combined SAS / RhodAF operation carried out internally from 21st April to 7th May 1972. There was a 'Nil Result' recorded in the Intelligence Corps Operations Table.

Explosive Decompression: 25 April 1972

I highlight this irregular emergency, because not many pilots ever experience such an unusual event. On 25th April 1972, my navigator Mike Ronne was exercising his Astro navex skills. These were boring sorties for the pilot, since it normally entailed only two turning points, flying at very high altitude, in freezing conditions I might add, in order for the navigator to shoot the stars. Towards the end of the sortie, we would drop a couple of bombs, from medium-level, on the range - that is if the navigator got close enough to find the Bombing Range after such a long flight by the stars.

Range Warden John McKenzie would have to sit up till late at night because the average Astro-nav was invariably in excess of three hours night flying. Being about 60 nautical miles off target was not uncommon - it would represent a mere one-degree error. The short duration descent to medium level was hardly long enough to thaw from the freezing levels experienced at altitude. The short leg from Kutanga to Salisbury would invariably be flown between 20 and 25,000 feet. On this particular sortie, we had also flown through a fair amount of cloud, and despite it being a night sortie and black as the proverbial "witch's tit"; I had by then logged an hour and fifteen minutes instrument flying including half an hour 'actual'. Anyway, as we were approaching Salisbury, there was a terrific bang as the Perspex nose cone fractured, blowing a gaping hole in the nose of our Canberra. Mike was still lying in the nose cone - the position he had taken up for our bombing run into Kutanga. With the explosive decompression all the pressurised air in the cabin blew out through the nose cone. Mike was literally sucked forward in his prone position. He lost some of his flying notes and the odd loose article lying around in the nose.

Once it was realised that he would not be sucked out of the aircraft, Mike was able to extricate himself from the bomb-aimer's station. It took a fraction of a second for the air pressure to neutralise itself, but the air swirling around the cockpit was making a terrific racket - so much so that I could hardly hear Mike or the control tower transmissions. I adopted a steep emergency descent to get below 10,000 feet pronto-pronto. I informed air traffic control of our problem and they gave us priority clearance to continue our descent for a straight-in approach and landing. Mike did not strap into his ejector seat for the landing, but remained on the rumble seat.

We landed safely without any further mishap. I, however, could add one more unusual occurrence to my list of flying experiences. Three days later, on 28th April 1972, I had another unusual sortie. I was tasked, with Flight Lieutenant Bernie Vaughan, to carry out a photo-reconnaissance task. Bernie was considered our expert photographer. What made this particular sortie unusual was that Group Captain John Mussell was rather a very senior Air Force officer to just "come along for the ride". I can't remember why the task was sufficiently important to warrant a Group Captain coming along, but regrettably the photo-task was aborted. The reason for the abort was a failure in the intricate fuel system, and we were venting fuel. The memory of my Hunter experience with Al Bruce (when he was forced to eject) was still fresh in my memory, so I took no chances and returned to base immediately. I could just imagine explaining to Air Staff why a Group Captain would have needed to don a parachute had we failed in our mission to get the Canberra safely back on the ground.

These border recces were important for two reasons – firstly to let the gooks know that they infiltrate at their peril; and secondly, to wave the flag for all the South African policemen guarding the border. In this instance, we flew with Sergeant Brown, and also landed at Victoria Falls to refuel (hence the reason for taking one of our ground crew along, to do all the dirty work). We then continued with our northern border recce, landing back at New Sarum.

On 9th May I was able to upgrade my instrument rating to "Green Card". Air Lieutenant Rich Beaver was my safety pilot the day before. It seems that our paths had crossed many a time. Rich Beaver was my OCU student on Provosts and Vampires, and here we were together again on No 5 Squadron, flying Canberras. On the 15th I had that memorable sortie to Beira, via the Zambezi Delta, with Bill Stevens, which I recorded under "jollies" to Moçambique. Our return flight was one of those dreaded 'Astro-nav' sorties – but the consolation was that we made the most of our time in Beira.

Pearce Commission

On 23rd May 1972, I was 'scrambled' to fly the Pearce Report findings to Bulawayo. My navigator and I had carried out a photo-recce task during the day when we were tasked to deliver the report pronto-pronto. Mike Ronne and I took off late afternoon, landing at Bulawayo just as the sun set. After handing over the documents to a waiting courier, we restarted the Canberra, and flew back to New Sarum at night.

The Pearce Report was bad news for the country. The whites had voted overwhelmingly in favour, but the commission found the settlement proposals unacceptable to the blacks. It was a farce (to quote Ian Smith - page 155 - "*The Great Betrayal*").

The Rhodesian Front had won all fifty 'A' roll seats for the second successive time since UDI. Contrary to predictions, the Conservatives won the British general election and Ian Smith concluded a successful agreement with Sir Alec Douglas-Home. Bishop Abel Muzorewa, who campaigned for a "No" vote, did a 180 - and conceded his mistake. But the die had been cast.
It thus transpired that I was the one selected to courier these historically important documents between Salisbury and Bulawayo. Had I known then what I know now, I should have chucked the biased report out of the window. It seemed that no one took Ian Smith's warning seriously regarding the effectiveness of black intimidation, and to "stampede innocent and unwary people."

Boeing Hijack

On 24th May, Mike Ronne and I had just returned from a routine 6 x 130lb low-level bombing exercise at Kutanga when we were told that our aircraft was urgently needed for a quick turn-round - to pursue a hijacked South African Airways Boeing. Canberra R 2156 was duly made ready and I joined the Squadron Commander Tol Janeke, with his navigator, Air Sub-Lieutenant 'Wedge' Brown to follow SAA Flight 029.

SAA Boeing 727, *Letaba*, was on a routine flight from Durban to Johannesburg as Flight SA 029 when it was hijacked by two Lebanese nationals. The hijackers, who had wrongly thought Gordon Waddell, then an executive director of the Anglo-American Corporation and son-in-law of billionaire Harry Oppenheimer, was aboard. Their intention, apparently, had been to kidnap Waddell and hold him to ransom for a million Rand. They threatened to blow up the aircraft unless the pilot flew them to the Seychelles or Tananarive in Madagascar, but he managed to persuade them that the aircraft could only make it to Malawi, provided a refuelling stop was made in Salisbury, Rhodesia. Having landed at Salisbury, the South African Government, which was in constant touch with Salisbury Tower via SAA's radio control in Johannesburg, vacillated when the Rhodesians requested permission to disable the aircraft to stop it taking off again. Permission to shoot out the aircraft's tyres was refused.

This would not have been difficult for although the aircraft had been parked away from the terminal building; the world's top Bisley and service shot-tist (BSAP Don Hollingworth) was only 200 metres away, his rifle loaded and awaiting the order to fire. The Rhodesian Government would not take the responsibility for doing so without South Africa's consent, so the aircraft was allowed to take off for Malawi.

We, meanwhile, had already got airborne in our Canberra, and were circling just south-west of the airfield, waiting for the *Letaba* to get airborne. We did not have long to wait. Salisbury Tower kept us informed, on a different radio frequency, so that the Lebanese hijackers would be unaware of our presence. Boss Tol expertly followed the Boeing Trijet as it climbed to altitude, and set course for Malawi. We followed Flight 029 to the Zambezi River and landed back at New Sarum an hour and ten minutes after our 'chase and escort' mission. Boss Tol promptly briefed Officer Commanding Flying Wing.

Ultimately it fell to Dr Banda's Malawians to take the positive action needed, thus halting any further journeying and ensuring the release of the hostages and the arrest of the hijackers. Regrettably, the Malawians, who were short of the likes of Rhodesian Don Hollingworth amongst their top marksmen, happily hosed the Boeing from nose to tail with bullets, causing enormous damage.

For South Africa it was an uncomfortably close call. For, if the aircraft had been allowed to continue to a state hostile to South Africa, with an insane leader (like General Idi Amin in Uganda or the cannibalistic Bokassa of the Central African Republic), there is no telling what might have happened to the South Africans on board. This had shaken the South Africans to the core, creating the resolve to never shilly-shally with terrorists again.

For me, it was just another noteworthy entry in my Pilots Flying Logbook.

Exercise Black Jack: 4 to 9 June 1972

Black Jack was a Forcex designed to test the operational efficiency of the Air Force squadrons. Flight Lieutenant Bernie Vaughan and I had flown on a photo-task mission on 27th May 1972, in preparation for the Forcex commencing on 31st May. Bernie and I took aerial photographs of Nyamasoto and Bumi Hills weapons ranges, which would be handed to pilots and crews to carry out airstrikes on specific targets. Nyamasoto was not new to me, because I had previously carried out airstrikes there in November 1970, during Exercise *Oxtail*. Bernie and I would thus be something of an advantage, knowing beforehand what the terrain looked like for the Forcex.

Two days later, Mike Ronne and I carried out a practice 6 x 130lb low-level FAC sortie, in preparation for the Forcex. A further bombing sortie was flown on 31st May 1972, in our allocated Canberra number R 2055 – which we would use for the duration of Exercise *Black Jack*.

On 4th June 1972 Mike and I got off to a flying start, dropping our two 130lb bombs low-level at Nyamasoto Range, landing back at New Sarum. After refuelling, we set off again for another 2 x 130lb at Nyamasoto, but this time landing at Kariba for a night-stop. The trip the next day was 'lekker' – after taking off from Kariba we headed for South Africa to drop one bomb at Roedewal Range north of Pietersburg, and continued to Moçambique, where we landed at Beira for our second night-stop, after having flown up low level, along the entire coastline. The concentrated flying programme for Exercise *Black Jack* did not dampen our spirits sufficiently to prevent us from hitting the Moçambique town and frequenting a few "places of ill repute". Our prawn supper was a lot better than could be said for the meals had by many of the other aircrews. Regrettably, this was my last 'flying visit' to this memorable town.

Then early on 6th June 1972, Mike and I got airborne from Beira to drop one 130lb low-level bomb at Kutanga Bombing Range, landing back at Kariba. After refuelling and re-arming, we set off again on a low-level timed exercise, and returning to bomb a water target that had been floated on Lake Kariba. Mike and I dropped our 2 x 130lb bombs on the water target and landed at Kariba. The next day, 7th June 1972, we had our first lengthy sortie of two hours forty minutes, returning twice to drop bombs on the Bumi Hills bombing range – this being the fourth different bombing range used during the Forcex.

On Friday 8th June 1972, we got off to another early start to drop another two bombs on the water target. After landing and refuelling, we then dropped one more bomb on the Bumi Range target and landed at Kariba for lunch and to wrap up the Forcex with a debrief. After lunch, Mike and I loaded our kit plus technician Sergeant Tony Brown for our recovery flight back to New Sarum. All in all, Exercise *Black Jack* was one of those excellent Forcexes with realistic operational exercises to test the preparedness and efficiency of the Rhodesian Air Force fighting capabilities. *Pride of Eagles* makes mention of and expands on this Forcex.

Canberra R 2055 – my aircraft (foreground) on Exercise Black Jack

On Saturday 9th June 1972, Mike Ronne, Sergeant Tony Brown and I were selected (with all modesty, I might add), to carry out a live demonstration at Nkomo Range, dropping 16 x 20lb fragmentation bombs. The demo was air orientation for the Brownjobs on a Coin-ops course. In retrospect, these Army co-operation exercises paid handsome dividends when the Bush War peaked, because by then the Brownjobs had had excellent schooling in the capabilities of the Air Force. They also enhanced the Rhodesian Security Forces reputation of being one of the finest fighting forces in the world – in its day.

On 13th June 1972, Mike Ronne and I flew down to Waterkloof on an Operation *Junction* mission. We returned late afternoon, dropping bombs at Kutanga Range, and getting some night flying in to boot. Then on 19th June, we flew down to Thornhill, dropping a couple of 20 pounders from high level via the Range, and also dropped off Sergeant Stuart. I then had two Operation *Junction* sorties, the first with Flight Lieutenant Bernie Vaughan, down to Pretoria, and the second with Mike Ronne, into Moçambique. On 17th July, I flew with Squadron Leader Tol Janeke in the dual-seat T 4, on a high-speed test run (flown at dusk – so as not to over stress the fragile airframe) and got in some night currency flying as well. We increased our low-level speed up to 450 knots, which was nearly double our normal cruising speed of around 250 knots. At this speed we could out distance the Vampires.

Exercise Chessman

My flying log records that I flew two missions with Air Lieutenant Mike Ronne on Exercise *Chessman*. Both sorties were flown in Canberra R 2504 – the first on 20th July 1972 (which involved formation flying); and the second sortie was flown on 14th September 1972. This sortie included dropping 6 x 130lb bombs.

What made the second sortie so interesting is that on the same day, I flew top cover to Cabora Bassa for the PM – the Honourable Ian Douglas Smith, Prime Minister of Rhodesia. I believe that this was one of those very top-secret missions of which only few people would be aware – our PM holding confidential talks with the so-called Front Line States. This top cover mission was flown in Canberra R 2055, with navigator Air Lieutenant Starry Stevens (who became a Lynx pilot – tragically later killed in the service of his country).

Operation Swordstick II and III: 29 September to 30 October 1972

These were SAS recce operations in Zambia – along the Zambezi Escarpment and old base camp. A fortnight later, from 10th to 11th November 1972 the SAS recce'd G Camp in Zambia. The Air Force was placed on stand-by in case it was called upon.

Operation Junction June 1972 and Operation Alcora June 1973
No 5 Squadron RhodAF and No 12 Squadron SAAF
The author is sixth from the right in the front row

Operation Junction

Operation *Junction* comprised Canberra photo-reconnaissance missions in Zambia and Moçambique. No 5 Squadron was also assisted by a detachment of South African Air Force Canberras from No 12 Squadron from Waterkloof Air Force Base. The South Africans focused their PR missions in Angola and western Zambia.

I flew four missions, logging a total of fourteen hours. I flew two sorties with my regular navigator Air Lieutenant Mike Ronne, on 13th June and 24th July 1972, in Canberra R 2504. The other two sorties were flown with the Photo Leader Flight Lieutenant Bernie Vaughan, in Canberra R 5203, on 12th July and 4th August 1972. The latter trip was a lengthy four-hour mission deep inside Moçambique.

My first trip, with Mike Ronne, entailed a trip down to No 12 Squadron at Waterkloof. To make the most of the mission, we returned via Kutanga to drop 6 x 130lb medium level bombs.

Commandant Gerry Coetzee commanded No 12 (SAAF) Squadron. The South Africans worked exceptionally well with the Rhodesians, and we enjoyed having them share our planning and crew rooms with us. Their interest lay mainly in Angola and Zambia who were openly supporting SWAPO infiltration into South West Africa. I suspect they were using Rhodesia in order to hoodwink any Angolan and Zambian agents monitoring Air Force movements over Southern Africa. What was somewhat unusual about Commandant Gerry Coetzee was that his advancement had been through the navigator profession. Also, Lieutenant Colonel Bob RH Preller had commanded No 12 Squadron during World War II. Bob Preller, and my father, Lieutenant A C F Preller Geldenhuys, served with the SAAF in the battles against the Italians in North and East Africa. It was thus significant that here I was, nearly 33 years later, flying a similar type of aircraft that was also being flown by No 12 Squadron, SAAF. Bill Jelley was appointed OCFW New Sarum in July 1972.

My first Canberra sortie with my best friend Richard Beaver was flown in the T 4 on 3rd August 1972. I was his safety pilot for instrument flying practice. I carried out a repeat for Beav on 8th August. Because of a night flying sortie that night, with Bill Stevens. Three days later, I flew safety pilot for Flight Lieutenant Murray Hofmeyr. It may be recalled that both Richard

Beaver and Murray Hofmeyr were with me during Operation *Nickel* – five years earlier. The three of us were indeed lucky to have survived the Bush War – a quick glance at the 'Roll of Honour' will show just how many of my close colleagues didn't make it.

August 1972 ended with a flurry of photo-reconnaissance missions to Livingstone, Bulawayo, Tuli Block, Bindura, and F96 trials in marginal weather conditions.

Operation Sable: 8 May to 11 November 1972

During September and October 1972, No 4 Squadron deployed four Provosts and a Trojan aircraft to Nyamasoto, to provide air support to the SAS and RLI, operating in the Tete Province of Moçambique. No 7 Squadron provided four helicopters. This operation was code-named *Sable*, and included the odd flight to Tete. The squadron had up to four aircraft on detachment. In the SAS attack, 7 terrorists were killed, 3 captured, and 2 escaped wounded. A further 12 others escaped.

Attending the Officers' Administration Course, run from 18th September to 6th October 1972; put a temporary hold on more exciting flying duties. By early October 1972 two navigator Officer Cadets, Paddy Morgan and Richard Airey, joined No 5 Squadron, to start their Air Force careers. I had the opportunity to fly with both of them soon after returning to the squadron from my Admin Course. On 8th October 1972, I flew Richard Airey down to Thornhill for the Air Force Open Day, and returned the next day with Paddy Morgan. On 26th October, I flew an interesting airtest on Canberra R 2504. A whole mainplane (wing), complete with Rolls Royce engine, had been changed. Several significant sorties were flown during November 1972. The first was flying down to Pretoria (Waterkloof) with Mike Ronne to uplift fellow No 16 Course pilot Flight Lieutenant Bruce Collocott and Air Lieutenant Ken Burmeister. On our return, we dropped Ken off at Thornhill and continued on to Salisbury with Bruce. On 4th November, Flight Lieutenant Schooling and I flew into Moçambique to photograph a FRELIMO terrorist base camp. FRELIMO were making major inroads in the Tete Province, and Special Branch was already keeping tabs on ZANLA terrorists, dressed in FRELIMO uniforms, seeking safe haven whilst establishing arms caches within striking distance of Rhodesia.

On 4th November we got four Canberras airborne for our air-to-air Christmas Card photographs- See photo, previous page. Boss Tol Janeke led the formation. I kept an original, and note with pride that my good pal Richard Beaver – flying number three, and I (as number two) had our picture dispatched to family and friends everywhere.

On 14th November, I got airborne at 03h15 in the morning for a surprise mock attack on Thornhill. We caught the Fighter Air Force Base literally with their pants down – I had a 9x500lb-bomb load, simulating a classical war scenario, with Mike Ronne and Paddy Morgan as the navigator and bomb-aimer. We landed at Thornhill, had a hearty breakfast, and flew back to New Sarum later in the day. The next day I flew with Phil Schooling, checking out Paddy Morgan, on Advanced Navigation School mission turning points at Lourenço Marques and Middleburg (Moçambique and Transvaal). On 16th November, I carried out a 450knot high-speed airtest on the Canberra with the wing and engine change. If the wing failed, I could only blame myself – I was the one that did the original wing and engine airtest. As mentioned, flying at almost double the normal cruising speed, is quite hairy – it can be likened to riding a bucking bronco – or even a jack-hammer. One made sure there were no loose articles in the cockpit, because the violent vibrations had items flying in all directions. The pilot did not have it so bad, with both hands on the control column. It was not comfortable for the navigator, and I knew that they dreaded this type of flying at low level.

Flying was becoming more interesting by the day. If November had been good, then December was even better and it started off with a bang. I flew three sorties on the trot with Flight Lieutenant Bernie Vaughan (as the Photo Leader) on target photography. Our targets were in hostile Zambia and three different terrorist base camps. We started with the furthest, deep inside Zambia, and worked our way closer to our border. The tactic was to diminish the time that the Zambian Air Force would have to scramble their MiGs to intercept us – that is, if they were capable. I still recall those early interdict missions, in the event of our being shot down, and surviving, the Rhodesian Government would disown us, and claim that we must have got lost on a routine navigational training exercise. Anyway, for me it was quite a challenge, as well as a wake-up call not to under-rate the serious twist that the ZANLA dissidents were taking now launching their murderous attacks on the "Jewel of Africa". Bernie and I flew into Zambia on 1st, 4th and 9th December 1972.

Paddy Morgan had also by now passed his navigational training, and been commissioned in the rank of Air Sub-Lieutenant. On 12th December 1972, he and I flew my third 'wing and engine' airtest – in Canberra 2085. A general handling sortie with Bill Stevens, as my nav, followed after my flight with Paddy. My third task for this significant day was a dispatch to Kotwa in the north-east corner, to relieve Squadron Leader Randy du Rand – on Operation *Tempest*, and the start of Operation *Hurricane* (the Bush War proper). Having done two sorties for the day, I hadn't much time to get my butt to Kotwa. My involvement on JOC *Tempest* lasted for a very brief, but highly significant, five days from Tuesday 12th to Saturday 16th December 1972. I was party to wrapping up Operation *Tempest* prematurely.

Then on 22nd December, the so-called "fertiliser hit the fan". Terrorists attacked outlying white farmers. Altena and Whistlefield farms in the Centenary area were attacked on consecutive nights. The news headlines flashed across the country. During that period, I flew twenty-one times, only missing two Saturdays in the process.

On Wednesday 27th December 1972 I flew down to Thornhill with navigator Bill Stevens and Armourer Sergeant Tony Brown, with 3x130lb bombs, to uplift other bigger 3x250lb bombs. We then carried out low level bombing trials, dropping all six bombs. There was basically no difference in the flight characteristics of the various weights. We landed back at New Sarum to report our findings. The next day I flew with my regular navigator, Mike Ronne, to drop another two bombs on a low-level timed navigational and bombing exercise.

Our 1972 Christmas Card photograph - Boss Tol Janeke, the author, then Richard Beaver.

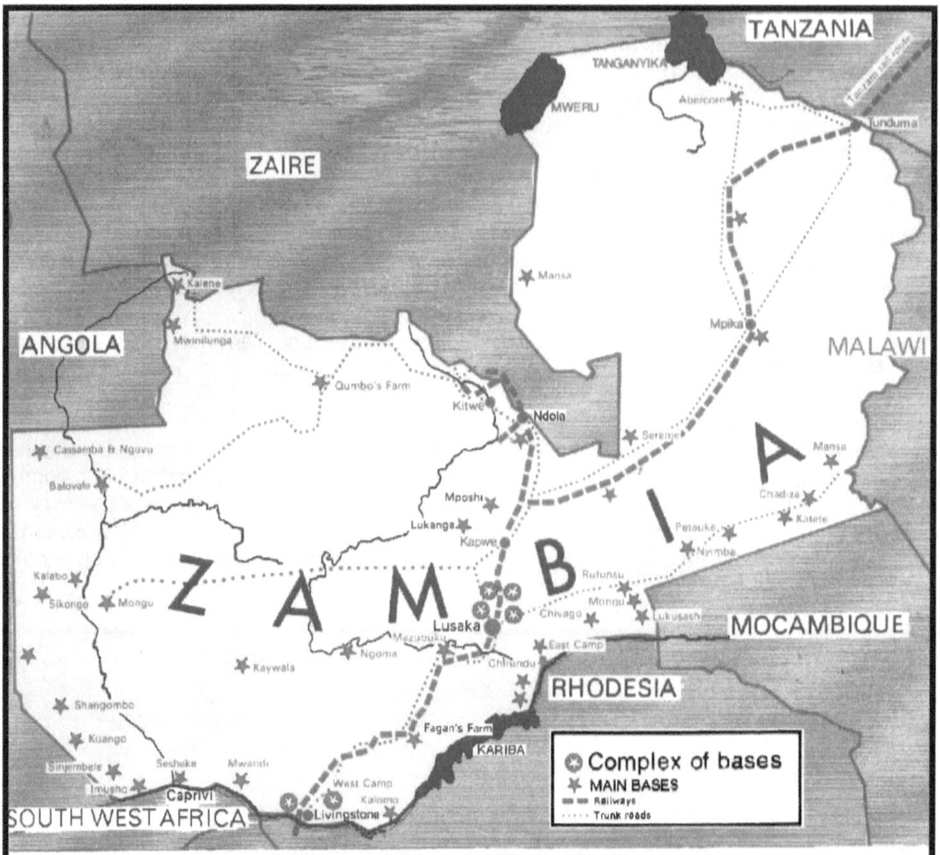

Swapo, ZIPRA, ZANLA, A.N.C. and Frelimo bases

Canberra Contrails at altitude – by Bill Jelley

On Friday 29th December, I flew the camera Canberra, R 2085, with Flight Lieutenant Phil Schooling, to photograph the Luanda road and Railway Bridge in Zambia. This was followed up with my first Operation *Hurricane* photo-reconnaissance mission in the Centenary area, on Saturday 30th December 1972 – also with Phil Schooling. But there was no peace for the wicked – on the Sunday I flew my first Operation *Hurricane* armed-reconnaissance sortie; this time with ace bomber Air Lieutenant 'Wedge' Brown. Our sortie lasted two and half-hours. John Brown and I were hyped up, and felt a little flat on landing, in that a suitable target had not presented itself during our somewhat lengthy presence in the operational area. If anything, our availability to the ground follow up troops must have had a reassuring effect, knowing that air support was just a call away.

I believe the object of the exercise was to provide a jet presence in the operational area to give the invading terrorists a very clear message – that the Air Force meant business. Besides, I had another sortie lined up on New Years Day, and needed my beauty sleep in order to remain alert. John Brown and I accordingly flew our second successive armed mission in the operational area.

The armed reconnaissance sortie was a rather short ninety minutes – I can't recall whether it was 'Wedge', or I, that was having hangover effects. Operation *Tempest*, and Operation *Hurricane*, are major stories on their own.

4 Hurricane

Hurricane

The lull in the Bush War showed signs of being over in the latter part of 1971. Intelligence reports coming in from the north-eastern areas indicated a terrorist presence in the border regions and fleeting contact was made with columns of porters passing southwards through Mazarabani and the surrounding areas. The terrorist presence and activity were not defined clearly enough for the Security Forces to react militarily, but the consistency of the reports was such that it seemed that terrorists were now living among the population. More and more frequently the words Chaminuka and Nehanda appeared in the reports. These were initially identified as names given to the ZANLA military zones which overlapped into Rhodesia from Moçambique. It was then realised that ZANLA had moved ahead in the spirit world by invoking the national spirit of Chaminuka.

Operation Tempest 1: 1 September to 1 December 1972

Op *Tempest I* started off as an internal SAS / RLI COIN operation against ZANU elements in the Chimanda TTL, Rusambo and Ngarwe. Before this Op was wrapped up, Operation *Tempest II* commenced in the north-east, in the Kotwa area.

JOC / Operation Tempest 2: 5 November to 16 December 1972

Operation *Tempest II* from 5th November to 16th December 1972 was the forerunner to Operations *Hurricane, Thrasher, Repulse, Grapple and Splinter* - in fact the Rhodesian War proper - but little did most Rhodesians know or realise at that time.

From subsequent research conducted, it was established that on the night of 4th December 1971 (i.e. a year earlier), two ZANLA terrorists, Justin Chauke and Amon Zindoga, crossed into Rhodesia from Moçambique 's Tete Province near Mukumbura on the north-eastern border. Their mission was to begin laying the groundwork for further infiltration. Their incursion was but a brief reconnaissance contact with a local schoolmaster who was sympathetic to FRELIMO guerrillas. (Author's note: both Chauke and Zindoga survived the war, but in radically different circumstances. Chauke rose to the ZANLA high command but Zindoga was wounded and captured in early 1973. He had one leg amputated and spent the next seven years in prison. Zindoga came from the Chilimanzi area - his real name is Sebastian Hore, and his terrorist nickname was Matsikachando).

During November 1972, intelligence came to light that insurgents had infiltrated from Moçambique into north-east Rhodesia, and an internal operation codenamed *Tempest* was launched on 5th November. The Air Force dispatched a FASOC - Forward Air Support

Operations Centre - Steyr Puch (compact, four-wheeled drive, highly mobile) vehicle to Kotwa in support of the civil defence, Police and Rhodesian African Rifles.

Three ZANLA terrorists were picked up by Special Branch ground coverage, during the earlier part of the operation and Pete Stanton sat them down in a little trench for a bit of privacy, shooed away the scorpions, and got them to tell all they knew. The three captives had been part of an original group of 27 men who had carried war materials from Zambia through Moçambique and into Rhodesia - and their huge arms cache was hidden north-east of Mtoko. Planning was well advanced and ZANLA had divided the northern portion of Rhodesia into Sectors called Nehanda and Chaminuka.

ZANLA had moved ahead of Rhodesian Intelligence in the spirit world. They invoked the national spirit of Chaminuka (the greatest Shona prophet at the time of the First Chimurenga in the 1890s) and by taking into Moçambique the spirit medium Mbuya (Mother) Nehanda, the 'reincarnation' of Nehanda (the powerful regional medium who had been executed during the First Chimurenga in 1898). The implications cannot be over emphasised. Many top brass could not be bothered with all this mumbo jumbo of witchcraft, but it was, and is still a very real and powerful force amongst the Africans. The simple fact was that the Bush War had now taken the Security Forces into the heart of the former Munhumutapa empire, the spiritual home of the Shona people and their allies across the border in Moçambique.

I had first come across the power of the spirit mediums during Operation *Nickel*. Although ZIPRA was involved in a semi-classical resistance then, the terrorists were led to believe that they would be immune to small arms fire. That belief accounted for the fierce resistance during the numerous firefights. It emerged during *Tempest* that terrorist tactics were more focused on avoiding Security Force contact - and when they did, it was more a case of hit-and-run.

Terrorist leader Urimbo took Mbuya Nehanda, an old woman, who lived in a village in the Musengezi area, against her wishes, to the training camp Chifombo earlier in the year. The terrorists constructed a crude stretcher from poles and blankets, and carried her to the Zambezi River, where they were forced to clap their hands before they were able to ferry the old women across the Zambezi in a dugout canoe. A house was built for her to bless the war materials and the terrorists infiltrating Rhodesia. The piece of black cloth that was wrapped around her body was to play a significant role in the indoctrination of her followers. Other spirit mediums used by the infiltrators included one called Chipfeni and another named Chidyamuyu.

It was difficult to believe that the front had advanced so far south. It seemed to have moved 200 kilometres (120 miles) virtually overnight. On 12th December 1972, I was detached to Kotwa to relieve Randy Du Rand as the Senior Air Representative on the JOC. My brief was that the ZANLA terrorists had infiltrated upstream of the Nyamandombo River and established themselves in the Ngarwe TTL north- east of Mtoko near a granite boulder kopje – these hills were fairly prevalent throughout the area. The infiltration route was believed to be from Magazine near the Zambia/ Moçambique border. From Magazine the terrorists trekked south-east to Chifombo, then on to Chicoa which was on the southern bank of the Zambezi River. Infiltrations into Rhodesia were through Musengezi, Mukumbura, Matimbe and Baobab Beacon. The terrorists were using a tree as a letterbox. Unbeknown to the RAR, SB and the captured informer, the kopje was the site of the sought-after arms cache.

The letterbox contained three letters, which were duly noted and subsequently ambushed by the RAR. Quite accidentally a mortar bomb was located which revealed a large quantity of arms, ammunition and explosives, necessitating several helicopter shuttle loads back to Kotwa. In addition - the Black Cloth was found of a female Nganga (ngangas - medicine men). SB Detective Inspector Bob Clegg briefed me to the effect that a group of twelve Gooks had infiltrated close to Baobab Beacon, north of Nyamapanda at a point that is the most north-eastern corner of Rhodesia. Their presence was exposed when one of the terrorists bought ten loaves of bread from a local store. The storekeeper blew the whistle, because it was most unusual for one person to buy so many loaves of bread in that remote area. Shortly thereafter, this group of twelve split into two sections, with one group tasked to abduct the witch called Ndau Marita (she hailed from Maremba, north of Mrewa on the Nyadiri river), and the second tasked to carry out a reconnaissance route into Inyanga. They were marching on high points on one of those free handout road maps that one obtained from petrol stations. They only moved at night, from one hill to another, and would lie up during the day. Tracking was made easier because of the familiar figure 8 prints made by their boots.

It needs to be acknowledged that Special Branch had a near impossible area of responsibility. Bob Clegg had it a little easier - because he also had Dennis Anderson to help him cover sixteen hundred square kilometres. The Police area stretched from the Nyamapanda border post, down to Wedza, and included Kotwa, Mtoko, Mrewa, Marandellas and Macheke. The Mount Darwin area was worse - they had one SB member to cover an area measuring some 8,000 square miles (20 500 sq. Km). Their modus operandi to establish whether the locals were apt to co-operate was quite ingenious at the time. They would dress up like gooks, blacken their faces, arm themselves with AK rifles and then call on selected kraals. A black member would meet with the kraal head, while the rest of the gang would make their presence known at a suitable distance (normally a tree or anthill, where the SBs sweaty white odour would not jeopardise the trap). The black member would ask for favours like beer, women or food. The same team would reappear by day, dressed normally, and query whether the kraal had been 'visited recently by any strangers. If the headman denied any visitors during the night, that particular kraal would be singled out as terrorist sympathisers. If on the other hand, the kraal members' admissions tied up with the SB antics the night before, they knew they would be able to develop known informers.

The same *modus operandi* would also be used in reverse. Sympathetic kraals would be visited by the SF during the day, then a couple of nights later the kraal would be visited again by the same pseudo SB, this time armed with AKs, to query security force movements. Obviously, as much information as possible of terrorist movements would also be extracted from the locals. These developments were later to result in the formation of the Selous Scouts.

An important realisation in this early stage of the Bush War proper was the favoured tactic of the terrorists to site their bases in the mountainous areas. Their preferences, in priority order, were: first, mountain bases; second, plain bases; and last, river and lake bases. They would coerce or force the locals to provide food, make tea and porridge, provide porters, furnish stretcher-bearers to carry the wounded, and employ mujibas (youths) to spy on Security Force movements. For our forces, it was all valuable experience in learning to apply counter-insurgency tactics to fight this scourge of Africa.

It was during Operation *Tempest* that I had the misfortune of co-operating with Major John "Fluff" Templar, one of the few army officers with whom I did not get along - and subsequently met again several times including during joint operations at Rutenga during Operation *Repulse*. We invariably ended up being at loggerheads with one another. Fortunately, the strength in the JOC concept lay in a collection of minds representing each branch of the Security Forces, and one was free to choose whose side one supported. This meant that if I disagreed strongly with say John's viewpoint, I could then opt to side with the Special Branch, BSAP or even the District Commissioner's (representing Internal Affairs) viewpoints. Alternatively, my argument would need to be good enough to persuade the others to come around to my viewpoint. It was all dependent upon one's powers of persuasion.

Four terrorists had been killed at the Letterbox Tree north of Kotwa, four were captured and interrogated (three were later sentenced to death by the High Court and subsequently hanged) and the balance fled back to Moçambique. The leader, Section Commander David Hani declared "We brought all those things to start a war to kill the Europeans and all those people who support the Europeans". I am not aware whether David Hani was related to Chris Hani of SA ANC / Umkhonto we Sizwe / Communist Party leader fame who was assassinated twenty-one years later in South Africa in April 1993.

It was soon established that the gang our JOC had accounted for, was responsible for the various abductions and rape of women, store breaking, the spread of cholera in the Baobab Beacon area and distribution of recruiting posters. Intelligence had also been gleaned that the terrorists intended attacking outlying Police Stations and government offices. We at the Tempest JOC, I must admit, tended to disbelieve the latter warning - possibly because we wanted to wrap up the operation before Christmas and most operations to date were indeed of very short duration. Our short sightedness at that time was clouded by our desire to return to our families in snug suburbia in time for the festive season. Our sub-JOC had in fact accounted for all 12 of the terrorists that had crossed at Baobab Beacon. The other fifteen from the original 27 had either passed through Inyanga or escaped back to Zambia via the Mount Darwin area. SB Superintendent Bob Clegg had confided in me that during their interrogation sessions (in the scorpion trench?), one of the captured terrorists had confessed that he had been on the outskirts of the Mavuradonha Mountain range at the headwaters of the Hoya River for over a year. The terrorists were engaged in subverting the locals and caching arms in the Darwin area. Bob also confirmed that dead terrorists were incinerated - their bodies were doused with petrol, set alight, and buried in shallow graves.

Most internal operations until this time seldom lasted longer than six weeks, to rounding up all the infiltrators. So foolishly, I went along with Fluff Templar and signalled the OCC - Operations Co-ordinating Committee to wrap up Operation *Tempest* - despite having come across the elusive Solomon Mutizwa, Chimurenga name for one notorious Rex Nhongo (later to command the Zimbabwe Army). Convincing intelligence pointed to the fact that the Rhodesian Liberation War was about to start in earnest. Little did I realise that I was in fact right in the middle of arch enemy Josiah Tongogara's MMZ zone, which was to become the Takawira Sector.

And so my FASOC set-up and I departed for base on 16th December. It transpired that it was the right decision. The terrorists had adopted hit-and-run tactics and were more inclined to concentrate on indoctrinating the masses as per their Chinese training in Tanzania and elsewhere. They had learnt the hard way that confronting the Security Forces head-on meant that they would only come off second best. The ZANLA terrorists, by their Chinese teachings, were thus more 'chicken' when compared to the Russian schooling of ZAPU's ZIPRA terrorists who confronted the SF head-on as in the case of *Nickel* and *Cauldron*.

For me personally, Operations *Nickel* and *Cauldron* had been fairly intense and lengthy, and I had no doubts the Security Forces would continue to enjoy military successes as in the past. No sooner had we returned home than all hell broke loose on 21st December 1972. Terrorists attacked tobacco farmer Marc de Borchgrave's Altena homestead in the Centenary area - and so commenced Operation *Hurricane* - only 5 days after my return from JOC Tempest.

While reading *The Struggle for Zimbabwe*, "The Chimurenga War", by biased authors David Martin & Phyllis Johnson, with *Foreword by Robert Mugabe*, I read with interest Rex Nhongo's involvement during Operations *Tempest* and the start of *Hurricane*.

Operation Hurricane

Just before and after *Tempest*, my flying highlights included:-
- A jolly to Waterkloof to uplift Flight Lieutenant Bruce Collocott and Air Lieutenant Ken Burmeister in a Canberra on Air Task 887. Bruce was later (31st May 1977) killed in action when he was taking off in a Dakota from Mapai airstrip in Moçambique.
- Canberra PR (photo-recce) of a FRELIMO terrorist base camp.
- 2 x 9 x 500lb Classical War exercise, attack Thornhill, Take-off at 03h15.
- Low level high-speed air tests at 450 knots.
- Port Elizabeth and Cape Town jolly, flying down along the East Coast.
- 25th Air Force Anniversary flypast on 28th November 1972
- Three PR sorties of Zambian terrorist base camps.
- PR of Luanda Bridge and first Operation *Hurricane* PR sortie on December 30th.
- First Operation *Hurricane* armed recce on Old Year's Eve and then New Years Day 1973.

Centenary: As previously mentioned, the War proper started on 21st December 1972 and lasted for eight years until late 1979. Looking back, no one could have realised the significance of Marc de Borchgrave's involvement in the history of Rhodesia - which resulted in the turbulent birth of Zimbabwe - and the demise of our beloved Rhodesia. Following the abortive attack on the Altena homestead in which one of his children received minor injuries during the brief skirmish, the de Borchgraves sought refuge at their neighbour Archie Dalgleish's Whistlefield farm. As luck would have it, Whistlefield was the next to be attacked two nights later and again one child of the de Borchgrave's received injuries during the terrorist rocket and grenade attack.

The terrorists also burned down the farm store as well as a nearby church (we ask, why a church?) as they hotfooted it back to their base in the Chiweshe Tribal Trust Land. The terrorist attack on the farm homestead was cowardly, carried out by a section of nine gooks led by Jairos, deputy to Rex Nhongo.

The first SF casualty of Operation *Hurricane* was a white soldier who died from a landmine blast whilst responding to the farm attack. Two landmines had been detonated, killing Corporal Norman Moore of the Rhodesian Light Infantry, and wounding another three soldiers.

It transpired that in November 1971, Tongogara went to Tanzania to collect the first forty-five so-called *guerrillas* i.e. terrorists who had been specially trained for the impending north-eastern offensive. In three trucks, supplied by the OAU Liberation Committee, and carrying food, clothing and weapons as well as cadres, they went to the FRELIMO farm outside Lusaka and then onto Kaswende camp. Their arrival at Chifombo was delayed because of a Portuguese attack on the camp at that time. When they got there, they were divided into two groups. Twenty-three began carrying armaments from Chifombo to the Zambezi, under the command of Chamunorwa (who later died in a contact). The remaining twenty-two, commanded by Thomas Nhari, portaged the arms on south to the Rhodesian border. Each leg took three days, walking some thirty kilometres a day. These arms were then cached in Rhodesia throughout 1972. Some of the caches were buried in the vicinity of St. Albert's mission school, north-east of Centenary, and through the Dande, Chesa, Mount Darwin and Centenary farming areas over a period of six months.

Rex Nhongo, Jairos and Hopedzichirira split their group in three sections of seven terrorists, because Nhongo was afraid of risking his entire force in a single battle should they be confronted by the SF. Nhongo is claimed to have taken the decision to attack Altena Farm. On hearing the news on Rhodesia radio on 19th December, intimating that *the group in the Mtoko area had run into difficulties with the security forces* (my quote, verbatim, referring of course to Operation *Tempest*). He claimed that he decided to act to take the pressure off them - little did he know that we had wrapped up *Tempest* three days earlier. He thus decided on the hit-and-run tactic in order "to hit farms so that we could destroy the economy of the country". They ran to their base in the Chiweshe, to await feedback from their *Mujibas* (their eyes and ears sympathisers) regarding Rhodesian response to their cutting the telephone lines, mining the roads, and their cowardly attack on isolated farmers.

The reaction, in fact, was a rapid deployment of troops, armoured cars, and helicopters from No 7 Squadron and reconnaissance aircraft from No. 4 Squadron. To my knowledge, Marc de Borchgrave did not live to see the end of the war. Despite surviving numerous terrorist attacks, he died during a hunting trip. If my memory serves me correctly, he was trampled by an elephant (how fortunate I was earlier in 1965 to escape a charging elephant - not on one occasion - but two - during my UDI stint at Kariba, with Polly Postance on Operation *Wizard*).

After my two successive Operation *Hurricane* armed reconnaissance sorties with Wedge Brown, I spent the first week of 1973 concentrating on medium-level and low-level bombing, for calibration, categorisation and operational conversion training for Rich Airey. Then on Sunday night, 7th January 1973, No 5 Squadron was called out to disperse its Canberra aircraft. Mike Ronne was waiting for me when I arrived at the Squadron, and we hurried to Thornhill. We spent the night there, returning to New Sarum on Monday. I guess we were being tested or exercised to iron out any contingency plan shortcomings in the event of a real threat arising.

The second week of January was spent completing Paddy Morgan's operational conversion unit training. Then on Sunday 14th January 1973, I flew my third Operation *Hurricane* armed reconnaissance sortie – this time with my regular navigator Mike Ronne, but also with Sergeant Tony Brown, possibly because we were flying with a full load of 96 x 20lb fragmentation bombs in the bomb-box. Then on Friday 19th January, 1973, Bernie Vaughan navigated for our second photo-reconnaissance mission. My next PR sortie was flown with Phil Schooling a week later. Operation *Hurricane* sorties were now coming up with monotonous regularity.

JOC Centenary

A Joint Operations Command or JOC was established at Centenary on 30th December 1972 to confront the most recent infiltration - and this was then the official start to Operation *Hurricane*. Although I got back from Operation *Tempest* seven weeks earlier, I was deployed to Centenary from Saturday 3rd February 1973 for a month.

The JOC was a further refinement of the FASOC concept - it consisted of the most senior representatives of all the Security Forces present together with the local District Commissioner and any other co-opted members who were able to contribute to the most efficient discharge of combined operations. Chairmanship of this mini-war council would rotate but all decisions were considered Joint responsibility. This held true for all successes as well as all failures....and let us not kid ourselves, some decisions taken collectively were not always the right ones. The idea being that no one person would be held liable for a Foxtrot Uniform (a foul up).

A FAF - Forward Air Field was set up at Centenary and the main JOC moved to Darwin. As *Hurricane* progressed, another Sub-JOC was established at Mtoko and the Army relocated their Brigade Headquarters to Bindura - which was then central to the other sub-JOCs at Centenary, Mt Darwin and Mtoko.

Eighteen days after the Altena farm attack, three land inspectors, Gerald Hawksworth, Dennis Sanderson and Bob Bland, with their two black messengers were ambushed on a road in the Mount Darwin area. Bland and Sanderson were killed - the first white civilians killed by terrorists since the Viljoens in May 1966. ZANLA took Hawksworth prisoner. The blacks escaped. SAS Captain Garth Barrett and Lieutenant Chris "Schulie" Schulenburg were paradropped by Air Force Dakota, from 11,000 feet, on either side of the Musengezi River, some 36km inside Moçambique. Their mission was an attempt to intercept the fleeing terrorists. Unfortunately, Sergeant Frank Wilmot's main parachute did not open and he spun into the ground. Helicopter pilot Peter Woolcock retrieved the body.

It was also during my detachment to Centenary that we got the sad news that well-liked Kevin "Tinker" Smithdorff was killed on active service in the Ruya Game Reserve, with Air Lieutenant John Smart, in an Alouette helicopter prang. Tinker was a member of 16 LAR, who attested into the Royal Rhodesian Air Force in January 1964. He was related to Mark Smithdorff, who did my Final Handling Test on Provosts, whilst I was a Cadet during Basic Flying School. Mark was the 'A' Flight Commander at that time.

When I got back to the Squadron on 5th March 1973, I had a change of navigator. Air Lieutenant Mike Ronne had been my navigator for some fourteen months, up to the end of January 1973 (since I had joined the Canberra Squadron in November 1971). I was then allocated fellow No 16 Course colleague, navigator Flight Lieutenant Doug Pasea with effect from 5th March 1973. On that day, my first day back on the Squadron, we flew my first airstrike, dropping a 96 x 20lb bomb-box load on a terrorist target. The Canberra for my first strike in anger, was R 2155. Aircraftsman Ullyett came along for the experience.

Doug and I had knitted well together – during March we had carried out no fewer than seven Operation *Hurricane* photo-reconnaissance sorties. Four of the PR sorties were flown in "Funnyland" – alias Moçambique, whereas the others were aerial reconnaissance for Army purposes. For the remainder of March 1973 our flying was mainly calibration, application and categorisation bombing. We also carried out one of those high-speed airtests, pushing the Canberra airframe up to 450 knots. All told, we put in nearly forty-seven hours flying for the month. That was well above average for a jet-jock.

April 1973 was interesting for several reasons. I rated ex-Squadron Commander Flight Lieutenant Ian Donaldson, who was flying with Starry Stevens as his navigator, a Green instrument flying standard. Both were destined to play historical roles in the Bush War. Then later in the day, Doug and I carried out a dusk medium-level bombing at Kutanga, dropping 4 x 130lb and 2 x 1,000lb high-explosive 'big daddies'. The thousand pounder bombs were a beauty to behold – in terms of the noise and the devastation they caused on the ground. They virtually reduced the target to a wasteland, leaving craters that were visible for miles around. Then the next day, 4th April 1973, whilst on an operational PR sortie deep inside Zambia en route to the Tanzam Railway line, one of our engines failed. I was unable to re-light the engine and was forced to fly asymmetrically on just one engine all the way back to Rhodesia, fortunately without further adverse event. I must say, though, it is a very uncomfortable feeling being deep inside enemy territory with one engine out and no 'reserve' should the other conk out.

Then I also carried out instrument rating tests for our Squadron Commander, Squadron Leader Tol Janeke and QFI Flight Lieutenant John Bennie. The highlight by far though, was my appointment as Flight Commander.

No 5 Squadron – March 1973
Paddy Morgan, Prop Geldenhuys, Starry Stevens, Wedge Brown, Rich Brand, Boss Tol Janeke, Glob Pasea, Father Dakyns, Jeb Bennie, Rich Airey and Vulch Beaver (Three navigators not shown – Phil Schooling, Bernie Vaughan and Mike Ronne)

No 5 Squadron – 'A' Flight Commander

13th April 1973 was a milestone in my career - I was appointed to the command post of 'A' Flight Commander on No 5 (Canberra) Squadron, Rhodesian Air Force. I trust that Bill Jelley had input, because he was still the Officer Commanding Flying Wing.

NO 5 SQUADRON INTERNAL ORGANIZATION

(with effect from)
1 May 73

Sqn Ldr F.D. Janeke	–	Squadron Commander
Flt Lt P.M. Geldenhuys	–	A Flight Commander/IRE
Flt Lt B.W. Vaughan	–	B Flight Commander/Tech Liaison/Nav Leader
Flt Lt D.W. Pasea	–	Photo Leader
Flt Lt J.E. Bennie	–	Ground Training/Survival
Flt Lt I.H. Donaldson	–	QFI/Standardization/ Chiredzi Liaison
Air Lt R.G. Beaver	–	Flight Safety/Intelligence
Air Lt J.J.F. Brown	–	Adjutant/Sqn Fund
Air Lt H.W.H. Stevens	–	Bombing Leader
Air Sub Lt W.R. Airey	–	Ops Briefing Room/Dep Bombing Leader
Air Sub Lt M.J. Delport	–	Sport/Dep Adj/Inventory
Air Sub Lt S.P. Morgan	–	Map Store/Publications

Many changes occurred during the short course of a year. Pilots came and pilots went. 'Father' Dakyns was posted to Dakotas, Rich Brand was posted to No 1 Squadron, Navigators Phil Schooling retired to go farming in the Eastern Districts in the Cashel area and Starry Stevens remustered to pilot training. Ian Donaldson packed up his co-ownership of a Lowveld newspaper and rejoined No 5 Squadron. Mick Delport was also posted to the Squadron during April 1973.

I replaced Rich Brand as "A" Flight Commander, and my fellow No 16 PTC colleague Bernie Vaughan replaced Phil Schooling as "B" Flight Commander. Ex-Squadron Commander Ian Donaldson replaced Father Dakyns as the Squadron QFI. I respected Ian for accepting his station in life and was guided by his wise counsel in the performance of my duties as the Flight Commander and Instrument Rating Examiner on the squadron that he had previously commanded before he left to go into the Lowveld newspaper business.

My first big challenge came around before the month was out. On the 27th and 29th April 1973, Bernie Vaughan and I flew two successive Operation *Hurricane* aerial reconnaissance missions on two terrorist base camps in Moçambique. On landing on the 29th, the Squadron mounted an airstrike on the first camp that Bernie and I had photographed. I got airborne in Canberra R 2519, which had been loaded up with a bomb-box with 96 x 20lb fragmentation bombs, and carried out the airstrike with Doug Pasea, plus Air Lieutenant Rich Beaver as passenger cum observer. The airstrike went in exactly as planned. By the time we landed, the photo-interpreters had had time to develop and study the prints of the second terrorist base that Bernie and I had taken earlier in the day. The decision was taken to attack the second target at first light the next day. That gave all the aircrews time to study their targets that night. And so, early on 30th April 1973, I got airborne again, in Canberra R 2502, with my navigator Flight Lieutenant Doug Pasea, and newcomer Air Sub-Lieutenant Mick Delport (as my passenger cum observer), for our second airstrike into Moçambique. We again dropped nearly two tons of fragmentation bombs from our bomb-box. In reality, it could be said that "this is where the rubber meets the road". This is what our training was all about – to bomb the hell out of the enemy, using the most powerful weapon available to the Air Force.

May 1973 was a month for a lot of trips to South Africa. The first jolly was a day stop to Pretoria on the 4th with Paddy Morgan. The next was on the 15th to drop off Rich Beaver and Bernie Vaughan to bring back a Canberra that had been fitted with the Doppler navigational aid. I then had a bombing sortie with Doug Pasea to Roedewal Range north of Pietersburg, and then that very memorable sortie to Hopefields, Langebaan and Cape Town when my inexperienced technician Senior Aircraftsman filled the wrong tanks first – making our nose-wheel Canberra a "tail-dragger". Other notable sorties were two airstrikes on terrorist targets and three aerial reconnaissance sorties on Operation *Hurricane*. The first airstrike was with Doug Pasea, on 5th May 1973, dropping 96 fragmentation bombs, and the second was on the 21st May, dropping 9 x 500lb bombs. Rich Beaver was my passenger cum observer on the latter – our target being a terrorist base in Moçambique.

Standing: Paddy Morgan, Mick Delport, Rich Airey
Sitting: Starry Stevens, Vulch Beaver, Glob Pasea, Ian Donaldson, Prop Geldenhuys, Air Vice-Marshal Mick McLaren, Sqn Ldr Tol Janeke, Gp Captain Stn Cdr, Bernie Vaughan, Jeb Bennie, Wedge Brown

No 5 Squadron did particularly well during 1973, so much so that we were awarded the coveted Jacklin Trophy as the best squadron in the Air Force - I believe our good showing during the *Black Jack* Forcex had made an impact. As was normal for the recipients, a formal parade was held at New Sarum. The Commander of the Air Force, Air Vice-Marshal Mick McLaren, presented the Jacklin Trophy to the Squadron.

When Rich Beaver was posted to No 3 Squadron, I took over his extraneous duty of writing the Squadron History. Rich presented the Squadron with leather bound covers in which to file the monthly History reports, and I did justice to this upgrade with my first write up concerning No 5 Squadron's 40 ton week. Air Lieutenant Keith Goddard was posted to No 5 Squadron to fill the pilot vacancy when Richard Beaver left. Officer Cadet Jim Russell replaced 'Wedge' John Brown, who had shown computer aptitude and re-mustered later on in the year. He was nicknamed 'Wedge' because that is the lowest form of tool known to mankind – a most inappropriate sobriquet.

The Rhodesian Herald headline – August 1973

The Rhodesian Herald headline – August 1973

Squadron Leader Tol Janeke, John Bennie and Prop Geldenhuys admiring the JacklinTrophy

Operation Alcora: 6 June to 19 August 1973

Operation *Alcora* started on 6th June 1973. This was deep penetration into Zambia on aerial reconnaissance with telephoto lenses. I flew the mission with Doug Pasea, and our flight time of three hours twenty minutes took us virtually to the Zairian border. *Alcora* is the subject of a separate story in its own right.

By mid-June 1973, our needs for more sophisticated navigational aids were satisfied with the installation of Doppler systems into the Canberras. On 18th June 1973 I flew down to Waterkloof with Flight Lieutenant Bernie Vaughan, and Flight Sergeant Mo Houston in Canberra R 2055 for Doppler trials. Doppler can be likened to dropping a pebble in a pond of water – Doppler radiates radio waves away from the aircraft – and the return signal is measured. The navigator is thus able to compute distance and bearing – either position travelled at that point in time, or distance and heading to reach a target. Doppler was thus a technological advancement for No 5 Squadron, at a time that we needed it most. Had Jim Stagman and Polly Postance had Doppler at their disposal, it is most likely that they would not have ejected from their Canberra. I was fortunate to be on the ground floor when this development occurred. Bernie was our most senior navigator, and Mo the radio fundi charged with the installation.

On 20th June 1973 Doug Pasea and I flew on a PR Survey of Paradise Island in the Moçambique channel. This was a special trip for me, having spent my honeymoon there over six years earlier. Santa Carolina Island was set in idyllic coral seas; the hotel had been expropriated by Samora Machel and turned into an island fortress. Socialism had robbed the Moçambicans of much needed capitalist foreign exchange. Machel was obviously more concerned with his own personal safety than what was good for the country. Anyway, our trip took us nearly three and half-hours to photograph the whole island, and to return safely to Salisbury.

On 29th June 1973, I ended the month with a close formation flypast over Salisbury with Bill Stevens. During the last week, I had flown with six different navigators – Bernie Vaughan, Doug Pasea (my normal navigator), John Brown, Bill Stevens, Paddy Morgan and Rich Airey. The sorties were mainly air tests, including one high speed run airtest at 440 knots. July 1973 was somewhat subdued – I flew a mere 13½ hours, mainly aerial reconnaissance on Operations *Polar* and *Hurricane*. From mid-July to end of August I stood in as Acting Officer Commanding No 5 Squadron, which possibly accounted for the low airtime put in.

The next significant change occurred when Squadron Leader Tol Janeke left, on promotion in June/July 1973, and I held the temporary vacancy as OC 5 Sqn for a couple of months.

Operation Onyx: July/August 1973

Some operations, like Operation *Onyx*, are so Top Secret that even the mention of the code-word raises eyebrows from those in the know. Very few aircrew that are air tasked on some top secret missions realise how their particular contribution fits into the grand scheme of things. A sortie may even be flown by an unsuspecting crew, which they treat as just another mission. Sometimes the penny drops, but more often than not, it does not.

Onyx was a very "Smersh" arrangement between Rhodesia, South Africa and Portugal, and entailed a tri-partite project that would normally be outside the scope or resources of just one partner or Country. I came across *Onyx* by chance while I was standing in as Acting OC 5 Squadron for July and August 1973. Squadron Leader Tol Janeke had been promoted to Wing Commander, with our new Boss Randy du Rand taking over in September. The Rhodesian Air Force was tasked with taking all the risks with our Canberra PR capabilities, Portugal was funding the project, and South Africa was using their expertise in developing (and cleverly copying, I might add) all the film. After South Africa had processed the film, they would dispatch their side of the bargain to Lisbon. When Angola and Moçambique went sour with the overthrow of Dr. Caetano by General Antonio de Spinola; the proverbial cat was out the bag. Spinola's broadcast of 27th July signalled the disappearance of Portugal from Africa.

The map I refer to was photographed by No 5 Squadron, South Africa had all the proofs, and Portugal was hurling in the towel - as well as shutting its purse. When Portugal demanded all the film, South Africa was forced to release it, but not before making damned sure that they had a duplicate of everything we had taken. I don't think we had the expertise, or resources to go it alone, and in the end were possibly the losers. Portugal no longer had any interest in the overseas Provinces, and just wanted to pull out - boots and all.

It may be recalled that air and ground co-operation between No 12 SAAF Squadron and ourselves, militarily speaking, was of the highest order, and that we had operated together on numerous ventures. However, once the politicians poke their noses into things military, a bugger-up becomes the result. I wait with interest, for this full story to be told, one day.

Squadron Leader Randy du Rand assumed command of the Squadron in September 1973. This necessitated further reorganisation resulting in me losing my navigator, 'Glob' Doug Pasea to the new Boss. Air Sub-Lieutenant Paddy Morgan became my new navigator on 25th September 1973. A new addition to the Squadron included Flight Lieutenant Rick Culpan – but I don't recall him staying very long before he was posted back to No 1 Squadron.

Operation Heup: 3 April 1973

Operation *Heup* was a SAAF operation, which entailed the transfer of six Alouette II helicopters to the SAP on 3rd April 1973. These aircraft were attached to No 7 Squadron and used in the roles of training and communication such as changeovers in the field, thus releasing much needed Alouette III helicopters for operational duties – due to increased terrorist incursions. All of them displayed the SA Police markings, but after the SAP were withdrawn, they were transferred to the Rhodesian Air Force. They all survived the bush war, and were returned to South Africa in 1980/81.

Operation Overload: 1973

Operation *Overload* was the movement of 60,000 people into twenty-one Protected Villages in the Chiweshe Tribal Trust Land. The movement of so many locals into security fenced and floodlit villages was carried out at enormous cost. The *Rhodesian Herald* noted "... brings Rhodesians to the sharp realisation of the extent of the terrorist infiltration despite the great success of the Defence Forces in active operations". More so, because Chiweshe was a mere one hundred kilometres from Salisbury. However, cost effectiveness had to be viewed against the cost in lives that the terrorists inflicted on innocent civilians for refusing to provide them their livelihood of living off the land.

In the first full year of operations, 300 terrorists were killed – 850 blacks abducted – eleven Europeans and 74 African civilians murdered in attacks on farms, settlements, villages and vehicles. 37 members of the Security Forces were killed. The total white population of Rhodesia, in 1973/74 was a mere 280,000. The regular armed forces strength was 4,700 (about two thirds Black). The country also had 10,000 Territorial soldiers, 8,000 BSAP and 35,000 reservists.

The RHU – Reinforcing Holding Unit were veterans of the community on reserve who were 38 years old or more. Manpower shortages resulted in more and more RHU being called up for service.

Mount Darwin & "No Go"

I did various stints at Mt. Darwin between November 73 and December 74. This part of the country was a notorious safe haven for terrorists that resulted in the establishment of PVs - Protected Villages.

During the early part of the war, Captain Dumpie Pearce, of Op *Cauldron* fame (when his stick was inadvertently bombed by the Canberras), formulated the frozen area concept whereby the Selous Scouts and pseudo troops could operate without fear of coming to grips with the SF. It was first used along the Ruya River where a famous pseudo operator, Andre Rabie of the SAS, met his death due to an incorrect location given. In hot pursuit of terrs the Support Commando of the RLI mistook Rabie for the enemy, and so he died in September 1972 without having claimed a kill.

Shortly before Rabie's death, he had picked up a gook named Kefas Mashangara. Rabie established that nine terrorists were moving from their Chibara hide-out. During the ensuing follow-up, contact was made at Mukaradzi Mine and three gooks were killed. Their commander

Kennedy Zvamutsana died from his wounds en route to a new camp in the Chesa African Purchase Area.

Enter Basil Moss. I got to know Basil when he was Flight Lieutenant Officer Commanding 'A' Squadron General Service Unit. I was OC Admin Wing Thornhill and involved with the GSU who were the forerunners of the Air Force Regiment. Unbeknown to me, Basil was secretly a 'star' pseudo terrorist because of his uncanny knowledge of the African language and a unique ability to imitate Africans. Every now and again Basil would 'disappear' for Special Forces duties he indeed features with distinction in Ron Reid-Daly's "*Selous Scouts, Top Secret War*", and his "*Pamwe Chete*" edition (published 1999). He was seconded to serve with the Selous Scouts in July 1973.

Basil, as one of the original pseudos, (together with Alan *(Stretch)* Franklin) was instrumental in a contact with two terrorist groups nineteen in number, in the Chesa African Purchase area. This resulted in four captures and three killed - including veteran gook Jakachaka, and two others who had arrived a scant 10 days earlier. Also, information was gleaned from captured gook Andrew Makoni that ZANLA was using the FRELIMO camp called Horteiro in the Matimbe area of Moçambique as a transit point. A little bit more about Basil later on.

My first deployment to JOC Darwin was from 25th November to 13th December 1973. Being a Bluejob I did not have to risk landmines or ambushes - we took the short cut and positioned by air. The JOCs certainly contributed to the fine teamwork amongst the various security branches and did much to engender an esprit de corps within one's own chosen profession. Captain Pat Armstrong, later Lieutenant Colonel Commanding RLI, made a significant impact on the day-to-day conduct of the war effort. I also take my hat off to those wonderful ladies who established the Forces Canteens in the forward areas.

It was during my time at Darwin that the gooks were caching arms and ammunition along the north bank of the Mukumbura River, and infiltrating gangs into the Gwetera and Fura areas of Mount Darwin. The Chesa African Purchase Area in the Centenary area was also a hive of terrorist activity. It is pertinent to point out the terrorist zoning of the various areas. The area straddling the Musengezi River (and the Umvukwes - Centenary road running northwards) was initially called the MMZ Sector - Zimbabwe- Moçambique zone. This zone later became the "Nehanda" zone. The Bindura - Mount Darwin road bisects the "Chaminuka" zone, lying east of the Nehanda sector. Then further east, east of the Mazoe River, lay the "Takawira" sector. The Takawira sector was bisected by the Mwera - Mtoko - Kotwa road bisecting the zone.

John Vorster's concept of "Détente" was well under way by this time. Under duress, Ian Smith reluctantly agreed to release the detained nationalists for talks. When Kenneth Kaunda's aide, Mark Chona came to collect the detained leaders for talks in Lusaka in early November, Ian Smith wagged a finger at him, saying, "If you can achieve unity, you can come back and cut this finger off." I believe Ian Smith realised the futility of the exercise - and his serious concerns, that the released detainees were to be given golden opportunities to intensify the war effort, were justified.

A week after I left Mount Darwin, on 20th December 1973, Air Lieutenant Dave Rowe was wounded whilst trooping in the operational area. While approaching a landing zone, his Alouette helicopter came under heavy terrorist ground fire and the pilot was seriously wounded in the right arm and right leg. Dave's helicopter technician, Sergeant Chris de Beer, immediately attempted to bind the wounds and to assist his pilot. However, it soon became obvious that Dave Rowe would not be able to fly the helicopter back to the base camp, and, a forced landing became imminent. Dave briefed his technician on the use of the collective pitch lever, which the pilot was unable to operate as he now needed his left hand to operate the cyclic control. The collective is the vital flight control for landing and taking off. With both members of the crew operating various flying controls, a safe landing was made, thus saving the aircraft and the lives of the troops on board.

Between ground duties and Field Force deployments, we Bluejobs enjoyed doing what we do best in the air. Some of my more noteworthy sorties included the following air strikes.

Zambezi: Two air-strikes were carried out on 19th and 21st February, dropping 2 x 96 frag bombs, with Navigators Air Sub-Lieutenant Richard Airey and Flight Lieutenant Bernie Vaughan

(Rich Airey was subsequently killed in action). According to my logbook, I had the 20th off - lucky me.

Moçambique: Another two air-strikes were carried out on 23rd February 1974 flying with Randy du Rand / Doug Pasea dropping 9 x 500lb medium charge high explosive bombs, and 9 x 500 HEI, again with Bernie Vaughan. An additional 9 x 500lb sortie was also flown on 11th January, but aborted because of low cloud over the target area.

JOC Bindura

I carried out numerous stints at Bindura - either passing through for briefings, serving as Operations Officer or as the Air Rep on the JOC. My first stint was from 6th to 21st March 1974.

Throughout 1974 the detainees were moved several times. Mugabe was detained in Salisbury, while Nyagumbo, Enos Nkala and Edgar Tekere were transferred to Que Que. It is there that the latter three hatched their plot to suspend and oust Sithole. The militants were not satisfied with progress made with Vorster's détente. In addition, Portugal's collapse favoured opening up the Moçambique front for the terrorists.

I met Brigadier John Hickman at Bindura and in my estimation he was one of the main architects of the Selous Scouts. I remember him as a ladies man especially in the posh Browns Pub. Very strict traditional rules of etiquette and dress applied as in all the Army field messes. To my knowledge, he was the only senior ranking Army officer who always wore a styled safari-suit type bush jacket.

I've always regarded Brigadier Hickman as a truly professional soldier and it came as no surprise later when he commanded the Rhodesian Army as a Lieutenant General. I recall talking to him in the pub and gaining the impression that he was a field man - not a desk bound career officer. It was rather through force of circumstances, when his rival, Major General John Shaw was killed in an Alouette helicopter crash, that Brigadier Hickman was destined for higher places. It was also ironic, for me anyway, that despite his belief in pseudo operations and subsequent support for the Selous Scouts, he fell from grace due to the unfortunate Mess incident involving Lieutenant Colonel Ron Reid-Daly (concerning the latter's telephone bugging incident).

Staying at Bindura, I should mention Group Captain Ken (KAS) Edwards (my No 4 Squadron Commander) and Volunteer Reservist Flight Lieutenant Dave Stephens of No 101 (Bulawayo) VR Squadron. Boss KAS, later as Air Commodore and Director General Operations, is another airman who had a great influence on my life and Air Force career. He was always approachable, stood by his subordinates' rights, and was prepared to shout the odds - but beware you did not "cuff" a requirement or reveal the full facts regarding any matter. When I lodged a complaint against a No 3 Squadron Dakota crew for poor airmanship, when they did their run up right in front of my Provost on a newly graded runway, Boss KAS followed through by reporting the incident to Boss Ozzie Penton - who was OC Flying Wing at New Sarum.

As Strike 1 at Air Force Headquarters, it was my co-responsibility with Tac 1 (Squadron Leader Peter Petter-Bowyer, my BFS flying instructor) to plan and organise the Field Rosters. With the escalating war effort, high-ranking Air Force officers were required to carry out field duties. Group Captain KAS Edwards did more than his fair share

Dave Stephens, who served with me under Groupie Edwards at Bindura (and for that matter on numerous other JOCs such as *Repulse*), was the person who introduced me to TM - Transcendental Meditation. Dave was indeed a remarkable man - somewhat highly strung but a pillar of strength with a cool head when under intense pressure. Many were the times when he would disappear for very short periods - only to be found on his bed in a TM state. Having awakened, he was as right as rain and raring to give it another go in the frequent hectic spells in the various Operation Rooms. (I would like to add at this juncture that nearly 20 years later, Technikon Natal Director, Department of Human Resources Mr Dave Stephens, B.A. (Hons) (RhU), Dip.Pers.Man. (RhU), NH Dip. (Pers.Man.)(TN), F.E.T.C. (CGLI), M.I.P.M. (SA), M.I.P.M., RPP, taught me Labour Economics).

Makombe Days: 1 August 1973 – 23 April 1974

'Makombe Days' will always be fondly remembered by many Air Force and SAS personnel who spent many a day fighting the Portuguese' war for them, while specifically tasked to harassing ZANU in the Tete Province of Moçambique. Makombe was a Portuguese aldeamento south of the Zambezi – and while the RAR worked south of the river, the SAS operated in the rugged, mountainous terrain to the north. A feature was the vast number of anti-personnel mines liberally scattered by FRELIMO, which tended to keep the Portuguese troops confined to their bases. Air Support, particularly fixed wing, tended to recover nightly to Mukumbura.

Makombe Pax Dakota

When Lake Cabora Bassa started filling up; Makombe would soon be under water. No 3 Squadron were tasked to evacuate the locals to Musengesi. This story came to me via e-mail from Bill Sykes when Bob d'Hotman was captain of the Dakota involved - and I quote:

"Cabora Bassa was filling fast and places like Makombe in western Moçambique (Tete Province) would shortly be under water so, together with the SAS, we were asked to uplift as many villagers as possible to the higher ground of Musengedzi, just within our border.

"On 11th and 12th March 1974, Bob d'Hotman and I took Dakota 7053 into Makombe airstrip which was just 800 metres long with barely-visible markers in the grass. Hundreds of villagers were waiting with as much of their worldly goods as they could carry. This included bicycles, blankets, boxes, baskets, boots and babies; not forgetting poultry in coops and some goats on ropes. The villagers comprised all sorts from the very, very old to the very, very young. One elderly woman had a most unfortunate deformity; Only half her face had a proper bone structure, the other half-hung down making a most grotesque appearance. Even more remarkable: she was obviously pregnant.

"Rob Warracker was the SAS Officer supervising the loading. This was the first time I had met him. His plan was to pile the worldly goods in a heap in the middle of the aircraft's cabin and then the owners of those goods were sat on and around those goods. After a quick pre-flight walk-round we found it more difficult to clamber over everything and everyone to get up to the cockpit. However, all was well and good and the sorties progressed throughout the two days although, admittedly, we noticed that the aircraft felt heavier each time we took off.

"On the last sortie on12th March, the same procedure was followed, except that Rob Warracker suggested that the pilots go "up front" sooner and let him finish off the loading. As it was getting late and time was of the essence with the fading light, we agreed. He eventually came under the cockpit windows and shouted up to us that our Engineer had managed to squeeze into the toilet and we were all set to go. Glancing back into the cabin we saw the usual mass of humanity and goods packet up to the ceiling. Sensible Engineer, we thought.

"Bob wisely used a quarter of flap to help with the take-off and ran-up the engines to full power before releasing the brakes. Well, every metre of the 800 was used for the take-off. As we lumbered off into the air, Bob said we must do a head-count when we land at Musengedzi.

"As I recall, 94 passengers were counted off at Musengedzi or was it 97? (I'm sure Bob will remember the number). The Engineer was squeezed into the toilet because there was simply no where else for him to go. Although we suspected that Rob Warracker was stretching our good faith in him, he obviously had more faith in the Dakota than the rulebooks had.

"The book "*The Dakota Story*" has a record of 111 Pakistani passengers on a Dakota but I think we came a good second, especially because of all the "Worldly goods"".

The above story occurred during my first stint at JOC Bindura. The actual tasking of the aircraft would have been done at the sub-JOCs at Centenary, Mount Darwin and Mtoko. Note – Centenary was FAF 4 and Mtoko became Forward Airfield 5.

Dealings with the likes of Brigadier Hickman certainly went a long way towards enhancing inter-service teamwork.

Air Strike 118. No sooner had I returned from JOC Bindura, than I teamed up with Air Lieutenant John Brown - Squadron Leader Tol Janeke's navigator - for an air strike in the Chiweshe Tribal Trust Land. John was a good navigator - he had to be - having teamed up with the Squadron

Commander on completing his basic training in South Africa. Canberra 2156 was loaded up with 96 Fragmentation bombs and we took off at 11h00 on 28th March.

Airstrike No 118: Date 28/03/1974;
Aircrews:
- Prop Geldenhuys / John Brown
- Randy Du Rand / Doug Pasea
- Mick Delport / Bill Stevens
- Ian Donaldson / Bernie Vaughan
- Rob Gaunt
- Vic Wightman
- Don Northcroft
- Ricky Culpan
- Chris Dixon
- Bill Sykes

Targets Targets at US061295, US077314, US023219
Ruya River, north east of Madombwe Mission, and 13 nautical miles south east of Centenary.

Canberra 2156 was in perfect condition because in late February Flight Lieutenant Bill Stevens and I had carried out a post Minor inspection air test followed by a second high speed run air test - at 450 knots low level. Little did I know that this would be the last time I would have the privilege of being navigated by Starry who - was the first Air Force Navigator turned Air Force Pilot and - destined never to return from an operational airstrike along the Eastern Border with Moçambique.

On 28th March 1974, 'Wedge', as Air Lieutenant John Brown was affectionately nicknamed, and I, took off loaded with our bomb boxes full of 96 frag bombs - target Chiweshe. The target details were somewhat sketchy - there were up to 50 terrorists based up in three different camps along-side separate kraals in the Tribal Trust Land, our target being Target Bravo, and another two designated Alpha and Charlie.

Wedge knew that target acquisition would be difficult. What little time he had for planning the bomb-run was put to good use - the target was in dense bush but more importantly, in a highly over-populated tribal area within Rhodesia. It was imperative that we avoid innocent civilians, especially children, albeit that Chiweshe was a hot bed of terrorist activity. Since October 1973, all our air strikes had been in Moçambique bar two in mid-February. These were below the Zambezi escarpment area (I might add, there was less regard for human life on transborder operations - but in Rhodesia, our targets were never the civilian population - only the communist terrorists against Rhodesia). Well - we never made it - during our run in, all hell broke loose on the intercom - and during the critical stage of our bombing run. There were shouts of "Go Charlie, Not Bravo." That was it - no ways do you tell the navigator who is about to press the "tit", and having painstakingly planned the run at short notice, and with duff gen (inaccurate or misleading information) I might add, to change his target at the last minute. I owe it to Wedge's professional approach that I recorded in my log book - DNCO - duty not carried out - for me a very rare occurrence - despite beating about the bush a wasted hour in trying to locate the correct target especially when the vital element of surprise had been lost.

However the war had to go on and that same evening I crewed up with Squadron Commander Squadron Leader Randy du Rand, and my old navigator, Flight Lieutenant Pasea on a 8 x 20lb medium level night bombing off-set trials sortie. We were rapidly perfecting the technique for operational use, and we determined that the optimum distance for the ground forces to set up the flare was 800 metres from the target (leeway was 2000 metres down to 800 metres).

It was only subsequently that I learnt that Ron Reid-Daly's men was responsible for the total "lemon" in Chiweshe. The Air Force had reacted in true tradition and very much to form - it was seldom that an all-out air strike could be put together at such short notice only to find that happy Africa was bombed out of sight - but with zero result. No small wonder I resented the

Scouts for the use, abuse and misuse they subjected airmen to. No 7 Squadron pilots used to have the same problems in the bush.

Mtoko

Both Intaf/DC and the uniformed branch of the BSAP, who had their Ground Coverage operative, reported a changing attitude by the locals. Ground Coverage was the main source of intelligence for the SB and consisted of a network of informers throughout the country.

JOC Mtoko decided to go for CVs – Consolidated Villages, as an alternate to the PVs practised in the Chiweshe TTL around Centenary. And so I was party to the establishment of the Consolidated Village, sometimes called 'Collective', concept in the Pfungwe and Ngarwe tribal trust lands. Hope Zichirira of a ZANLA reconnaissance group had been tasked to prepare the ground for a large-scale terrorist incursion scheduled for the end of 1974. Thus the CVs were decided on, because of the cost factor, in order to make SF contact with the locals easier, reinforce declining Ground Coverage and reduce the advantages the terrorists had with widely dispersed kraals. CVs effectively negated the enormous costs associated with Operation *Overload*.

The deteriorating situation in Moçambique was cause for serious concern. FRELIMO was rapidly replacing Portuguese control. The Portuguese practised a form of scorched earth policy commonly known as *Aldeamentos*. This was a policy of building fortified villages, while all other local shops and schools were razed to the ground - so as to deny home comforts or a source of food for infiltrators. In 1962 their main lines of defences were generally along west to east flowing rivers, starting on the Rovuma river between Tanzania and Moçambique. Aldeamentos were the Portuguese strongholds, but they had a poor infrastructure to support these strongholds. By 1971 ZANLA was given permission to cross Zambia and Moçambique. In effect, FRELIMO out-flanked, out-manoeuvred and out-fought the Portuguese. As the Portuguese abandoned one stronghold, they would pull back to the next river, or retreating line of defence. FRELIMO had it made - they just promptly occupied those Aldeamentos abandoned by the Portuguese. As would be the case by 1974, the southerly withdrawal by the Portuguese resulted in FRELIMO finding itself on the steps of Lourenço Marques. They had in fact advanced in to the soon to be named Maputo itself.

Operation Alcora

My first sortie on Operation *Alcora* was flown with navigator Flight Lieutenant Doug Pasea, on 6th June 1973 in the dedicated photo-reconnaissance Canberra R 2519. My logbook records the details as "PR Swartland FTS - Op *Alcora* - A to Z^2". (Trying to decipher the secret code taxed my feeble brain 27 years later). Whereas PR Swartland is obvious photo-reconnaissance Black States and 'A' stands for Angola plus 'Z squared' for Zaire-cum-Tanzania and Zambia, I guess FTS is interpreted as F96 camera for *Target Sites*. The three hours twenty minute duration of the sortie certainly meant very deep penetration into Zambia, flying at very high altitude where the Canberra was still capable of out-performing anything the Zambians or Zaireans could intercept us with.

Glob Pasea and I flew our next Operation *Alcora* sorties on August 10th, 14th and 19th each ranging up to four hours in endurance. That is a pretty long way, at altitude, in a Canberra. The four sorties were thus all across the border and over enemy terrorist territory. Total time amounted to nearly fourteen hours. I believe it was during one of these trips that one of the Rolls-Royce Avon engines flamed out - and we could not afford a descent to 20,000ft for the re-light, otherwise we would not have had the necessary fuel to make it back to base.

Terrorist camps were springing up like mushrooms. JSPIS, the Joint Service Photographic Interpretation Section was having their work cut out for them, and meanwhile the Canberra pilots were having a field day photographing all sorts of targets. Those that come to mind were Angola camps at Luso and the Benguela railway - Zambia's western route to the Atlantic at Lobito, bridges were the Chambeshi (on the Tanzam railway) in Northern Zambia, the Chongwe River bridge, approximately 40 kilometres from Lusaka, Tanzanian terrorist camps that attracted a lot of interest, Mgagao near Iringa, Nachingwea (in southern Tanzania), Kingolwiro and Mboroma. Zambian camps were at Magazine, Ngwemanzi, Pea, Mkushi, Lusuto, DK 1 & 2, and the infamous Westlands Farm of Green Leader (Chris Dixon) fame.

Moçambique camps were too numerous to list, but included Mpima, Tembue (north of Cabora Bassa), Dondo, Chicoa, Chioco, Chifombo, Chimoio. Madulo Pan (the operation in which Ian Donaldson was shot down), Chicombidzi, Chigamani, Caponda, Matimbe, Maxaila, Jorge do Limpopo, Massangena and of course Nyadzonia/Pungwe plus various staging posts.

Whilst Operation *Alcora* focussed mainly on all the long range Trans-border targets, the other PR operations that followed achieved similar successes and results. Tribute needs to be paid to navigators such as Bernie Vaughan and Doug Pasea who had to find these pinpricks like a needle in the African haystack - and then also operate the sophisticated cameras with which Canberra R 2519 was fitted. Bernie and Glob also have a tale to tell. The Photographic Section at New Sarum played its role too, and distinguished itself in the top secret Operation *Onyx* that was to follow.

I wish to make special mention of the excellent co-operation we had with No 12 (SAAF) Squadron, and the Tri-Partite agreements between Portugal, South Africa and ourselves.

Exercise Cauliflower: June 1973

Exercise Cauliflower was an extension of Operation Alcora – the tri-partite agreement between Rhodesia, Portugal and South Africa. The good political and inter-service relationships extended over a very wide field and entailed the establishment of several committees to address issues like airfields, mapping, radio communications, vehicle mine-proofing and so on. PB writes about his and Peter Cooke's visit to Cabo Del Gado, in his *Winds of Destruction* autobiography.

Hot Pursuit: Pete Simmonds – 4 July 1973

The following insert concerns the story as told by No 4 Squadron pilot, Air Lieutenant Pete 'Simmo' Simmonds, whilst flying a Provost, in support of the Rhodesian African Rifles, on hot pursuit operations after a terrorist gang north of Mukumbura, in July 1973. Simmo relates his war story thus:

"I had been getting up before first light in Centenary and flying down to Mukumbura in a Provost, to be on stand-by there from sunup to sundown for a few days. We could not stay there overnight, as there were no guards for the aircraft and FAF 4 at Mount Darwin still had not opened.

"Lieutenant Mike Wilson, of the Rhodesian African Rifles, had picked up tracks at the site of a landmine or ambush and found that these tracks went straight over the border into Moçambique. He had walked off his map of Moçambique with his stick of about ten men and neither he nor I were too sure of exactly where he was. After a day or two we had only a general idea of his position, but if he had caught up with the terrs, the plan was that he would guide me in from high level in order to support him with my guns and frantan. Each day he got closer to the enemy and then fell behind whilst he and his stick slept on the tracks during the night. His Major, in Mukumbura, was in a dilemma about whether or not to send me over the border to find him and drop him some maps. We didn't want the enemy to know we were following them by letting them see my Provost, but the further he tracked away from Rhodesia the more pressing it became that we should know exactly where he was. This went on for three days and on the fourth it was decided that since he was running low on radio batteries I would have to find him at last light and drop him both batteries and maps. It was July the 4th 1973.

"At about 5pm a package of maps, batteries and personal mail was tied up and I set off in the Provost with Mike Guy, my very trusting technician. I flew east into Moçambique for about 20 minutes at 2500ft until Mike Wilson could see me whereupon he then directed me overhead his position. He estimated that he was about 12 hours behind the terrorists at this stage and he was around 30 miles from the Rhodesian border. He had obviously been tracking hard for the previous few days. When I found him I pulled out the correct map and put a large X on it with 'YOU ARE HERE' written next to the X. I also wrote a suitably rude comment about 'Brownjobs' always being pulled out of trouble by 'Bluejobs'. I then used it to wrap up the package before tying all with string. We descended to 50ft, lined up with Mike on the ground, put down full flap and slowed down to just above the stall with the canopy wound back. As his troops disappeared under the nose of the aircraft, I was about to chuck the package out of the cockpit when there were two very loud bangs as if the engine had backfired. I was sure it was the aircraft engine and looked at the engine instruments while pushing the throttle forward. I was always very worried about having to force land in Moçambique and therefore tended to watch the engine instruments of the single engine Provost constantly whenever I was far from home. I was surprised then when I saw the engine instruments performing perfectly well and heard the engine responding normally to the throttle. I looked at Mike Guy quizzically in case he had the answer to the bangs. But his eyes were firmly focused on my legs with a very surprised look on his face. Realisation hit me that I had been shot through the left thigh. My left femur was broken and the bullet had stopped in my right leg. The second bang was another bullet going through the fuselage behind the cockpit. Mike Wilson was as surprised, as we were that he had caught up with the terrorists who had in fact been watching him from their resting place on higher ground before I arrived. I turned the Provost back to Mukumbura and told him what had happened to me. I then asked Mike Guy to fly the aircraft straight and level while I tried to sort myself out. There was little pain and a lot of adrenaline but I could do no more than block the holes in my left leg with my fingers.

"I was terrified that the loss of blood would cause me to flake out and knew if that happened, Mike Guy would not have been able to stand a fighting chance of landing the aircraft on his own with me hanging all over the control column and rudders. I am sure it was the adrenaline brought on from this thought that kept me awake and flying. As we flew back I remember willing the Mavuradona Mountains in the distance to come closer, faster. It took 20 minutes to fly back to Mukumbura and by then the RAR major had organised a reception party for me at the airfield with a medic. I may have had bad luck in being shot that day but I was very lucky in other ways. I was unable to get my left leg off the rudders but my right leg was still able to pull and push the rudders a little due to the toe strap across the top of the rudder. That toe strap made the difference between being able to land the aircraft and crashing it on to the ground without the ability to stay straight on the runway. The Provost is the only aircraft I have flown that has these toe straps on the rudders and a brake handle on the control column. The rough rubble surface of the runway at Mukumbura was also in my favour as it was ideal for sliding sideways in a ground loop. I landed gently and was able to keep the Provost straight on the rudders whilst slowing down and braking with my hands until about 30 knots. We then ground looped through 270 degrees with full brakes and the Provost lurched to a stop.

"The flight was over. The priority of landing safely was now behind us and a wave of immense pain hit me even before the dust had settled. There is no point in trying to describe the pain I felt because I don't believe words can express it. After switching off the engine there was another problem though, I was unable to get out of the cockpit on my own and was stuck there. The biggest RAR soldier I had ever seen volunteered to fix this. He thrust his arms underneath me, plucked me out of the cockpit in a second and carried me off the wing on to a stretcher while I screamed and yelled. My broken leg seemed to have a mind of its own as it flailed about in the air until I was settled on my back. .

"I always remember how calmly Mike Guy took his predicament while with me in the aircraft and terrified as he may have been he never showed it. Pete Wilcox flew a chopper without a horizon that night to get me back to Centenary with a doctor for this. I have always been grateful to both. By then I was as high as a kite on Pethadine and time meant very little to me. My squadron friend, Alf Wild, took me in a Trojan to New Sarum and an ambulance delivered me to the Salisbury General Hospital. The doctors fixed my leg up and six months later I returned to operations but this time on helicopters.

"The Army Major made some excellent decisions during the chase to close with the enemy and certainly did a marvellous job in getting me back to Salisbury alive. He also backed me up fully during the subsequent Air Force enquiry but the powers that be were in no mood to blame anyone else but myself for being shot and for endangering my aircraft and the lives of my Tech and I. I was astonished at their attitude at the time. When it was suggested that I was 'just out there dropping mail to my buddies when I got myself shot' I was angry for years, especially because I had specifically been sent to Mukumbura in support of our troops operating across the border in 'hot pursuit'."

Then in December 1975, Phil Malan had another "holiday camp at Mukumbura by the Sea". They were sent to Inkomo Barracks for a three-day refresher stint, spent one night at Mount Darwin – and then the rain came down. All seven inches of it. The TF Company was bundled into the back of an Army Bedford RL truck that set off for Mukumbura, through all the mud, muck, and more rain. By the time they arrived at the so-called 'seaside resort', they, and their rat packs, were swimming and dancing in the rain. False teethed old ladies could even chew the dog biscuits. The fresh ration truck, dispatched on the 23rd to supply the Company, only arrived on the 29th – too late to enjoy it as Xmas fare. Phil's patrol had meanwhile stumbled on an African village, whose Headman kindly offered some shelter from the incessant rain – but also generously administered a potent Marula juice home-made "rot-gut" brew. Just a sip of the rotgut was a cure all, which turned out to be 86 proof. The brew was more than sufficient to drown the Brownjob sorrows during this particularly rain drenched border patrol call-up.

When Simmo was shot and Phil was drinking elephant urine, I was on my way to Nampula, in northern Moçambique, with Bernie Vaughan in Canberra R 2055. Our passengers were Squadron Leaders George Baverstock and Rex Taylor – for the start of Operation *Polar*. However, to set the scene, some background regarding Détente and the release of the terrorist leadership warrants mention.

No 5 Squadron – March 1974
Pilots Keith Goddard, Mick Delport, John Bennie, Ian Donaldson (QFI), Sqn WO George Heron, Prop Geldenhuys ('A' Flt Cdr), Randy du Rand (Sqn Cdr), navigators Bernie Vaughan ('B' Flt Cdr), Glob Pasea, Starry Stevens, Paddy Morgan, Rich Airey and Jim Russell

Operation Polar: 4 July 1973 to 2 September 1974

Vorster's Détente exercise backfired on the Rhodesians. Julius Nyerere of Tanzania, Zambian Kaunda, FRELIMO's Samora Machel and Seretse Khama of Botswana backed Nkomo and Sithole. Ian Smith knew otherwise. The detainees schemed to replace Sithole with Mugabe. When Mugabe was released and arrived in Zambia for the pre arranged talks, Nyerere was furious and dispatched Mugabe back to detention (Mugabe had the foresight to realise that Sithole would buy him time, and before long, would hang himself, so to speak, given enough rope) and replaced by Sithole. By mid-December 1974, Mugabe, Nkomo, Sithole and Bishop Abel Muzorewa, were released from detention as Ian Smith announced a cease-fire.

It is small wonder that Ian Smith, in his Betrayal autobiography, was left a very bitter man. The following quote from Mugabe's autobiography puts the issue into perspective. It reads, "We had decided to accept détente purely as a tactic to buy the time we needed to organise and intensify the armed struggle. In short, *détente*, in Mugabe's case, was just another word for freedom. *Freedom to wage war.*" (emphasis added). Let the bloodshed be on the hands where it is deserved. It is no small wonder that Ian Smith sincerely distrusted the terrorists and their motives. He who lives by the sword shall die by the sword. Mugabe was about to reap the fruits of his dishonesty in the intensified war effort that was about to fall upon the so-called liberation movements.

Rhodesia and Moçambique cooperated fully on a combat level. Rhodesian troops operated in close support with Portuguese units on both sides of the undefined Tete frontier. A number of Rhodesian forces spent extended periods operating with the Portuguese in Moçambique – and it was exactly this disclosure that caused the arrest and trial of newsman Peter Niesawand in 1973. My own PR operations out of Nampula, along the Rovuma River border with Tanzania, and down along the east coast to Nacala, were memorable Canberra missions. The Niassa and Cabo Delgado areas of northern Moçambique were very sparsely populated. Porto Amelia was a very pretty area, and sported pristine coral beaches.

The survey photographic sorties, from Nampula, entailed long east to west, and return legs, from Lake Malawi to the Indian Ocean. Flying along the east flowing Rovuma River also provided the opportunity to photograph the FRELIMO bases at Newela and Mtwara. The camps were just across the border into Tanzania, but we generally felt safe taking off and landing at Nampula, situated centrally in the northern '' province, which was some distance away from the northern provinces of Niassa and Carbo Delgado, bordering Tanzania. One memorable sortie was a low-level flight to Nacala up to Porto Amelia. The entire area between the Rovuma and the Rufiti Rivers in Tanzania, about 150 kilometres south of Dar es Salaam was regarded as a militarised zone.

Whilst flying parallel to the Tanzanian border, we were constantly aware that there was a strong possibility of interceptions by the Tanzanian Air Force MiG-17 and MiG-19 aircraft. The Tanzania's People's Army had built up a formidable strength of 14,600, and were equipped with Red Chinese T-59 and T-62 tanks and Chinese aircraft. Things had come a long way since the days when it had little more than one infantry battalion of the Kings African Rifles. However, we knew that our Canberra could still out-turn the Tanzanian aircraft at altitude, but it was up to the pilot to keep a sharp lookout while the navigator was map-reading and operating the survey cameras.

Canberra Vic Formation

The accommodation in Nampula was above average by normal Moçambique standards. We stayed in a 10 to 12 storeyed building, the highest in the town. It resembled a cross between a posh hotel and an upmarket Officers' Quarters. Portuguese Air Force liaison officers were assigned to attend to our every need, and we were entertained royally taking meals at the best restaurants in town, like the Baghdad night-club. Favourite meals were fresh lobster, crayfish and LM prawns. Their forces canteens also sold heavily subsidised liquor, cashew nuts and liqueurs.

It was normal practice for us to stock up our bomb bays with cases and more cases, and then fly back to Rhodesia, and by-pass customs clearance.

An interesting side issue, unbeknown to me at the time, was the underground operation of "The Group of a Thousand". This was a secret organisation whose aims were the complete elimination of FRELIMO and all other forms of communism in southern Africa. Planning a successful revolution took time, so they set 30th September 1974 as their date for a unilateral declaration of independence. They intended to install a black but sympathetic government under Dr Miguel Murrupa from Quelimane. Formerly FRELIMO's foreign minister, he became disillusioned, and defected. After adopting a fervently anti-communist stance, he acted as an adviser to Moçambique's army chief of staff, General Kaulza de Arriaga, until 1973. The Group had its headquarters in Nampula, but apart from token resistance, it was not a force of substance. Peter Stiff unearthed evidence to suggest that Rhodesia's CIO head, Ken Flower, was in with the conspiracy, indicating that the CIO had communications with the Group of a Thousand. Flower also said Rhodesia would have given practical assistance if the revolt had progressed beyond the first stage. Just my luck – I left Nampula on 2nd September 1974.

Canberras, Vampires and Hunters – Rhodesians main strike aircraft used during the Rhodesian War 1965 to 1980

Angola: Exercise Luanda

Glob Pasea, my navigator, together with Sergeant Tony Brown, flew with me to the Portuguese West Coast City of Luanda. We flew to the Caprivi Strip and headed northwest across the Angola Cuando Cubango province towards the Portuguese capital Luanda. After crossing the Benguela railway, we descended when the Atlantic Ocean became visible, and had a good look at Luanda from the air. What struck me the most was the large number of squatter camps in the prime built up areas. We landed without event, beating the sun by an hour.

The Portuguese military were professional. That is, especially when compared to their east coast Moçambicans. The Angolan Portuguese were generally neat and tidy, well organised, and perfect hosts. The Base Commander entertained us to brandy and black coffee, served in miniature cups, half of which I spilt down my safari suit. After checking into our Hotel for the night, a Portuguese Air Force escort showed us the sights of the city. I was particularly impressed with the long spit of land that curved out clockwise from a beautiful esplanade. That night we

frequented all the haunts, where a transvestite fooled our technician. We saw a really good night club striptease, tastefully performed albeit completely starkers.
After our enjoyable night out, we departed for home the next afternoon, flying east and adding one-hour real time to our 3 hour 10 minute return journey.

Cape Town

The Cape Town jollies were very much sought after affairs. I was privileged to enjoy quite a few. On 6th November 1973, Air Commodore Dickie Bradshaw joined Paddy Morgan and myself in Canberra R 2516 for the three and a half-hour flight to South African Air Force Base Langebaanweg. We had loaded up with 4 x 130lb bombs for low-level bombing on Hopefields Range. After dropping our bombs on the South African bombing range, we landed at Langebaanweg to refuel, which my navigator Paddy and I quietly attended to while the Air Commodore relaxed and enjoyed coffee refreshments with the base OCFW. Once the Canberra had been turned round we flew the thirty-minute leg low-level along the coast to DF Malan airport in Cape Town. After two nights in the Mother City, we flew back to Salisbury for a night landing. However, the return sortie was not without its excitement. As was normal, we were intercepted en-route by two South African Air Force Mirage supersonic interceptors. It was good air experience for the Air Commodore - to satisfy Air Staff at the Glass Palace that the jolly to Rhodesia's friendly neighbours produced constructive inter-Service co-operation and tested pilots' skills in the defence of sovereign airspace. Dickie Bradshaw passed away in February 2002.

Operation Marble: 20/40 Ton Week

April 1974 was a disastrous month for the Air Force. The month started off OK with a Master Green Instrument rating for Flight Lieutenant Ian Donaldson (killed 1977), with his navigator Flight Lieutenant Bernie Vaughan. The next day, the 2nd, a Green Instrument rating test was flown with Flight Lieutenant John Bennie (died of cancer) and my navigator Paddy Morgan. Then on the 3rd, Paddy and I dropped 6 x 20lb Low Level Bombing and returned for a GCA PPI letdown (Radar ground controlled approach and landing), in view of our thirty minutes flying in cloud.

Operation Hurricane – 20 Ton Week – February 1974
Aircrews: Bernie Vaughan, Starry Stevens, Rich Airey, Mike Delport, Keith Goddard, John Bennie, Prop Geldenhuys, Glob Pasea and Squadron Commander Randy du Rand

(Authors note: The left-hand bomb trolley is loaded with 500lb High Explosive bombs. The bomb box rack, on the right, would hold up to 96 x 20lb Fragmentation bombs. It was the latter that malfunctioned, and resulted in the death of Rich Airey and Keith Goddard)

Operation Marble – No 5 Squadron, after dropping 20 tons of bombs in a week. Keith Goddard and Rich Airey were killed shortly after this photo was taken

Then the fateful 4th April. Air Sub-Lieutenant Mick Delport joined Paddy and me in Canberra 2155 for an Operation *Hurricane* 96 x 20lb-frag bomb-box airstrike in Moçambique, across the Zambezi River. Canberra 2156 was similarly being armed for a further airstrike. As the Flight Commander, I authorised Air Sub-Lieutenant Keith Goddard, together with his navigator, Air Sub-Lieutenant Rich Airey to carry out the airstrike. Having just completed my attack, I was able to brief Keith on what to expect on this, his first operational sortie since the successful completion of his OCU. Keith and Rich did not survive his first Canberra airstrike - they perished with Canberra R 2156. One month earlier, on 4th March, I had carried out Keith's White instrument rating test, with Rich Airey, in Canberra R 2175.

This actual Airstrike, with Rich Airey, dropping 96 Frag bombs the day before my birthday (on19th February 1974) graphically illustrates my own lucky escape! Note the haphazard flight characteristics of the 20lb fragmentation bombs. With careful observation, three lots of bombs will be noted. At the bottom of the photograph, the first lot of 20lb Frags can be seen way below the aircraft, albeit very tiny. These have had a "white border" drawn around them in order to distinguish the height differential between them, and the later bombs. The next lot appears to have shiny nose cones, which are as a result of the sun reflection after clearing the aircraft's shadow. The last lot, with the "black squares" drawn around some, illustrates 'floaters' that tend to hang-up in the air disturbance in the bomb bay.

I had authorised the airstrike when Keith Goddard and Rich Airey were killed on 4th April 1974. The initial speculation for Keith and Richard's death was that ground fire had detonated a frag bomb. The lead Canberra had reported that the bombs were no more than 50ft below the aircraft when it was engulfed in a huge ball of flame, much larger than the aircraft itself. The nose section of the fuselage was seen tumbling out of the fireball towards the ground, followed by a trail of other debris and burning fuel. The crews had no chance of escape and were killed instantly. A Board of Inquiry was convened and preceded to the scene of the aircraft crash. After taking the necessary photographic evidence, the bulky items like the engines, fuselage, wings and tailplane were dumped by helicopter into the Zambezi River.

The Board of Inquiry concluded that the only explanation for this accident was that one of the spin-off caps had detonated a bomb, causing a chain reaction throughout the entire bomb load and destroying the aircraft. Trials of the bomb box, with its 96 x 20lb fragmentation bombs, were filmed using a bomb bay mounted F 95 camera. It was apparent that the bombs were affected by the turbulent airflow within the bomb bay. Upon release, the front bombs tended to hang for a while in the vacuum created by the forward bulkhead of the bomb bay and upset the orderly fall of the bombs from the aircraft. It could be seen that, due to the random departure of the bombs from the aircraft, it was possible for one of the caps to come in contact with the now exposed diaphragm of a following bomb and thus cause it to detonate prematurely.

The 20lb Mk 1 fragmentation anti-personnel aerial bomb was stubby in shape, bound with coils of steel and designed to detonate just above the ground. This was achieved by a diaphragm in the nose that reversed due to the build-up of air pressure as the bomb neared the ground, initiating the firing mechanism. A metal cap that spun off the front of the bomb, once it was clear of the aircraft protected this diaphragm. The finding by the Board resulted in the immediate suspension of the bomb box and the Mark 1 frag bomb was taken out of service. Phew - another lucky escape for me because of my own airstrike that very morning that had also entailed dropping a full bomb box load of 96 frags. A quick check of my pilot's logbook reveals that I had done no fewer than eight sorties, dropping a total of 8 x 96 = 768 20lb Mark 1 fragmentation bombs. I trust that the Good Lord had his Guardian Angel's hand upon me.

Like the proverbial cat, I had survived my eight lives. By the time I was posted off No 5 Squadron, I had dropped nearly one hundred and sixty tons of bombs, made up of 768 fragmentation bombs, 637 by 130lb bombs, 360 by 20lb bombs, 63 by 500lb bombs, 20 by 1000lb 'big bang' bombs and 9 by 250lb bombs.

The Squadron had thus been reduced to five crews, necessitating a reallocation of squadron duties and responsibilities. Fewer people needed to shoulder additional workloads, and it was a source of pride that there was no grumbling as everybody put their shoulders to the wheel, and just did what was expected of him. Specialist navigator appointments included Navigation Leader, Bombing Leader and Photo Leader – these were allocated on the basis of knowledge and skill. Because Bernie Vaughan was a mathematical genius, he retained the Lead Navigator portfolio, and shed the Photo Lead portfolio to my ex-navigator – Doug Pasea. Wedge Brown, who had been Boss Tol Janeke's navigator, retained the Bombing Lead portfolio, pending his transfer to the Computer Bureau, and also pending special training for my current navigator Paddy Morgan to assume full responsibility for the Bomb Leader portfolio.

Following our Squadron losses, No 5 Squadron internal organisation read, with effect from 9th April 1974, as follows: -

Sqn Ldr J.F. du Rand   Squadron Commander/Tactics
Flt Lt P.M. Geldenhuys 'A' Flight Commander/IRE/Squadron History
Flt Lt B.W. Vaughan   'B' Flight Commander/Tech Liaison/Nav Leader/Dep Photo Ldr/Aircraft Inventory
Flt Lt D.W. Pasea Photo Leader/Dep Nav Leader
Flt Lt J.E. Bennie Ground Training/Flight Safety/Intelligence/Survival
Flt Lt I.H. Donaldson QFI/Standardisation/Chiredzi Liaison/Dep Flight Safety
Air Lt J.J.F. Brown Bombing Leader/Barrack Inventory/Dep Adj
ASL M.J. Delport Sport/Adj/Monthly Returns/Sqn Fund
ASL S.P. Morgan Map Store/Publications/Dep Bomb Ldr
Off Cdt   J. Russell   Dep Map Store/Ops and Crew Rooms

There was a break of a week after the squadron loss. Then on the 10th I carried out an engine change airtest on Canberra R 2514. The next day Canberra R2155 was loaded up with 6 x 500lb bombs for my Operation *Marble* airstrike - with Paddy Morgan as my navigator.

Three days later, on the 14th, Flight Lieutenant Chris Weinmann was killed in action whilst flying a Trojan. Chris was a tragic loss to the Air Force. He had been one of my earlier students, and had shared some really hairy moments with me, especially our middle of the night Battle of Inyantue sorties during Operation *Nickel*. Chris was shot down in Trojan R3244, near Rushinga, and had his aircraft cleverly camouflaged by the terrorists. About a week later, on 20th April 1974, while conducting an aerial search for the downed camouflaged wreck, Air Sub-Lieutenant R. Wilson in Trojan R 3427 was shot down and killed in action by a SAM-7 missile.

Special Joint Services Coin Course: May 1974

1974 proved to be quite an eventful year. I considered myself fortunate to be selected to attend a lengthy Special Joint Services COIN Course during May 1974. There were eighteen of us – two from the Air Force (my ex-1 Squadron Commander, Roy Morris and I) and the rest were either Rhodesian Army or South African Defence Force personnel. Amongst the Brownjobs was Lieutenant Colonel Peter Hosking of RAR fame, Ian Bate and Pat Hill.

The course was most useful when it came to exchanging ideas on joint force co-operation and tactics. I would like to think that the South Africans had learned a thing or two from their much smaller neighbour. A course photograph was taken during a tour of the Air Force squadrons – and I was able to give my input when it came to the weapons capabilities of the Hawker Hunter – having served on the Hunter Squadron in 1970. Techniques were evolving all the time, and it was good to be exposed to current South African thinking as well. My attendance on this "Special" course also stood me in good stead when a couple of years later I attended the SAAF College Course in Pretoria. The following photograph was taken in front of a Hunter, with its armaments displayed around the aircraft.

Hawker Hunter – COIN Course - May 1974

Photo Reconnaissance - PR

PR was a specialised function of both the Hunters and the Canberras, but more so on the latter. Camera configurations varied depending on tactical and strategic requirements. Whilst survey photography could be boring at times, it did produce a great sense of satisfaction to supply the Surveyor General with up to date prints of Rhodesia, as well as of the neighbouring states. Target photography was just as rewarding, especially in planning of offensive operations and airstrikes.

Targets would include bridges for demolition, terrorist bases and camps, national key point areas, monitoring the construction of Cabora Bassa dam, Tanzam railway line and such like. A point of possible interest is that during construction of the hydroelectric scheme, the dam was known as "Cabora" – but was changed to "Cahora" by the FRELIMO regime. They were hell-bent on destroying the dam because of its natural barrier across the Zambezi. However, with their independence, they soon realised the dam's economic significance, and renamed it because it more closely approximates the local people's pronunciation of the site.

It will be recalled that the Special Air Service had a Tactical HQ at Makonde aldeamentos, and by January 1974, the South African Recces joined the SAS at Mozangadzi Mission – north of the Zambezi River and west of Tete. The South Africans worked operational tours of six weeks at a time. If not on patrol, they manned Observation Posts. When they saw terrorist groups they called for support from Rhodesian Canberras from New Sarum, and often talked the bombers in for bombing runs. Round about this time, Radio Activated Marker Services – RAMS – were being developed and the ground units would place these aids for offset bombing techniques employed by No 5 Squadron.

Terrorist camps that come to mind include Binda, Horteiro, Chamboko and Chifombo in Zambia; Itumbi, Lukwila, Mgagao, Newela and Nachingwea in Tanzania. Often, en route to or from Nampula in Northern Moçambique, opportunities would be grasped to photograph anything out of the ordinary or of interest. The Tete province in Moçambique became a hotbed of terrorist infiltration. FRELIMO were making major inroads on the Portuguese strongholds. The main FRELIMO camp was at Nachingwea, with two large centres at Mtwara and Lindi. They had numerous staging posts at Songea, Tunduru and Chamba, which were in addition to those others already mentioned.

By 1973, ZANLA were infiltrating into Rhodesia from camps at Mzarabani and Sundi. Operation *Blanket* and *Polar* provided convenient opportunities to photograph known camps at that time.

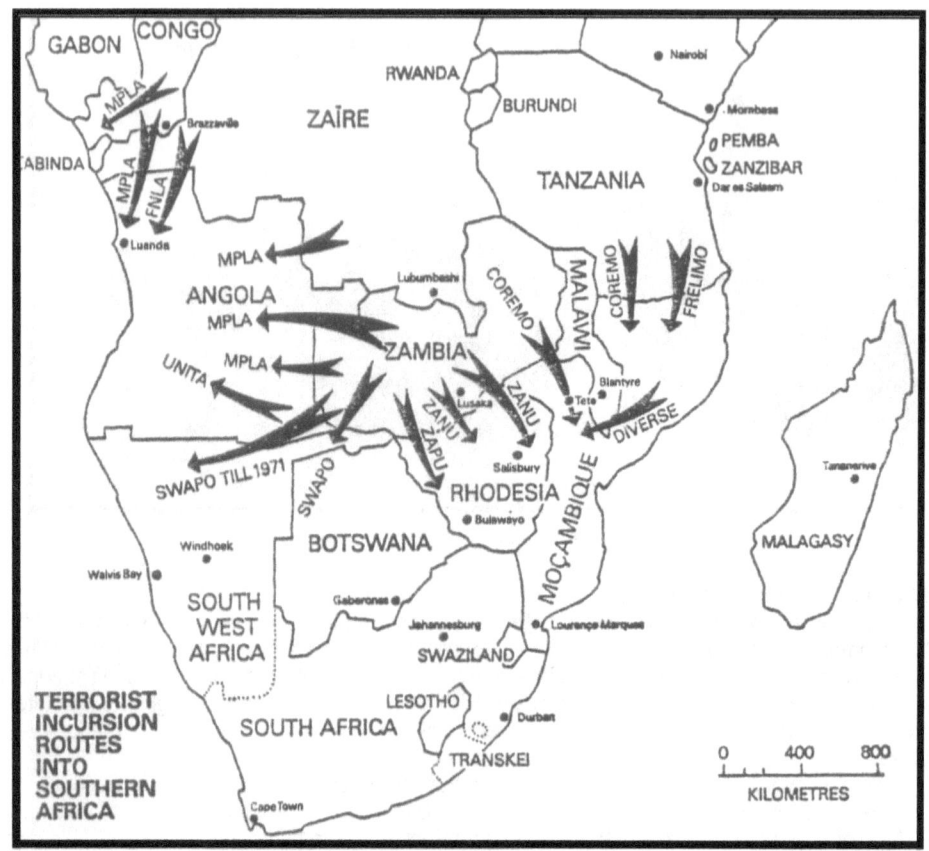

Terrorist incursion routes into Southern Africa – and whose camps were within range of Rhodesian Air Force Canberra Aircraft

Exercise Vanguard: 31 July 1974

Exercise Vanguard, staged in July 1974, was a Forcex that included all the Squadrons as well as the VR Squadrons. The RTV publicity film "Pride of Eagles" was produced – and much later made into a DVD which also included "Bateleur Eagles". In the earlier film when AVM Harold Hawkins was the Chief of Air Staff I was featured briefing 4 Squadron crews on Air-to-Air quarter attacks and Battle Formation; and in the latter film I dropped six 130lb bombs as well as carrying out several Canberra take-offs and landings.

Operation Big Bang: 9 August to 1 October 1974

Operation *Big Bang* entailed three ground reconnaissance missions into Zambia to establish the whereabouts of a ZIPRA Pondoland East A-camp north of the District Commissioner's camp on the Zambezi River. The DCs camp, Sidinde Island, was below the Falls, and upstream from Deka. I flew several photo-reconnaissance sorties between July and October 1974, but air photo interpretation of the most likely base at Ngwemanzi indicated that it appeared deserted. Most of the PR missions were also flown as Operation *Polar* sorties, but for the purpose of this story, I intend reporting mainly on the Special Air Service activities. The SAS established their tactical headquarters base just within Rhodesia, and which I would become well versed later on when I was posted onto Lynx aircraft. But in 1974 I was quite content to be in the high flying Canberra, recovering back to New Sarum, rather that prolonged deployments to FAF 1 at Wankie.

Aerial reconnaissance was flown on 5th July 1974. I was piloting Canberra R 2085, and my navigator Glob Pasea selected split pair cameras for the sortie from Chete to Deka. The photographic interpreters felt that the Ngwemanzi River camp, some eleven kilometres inland, could be housing as many as twenty people. Special Branch sources considered that the camp could well be the headquarters of a number of ZIPRA satellite camps. Documents that had been captured on a Pondoland East "B" camp attack told of another camp a day's walk to the west. Thus came about the renewed interest in the area of Ngwemanzi. On 30th July, I was back. This time with navigator Air Sub-Lieutenant Paddy Morgan, using our F 96 PR camera.

On 3rd August 1974, the Squadron was tasked to carry out a Search and Rescue for a missing South African Z-Car. The task was given to me. Paddy Morgan and I got airborne in a Canberra to join the other aircraft that were already out looking for the missing Alouette crews. However, we were no sooner airborne from Salisbury than we were recalled. The Z-Car had been located and our assistance was not required. This would have been my second Canberra call-out on Search and Rescue missions. It was reassuring to know that the Air Force pulled out all the stops whenever an aircraft went down.

Then on 9th August 1974, SAS Lieutenant Chris 'Schulie' Schulenburg conducted a ground reconnaissance of the ZIPRA camp. The camp appeared deserted, but he did come across signs of terrorist boot prints and vehicle tracks. It appeared to him that the main activity was further east. He was recalled before the re-sited camp was located. Meanwhile, aerial photography picked up a suspicious looking hole in the ground in the vicinity of the Mazanga River.

Towards the end of August, early September, Schulie was back again, this time with SAS Sergeant Bob McKenna, for his second ground recce of the area. They observed larger military truck movements, in the order of four-tonners, that were well shielded, operating in the vicinity where aerial photography had picked up the large hole. On 23rd September 1974, Paddy Morgan and I were back in Canberra R 2519 to monitor developments – concentrating on the area to the north of Deka. The SAS had also planned to attack the camp and assembled a ground force of 43 SAS chaps and crossed the border on the night of 3rd October 1974. This was the biggest number of Rhodesian security forces to go external on a single operation into Zambia since the start of the bush war. Two days later, the troops were in position to launch their assault on the ZIPRA camp.

During the early hours of 5th October, the SAS assault force advanced from the north and overran the still sleeping gooks. Fleeing terrorists tried to make good their escape running southwards, but ran straight into stop groups manned by Captain Garth Barrett. Within five minutes, some 2,500 rounds had been directed at the fleeing ZIPRA. All told, nine ZIPRA, the only ones there that morning, had died in the attack. The 'big hole' in the ground turned out to be a massive weapons cache, including limpet mines and two-metre-long 122 millimetre rockets – arms that the SAS had never seen before. There was also a 12,7 millimetre anti-aircraft gun. Also included were millions of rounds, some 5,000 detonators, Tokarev pistols, 200 Garand rifles from America (never again seen during the war), 12,7 millimetre heavy machineguns, light machineguns, 100 boxes of anti-tank mines, dozens of boxes of anti-personnel mines, AK-47s, SKSs, RPG-7 rockets, 75 millimetre recoilless rifles, bayonet, shells, and much more. Demolitions expert Rob Warracker reckoned there had been three tons of explosives, as well as large quantities of webbing and clothing. The SAS helped themselves to some of the limpet mines, AKs, bayonets and Tokarevs. The rest, including above ground 12,7 millimetre anti-aircraft gun, 75 millimetre gun, detonators, and rolls of detonating cord and safety fuses were dumped in the bunker. Rob Warracker then set the charges and blew the arms cache sky high.

When the SAS got back to their base camp, they found that ZIPRA had carried out a simultaneous attack on their own base while they were attacking the ZIPRA base. Corporal Willie Erasmus had been seriously wounded – but they had not alerted Garth Barrett, believing he would have called off the assault on the ZIPRA camp, had he been informed. In any event, Operation *Big Bang* was rated highly successful; with ZIPRA no doubt the losers. Schulie was awarded the Silver Cross of Rhodesia for the part he played, and Garth Barrett received the OLM – Order of the Legion of Merit.

On October 20th, Paddy Morgan and I were back again – in Canberra R 5203, for our follow up on the devastation caused to the ZIPRA PEA base – Pondoland East "A" – and our operational PR of Deka to Chewore. It transpired that the PEA base had been the central logistical base for the whole of ZIPRA's operations into Matabeleland. The cache was being built up to feed the small local caches dug in the Matabeleland TTLs. The internal network had been smashed; now all the ammunition for the internal caches had been blown to smithereens.

Paddy's reward was his promotion to full Air Lieutenant. Mine was the variety of operational missions in the making – such as Operations *Polar* and *Blanket*, survey and target PR, and the No 3 Army Co-op Coin Course that was on the go during the SAS incursion into Zambia.

Crash of Alouette III 28 (5674)

Told by Peter Booth "As a slope (South African) chopper pilot I was based at Wankie (FAF 1), on that particular typically warm sunny day, 10 July 1974. I had elected to do a double tour of duty to earn extra money my fiancée and I needed to be married. I was tasked to fly over to the Zambezi ravine to locate and supply a SAP patrol. As we would be light and 28 was equipped as a k-car, and it being a beautiful day I decided to give three privates of the FAF's GSU security guards a flip. I had as Flight Engineer Sgt. Dave Noakes.

Take off was at 1330 and all proceeded without mishap for the first 15mins, until I decided to do an unauthorised manoeuvre known at the squadron where I flew as a "handstand". This was a manoeuvre that I had developed and which unknown to me was highly dangerous. Usually I had carried it out from ground level. It entailed climbing vertically in the hover normally to 200 ft agl and then with .8 power setting on the collective you nose over until the Alouette is vertically nose down and then flies it out the bottom at about 50ft.

On this occasion without prior thought I started the manoeuvre at about 800ft above ground level from cruise flight. I climbed with about a 45 degree nose up attitude to lose speed, nosing over to the vertical as the ASI came down to zero airspeed. What I had forgotten was that this was an ideal vortex condition. This occurs when the airflow up through the rotor disc caused by the vertical descent of the helicopter equals the downward airflow created by the lift of the rotor, i.e. zero airflow up or down through the rotor. When this condition occurs it can take up to 800ft vertically to recover control of the aircraft, irrespective of how much the collective pitch is altered, or cyclic moved around, and there was much of both going on.

Curiously although the nose was vertically down the airspeed never rose above 80 knots! I recovered a level attitude in a valley, only problems being I was below the level of surrounding ground, going up the very highest part of the valley, with a ridge towering above the machine. Although I had pulled up emergency power and had a considerably nose up attitude to try and climb and reduce airspeed, as it was obvious to even me, that an unintentional landing of some sort was imminent. Needless to say we did not clear the ridge, and the tail rotor struck a tree.

Unfortunately I lost not only the tail rotor, but the entire gearbox and rotor decided to look for own LZ without permission or direction from me. With emergency power on and low airspeed, (down to about 40 kts), the new flight envelope of the Alo was confined to doing high speed hover turns. In fact I remember the only way I could maintain a level flight attitude was to keep the nose between the green and blue of the horizon, i.e. trees and sky! Had I maintained forward speed I would not have cleared any of the trees. Had there been more forward speed I may have been able to maintain some semblance of direction due to the weathercock action of the fuselage. Oh well life is full of choices.

You cannot believe how fast you lose control in this kind of situation. I remember saying to Dave as the Alo started to rotate, "I think we have lost the tail rotor." I don't recall reducing collective so we must have been climbing at that stage. I remember being pushed to the cabin door side of the seat by the "g" force of the rotation. I'm not referring to centrifugal force but that caused by the anti-torque action of one's body. (The body's resistance to the rotational acceleration.) Maybe with the same happening to Dave, he may have leant on the collective and thus reduced power to the engine.

I have no idea how we ended up on the ground, or what stopped the Artouste III engine but believe me it was more enviable that being in the air situation. The blades cut down the few small trees that were within the impromptu LZ. Somewhat dazed we climbed out of the now silent chopper. I had lost several teeth to the instrument panel. My back was extremely sore, as was my chest. On investigation Dave had a slight cut on his knee. One of the fellows in the back, (Dave Palmer), had hurt his back that turned out later to be a crushed vertebra. I no longer remember what the other chap's injuries were, but remember that mine were the worst. I had a crushed vertebra, several broken ribs, and a broken sternum, (breastbone). That meant no matter what position I was in something hurt!

The Alo's blades looked remarkably good considering that they had been used as their namesake, "chopper". The undercarriage had collapsed, the tail boom looked tired, and the cabin had slightly less headroom than was normal although the sliding doors still opened. The engine mountings had bent, and in general it looked a write-off. It could only have been divine intervention that put the helicopter in the LZ and the right way up. How many choppers have you heard of landing on their undercarriage whilst spinning violently without a tail rotor? I have no idea whether I reduced power as the Alo started to rotate; I doubt it, as it would not have rotated so fast. There had to be someone looking after us.

We tried making contact on the radio with an airliner overhead, but to no avail. As I thought it would be a considerable while before we were noted as being overdue I suggested that we take out the compass, Very cartridges and pistol, then head toward the south as the main road to Vic Falls couldn't be too far. Dave removed the compass and we started walking slowly due to our injuries. We soon found that was a mistake, as there were numerous round pebbles on the ground and the ground undulating. The consequence was that we were sliding on these pesky pebbles. Progress was dreadfully slow because every movement I made was painful and sudden movements caused by the pebbles were from the pits.

I was entirely wrong about how long it would take for search aircraft to put in an appearance. I recall a RhodAF Alo was called across from Binga and came and searched. It appals me that I cannot remember either the pilot's or the engineer's name especially when I am extremely grateful for their help. The first two Very cartridges were so swollen they could not fit into the gun. The third worked and fortunately the Alo driver saw it immediately. Soon the Alo put in an appearance and all I remember of the pilot was that he had fair hair, had recently come across from fixed wings, and I think had also been involved with a crash.

To my disgrace I will tell you I asked everyone to lie to the board of inquiry, to say we had seen a buck on the ground and went and had a closer look. That I then turned the tail into a tree and lost the tail rotor. That is what stands in the records! People may have learned something out of the real truth. My life has since come under new management, and Jesus helps me conduct my life differently.

I spent a few days in Wankie hospital before being flown down to the RSA to face the music and convalescence. I was back in the bush six weeks later trying to earn that extra funding and made it back in time for my marriage, still sore. My back took a further 4 years to return to a modicum of its former self. I never did hear anything more of what happened to my passengers. I remember one's name was Dave Palmer, another Llewellyn and the third I can remember nothing. Dave Noakes left the South African Air Force a few years later and joined Kentron a division of Denell. Alouette III 28 was flying again six months later – truly a credit to our magnificent technicians."

Operation Blanket

For me, Operation *Blanket* started on 10th August 1974, with Doug Pasea in Canberra R 5203, which was a two hour thirty-minute photo-reconnaissance sortie on survey work - for mapping purposes.

A further seven missions were flown between the 18th and the end of the month. The navigators on these trips were Bernie Vaughan, Glob, Mike Ronne and Paddy Morgan. Duration varied up to four hours per sortie - the navigators could spread the load but we poor pilots had to grin and bear the cold, boring challenges of flying perfectly level for this type of photography. Operation *Blanket* missions were flown on August 10, 18, 19, 21, and 25th. Survey photography demands cloudless skies, and is invariably flown in the dry spring season, prior to the ITCZ moving down the continent.

RAMS

Our 5 Squadron Commander Randy du Rand perfected offset bombing technique during March 1974. This method was code named RAMS - Radio Activated Marker Service. RAMS proved a major breakthrough for day and night bombing in insurgency operations. The advantage of pilots undertaking Field Force Unit (FFU) duties such as at Bindura included appreciating ground forces' *modus operandi* and also improving inter-service liaison and co-operation.

My last sortie on No 5 Squadron was flown with Mike Ronne in Canberra R 2519; on a 6 x 130lb medium level offset bombing trial on Thursday 14th November 1974. I cleared the Station on the Friday, in preparation of my posting to the Glass Palace (Air HQ, Milton Buildings) as Strike 1. It would be a number of years before I would get my bum in the air again - something like another two years, nearly to the day (10th November 1976).

As a matter of interest, Peter Stiff determined that ongoing operations in Moçambique, between 1970 and the Marxist take-over in 1974, resulted in the Rhodesians killing more FRELIMO than the Portuguese did. Whilst hot pursuit operations were the norm during those times, it was hardly a correct designation. The SAS, with support from the South African Recces, operating in small groups, contributed greatly to locating terrorist camps and winkling out the gooks.

In November 1964, six months after the Lisbon coup, pressure was brought to bear on the Rhodesians by the South African Government because of John Vorster's détente exercise, so Rhodesia reluctantly withdrew its 'hot pursuit' troops from Moçambique. The Recces operating with them also withdrew. It appears unlikely that Prime Minister Vorster knew that his troops had been assisting with the Joint Defence of the Zambezi River Line.

Operation Biscuit: 9 September 1974

This was a short SAS recce operation of Chete Island, a precursor to Operation *Mica*.

Operation Mica: 9 to 11 September 1974

Like *Biscuit,* this was a short, three-day recce of Chete by the SAS. The objectives were to thwart known crossing points used by the terrorists, as well as prepare the groundwork for future cross-border operations.

Airstrike Log 207
Aircrew:
- Roger Watt / Garry Whittal
- Trev Baynham / Roy Stewart
- Solo van Rooyen / Bill Riley

Target: Nine to ten Terrs at US735630, 11 n.m. west of Rushinga. Terrs scattered along riverbed
Result: Two wounded, seven killed. Tenth wounded, captured later. Roger and Garry awarded SCR – See Pride of Eagles, pages 576–577.

Roger Watt recalls "Having just resupplied a radio relay station in the Marymount area, Garry and I spotted eight to ten terrs sprinting for cover close to a dry river bed. The gang bombshelled, splitting into three groups. After only firing one shot the MAG had a stoppage, with Garry having to re-cock the gun after every shot. I radioed FAF 5 for the Fire Force, and continued engaging the enemy who kept up fairly accurate ground fire at us. After about 25 minutes Trevor Baynham arrived with the K-Car, with Solo deploying stop groups. An RAR call-sign, who was about eight miles away, made a gallant effort to reach the contact area, running all the way and arriving shortly after the fireforce. The ten terrs we had sighted were all accounted for"

Despite Roger's rather modest account, a more detailed write up will be found in Pride of Eagles – and the SCR gallantry awards that were subsequently made.

Operation Market Garden: November 1974

Operation *Market Garden* involved Flight Lieutenant Basil Moss while he was serving with the Selous Scouts. The Scouts were using village contact men and it soon became evident that the Scouts' operations in the Mavuradonha Mountains area were taking a nosedive. Their problems were traced to an extremely crafty and wily old man that became a double agent – not only was he leading the Scouts up the garden path, but was also passing on Security Force movements to the terrorists. It transpired that the old man soon realised that the pseudo groups operating in his area were "*Skuz'apo*", and as a result of his passing this information onto ZANLA, the Scouts started taking heavy losses.

Basil was sent to sort out the crafty headman. They designed a scheme whereby Basil, in pseudo garb, met up with the old man and gave him a Post Office Savings Account deposit slip to sign – and flashed four hundred dollars. Basil explained that the money was for him and the signature on the deposit slip would mean that the money that he was shown will be deposited in his name, in his own Savings account. The old man duly obliged. Basil then got the contact man to sign another piece of paper. Basil then told the 'informer' that the second piece of paper was in fact a receipt for the money from the British South Africa Police. It was explained to him that if he should try his monkey business again, the *Skuz'apo* would not hesitate to forward the incriminating evidence to the ZANLA High Command in Moçambique.

It did not take too long for the old man to realise that he had fallen for the blackmail trick, hook, line and sinker. He knew only too well what ZANLA would do to him as a 'proven' sell-out. Not only was his own safety at stake, but his family and property. There was an immediate improvement in Security Force successes in the Mavuradonha Mountain area – the RLI had a field day when the terrorists were led into one trap after another. In a matter of eight weeks, thirty-two terrorists were killed, after being set up by the compromised contact man. This same tactic was used until, like all good things, it comes to an end. The old man's nerve snapped and he fled his village – with his entire family but minus his large cattle holdings and all his other possessions. Another likewise-compromised contact man came to an untimely and sticky end at the hands of his terrorist friends, who grew irritable and suspicious when they noticed all the ZANLA sections operating the areas around them, were systematically getting wiped out.

A month after my last sortie on Canberras, Air Lieutenant Brian Murdoch was killed at Mashumbe Pools airstrip in a Trojan. Brian had been Bruce Smith's OCU student on Vampires, but I had also instructed Brian on numerous occasions. It was a tragic loss. Brian had gone in to the short airstrip to uplift Lance Corporal Povey of 2RR (who had been injured in a landmine blast), but they did not have sufficient gooseneck flares to light up the runway for Brian's take-off. Instead, the Army positioned a couple of Land Rovers down along the airstrip, using their headlights in lieu of flares. During the take-off run, the Trojan collided with the vehicle at the end of the runway. All on board were killed. The Trojan was notorious for its poor take-off performance – as well as its very short landing runs. Whether the accident was a matter of poor judgement by Brian, or operational necessities demanding risking life as well, I can't say for sure. I would like to believe that most Air Force pilots were committed to flying to the utmost limits of both the aircraft, and the ability of the pilots, one may wonder whether such risks would be contemplated now-a-days.

My time on Canberras came to an end. It was probably one of my more rewarding postings, and it had been a great privilege to serve with a very fine bunch of airmen.

Summary of Writers No 5 Squadron Offensives

The following summary shows the number of Canberra airstrikes that I carried out during the Rhodesian War. Listed by Date, Aircraft Number, Navigator, Passenger, Bomb load and target area:-

5 March 1973; 2155; Doug Pasea + Ullyett; 96x20lb Frag bombs; Hurricane
29 April 1973; 2159; Doug Pasea + Rich Beaver; 96x20lb Frags; Moçambique
30 April 1973; 2502; Doug Pasea + Mick Delport; 96x20lb Frag; Moçambique
5 May 1973; 2519; Doug Pasea; 96x20lb Frag; Hurricane
21 May 1973; 2519; Doug Pasea + Rich Beaver; 9x500lb HE; Moçambique
7 September 1973; 2504; John Brown; 96x20lb Frag; Hurricane
12 October 1973; 2055; Doug Pasea + Paddy Morgan; 6x1000lb HE; Hurricane
13 January 1974; 2504; Doug Pasea+ Randy du Rand; 9x500lb HE; Moçambique
19 February 1974; 2519; Rich Airey; 96x20lb Frag; Hurricane/Moz
21 February 1974; 5203; Bernie Vaughan; 96x20lb Frag; Hurricane
23 February 1974; 2504; Bernie Vaughan; 9x500lb HE; Hurricane
28 March 1974; 2156; John Brown; 96x20lb Frag; Abort-Wx-Op
4 April 1974; 2155; Paddy Morgan + Mick Delport; 96x20lb Frag; Zambezi

11 April 1974; 2155; Paddy Morgan; 9x500lb HE; Marble
Canberra bombing wreaked death and destruction on all living creatures in the target area.

Summary of Operational Aerial Reconnaissance Missions
27 May 1972; 2502; Bernie Vaughan; Op Black Jack - Nyamasoto
12 July 1972; 5203; Bernie Vaughan; Op Junction - Moçambique
14 August 1972; 2085; Bernie Vaughan; Target Livingstone - Zambia
12 September 1972; 5203; Phil Schooling; Livingstone airfield - Zambia
4 November 1972; 2085; Phil Schooling; Frelimo Ter Base Camp - Moçambique
1 December 1972; 5203; Bernie Vaughan; Ter base camp - Zambia
4 December 1972; 5203; Bernie Vaughan; Ter base camp - Zambia
9 December 1972; 5203; Bernie Vaughan; Ter base camp - Zambia
29 December 1972; 2085; Phil Schooling; Luanda Bridge - Zambia
30 December 1972; 2085; Phil Schooling; Hurricane armed Recce
19 January 1973; 2502; Bernie Vaughan; Op Hurricane
2 February 1973; 2085; Phil Schooling; Op Hurricane
20 May 1973; 2085; Doug Pasea; Op Hurricane - Moçambique
21 May 1973; 2085; Doug Pasea; Op Hurricane - Moçambique
22 May 1973; 2085; Doug Pasea; Op Hurricane - Moçambique
23 May 1973; 2085; Doug Pasea; Op Hurricane
24 May 1973; 2085; Doug Pasea; Op Hurricane
27 May 1973; 2085; Doug Pasea; Op Hurricane
4 April 1973; 2085; Doug Pasea; Op Hurricane - Zambia
27 April 1973; 5203; Bernie Vaughan; Hurricane - Moçambique
29 April 1973; 5203; Bernie Vaughan; Hurricane - Moçambique
2 May 1973; 5203; Doug Pasea; Hurricane - Moçambique
18 May 1973; 5203; Doug Pasea; Hurricane - Moçambique
6 June 1973; 2519; Doug Pasea; Op Alcora - Zambia
4 July 1973; 2055; Bernie Vaughan; Op Polar - Moçambique - Nampula
5 July 1973; 2519; Doug Pasea; Op Hurricane - Moçambique
9 July 1973; 2055; Bernie Vaughan; Op Hurricane - Moçambique
10 August 1973; 2519; Doug Pasea; Angola - Zambia - Zaire
14 August 1973; 2519; Doug Pasea; Op Alcora - Zambia - Zaire
19 August 1973; 2519; Doug Pasea; Op Alcora - Zambia
16 January 1974; 2519; Doug Pasea; Op Alcora - Zambia
7 June 1974; 5203; Doug Pasea; Op Hurricane - Chete-Deka - SAS Ops
13 June 1974; 2085; Doug Pasea; Deka - Feira - Mana Pools
5 July 1974; 2085; Doug Pasea; Op Big Bang - Chete-Deka - SAS Ops
6 July 1974; 2085; Buff Phillips; Op Polar - Moçambique - Nampula
15 July 1974; 2085; Doug Pasea; Op Polar - Moçambique - Nampula
17 July 1974; 2085; Doug Pasea; Op Polar
30 July 1974; 2055; Paddy Morgan; Moçambique - Ter Base Camps - Zambia
6 August 1974; 5203; Paddy Morgan; Op Hurricane
10 August 1974; 5203; Doug Pasea; Op Blanket
12 August 1974; 2085; Doug Pasea; Op Polar - Moçambique - Nampula
12 August 1974; 2085; Doug Pasea; Op Polar - Moçambique - Nampula
18 August 1974; 5203; Paddy Morgan; Op Blanket
18 August 1974; 2085; Doug Pasea; Op Blanket
19 August 1974; 2085; Doug Pasea; Op Blanket
21 August 1974; 5203; Bernie Vaughan; Op Blanket
25 August 1974; 5203; Mike Ronne; Op Blanket
25 August 1974; 5203; Mike Ronne; Op Blanket
30 August 1974; 5203; Mike Ronne; Op Blanket
2 September 1974; 2085; Doug Pasea; Op Polar - Moçambique - Nampula
2 September 1974; 2085; Doug Pasea; Op Polar - Moçambique - Nampula

23 September 1974; 2519; Paddy Morgan; Op Big Bang - Deka DK Camp
14 October 1974; 2519; Doug Pasea; Hurricane - Colour survey
20 October 1974; 5203; Paddy Morgan; Big Bang - Deka Chewore - Ngwemanzi
28 October 1974; 5203; Paddy Morgan; Hurricane - Mt Darwin - Mtoko

Aerial Reconnaissance contributed a significant, if not more important, role in the Rhodesian Bush War. Had it not been for photographing target details, many of the airstrikes and Army cross-border raids would not have been possible. In many instances, the intelligence gained by photo-reconnaissance took several years of planning, rehearsals, and co-ordination of combined operations in order to mount external offensives. The role played by the No 5 Squadron navigators should never be under estimated. I had the highest regard for our navigators who were able to find well camouflaged camps in the middle of "no-where" – and the photo-interpreters, whose scrutiny of our photography enabled us to build up intelligence from the scant evidence that the Canberra crews brought back. Cognisance needs be taken that the navigator had to direct the pilot to the target area in the first place, roll the cameras at the right time, mark up the film, and often return to bomb a target hidden in featureless areas.

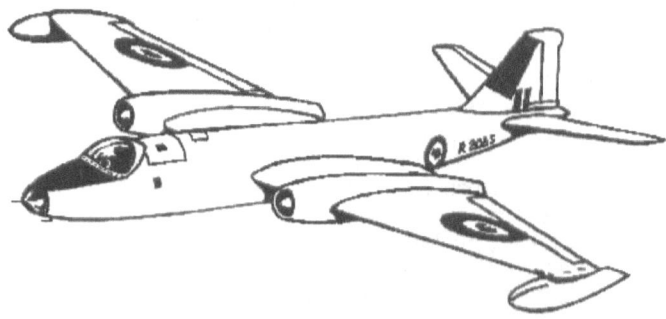

The "Graceful" Canberra

As previously mentioned, photo-reconnaissance took two main forms – Survey PR, and Target PR. I found the latter a lot more rewarding. Perusal of my flying log reveals a page long history. I flew a total of 56 operational aerial reconnaissance missions, more than half of which saw me teaming up with Doug Pasea. It was also significant that the various navigators had their own preference for specific aircraft and configurations. A breakdown, by navigator, with total sorties flown, and Canberra preference, is: -

- Doug Pasea - 29 Missions - Canberra R 2085 [17]
- Bernie Vaughan - 12 Missions – Canberra R 5203 [7]
- Paddy Morgan - 6 Missions – Canberra R 5203 [4]
- Phil Schooling - 5 Missions – Canberra R 2085 [4]
- Mike Ronne - 3 Missions – Canberra R 5203 [3]
- Buff Phillips - 1 Mission – Canberra R 2085 [1]

Canberra R 2504 was put on static display at the Zimbabwe Military History Museum in Gweru in 1989. This Canberra was built by English Electric in 1952. It served with No 44 Squadron, Royal Air Force Honington (1954 to 1958) and ferried to Rhodesia on 4th May 1959. Pete Woolcock hit power lines while flying it in September 1968, but landed safely, dragging miles of hy-tension electric cables behind him. I flew this Canberra on 42 sorties (29th December 1971 to 26th June 1974). It was the first aircraft to drop live Alpha bombs in October 1976. It was hit by a SAM-7 heat seeking-missile, in the port engine, in October 1978. The aircraft landed safely, using only the starboard engine.

Brown-Job: School of Infantry

Re-enter Herbert Chitepo and Josiah Tongogara, and their lust for power. In November 1974 there was a rebellion. In a ZANU camp at Chifombo on the Zambia- Moçambique border, a group of terrorists arrested their commanders, took control of the central command, and appointed one Thomas Nhari (a law graduate from Salisbury who had joined ZANU five years earlier) as their leader. All of them were Manyikas (from Manicaland / eastern highland tribes) and they were quick to denounce Tongogara, a Karanga, for their failures in the field. In contacts, the terrorist losses were ten killed for every one SF casualty.

On 9th December Nhari arrived in Lusaka with a gang of 20 freedom fighters. They abducted Tongogara's wife and brother-in-law, then kidnapped three ZANU party leaders: Mukudzei Mudzi, executive secretary; Kumbirai Kangai, welfare secretary, and Henry Hamadziripi, treasurer. The rebel convoy was heading for Tongogara's house when it was spotted, and the police were called. Most of the rebels were arrested. Tongogara was dispatched to the 'front' to crush the rebellion. Early in the New Year he stormed the camp at Chifombo: 45 people were killed. His own forces regained control.

On 22nd January 1975 a committee of three, headed by Chitepo, tried the rebels at Chifombo. Those convicted - it only took a matter of minutes for some - were executed a few hundred yards from the hearings. That wasn't the only summary so-called justice meted out. Convinced that the Manyika group had started the rebellion against them, the Karanga faction launched a wave of revenge kidnappings and executions. Some were murdered in Moçambique, others in Zambia. More than a hundred were killed. And this without a shot fired by the SF.

The above was blamed as the cause of Chitepo's assassination. ZANU labelled this insurrection within their own ranks as the Nhari Rebellion.

Flying Days Numbered - Strike 1

For the sake of continuity, and correct a perception of Security Force skulduggery, Herbert Chitepo's demise warrants mention. On 16th March 1975, he had confided in Kaunda that he feared for his life. Thirty-six hours later, as Chitepo was starting his car up at his house in Lusaka, a bomb exploded inside the vehicle. It killed him instantly. The incident created disarray within ZANU and ZANLA. Tongogara fled to Moçambique, his allies to Tanzania. Kaunda was furious. A special commission took a year to find Tongogara implicated. He was returned by Moçambique and was found guilty.

Tongogara, to the day of his own death (in 1979), was to deny the charge. At the time he accused Ian Smith, Vorster and Kaunda, insisting that Chitepo stood between them and the success of their policy of détente. Mugabe later agreed, in 1976, that Tongogara was guilty. Tongogara was imprisoned for 18 months. For me, the murderers of the Viljoens had been avenged.

SWAPO had been banned in South Africa in 1963 and turned to armed struggle in 1966. They operated from bases in Zambia and, after 1975, Angola. SAAF crews operating from Thornhill had been involved in the construction of the Katima Mulilo base in the Caprivi Strip.
Our exercises of South African troop deployments, through Grootfontein to Tsumeb and Rundu were obviously pre-planned strategic attacks against Sam Nujoma guerrillas inside Angola. Likely outcomes were Operation *Reindeer* in 1978 with the South African airborne assault on Cassinga, where a SWAPO settlement in the south of Angola was established. Six hundred Namibians died at Cassinga.

By the time I attended the SAAF College in Pretoria, I was no stranger to Angola. I had already experienced a memorable weekend at Luanda - having flown over Masvingo and Cuito Cuanavale in the Cuanda Cubango province, and between Huambo and Kuito on the Benguela railway. Portugal was still in control, but by 1974, when revolution in Portugal made independence in Angola inevitable, the prospects of the three rival factions of MPLA, FNLA and UNITA, sharing power was remote.

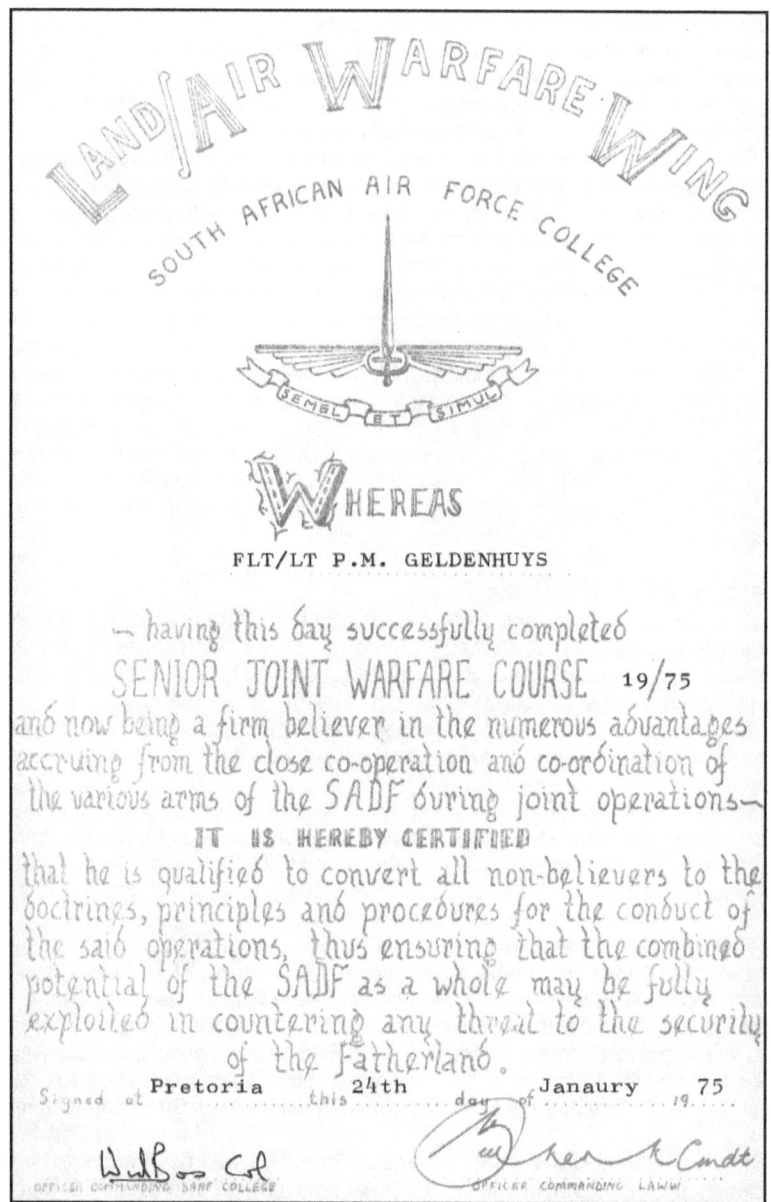

Agostinho Neto, the prominent intellectual leader of the MPLA sought favour with the Russians and, through Che Guevara, with Cuba. MPLA's rival in Angola was Holden Roberto and Jonas Savimbi's FNLA who was recognised by the OAU, with support from the Chinese and Romanians. Jonas Malheiro Savimbi later broke away from FNLA to form his own UNITA movement. The ruin of Angola was well under way on the eve of independence in 1975.

Operation *Carlota* concerned the dispatch of Cuban troops to Angola, which according to Gabriel García Márquez 'was not a simple expedition by professional soldiers, but a genuine people's war'. Márquez argued that the Cubans were coming to the rescue of a people 'with a magical dread of aeroplanes' who were 'convinced that bullets could not pierce white skins'.

With troops from South Africa, Cuba and Zaïre deployed throughout Angola, it was already hostage to external forces. A month before independence was due to be declared a column of

South African armour crossed the South West African border and made its way up the country - not unlike the battle exercises I had conducted at the Staff College. The South Africans had every intention of entering Luanda but they were drawn up short by the resistance from a Cuban expeditionary force. Cuban officers had been training MPLA troops in Angola for several months, and Fidel Castro had sent reinforcements in response to the news that South Africa was about to enter the field.

The result was a stand-off. However, the South Africans were still in the country in November, when the MPLA proclaimed the independence of Angola under its sole leadership - and installed Agostinho Neto as the president of the People's Republic.

The collapse of Portuguese colonialism meant an increase of ZIPRA, ZANU, ANC and SWAPO activity along a vast stretch of hostile borderland facing Rhodesia.

Glass Palace

My posting to Air Headquarters, Milton Buildings, Jameson Avenue, reporting to Director Operations Group Captain KAS Edwards meant that I was privy to what was going on militarily. I made it my hobby to note the various operations - past, present and future - that had a bearing on the history-in-the-making of the Rhodesian Air Force. Admittedly, there were many gaps in the puzzle, and it was only years later that others came to mind, as well as many past and present operations that were classified too secret for my eyes.

As Strike 1, my office was right next door to Air Force Headquarters operations room. I was invariably involved with, or aware of, all day to day air movements. Flight Lieutenant Dave Clements was OPS 2 – Operations No 2, reporting to Ops 1, and SOOPs – Staff Officer Operations (Wing Commander Wally Heindriks). Dave and I got on very well together. With Dave being responsible for the day to day running of the Air Force Headquarters operations room, I was invariably taken into his confidence. I was thus in a position to be kept abreast of all the Air Tasks that were issued, and I caught sight of the MisReps – Mission Reports – that the pilots had to report back after returning from their respective tasks. Dave was also father-in-law to John Annan. All of the Air Staff was required to carry out 24-hour Duty Officer duties, necessitating sleeping over, in a specially furnished room next to the Operations Room. Dave Clements also prepared a weekly Brief for senior staff officers. During my tours of duty as the Duty Officer, I would catch sight of the daily Briefs from Dave. It was while I was Strike 1 that I started documenting all the various operations that the Air Force was involved with. (Dave Clements retired to Natal, and died at Hilton in November 1998).

Operation Newton: 18 to 25 June 1975

Operation *Newton* was a combined forces operation in the Kandeya Tribal Trust Land that fell within the jurisdiction of the main *Hurricane* JOC at Bindura. As Strike 1 at Air Force Headquarters, and scheduled to do my fair share of Bush Duties, it was indeed my pleasure to rub shoulders with the likes of Brigade Major Mike Shute, and the highly proficient Regimental Intelligence Officer, Lieutenant Alan Lindner. Alan was aware that senior members of the ZANLA Nehanda Sectoral Operations Commander, a Kenneth Mabunu (I suspect it was Peter and not Kenneth) was meeting his subordinates at a local kraal known as Mausa village.

A plan was put together that would involve sixteen helicopters, three Provosts, seven Trojans and four Dakotas. Troops from the RLI and RAR would be used to make up the Fire Force elements. A cordon and search operation involving twelve companies of troops was deployed around the anticipated meeting place. These included elements of 2 Independent Company, and four Rhodesia Regiment territorial force companies, as well as support from 2 Engineer Squadron. Three Fire Forces were made up – the first consisting of a K-Car with five G-Cars; and two of a K-Car and four G-Cars each. Special Air Service and Selous Scouts were deployed to suitable OPs to observe terrorist movements, and initiate the Fire Force call-outs.

The first call came at 10h00 on 24th June 1975, when a large group of terrorists was seen, but nothing of substance came from this call. Later the next day, another three contacts with terrorists occurred and a total of six were killed and one captured. A group of ten terrorists surprised a stop group of five men, and were able to escape the net. The captured gook revealed that thirty-three terrorists had been within the cordon, and had managed to escape the clutches of the Security Forces. In total, 33 terrorists were killed and six captured. Despite not accounting for all the gooks, this operation was rated a success. However, such a large concentration of air support was not repeated – our limited resources were needed to cover the whole of Rhodesia, as well as lending vital air support to the cross border raids.

Operation Dirk: December 74 to August 1975

Operation *Dirk* was the South African air assistance programme consisting of two Dakotas and numerous SAP Alouette III helicopters, during the period December 1974 and terminating about 24th August 1975.

During mid December 1974 a Dakota arrived at New Sarum and was attached to No 3 Squadron. It flew its first operational supply sortie on 19th December, and was used mainly for the re-supply of SA Police camps, and other SAP support. A second Dakota supplemented it, and a change-over of aircraft took place on 11th July 1975, when the first aircraft returned to Swartkop. The two Dakotas remained in Rhodesia until the withdrawal of the Police.

The much-needed helicopters did sterling work, and served the country well. They sported SAP markings and were easily recognisable in that the aircraft numbers only ran to three digits. However, Premier Ian Smith was aware of the South African interest in Angola, where a large-scale incursion (by South Africa) was planned – with the blessings of the Americans. By October 1974 John Vorster made his famous cross-roads speech and further pressure was applied to the Rhodesians to reach an agreement with the gook leadership. When Ian Smith complied on 11th December 1974, the SAP Commissioner General Theo Cous personally informed the Rhodesians that the SAP would withdraw immediately the cease-fire came into effect.

Hilgard Muller, the South African foreign affairs minister announced on 11th February 1975 that the SAP had been removed from their forward positions, and by 1st August the remaining policemen were finally ordered out of Rhodesia. Lieutenant HT Paine is on record as flying the last operational sortie on Operation *Dirk* on 24th August 1975 – with Alouette III, number SAP 107. However, the bush war was far from over and more than 50 South African pilots and technicians remained – under the code name Operation *Polo*.

Operation Bluebolt: 29 to 31 July 1975

Bluebolt was a combined Internal Affairs and Army exercise, with Air Support, in the Mukumbura Tribal Trust Land area. Cyril White and Danny Svoboda, flying two Provost's, carried out frantan, sneb rockets and Browning front gun attacks on 29th July 1975. Targeted cattle were killed – to deny foodstuffs for the terrorists. Two days later, Danny led Norman Maasdorp on a second frantan and front gun airstrike, successfully burning a hut and a small surrounding area.

Air Strike No 256 and 257

Aircrew:
- Cyril White
- Danny Svoboda

Target 29/07/1975: UT405086 and UT425065, 8 to 10 n.m. west and south-west of Mukumbura
Result: Cattle killed and burnt. Bluebolt Operation in conjunction with Internal Affairs and Army.
Comment: small-scale air proscription must be carefully controlled and co-ordinated to prevent them from becoming counter-productive.

Aircrew 31/07/1975: Danny Svoboda, Norm Maasdorp
Target: UT403068 in the Mukumbura Tribal Trust Land
Result: Hut and small surrounding area burnt. Comment: useful training for Air Sub-Lt. Norman Maasdorp

Operation Polo

Operation *Polo* was a secret assistance programme in which fifteen South African officers were attached to Rhodesian military headquarters and fifty helicopter pilots and technicians with the Air Force until August 1976.

When ANC terrorists were engaged during Operation *Nickel* in 1967, after infiltrating from Zambia via the Wankie Game reserve, with their ZIPRA counterparts, South Africa responded by deploying up to 2,000 paramilitary policemen for border control duties. South Africa subsequently used the military pawn in the political chessboard context to squeeze concessions out of the Rhodesians. After the Vorster, Kissinger and Smith agreement of September 1976, things went horribly wrong for Rhodesia - American promises evaporated with the demise of Kissinger, South Africa put the screws on Smith, and Rhodesia, true to her word, was the only partner to carry out her side of the bargain.

In February 1975 a Rhodesian government spokesman announced that SAP elements were withdrawing from forward positions along the Zambezi. He added that seventeen SA police had been killed in the war since December 1972. Most of them died in 1974. In March, a ZIPRA unit surprised a patrol swimming in the Zambezi, upstream of Victoria Falls, and killed five. ZIPRA killed two more SA police in early October, during five clashes in ten days along the Zambezi. The Zambian government rejected a formal protest note over the use of its territory for infiltration, and *suggested instead that Rhodesian forces had killed the policemen to enlist sympathy in South Africa*. As if we would be so naive as to shoot ourselves in the foot. Then in late December, less than two weeks after the so-called cease-fire, six more SAP died in an ambush that became a legend among the local police. A senior ZANLA commander, Herbert Shungu, had sent an emissary to a SAP camp with a message that he was willing to discuss surrender terms. A SB officer reported "The SAP, somewhat naïvely, accepted the invitation and were ambushed on the Mazoe high level bridge where six of them were killed. So much for the cease-fire."

The killing of the six SA policemen so soon after the Vorster/Kaunda Lusaka Agreement, the death of another a few days later, and the wounding of five more, infuriated Vorster. Vorster then confined his paramilitary police to their base camps in Rhodesia, and by early August 1975 they had all been withdrawn from the country, *despite an earlier undertaking that this would not occur until a cease fire had been effected (as per his failed détente agreement)*. The Italics are mine.

SAP border control Operation *Dirk* was withdrawn in August 1975, followed by my own experience a year later when the SAAF helicopter - "Z-Car" crews were summarily evacuated whilst I was OC FAF 7. No wonder Ian Smith entitled his autobiography *The Great Betrayal*. And so Operation *Polo* came to an end with the final withdrawal of SAAF pilots in August 1976.

Operation Sand

In a highly secret operation, Rhodesian pilots and technicians were attached to the South African Air Force, to fly and service Impala and Mirage III aircraft. They wore SAAF uniforms and badges of rank at the exclusive flying training school at Louis Botha, Durban. The flying training was conducted on the Impala, the South African version of the Aermacchi MB 326M, built by the Atlas Corporation adjacent to Jan Smuts Airport, Transvaal. The Impala training became necessary in order to maximise Vampire T11 availability to prosecute the war effort. Squadron Leader Keith Corrans commanded the Mirage squadron, on "Special Duties" as OC 1, from 15 to 31 January 1971. Those fortune enough to fly Mirages included Rick Culpan, Jim Stagman, Alf Wild, Spook Geraty, Paddy Bate, Doug Reitz, Pete Mason and Mark Aitchison.

For the record, it should be noted that Canberra navigator *ab initio* training was also carried out at the SAAF base at Langebaanweg on the west coast of the Cape. At various stages Alouette helicopter pilots also trained at Ysterplaat, Cape Town, and mountain flying training was done in the Drakensberg. Rhodesian Air Force / South African Air Force co-operation remained of the highest order before, during and after the war.

The RhodAF had fairly high ranking officers based at SA Defence HQ in Pretoria, with diplomatic immunity (refer my escapades during Operation *Hottentot* - but see also Operation *Onyx*). These ranked from Group Captain to Air Commodore - or equivalent to Brigadier rank. Obviously, the South Africans reciprocated - and what a fine bunch of ambassadors they were too. Flight Lieutenant van den Linden, Squadron Leader Kon van Heyningen and Tony Geldenhuys to name but a few - for they adopted our ranks and uniform and could not be distinguished from their Rhodesian counterparts, except by their superior transport in the form of Mercedes cars.

Hunter and Canberra – Nos 1 & 5 Squadrons – two of the jet strike aircraft that fell under the Strike 1 portfolio at Air Headquarters

Then there was co-operation at various other levels too, such as photo interpretation, mapping, Council for Scientific and Industrial Research (CSIR) and National Institute for Personnel Research (NIPR) in psychological aptitude testing of aircrews. No doubt there were many intelligence interchanges, weapons developments, while using the Rhodesian situation as an ideal testing ground for South African purposes.

Speaking of jollies - then there were those glorious sorties to Pietersburg, Waterkloof, Bloemfontein, Durban, Port Elizabeth, East London, Langebaanweg and of course Cape Town.

But Operation *Sand* came to an end after the bush war because the South Africans were too shrewd to fall into the Zimbabwean trap. Prime Minister Robert Mugabe insisted that the Air Force obtain South African Cabinet endorsement that the SAAF was in fact training White Zimbabwean pilots in South Africa. That was the condition for Op *Sand* to continue so that Messrs M'nangagwa and Mugabe would hold the trump card, and so forcibly end the career of Air Vice-Marshall Hugh Slatter.

I should mention that Hugh Slatter was promoted to Air Vice-Marshal in February 1982 when Len Pink retired as Chief of Staff.

FAF 5 - Bedouins

Forward Airfield 5 - FAF 5 - was established at Mtoko as a strategic base in the middle of the Operation *Hurricane* area. The Sub-JOC Mtoko reported directly to JOC *Hurricane* at Bindura. The rural village of Mtoko served a small commercial farming community and the tribal districts of Mudzi and Nyamapanda. Being in the north-eastern corner of the country, the Mtoko district became an important infiltration route for ZANLA terrorists – especially after mid-1975s – after FRELIMO came to power in Moçambique.

In February 1975, fresh from the two week South African Air Force College (Pretoria) "Senior Joint Warfare" course, and sporting my Squadron Leader scraper, I was dispatched forthwith for a tour of border operations with Sub-JOC Mtoko. The Sub-JOC was jointly commanded by five representatives - one each from the Army, Police, Special Branch, Internal Affairs District Commissioner, and me as the Senior Air Representative. We were charged with the responsibility of prosecuting the war effort in our designated area.

One of the highlights of this particular period was the Sub-JOC recommendation for Consolidated Villages (CVs) to take over where the Protected Villages (PVs) concept had run into economic snags in view of their great financial burden on the State coffers. CVs differed substantially from the PV concept in that they were based on the principle of self-sufficiency and self help independence - versus continuous handouts.

The protected village idea, whereby the vulnerable, unarmed local population were moved and resettled into villages in order to deprive the enemy of his target and means of support, while providing better community facilities and a more sophisticated infrastructure, was started in the Chiweshe TTL at the beginning of Operation *Hurricane*. This counter-insurgency concept had its origin in the 1951-1954 Malaya Campaign, and was also extensively used in the Portuguese Provinces where they were known as aldeamentos.

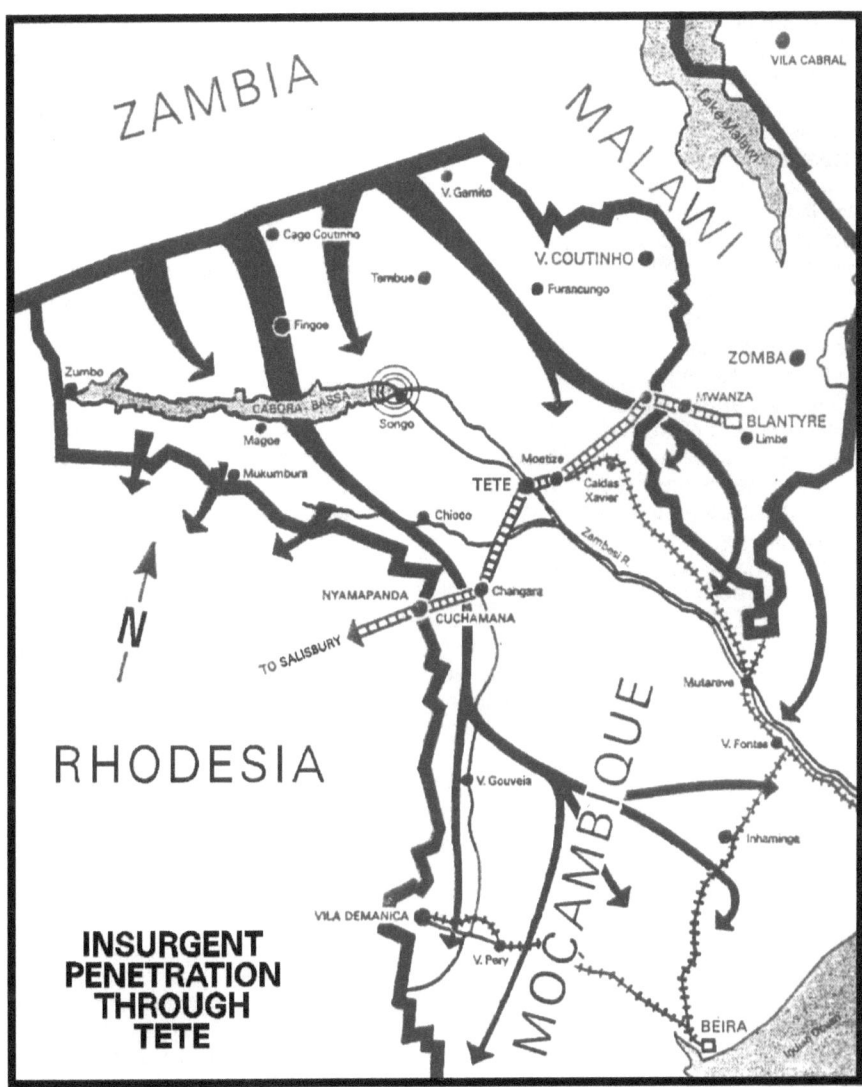

INSURGENT PENETRATION THROUGH TETE

In any event, the CV concept owed its origin to the Sub-JOC Mtoko formulation, and I consider myself privileged to have been part of this new counter-insurgency development, albeit from a purely historical viewpoint. The significant deviation for CVs from PVs were the fact that the villages were not fenced, they moved voluntarily, the villagers could choose their own sites and only very basic building materials were granted as were bare essentials regarding infrastructures. 20,000 tribal Africans living in the remote areas were resettled. Its purpose was to deny the insurgents the support of the civilian population for food and water.

A brief comment on the *Cordon Sanitaire* warrants mention. This was a programme implemented along the entire border with Moçambique, which involved the double fencing and mining of a wide swathe of real estate to deny access to the infiltrators. De-foliant chemicals were also sprayed along the border to stunt vegetation growth. The Cordon facilitated easier identification of the gooks crossing into Rhodesia.

I first came across the programme during my days at Kotwa on Operation *Tempest*. The JOC would get updated briefs on progress by the Internal Affairs department representatives –

or the Guard Force, which was established to provide some means of protection to the locals in their PVs/CVs. The denial of food sources to infiltrators was also known as Operation *Turkey*.

As the most senior Air Force Officer present, I was privileged to live in a caravan – as opposed to roughing it in tents and stretchers. The caravan was equipped with all mod-cons, including gas lighting whenever the electric lights diminished with "lights out", luxury bunks with foam rubber mattresses and minimal creepy-crawlies.

It is not my intent to be unkind to the gentler sex. However, there is also the story of a particular lady who would not be amiss amongst the best of them. Regarding aircraft fuel consumption, one can imagine the large quantities needed to keep operational aircraft in the air - necessitating large storage tanks. In the initial stages, aircraft fuel was supplied via 44 gallon/200 litre drums. As FAFs became more established, the 500 gallon/2500 litre tanks often seen on farms, replaced fuel drums. One would normally expect this construction job to be carried out by burly men. In the case of FAF 5, a fairly good-looking lady carried out this job. As the FAF Commander, it was my duty to instruct the contractor as to where and how I wanted the tanks erected and installed.

After a couple of weeks in the bush, anything that looks good in a dress affects male's hormones. I admit that I was no exception. A bit of graffiti found on one of the toilet doors put it well: "Absence makes the heart grow fonder, but in the bush it makes the Blacks go blonder". Rushing into the caravan to make myself presentable, I wasted no time in introducing myself to this luscious looking female. Imagine my surprise when every second word was a four-letter word. She could certainly hold her own amongst the best (swear like a trooper, that is) - as well as her ability to erect fuel tanks. So much for the glamour one experienced in the bush.

Speaking of temptation, a reader may be tempted to question the choice of "Bedouins" as a sub-heading. The answer is I was tempted to add credibility by quoting verbatim from a newspaper report which appeared in the Rhodesia Herald which gave due credit to the invaluable contribution to the war effort by our Volunteer Reserve.
Herald Reporter John Kelley published the following article in *The Rhodesia Herald* on 17th February 1975: -

'Bedouins' of Air Force

The Coffee crop is ripening nicely down at Chipinga. And there is not much Robin Fennell can do to help it. So he is doing his Call-Up - and the other services for that matter - is very good about the timings of such things. So the volunteer reservists who have seasonal work of importance to the country can more or less pick their times of service.

"There aren't many problems on the estate at this time of the year," said Robin, "although I have had a new tractor overturned and they're not keen on taking orders from my wife." As soon as his five to six week stint is over, he will be back in Chipinga picking coffee until November. Robin is doing his service this time at Forward Airfield No. 5, a cosy little canvas and caravan operations centre and airstrip. He helps run the centre with six different means of communication. His fellow officers and men appear relaxed with their music, their games and their good grub.

But the planes and helicopters that come and go, the weapons and paraphernalia of war parked menacingly around, and a sharp-end (military) stint in the north-east instead. Robin is one of a large number of people who down pens and pliers, put on uniform and leave the cities and farms for the temporary post of combating terrorism. For there is still an awful lot of work in that direction. The Air Force eyed a lot of the Air Force Territorial doing guard duties, which should dispel any impression of idleness. The camp is close to an area where there is still plenty of activity. Terrorists have been mining vehicles and ambushing others not very far away.

The camp is run by Squadron Leader Preller Geldenhuys, South African born, but Rhodesian by choice. His friends call him Prop to go with propeller. In seconds he can be in contact with the right people through air traffic control, three different radio systems, tele-printer or telephone. He can have a plane or a helicopter over an area within a few minutes. Prop's only other regular Air Force staff is the cook, the equipment NCO and the telephonist (radio operator). The remainders are Reservists or Air Force Territorial Force. His Camp Commandant is a marketing manager for the Rhodesian Wattle Co. There is another farmer in the Operations room, by co-incidence also from Chipinga.

Forward Airfield 5 can be packed up and spirited away somewhere else within 24 hours - lock, stock and barrel and everything else except the shower, the only permanent structure on the place. (Authors note: The reporter had taken and published a picture of a TF taking a shower. The caption read "The shower at FAF 5 is Heath Robinson. But it works well. Taking the heat out of life at FAF 5 with soap and water is one of the Air Force Territorial's").

This small forward airfield is as close as the Rhodesian Security Forces can get to the Bedouin Arab tradition. It has not happened yet. But if military policy demands it, the first thing that the locals will know is when they see a shower, an airstrip and some concrete slabs getting covered by blown sand. Between the action going on at present there are new paperbacks to read - the Air Force buys them every month - and a tape recorder with new cassettes to use. But, best of all, perhaps, comes the occasional bottle of wine. It all depends how the accounts are organised, for the Air Force messing is on a cash basis locally.

Being away from the farm cannot be that bad, can it?"

From its early humble beginnings, FAF 5 developed rapidly into one of the many formidable bases established by the Air Force to serve the security needs of the country. With its early beginnings, the Air Force wisely selected the best sites to feed, house, and accommodate personnel, and construct operational centres. With time, the other arms of the Security Forces also constructed semi-permanent structures to accommodate their personnel. The Scouts built their 'fort' and the other Brownjobs like the RAR and RLI also based themselves at the FAF. FAF 5 thus became a prime site from which hot-pursuit operations were launched into Moçambique, as well as the preferred operational centre for the highly mobile Fire Forces that evolved as the war progressed.

I was privileged, and felt honoured, to have contributed to the early establishment and development of the Forward Airfield.

Operation Turkey

Operation *Turkey* had been introduced with the objective of limiting quantities of food going to the rural areas. It was a form of rationing to ensure that local subsistence farmers had little or no surpluses to spare to feed infiltrating terrorists. It was particularly effective along the *cordon sanitaire*, as well as along the long, inhospitable Botswana, Zambia and Moçambique border areas.

A mute point among the so-called liberation movements was the Rhodesian Martial Law, which empowered state structures to destroy crops whenever evidence was found that remote kraals were collaborating with and sheltered terrorists. As already mentioned, de-foliant chemicals were also used to inhibit large tracts of arable land being used to grow crops specifically for feeding the gooks.

The operation was largely administered by the Department of Internal Affairs, with wide powers conferred on District Commissioners. As and when needed, the security forces would be called upon to co-operate with the civil power. Whilst the ravages of war caused displacement of the rural populace, it also resulted in more effective and efficient development of the Protected and Consolidated Villages concepts.

Air Strike Log 273 – 18 October 1975

Aircrew:
- Michael Borlace – Tony Jordan

Target: React to Landrover ambush VQ7111, 4 n.m. north east of Umtali – Penhalonga
Result: Fire returned at Frelimo inside Moçambique. No casualties. Excellent shooting by Jordan – gun kept jamming.

Mike Borlace recalls: "This was to assist a police Landrover that had been ambushed on the border. The whole story is quite comical in its own way. It included a one-sided interview with AHQ as - and these words are verbatim - "We're not at war with these people you know" - and, verbatim also after I said that the reason we had engaged the Freds was because they were shooting at us - "Were the bullets coming close?"   Far from there being no casualties, we learned a few days later, at that time we just had the one helo (helicopter) at Adam's

Barracks, that there were several Frelimo dead. We had in fact, as part of the plan to extricate the vehicle gone over the border and a pretty fierce fight took place, which was suitably edited for the airstrike report. Tony Jordan did some excellent shooting, particularly as the gun kept jamming."

FAF 2 - Kariba

I was posted and appointed OC FAF 2 on 15th December 1975. I owed my plum posting to the Director Operations – Group Captain Ken Edwards. As Strike 1, I was able to speak my mind freely with my old No 4 Squadron Commander.

My FAF 2 posting was a holiday camp. The Air Force provided my family with a really super four bed-roomed house on Yellow Tree Ridge. I was given a staff car to commute daily between Kariba airfield and the township. Kariba sunsets were something to behold. Work duties entailed helicopter trooping for No 2 Independent Company soldiers on border control reconnaissance excursions and the weekly relay station changeover on the Bumi Hills mountain range. I went on the odd relay changeover and often marvelled at the massive crocodiles lounging at the mouth of the Sanyati Gorge.

The fjord-like Gorge extends more than 20 kilometres inland from Lake Kariba, and teems with enormous tiger fish (which probably explains the size of the crocodiles). On more than one occasion the helicopter pilot would hover over the reptiles. I recall that an Alouette helicopter measures some thirty-five feet from nose to tail. Without exaggeration, some of those crocodiles in the Sanyati Gorge were longer than the helicopter. Visibility from the air is perfect; one can see quite a way below the surface of the Lake, which is not possible when floating in a boat. Even the local crocodile farm sported reptiles that were very old and massive in size.

The Matusadona lay between the Sanyati and Ume rivers (Ume for Bumi Hills). This area was later developed into a National Park, renowned for its African elephant. They were just about everywhere. Watching elephant swim across the Lake to Snake Island was a sight to behold. The elephants would use their trunks as snorkels. Calves would hang on for dear life - their trunks intertwined with their mothers' tails – the mothers seemed at ease towing their offspring over the large expanse of water to the various islands. Buffalo, waterbuck, zebra and various antelope and impala were plentiful.

No 2 Indep. Coy was also responsible for the protection of the dam wall and power station. The risk of sabotage was possibly slim because the Zambian Copper Mines were dependent on the electricity supply. Being the milch cow propping up the Kenneth Kaunda economy, while the risk was low, this did not hinder the opposing sides' eye-balling each other. Our guys had their binoculars scanning the Zambian sprawling Siavonga Township, as well as their eyes peeled for movement on Sampakaruma Island. Regular boat patrols were carried out from the harbour, and were also the forerunner of Special Forces marine operations when Operation *Splinter* was opened up later on during the bush war.

Gambling at the various casinos was a popular pastime. One particular SAAF pilot was Olla Grinaker, whose father owned the massive South African consortium. Olla was never short of cash and we spent our idle time devising various schemes to maximise our returns. Based on the law of averages, we developed a game plan on the roulette tables that minimised one's losses. At various stages, fairly handsome winnings tended to reinforce the addiction one becomes liable to when frequenting the gambling houses. I might add that Olla left behind a fair investment by the time he returned to South Africa. There was no way of beating those gaming machines - in the end they just gobble up your hard-earned cash.

Before I leave Olla, I wish to mention his claim to fame. I knew him as a Kiewiet pilot. As a SAAF helicopter pilot he was wounded in Owamboland and transferred to SADF Special Forces Headquarters staff, and also received an Honoris Crux for his deeds. Bill Sykes recalled an interesting story worth repeating: "A call sign in the Beit Bridge area was being chased by a platoon of gooks. There was no one in radio or even reaction distance as the nearest choppers and Lynx were at Rutenga? Olla was flying around Messina with his thumb up his fundament and his mind in neutral when he tuned into Channel X to listen out for any action from our side of the border. The high pitched squeals for help were heard strength ten and he, against all regulations except human instinct decided to help out. He asked for a grid ref. and flew to the area. I don't even think he was armed. As he flew over the call sign the gooks all gave him a full magazine of 'intermediate', plus a few from the RPDs, no doubt. He made like a turtle as he did not have an armoured seat - did not need one in RSA. His tech was 'asleep' in the back seat relaxing with his feet crossed. The whole chopper was riddled with bullets, so much so that all the plexiglass was smashed. When Olla landed his new sports model at Beit Bridge they threaded string from all the entry holes to the exit holes. Then they tried to get Olla into the pilot's seat. There was simply no room for the pilot because of all the string! The only bullet that did any harm was the one that went through the tech's two crossed feet."

The other popular pastime was pub crawling to all the various lake side resorts. Favoured haunts were the Cutty Sark Hotel, Carribbea Bay, Kariba Breezes, Lake View and sailing on the Lake (that is where my interest in catamarans was roused).

No mention of Kariba will be complete without mentioning the kapenta operators. In the early days, kapenta fishing was still in its infancy. Tiger fish thrived on these tiny sardines. Nowadays, the kapenta fishing fleet baffles the imagination, in its ingenuity, size and methodology.

It was not all play and no work at Kariba. The war was hotting up and infiltrations from Zambia became rife during the latter stages of the bush war. However, by that time, we had already plotted all the most likely crossing points, such as the Kota Kota and Sebungwe Narrows, as well as Chete Gorge where the border line runs close to our mainland. Look out on island 126 was well surveyed, with a concealed military presence kept there, as long as I remembered.

On 3rd March 1976 President Samora Machel announced he was closing Moçambique's border with Rhodesia to comply with UN sanctions and putting his country on a war footing. This could only have had one interpretation in the circumstances - that Moçambique was declaring war against Rhodesia. FRELIMO confiscated Rhodesia Railways' rolling stock stranded within Moçambique along with cargoes. Virtually overnight, we found ourselves defending a hostile frontier running north to south for some 900 km of mostly un-demarcated bushveld. I was given two weeks to wrap up FAF 2, put it on a caretaker basis and get my butt over to FAF 7 at Chiredzi (and move the FAF to Buffalo Range). In all honesty, I was not caught unawares – I had suggested to D. Ops that moving the 'holiday camp' to the eastern border was more in the national interest, with the war hotting up along Moçambique.

SWO Tony Verster and Storeman Alan Readings were given their orders to pack up and ship out by 15th March latest.

Defence Minister: September 1975

The Minister of Defence, P K van der Byl, was an eccentric parliamentarian much respected among the Security Forces. 'PK', as he was affectionately known to the Rhodesians, was flamboyant and frightfully British, and 'old school tie'. He was a master of the Churchillian phrase and the troops thought he was magnificent. There was no one quite like PK in his or her eyes; and indeed no other Defence Minister had such a rapport with the troopies. PK wanted to meet the troops in the bush and the Air Force tasked No 7 Squadron to fly him around the border area.

Air Lieutenant Pete Simmonds was detailed to do the trip and this is Simmo's side of the story, as humorously told by him:

"I had just completed a 4-week trip on operations at Mt Darwin and was looking forward to ten days rest at home away from the war. On my first day back at New Sarum I wasn't pleased when Squadron Leader Eddie Wilkinson told me that an Air Task had come in and there was no one left on the Squadron to do it but myself. There had been a recent cabinet reshuffle and P K van der Byl had just become our new Minister of Defence. PK had decided that the best way to get to know the military and to show how serious he was in his new portfolio was to tour the front line. My Air Task was to fly him around the north-east operational area over three nights and four days from the 2nd to 5th September 1975. "

"The war had not escalated much at this stage and we only had fire forces from Mt Darwin eastwards and south down to Fungwe in the Mrewa district. I had been tasked to spend one night each in Mount Darwin, Marymount Mission and Fungwe with PK, while he got to know the various army commanders and their men in each place. Eddie Wilkinson, "Wilkie", briefed me to take an Alouette II for the job, to fly low in the operational area so as not to be shot at but not so low as to frighten the Minister. I was then to drop him back at the Squadron where the Commanding Officer of New Sarum would be waiting to greet him, before he drove home on Friday 5th. I hadn't met PK before but had seen him on television and was therefore aware of his eccentric character but I can't say I was ready for him when I did meet him for this trip. On Tuesday 2nd, Steve Stead, my technician and I prepared the Alouette II with enough fuel to fly us safely to Mt Darwin. Steve and I had a tiny bag each with clothes and toiletries for three nights in the bush, and a stretcher each, packed under the back seat of the aircraft. The two of us took up very little space in the aircraft. PK duly arrived on the Squadron with Wilkie in attendance. His car drove up to the helicopter while introductions and handshakes took place. I noticed that the new minister had somehow managed to find a full set of camouflage clothing for the trip. His attire was conspicuous in that he wore no rank on his shoulders at all, but his green and khaki longs were different because he held them up with a brightly coloured stable belt he had kept from his earlier days as an officer with the Hussars. He must have dug deep in the attic for this belt. Then his bedroll was hauled out of the car boot and I wondered if we would ever get it into the tiny Alouette II. It was bigger than the size of a 44-gallon drum and it was obvious he intended being comfortable in bed while on this trip.

"Then two large bags came out of the car. One must have had clothes in it and the other, much heavier, clinked with full bottles, as we somehow managed to squeeze it all into the cabin of the aircraft. He was also hanging on to what looked very much like an elephant gun. He was well known for his elephant hunts in Rhodesia with visiting dignitaries from other parts of the world but inappropriate as this weapon might have been for fighting terrorists PK seemed delighted with it. No-one suggested he change it for a better fighting weapon when he mentioned that he was hoping to put it to good use on this trip. The chopper was frightfully heavy but we managed to take off and flew away north over Borrowdale. We then passed over the granite hills and valleys of Dombashawa and on to Bindura, before descending to 50 ft. above ground level for the rest of the trip to Mt Darwin."

"Right from the start PK was chatty and excited but he let me know within 10 minutes of leaving New Sarum that he was to be dropped in the Botanical Gardens near his house, off Second Street Extension, when we returned on the following Friday. Wilkie had been explicit that he must be brought back to New Sarum; but PK was insistent that he would be dropped near his house and wouldn't accept the instruction I had been given. I thought it was odd that he should be worrying about the end of his trip before it had begun but as he said in his very English accent "It's all been organised, Peter. I've arranged for people to meet me there, so it cannot be changed, we must land in the Botanical Gardens."

"Ten minutes from Mt Darwin, I warned Operations on the radio that we would be arriving soon and discovered that a contact was in progress to the west of FAF 4. Colonel Dave Parker was running operations in Mt Darwin and suggested we change frequency so that the Minister could hear the punch-up going on. We changed over to Channel Two and PK immediately started pushing me to let him join in the contact. He wanted to be put down on his own in the contact area with his elephant gun "on high ground please, Peter, as I like to attack downhill. I'd like to bag one of these chaps and this is the ideal opportunity, don't you think?" All this was said seriously in the plumiest of accents and Steve Stead suppressed a smile while continuing to survey the bush around us from the back of the aircraft. There was no chance I could possibly carry out his bidding of course but I felt I owed it to him at least to ask the Colonel if we could fly at height over the contact area for a look see.

"Colonel Dave Parker was adamant in his next instructions. "Get the Minister to Mt Darwin, now, Simmo. He is not to be allowed anywhere near the contact – I will get him as close as he needs to be on the map in my Ops Room when he lands." PK heard the transmission and looked disappointed while Steve continued to watch the bush going by without a word, seemingly oblivious to the goings on of pilots, officers and ministers around him.

"After we landed, PK saw out the rest of the contact in the Ops Room and spent the afternoon poring over maps, tactics, and strategies and getting to know the men involved in the war. He enthusiastically chatted to soldiers and managed to attract even the roughest troopies attention with them saying they wanted to "kyk this new oke." (See the new guy). That evening he endeared himself in the Officers' Mess with his quaint stories – and three bottles from the clinking bag. The Minister knew a thing or two about winning us over and we were well lubricated by his Scotch whiskey, fine wine and beguiling character.

"The following day he wanted to visit Karanda Mission, on the way to Marymount Mission. The Colonel had told him that we had taken some seriously wounded soldiers there recently and that the renowned American surgeon at the Mission had kindly patched them up before sending them on to the Salisbury General Hospital. He had probably saved the soldiers' lives and since we were never really sure whose side any of these missionaries were on, it was considered a good idea to encourage them by sending the Minister to thank them personally for their action. We were not expected, and landed unannounced at the airfield where the Karanda Mission pilot was attending to his Cessna. When our blades stopped turning he wandered over and I persuaded PK to leave his gun in the aircraft. The pilot didn't know who PK was so I told him this was the new Minister of Defence for Rhodesia and explained why we were there. He was most impressed with all this and insisted on calling PK "Your Highness" for the rest of the visit. Steve Stead didn't blink and it seemed PK had no intention of putting the pilot right. He obviously preferred to maintain his 'no rank on the shoulders' stance and his new "Your Highness" title. It seemed to me that it actually suited him. The pilot showed us to the surgeon who was appropriately thanked with a little pomp before we moved in a cloud of dust for Marymount Mission.

"Halfway there we flew over a couple of African women carrying huge suitcases on their heads as they walked along a lonely path in the middle of nowhere. PK immediately wanted to check them out "in case they were carrying weapons of war". This was a Minister like no other we had seen before. He was determined to be directly involved and he was a contact looking for somewhere to happen. No other senior politicians had been this far into the bush before and frankly, even the good ladies from the Border Patrol Welfare Fund had ventured deeper into the Operational Zone than any of the Ministers I could remember. I felt there would be no harm in letting him have a look in the suitcases and who knows, they may have contained something they shouldn't. I landed nearby and asked the ever suffering Steve Stead to accompany PK for the suitcase inspection. Steve's face gave away nothing as he galloped away with his FN after the Minister who was by now bounding through the bush with his enormous gun held menacingly at the ready. By the time I got airborne and overhead them, the offending suitcases were open on the ground and the African ladies were standing nearby with their hands up in the air. PK was hoiking colourful clothes out of the suitcases with the barrel of his gun. There was clearly nothing sinister hidden away in the suitcases and PK's disappointment with the lack of war booty was obvious, even from the air. We left the ladies to continue their haulage and moved on to Marymount Mission.

"If Karanda was a mission prepared to treat our troops in an emergency, Marymount was a different kettle of fish. The missionaries were particularly anti us and openly hostile to our presence. This was most unfortunate because with the large pile of dollars sent to them from America that they had built a 30 by 20-meter swimming pool on their grounds, which we weren't allowed to use. A certain Father Ignatius refused to let us near the most enticing pool tucked away in this hot, dry and dusty north-east corner of Rhodesia. He was well known to many of us for marching angrily about in his white socks and sandals, constantly complaining about the many inconveniences of having military people around his mission. He never missed a chance to send numerous letters of complaint to the ever-suffering army commanders unfortunate enough to be camped nearby on the airfield.

"Major Brian Robinson, (Robbie) in command of the Special Air Service, was based there when we visited on this occasion, and his men were operating over the border in Moçambique. It crossed my mind that the Minister may not win over as many hearts and minds at this place as he had the day before. The SAS had lost one of their men the previous day. SAS Corporal Storie had been killed in action and no matter how professional the SAS were about their specialised job, they were still a tight-knit force of human beings. Having lost one of their men, they would have been in no mood for nicety visits and polite chats with strange ministers. Brian Robbie was a tough master and the type of man who would have normally preferred that politicians stay in Salisbury with their suits and lengthy discussions while he was left unencumbered to fight the war. I couldn't have been more wrong and was underestimating PK's charm. He was fully aware of Corporal Storie and whilst sensitive to this he was determined to let these soldiers know they had a supportive representative in government who was thoroughly on their side. When we landed he wanted to address the few men in camp and he did this sensibly. PK then mentioned to Brian Robbie that he was tired of his camouflage longs and he wanted to look more like the rest of us with the standard khaki shorts, no socks and veldskoons. Robbie summoned the Quartermaster - and a short while later the Minister walked back into the Ops tent wearing a particularly tight pair of short shorts and was now sporting spindly white naked legs. Brian Robinson saw the shorts and suggested that perhaps they were a little too short and that he might want a larger size. In front of all the assembled men, PK looked down and announced "you are quite right, Brian, my cock sticks out of this one". It certainly lightened the mood and he was winning them over fast. After more discussions about tactics, strategies and troop movements, he insisted on spending the night on ambush somewhere in the bush yet again, hopefully to "bag one of those buggers". We had an early meal with him in the Mess tent and again a few more bottles came out of the musical bag. He then set out with a Stick of Rhodesian African Rifles men to ambush a likely track that had been used by terrorists to leave the country on a previous occasion. It rained that night and I really hoped, whilst I was tucked up in my dry bed, that PK would get a chance to finally use his gun. It didn't happen and yet he still returned chirpy and unfazed by the wet night he had had in the bush. He had found a 'demmo' (African axe) whilst out there which he had decided to keep as a memento and "a rather good specimen, don't you think?" He then had breakfast and a rest, before we were supposed to leave at midday.

"Brian Robinson had somehow managed to succeed with Father Ignatius where previous commanders had failed. Through all of Ignatius's rude bossiness and a very tight roster as to who could use the coveted swimming pool, Brian had amazingly cajoled him out of a precarious half hour from 5 to 5.30 each evening during which a few troops would be allowed to swim. This privilege was to be temporary and all pool rules had to be "strictly adhered to". The rule list was exhaustive and barely allowed swimmers to get wet. Staff at the mission had pool access most of the day. Students had a couple of hours under supervision and a restricted number of thoroughly washed soldiers were allowed in from 5 until 5.30pm with "no noise please". After his rest PK was outside the Ops tent looking a little tired when he asked about 10 or 12 SAS men around him if there was anything more he could do to help them before he left. The question was asked in the context that he might do something for them back in Salisbury as the Minister of Defence and most people present were content to say that no more was required.

His actions the previous night had already won their respect. However, one of the troopies was clever enough to see an opportunity and he explained the swimming pool situation whilst describing the difficult Father Ignatius as a member of the enemy. PK understood the situation immediately and his answer was simple. He said, "Corporal, go to Ignatius, send him my regards and explain to him that from now on my troops will have free access to the pool, he will be allowed to use it from 5 to 5.30pm and if he doesn't like the new rules, I'll deport the fellow". We left Marymount Mission a couple of hours later much to Father Ignatius's relief, but with the complete support of every soldier within a hundred miles.

"A Rhodesian Light Infantry Commando led by Major Bruce Snelgar, with two helicopters at his disposal, manned Fungwe. The camp was based on a low granite kopje at the western end of the Fungwe airfield. I radioed ahead that I was landing there in ten minutes with a VVIP on board. I had elevated PK from VIP to VVIP in my radio transmissions and as we flew over the camp, Joe Syslo, who thought I was bullshitting about my passenger, had assumed I was trying to make myself sound important. He lined up five bored men to give me a formation "brown-eye". PK saw the bare bottoms facing sky-wards as we flew by before landing and asked me disdainfully if my compatriots always welcomed me like this. Bruce Snelgar looked after PK for the rest of the day and the last of the clinking bottles was gratefully consumed on top of the granite kopje as the sun went down that evening. It was a particularly red sunset and we were comfortable late into the night with the heat radiating out of the granite rock on which we were camped. (Authors note: I had also known, and flown with Bruce. He was a fine Fire Force operator, but was killed in a K-Car).

"I sent a message back to my Squadron Commander saying I would be dropping the minister off, at his insistence, near his house in the Botanical Gardens. The next morning Bruce gave me a ziff – a brief, telegram type message - saying that this would not be allowed. The Commanding Officer at New Sarum had planned it all and he was to be dropped in front of the reception arranged for him in front of the HQ building at New Sarum that afternoon at 5pm. I wasn't going to argue with PK about this and by now I was sure as Minister of Defence his order out-ranked everyone else's anyway. We left Fungwe at 4pm and flew back over Avondale to PK's chosen triangle off Second Street Extension in the Botanical Gardens. Air Traffic Control had been warned of my flight and asked me if I was proceeding to New Sarum, which they were expecting. I told them that I most certainly was going to New Sarum, but would be landing in Avondale briefly on the way. They didn't bother informing New Sarum of this stop, so no one had the chance to prevent me from landing at the Minister's preferred landing zone. When we touched down at PK's landing spot, all became clear. The adjacent 4-lane highway was packed solid with the Friday evening slow moving 5 o'clock traffic. This traffic all but stopped with the arrival of our helicopter and two servants dressed in freshly ironed and starched whites were standing to attention waiting for us at the side of the LZ.

"The enormous bedroll went on to the head of the first servant and the bags were carried by the second, while PK led the entourage away from the chopper. He was wearing his newly acquired shorts and a fair amount of soot from marching through the bush and sitting in ambush, the "demmo" was hanging off his left shoulder and his elephant gun was prominent in his right hand. He threaded his way through the traffic waving to the drivers as the new Minister of Defence was seen to be doing his work. He must have won many votes that day and mine was one of them; but I was also in the quagmire for not having taken him to New Sarum. It was a fantastic trip during which Steve and I had many laughs and we both found ourselves missing him by the time we took off for New Sarum."

The story is reproduced by kind permission of Simmo, who was in Singapore at the time, and who also mentioned to me that "PK had gone to the great elephant hunt in the sky" a few days before he was able to forward the story to the late Minister.

Lynx Ferry

Eighteen Reims Cessna 337G twin-engined Skymaster aircraft were acquired from France in January 1976. As early as 1973 the Commander of the Rhodesian Air Force Air Marshal Mick McLaren visited the Reims Aircraft Company after attending the Paris Air Show. The Cessna Corporation of America had developed the 337G for use in Vietnam. French designers Engin Matra, in collaboration with Reims, introduced a weapons system, ready for use and essential for all types of total cohesion between ground and Air Forces. Its twin push-pull engine configuration limited vulnerability and facilitated piloting. The power plants were two Rolls-Royce Continental 210hp engines, and with its high wing for a variety of weapons, as well as providing good visibility from the cockpit, made it an ideal armed reconnaissance and surveillance aircraft for the Air Force.

Director Equipment, Group Captain Alec Thompson was tasked with the procurement of the aircraft and the necessary spares. In order to confuse the sanctions enemy, a cover organisation was registered in Spain, called *Sociedad Estudios y Pescas Maritimas* – SEPM – "The Society for the Study of Sea Fish". French-speaking pilots were recruited to aid the deception that the aircraft were not going to Rhodesia. The first ferry of ten aircraft, led by Squadron Leaders Rob Gaunt and Eddie Wilkinson departed from Reims Prunay airport at 02h00 on Thursday 15th January 1976, with a full moon. The West Coast of Africa route was decided on. They flew to Malaga and landed at Las Palmas to night-stop. On Friday they flew to Abidjan and the next day to Port Gentil, flying via the island of Fernando Po. On Sunday, the flight routed to Ruacana via Mayumba, Mocamedes and the Cunene River mouth. All ten aircraft arrived successfully in Salisbury on the Monday, 20th January, after just over 44 hour's flight time.

The second ferry, consisting of eight aircraft, led by Wing Commanders Mike Gedye and Keith Corrans flew the East Coast route – from Reims to Majorca, Crete, Djibouti, Mombassa, and then on to Salisbury. Departure was on Wednesday 28th January. The ferry from France to Kenya was accomplished without any problems, but while flying along the east coast of Moçambique, one aircraft piloted by a Frenchman force landed at Memba in hostile territory, snapping its nose wheel in an ant-bear hole. The other seven aircraft landed at New Sarum at 17h30 on1st February. Jack Malloch had meanwhile arrived on 30th January, flying his *Affretair* DC 8, loaded with Lynx spares from Reims. A RUAC - Rhodesian United Air Carriers - aircraft from Charles Paxton was chartered, with two Airwork technicians. They loaded up with the requisite spares and flew to Beira. From there, a TAT - *Transportes' Aeroes de Moçambique* - Islander flew the recovery team up to Nampula and then on to the crash site where the necessary repairs were carried out on the stranded Lynx. After due repairs, the last of the ferry Lynxes were all back safely in Air Force New Sarum hangar number 3 - where all 18 brand new aircraft took on Rhodesian Air Force colours.

The Lynx has landed. The ferry coup raised the spirits of the beleaguered Rhodesians – to survive and perform as well as they did – without the self sacrifice of the Rhodesians who left their families at home for months on end as they fought their own kind of war in the rest of the world. On arrival, Air Marshal Mick McLaren introduced the Lynx to a grateful Prime Minister, Ian Smith, himself having been a wartime pilot.

Operation Underdog: 17 January 1976

Operation *Underdog* was a helicopter support deployment of Selous Scouts to attack the ZANLA Chicombidzi base in Moçambique following a FRELIMO capture who had attempted to cross the border minefield. FRELIMO had tried to infiltrate Rhodesia on New Year's Day, and left one of their kind to the mercy of the Rhodesians when the poor fellow stepped onto an anti-personnel mine in the mine belt that formed part of the border control measures. His comrades fled in disorder, and the Rhodesians were able to extract valuable intelligence from their capture.

The capture revealed that a ZANLA transit camp was located nearby Chicombidzi, which was in almost continuous use by ZANLA. The Selous Scouts assembled an assault force of 15 under the command of Lieutenant Tim Bax. At 18h45 on 17th January, No 7 Squadron Alouette helicopters dropped Tim Bax and his men on the Moçambique side of the border. The Scouts then foot-slogged, on compass bearing, to where the ZANLA camp was located, arriving at about nine o'clock that night. Having recognised Shona being spoken, they waited until the enemy hit the sack and a deathly hush settled over the camp.

As Tim advanced under cover of darkness, a sentry must have seen them, and opened up with a burst of gunfire. The Scouts fired 1000 rounds of small arms ammunition at two grass bashas, and a larger structure that appeared to be a dining room or grass conference shelter. They also fired an RPG-7 rocket and ten mortar bombs. Whilst conducting a sweep, they found a further five bashas, but no enemy bodies were found. A large quantity of weapons, kit and equipment – too much to recover - was thrown in the grass structures and set alight.

At first light the helicopter G-Cars arrived to uplift the call-sign, ending this "shoot and scoot" raid into Moçambique.

5 Operation Thrasher: February 1976

The *Thrasher* operational area officially opened in February 1976 – and was charged with the responsibility for the Eastern Districts; from north of Inyanga to south of Mount Selinda. FAF 6 was established at Chipinga, and FAF 8 at Grand Reef [FAF 7, initially at Chiredzi and later moved to Buffalo Range, was established before FAF 8 Grand Reef / Umtali].

The so-called ZIPA, which was a failed attempt to unify the ZANLA and ZIPRA terrorists, was formed on the 12th November 1975, and commanded by Rex Nhongo. Under duress from the Front Line States, particularly Samora Machel, the renewed offensive should have commenced before Christmas Day 1976. This did not get off the ground until January when 400 terrorists were deployed in Tete (Op Hurricane area). 150 were deployed in the Manica Province and somewhat less than 150 into Gaza. 90 terrorists crossed into Rhodesia on 21st January 1976 south of Nyamapanda. The Rhodesian forces made contact the next morning, killing four and capturing one. The capture revealed that he was part of the "simultaneous" three-pronged infiltration. The plan did not work in that the second assault in the Melsetter area by 130 terrorists took place some five weeks later (and the third lot in the south-eastern area – Operation Repulse area – took place seven weeks later).

This also explains why FAF 6 was established before FAF 8.

Air Strike Log No 284 February 1976

Aircrew
- Trevor Troup /
- Boertjie Becker
- Pete Simmonds / Doug Sinclair
- Karl Volker / Maplot Pretorius

Target details: Ten terrs at VS740333, 7nm northeast Kotwa – and west of Nyamapanda. (Choppers based Kotwa)
Aircraft: Alouette III; G-Car 7514; Alouette III
Weapons expended: 160x20mm cannon, 750 7.62mm MAG, 75x.303
Results: The terrs opened fire on the helicopters. Six terrs killed, two wounded and captured. Simmonds slightly wounded (after relay change Nyamapanda – Police hit landmine). 10 RR pax also hit and wounded by ground fire. Aircraft moved from Kotwa to Mudzi on 8 February 1976.

Pete Simmonds writes: "My tech was Doug Sinclair and we were based at Kotwa. I was called to do a relay change on a huge granite 'gomo' (hill) by the border, just north of Nyamapanda. A map will show you which one because it is so big and stands alone. On the way back to Kotwa I saw a Police Landrover carefully driving along the border road beneath the gomo and remarked to Doug that they were on a dirt road and must be shitting themselves worrying about land mines. We landed at Kotwa about 15 miles away a few minutes later and we heard the land mine that took them out go off just after our engines wound down. We both knew exactly where the next call out was going to be and a few seconds later the siren went off in the ops tent. I didn't need to go to the ops tent to get the grid reference and we were hurriedly refuelling when the other crew came galloping out to the soccer field where the aircraft were all parked. They took off with the available browns onboard that were from 10th Battalion (Bulawayo). They were a very upbeat and aggressive bunch of guys, looking for a war to fight. Trevor Troup, flying the K-Car, led the formation out to the Landrover and put trackers down.

"Doug and I eventually finished refuelling and couldn't find enough soldiers to take from Kotwa out there until the 2i/c, a Captain, managed to get a cook, himself and a couple of hangers-on together, one with an MAG machine gun. We then caught up with the rest of the formation going round in circles while the trackers tried to find a direction of flight. I decided not to go all the way to the landmine site and as I had heard that the tracks were initially heading north I tried to put myself into the minds of the terrs and guess where they would have gone. They couldn't go east out of the country because that was where the gomo was. They were unlikely to carry on north because their tactic was never to keep going in the same direction as their initial line of flight. South had some open land and the main road to Moçambique for them to cross and west, deeper into Rhodesia, had a tree filled river line that would have given them a bit of cover. I followed the river West at low level with my cook and bottle washers.

"The 2i/c was under strict doctor's orders to do no heavy physical work while on his call up because he had a bad knee that continually popped out of its joint when he tried to run or jump - so we were trying to be the last chopper called upon to put troops on the ground. He had been assigned to taking care of the ops room for the duration of their call up. Since there literally wasn't anyone else available to make up the 4th member of the stick he decided to go against his doctor's orders. As we were flying along the river line at about 100 kts and 100 ft AGL the machine gunner with the MAG saw the group of terrs and promptly opened fire which was against all his training and orders. It gave Doug and me the fright of our lives but by then we were coming under heavy fire from the terrs that had been waiting for us to fly over them.

"Two bullets came through the cockpit, one went through the perspex in front of my feet and the other came from behind on my right. 7 Sqn had very recently installed a more protective seat that was made of 1/4 inch solid steel and gave protection from under the thighs just behind the knees around the important parts if you like 'wimmin', and up the sides to include the small of the back. I was thrown forward as the bullet hit the seat about one inch below the lip inline with my spine and bounced off into the knee of the trooper sitting in the centre rear seat. He naturally began making a few complaints and Doug plus the machine gunner blasted away while I called Trevor Company over. Some shrapnel went over the seat into my back. As Trevor arrived overhead and was able to bring his K-Car 20 mm cannon into use, I was landing 1/2 a mile further West where the terrs were moving. The three remaining 10 Battalion guys jumped out of my chopper and the 2i/c's knee joint popped out as he deplaned next to me. The terrs were very close and about to come over a rise when one of the soldiers grabbed his Captains leg, put his foot into the Capt.'s crotch and hauled the leg back into alignment. They then got up and went hobbling into ambush positions.

"I left with my casualty who amazingly was not complaining much and wanted to be on the ground with his pals. The bullet was deep in his knee joint and must have been bloody sore. We got him to a doctor quickly and in the meantime Trevor and his Tech/gunner were having a field day along with my stick that had the terrs running past their position. I can't remember the kill and capture count but when it was all over everyone was full of shit about the punch up. In fact Karl Volker was so excited during one of his refuels in Kotwa that he decided to give the very few people left there a bit of a beat up and a fancy turn at low level across the soccer field. Unfortunately he was too low and collected a wooden goal post with one of his blades. The chopper didn't like flying with the imbalance in the blades and as it came round to land on the field it sounded awful. I also noticed he was giving his Tech 'a very severe listening to' while they touched down and until well after the blades had come to a halt. Trevor's Tech was beside himself with excitement and was able to claim at least a couple of the kills. As for Doug and I, we were just very lucky that the MAG gunner opened up on the terrs ahead of them firing at us because it kept their heads down long enough to prevent any real damage to our chopper. The shrapnel in my back has come out a piece or two at a time every few years but if it hadn't been for the new seat which I was using for the first time, the bullet would have cleanly gone through my spine. A very close shave indeed!"

Airstrike Log No 287 – 7 February 1976
Aircrew:
- Mike Litson / Hansi Steyn
- Dave Johnston / Roelf Oeloffse
- Kevin Peinke / Steve Stead
- Dick Paxton / Steve Russell
- Ken Newman / Frank Robinson
- Michael Borlace / Pat Graham

Target Details VN685273, 23 n.m. south of Chipinga – in Moçambique
Aircraft: K-Car + 5 G-Cars.
Results Intensive fire from terrs. Four terrs captured. Terr on bicycle should have been in the Olympics because he pedalled so fast!

The above airstrike was recalled thus by Mike Borlace: "This was an external attack on Espungabera. I'm pretty sure Baldi Baldwin was involved in this in a K-Car - probably there were two fireforces brought together - as he made the comment in his report that some gook on a bicycle that he was firing at should have been in the Olympics he was pedalling so fast".

Operation Small Bang: February 1976

Operation *Small Bang* was a Fire Force assault, with Hunter airstrikes, on a ZANLA base at Pafuri on 24th February 1976. Special Branch intelligence stated that the south-west of Rhodesia was targeted by ZANLA as a vital supply route for Rhodesia because of its road and rail connections with South Africa. ZANLA, with its Moçambique connections, was anxious to capitalise on the railway and road running from Lourenço Marques to Malvernia, as an infiltration route. The route favoured by ZANLA to get to the Sengwe and Mtetengwe Tribal

Trust Lands in the Beit Bridge area, was a dirt road running from the railway line to Pafuri where the borders of Moçambique, South Africa and Rhodesia all met. The Special Branch had information from a recent capture that ZANLA had a transit camp sited just north of Pafuri that contained about thirty terrorists.

By 23rd February 1976, the assault force consisting of one K-Car and three G-Cars with an infantry force of Rhodesian African Rifles moved to Mabalauta – about thirty five minutes' flying time from Pafuri. A Selous Scouts reconnaissance team was tasked to take the RAR stop groups to the vicinity of the camp. The plan called for a surprise airstrike by the Hunters, with close air support from the Fire Force, with the intention of netting any escaping gooks by the RAR/SS stopper groups. During the early hours of the 24th, the reconnaissance groups led in ten stop groups, each comprising four soldiers, and pre-positioned them on the outskirts of the transit camp. However, as the Selous Scouts were in the process of setting up electronically detonated flares as target markers for the Hunter airstrike, the Scouts encountered two sentries. When challenged, the Scouts fired at the sentries, who then dropped their weapons and fled. Having been compromised, with the element of surprise lost, the Scouts had no option but to call for the Hunter airstrike to commence sooner than planned. Also, the helicopter-borne force could do nothing to arrive any earlier, in view of their flight time from Mabalauta. A sweep of the area located three dead terrorists, five firearms, a large amount of ammunition and a quantity of useful documents.

Radio intercepts established afterwards that the raid had disrupted the planned incursion. Forty-one terrorist survivors had fled into the bush in disorder, and independently made their way back to the ZANLA headquarters in Mapai. Operation *Small Bang* was thus not as successful as the SAS raid of the ZIPRA PEA base in Zambia during Operation *Big Bang*. However, I trust that the developments in the south-east prompted the Air Force to move me from FAF 2 Kariba to FAF 7 at Chiredzi/Buffalo Range.

Mavue Attack – 24 February 1976 & Air Strike Log 306 – 28 February 1976

This was a successful external attack by the Air Force, SAS, 1RAR and the Mortar Detachment School of Infantry (Gwelo) in the Gaza Province of Moçambique. The target was a ZANLA camp at Mavue, grid ref VM 398428, the attack resulted in 17 ZANLA terrorists killed, 8 wounded and one captured. The radio and radio room was totally destroyed and various weapons and equipment captured. This *Repulse* operation was followed four days later by an equally successful *Hurricane* operation, as detailed by the Air Strike Log below.

Pete Simmonds recalls: "On 28/02/76 my K-Car was 5701, with my Tech Allan Hutchings. This was our biggest Op to that stage in the war. I remember it well. I was on bloody standby that day so when shots were heard coming from a village in the night, it was I who had to get up at 4am and fly the trackers to the village and reach there as the dawn cracked. The tracker's name was Smith and he was from the Game Department on call up. After dropping him with his team at the village, Hansi Steyn and I came back for breakfast by way of a little hovering and unnecessary farting about near the sleeping billets. It was a nasty, irritating trick but everyone did it for a while so it was my opportunity for some pay back time. There is no mention in the strike report that day of the Lynx pilot who I seem to remember was Phil Haigh. Throughout the day Phil was busy scouting around in liaison with the trackers, trying to read the 'line of flight' and doing a good catching up job by leapfrogging two sets of trackers along various paths with the help of a G-Car. The other tracker group, also made up of Game Dept bods, was led by a good friend of mine from school called Howard Shackleton.

Airstrike Log No 306 - 28 February 1976
Aircrew:
Target Details: US673678, 17 n.m. north east of Mount Darwin
Aircrew
- Pete Simmonds / Hansi Steyn
- Ray Fitzpatrick / Thomas
- Baldy Baldwin / Frank Robinson
- George Sole / Pat Graham

- Mike Litson / John Britton
- Allan Hutchings / Eddie Strever
- Gavie Venter / Stapelberg
- Reynolds / Jakes Jacobs (SAAF)

Aircraft: K-Car 5701, K-Car, 4xG-Car, 2x Z-Car
Weapons used: 170x20mm 215x20mm cannon shells
502x7.62mm MAG
Result: 17 killed and one wounded captured. Comment: An extremely good show and team work superb. See also write-up below by Pete Simmonds

"By 2pm we were getting close to a group of what we thought were 12 terrs so I was sent up in the K-Car by OC FAF4, Tol Janeke, to be on hand if needed. The Army Boss with Hansi and I in the K-Car was Maj. Matkovitch of 1RLI and he decided to bolster the trackers with two sticks of 1 Commando troops. Baldy was looking after the G-Cars on the ground at Karanda Mission airstrip, which was nearby. When the trackers decided we were within 5 minutes of the group it was obvious a contact was imminent so I asked Baldy to bring in Yellow formation and their fire force. He took only ten minutes to reach us but our troops on the ground had already run into an ambush right in front of my eyes. I had been drinking with 1 Commando the night before and could easily recognise the men whom I had been with. It was awful to watch some of them go down obviously badly wounded. We opened fire and the terrs began to break up and leave the ambush area by the time Baldy brought in more troops and provided the casevacs we needed for about 6 badly wounded men. The extraction from the ambush area was fraught with danger due to the proximity of the terrs but Baldy and his team got the casevacs out fast while Hansi blasted away at the moving targets.

"Then our firing pin broke. We lost 4 soldiers in that ambush including the tracker Smith, Cpl Cookson, Tpr Dietricks and Colour Sgt Pete (Bronzi) White. One of them died in Baldy's aircraft while he was flying him to Karanda Mission. Ray Fitzpatrick brought in a spare K-Car from Darwin and took over from me, as I was low on fuel. The Army continued the follow up and Ray and his Tech had a field day with their 20mm cannon. When he was low on fuel I went back to the contact area and as we landed in a mealie field nearby to get the firing pin from Ray's cannon, we flew right over a terrorist no more than 20 feet below us. Ray was coming into land just behind me and he saw the terr put his hands up when he came into the hover next to me. Ray hovered so that his gun was pointing at the terr and for some reason the terr picked up his AK47 from the ground and pointed it at Ray. Before he could pull his trigger, Ray's tech, du Preez, had planted about 10 rounds in him and he was gone in a second. Hansi collected the firing pin from Ray's aircraft and we went on with the contact. Dave Bourhill put in some strikes with the Provost on one target and at another stage I noticed a terrorist doing about 40 miles an hour along the ground quite far from the original contact area. We had been told to use our 20 mm shells sparingly so I asked Mike Litson to come in with his Tech John Britton and to see if they couldn't do something about it. I thought that they would have a go at him with the MAG to induce a surrender so I was very surprised when I saw Mike land near the now exhausted gook. John Britton came out of the G-Car before the chopper had landed properly and rugby tackled the terr. from the side.

"This was our only capture from the contact which we needed badly for the intelligence he could give us and I always have felt that JB deserved a commendation for his brave efforts. The terrorist later told us that the original group of 12 that we had been following all day had joined with a further 30 terrs just before we made contact with them. This meant there had been over 40 of them waiting for us in the ambush. The contact was deemed to have been a success but we had lost 4 of our friends and comrades from the RLI so the contact really had a very bittersweet ending".

Air Strike Log 318 – 27 March 1976
Aircrew
- Cocky Benecke
- Mark McLean / Bert Keightley
- Perry Childs / du Preez

- Michael Borlace / Mike Upton
- Hutchings / Eddie Strever
- Slade Healey / Kreil (SAAF)
- Daryl Squance

Target Details: VS534739, 12 n.m. north east of Marymount – on Moçambique border
Aircraft: Provost 3601, G-Car 5719, K-Car 5637; G-Car 7524, G-Car 5773; Z-Car 5771, Lynx 3401
Results: Several signals received. Major Ainslie killed by ground fire. Perry Childs wounded by flying shrapnel. Mike Borlace / Mike Upton shot down, rescued by Dick Paxton

This airstrike is described by Mike Borlace: "This started off with the "Mudzi" fireforce being called to a perfect Scouts' set-up. It had been requested to get the Darwin fireforce joined up but this was denied. Ainslie got shot during the talk-on - only two bullets hit the K-Car both of which hit Ainslie and killed him and either shrapnel from them or one of the rounds also wounded Perry Childs. Mike Upton and I were in 7524 which had about twenty hours total time on it and were involved in a very fierce low-level gunfight with the gooks that were trapped on a small feature surrounded by open ground. Upton used all of our ammo and then that from the army MAG and the K-Car flew off with Ainslie and for some reason the other (SAAF) G-Car went with them. We eventually got shot down and Darryl - I think it may have been his first contact - tried to keep the gooks contained putting in rocket attacks, until eventually the Darwin fireforce arrived, far too late to be of any effect. Paxton saw our helo on the ground and assumed it was some sort of refuelling point, came into land and was amazed to find myself and Mufti leaping aboard before he touched down almost, with big eyes and exhortations to Foxtrot Oscar out of here."

Operation Repulse: FAF 7 - Buffalo Range: 16 March 1976

I reported for duty on 16th March 1976 as Officer Commanding FAF 7. My appointment as OC FAF 7 lasted till November, and I was fortunate to witness the rapid development of field operations, as well as some historical external offensive joint-services co-operation. Had I jumped the gun? Most sources give 1 May 1976 as the start of Operation *Repulse*. My posting was thus some six weeks prior to the event! My reporting was to Boss Tol Janeke, based at Air Detachment *Repulse*, Fort Victoria. It will be recalled that he was my 2 Squadron Vampire, and 5 Squadron Canberra boss.

FAF 7 was hard work. No 107 VR (Lowveld) Squadron, commanded by Squadron Leader Steve Fenton-Wells, was based in Chiredzi. Their personnel provided the FAF with the bulk of the Voluntary Ops officers, whereas the Bulawayo VR Squadron provided mainly Camp Commandants. My work was made a lot easier because of the highly competent Air Force volunteer personnel.

The FAF was still at Chiredzi when I arrived to take up my new challenge. I took over from Squadron Leader John Digby, who then returned to Thornhill after his six-week stint. My appointment would last several months. I was instrumental in the decision to accelerate our move to Buffalo Range - much to the dislike of Camp Commandant Squadron Leader Peter Corbishley. Peter was the OC 101 (VR) Squadron - based in Bulawayo. The reason for our disagreement was that the new Air Force base constructions taking place at Buffalo Range had not yet been completed. I contended that the sooner we got there, the sooner we would settle in and establish ourselves. Works 1 at Air Force Headquarters, Squadron Leader Murray Hofmeyr, was doing a sterling job with the erection of pine constructed buildings as well as building brick and mortar billets, plus decent ablutions. I also felt that we would be better able to provide recreational facilities the sooner we occupied Buffalo Range. Top of the list was to build a pub from bar profits. We commissioned local builder Tom Preston who was quite happy to deploy his building gang to the FAF whenever sufficient funds were in the kitty. Tom even carried our debt, and would continue the work even though the cash had not come in yet. Tom Preston survived the war, and became rich in the process – even establishing his own private air charter business.

I might add that the managing director of Triangle Estates, Terry Goss, funded the roof of our FAF pub. We had invited all the local dignitaries to the opening of our self-help project – hoping that some kind sponsor would come forward. Terry Goss was so impressed with our initiative in raising non-public funds, that he did not bat an eyelid when we hinted that donations from local business would be most welcome. The developers of the Buffalo Range Township, Rod and Clive Styles were also local personalities of note. It also needs to be said that all the Volunteer personnel contributed with their excellent powers of persuasion – like Camp Commandants Peter Corbishley and Ernie Deysel. Ernie was the elder brother of Air Force 'jam-stealer' Dux Deysel – they were both national rugby heroes.

I wish to single out one particular VR Operations Officer, Peter Hingeston, who was a very successful sugar cane farmer in the Triangle area. He came from a military family (son of the well-known Brigadier Hingeston), and took to his duties like a duck to water. I felt quite comfortable for Peter to make operational decisions in my absence. John Fairlie, Steve Duvanage, Ian Stein, Titch de Waal, Jeremy Baldwin, and a host of other 107 (VR) Squadron personnel made a significant contribution to the war effort. In addition to the VR, we also had, and made good use, of local PRAW – Police Reserve Air Wing pilots. I recall Alistair Davies, a private sugar cane farmer at Mkwasine, who owned a Cherokee Six aircraft, which came in very useful for stretcher casevacs. Alistair also shared the Telstar roles with another Mkwasine PRAW pilot named Eric Harrison. Eric owned a Mooney. The FAF also had its fair share of Air Force aircraft – and I took a lot of pride when the special aircraft revetments were constructed at the FAF – providing protection against mortar and RPG-7 fire. These consisted of 44-gallon drums filled with sand, two rows of two drums about forty feet apart (to hangar Provost and Trojan aircraft, as well as the Alouette helicopters), with another single row of drums on top. These high walls then supported two layers of wire netting to catch any mortar bombs in the event of the FAF coming under terrorist attack. The hardstanding was soon littered with these neat rows of aircraft revetments. Gun pits were also constructed, and manned initially by elements of the Volunteer Reserve, and later by the Air Force Regiment, supported by AFVs – Armoured Fighting Vehicles.

Airfield defence took up a fair amount of time and energy. I recall doing a perimeter patrol one night and stopped to chat to one of the security chaps. This particular Volunteer Reservist, with the lowly rank of Aircraftman, turned out to be none other than a very senior manager with the Cold Storage Commission. When I volunteered to support a military deferment at best, or possibly even a military exemption at least, the fellow pleaded in the strongest of terms. Despite my argument that it would be in the national interest for him to continue his sanctions-busting activities in exporting Rhodesian Beef, he maintained that his bush trips to guard aircraft was in fact a tonic to his hectic lifestyle. He had no qualms patrolling airfields and guarding aircraft in the middle of the night – it was a complete change to the stressful challenge of devising schemes to get our Rhodesian beef into Europe, North Africa and elsewhere. Having a military job to do that carried no responsibilities (or 'rank', for that matter) made no difference to him. I could only respond and say "Sir, I salute you."

Steve Fenton-Wells was also a local sugar cane farmer and was very partial to supporting the Selous Scouts, who were also building their 'fort' at Buffalo Range. If anything, Steve was somewhat biased towards the Scouts, and started to fall from favour as the appointed Volunteer Squadron Commander. The local chemist, Dave Sinclair, duly replaced him. Steve followed all the pseudo operations with keen interest, and his contacts with Special Branch Intelligence proved to be a valuable resource. I got more intelligence information from Steve than I was able to glean from the regular soldiers. Unfortunately, Steve did not survive the Bush War – he died of a heart attack some time after I left the FAF. Operation *Detachment* commenced shortly after my arrival at the FAF, and was but one of many during my tour of duty that lasted until mid November, early December.

In fact, quite a lot happened during my couple of months as OC FAF 7. In many respects, it represented a turning point in my Air Force career, as well as a turning point for Rhodesia, as a country we knew and served loyally. We certainly were living in significant and historical times.

I was also on the spot to witness the transition of a respectable "civilian airport" into a rugged military establishment. The Air Force built its camp quite close to the Air Traffic Control Building cum Tower. We could easily get meteorological info and get our flight plans done. The

Selous Scouts built their fort further away, to our west. When the Army guys eventually settled in, they unfortunately chose the extreme western area, near the threshold of runway 13, and it meant quite a footslog to attend the daily JOC meetings and briefings. Their disadvantage was the distance to the aircraft. However, as the Fire Force concepts developed during the course of the bush war, it was essential that the aircrews were near the main Ops Rooms for their deployment briefings. Because of the vastly superior Brownjob numbers on the FAF, the Forces Canteen was eventually constructed near the Army camp.

One No 4 Squadron pilot who served FAF 7 with distinction was Air Lieutenant Kevin "Cocky" Benecke. Cocky had qualified as an IS Pilot in April 1973 and by April 1976 had gained the justifiable reputation as an exceptional air reconnaissance pilot. His perseverance and determination provided accurate intelligence, which led to numerous successful contacts with terrorists. He was also an outstanding close support, ground attack pilot, and his FAC – Forward Air Controlling skills in directing jet aircraft strikes on to enemy positions became legendary. But I also remember Cocky as a handful – he had an airhostess girlfriend who used to visit him during scheduled Air Rhodesia flights into Buffalo Range.

As OC FAF 7 I had the unique opportunity to meet and work with a large variety of military personnel and Brownjob units. On occasions Generals Peter Walls and Sandy McLean would accompany senior Air Staff officers during flying visits to the various units in the field. Brigadier Barnard was also a personality of note, and I remember him as a professional soldier who listened to grass roots opinions (my one discussion that comes quickly to mind was the temporary siteing of a sub-JOC (Joint Operations Command) at the Rutenga rail-head). Army Units that one came into daily contact with included the SAS, RLI, RAR, Artillery, Engineers, Rhodesian Regiments, Grey Scouts and the thorn in my side (for Op *Parker* abuse), the Selous Scouts. It is perhaps opportune to mention, in particular, the second Battalion of the RAR – Rhodesian African Rifles. They had established their battalion headquarters at Fort Victoria, and as a result thereof, tended to deploy their Companies essentially in the Operation *Repulse* sphere. Ever since my Operation *Nickel* days, I have held the RAR in high regard. Here I wish to single out the men of "A" Company, 2 RAR, ably commanded by Major André Dennison. Factually, "A" Company was the best Fire Force produced by the RAR during the war. During the period September 1976 to June 1978 this Company killed 364 terrorists and captured 39. Most, but not all, of these kills were as a result of fireforce actions. I got to know and respect André Dennison for his dynamic leadership of his white-officered black soldiers. André regrettably did not survive the war – he was killed in a skirmish.

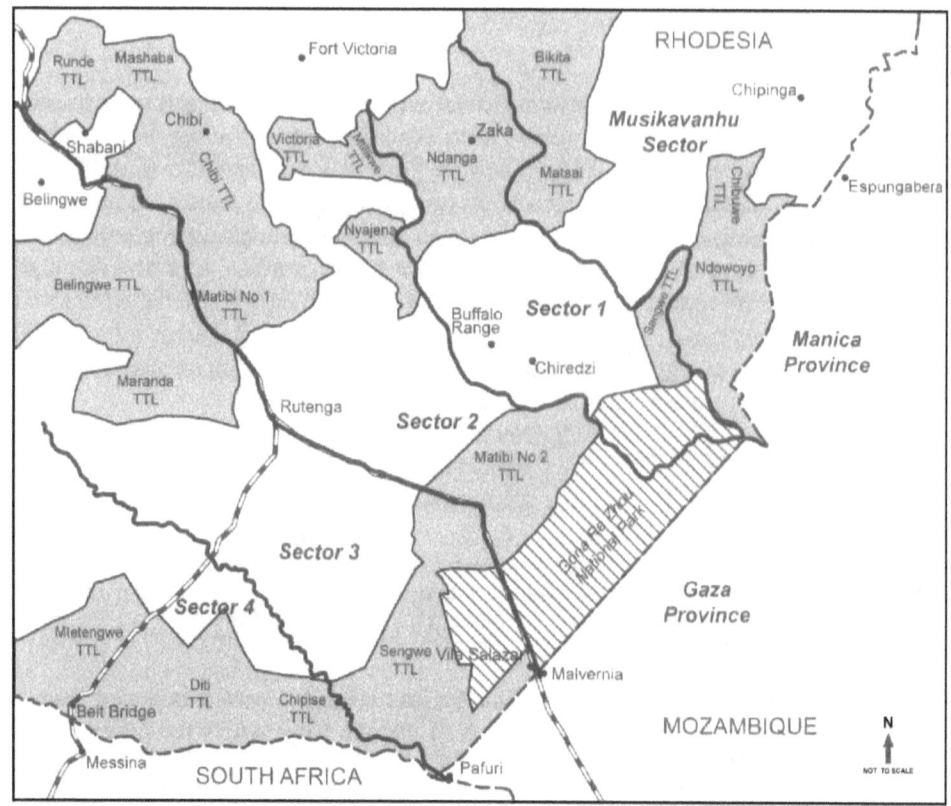

Detailed map of ZANLA's Sectors 1 to 4 and part of Musikavanhu Sector.

During the winter of 1976, No 3 Commando of the RLI was deployed in the vast Gonarezhou game reserve to the south of FAF 7. The terrain between the Lundi and Nuanetsi Rivers is flat and parched. However, along the rivers the foliage is lush and thick with buffalo grass and majestic mahogany trees. Water, in general during the winter months, is in short supply, both for the gooks and our security forces. The Commando had been despatched there to patrol the reserve and search for terrorist entry points into the country. Our Ops Officers at the FAF would be kept informed as to security force movements, in the event of air resupply or Telstar duty needs. The Army used A63 radios, which proved reliable during Operation *Nickel* and *Cauldron*; but they were now also starting to use the longer-range TR48 radio sets.

Gento Attack: 20 & 31 April 1976

The SAS successfully attacked a FRELIMO stronghold at Gento, grid ref VS 502843 in the Tete Province of Moçambique on 20th and 31st April 1976. 5 FPLM were killed, one wounded and three reported missing. On the day before the latter - 30th April – two FRELIMO were killed and six wounded in an SAS attack at an FPLM Central Base at Seçuranca, also Tete Province.

Operation Traveller: 25 to 27th April 1976

Operation *Traveller* was a Selous Scout attack on the Caponda Base, about fifty-five kilometres north of the Rhodesian border. The Scouts didn't fancy a long foot-slog and were granted a concession to use helicopters to take them, plus two forty-four gallon drums of water, to a point half way to the target.

A first abortive attack on Caponda was carried out during March 1975. However, a recently captured contact-man squealed to the Special Branch that the Caponda ZANLA staging post had again been brought into use. Granting the Scouts the use of helicopters to save them some boot leather eased limitations as to Air Force air support. A further restriction was that no evidence was to be left behind which could pinpoint Rhodesian involvement. A twenty-man shoot and scoot strike force was decided on – get in quick, get out quick – and minimise the risk of enemy follow-up.

On 25th April 1976, No 7 Squadron flew the Scouts into Moçambique, to the agreed drop zone. From there, the soldiers marched to the target area, arriving on the evening of the 26th. Whilst most of the call-sign caught a bit of shut-eye, a small reconnaissance group was sent to see whether any changes had taken place. None had. The attack was launched at 05h50, with the Scouts directing their fire at a brick building believed to contain the ZANLA armoury cum-command element, and eight thatched bashas. During the sweep, one terrorist mistook the pseudo Scouts as one of their own, and was shot. Forty SKS rifles, a number of sixty-millimetre mortar bombs, clothing, blankets, camouflage uniforms and medical supplies were destroyed. A register listing the names all the terrorists who had passed through the base, and the serial numbers of weapons issued to them, and their destinations, plus the names of contact men in the Nehanda sector was a major find. The task force returned by helicopter to Rhodesia, without further incident.

A subsequent radio intercept stated that seven ZANLA terrorists had been killed in the attack, and another sixteen who were wounded, were treated medically at Mague village.

Air Strike Log 346: 14 May 1976
Aircrew
- Michael Borlace / Dave Boyce
- Perry Childs / Chris Hoebel
- Dave Atkinson / Vorster
- van Vuuren / Wayne Ferreira
- Cocky Benecke
- John Bennie

Target US379692, 15 n.m. north west of Mt Darwin
Aircraft: G-Car 5770, G-Car 7524, G-Car 5773, K-Car 5674, Prov 3601, Prov 3163, Lynx 4301
Weapons expended: 38x20mm cannon, 8 frantan, 140x37mm SNEB rockets, 300x7.62mm MAG
Results: Six Terrs killed, one captured. G-Car 5773 was hit twice by ground fire. Provost 3163 was also hit. Captain Len Pitch wounded, but died subsequent to his casevac.

Recalled by Mike Borlace: "Alouette 7524 had just been rebuilt from its previous prang. The RLI had taken severe casualties and were pinned down close to the gooks. Having told the K-Car to move aside, Cocky and I devised a plan to extricate these guys and we landed the G-Car to coincide with his airstrike, which was about ten metres from us. I have an idea this may have been one of the last strikes of the war from a Provost. (This particular helicopter which we had acquired brand new in early 1976, had great difficulty building up hours, it seemed to be an absolute magnet for bullets). The air strike was an early morning callout from Darwin. We basically aerial-tracked a group, dropped some troops to move into an area of bush and the (SAAF) K-Car driver refused to put flushing fire into the bush prior to the troops advancing. At that time only SAAF pilots could fly SAAF aircraft - and the K-Cars were often being piloted by the most inexperienced pilots in the fireforce. Very shortly afterwards, there were two very reasonably successful fireforce actions. Unfortunately one of the casualties - Captain Len Pitch - who had been kept alive in the helo going to Bindura by some major surgery by the RLI doctor - subsequently died of an embolism during an ambulance transfer to Salisbury a few days later. I have to say that this incident coloured my own attitude towards "flushing" or "covering" fire in all future actions, and I would always use the twenty mill cannon despite the ridiculous directives emanating from AHQ about cost and the like.

Operation Detachment: May 1976

Major Butch Duncan was the Selous Scouts Liaison Officer at Chiredzi and was one of the many soldiers whom I got to know during my stint as OC FAF 7. He was tasked to send a mini flying column to attack Chigamane on 13th May 1976 - code-named Operation *Detachment*. It was also intended to test-run the pseudo Unimogs that resembled FRELIMO transport.

Chigamane is a small village and was situated within Moçambique some hundred and eighty kilometres from the Rhodesian border. It was due east from Malvernia as the crow flies. Tim Bax, whom I also got to know quite well, commanded the raid, and blew up an Isuzu truck on the outskirts of the village. They also laid a scattering of Russian TM-46 mines at various points along the route. The Air Force involvement was to provide Telstar radio relay support during their cross-border attack on the ZANLA camps on the fringe of the town.

This operation lasted only a day, and Tim Bax was able to cross back into Rhodesia and link up with Major Duncan in the early hours of the following morning. It was typically a *Shoot and Scoot* exercise. On 28th May 1976, the Scouts mounted another hit and run mission to ambush ZANLA terrorists in transit between Chicualacuala and Malvernia. A five-man patrol set up an ambush on the road leading north-east along the Rhodesian/ Moçambique border inside Moçambique. Their task was to harass ZANLA being transported to infiltration points.

Early in the morning a Berliet troop carrier was spotted coming from Malvernia; its occupants were a FRELIMO driver and one guard, so the vehicle was allowed to pass through the ambush killing ground. About five hours later, the six-wheeled troop carrier was again spotted, this time returning with a load of ZANLA terrorists. The ambush was duly sprung, with the activation of a claymore mine. The vehicle was seen to carry on driving, and the Scouts scooted back across the border since they expected immediate follow up by FRELIMO troops.

A radio intercept later credited the Scouts with a badly wounded FRELIMO driver and a tally of fourteen ZANLA terrorists killed. Two days later, a Trojan reconnaissance pilot from No 4 Squadron landed at the FAF and reported that he had spotted a large truck, apparently abandoned, in the bush, nearby the scene of the recent ambush site. A Scout patrol re-crossed the border and, working from the directions given by the Air Force pilot, soon located the truck. It was evident that the FRELIMO driver had kept going about three kilometres past the ambush site and was forced to stop because of a puncture from gunfire. Tracks found in the vicinity showed that FRELIMO had sent vehicles to carry away the casualties, but had not bothered to recover their vehicle. It transpired that the only damage was the puncture, which the patrol duly repaired, and drove "Brutus" the Berliet troop carrier back to Rhodesia. Brutus was used for subsequent pseudo operations into Moçambique – with a FRELIMO olive green vehicle that could be easily mistaken for "friendly" transport within Moçambique.

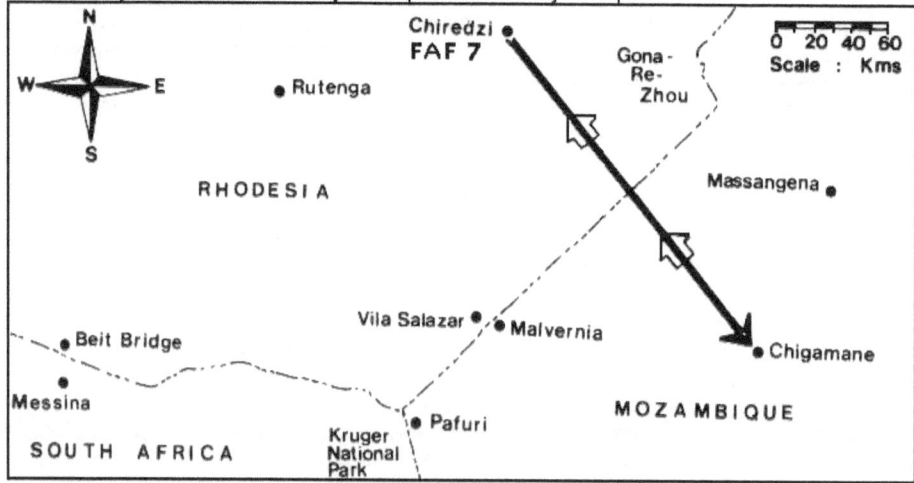

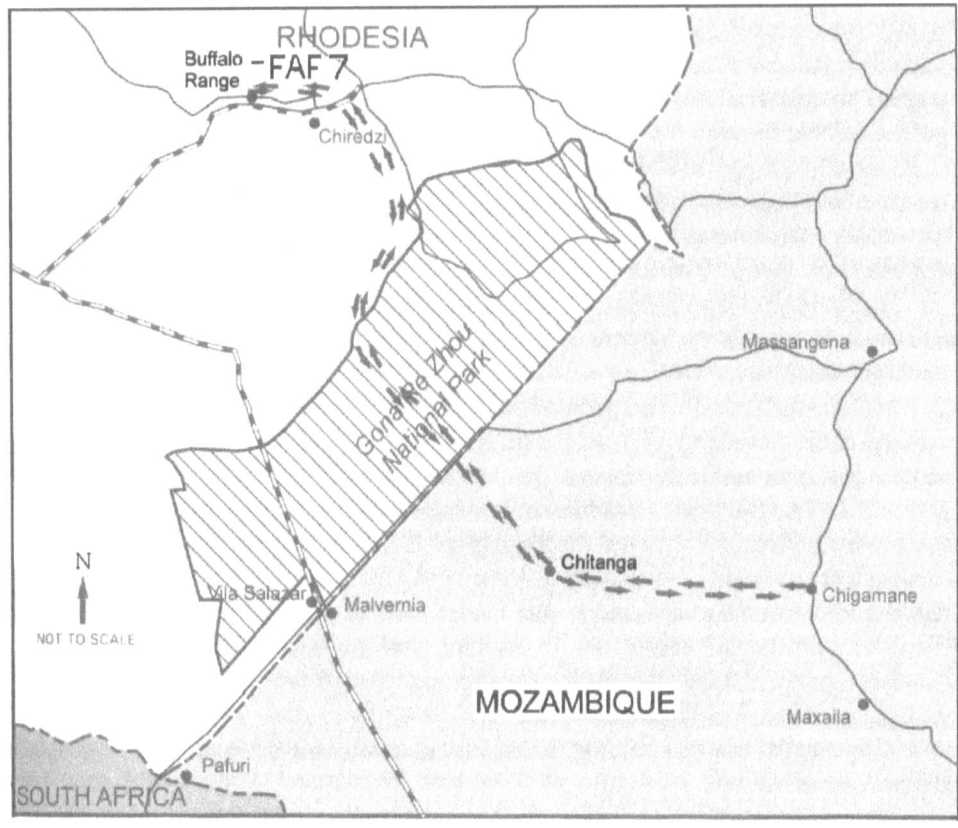

Operation Detachment. Map showing first flying column raid by Selous Scouts into the Gaza Province of Mozambique. It targeted ZANLA bases at Chitanga and Chigamane.

Aside from Operation *Detachment*, numerous other actions were taking place. These included the following short "war stories".

During February 1976, Air Lieutenant "Baldy" Baldwin casevaced wounded security force members during a contact against a large group of terrorists. This was done despite very tight landing zones and whilst under heavy enemy fire. In the same month, Flight Lieutenant Rob McGregor was mentioned in dispatches – as a K-Car commander of a Fire Force action, Rob skilfully directed the positioning of troops as well as directing effective airstrikes during a contact in which a large number of terrorists were killed and others captured. In a separate incident, he gave accurate top cover while another Alouette carried out a tricky casevac. He then returned at night, again under fire, to resupply the ground troops with ammunition.

On 28th February 1976, Major Roy Matkovitch, of the 1st Battalion, Rhodesian Light Infantry, was deployed with a Fire Force action against a group of terrorists in the north-eastern operational area. Contact was made in the afternoon, in dense bush, and in the initial clash the Fire Force suffered fairly heavy casualties. Roy maintained a cool head, effectively controlling the air effort, evacuating the casualties, and accounting for seventeen terrorists killed. Roy and I had been at school together (Guinea Fowl) and our paths crossed quite frequently during the course of the Bush War.

On Easter Sunday evening 18th April 1976 a group of armed terrorists stopped and robbed two South African tourists, about twelve kilometres south of Nuanetsi, on the Fort Victoria - Beit Bridge road. Whilst the robbery was in progress, four more South African tourists, who were mounted on two motor cycles, arrived on the scene of the hold-up from the north. The terrorists opened fire on the motor cyclists, killing two outright and wounding the other two, one critically. In the confusion, the two motorists managed to get away. Shortly thereafter, a Mr Douglas Plumsteel and his wife Margaret (of Randburg, Johannesburg), drove up. They thought at first that there had been an accident, but a wounded Miss Vonda Davis told them what had happened. Douglas Plumsteel had the presence of mind to turn off his Land-Rovers lights, armed his wife with a revolver and fetched his rifle, and fired into the bush on both sides of the road. While Margaret kept on firing, Douglas lifted the wounded Miss Davis into the Land Rover. When another car drove up, Douglas provided covering fire while the remaining wounded and dead motorcyclists' bodies were lifted into the vehicles. By now a police patrol had arrived and it escorted the parties to Nuanetsi Police Station, where arrangements were made to fly Miss Davis to Fort Victoria. The critically injured motor cyclist died before reaching Nuanetsi. Douglas and Margaret were awarded the Rhodesian Meritorious Conduct Medal for their bravery – the award being presented to them by the President and Mrs Wrathall.

In other contacts, the brave action of Corporal James Makuwa (of 1st Battalion RAR) needs recognition. Corporal James was part of a Fire Force that responded to a call on 30th April 1976 when an Army sub-unit was in contact with about twenty terrorists (three of whom had been killed). James sighted thirteen terrorists attempting to escape from the contact area, called one of the G-Cars and successfully directed air power onto the target. A further two terrorists were killed. Then during follow up, contact was again made and another four terrorists were killed. While regrouping and moving to their rendezvous, Corporal James' stick came under fire from two terrorists. The fire was returned, resulting in the wounding and capturing of the two terrorists. Corporal James was recommended for immediate promotion to sergeant, but this fine Rhodesian African Rifles soldier was wounded during a follow-up and died of his wounds on 9th May 1976.

Another contact occurred on 16th May 1976, involving the BSAP CID and elements of the Rhodesia Regiment. Two members of the Criminal Investigation Department, together with Lance Corporal Malcolm Forsyth of 4th Battalion RR, were investigating damage to a civilian vehicle in the Eastern Border operational area, when they located the spoor of a number of terrorists. The three of them followed the spoor for a short distance and came under fire from about five terrorists just as they were crossing a river. Air support was summoned and with a 7 Squadron Alouette helicopter soon on the scene, with Fire Force gunfire, another successful contact was concluded.

Second Lieutenant Dennis Passaportis comes to mind as a very competent and respected Fire Force operator. Dennis also served with the RAR, which I personally had a high regard for. On 13th May 1976, he dropped his stick in an area where about ten terrorists had been contacted. He was superficially wounded and one of his soldiers mortally wounded during a series of running contacts. Despite his predicament, he was able to give calm and accurate target identification for all the aircraft called to carry out airstrikes. Five days later he was involved with another Fire Force callout.

On 18th May 1976, the Fire Force commander dropped Dennis's stick close by the contact to effect a capture, as the terrorist had dropped his weapon some distance away. The terrorist threw a grenade and Dennis and another soldier received serious injuries – the remainder of the stick killed the gook. Despite receiving sixty-two shrapnel wounds from the grenade, Dennis Passaportis was back in the operational area within five weeks.

On 17th August 1976, Air Lieutenant Mick Delport was under OCU instruction when the pilot and captain of his aircraft (Cocky Benecke) was injured during an airstrike on a terrorist target. The aircraft sustained aileron damage affecting roll control, and Mick, despite his limited experience on type, took over control of the crippled aircraft and flew it back to base for a safe landing. In order to do justice to this short 'war story', I felt it necessary to repeat Cocky's side of the story (with thanks to Eddy Norris and his ORAFs circulation). Cocky reports thus: - "Grey Scouts were on tracks north-east of Mount Darwin of a group of 40 plus gooks who had crossed the mine field. I was training Mike Delport in Recce, and we went out in a Lynx to see if we could help with some aerial tracking. Normally the student sat behind me so we could both look out of the same side for instructional purposes, but as it turned out, Mike very fortunately strapped himself into the front seat next to me. We estimated that we were about five kilometres from the Grey Scouts when I heard the familiar sound of bullets flying past the canopy and I knew the gooks had found us.

"I went into a left hand orbit and immediately saw one of them running across an open field. As I turned into the attack we both saw a large explosion on the ground and then about six seconds later, what appeared to be six or eight airbursts in front and slightly lower than we are. I pressed home the attack and it looked as though we hit a few of the gooks on the first dive. We then climbed back into the orbit to tell Mount Darwin to send the Fire Force and we continued in the orbit looking for more gooks. Again we saw a large ground explosion followed by seven or eight airbursts.

"We then saw about 20 gooks running through the trees and as I banked we came under very heavy ground fire. I heard rounds going through the fuselage, some very close to my head. It turned out that one of the rounds had come through the top of the cockpit, passed through the back right hand seat and exited through the side of the fuselage. It just missed my head because I had been craning my head to the left during the turn in for the attack.

"I continued with the attack and as I fired the rockets and started my pullout I was hit in my left thigh by a bullet. I shouted to Mike that I had been hit and he took over the controls. I was looking at my leg when I heard Mike shout, "We've got no ailerons."

"I looked up to see the aircraft in a right hand bank 50 feet above the trees. The aircraft started rolling to the left and I instinctively started pushing right rudder to stop the roll. I then noticed out the corner of my eye that Mike's leg was juddering on the left pedal and I realised that we were now fighting each other. I slowly removed my leg from the rudder pedals so that it didn't cause a sudden roll. The control wheel was completely useless and could rotate freely, although we still had elevator control. We were at treetop height with rising ground ahead of us so I pushed full throttle and left Mike to control the rudder pedals and elevator. I jettisoned the frantan and rocket pods, as we didn't want those with us in the event of a crash. When I looked out of my side of the aircraft I did a double take – the aileron was completely deflected for a left roll. When I looked at the right aileron it was completely deflected for a right roll. I then realised what had happened – a round had severed the aileron cable and the low-pressure area on the top of the wing had sucked both ailerons into the vertical position. This accounted for the low airspeed we were encountering due to the extra drag.

"Mike was doing a magnificent job at controlling the aircraft and we managed to claw our way to a reasonable altitude of about two thousand feet. It took us a few seconds to gather our senses before we called Mount Darwin to tell them of our predicament. There were numerous dirt runways in the area but we didn't want to attempt a landing in case we crashed and there were no fire-fighting or medical facilities. The nearest place which had good medical facilities was Mt. Darwin but they only had a small fire jeep so we decided to continue to Salisbury which had the longest runway in Africa as well as fire-fighters and a station sick quarters.

"We were not issued with parachutes in the early days of the Lynx so baling out was not an option and Mike and I both said that we wished we had parachutes. In addition to these problems we were now presented with a further potentially catastrophic situation – there was a strong smell of fuel in the cockpit and I was getting very dizzy. Mike kept asking if I was okay. Then my feet started slipping on the floor. Mike thought it was blood but when I looked down I noticed fuel was leaking out of a non-return valve. The round that had hit me in the left leg had damaged the non-return valve before ricocheting into me. We now had a huge fire risk. We were also leaking fuel from the left tank and were getting right wing heavy. We couldn't be able to keep flying if we continued to lose fuel so I did a cross-feed to the front engine, which normally feeds from the left tank. This worked and we were able to keep the aircraft in balance.

"Our next problem was the undercarriage. When the Lynx undercarriage is activated the doors and wheels open at different rates causing quite a bit of rolling action until the gear is down and locked. It is not a problem when you have ailerons, but in our case we didn't. Mike and I discussed having the runway foamed and that we would do a wheels-up landing, working on the premise that it would have been a shame to have got all the way to Salisbury and then lose control at the last minute. However there was a chance of missing the foam and all that was needed was a small spark and I don't think any fire engine would have been able to save us.

"We contacted Salisbury Tower who had already been notified by Mt. Darwin. Leon Keyter answered, which was ironic, as Leon had been a trainee ATC on Mike and my pilot's course. Here were the three of us working our butts off to try to land safely.

"We went for broke and with bated breath selected the wheels down. After what seemed eternity we had three green lights. We then discussed using flaps but we were unsure of their condition. The flaps are connected to the ailerons to form flaperons and we didn't want to select the flaps in case only one moved. That would have been bad news. We also needed added speed to provide airflow over the rudders, as they were our only means of directional control. Because Mike had been doing such a great job of controlling the aircraft up till now we agreed that he should do the landing. He did a superb job and brought the aircraft to a halt. We opened the door and ran like hell to put as much distance as possible between the plane and us.

"I remember standing at the edge of the runway looking at the aircraft with fuel pouring out of the bullet holes and the fire engines foaming it down. Air Commodore McLaren, who had been airborne in a Dak, had been informed of our predicament. He landed shortly after and came across to talk to us.

"I paid a quick visit to SSQ to have my leg checked out (it was only a minor flesh wound, thanks to the NR valve) after which Mike and I went to the Officers' Mess for a few well-earned beers.

"It turned out later that when Fire Force arrived at the scene of the contact the gooks were waiting for them and it was one of the few contacts that we came second in. I believe a number of gooks were killed from our original attacks but I think we lost a few troopies in the ensuing action. The explosions and airbursts that we saw during our attacks were very interesting. When the terrs crossed though the minefield they lifted some of the mines and brought them with them. They then set up an aerial ambush by burying a land mine in the ground and laying six to eight stick grenades on top. The stick grenade pins would be attached by wire to a stake in the ground and a hand-cranked generator would detonate the mine. All they had to do was entice an aircraft overhead. The stick grenade would be propelled into the air and explode, and the aircraft would hopefully fly through the shrapnel. Fortunately for us their timing was a little out, so while it looked very intimidating it proved to be relatively ineffective.

"Mike was awarded an MFC (Operational) for outstanding flying in bringing back a valuable aircraft."

Operation Long John: 25 June 1976

Operation *Long John* was a cross-border raid into Moçambique for a strike against a ZANLA base at Mapai and a staging post at Chicualacuala in June 1976. Casualties were some nineteen killed, and eighteen wounded for the loss of Sergeant Major Jannie Nel and permanent paralysis of Lieutenant Dale Collett.

The operation was mounted from Chiredzi while I was OC FAF 7. Air support consisted of Trojans and Alouettes to support the 58 ground troops who crossed the border on 25th June. The Trojan was used for Telstar (radio relay, at high altitude), ground attack and subsequent casevac. The helicopter was on standby for hot-extraction and casevac.

Meanwhile, enter Flight Lieutenant Basil Moss - who was the OC 'B' Squadron, General Service Unit at Thornhill. Basil was recruited by the Selous Scouts because of his skills, abilities and knowledge of African culture. Basil was sent into the Kruger National Park, in a civilian Land Rover, to drop off a two-man patrol to trek the thirty kilometres due east to Mapai. Their mission was to reconnoitre Mapai before the mobile column was committed to the trans-border raid. The Scouts had intended using the Danie Theron Boer War dual bicycle - or quad cycle, which could be pedalled on the railway tracks - but had to be abandoned when it was discovered that there was insufficient ballast on the Moçambique sections of rail.

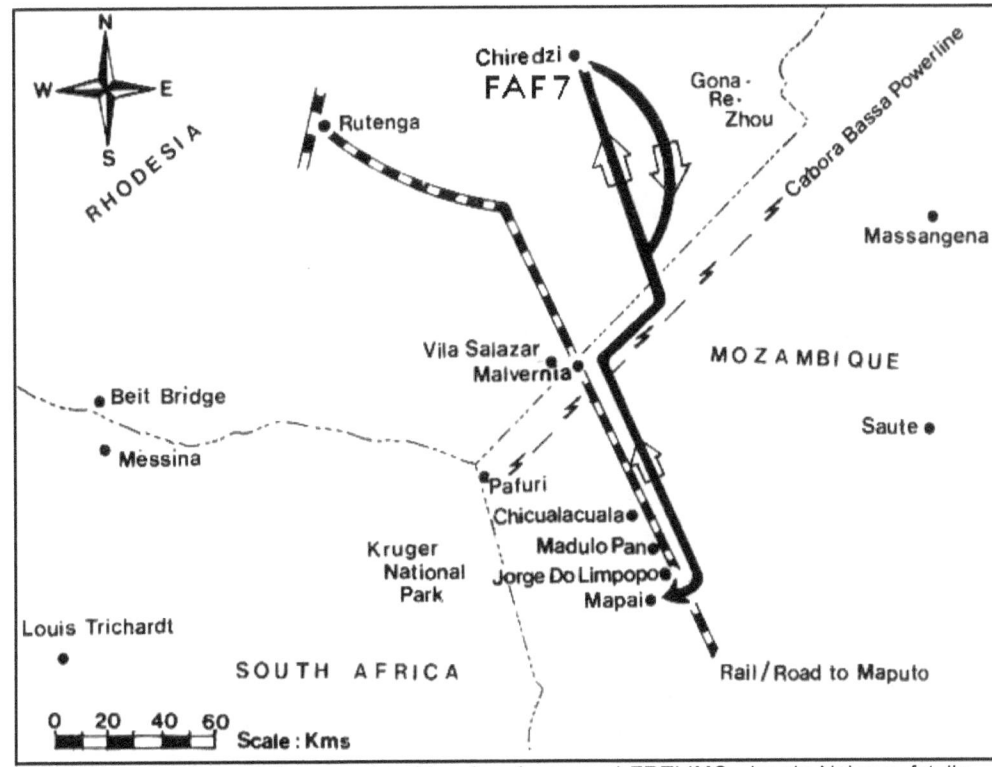

When the Special Forces got to Mapai and engaged FRELIMO, Jannie Nel was fatally wounded. The armed Trojan was called in to fire its rockets, which the pilot did with pinpoint accuracy. The fierce fire which immediately erupted in the arms-store building soon engulfed and killed all the enemy who had been resisting with such determination. The Alouette was then called in to pick up the casualties at Mapai, allowing the column to reform and retrace their steps for the return journey. The Scouts had salvaged a 50-seater Mercedes bus, and used it to take the lead in surprising the ZANLA gooks in hiding at the Chicualacuala staging post. The compound of prefabricated tin huts was subjected to effective ground fire.

Operation *Long John*, with air support, was rated successful. Morale at FAF 7 was extremely high. However, abuse of air power on the contrary, was very demoralising as seen below.

Operation Parker

Standard SS procedure was to load "funnies", pseudo groups, in covered trucks, and take them to the far end of the runway where they would deploy in fixed wing or choppers.
Through the use of Operation *Parker*, or misuse thereof, the SS discovered that deployment by road was too cumbersome and they had found a better system of deployment (why not use helicopters, which were in short supply?). At first they kidded themselves that they could only use a few trusted helicopter pilots. But as soon as the pressure built up, it became impossible to restrict the piloting of helicopter borne deployment to only a select few and it was not long before every helicopter pilot helped the SS out to satisfy their so-called Smersh taxi service requirements.

The frequent and unjustified misuse of Operation *Parker* disillusioned me to the point that I acquired an extreme disrespect for the Selous Scouts. In my view Lieutenant Colonel Ron Reid-Daly's lieutenants contributed much to the large number of "lemons" caused by Operation *Parker* misuse.

Many years later – in 2005 in fact, I came across a very interesting SB Scout named Jim Parker who had written "Assignment Selous Scout". His novel set my mind to wondering whether he was not the bugger who had given me all the grief at FAF 7? He was a Lowveld farmer who served most of his call-ups in the *Repulse* area and knew the Buffalo Range SS fort intimately. He often referred to Scouts like Bert Sachse, Rob Warracker, Athol Gillespie, Steve Fenton-Wells – and every other Scout who shouted "Op Parker" whenever they could not get their way with me. In retrospect, it wouldn't surprise me if in fact the last laugh was with Jim Parker all along! It seems if I had been truly duped all along – because no other Bluejob ever mentioned that they were hassled by Op *Parker*.

Air Strike Log 363 – 366 (Operation Thrasher) 01/06/76
Aircrew:
- Michael Borlace / Henry Jarvie
- Chris Dickinson / Philip Tubbs
- Dave Atkinson / Griffon
- Ray Bolton

Target: VP506534, Odzi river, 15 n.m. north of Hot Springs and 28 n.m. south of Grand Reef. VP502542 – slightly further south of above.
Result: 13 terrs killed. Griffon shot in both feet.
Date 03/06/76
Aircrews:
- Ray Bolton
- Michael Borlace / Henry Jarvie
- Chris Dickinson / Philip Tubbs
- Dave Atkinson / Chris Rademan

Target: VP638779, Mpudzi river, 10 n.m. west of Burma Valley and east of Umtali-Birchenough Road
Results: Results not confirmed.

Air Strike Log No 363 – Mike Borlace recalls: "I think that this was the first fireforce success in *Thrasher*. We had had several lemons, it was a Sunday; SB turned up with a village headman, and the army company commander decided the intelligence wasn't up to much so declined to mobilise. But he agreed that we could take two sticks on an "armed recce", with the SB guy and the headman both carried in the K-Car. We hit the "coke" and had a duck shoot, the village headman made a fortune in bounty money and poor old Captain Morgan-Davies was kicking himself for days. Dave Atkinson's helo got revved and one round went through both the techs feet - apparently he used to sit with one foot resting on top of the other. Another round came off the top of the cyclic and I think hit Dave's cigarette case or something, which was yet another excuse for him to continue smoking like a chimney".

Airstrike No 365 – 02/06/76: I don't think we scored.

Airstrike No 366 – 08/06/76: "This was in the Honde valley, and we got a real snot-squirt. When the K-Car got revved, apart from my leg, Henry jumped out of his seat when a round hit the seat pan, and smashed the gunsight with his nose".

Détente

The collapse of Détente at Victoria Falls spawned a truce between Nkomo's ZIPRA and ZANU's ZANLA - and their combined forces formed ZIPA (Zimbabwe People's Army) under 27 year old Rex Nhongo. Russian rifles and ammunition, originally destined for Nkomo, arrived through Moçambican ports, together with Chinese weapons as well. Nearly a thousand terrorists infiltrated early in 1976. Many were raw and fresh from training camps in Tanzania. Their mission was to attack white farms and stores. But it was a military fact that the SF claimed many enemy dead for each one of ours. In February 1976 the Front Line presidents Machel, Nyerere, Kaunda and Seretse Khama met Mugabe at Quelimane for a summit. Mugabe stated, "The worst they (the Rhodesians) have feared all along - the factor of Marxist Communism - must now inevitably be introduced in Zimbabwe because majority rule must now be decided on the battlefields." Peter Walls was quick to reply. "We will not be pushed around or surrender to any Marxist-inspired land grab," he said. "We are going to fight." Days later, the Rhodesian Air Force attacked a village inside Moçambique, and Machel closed the border. Machel also gave Mugabe permission and full support for the northern province of Tete to be used as a base for military strikes on Rhodesia.

Mugabe sought and got a handout in Zurich. The Kampfendes Afrika presented him with 10,000 Swiss francs. He vacated Quelimane and relocated to a Portuguese-style villa in Avenida Dona Maria Segunda in Maputo, where he was then based for the next four years.

During April 1976 more than 500 terrorists infiltrated from Moçambique into the Eastern Districts. In June, a further 300 were dispatched, to the south-east and Lowveld areas. The terrorists were generally pinned down in the border areas - but as their training and organisation improved, they were able to make some inroads. Now for the first time, by their own admission, they started succeeding in subverting the local population. In the sugar and wheat-growing country around Chiredzi and Chipinga, they started issuing orders to plantation workers to stay away from work: if they were disobeyed, the terrorists ambushed company buses en route to work. They mined the roads, even used mortars on mills and pumping stations.

Mike Borlace - Butch Graydon
Alouette R5076 - Hit trees near
Rutenga - 25 July 1976

The reply from Salisbury, in August, was a large-scale raid into Moçambique itself. There had been hit and run attacks in the months before and by the time the Rhodesians attacked a camp at Nyadzonia, about 35 miles from the border, our SF were well rehearsed. They advanced in convoy, wearing FRELIMO uniforms, with FRELIMO insignia on the trucks, even singing FRELIMO songs. 700 terrorists, who were in the camp, gathered to welcome the invaders. The SF had a field day. The so-called guerrillas were quick to cry 'foul.' The SF were adamant that it was a guerrilla training camp. Mugabe and Machel insisted it wasn't. The United Nations envoy sent to investigate told the press that 670 refugees had been killed – but note the subsequent admission that "there were also about 700 guerrillas", in the David Smith and Colin Simpson biography of Mugabe.
The abortive Geneva Conference followed.

Hot Extraction: 1 August 1976
The Air Force was called upon to extricate a four-man SAS recce call-sign who found themselves being pursued by a group of about 100 ZANLA in the vicinity of Zamchiya Business Centre – in the Manica Province of Moçambique. The writer was not able to establish which pilots carried out this hot-extraction on 1st August 1976.

Operation Eland: 8 to 12 August 1976
Operation *Eland* owes its origin to my old No 5 Squadron Boss, Randy du Rand who photographed the massive ZANLA terrorist base camp known as Nyadzonia/Pungwe. Actually, it was a rather switched on Canberra navigator who spotted the camp from the air, some fourteen kilometres from where ground intelligence had said it was.

No 5 Squadron had been sent on numerous lemons along the Pungwe River, where the river bisected the main road from Chimoio to Tete, in Moçambique. The base was used for infiltration into the Operation *Thrasher* area. I was still at Buffalo Range, as OC FAF 7 - with my area of operations being *Repulse*.

The Canberra flown by Randy was on an unrelated photographic mission, and in view of excessive cloud over their Moçambique target, was forced to abort the mission. It was then that the eagle-eyed Navigator picked up the details of a large complex in the bush below, pressed the camera 'tit', and photographed about eight hundred terrorists on parade. This made it the largest single concentration of gooks that had ever been seen in the war until then.

The Special Forces commanders were summoned to appear before the Special Operations Committee to do a feasibility study on methods of mounting an attack on the base. Both Officers Commanding SAS and Selous Scouts could not come up with a plan without air support. They were not content with just casevac only restrictions, but had to rely on the Air Force completely, to stand any chance of getting over the border and to the base . . . then getting back home after the attack. Plans to attack the camp were shelved.

The Air Force, meanwhile, continued to photograph the camp regularly to monitor developments, and reported its growth to at least 1,000 terrorists. Shortly thereafter, a captured ZANLA Detachment Commander, Livisoni Mutsati confessed that the Pungwe camp was indeed the main logistics base for infiltration into the Eastern Districts - and that there were many more than 1,000 ZANLA gooks based there - in fact 5,250 - at least (which included 604 "Povo"). This development was again confirmed by Canberra missions, and renewed ComOps' interest in carrying carry out airstrikes on the base.

Then on Monday 9th August 1976, the Special Forces armoured column (with Vampire Hispano 20mm cannon, I might add) carried out a daring *Shoot and Scoot* raid on the ZANLA base. However, as soon as they were subjected to mortar fire, the Air Force was called in for a 'rescue' mission. A pair of Hunters was scrambled and arrived over the column. After a little guidance from the ground, the 30mm cannon from the section of Hunters quickly neutralised the FRELIMO mortars. Noticing that return anti-aircraft fire was being directed at them from the 12,7mm gun that the Scouts had spotted earlier, the Hunters pursued their airstrikes. Their target was a roofless hut where the ack-ack gun was emplaced, as well as a nearby store. Direct hits were scored on both, and enormous explosions erupted where the store had been, indicating that it had been an ammunition store.

Once the fire had died down, an Alouette was summoned to drop off picks and shovels (for the convoy to bundu bash their way back to Rhodesia), and casevac one serious battle casualty. A Lynx was also requested for top cover, to plot their position and progress, as well as indicate the easiest cross-country route to the border.

Early the next morning, No 5 Squadron sent a Canberra to do photo-reconnaissance of the camp. The photographs, once they had been developed and scrutinised by the photo-interpreters, showed hundreds of bodies strewn around the whole area of the devastated camp. The figure of 300 terrorist casualties was put out in a press release.

After a roll call it was discovered that two soldiers were unaccounted for. A Lynx was called in for a search and rescue mission on Wednesday 11th August, but failed to find any trace of the missing soldiers along the columns exit route. The good news, however, was that the two missing chaps had walked their way out by a more direct route, arriving back in Rhodesia on the 12th.

Terrorist documents subsequently captured (at the Air Force, SAS and RLI attack on Chimoio on 23rd November 1977), gave the ZANLA casualty figure as 1,028 killed, 309 wounded in hospital and a 1,000 missing – 14 were captured and 200 believed drowned. Operation *Eland / Thrasher* certainly could boast of a successful cross-border raid. This was despite the Selous Scout claim that they were without air support.

Operation Prawn: August 1976

As OC the SS fort at Chiredzi/Buffalo Range (where I was OC FAF 7), Major Bert Sachse successfully derailed two trains on the Malvernia railway into Moçambique. That is, with the use of forward airfield Alouette helicopters. With this success it was decided to paradrop the Scouts by helicopter further south, towards the Barragem rail head - and thereby achieve the objective of taking out another three trains at different places along the line - and possibly Moçambique's only steam crane when it came to re-rail the trains.

The plan depended on the helicopters to deploy teams tasked with demolitions. It also so happened that the Moçambicans also operated a yellow-painted Alouette to fly a Maputo engineer on a weekly line inspection. They would fly up the line of rail to the Malvernia rail and road junction, from where they would then fly north-east and follow the Cabora Bassa power line to the Troposcanner, some twenty-five kilometres away. Radio intercepts confirmed that these flights occurred weekly on Tuesdays - and thus it did not take a rocket scientist to hit on the idea of the Air Force painting one of our own Alouettes the same colour. The deception proved successful for several weeks.

As pilot of the *Yellow Submarine*, Flight Lieutenant John 'Planks' Blythe-Wood was tasked to fly Special Forces demolition teams to a point on the line of rail between the power-lines and Chicualacuala. Rob Warracker had boarded a FAF 7 Lynx and was flying at high altitude to watch the westward progress of the train, which was pulling several large water bowsers. Bowsers were the only means by which Malvernia could be supplied with water. Plank's demolition team stayed under cover while the train passed on its way to Malvernia.

Our telstar Lynx then warned the demolition-cum-ambush party of the return journey of the train that had delivered its water bowsers to Malvernia. It was travelling at speed, with empty bowsers and coaches loaded with FRELIMO soldiers. The explosion that followed completely derailed the entire train, including all the coaches containing the enemy soldiers.

Rutenga Detachment

For a short time during the winter of 1976, I was deployed to Rutenga as the Senior Air Representative on the mini-Sub-JOC. For my sins I was once again obliged to work with my Army counterpart – Major Fluff Templar. Somehow, he and I just did not see eye-to-eye, and invariably ended up having diametrically opposed opinions as to how the bush war should be prosecuted in this part of the country. The line of rail from Vila Salazar to Shabani was an essential communication and transportation link to keep imports and exports flowing to and from landlocked Rhodesia. The railway line was being sabotaged and blown up with increasing regularity. Additionally, the main road convoys between Fort Victoria and Beit-Bridge routed through this vital railhead. Although the BSAP escorted the vehicular traffic, I remain convinced that the military presence at Rutenga provided a measure of reassurance to civilians and other motorists.

Who can forget the sterling job these BSAP Reservists did to keep the wheels turning? The convoys were led by a police Mazda pickup, with another at the back and on occasions a third in the middle of the convoy, depending on how large the convoy had 'grown' by the time of departure. The vehicle at the back was manned by (often elderly) police reservists, armed with a Browning machine gun – providing the retaliatory firepower in the event of the convoy being ambushed by terrorists en route. The slowest vehicle regulated the speed of the convoy, but more often than not the odd motorist had no option but to travel flat-out to keep up. I recall providing top cover for one such convoy run, where a poor caravaner ended up with a wrecked caravan. He either got a fright when he saw the aircraft, or travelled too fast and lost control. So much for his holiday. In the event of being ambushed, drivers were pre-briefed to get out of the killing ground, keep left, pull over and dive for cover into the nearest gully or culvert. The Mazda support vehicles would then engage and hopefully cause the gooks to "take the gap".

While at Rutenga I remember our world class golfer, Nicky Price, serving his National Service in the Air Force, driving his golf balls down the grass runway. He had envious admirers wondering how he could drive a golf ball so far - several hundred metres! I was also reminded of my stint at Rutenga, and Brigadier Barnard – who possibly took note of an earlier comment I had made during one of his frequent visits to the front. When asked where I thought a good site would be for military operations, I had replied that the rail intersection and road infrastructure would favour Rutenga (I was thus not surprised that FAF 9 / Rutenga came into frequent use).

I also remember one "hairy" Trojan sortie from Rutenga to FAF 7. The cloud base was very low during the odd winter guti (low cloud base associated with drizzly rain), and I pushed the No 4 Squadron pilot to take me home for some R and R. This was also one of those stupid but lucky occasions of flying very low-level into eight eighths cloud, pulling the aircraft into a steep climb and hoping that there were no gomos looming directly in the flight path.

The good work that the Grey Scouts did in the south-east also warrants special mention. On 27th August 1976, Sergeant David Scott was in command of a small group of horsemen when they located the tracks of a large party of terrorists and recruits. The horse-mounted infantry were in a natural environment for rapid follow up and could cover great distances in short periods of time.

The Grey Scouts were thus able to follow the tracks for a considerable distance with determination and speed, and this resulted in a most successful contact.

But bush life in the forward areas was not all wine and roses. Dark clouds lay ahead. Demoralising political developments were to follow.

Capitulation: 24 September 1976

24 September 1976 is a day I will not easily forget. As Forward Airfield Commander of Buffalo Range - OC FAF 7 - I was summoned, together with all the other Air Force and Army field commanders, to New Sarum for a briefing by General Peter Walls.

PRAW Pilot and Flight Tasking Officer Sheila Anderson (the first operational woman pilot in the BSAP) arranged my flight to Salisbury - I did not want to take any of my own allotted aircraft, which were needed to prosecute the local war in the Chiredzi Sub-JOC area.

Henry Kissinger, the American Secretary of State, nicknamed 'Super Kraut' was determined to pull off a diplomatic coup to enhance Gerald Ford's re-election to the White House in November - and the only way of getting Ian Smith to bend was through South Africa's John Vorster. With threats, bribes, promises and lies, Kissinger cajoled the South Africans into "reading the riot act" to Salisbury. Already strange delays - "congestion in the Transvaal" it was called - had been disrupting Rhodesia's vital oil and armaments lifeline to the South. Air Support was suddenly withdrawn without reason. 50 South African pilots and technicians were recalled to South Africa.

Ian Smith had gone down to Loftus Versveld to watch rugby with John Vorster - but it was Smith and Kissinger who talked, whilst John Vorster was closing the tap. It was a time of trial for the Rhodesian premier; he was required to accede to black majority rule in his country within two years - something he had always opposed ("Not in a thousand years - not in my life-time"). But he was over a barrel – The South African Foreign Minister, Dr Hilgard Muller, stated on 9th August 1976, that he supported majority rule in Rhodesia.

The record needs to be put straight about the 1,000-year statement. Smith has always been misquoted on this, and wisely, he has never tried to justify it. What he said was true – what he meant was that he was opposed to "majority rule", not to a black government. A competent black government was acceptable, but not simply because they were in the majority.

General Walls briefed us, psychologically persuading the field commanders, simultaneously while Ian Smith was meeting with his full Cabinet. I can unashamedly record that the tears ran down my cheeks - the end was in sight – it was capitulation.

All the Commanders returned to resume their duty in the field - to await the outcome of Smith's mammoth Cabinet meeting. But there was no other option. Having been pre-briefed, I assembled the FAF together for OC Air Det *Repulse* Group Captain Tol Janeke to break the news to the fighting airmen.

On 24th September 1976, Premier Ian Douglas Smith gave a solemn 24-minute address to the nation - he dressed up what was in fact a stark ultimatum; he said, " The alternatives to acceptance of the proposals were explained to us in the clearest of terms which left no room for misunderstanding..." The Sunday Mail's editorial read "..no choice. Accept a majority rule constitution or you will be crushed, economically and militarily."

The tap had been turned off. Let history record: -
(1) Ford lost the November 1976 Presidential elections and Kissinger was out of a job.
(2) Ian Smith stuck to his word - he introduced black majority rule.
(3) The British failed to recognise Zimbabwe Rhodesia.
(4) South Africa recalled 50 pilots and technicians.
(5) John Vorster did not last long. In retrospect, I felt feathers for his infamous "Too ghastly to contemplate" speech.

We capitulated - the trade-off was that the tap was suddenly opened again - but it was indeed a time for tears. The Rhodesians were brave but they could not fight the entire world. "Battles were won, but the war was lost".

1976 certainly proved to be one of the most eventful years of the entire Rhodesian Bush War for me. Operation *Thrasher* was opened in the Eastern Highlands in February; Operation *Repulse* in the south-east in May, Operation *Tangent* in August, for the length of the Botswana border (including the Victoria Falls and Wankie areas); my deployment as OC FAF 7; capitulation; and my return to operational flying duties.

~~~OOO~~~

With the recall of all the SAAF pilots, the Air Force was faced with covering a much larger area than hitherto, and could no longer afford to make permanent Air Force field deployments – like OC FAF 7. There was a need for me to help with relief flying duties on No 4 Squadron. Squadron Leader Chris Dixon flew in to Buffalo Range in order to take over the FAF from me (on a temporary basis), and I returned to Thornhill to commence conversion onto two types – the Trojan and the Lynx.

Squadron Leader John Bennie gave me my conversion to the Trojan, No R3248 on 10th November 1976. The next day, we celebrated our 10th year of Independence post UDI and I was thus only able to record my first solo to type the day thereafter. Boss Peter Cooke was not keen for me to fly the Trojan when he had taken command of No 4 Squadron way back in 1967. Now, at last (even though it was nine years later), I was able to add the Trojan, as well as the Lynx, to my list of aircraft types.

Airstrike Log 538: 23 November 1976

Hugh Bomford recalls: "I was part of the ground troops - all 4 of us - a Cpl Roy Orchard, L/Cpl Al Currie, Rfn Gary Kenny and myself as Rfn H Bomford. There was a sighting on an island in the Zambezi. Why I remember it was that we set ourselves up to be picked up as we had been trained (and done before) with the wind to our backs. The G-Car landed with its tail to us so round we went and emplaned. The chopper could not take off so we were deplaned and had our gear checked - we only had webbing - no packs as we expected to be in and out. Back in and we did these bunny hops until we were facing into the wind, then off we went. The pilot had a picture of a nude woman in a rather welcoming posture on the back of his helmet. I wondered to myself as to how many stick leaders this was the last woman's fanny they ever saw and why the pilot seemed to my non-flying expertise to have made such a tadza of the landing and take-off. My stick leader Roy Orchard did actually get killed but that was 6 months later on 22nd July 1977 in a land-mine explosion.

"Anyway this all stuck in the memories until I came across Joe Syslo who said that he had a helmet like that. The result of Ian Armstrong's airstrike was un-ignited napalm all over the reeds which we had to pick our way through and no sign of the gooks although we suspected they may have been a couple of very frightened fishermen. We destroyed the dugout we found – by shooting the bottom out".

Casevac

27th November 1976 was an eventful day. I had just gone solo on the Lynx the previous day when I was tasked to carry out an urgent courier flight on the Trojan. My mission was to take Flight Lieutenant Tudor Thomas and Sergeant van Rooyen to FAF 8 - Grand Reef. The three of us got airborne quite early on the 27th in Trojan R 4320 and I duly dropped off my passengers. However, instead of heading back to Thornhill as expected, I was then directed to proceed to FAF 7 - Buffalo Range for an urgent Casevac. I duly complied and hastened to my diversion destination, which I knew quite well. On landing, and refuelling, I awaited the arrival of the patient that needed to be taken to Andrew Fleming hospital in Salisbury.

I was soon advised of a delay, because the terrorist ambush victim, Mr Colin Williams, had taken a turn for the worse and needed the best medical attention available locally. After a short while Dr Paul Canter arrived, with Colin Williams, and requested that he accompany his patient to Salisbury. We took off at about 5 o'clock in the afternoon and headed for New Sarum as quickly as the Trojan could make it. We encountered a headwind, and despite flying at near full power, the flight took two hours - unfortunately all in vain. As dusk fell, at ten minutes from landing, the doctor was not able to revive his patient, and Colin Williams died from his wounds.

There was thus no need for Doc Paul Canter to accompany his patient in the awaiting ambulance - we instructed the ambulance to deliver the body to the city mortuary instead, boarded the Trojan and we then cruised back to Buffalo Range to drop off the Doctor. Our return journey, at economic cruise settings, consumed half the fuel it had taken us to Sarum, and even our flight time reduced by fifteen minutes. It was nearly midnight when we landed at FAF 7, so I decided to night-stop.

Just as well. Another unscheduled airtask awaited me. I had to borrow shaving kit and chewed on a toothpick in the absence of any toiletries. Then on 29th November I uplifted Special Air Service Captain Martin Pearse on a courier mission to the School of Infantry in Gwelo. I had got to know Martin quite well during my FAC courses, and had a high regard for the professional soldiers, that the SAS were. It was thus with profound regret that I learned of his death, killed in action in June 1979. Soon after landing at Thornhill in the Trojan, I flew my second solo sortie in the Lynx aircraft, as part of my conversion to type. I ended the three-week month with over 36 flying hours - so much for No 4 Squadron not permitting me to convert to type shortly before my posting from the Squadron nine years earlier.

The following month I had another casevac with Doctor Paul Canter from the Lowveld. On this second occasion we moved civilian David Voster with spine and abdominal injuries sustained in a landmine incident in the Matsai area. The good doctor was getting in a fair amount of night flying with me, in addition to treating patients with war inflicted injuries.

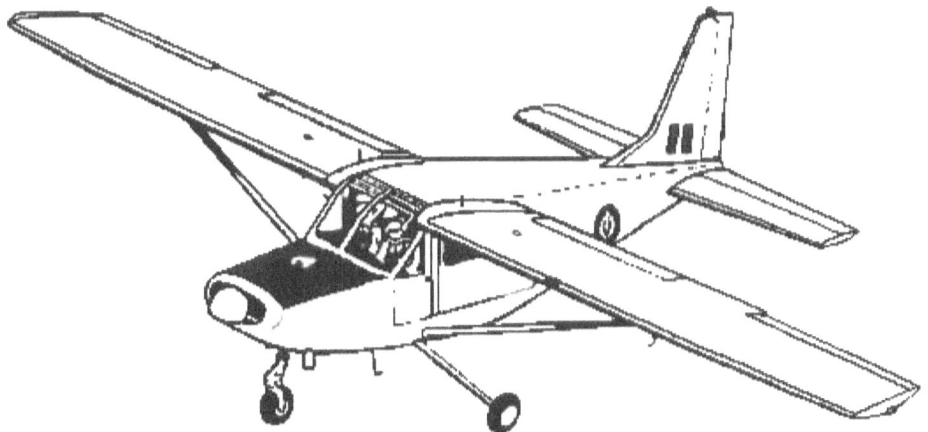

No 4 Squadron Trojan – Close air support aircraft

Forward Air Controlling

Forward air controlling has been mentioned quite intensively so far, mainly because the Air Force was at the cutting edge of developing tactics. It would have been noted that the first formal training of the Rhodesian Army professional soldiers was held as early as April and June 1965 (for Captain Peter Burford and Lieutenants Meyer, Lockley, Ian Pullar and Thorne), which was well before the commencement of internal hostilities against infiltrating terrorists. The Army FAC Course that ran during June 1966 for Captains Geoff Atkinson, Peter Hosking (later Colonel, commanding the RAR Regiment) and Bert Sachse (of SAS, then Selous Scouts and finally of South African Special Forces fame) resulted in subsequent spectacular air-to-ground strikes.

While the earlier courses entailed air orientation and demonstration solely with Provost aircraft, this was later extended to involve and include all strike aircraft - Vampires, Hunters and even Canberras. I personally flew some 39 Brownjobs on both simulated FAC attacks as well as on live airstrikes and target marking missions. Some of the Brownjobs that performed particularly well include the likes of Graham Wilson, Martin Pearse and Colin Willis (SAS), Bert Sachse, Dale Collett and Gisseppie Gillespie (Selous Scouts), as well as numerous others like Majors Peter Matkovitch, Pat Mincher, and Parker.

The vast majority, at some stage of their military careers, passed the stringent selection for Special Forces duties during which very effective use was made of air-power in both Coin-Ops and conventional warfare roles. They appreciated the significance of air support use in combined operations. Graham Wilson and Bert Sachse were exceptional soldiers. Graham Wilson, known by the *nom de guerre* of Dave Dodson, sometimes as the 'Phantom Major', was only the second soldier to win Rhodesia's VC, the Grand Cross of Valour. The first was Captain Chris 'Schulie' Schulenburg of the Selous Scouts. Unfortunately for Graham Wilson, although he wore the medal and everyone knew he had won it, the award was not gazetted. (Possibly due to ZANU PF winning the 4 March 1980 elections, or more likely because of his abortive attempt with South Africa's 4 Reconnaissance Commando in February 1979, to assassinate Mugabe in Maputo). I also recall a Zambian cross-border SAS raid with Graham Wilson that necessitated a hot extraction across the Zambezi, with us providing top cover for the helicopters, and at the same time dodging SAM-7 surface-to-air missiles. Graham was all "a bok for stonking the gooks".

I will mention Bert Sachse later, as related to Operation *Manyatela*, during late December to mid-January 1976/77. The natural professional soldiers also quickly appreciated the value of having the ground commander airborne – and hence the development of the Command Lynx (as forerunner of the Command Dakota). This technique was immeasurably better than the Lynx pilot performing purely telstar functions relaying messages between all the ground units. The airborne Army commander could thus direct his ground deployments more efficiently. Graham Wilson, Bert Sachse, Martin Pearse and Colin Willis certainly made maximum use of my services whenever they flew with me.

Operation Ignition: November 1976

Operation *Ignition* entailed the destruction of ZIPRA House in Francistown by the Selous Scouts, without the need for Air Force support. A group of nine Scouts drove into Botswana in two Land Rovers, with appropriate vehicle number plates, and using little-frequented dirt tracks, they cut inland until they bisected the main road. The operation was carried out during the night of 18th September 1976.

The trip to Francistown was uneventful, and the men arrived at their target at 01h15 hours. Having fed the security dog's poisoned meat, the sabotage party placed suitcase bombs outside the ZIPRA house. An occupant who was roused by the barking dogs happened to open a window and spotted the Scouts outside. The window was slammed shut, followed by a pandemonium of shouts. As the raiders made good their escape, three satisfyingly loud grumbling explosions erupted behind them. A team member had been left behind, and when the missing Scout failed to arrive at the crash rendezvous, they feared the worst – their mate had either been killed or captured. The main party arrived safely back in Rhodesia at 04h45 – some seven-and-a-half hours since entering Botswana. To everybody's surprise, the missing Scout walked his way out, arriving at the border around mid-morning.

The result of the operation was five occupants injured in the blast, and ZIPRA's safe house in Francistown demolished (despite one suitcase bomb failing to detonate).

Operation Repulse

On 26th September 1974, Air Sub-Lieutenant Paddy Morgan and I had carried out a two hour photo-reconnaissance sortie of Chiredzi in Canberra R 2519 for JSPIS - the joint services photo-interpretation section, in order to permit future planning as a result of Portugal abandoning Moçambique. This was still nearly two years prior to opening the south-eastern front in May 1976. It was prompted by the major incursion of somewhat less than 150 terrorists from Gaza a month earlier.

The main JOC for Operation *Repulse* was based at Fort Victoria, and controlled all combined Security Forces operations in the south-eastern region of Rhodesia. The second Battalion of the Rhodesian African Rifles had also established its base there - to the north-east of the town and in close proximity of Fort Victoria's airstrip. The senior Brownjob was Brigadier Barnard, with Group Captain Tol Janeke spending a fair amount of his time serving on the JOC. A Sub-JOC was established, initially at Chiredzi, but this was later moved to the all-weather tarred runway at Buffalo Range.

I recall a couple of ground stints at the Main JOC, with VR Dave Stephens (of Sub-JOC Darwin and transcendental meditation fame) as the Operations/Intelligence Officer.

~~~OOO~~~

Following my posting from FAF 7 to No 4 Squadron, to resume flying duties, I flew fellow No 16 PTC Course mate Squadron Leader Chris Dixon to Buffalo Range in Trojan R 3248 on Friday 19th November 1976.

My return to Thornhill also entailed conversion onto the Lynx aircraft, going first solo on type on 26th November 1976. My first operational sorties in the Lynx on Operation *Repulse* started shortly thereafter, with armed reconnaissance, weapon demonstration, air escort of road convoys, casevac, transborder and target marking for jet-airstrike sorties. Details of missions flown will be covered under the numerous operations, which I participated in - such as Operations *Mardon* and *Manyatela*.

Meanwhile, also during December 1976, ZANLA terrorists murdered twenty-seven black workers at the Katiyo Tea Estates, near the Honde Valley in the Eastern Highlands. The terrorist gang entered the workers' compound one night and rounded up most of the men folk, many of them migrant workers from Moçambique, which made the massacre all the more inexplicable. They forced the wives and children to watch, while they systematically shot or bayoneted the workers to death. The terrorists struck 'soft targets', mostly where the locals saw their power as omnipotent. Atrocities committed during the war were sickening. Then, in early 1977, in the Mudzi Tribal Trust Land, just south of Mtoko, near the All Souls Mission, another sickening rape and murder was committed. It is best described by a survivor who relayed the following story: -

"The *vakomwana* (people) came last night and demanded food and beer. The village is poor with barely enough food to keep us alive through the winter. We were frightened so we did as we were told. The *vakomwana* got very drunk and began smoking dagga. The leader shouted at the headman, who was very frightened. They then forced the villagers to gather around by the fires and watch while they tied the headman up with wire and forced him to kneel.

"Then the terrorists killed him, but they did not let him die quickly. First they cut off his ears, and after that his nose which they made him eat. Finally they cut off his lips. When they had done, they stabbed him many times with their bayonets. The people were too afraid to make a sound.

"Then they got hold of the headman's youngest wife. She screamed pitifully as one of them pulled her baby away from her. He then gave another woman a stick and ordered her to batter the infant to death. What could the woman do? She smashed the baby with a stick and killed it because she had no choice. When the baby was dead they took the mother and raped her many times in front of every man, woman and child in the village. When they had had enough they bayoneted her to death.

"They then killed the headman's' relatives and shot his cattle. The cattle were innocent and they did nothing. The people were also innocent and they did nothing…. I do not know why they were killed."

~~~OOO~~~

I know of at least two occasions when our troops committed atrocities. The one relates to a machine gunner in Support Commando of the RLI who came across a group of small children playing by a stream in a rural area. He shouted to them, trying to entice them with sweets to come over to him. Most were too afraid, but one little chap braver than the rest, approached him. For no apparent reason the machine gunner raised his weapon and shot the child dead.

The second occasion I actually overheard while on Fire Force duties. A captured Gook was interrogated following a successful contact. I was the Lynx pilot who relayed news of the capture to the FAF, for inclusion in the daily Sitrep.

That night I was surprised to hear that the prisoner had been shot whilst trying to escape. The truth came out in the pub. The RLI Major relayed how the poor capture had been beaten about the head and shoulders to reveal where the now-scattered gooks intended to rendezvous. Having given whatever information the prisoner could give in order to effect an immediate follow up, he was invited to get himself a drink of water. No sooner had he turned to see where the water bowser was, when a pistol was drawn and the poor fellow flopped down with a wound to the back of the head. Sunray Major was heard to mutter ,"Look, the silly bugger was trying to escape. I had no other option but to shoot the fellow." Sickening. Small wonder that many civilians (and prisoners) become victims in war.

Operation Mardon: 30 October to 16 December 1976

Operation *Mardon* was a trans-border operation in Moçambique, involving the Air Force, SAS, RAR, 1 Indep Coy and Selous Scouts. The Scouts' column crossed the border in the Gonarezhou area and penetrated some 350 km into Moçambique in four days. They moved south-west, south and then north, cutting and slashing at ZANLA's and FRELIMO's soft logistical underbellies and lines of communication. They successfully attacked ZANLA bases at Chigamane, Maxaila, Jorge do Limpopo and Massangena. 2 RAR together with 1 Indep were tasked to take out the ZANLA / FRELIMO Chitanga base camp. My task was to support the transborder operations for the latter in the south-east, including target marking for the Canberra Air Strike.

In the north-east the SAS and RLI, using the horses of the Grey Scouts to carry 81mm mortars and ammunition, crossed into the Tete Province on foot and attacked primary targets. Afterwards, trucks were driven into Moçambique to pick up the troops. They then thrust 100 km north towards Tete, attacking FRELIMO and ZANLA military targets and capturing or destroying tons of arms and ammunition. At Nura (grid ref VS 058908), the SAS and 5 Battery Rhodesian Artillery accounted for 9 FRELIMO, 5-8 terrorists killed, as well as one AMA (African Male Adult) and one AMJ (juvenile) killed, for the loss of Trooper E. Lotringer killed and one SF wounded.

Chitanga was known to be one of the main staging posts into the Matibi 2 area, and reports that it housed groups up to forty gooks at a time, with the odd sprinkling of FRELIMO, were not uncommon. In fact, Andre Dennisons' 'A' Company 2 RAR, had carried out two earlier hot pursuit and assault missions on the camp. The first was on 31st August 1976, when four FRELIMO were killed, a dozen tents and a Landrover with water-trailer was destroyed, plus the recovery of a wide range of weapons and ammunition effected. The second raid was carried out two months later at the end of October 1976, when six gooks were killed (a group of ninety had passed through the camp a mere twelve hours earlier). The JOC had taken the decision to mount pre-emptive strikes against all known Moçambique camps in the 2 Brigade area. On the way back from Chitanga II, the RAR vehicle hit a TMB3 – Russian anti-tank mine – flanked by three AP – anti-personnel mines – resulting in the wounding of nine soldiers, six badly.

The current action called for the 2 RAR call-signs to cross the border after dark on the 15th, and be in position just prior to the Canberra airstrike that had been laid on for first light. 1 Indep stood by with the FAF 7 Fire Force helicopters to react to any significant contacts.

On 16th December 1976, whilst flying with Captain Irvine and Sergeant Price in Lynx R 3154, I marked the Chitanga terrorist camp with two frantans for the Canberra airstrike. My 16 PTC colleague Al Bruce was flying the Canberra, and his navigator was Jim Russell. They dropped their bomb load of 100 Mk2 Alpha bombs. After frightening the hell out of any occupants, the Fire Force swooped in with their two K-Cars and two G-Cars. The K-Car pilots were Planks Blythe-Wood and Ginger Baldwin, with the troop-carrying pilots being Mark Knight and Chris Dickinson. Meanwhile, 2 Platoon had an inconclusive contact with a group of CT's at first light, getting a mean "snot squirt" (stonking) from a 7.62mm long MMG – Goryonov medium machine gun. However, three gooks tried to break clear while we stonked (mortared) the camp, but they were brought down by joint air and ground actions. The K-Cars were effective in the use of 20mm cannon – JR firing some 54 cannon shells and Ginger some 42 cannon shells

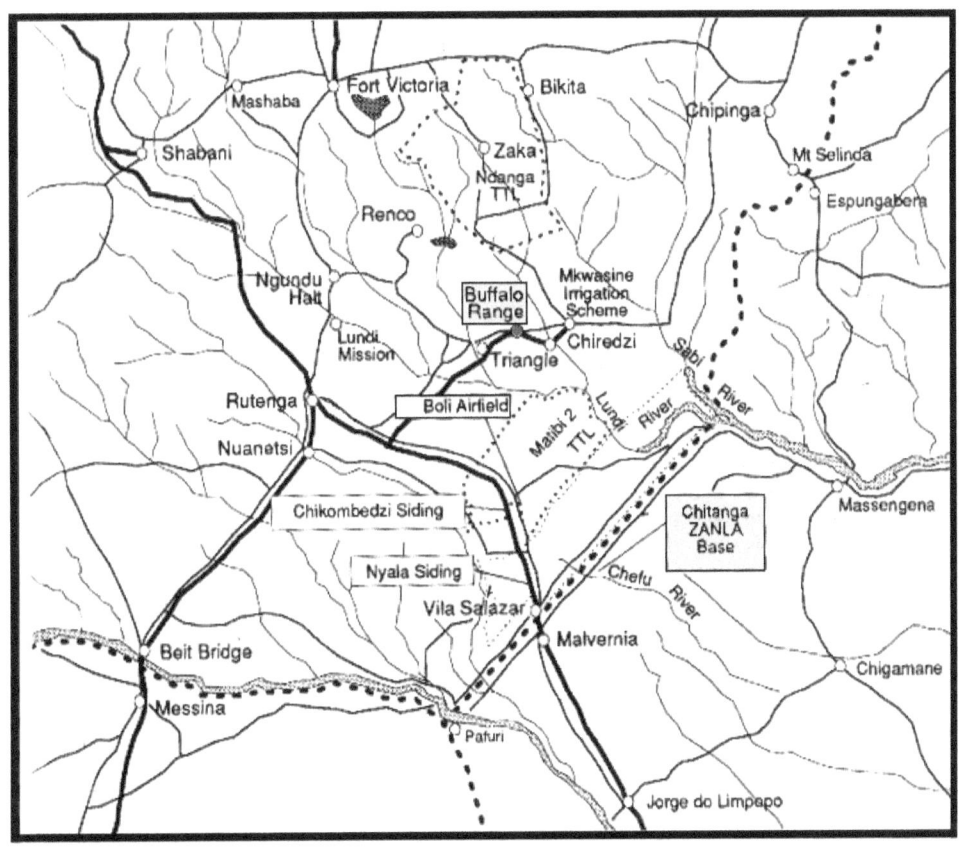

Chitanga Air Strike – 16 December 1976 (map by JRT Wood)

Air Strike Logs 560, 561, 564 and 565: 16 – 19 December 1976

Date: 16/12/1976
Aircrews:
- Prop Geldenhuys / Capt. Irvine
- Al Bruce / Jim Russell, John Blythe-Wood / Doug Sinclair
- Malcolm Baldwin / Alan Shields
- Mark Knight / John Chamberlain
- Chris Dickinson / M. Summersgill

Target: UL921754 Moçambique – Chefu River, Chitanga terr base, north east of Malvernia
Result: Four terrs killed - one by K-Car 5178, three by ground forces. Chitanga terr camp in Moçambique – Op *Mardon* – with 'A' Coy 2 RAR and 1 Indep Coy

Date: 17/12/1976 ASR 561
Aircrews:
- Prop Geldenhuys
- John Blythe-Wood / Doug Sinclair
- Baldy Baldwin / Alan Shields
- Mark Knight / John Chamberlain
- Chris Dickinson / M. Summersgill

Target: UL915854, UL938845
Moçambique, north of Chefu river, 22 n.m. north east of Malvernia and 38 n.m. south of Chipinda Pools

Result: Two terrs and one African man killed and one African man casevac'd.
Date: 19/12/1976 ASR 564
Aircrew:
- Prop Geldenhuys

Target: TL540468 Approx. 5 n.m. north of Limpopo and 35 n.m. east of Beit Bridge.
Result: Tshiturapadzi – Matsai contact, casevac'd one AMJ. Flew with SAS G. Wilson
Date: 19/12/1976 ASR 565
Aircrew:
- Prop Geldenhuys / Capt. Wilson
- Baldy Baldwin / Alan Shields
- Mark Knight / Beaver Shaw
- Chris Dickinson / Rob Nelson
- Rick Culpan

Target: Four juveniles at UN 8738, 4 n.m. east of Matsai and 40 n.m. north east of Buffalo Range
Result: Tshiturapadzi - 1x37mm SNEB, 73x20mm cannon shells

We remained airborne just short of six hours, landing back at FAF 7 after dark. That night, five FRELIMO snivelled back into the camp but were ambushed by the Brownjobs (Lt Schrag), who accounted for two dead and a fair amount of gook equipment - including a large wet battery and an array of aerials (but no radios). The next morning I flew back into Moçambique, this time with Bluejob Flight Lieutenant Eric Bone (VR), where we found a new looking tractor and trailer partly camouflaged under a tree. We duly dropped one frantan and fired five sneb rockets at this opportunistic target. Although there were kraals nearby, it appeared abandoned - it was probably used to transport the enemy and/or supplies to inaccessible places.

2RAR remained in the area for the next two days finding several rest areas and assorted items of kit. The ground assault forces withdrew to Chikombedzi siding, just west of Boli, at the completion of my involvement on Operation *Mardon*.

The next day, after a Lynx change, I carried out an armed reconnaissance sortie of the Operation *Repulse* Sengwe area. Then on December 19th, I had another lengthy sortie with SAS Captain Graham Wilson, and an AMJ - African male juvenile, for casevac. We had a contact at Tshiturapadzi in the Matsai area, fired one 37mm sneb rocket, and recorded a casevac in Mashoko. Then on the 21st I flew with Major Pat Hill on an Operation *Repulse* HDF - high-density force reconnaissance sortie in the Nyajena area.

The Battle of Bangala – 22 December 1976

On 22nd December 1976 Brigadier Barnard and SAS Squadron Commander Captain Graham Wilson joined me on a successful airstrike. On this particular mission, we flew for a mammoth six hours ten minutes in Lynx R 3407, fired 33 x 37mm sneb rockets, dropped our two frantans, and claimed five CT killed and one wounded. But we did not come away unscathed - the Lynx was also hit by ground fire, fortunately without casualty to my high powered Brownjobs.

Beaver Shaw recalls: "On 20th December 1976 we positioned at Bangala for a HDF – High Density Force deployment. It took the fireforce 40 minutes consisting of a Lynx R3407 flown by Prop Geldenhuys, K-Car R5178 with John Blythe Wood and Doug Sinclair, K-Car R5817 crewed by Ginger Baldwin with Alan Shields as gunner. Two G-Cars followed, crewed by Mark Knight with me as gunner and Nick Meikle with Mario Venutti as his gunner. Flying time to Bangala dam Airstrip was about forty minutes where we found the Air Force security section and the army had prepared a camp for us blues next to the SAS camp which was close to the gravel airstrip. Bangala dam airstrip was surrounded by high kopjes and was close to the TTL surrounding the white farming area. Conditions at camp were quite rough as it was the rainy season and everything was wet and muddy."

The Nyagena TTL south of Fort Victoria was a hot-bed of terrorist activity, and a major incursion route to the Chibi and Belingwe areas. A HDF was planned by the main Repulse JOC (Joint Operations Centre) and involved the Buffalo Range Sub-JOC / FAF 7. The HDF in Matibi 2 TTL, south east of FAF 7, was drawing to a close, but elements of 2RAR (Andre Dennison's A

Company) was tasked to remain in the Boli / Chikombedzi area - and with back-up by elements of 1Indep Company to recce and re-locate the Chitanga III base camp just across the border in Mozambique. The HDF force for the Nyajena TTL assembled at strategically appropriate 'locstats', Fort Victoria, Rutenga, Ngundu Halt, Morgenster Mission and naturally FAF 7 - Buffalo Range. While flying with Brigadier Bertie Barnard he mentioning to me that the Nyajena HDF involved something like 14 to 16 Companies, a whole Brigade strength. Its aim was to disrupt the terrorist stronghold in the Tribal Trust Land completely.

On the 15th December I had carried out a recce of Belingwe for E Company 2RR. [The next day I target marked the Chitanga Camp for a Canberra airstrike]. On the 19th December I flew with the 2 i/c SAS Captain Graham Wilson on an airstrike at Tshiturapadzi. Two days later, with the HDF well under way, I flew a lengthy armed recce with Major Pat Hill. We circled and covered the whole of the Nyajena TTL, but especially the northwest corner were a Hunter airstrike had been carried out a month earlier (see map below - Airstrike # 514 - 10 n.m. north-west of Bangala Dam).

The Battle of Bangala was fought the whole day on 22nd December 1976. I took off from FAF 7 with the Brigadier and SAS Captain on-board. Sightings were reported from OP's for ground and air elements tasked to check out all suspicious areas. The Lynx was used as a form of army airborne 'command cyclone', because keeping track of literally dozens of call-signs was no easy matter. Our Army colleagues were conducting tracking, sweeps, ambushes, hut searches and things they do best. The odd sighting and skirmishes / contacts were taking place here and there. The gooks by and large would shoot and scoot. They generally avoided coming into contact, but there were exceptions. Before long, the Lynx was called in to strike a rocky outcrop next to a tributary of the Nyamawanga River which runs into the top end of Bangala Dam. The GAC (Ground Air Control) went something like this: "From my Tango / Smoke, go left 10 O'clock 300 metres is a waterhole in river, from river go 12 O'clock 200 metres is rocky, wooded outcrop. The rocky outcrop is your target!" From my perch I would see hundreds of outcrops, so choosing the nearest one to about 200 metres north of the stream I fired off a couple of 37mm Sneb rockets. At best I would get an excited "On Target", or "Add 100 (or Drop whatever)". Once positively identified, I emptied one rocket pod, and dropped a frantan on the target or immediate surrounds. The second rocket pod would be kept in reserve and used as dictated by circumstance.

Beaver Shaw relates his side of the story: "After sorting out our sleeping arrangements and helicopters Mario Venuitti and I went to chat to the SAS troopies and compare ration packs with them as the SAS troops were issued with better rat packs than the Blues (we preferred the pilchards to the Bully beef). We sat and chatted to Gary Seymour and some other troopies and compared notes about things in general before calling it a night.

"We woke up early on the morning of the 21 December and spent most of the day moving troops from RAR and Selous Scouts to O.P. and ambush positions in preparation for the H.D.F. It was a wet and rainy day and must have been really miserable for the troops in the bush. Then the morning of 22nd December started off quietly with us Blues hanging out at the operations tent listening to the radio chatter and drinking tea waiting for a call out. Some time during the day an O.P. reported sighting a group of ten to twelve terrorists moving along a ridge line at the base of a big kopje about 10 nautical miles from our Bangala Airfield base camp at UM015235. We scrambled to the aircraft and emplaned our SAS fireforce troops before winding up and scrambled down the wet gravel runway to the terrorist sighting with John Blythe-Wood and Doug Sinclair K-Car 1 (*I can clearly remember that John commanded this contact himself from the K-Car as the SAS commander Captain Wilson was in the Lynx with Prop Geldenhuys and Brigadier Barnard see comment by Prop*).

"K-Car 1 pulled up into the contact area and threw smoke to mark the target. Pink Section which consisted of three G-Cars and the Lynx circled the contact area with our SAS stop groups. The stop group in my G-Car was Andy Chait, Torty King, Gary Seymour and a Lance Corporal Boet Nel. After some time in the orbit we turned into the contact area to drop our stop on a slope on the side of the kopje. The troopies debussed and ran into their defensive positions as we blasted off overhead them and back into an orbit around the kopje.

"I had fleeting glimpses of the terrorists running along the side of the huge kopje and heard the crack of small arms fire as they took pot shots at the helicopters. (*After the contact I found a bullet hole going through one of the G Car's elephant ears for the sand filters*). John moved the stop group higher up the kopje and when he was happy with their position told them to hold a position next to a large log and wait for the enemy to run uphill into their stop group. As we orbited the contact area we could hear John calling over the radio and warning the SAS Stop that the terrorists were heading toward their position, he kept repeating that the terrorists were moving up the kopje and for the stop to keep their eyes peeled as the bush was too thick for K-Car to put down suppressing fire. Suddenly the radio came into life and someone was yelling "I'm hit, I'm hit!" over and over again (*The troopers in the SAS Stop group had stood up to see if they could see the terrorists as the terrorists ran into their Stop position and the terrorists opened fire killing Gary Seymour and L/Cpl Boet Nel instantly, Torty King had been shot in the arm and a round had smashed his nose and destroyed his eye, only Andy Chait was untouched by the ferocity of the attack*).

"John immediately spoke our G-Car on to a small LZ downhill from the Stop position on the side of the Kopje. As we were flaring Willie yelled at me to deplane and assist Andy with the wounded. I grabbed my FN and cocked it only to find it jammed with dust from the previous landing. (*F_ K what now, I don't want to f _ _ _ g go out there the friging gooks are going to shoot the S- -T out of me. Look what they bloody well did to the SAS!!!*)

"I told Willie my FN had jammed and he threw his at me yelling to get the f- -k out there and sort it out. I took off in the direction of the firefight and ran into Andy who had moved a short distance from the kill zone, the two of us ran to the smashed up troopers on the ground. I could clearly hear RPD and AK 47 fire and the occasional thump and explosion of the K Car 20 mm cannon firing as the contact continued up the kopje. During the entire contact K-Car 1 fired 36 cannon shells and K-Car 2 fired 5 cannon shells. I was still wearing my bone dome but the noise was tremendous but there was no time to f- -k around thinking or even being scared. The sight of the Stop group lying in their positions all shot up was chilling. Gary Seymour and L/Cpl Boet Nel were laying face down dead from gunshot wounds; there was not much blood, just clear mucus mixed with twigs and grass sticking to their weapons and kit.

Air Strike Log No 568, Date 22/12/1976
Aircrew:
- Prop Geldenhuys / Brigadier Barnard / Captain Wilson
- John Blythe-Wood / Doug Sinclair
- Baldy Baldwin / Alan Shields
- Mark Knight / Beaver Shaw
- Nick Meikle / Mario Venutti

Target: Ten-twelve Terrs at UN015235, 10 n.m. north west of Bangala Dam, Lowveld
Result: Five terrs killed and one captured. SAS Boet Nel and Gerry Seymour killed. Torty King shot and badly wounded. Lynx hit by ground fire.

"Torty was in a terrible state and looked like he was dying with blood spurting from horrific wounds where a round had smashed the bridge of his nose and gouged his into his right eye, his right arm and right leg and thigh and it looked like his right elbow was severed by a round. The SAS stick had been shot to shit. We had no time to return to the LZ to get stretchers so we removed the dead and wounded trooper's sleeping bags and made makeshift stretchers to move them out of the contact area in a hurry. Andy and I did what we could for Torty under the circumstances and hurriedly placed Torty onto his sleeping bag and dragged him down the Kopje with us taking fire from further up the kopje to the G-Car where Willie was waiting with rotors running. I could hear the rounds snapping and zipping through the bush all around the path down the side of the kopje as we moved towards the waiting helicopter. There was also the distinctive whine of the Alouette engine as the K-Car continued its orbit above us. Everything happened at such a fast rate yet at times; like when I first saw the wounded and dead SAS troops; time wound down to a stop, even now 31 years later it's like looking through blood stained shattered glass. We loaded Torty on to the G Car and headed back up the Kopje to collect Boet Nel and Baldy in the same manner. Once we had all on board Willie blasted out of the LZ with K-Car giving cover and set a hasty course for Bangala Dam airstrip to unload our casevacs to a team of medics awaiting our arrival. As we touched down the medics approached the helicopter and moved the dead and wounded to a spot where they could do what they could.

NYAJENA HDF - Battle of Bangala (# 568) - 22/12/1976

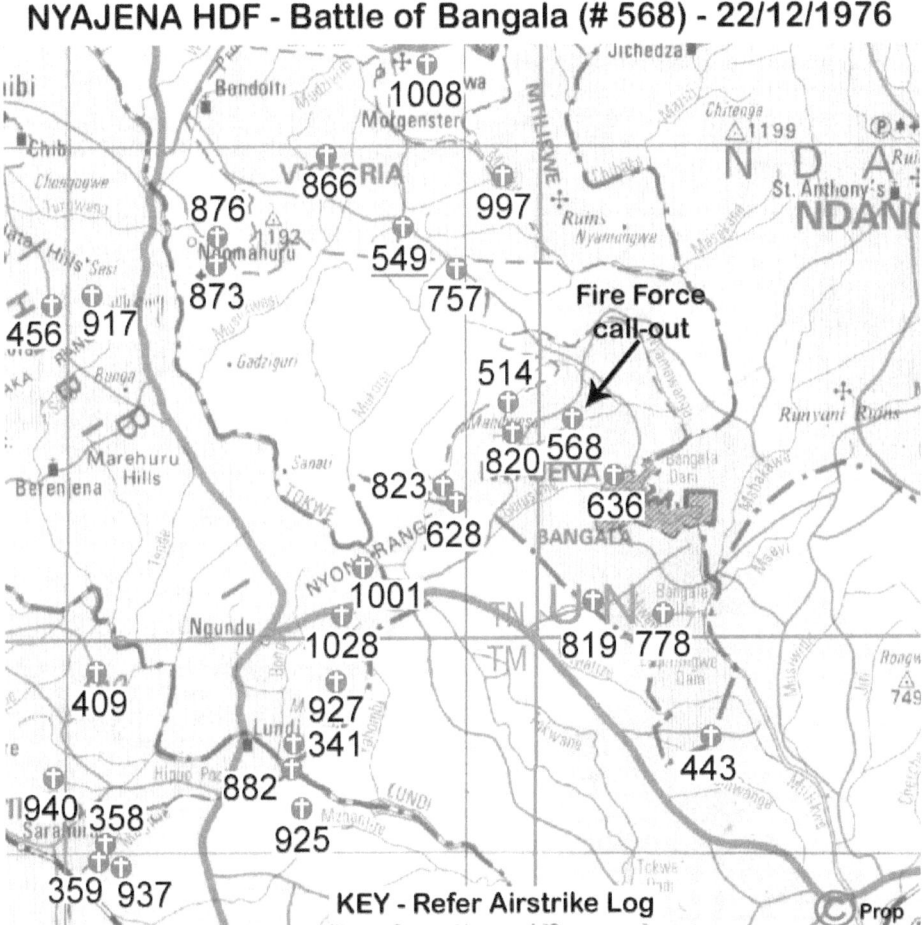

"There was nothing anyone could do could do for Steve or Lance Corporal Boet Nel.
"After we had shut down I removed their gory weapons and kit from the G-Car with a heavy heart, I could still feel the adrenalin dashing through my veins as I attempted to calm down make sense of what had just gone on. I looked at Willie and my jammed FN there was nothing to say, I just shook my head. I walked over to the fuel dump and just about carried the 44 gallon drum over to the G Car on my own; my eyes were smarting with sadness and anger. As I refuelled someone offered me some tea, I just turned my back on him as my emotions were running high. As soon as we refuelled we headed back to the contact area and were told by the K Car to patrol in an orbit at the back of the contact Kopje.

"Willie over flew a village and shook his fist violently at the villagers. We saw some unusual movement in a thicket near the village and Willie told me to put down some flushing fire into the suspect area. I fired a burst of .762 MAG at the area to no result. I had fired my first shots in anger and had seen the first of many of the horrors of war. After that things became a blur but I do recall seeing the five dead terrorists lying on the runway with their weapons nearby being inspected by SB. There was one capture with a hood over his head being shoved into the SB Landrover.

"(Torty King's cousin Pat King joined Seven Squadron some time after this incident and I understand Torty survived his wounds but lost his eye.)

"The contact had lasted until last light and when Prop Geldenhuys landed that night Ken Turner his technician reported that the Lynx had been hit by small arms fire in the tail plane. My whole attitude towards life changed that day and from then on I ensured that my FN was cleaned daily and the working parts covered with mutton cloth as it was difficult to keep a weapon clean while working from a G-Car.

"I was not going to get caught up in an incident like that again, even though it was a constant battle to keep our weapons clean. To this day I still think that aircrews should have been issued with AK 47 assault rifles as they were ideal for our situation. The HDF lasted until December 25 1976 where we repositioned back to FAF 7 and Chris Wentworth took over from Willie Knight as my pilot."

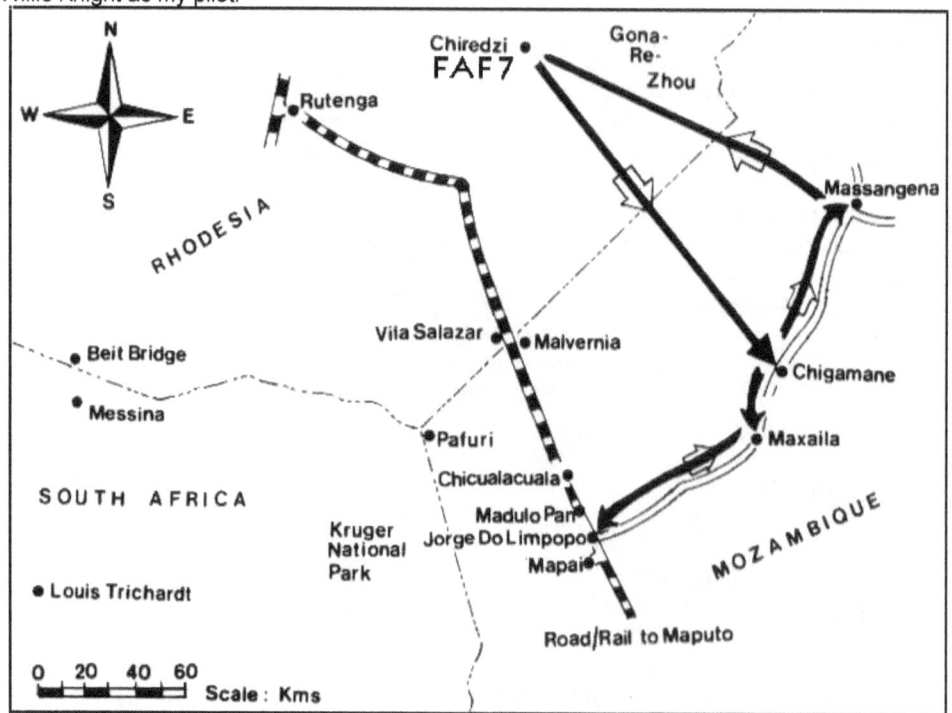

Operation Mardon – I marked the Chitanga target for the Canberra airstrike on 16th December 1976

The author met Torty in July 2007 just before his departure for Sierra Leone and was pleased for him to re-connect with the helicopter technician who had carried out his casevac so very long ago. He gave me his side of the story, and for the record book, recalls: "Andy Chait was not in that contact - he was on the airfield on standby in the para role with Daks as far as I remember. Boet Nel and Gary Seymour - both killed were in Ken Roberts' callsign. I was the only casualty in mine. We were in extended line with Ken on the far left flank, and me in the middle with my men on my right, Gary was on my immediate left, and next to him was Boet) They were shot through the back from an RPD from behind us, and I think what saved me from the same fate was that I spun around and faced him; that's when my elbow was shattered and a bullet went through my right thigh, unable to use my rifle, and with no cover, I ran towards the bastard hoping to use the ground as leverage for my left arm in some cover on his right (rather be a moving target than a static one). I basically ran through a wall of lead an as I got next to him I was felled by a bullet that passed through my right eye, rupturing it and then through my nose. I must add that if it was not for the excellent medical aid given to me in the field by Ken

Roberts, and the unbelievably quick casevac by the Air Force I would not be here today. I am eternally grateful to you all".

The SAS paratroops based Bangala airstrip was also dropped by Dakota into the contact area. Amongst these were Joubs Johan (also called JJ) Joubert, who many years later, befriended the writer and gave me his side of the story, which he is putting pen to paper. That, to coin is phrase, is another "fact-story"! So ended the Battle of Bangala. But the war had to carry on.

The next morning, while my aircraft was being patched up, I got airborne again, this time in Lynx R 3048, and with Colonel Peter Hosking for a Nyajena high-density operational reconnaissance.

Then on Christmas day, I was tasked on a transborder telstar mission and relayed the message that three terrorists had been killed. On Boxing day the Selous Scouts called for a night telstar in the nearby Matsai area. My next sortie was also a night mission, but this time for three SF casevac's that nearly cost me my life.

Three civilian soldiers from D Company, 5 Rhodesia Regiment had been injured in a landmine explosion in Matibi 2 TTL and were being taken to the nearest airfield which was Boli in the Gonarezhou area where Joshua Nkomo had been interned. When I landed at Boli, the petrol that the ground forces had thrown on the ground for my night landing ran out before I could bring the Lynx to a stop. I was not very charmed - Christmas and all - with my wife and children in Gwelo. And here I was, in the middle of the night, with no runway lights, no gooseneck flares, and only a bunch of Territorial Force soldiers trying to siphon fuel from their vehicles so that I could casevac their mates out of this hellhole.

I duly loaded stretcher cases Captain Irvine and Rifleman Johnson, with Rifleman Erasmus, an enormous overweight farmer sitting on the floor. Despite my appeal to the Brownjobs for a decent flare path for take-off, I found to my horror running out of lights with the overloaded Lynx just managing to scrape the trees on the far end of the runway. I was barely able to climb, and any attempt at turning 180 degrees for Buffalo Range, meant losing precious height. Anyway, I survived the trip, just!.

Air Strike Log 557 & 569: 17 and 26 December 1976

Mike Borlace recalls: "The gunner's name was SAC Brian Booth. I think there may be a mix up here. We had a contact on the 17th but it was near Marymount. I think the one you have is one we had on the 26th - Boxing Day - on the escarpment. All the farmers and their families drove up and had a braai on the escarpment whilst the air show went on. At one stage they had to move back as rounds were coming up the escarpment - the gooks were trying to get down and we caught them just below the rim.

Date: 17 December 1976
Aircrew:
- Cocky Benecke
- Michael Borlace / Brian Booth
- Trev Baynham
- Nick Meikle

Target: US262648, 17 n.m. north east of Centenary
Result: One terr killed.
Date: 26 December 1976
Aircrew:
- Michael Borlace / Doug Sinclair
- Nick Meikle / Billy Watt
- Mark Dawson / Marty Hulbert
- Leon du Plessis

Target: Ter position at US1580, 8 n.m. south of Hoya in Mavuradonha mountains
Result: Two terrs killed

Operation Manyatela: 30 December 1976 to 17 January 1977

Operation *Manyatela* was a trans-border airstrike of a ZANLA transit camp in funny land Moçambique. Special Branch intelligence intercepted FRELIMO radio transmissions indicating that ZANLA had re-established their transit base near Madulo Pan, some 80 km south of the Rhodesian border and to the west of the Malvernia-to-Maputo railway line. Canberra photo-reconnaissance confirmed evidence of the staging camp for terrorist infiltration into the *Repulse* area.

I had been detached to FAF 7 since 8th December 1976. The day after my hairy casevac of D Company 5 RR soldiers from Boli, I was called out for an armed recce with top cover for troops following up a terrorist presence in the Matsai area. This led to an airstrike when contact was made; I fired 18 x 37-mm Sneb rockets and dropped two frantans - logging one CT killed.

The next day, 29th December, I was airborne again in my Lynx when there was a report of another landmine in Matibi 2 TTL. I was still hopping mad from the earlier night casevac and felt the need to take revenge. I noted a nearby village to the second landmine scene and was about to attack the village occupants standing around, when the Sunray Major suggested that I "Cool it." Villagers were standing around, purposely ignoring my flying antics, and despite suffering some battle fatigue, I was able to restrain myself and reserve my weaponry for confirmed military targets. I did not need to wait too long.

On 30th December 1976, I flew my first Operation *Manyatela* mission. Special Forces Selous Scout Captain Athol Gillespie and I flew into Moçambique for telstar duties in support of their ground call-signs engaged on pseudo operations in the so-called "Russian Front", aptly named because of the presence of Russian advisers within ZANLA and FRELIMO. The pseudo call-signs carried target acquisition marker flares for a RAMS - radio activated marker system - that had been perfected by Squadron Leader Randy du Rand whilst I was still on No 5 Squadron. The sortie was uneventful and we landed back at FAF 7 after our four-hour-ten-minute sortie. After a quick lunch, my return to Thornhill for some well earned R&R was authorised - just in time to celebrate the New Year back at base. My relief had arrived in Lynx R 3094 so my tech Flight Sergeant Ken Turner and I duly returned to Thornhill.

I might add that the Air Force was considerate when it came to looking after the welfare of the aircrews. My R&R for the New Year was pre-arranged in view of my Christmas deployment. Whilst I was not able to spend Xmas with my family, New Year was the next best thing. The brief R&R was just long enough to do my laundry and repack my IS kit for my next return trip to FAF 7 – and Operation *Manyatela*.

Although I had not flown a Trojan for nearly a month, Squadron Commander DAG Jones roped me in as his safety pilot. I ended the month with a whopping 89 hours 25 minutes flying - all on the Lynx except for the two Trojan sorties totalling less than two and a half hours. That was no mean achievement – for any, not only current bush pilot. My R&R lasted until 10th January 1977, when I was again called upon as the safety pilot for Air Lieutenant Phil Haigh. This proved to be my last sortie with Phil - he was posted to No 2 Squadron, only to be killed in a Vampire later on in the year - with my unpleasant duty of notifying his wife Dot. I will cover the details later.

On 12th January 1977, I positioned at FAF 7 again in support of Operation *Manyatela*. I flew down in a Trojan with Air Sub-Lieutenant Darrel Squance - on what turned out to be a tragic day for the Air Force. I had hardly settled down when I was summoned by Group Captain Tol Janeke to scramble to the Moçambique border to conduct a search and rescue mission for downed Echo Five - Ian Donaldson, with navigator David Hawkes and Selous Scout Rob Warracker.

The planned Operation *Manyatela* airstrike had gone in during the early hours of the 12th. Special Branch intelligence reported that the Madulo Pan camp would be occupied by a large number of terrorists between 10th and 12th January. This intelligence was also verified by the Selous Scouts pseudo operators when I had flown Gillespie on special duties on December 30th. Reports had filtered in that food and ammunition was cached in a wide area of the surrounding bush at Madulo Pan. Infiltrations were resupplied from these transit camps. The JOC had decided in favour of an airstrike because a ground attack would probably be less successful. Surprise was essential, because any early warning would result in the gandangas (gooks) "bomb-shelling" at the first signs of a ground assault. On 10th January the Selous Scout recce team was parachuted by Dakota about 12 kilometres west of the target and proceeded to position the inner RAMS marker 800 metres from the camp and withdrew to their safe distance of 2 to 4 km with the outer marker. The plan called for the Scouts to activate their flare manually, the pilot to line up his run-in and the lead Canberra navigator to activate the inner marker remotely. The Canberra RAMS airstrike was targeted for 04h00, to be followed by a heli-borne sweep at first light, with close support provided by a pair of Hunters if needed.

Flight Lieutenant Ian Donaldson, with his navigator Air Sub-Lieutenant David Hawkes and Selous Scout Rob Warracker were orbiting at altitude, as reserve Canberra with its full load of Alpha bombs, and Rob communicating with his ground call-signs. The Canberras carried out their high-speed low level airstrike right on target. But when the helicopters arrived at first light, they encountered heavy anti-aircraft and small arms fire - by heavily armed FRELIMO who had reacted to assist their ZANLA shamwaris (bosom friends). The helicopter-borne troops were outnumbered and so the Hunters were called in to fire their 68mm Matra rockets and 30mm cannons. Then Ian Donaldson was called in to drop his load of Alpha bombs.

Ian descended through the layer of clouds, breaking through right over Malvernia. The Canberra was immediately subjected to intense ground fire. No one saw what struck the aircraft, but it suddenly banked steeply, flipped over and flew straight into the ground, exploding on contact and sending up a pall of smoke. The crew were killed instantly (the wreckage of R 5203 and the bodies of the crews were later displayed for public viewing in Maputo. FRELIMO claimed a hit by SAM, but this was never confirmed). Both Ian and the B2 Canberra were now no more. Both will go down in history as casualties of Operation *Manyatela*.

I, meanwhile, continued my search for Echo Five for another two hours forty minutes, without success, landing at the Mabalauta forward base. After a bush night-stop at the Scout camp, with Major Bert Sachse (Manyatela commander), I was tasked to continue with the search for the downed crews. I might add, the Army placed armed guards at the airstrip to guard my Lynx; I then got aboard one of their RL trucks, and set off along a sandy-softened land mined track, for their hidden bush camp. I must admit, I felt a lot more comfortable facing the enemy from the air, rather than being liable to getting caught in an ambush or detonating one of the enemy landmines. Anyway, my night-stop was uneventful - except that I pitied my old instructor Peter Petter-Bowyer who (as another 're-called' pilot like me) had been intimately involved since the start of Operation *Manyatela*.

Both Group Captain Tol Janeke and I continued with our Echo Five search on 13th January. I think he was flying in a Trojan, while I piloted a Lynx. Sergeant Mike Guy was my passenger cum air-observer for our two hour twenty minute search. Boss Tol radioed me to be wary of SAM-7s and be on the lookout for the give-away white pigtail when the heat seeking guided missile is fired. I maintained a healthy altitude, ensuring that I kept the bright sun in line with the known enemy fortified positions. Evasive tactics included a steep wing over into the sun so that the surface-to-air missile either latches onto the sun or airbursts out of range. However, after a while, I was recalled to FAF 7 for an urgent casevac.

Rifleman van Schalkwyk, from No 1 Independent Company, was uplifted, together with a Doctor Hale, and flown to Salisbury. I had left my night-stop kit behind at the FAF (to make room for the stretcher case), so then flew back to Buffalo Range, landing at about half past eight at night - too late for supper and too tired to eat anyway. On 12/13th January 1977 I had flown over nine hours. My short R&R spell had spoilt me with a more casual and relaxed lifestyle.

January 15th was another long day. My mission was top cover in the Belingwe/Pande area when the BSAP made contact with a group of terrorists that had penetrated inland. Two African and one European policemen had been killed, as well as one terrorist. The next day I was called upon to carry out top cover for two contacts in the Matsai and Mashoko areas. These resulted in one terrorist killed and two captured, wounded. I uplifted one Army stick consisting of Riflemen Hall, Freeland and Mdlulu. That night I provided top cover and escort duties for a K-Car to the Mwagazi Gap. For these two days I had flown four sorties for a total of over twelve hours.

The 17th brought mixed fortunes. Major Bert Sachse and I carried out a telstar for a Selous Scout contact at MacDougal. Bert was one of the few Scouts that I got along with. As a professional soldier, he served the country well, and carried out some "very hairy" operations for the South Africans following the disbanding of the Scouts. Bert was also the main ground commander for Operations Prawn and Manyatela. He commanded the Chiredzi Fort while I was

OC FAF 7. The other good fortune for the day was my appointment as OCAW Thornhill - I packed my bags and returned to the Air Force base with Sergeant Grant Domoney.

During January 1977, 3 Commando RLI manned the FAF 5 Fire Force. A Selous Scouts OP – Observation Post sighted a column of over two hundred ZANLA terrorists infiltrating the country just north of the Nyamapanda border post. The siren wailed and soon helicopters deployed the first waves of troops. As was normal at this stage of the war, support troops would deploy by road for uplift nearer the contact area. In this case, a Dakota was also used for paradropping elements of the SAS. In view of the large sighting, Comops also tasked the Canberras of No 5 Squadron to put in an airstrike ahead of the Fire Force arrival. Elements of the RLI were dispatched to the Kotwa airstrip, as the sighting was just outside the border, near the Mazoe River, for stop group purposes to ambush terrorists. Unfortunately, the terrorist columns were too strung out for the Canberra airstrike to be effective, but fifteen gooks were killed.

It was not always a case of all work and no play at the FAFs. I remember seeing my first blue movie at FAF 5. I can't recall the date, but it must have been early 1977. Although I was quite disgusted with the pornography and the weak story line, it was more amusing to see the effects that the blue movie had on some of the younger bush fighters. The movie only lasted about 20-minutes, but it was quite hilarious to watch the Brownjobs who remained seated at the end – too embarrassed to stand up from their cross-legged stances so as not to reveal their rampant erections.

Then there was also the occasion of flying a troupe of strippers down to FAF 7. I can honestly state that I was no longer the OC, but a regular retread (i.e. re-called to active duties) pilot doing a bush stint at the sharp end at that time. NCOs tended to scramble for the front row seats, while Officers tended to take a more respectable position at the back of the FAF 7 pub.

The buxom ladies certainly knew their stuff and soon had the lads roaring approvingly as bits of clothing were sexily shed. Provocative gesturing had the crowd roaring, "Take it off. Take it off." The chants even persisted when the peroxide blonde ladies had bared all. They had no qualms dancing off the makeshift stage and mingling among the airmen and troopies. I did not escape their attentions, and became a victim of having my face smothered by oversized wriggling mammary glands. Fortunately, I was spared public embarrassment because the bulk of the audience was engrossed in watching a feat beyond description. A second stripper performed a disappearing act with a beer bottle. The performance left a lot of macho men feeling somewhat totally inadequate. Enough said.

Air Strike Log 591: 16 January 1977
Aircrew:
- Prop Geldenhuys
- Michael Borlace / John Britton
- Tudor Thomas / Bob Thompson
- Mark Aitchison / Harding
- Bill McQuade / Doug Sinclair

Target: VN8250, 6 n.m. north east of Espungabera, in Moçambique
Result: One terr killed, one captured.

Air Strike Log 592: 16 January 1977
Aircrew:
- Prop Geldenhuys
- Michael Borlace / John Britton
- Tol Janeke

Target: VN3927, 18 n.m. north east of Chisumbanje and 15 n.m. south east of Sabi Experimental Station

Airstrike Log 594: 19 January 1977
Aircrew:
- Michael Borlace / John Britton
- Mark Aitchison / Mario Venutti
- Bill McQuade / Doug Sinclair
- Dick Paxton / Ronny Scott

- Daryl Squance

Target: UM8505, 26 n.m. south of Chipinda Pools and 7 n.m. north west of Chalanda (on Moz border)
Result: 19 terrs and recruits killed, 16 terrs and recruits captured. Good shooting by John Britton.

ASR 591/592 – 16/01/77, Mike Borlace recalled:"The day was spent with an external, and then Tol came up with some target at night that he wanted the K-car to have a crack at. We went over and made some holes with the twenty mills in the dark. I remember it was 'black as the proverbial witch's tit' and there was a lot of smoke in the air so we were having trouble keeping the world the right way up, and then began to run desperately short of fuel trying to get back to Chiredzi. I was preparing to put down in the cane fields for the night, when the Ops Officer at Chiredzi, Ian Stein I think, who had been following the exchanges between myself and Tol, got Alistair Brown to turn his lights on at his farm. We snivelled in there on about seventeen minutes' red light and spent the night in some very convivial company."

ASR 594 – 19/01/77: "There were actually two K-Cars that were involved in this punch-up. We arrived in 5178, which collected a snotty as we came overhead and put all the radios out – we also had used up all our ammo. We got straight into a sort of GT model we had at Chiredzi for some SAS externals we were covering at the same time, whose number was 5817 - it had extra ammo trays but no commander's seat. The ground troops involved in this included a troop of armoured cars that was cavorting around in the bush like Daleks, and Greys' Scouts, and from the air the whole thing was like a three ring circus. I remember JB's shooting was exemplary, and the donkey wallopers (Grey Scouts) were rounding up horses for about a week afterwards."

Operation Virgo: January to July 1977

Operation *Virgo* was an extension of Operation Polo, whereby Rhodesian crews trained on and flew South African Air Force Impala aircraft, based at SAAF AFB Durban. Amanzimtoti, with its golden beaches and holiday atmosphere, proved a popular rental location for the wives of servicemen. Advanced flying training was carried out on Impalas, before progression to the supersonic Mirage aircraft.

Operation Bluebell: 16 January to 19 February 1977

Operation *Bluebell* was an SAS canoe Operation on Cabora Bassa Lake, Tete Province, and Moçambique. The initial deployment was 12 men on 16th January to carry out recces and mine-laying. Ten days later a mine exploded north-east of Caponda, at grid ref UT 624478, followed by a night attack on Nhende Aldeamento (UT 8675) in which one vehicle was burnt and houses and barracks raked by fire on 31st January. Mines were also laid on the roads to Chinhanda and Chioco. The mine on the latter was detonated on 12th February. Then later the same day a successful ambush was carried out by the SAS in which 11 FPLM were killed, one wounded (who managed to escape), and a tractor, trailer, and a large quantity of supplies destroyed. A FRELIMO casevac vehicle detonated a mine placed on the road.

Operation Kodak: January to March 1977

Operation *Kodak* was a battle of wills, in south-east Rhodesia, at Malvernia, between January and March 1977. Air support and resupply was provided from FAF 7 Chiredzi/Buffalo Range. Territorial Army Captain John Murphy was tasked to bombard the FRELIMO garrison there, and to lay mines and ambushes with the objective of denying a safe haven through which the terrorists could infiltrate the *Repulse* operational area. With FRELIMO's support for ZANLA, the gooks had a safe haven in Moçambique, food, shelter, arms and ammunition. It was hoped that the FRELIMO garrison would abandon the town and withdraw to Mapai. The Rhodesian Artillery had also taken up positions about six kilometres from Vila Salazar, and would fire their long-range 122mm shells during the night. I had the odd occasion to visit their camp in a helicopter, and partook of that dreadful tea concoction that was brewed in a galvanised bucket - with bits of sadza floating about (the same receptacle would be used for all their meals – be it cooking mealie meal, bully beef or brewing their tea!).

The Selous Scouts sulked when the use of air support was denied them for their landmine laying parties into Moçambique. The Scouts were weary of the sandy soils in the area, which made anti-tracking difficult. A casualty of Operation *Kodak* was Sergeant Clive Mason - he was shot in the head during an early morning attack on an outpost outside Malvernia - but he also accounted for six Freds (FRELIMO).

Operation Cowboy: 2 to 6 March 1977

Operation *Cowboy* was a No 7 Squadron helicopter insertion of a 4-man SAS stick to carry out a recce of the Mungari – Luenha road in the Tete area of Moçambique (grid WR2496). I can't recall whether the helicopters were used for extraction, which ran the risk of compromise - but I would think the SAS would have called for helicopter uplift as well.

Operations Wrestler, Stripper and Starjump: 2 March 1977

These three operations were all launched on the same day. On *Wrestler* the SAS carried out a recce and ambush of the Chioco Crossroads, Tete Province, and Moçambique. For *Stripper* a helicopter insertion was required for the 8-man, 7-day ambush of the Choa-Catandica (Vila Gouveia) road in Manica – at grid ref WR 125187 (see the map section, at the end of the book). *Starjump* was a one-day recce and ambush of the Manica Guru-Gaerezi road.

Operation Hustler: 7 March 1977

This was a successful SAS ambush with land-mine detonation by a Land Rover on the Changara – Chigwara road, Tete, which resulted in 2 FRELIMO killed and four wounded.

Lynx 4312 Crash At Faf 5, Mtoko: 15 March 1977

FAF 5, Mtoko, was not the easiest of runways. If you were taking off on runway 23, then all was in your favour as the end of the runway just fell away into the Tribal Trust Land. Not so with runway 05 - the last 500 metres was a downhill slope towards the stream and the overshoot was a gradual incline - certainly not the ideal situation for night take-offs, especially if there was no moon. Major Brian Robinson of the SAS had arrived at Mtoko so that he could be uplifted by Lynx to fly out over Moçambique to talk to one of his call-signs that was in contact on a covert mission.

At just after 20h00 on 15 March 1977, Lynx 4312 with Air Sub-Lieutenant John Kidson at the controls got airborne. It was a particularly dark night and Kidson was new to this type of flying, having completed his conversion onto the Lynx a mere couple of months ago, and only done a few bush trips.

Max 'Sticks' McKersie, an ex co-student on John Kidson's flying course, was at Mtoko in his new role as an Intelligence Officer with Special Branch. This is his story: - "As I was interested in aircraft I approached the Lynx, got into a conversation with John and caught up with news of other pilots from No 28 Pilot Training Course. He did not recognise me at first, but he soon remembered me and we chatted about our antics on selection course. I hinted at the possibility of a flight around my area of jurisdiction (Mudzi/ Mayo). The Major finished his meeting and so I hopped out of the Lynx and wished John farewell. I was certainly very envious of him and the other successful pilots from our cadet course. Then I made the usual 'friendly' remarks like "You will never get this plane off the ground. You need experienced pilots like me to show you how. Don't forget to set your flaps on take-off and watch out for the gum trees at the end of the airstrip". With these 'callous' remarks echoing in his ears, John started up his aircraft and I went back to my intelligence caravan, sulking because I was not flying his aeroplane.

"I took off," said John, "and was in the process of raising my undercarriage when there was a loud scraping sound and we were thrown forward in our seatbelts. I knew immediately what had happened – having raised the undercarriage too soon. The aircraft came to a halt in a few yards and I shouted to Major Robbie to get out. As we exited the doors the aircraft burst into flames."

Brian Robinson takes up the story "My guys had a contact in Mozambique at last light. When we got airborne, it was pitch black. I glanced at the VSI (vertical speed indicator) and saw it pointing in the six o'clock position – we were heading straight for the ground! I shouted to John 'What the hell are you doing' (or words to that effect – quite mildly?)", while apparently adjusting his engine synchronisation.

"I heard the Lynx take off," continued McKersie, "and then there was suddenly a great commotion as people were rushing to vehicles and driving away down the airstrip. I didn't know what was going on and certainly did not think that John had crashed the Lynx, so I didn't join in the initial exodus. When I heard the news of his accident I burst out laughing (I suppose we were a little bush-whacked by that stage of the conflict), not knowing whether anybody had survived the accident or not. I jokingly thought: 'The stupid idiot didn't remember my valuable instructions about setting the flaps'. By the time I had mustered up some transport to get to the scene of the accident, everything was under control and the Dakota crew were being readied for casevac. Major Brian Robinson and John Kidson were put onto the Dakota and were flown to Salisbury by Flight Lieutenant Bob d'Hotman for the mandatory check-up by the Doc."

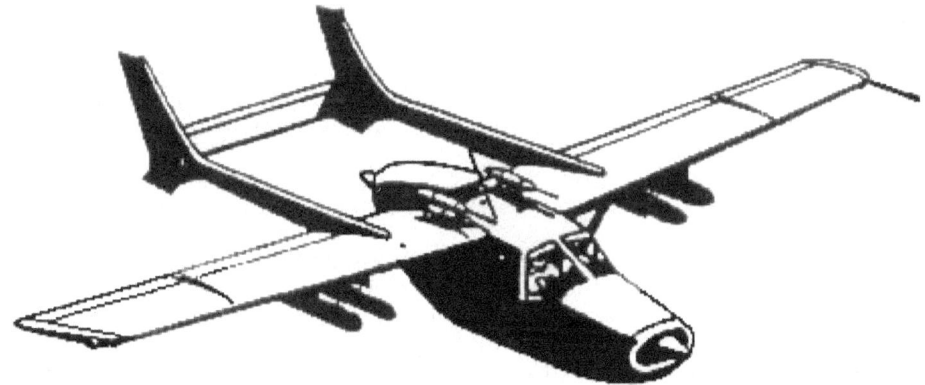

The 'Push-Pull' Lynx

Lynx 4312 was destroyed in the ensuing fire. Brian did confirm with the author, many years later, that the accident was pilot error (and not technical defect), and that they both were indeed lucky to be alive. Brian concluded "The crash impact was on the other side of the Mtoko road. Several hundred metres from runway 23 threshold. I have a photograph in my study".

Air Strike Log: 23 March 1977
Aircrew:
- Michael Borlace / Lionel Davel / Willem Joubert

Target: Rutenga area
Result: Assisted in contact initiated by Ian Harvey

ASR 657 – Mike recalls: "I think I called en-route to assist at this, and the contact was initiated by Ian Harvey from Rutenga, where he got a couple of scratch sticks together of cooks and bottle washers, and the Chinese cook or laundry man or someone slotted (shot) a gook."

Operation Driver: 9 to 29 May 1977
This was an SAS operation in the Tete Province of Moçambique. It started off well when on the first day contact was made by call-sign 19 and a FRELIMO was killed. Meanwhile call-sign 21 carried out a jitter (to scare the enemy) raid on Chioco with small arms, mortar and RPG harassment. With the reinforcement of six call signs, the attack on Chioco was carried out on 13th May – one FRELIMO was killed during the attack on the SAS mortar position, another wounded – and the entire settlement was taken without resistance. Seven .303 rifles, 9 AK's, 54 SKS, 11 RPG2 rockets, 28 B10 heat projectiles, 81 and 82-mm mortar base plates, 82-mm mortar bombs and 60-mm mortar bombs were recovered. Also small arms and ammunition, grenades and medic packs.

Call-sign 19 also had a successful day on 13th May – two FRELIMO were killed in a contact, four ferries and four boats were destroyed and a night attack was carried out in the vicinity of grid ref VT 3675. On the 22nd call-sign 32 carried out an ambush, killing one terrorist. Call-sign 19 had better luck the following day, the 24th, with their ambush accounting for nine terrorists killed at grid reference VT 3948. On the 27th call-sign 21 made contact with a group of 40 at VT 4248, killing one FPLM, four terrorists killed, and 4-5 terrorists wounded, for one SF wounded.

On 29th May 1977 call-sign 19 did the Air Force a favour by attacking an anti-aircraft gun position at Mague, UT 664524, Tete, capturing one 14.5-mm HMG, one 82-mm mortar, 5 AK's, 3 AKM's, ammunition and destroying a camp. The SAS also reported that the enemy were doing the job for them, by firing on each other!

Then in another country – on 1st June 1977, the SAS scored a victory by attacking Nyamuoba Farm, Zambia, and killing 17 terrorists.

Operation Aztec: 28 May to 2 June 1977

Operation *Aztec* was a combined forces' attack on Jorge do Limpopo, Madulo Pan and Mapai, in Moçambique, from 28th May to 2nd June 1977. It was a sad day for No 16 PTC - because it was on this operation that the first pilot from No 16 PTC was killed on operations - Flight Lieutenant Bruce Collocott. I had carried Bruce as a passenger in a Canberra trip flown nearly five years earlier - on 13th June 1972.

Operation *Aztec* involved sending the Rhodesian Light Infantry to clear Madulo Pan while the Selous Scouts were tasked to take out Mapai and demolish sections of railway in the Gaza Province.

Helicopters of No 7 Squadron trooped the RLI assault force into the ZANLA complex known as Rio, on the Nuanetsi River. Another group of RLI was para-dropped into the Madulo Pan ZANLA base area - the same area that had been previously neutralised by the Air Force. The Selous Scouts, meanwhile, launched a motorised column assault towards Jorge do Limpopo. Major Bert Sachse commanded the Scouts, from their fort based at FAF 7.

On 29th May 1977, at 11h00, a pair of Hawker Hunters from No 1 Squadron attacked the ZANLA terrorist base at Madulo Pan. The airstrike was followed by the para-drop of forty RLI commandos. As the RLI chaps swept the area, they came across a vast litter of skulls and human skeletons, which could only have been the relics left over from the Canberra bomber raid. Meanwhile, the Scouts, en route to Jorge do Limpopo, encountered scattered rocket and mortar fire on the outskirts of the town, and called for air support. A second pair of Hunters was scrambled and duly neutralised the enemy positions. A large quantity of enemy stores, equipment and vehicles was captured. Having cleared Madulo Pan, the RLI assisted the Scouts to garrison Jorge do Limpopo.

At the Mapai airstrip the Scouts encountered a large contingent of FRELIMO and ZANLA, well dug in, and equipped with 60mm mortars and 14,5mm anti-aircraft guns. A brief firefight ensued. By now night had fallen and the ground troops had to wait through the night to commence their assault on Mapai town itself at first light on the 30th.

Once again the Hunters from No 1 Squadron were called upon to carry out dawn strikes on the ZANLA and FRELIMO strong points forming a defensive perimeter around the village. After they had been softened up, the Scouts advanced. As they did so, they came under a severe mortar barrage, and the Hunter air support was again called for. Unfortunately, the Scouts couldn't pinpoint the mortar positions for the Hunter pilots. However, the mere presence of the Air Force made it easier for the Scouts to take the village - but the bulk of the ZANLA arms and ammunition had by now been dispersed into small dumps around the village.

Because the Mapai airfield was still in a serviceable condition, Ron Reid-Daly (OC Selous Scouts) called for a Dakota to airlift in a team of mechanics. He wanted the mechanics to make repairs to some of the captured ZANLA vehicles which were non-runners, because of neglect or mechanical ignorance. He then later called for a further Dakota to fly in an extra demolition team. Then during the afternoon the Scouts were running low on explosives and mortar bombs - and they wanted extra men – so a third Dakota resupply was called for. By the time all the arrangements were made, it was already late and the ill-fated Dakota, co-piloted by Bruce Collocott, arrived after sunset.

At 20h00, after having been unloaded, the Dakota pilots prepared for their night take-off with the aid of truck lights and strobes for runway lights. They taxied to the end of the runway, and had just commenced their take-off when an RPG-7 rocket slammed into the starboard engine, immediately setting it alight. The aircrew had no option but to abort the take-off, but had no control as the aircraft ground-looped, ripping off the undercarriage. In no time, the aircraft was ablaze, and everyone aboard, except Bruce, abandoned the burning Dakota. It was evident that Bruce had been shot - he was killed by the first burst of terrorist tracer fire (according to the Scouts' report).

~~~OOO~~~

At first light the next morning, the Air Force salvage team arrived by No 7 Squadron helicopter, and salvaged what they could from the almost totally burned out wreckage. Then ironically, explosives that had been airlifted in, were used to destroy what was left of the Dakota. The Air Force maintained flying patrols in order to keep a watchful eye on the possibility of enemy reinforcements being moved up from Barragem.

The Air Force strategy paid off. Six FRELIMO vehicles loaded with troops were destroyed in airstrikes. The result was that FRELIMO made no more attempts to send up relief forces. This gave the ground forces the respite to blow up a steam crane and massive concrete culverts under the railway line which effectively immobilised rail traffic until after the war.

The Air Force lost a valuable pilot, and aircraft on Operation *Aztec*. Estimated terrorist losses were reckoned on sixty plus, as well as the final elimination of the Moçambique railways in the Gaza Province along which the ZANLA terrorists, their equipment and stores had been moving to the Rhodesian border. The destruction or capture of a large number of military vehicles being used for the same purposes, and the capture of a vast quantity of terrorist war material were added bonuses.

No 5 Squadron – March 1974
Seated: Pilots Keith Goddard, Mick Delport, John Bennie, Ian Donaldson (QFI), Sqn WO George Heron, Prop Geldenhuys ('A' Flt Cdr), Randy du Rand (Sqn Cdr), navigators Bernie Vaughan ('B' Flt Cdr), Glob Pasea, Starry Stevens, Paddy Morgan, Rich Airey and Jim Russell

Canberra Vic Formation

No 5 Squadron 1974
George Heron, Prop Geldenhuys,
Sqn Ldr Randy du Rand,
Bernie Vaughan, Doug Pasea

Canberras, Vampires and Hunters – Rhodesians main strike aircraft used during the War

*Operation Hurricane – 20 Ton Week – February 1974
Aircrews: Bernie Vaughan, Starry Stevens, Rich Airey, Mike Delport, Keith Goddard, John Bennie, Prop Geldenhuys, Glob Pasea and Squadron Commander Randy du Rand*

(Authors note: The left-hand bomb trolley is loaded with 500lb High Explosive bombs. The bomb box rack, on the right, would hold up to 96 x 20lb Fragmentation bombs. It was the latter that malfunctioned, and resulted in the death of Rich Airey and Keith Goddard

Operation Marble – No 5 Squadron, after dropping 20 tons of bombs in a week. Keith Goddard and Rich Airey were killed shortly after this photo was taken

Hawker Hunter – COIN Course - May 1974

Operation Polar - Mozambique

Lynx Aircraft – No 4 Squadron – Operation Mardon

An impressive RAF No 111 Squadron Hunter formation flypast at the Farnborough Air Show – led by Squadron Leader Roger Topp – in 1956.

The barely recognisable remains of Bruce Collocott's Dakota at Mapai in the 'Russian Front". The Fin and engine cowlings, with propellers, of what was Dakota R 3702 can be seen. Bruce Collocott was the only No 16 PTC pilot killed on air operations during the Rhodesian War 1965 to 1980

Fire Force fire-power Aircraft

Lynx and Alouette K-Car

(Photos: from Eddy Norris of ORAF's – acknowledged with thanks)

Hunter and Vampire's arsenal of weapons

6 Mahogany Bomber

Mahogany Bomber / Seek and Strike

    I was appointed OCAW Thornhill on 17th January 1977, whilst still at FAF 7, as a Lynx jock on No 4 Squadron. I still had two operational sorties to fly with the Selous Scout Major Bert Sachse, who commanded Operation *Manyatela*. An attack had been carried out on Madulo Pan, and Bert wanted a current Sitrep (Situation report). On landing, I handed over the Lynx that I had used ever since my search mission for the downed Canberra crews of Ian Donaldson and David Hawkes.

My ferry flight to Thornhill was with Sergeant Grant Domoney. After handing the Lynx aircraft back to No 4 Squadron and changing from IS kit into Air Force blues, I duly reported to the Base Commander, Group Captain Tol Janeke. OC Thornhill briefed me on my duties, saying that I would be accountable to him and would be held responsible for all the administrative functions. These included the Accounts Section, PARO - Pay and Records Office, 'B' Squadron General Service Unit (GSU), Security, SWO - Station Warrant Officer, Guard Room, SSQ - Station Sick Quarters, NCO Messes, Gardens, Canteen, and all Department of Defence dealings regarding Estimates Submissions such as Major and Minor Works. I would also be the link man between Headquarters and Station on all administrative matters.

This seemed a formidable task, but very competent personnel that made the challenge quite exciting headed each Section. The beauty of this Mahogany Bomber staff position was that I would still be required to maintain my flying currency in case of operational needs. I did not have long to wait. On 22nd January 1977 I was tasked to uplift the Rhodesian Army Commander in a Lynx. I duly positioned Salisbury airport to uplift Major General John Hickman plus his Aide De Camp Major Harrison and flew them to Gwelo. Once they had finished their business at the School of Infantry, I again flew them back to Salisbury. Two days later, I flew two passengers down to FAF 7 Buffalo Range in a Trojan. This OCAW job certainly had its benefits - a desk-cum-flying job. I found myself flying some 108 sorties, as OCAW, logging more than 278 hours. Whilst my first love was still flying, the Mahogany Bomber also had its ups and downs.

My Mahogany Bomber was going nowhere - but an administrative posting is a fact of life in the GD/P mustering - general duties/pilot meant Mahogany responsibilities sooner or later. Flying a desk instead of an aircraft comes in various forms. I was privileged to land the plum OCAW Staff Appointment job because there were only two such posts in the Air Force: New Sarum and Thornhill. Both bases had three wings - OCFW, OCAW and OCTW - for Flying, Administration and Technical wings respectively. The three "wing" commanders reported to the CO or Station Commander. GD/Ps of Wing Commander rank commanded the senior wing, OCFW, whereas the other two wings were commanded by Squadron Leader-ranked officers. The other Squadron Leaders on the base, as Squadron Commanders, reported to OCFW. As OCAW reporting directly to the CO, I would be considered part of senior management as far as all administrative matters were concerned.

The SWO - Station Warrant Officer, equivalent to the Army Regimental Sergeant Major, is THE most powerful, and often feared, non-commissioned officer on the base. When he bawled "Jump." everybody responded with a "How high Sir?" - even most commissioned officers! I had Warrant Officer Class I Wally Jefferies as my SWO. The SWO was also responsible for Parks, Gardens and Recreation. Flight Sergeant Hennie Pretorius and Sergeant John Childs assisted Wally. I often had to be wary of sticking to the proper chain of command in relaying my orders to Hennie and John through Wally. Because if not, the SWO would make damn' sure my orders were ignored whenever I by-passed him. Needless to say I got on extremely well with all my staff and we even strengthened our own *esprit de corps* and traditions.

The Security Branch headed by Flight Lieutenant Peter Cowan and assisted by John Cox and Ted Barnard commanded the largest number of airmen on the base - the GSU - General Service Unit ground staff. Air Lieutenant Basil Moss commanded OC 'B' Squadron GSU. Squadron Warrant Officer 'Danger' Ncube ably assisted Basil - a highly respected Ndebele who was likened to Shaka Zulu.

SSQ - Station Sick Quarters - controlled by the MO - Medical Officer - included an eight-bed Station Hospital with separate ward facilities for Officers and ORs - Other Ranks. The MOs were Aviation Medicine experts who carried out annual flying medical examinations on all pilots. Thornhill also boasted the only decompression chamber in the Force. Experiencing the effects of anoxia or explosive decompression are career events, which all pilots are subjected to. Pilots would be grounded when they failed their annual medical and the MOs could determine within minutes whenever pilots' physical and mental fitness had slipped. I had full confidence in their methodology of measuring heart beat after only a couple of jumps up and down the dreaded 'box' in the examination room.

Flight Lieutenant Bryan Byars was in charge of the Accounts Department, which also included the Pay and Records Office, Typing Pool, Registry and Telephonist. I was a co-signatory for all cheques concerning public money expenditures. A Warrant Officer was also in charge of the MT - Motor Transport Section and I was required to authorise all Forms 658 requisitions - Request for Transport.

The management of the base Canteen (in effect a medium sized Supermarket) and specifically the Warrant Officers'/Sergeants' and Airmen's Mess were also my specific responsibility. As already mentioned, I was also solely responsible for all Major and Minor Works preparations and submissions to the Secretary for Defence and co-ordination-cum-liaison with PWD - Public Works Department. I then also had co-responsibility for Stores - controlled by the SEO - Station Equipment Officer. One 'jam-stealer' who readily comes to mind was the all-round ball player and national Rugby Team player Dux Deysel who could kick like a donkey - and all perfect 'torpedoes' too!

These wide-ranging responsibilities meant never a dull moment. That was so in my case and I thoroughly enjoyed my stint as OCAW - and appreciated the excellent "grounding" (to coin a phrase) that the Air Force equipped me with. It was a real handful when I started, but I owe Tol Janeke a debt of gratitude for imparting his Staff College skills to me.

Operation Peptic: 27 June to 2 September 1977

Operation *Peptic* was carried out in the Tete Province of Moçambique and consisted of recces, ambushes, mining and general harassment of the enemy by the SAS. Areas concentrated on included Chintopo, Zumbo and Seçuranca – where a large quantity of terrorist arms and ammunitions was destroyed. These included 150 82-mm mortar bombs, 150 60-mm mortar bombs, 12 RPG7 rockets and 10 boxes of 7.62-mm rounds destroyed on site. This also led to the Air Force carrying out an air strike by Lynx, Canberras and Hunters on the latter on 8th September 1977.

Air Strike Log 724 - 8 September 1977

Aircrews:
- Glen Pretorius
- JR Blythe-Wood

Target: Air Task 900 – Seçuranca, Tete, Moçambique
Result: Unknown casualties, cache destroyed. SAS ground sweep

No 724 – 08/09/77. This related Air Force and SAS operation was pieced together when I came across an "Operations Table, by Captain JRT Wood, Rhodesian Intelligence Corps", which appeared in an SAS book. It is apparent that towards the end of Operation *Peptic,* the SAS destroyed a large armaments cache on 2nd September. Wood's Operations Table lists the Air Force as having carried out a camp attack at Seçuranca, Tete, Moçambique, resulting in unknown casualties. The Lynx, Hunter and Canberra strike was followed by an SAS ground sweep. The cache destroyed included 6,000 7.62-mm rounds, 150 60-mm and 150 82-mm mortar bombs, and 12 RPG7 rockets.

Operation Brisket: 29 June to 29 July 1977

Operation *Brisket* was a recce of the Kavalamanja – Feira roads, Ditande area of Zambia by the SAS (see also Operation Turmoil for more detail).

Operations Grapple and Tangent: 1 August 1977

Operation *Grapple* was situated in the Rhodesian Midlands province. Thornhill Air Force base was bang in the middle. As OCAW my duties were essentially administrative. The operations personnel were responsible for prosecuting Coin operations from the Gwelo School of Infantry base. Every now and again I would find myself involved with various Operation *Grapple* functions.

In June 1978 a Hartley PATU - Police Anti Terrorist Unit of Reservist farmers made contact with a pseudo group, killing Selous Scout Corporal Obasi and his group of three Scouts, mainly because Inkomo (now called the Andre Rabie Barracks) had failed to communicate a frozen area to the *Grapple* JOC. It was a tragic failing of the need-to-know principle whereby it unnecessarily cost the lives of ground forces fighting on the same side. I for one did not blame the farmers - they could not afford to take any chances after the murder of the Hartley couple Johannes and Barbara Viljoen during Operation *Pagoda* in June 1966.

Operation *Tangent* covered the south-west border area next to Botswana, and specifically Matabeleland. Operations were conducted from Brady; the Army's No 1 Brigade Headquarters. With more operational areas opening up, the Air Force was being stretched to its limits.

Operation Terminate: 19 September to 21 October 1977

Operation *Terminate* with an attack at Cangudzi, Tete in which 1 ZANLA, 4 FPLM and 17 recruits were killed. Then eight days later, on the 27th, an opportune target presented itself to the SAS at WS 158804 in which a further 19 terrorist recruits were killed, as well as two incriminating AK weapons recovered. The next day an ambush on a vehicle column resulted in 2 FPLM and 17 terrorists and recruits killed. Ambushes sprung during early October added to the bag.

On 12th October the Air Force was called upon to air strike a FRELIMO vehicle column on the Mague – Mukumbura road, near Mague in the Tete Province of Moçambique. Planks Blythe-Wood and his wing man did pretty well.

Air Strike Log 736 - 12 October 1977

Aircrew:
- JR Blythe-Wood

Target: Convoy of three trucks in the Russian Front: Mague-Mukumbura Rd
Result: Merc, Toyota and Isuzu destroyed. 3+ FRELIMO killed, 14 wounded and 3 missing.

Richard Wood, from his position in the Rhodesian Intelligence Corps logged that 3+ FPLM killed, 14 seriously wounded, 19 slightly wounded and 3 missing. Destroyed Mercedes-Benz, Toyota, Isuzu, food, war materials and medicines. The SAS engaged on Operation *Terminate* enjoyed further successes on the 19th, 20th and 21st October 1977. *Terminate II* was carried out from 15 March 1978 and ended 15 August 1978.

Air Strike Log 735 - 11 October 1977

Aircrew:
- Rich Beaver

Target: Attack on Terrs
Result: Night air to ground attack

ASR 738 - 18 October 1977

Aircrews:
- Rich Beaver
- Spook Geraty
- Rich Brand

Target: Zambezi Gorge crossing
Result: Boat with terrs sunk. FAC for jet strike across river

It was during early October 1977, on 11th, to be exact, that my old Air Force buddy Rich Beaver acquitted himself rather well. He was rewarded for his bravery with the award of the MFC - Military Forces Commendation (Operational). His citation reads as follows - "As a (Lynx) pilot on No 4 Squadron, he assisted ground forces to withdraw from an untenable position by delivering a hazardous air to ground attack on terrorists by the light of flares which he had dropped. On 18th October, over dangerous terrain in the Deka - Zambezi River Gorge, he successfully attacked terrorists attempting to cross the river by boat, and then provided highly effective control for a strike by jet aircraft on a terrorist position adjacent to the crossing point."

According to Beav, he had been scrambled from FAF 1 and was given an in-flight briefing by the PRAW aircraft flying at altitude on border patrol duties. After plotting the boat crossing point on his map, he realised that attacking from the west, over the mountainous terrain, would jeopardise the element of surprise. He accordingly elected to remain low-level, and approach from the east, pulling up at the last minute to his 'perch' position. This plan was duly executed to perfection. Rich fired his front guns on his FRA - first run attack - in order to keep the terrorist heads down, and then fired a salvo of rockets at the boat, which was in the middle of the Zambezi river. Because he was flying the Lynx straight towards the rising mountains on either side of the river gorge, he was forced to pull up steeply as soon as he had fired his Sneb rockets. The boat was no more. Because he could see no sign of movement, he queried developments from the PRAW pilot circling overhead the airstrike. The PRAW pilot confirmed that the boat had sunk. It was only then that Rich noted numerous bodies being swept downstream by the fast flowing current of the Zambezi River. Rich remained in the vicinity and successfully directed jet pilots Spook Geraty (who had just returned from Operation *Sand* in South Africa) and Rich Brand onto the terrorist position adjacent to the crossing point. I might add that Rich Beaver also excelled during Operations *Modular*, *Hooper* and *Packer*, as a pilot with the SAAF.

During August 1977, on the 2nd, a mortar bomb attack was carried out on Zimbabwe House in Lusaka. A victim in this attack, suffering "hearing damage/impairment.", was a certain Chenjerai "Hitler" Hunzvi – who subsequently became the self-styled leader of the so called 'War Veterans' that spearheaded the white farm invasions in the mid 2000s, and thereby averted a narrow defeat for Mugabe's ruling ZANU P/F party. Hunzvi was also in Botswana, during either 1977 or 1978, when he again sustained injuries during a Rhodesian attack. A pity he wasn't knocked off.

Operation Dragon: 21 September to 13 October 1977

The SAS recce'd DK and Kafwambila camps in Zambia, presumably with photographs taken by No 5 Squadron.

Operation Grinder: 18 To 24 October 1977

Operation *Grinder* resulted in 16 terrorists killed when the SAS attacked the Nyamuomba Camp in Zambia.

Air Strike Log 737 - 15 October 1977

Aircrew:
- JR Blythe-Wood

Target: Op Melon – Convoy VK270500 Gaza Moz.
Result: 3 vehicles destroyed. 2 SAS wounded (JRT Wood)

Captain JRT Wood, of the Rhodesian Intelligence Corps, records that the SAS made contact at Grid Ref VK 270500, Gaza, Moçambique, on 15th October 1977. He states that there was an "airstrike on convoy", and noted that "2 SAS wounded. 3 vehicles destroyed". John Blythe-Wood is the only pilot known to have carried out an airstrike on that day, and author's licence is taken to draw obvious conclusions with regard to Air Strike Log No 737.

Mohogany Bomber Trade-Off: October 1977

To get back to some more of my own flying experiences - because I enjoyed the best of both worlds, I could trade in my Mahogany Bomber for a real flying machine. My flying currency had lapsed because I had not flown for quite a while. As mentioned, the Air Force was being stretched as more operational areas were opening up - and the need arose to fully utilise pilots, even those holding down desk jobs. We "retreads" could thus provide a small measure of relief to Squadron pilots who were in dire need of some R&R. Trading in my OCAW desk for a Lynx on operational duties injected a lot more variety and challenge into this GD/P - general duties pilot.

At the end of October 1977, Officer Commanding No 4 Squadron, Squadron Leader Dag Jones, gave me an urgent, quick, re-familiarisation and standardisation sortie on the Lynx aircraft. I had not had my bum in the air since my return from FAF 1 in the latter part of the month before. My solo general was a disaster - I experienced undercarriage failure and had to cut my sortie short, but was able to land successfully without any mishap. The Squadron technicians did what they could to clear the snag. Dag Jones then came up with me to check out the aircraft (Lynx R 3417), but we had to abort the sortie because of another undercarriage failure. The only other aircraft available for my instrument and night flying currency was Lynx R 3411. I logged a respectable four hours flying for the day.

The following day, 1st November 1977, Dag Jones flew safety pilot for me while I got in over two hours of simulated instrument flying. That night I flew a solo single line flare sortie with instrument flying letdown. There was obviously some urgency to get me fully operational on type as soon as possible, and so it came as no surprise that my next sortie was flown with a very, very senior pilot indeed - as my safety pilot. I needed to be instrument rated in order to undertake field deployments.

On 2nd November 1977, Group Captain John Mussell was my safety pilot whilst I practised a VDF and NDB simulated instrument/cloud flying letdowns. This certainly was the most senior Air Force GD/P officer I had been privileged to have as a safety pilot. John Mussell had been my Squadron Commander when No 4 Squadron moved from New Sarum to Thornhill way back in 1964. Looking back, this was only the second occasion on which I had flown with him (the previous was in a Provost). John's elder brother, Frank Mussell, was the current Air Force Commander. On 2nd and 3rd November, I flew the Lynx with Flight Lieutenant Tony Oakley and OC 4 Squadron to round off my minimum instrument requirement. Then early on 4th November Dag rated me White Card and I flew to Kutanga with Mick Delport for a quickie weapons re-familiarisation, firing 700 x ·303 rounds front gun, dropping 12 Bubs (break-up bombs frantan profile) and 10 x 37-mm Sneb rockets. This rushed mini OCU re-familiarisation was indicative of the urgent need to get as many pilots as possible ready for field deployments at short notice. I was now ready. My quick conversion had taken a mere five days.

A four-day detachment to FAF 1 for Operation *Tangent / Ranger* duties followed immediately after my Lynx conversion. I uplifted Sergeant Kevin Nelson from Thornhill and positioned Wankie late on 4th November 1977 - having flown six sorties for the day, and logging a total of six flying hours for the day. Kevin's younger brother Rob had been killed in action earlier in the year - on 8th May, and as fate would have it, his turn would come a mere seven months after my sortie with him. Kevin was killed in action in Moçambique in a South African Z-Car (on 28th July 1978. A tragic sequel was that his mother, who had now lost two sons killed in action, committed suicide). I obviously felt very much at home at Wankie, due to my Operation *Nickel* days. The purpose of this trip was to use the Air Force re-tread pilots for maximum effect and release the battle weary squadron pilots for well earned R&R, or even for re-deployment duties elsewhere.

My Operation *Tangent* detachment had its own highlights. Early on 5th November 1977 I was tasked with armed border reconnaissance cover from Kazungula to Victoria Falls, landing and operating from Sprayview airstrip. Later in the day, I got airborne again. I recorded one Zambian soldier killed. Kevin Nelson accompanied me on this one hundred-minute recce in Lynx R 3048. South African forces were conducting offensive operations against SWAPO in Zambian bases. I was not aware that the South Africans were operating out of Katima Mulilo in the Caprivi Strip of South West Africa - later Namibia (Special Force Recces were based at Fort Doppies). I landed at the new Victoria Falls Airport.

There was not much activity the next day, so I practised night flying and non-directional beacon letdowns, with circuits at FAF 1. The FAF had certainly developed over the years and the Wankie airfield could now be considered an all-weather airfield, boasting its own Rhodesian-developed glide-path approach lights. These lights were positioned at the touchdown point and would either glow red if the pilot is low on glide path, or orange if okay. It consisted of slits in a box, through which beams of coloured lights were projected at the exact angle of the glide path to aid pilots approaching the runway.

On 7th November my relief arrived and I returned to Thornhill in Lynx R 3094. Then it was back to the grindstone, and my rather enjoyable, albeit mundane OCAW duties. Any spell away from Thornhill invariably meant catching up with unattended business. I didn't mind. The fly boys were doing a splendid job. The Mahogany Bombers had it easy in comparison to the long hours demanded from those at the sharp end.

On 23rd November, I was tasked to conduct ground air control training for the Army Cadets, in the Bulawayo area. Sergeant Curwen accompanied me on the three hour Lynx flight to the 1 Brigade area. On the same day, Operation *Dingo* got off the ground.

Operations Ranger and SALOps

Operation *Ranger* covered the North-west Border area, stretching from the Tuli area in the south, through Kazungula on the north-west corner of Rhodesia, and up to approximately Binga on Lake Kariba. Although operational headquarters was originally centred at Bulawayo, Operation *Ranger* took over from the Matabeleland-focused Operation *Tangent*, and concentrated its activities mainly around Wankie – thereby exercising control mainly on north-west border operations. Its establishment coincided with Operation *Grapple* (Midlands) Salops concentrated on Salisbury and Districts. These structures facilitated command and control by Comops.

Operation Dingo: Wednesday 23 to Saturday 26 November 1977

Operation *Dingo* was a major air-initiated cross border strike against the Chimoio terrorist base in Moçambique, involving every serviceable operational aircraft the Rhodesian Air Force could muster. It was the biggest attack so far mounted in the war, and necessitated putting even the highly suspect Vampire FB 9 (i.e. without ejector seats) in the front line.

Chimoio Base, to the north of the town of like name, housed eight thousand inhabitants, and had become the official headquarters for all the ZANLA forces led by Robert Mugabe. The huge complex was situated three hundred and twenty kilometres from New Sarum, and its administrative core was well established with offices, great stores of arms and ammunition, vast stocks of food, a hospital, two schools and several substantial buildings roofed with corrugated iron, and concrete floors. It was a military base heavily defended with 12.7mm and 14.4mm anti-aircraft batteries. War refugees, numbering about twenty thousand at the time, were concentrated at Doeroi, some fifty-five kilometres further east.

The raid against Chimoio was to be followed by over thirty cross-border strikes before the end of the war.

The operation got off the ground late due to guti (drizzle) conditions, filthy weather for airmen. The cloud base at Chimoio was barely three hundred feet. This however, was no problem for the large ground forces that also took part - the whole of the Special Air Services and almost the whole of the Rhodesian Light Infantry.

Six No 5 Squadron Canberras, each armed with three hundred anti-personnel Mark II Alpha bombs, took off from New Sarum at 07h05 on that Wednesday morning, 23rd November 1977 and joined up with the Hunters from Thornhill before crossing the border. Half an hour after take-off, and with nearly five minutes to target, the Hunters of No 1 Squadron accelerated to four hundred and fifty knots and pulled up to their perch position for their first run attacks. The Cans followed at three hundred and thirty knots dropping their bomb load, landing back at New Sarum an hour twenty minutes after take-off to load up with more Alpha bombs.

Meanwhile the K-Cars went in with their 20mm cannons while the Dakotas from No 3 Squadron dropped their paratroops and the G-Cars landed their sticks of soldiers. Then six Vampires from No. 2 squadron followed, attacking their specific targets, including anti-aircraft emplacements, with their three-inch rockets and cannon. Other strong points were attacked when called upon to do so by the ground forces. Because Chimoio was on the limit of the Vampire range, they were also operating from New Sarum. Despite this, one of the Vampires did not make it back - see later. The Lynxes of No 4 Squadron were also in the thick of things. They took off from the FAF at Grand Reef. Armed with 37mm Sneb rockets and mini-Golf bombs, their task consisted of target marking for the strike aircraft and close air support of the army units. Being the most vulnerable, two Lynxes were hit by ground fire. A counter-insurgency tactic developed was the use of code names when communicating with the various aircraft types such as Panzers for the Hunters, Goblins for the Vampires, Hornets for the Lynxes, Kiewiets for the Cessnas and Spiders for helicopters. "Cyclone" was used by the ground troops to call or attract any of the various aircraft types.

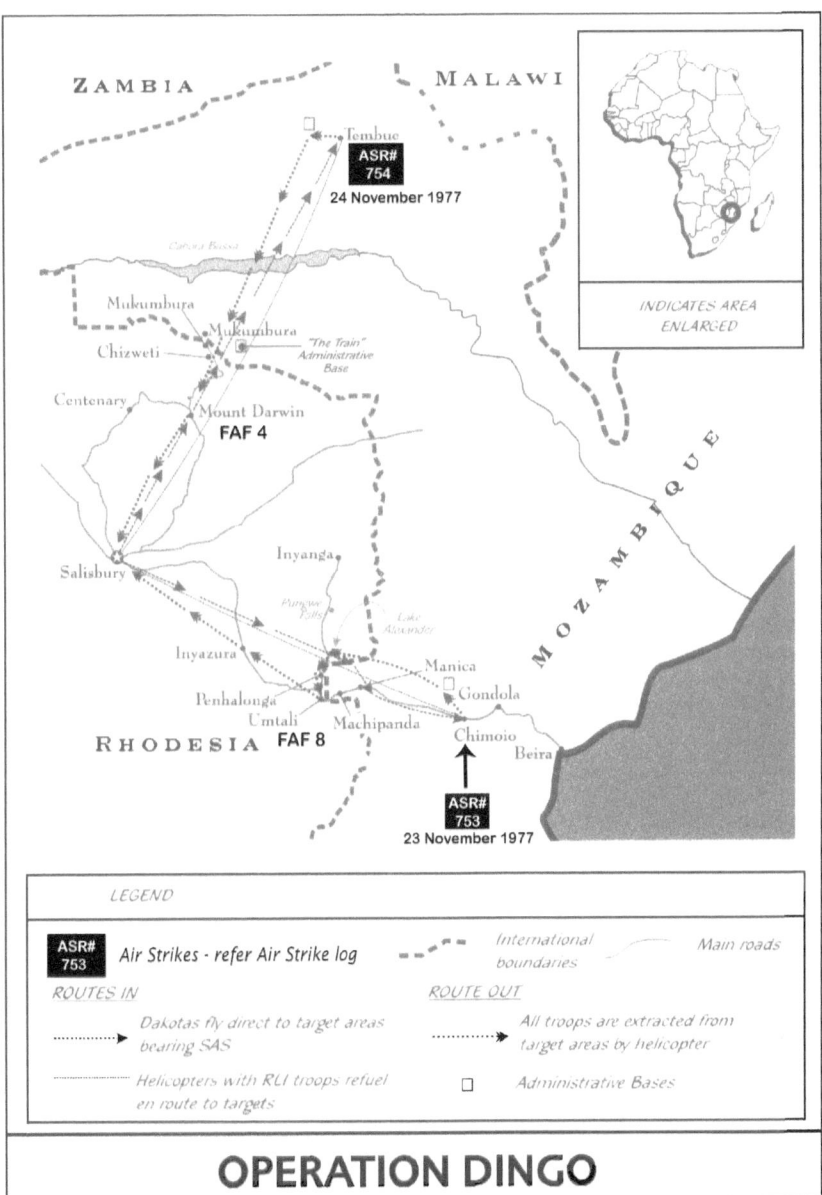

OPERATION DINGO

(Note: Refer to the Air Strike Log section – see # 753. Map kindly reproduced by permission of Covos Day books)

I was Officer Commanding Administration Wing of Thornhill Air Base at the time, and my Station Commander had "jammed" (connived to obtain - in Air Force jargon) himself a Vampire T 11, with the result that I was left behind to hold the fort. Unfortunately, Air Lieutenant Phil Haigh, flying a Vampire FB 9 without an ejector seat, had an engine failure on the way back from Chimoio, having sustained a hit in one of the bottom gas burners of his Goblin jet engine. Phil put the Vampire down, well inside Rhodesia, with a good wheels-up belly landing. But by sheer bad luck the Vampire slid into a gully and exploded. Phil was killed. The responsibility then fell on me to inform his wife Dot that her husband had been killed.

Op Dingo Airstrike Log
Air Strike Report 753 - 23 November 1977
Aircrews:
- Rich Brand
- Vic Wightman
- Steve Kesby
- JR Blythe-Wood
- Randy du Rand
- Glen Pretorius
- Tol Janeke
- Varky Varkevisser
- Ken Law
- Phil Haigh
- Vic Cook / Jeff Dartnall
- Harold Griffiths
- John Annan
- Bill Sykes + whole of 7 Sqn
- Mark McLean
- Chris Tucker
- Bob d'Hotman
- Norman Walsh
- Jack Malloch / George Alexander

Target: Chimoio – Vanduzi Camp WQ030525 Manica and Tembue Camp, VU815525, Tete Province north of Cabora Bassa
Result: Phil Haigh killed, during forced landing in Vampire. Vampire targets were the northern part of the Chimoio training element, anti-aircraft weapon sites and barrack blocks. JRT Wood tabulates 800 terrorists killed, 750 wounded. In addition to Haigh, Trooper G.J. Nel killed and 6 RLI wounded. Camp and all equipment destroyed.
See also Peter Petter-Bowyer's *Winds of Destruction*, pages 457 to 465

ASR 754 - 24 November 1977
Aircrews:
- Vic Wightman
- JR Blythe-Wood
- Glen Pretorius
- Varky Varkevisser (top cover)

Target: Tembue base – VU 815525
Result: (JRT Wood logs 400 terrorists killed at Tembue, VU 815525 on 26.11.77)

ASR 755 - 26 November 1977 Operation Virile
Aircrews:
- Chris Tucker
- Vic Wightman
- JR Blythe-Wood
- Rich Brand
- Spook Geraty
- Tol Janeke

Varky Varkevisser
Target: FRELIMO – ZANLA convoy Espungabera / Dombe road, Moçambique
Result: Support of Scout column, against enemy convoy and targets – over 1000 Terrs strong.
(JR – 3 sorties, Tol – 2 sorties)
See Peter Petter-Bowyer's book, page 470.

ASR 756 - 27 November 1977 - Operation Virile
Aircrews:
- Vic Wightman
- JR Blythe-Wood

Target: Op Virile: Clear Dombe – Espungabera road for Scouts flying column.
Results: Destroyed several vehicles – See page 289 Selous Scouts Top Secret War

Vampire FB 9s had been built before ejector seats became standard. Had he tried to bale out, there was a strong danger of him hitting the tail plane. Many years later, while doing research for this book, I established that the Vampire was in fact hit by FRELIMO anti-aircraft fire at Vanduzi cross roads after attacking Chimoio. Phil Haigh is also listed on the Roll of Honour as published on the Internet, and connected with Chas Lotter's *"Echoes of an African War"*.

Advising next of kin of a fatality is a job I would not wish on my worst enemy. I had to pick the right time and place, but also needed to do it as soon as possible, before the news leaked out. Staff Officer Personnel at Air Force Headquarters, Wing Commander Peter Knobel, had called me on the secra-phone. After having done the 'deed', I was then required to confirm my 'duty carried out'. I was fortunately able to establish that Dot was not at home - but had just completed her shopping at the base canteen and was on her way to visit a friend at the Security section. As soon as she came out of the building, I intercepted her with idle chatter, escorted her to her motor car, and told her I had bad news and that I would be driving her home. Once inside her car, I broke the news to her. I must add that she took the news very well and only broke down in the privacy of her own home. I had meanwhile arranged for the Station Medical Officer to follow a short distance behind us - with the intention of administering a sedative to offset the subsequent shock.

I then had to arrange a Committee of Adjustment, to wrap up Phil Haigh's affairs, and also helped Dot to make her travel plans back to Britain. I managed to get financial assistance from the Victims of Terrorism Relief Fund, which enabled Dot Haigh to return to the United Kingdom.

In addition to Phil Haigh being killed, one Rhodesian soldier was killed and eight wounded. The price of the Rhodesian casualties was 2000 enemy killed (admitted by the guerrillas themselves), while unofficial estimates put the figure nearer 3000. The Rhodesians occupied Chimoio for about thirty-six hours, returning to their bases by dusk on 24th November.

An account, from the receiving end, warrants repeating. It comes from Anne Tekere, as mentioned in Mugabe's autobiography by David Smith, published 1981. "It was about 7.30 in the morning of 23 November when the Rhodesian squadrons reached Chimoio. There were jet bombers, fighter planes, and helicopters carrying paratroopers from the Air Force base at Umtali about 60 miles away. They strafed the camp, and then bombed it; finally the paratroopers were dropped to finish off whoever and whatever remained.

"Anne Tekere, Edgar Tekere's wife, was found by Tongogara three days later in a 'long drop' latrine pit, where she stayed out of sight from the units of the Rhodesian African Rifles who stayed for 48 hours after the first attack. Her account of the raid is worth recording here not just for its gruesome testimony - but also for the deep-rooted hatred of the white government it engendered in her husband and some of his colleagues on the ZANU Central Committee.

"The attack began just as we were gathering for morning assembly. We heard first one aircraft (possibly the decoy), but the sky was overcast and so we did not see the bombers until they came above our heads. We were trying to disperse when there were explosions all around us and on top of us. The children were told to run into the bush.

"From then on it was impossible to gather the children in one place. We were not trained in military operations and we did not know what to do. There were smaller planes as well as the jet bombers, and some of them dropped paratroopers. And there were helicopters which machine-gunned people as they ran away. We had a security force of about 100 soldiers who fought back with machine-guns, but their ammunition ran out after a few minutes. The bombs seemed to be a kind of acid or inflammable. They burned the people and set fire to the bush.

DINGO BATTLE PLAN SKETCH

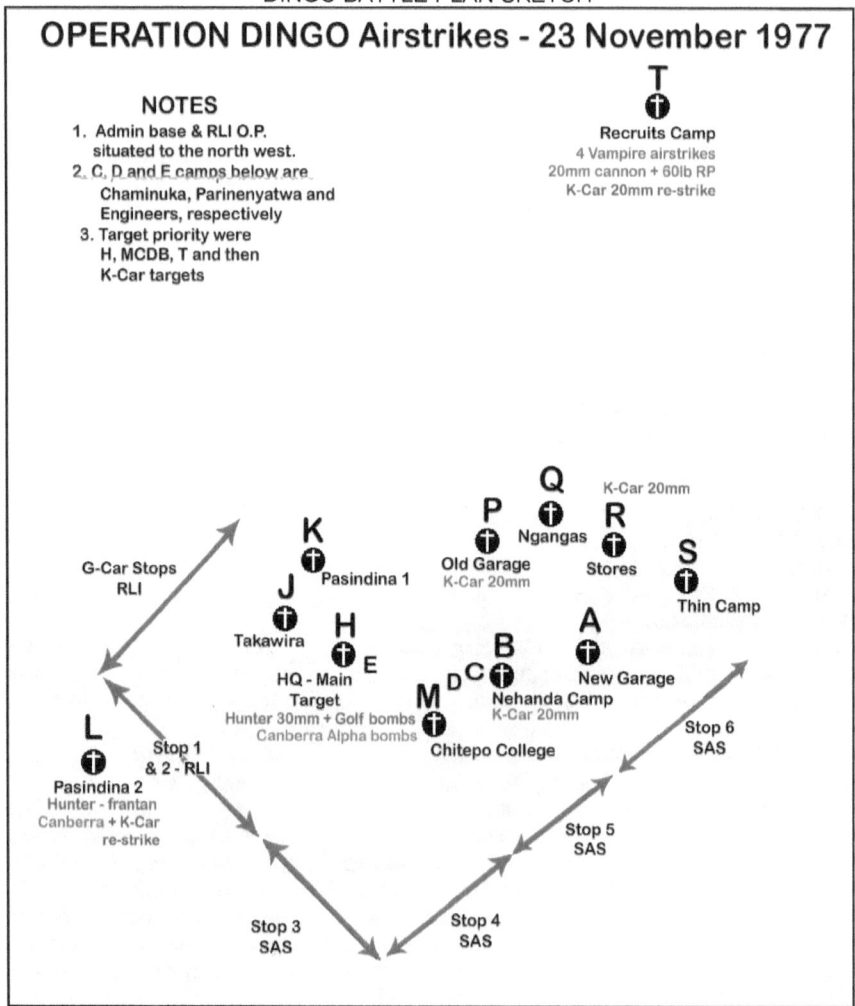

"I knew I could not run very much. When I looked towards Chimoio town I saw paratroopers landing and I decided to run and hide in a pit latrine. The sewage came up to my waist. Worst of all were the worms that crawled around me, but I felt safe because the bombs did not destroy the pit. All the time I was in the pit I heard explosions and shooting and I was too frightened to come out. I was afraid that if they had dogs they might find where I was and when I heard voices I was too frightened to call out.

"Then I heard an engine, a long distance away, and later recognised people speaking in Shona. I called out and they found me. They tried to haul me up with a rope, but I had hurt my arm getting into the pit and could not tie the rope around me. They broke the pit, removing the log."

The above sketch was drawn by the author and is intended to show the positioning, to scale, of the various complexes that constituted the targeted areas. The obvious 'out of the box' targets T for Tango and L for Lima – the Recruits and Passindina camps respectively, received special attention. The Recruits Camp (T) was struck by four Vampires with mopping up by two K-Car gunships. Passindina 2 was struck by Hunters with frantan, followed by a Canberra with

Alpha bombs, and then a couple of K-Cars. Space and complexity considerations do not, unfortunately, warrant further elaboration here. *Winds of Destruction* and *Pride of Eagles* do more justice in documenting this brilliantly executed battle plan.

~~~OOO~~~

Another account is documented in Cowderoy and Nesbit's *War in the Air*, where a terrorist survivor stated: "Within a few seconds planes were moving about in the air and we were all scared. We couldn't think what to do except run. I rolled and rolled across the ground and hid under a bush. Then a bomb dropped on the spot where I had just been. I rolled again and fell into a pit and broke my arm. I had to leave my gun. Now people were running in all directions and helicopters were firing at random and the jets were moving up and down. The attack seemed to start on our headquarters and on Base number two simultaneously. We walked and walked." Cowderoy and Nesbit also relate several first hand accounts regarding the Rhodesian Air Force. They concluded that by any standards, Operation *Dingo* must be considered a triumph for the newly created Comops and the exceptionally high quality of the security forces.

As was par for the course, the victims claimed that it was not a military camp, but a refugee camp. You be the judge. I question terrorist Josiah Tongogara extricating Anne Tekere from the long-drop, Edgar Tekere's war mongering reputation, admission of 100 soldiers, presence of 12.7 and 14.4mm anti-aircraft batteries, ZANU admission of their 'Chitepo College' at Chimoio (where military trained cadres of above-average ability were given intensive political courses), and even the subsequent finding of the Tanzania/ Moçambique critique. Surely, there was adequate evidence that it was indeed a terr camp, and not only a refugee camp.

The raid did give Ian Smith breathing space to pursue a settlement independent of Washington, London and Pretoria. An additional spin-off was the rift the attack created amongst the ZANU leadership. The raid also prompted Mugabe's own dissidents to overthrow him. For some time leading members of the ZANU Central Committee had questioned Mugabe's leadership on ideological and military grounds. They now tried to feed on the disarray and discontent created by the Chimoio raid to stage a coup against both Mugabe and Tongogara. Rugare Gumbo, information secretary, and Henry Hamadziripi, manpower secretary, led the 'dissidents'. Several capable ZANLA commanders in the camps supported them. In trying to gain support, they made Mugabe's leadership and the direction he was taking the main issue. He was attacked for lack of military knowledge, for reluctance to go into the field with the so-called guerrillas, and for even allowing himself to be seen to negotiate with the likes of Owen and Young. Mugabe and the High Command were blamed for the Chimoio debacle. According to the rebels, the Chimoio camp was pitifully short of a decent defence system (even the Tanzania and Moçambique governments were appalled) Above all, they accused the leadership of failing to foster seriously the "Marxism-Leninism-Mao Tse Tung thought" as laid down by the Chimoio Central Committee meeting the previous September. They wanted greater political power for the guerrillas themselves.

The operation was rated a great success, even though ZANLA commanders Josiah Tongogara and Rex Nhongo escaped the net and . . . . the Vampire FB 9s were thereafter taken out of service.

Chimoio Memorial

In August 2007 Bob Manser forwarded to the writer pictures of the Chimoio Memorial that had been constructed by his civil engineer landlord Kevin Tidy after the end of the war. The Memorial commemorates the day that the Rhodesian Air Force initiated Operation *Dingo* – 23 November 1977. Up until then, the main battle casualties occurred firstly during Operation *Eland* – 8 to 12 August 1976 (base camp known as Nyadzonia/Pungwe). ZANLA casualty figure was determined as 1,028 killed, 309 wounded and a 1,000 missing – 14 were captured and 200 believed drowned; and secondly during Operation *Dingo* – 23 to 26 November 1977. Casualty numbers were very conservatively estimated at 800 Zanla killed and 750 wounded (some sources says it varies from 2000 to 3000). In addition to RSF airman Phil Haigh killed, Trooper GJ Nel was also killed and 6 RLI wounded.

These were not the only Chimoio casualties. More than thirty cross-border strikes were carried out against Chimoio and surrounds, before the end of the Rhodesian 'Bush War'. Kevin

Tidy was commissioned by the Zimbabwe Government to construct the war memorial designed by architect Peter Jackson in 2000 at the site of the mass graves at the old Tembwe (not to be confused with Tembue, north of Tete) camp about 20km north west of Chimoio town. Construction was held up until the head of the National Monuments and Museums in Mutare, Mrs. Traude Rogers, devised a scheme for funds to be channelled through the Zimbabwe Beira Consulate. Kevin reiterated that visa payments were made over a two year period. Bob commented: "In some of the photos you will see the mass graves plus marble plaques engraved with many hundreds of names. It is estimated that there are about 4000 bodies interred there but no one really knows. A Zimbabwe army officer said during the construction that there was about 14000 bodies, this seems overly high as there seem to be about 2000 or so known names on the marble plaque, naturally many of the deceased were mujibas and were not on any register. It was said that there were about five mujibas to one armed trooper. It is however estimated by others that there may be 4000 or so bodies in the graves. Not all were casualties of Rhodesian attacks, many died of malaria and dysentery so the Zimbabwe army officer said".

Rhodesian Intelligence were aware that so-called war refugees, numbering about twenty thousand at the time, were concentrated at Doeroi, some fifty-five kilometres further east. It is very likely that burials there have been re-interned at this memorial site.

The Chimoio notice board below, reads: "Chimoio – Zimbabwe Liberation War Shrine • Here lie the remains of freedom fighters who fell during Zimbabwe's liberation war. These brave men and women were killed during a Rhodesian air and ground attack on Thursday 23 November 1977. National Museums and Monuments of Zimbabwe".

Chimoio Notice Board in Mozambique

Chimoio Memorial constructed by Kevin Tidy

The base was heavily defended with 12.7mm and 14.4mm anti-aircraft batteries – evidence of which was unearthed at the site and placed on the properly constructed mass graves – as can be seen in one of the pictures below.

A List of Names

Chimoio Anti-Aircraft Weapons and Guns

Mass Graves

Wall Murals - Photographs of two colourful wall murals by local artists and shows how they depicted the military events of the past. One is on a wall at a roundabout in Chimoio Town and the other on the wall of a 'waterhole' at Inchope.

Wall Mural – Armed Fighters or Attackers

Mural – Aerial Attack

The success of Operation *Dingo* has attracted USA military interest, and is believed studied for its strategic planning and brilliant execution in cost effectiveness.

Operation Melon: 26 October to 11 April 1978

Operation *Melon* was carried out in November 1977 in the 'Russian Front'. It was a highly successful airstrike on FRELIMO's 4th Brigade HQ (Mobile) and a couple of ZANLA trucks. The SAS were initially tasked to ambush the expected ZANLA convoy, which was on its way from Maputo docks to Mapai, the major military garrison in the Gaza province of Moçambique. The area was well known to the SAS – as the month before Jack Malloch had dropped 22 paratroops free-fall, from his DC-7 aircraft, just east of Mapai. The Russian presence and support for the terrorist forces had resulted in the SAS dubbing the region "The Russian Front".

On 1st November a No 3 Squadron Dakota uplifted 16 SAS paratroops under the command of Captain Colin Willis from Mabalauta and dropped them after dusk, some 120 kilometres (75 miles) into Moçambique. On the return journey, the Dakota came under a barrage of 23-mm anti-aircraft cannon and 12,7 millimetre heavy machine fire from Mapai – sustaining no fewer than 23 hits (with some holes as big as a man's fist). Fortunately, nobody was injured.

During the night Colin Willis trekked the 15-km to the Mapai-Maputo road and laid landmines and claymores in the road. Despite a brief skirmish with two FRELIMO and one ZANLA – who were shot – the sound of an approaching convoy was heard, apparently of much greater strength than originally expected. The SAS withdrew to a safe position so as not to compromise their position as a result of the three dead enemies left at the ambush site. As luck would have it, the lead vehicle was an ammunition truck – and it went up in a blazing fireball when it struck the landmine that had been laid by the SAS. This effectively blocked the road, preventing the other convoy vehicles continuing to Mapai. The decision was then taken by Comops to send in the Hunters at first light the following day.

Flight Lieutenant Giles Porter (one of my earlier OCU students), piloting a No 4 Squadron Lynx, had the SAS 'A' Troop commander, Captain Bob McKenna aboard in order to get the latest Sitrep from the ground forces. The ammunition truck was still ablaze, but the pilot could see the remainder of the convoy vehicles hidden under dense trees. As Giles flew lower, he was greeted by the deafening roar of some 400 automatic rifles, several 23 millimetre anti-aircraft guns, machineguns and assorted missiles including the dreaded Strela. Colin Willis was heard to comment: "I rate that as the heaviest concentration of firepower that I have witnessed". Amazingly, neither the aircrews nor the Lynx had taken a single hit. Just as well, because shortly thereafter,

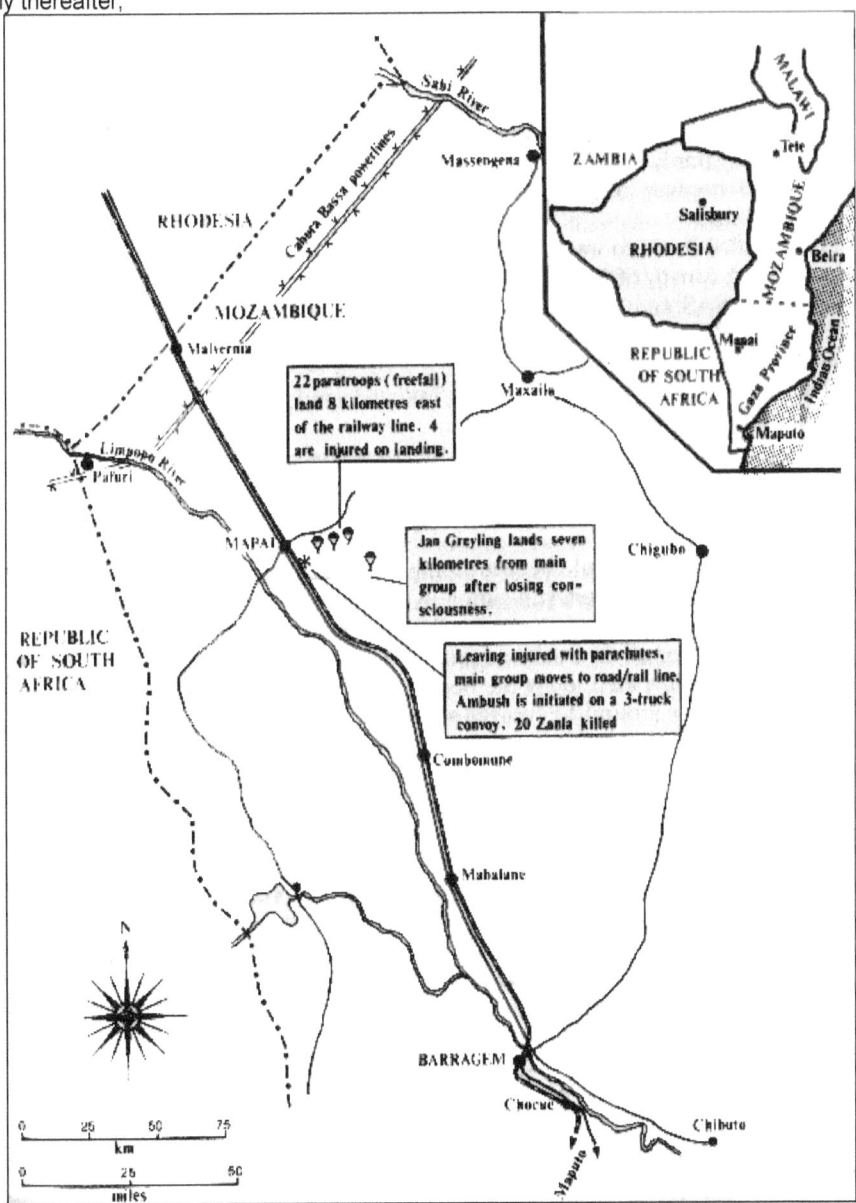

No 1 Squadron came to the rescue.

The Hunters swept in, locating their targets from the muzzle flashes of the weapons firing at the Lynx, and from the windscreens reflecting in the early-morning sunlight – a point the enemy had overlooked when attempting to hide their vehicles. By the time the Hunters had carried out their first few strikes, the scene below them resembled something out of a Vietnam movie. Ammunition trucks were burning and exploding terrorist rockets were zigzagging all over the show, the wrecks of vehicles were cart-wheeling in every direction and there were massive fireballs everywhere.

The smoke from the Hunters' 30 millimetre cannons added to the spectacle and often, as one Hunter swooped in to attack and a truck blew up behind it, the second Hunter would be flying through the debris from the first strike. For the next five hours an intense and spectacular land/air battle raged. The Hunters kept up the momentum, making strike after strike, hitting the vehicles, with one pair of aircraft replacing the next as their weaponry was exhausted and their time over target ran out; and they had to return to base to rearm and refuel in readiness for their next strike. And the defenders grimly hitting back with everything they had.

After the fourth airstrike, the Browns raiders decided discretion was the better part of valour and leaving the Blues to sort out the convoy, they vacated their foxholes and quickly made good their departure. However, Comops ordered the Browns back to make a full report on the damage inflicted.

Operation Melon Airstrikes (Log Extracts)
Air Strike No 736 - 15 October 1977
Aircrews:
- JR Blythe-Wood

Target: Op Melon – Convoy VK270500 Gaza Moz.
Result: 3 vehicles destroyed. 2 SAS wounded (JRT Wood)
Air Strike No 745 - 31 October 1977
Aircrew:
- JR Blythe-Wood

Target: Air Task 1181
Result: Take over
Air Strike No 746 - 1 November 1977
Aircrew:
- Giles Porter

Target: Lynx FAC for Hunter strike; Moçambique – ZANLA convoy Mapai / Maputo Rd
Result: Airstrike on FRELIMO Fourth Brigade HQ (Mobile)
Air Strike No 748 - 3 November 1977
Aircrew:
- Glen Pretorius

Target: Op Melon, with Hunters
Air Strike No 749 - 7 November 1977
Target: Air Task 1216, with Canberras
Air Strike No 750 - 13 November 1977
Aircrew:
- Vic Wightman

Target: Convoy Mapai – Mabalane Rd, Gaza
Result: 17 vehicles destroyed. Tank spares, ammo and Russian dictionary found

After the apprehension of returning to the scene, the SAS to their relief found the place totally devoid of the enemy. Around them lay the remains of what had been a convoy of brand new vehicles. All told, there were 21 damaged vehicles. Only one had managed to escape the carnage. They found a mobile operations centre, and the more they looked around, the more obvious it became that the Air Force and their Brownjob friends had taken on the whole FRELIMO 4th Brigade Headquarters. They had been moving up to Mapai in compliance with their orders to supply closer support to ZANLA and to set up a forward base to conduct the war against Rhodesian Security Forces. The security forces found enough evidence to convince them that the convoy was led, managed and organised by Russian advisers. It was the first time that the Rhodesians had seen definite proof that the Russians were operating in Mapai. The damage inflicted by the airstrikes was virtually complete – it was gratifying to see the amount of brand new Russian trucks, trailers, fuel and water bowsers, operations and command centres, support weapons and spares which had been rendered useless on their first trip from the Maputo docks. There were also bogies, track and ammunition for T34 tanks, making it the first indication of tanks in the Gaza Province – and the first time tanks had been found so close to any Rhodesian border. A ZANLA presence was also found in the form of two trucks, the remains of which carried ZANLA literature, uniforms and documents.

Because it was assessed that a few of the vehicles could be repaired and just to prevent that happening, the Hunters screamed in a few days later to put them out of action for good. There was only one body, but the evidence of used medical equipment, bloodied uniforms and helmets with skin attached to them, indicated that many had been wounded or killed. Subsequent intelligence confirmed that there had been fifty casualties.
The enemy, and their Soviet advisers in the *Russian Front*, had been dealt a very severe blow indeed.

Operation Partisan: 29 October to 5 November 1977

Operation *Partisan* consisted of mining ZIPRA routes in Zambia. The operation accounted for one Zambian National Defence Force officer and 1 ZNDF soldier killed, and 5 ZNDF injured (one of whom died later).

Operation Virile: November to 19 December 1977

Operation *Virile* entailed the blowing up of six road bridges, between Espungabera and Dombe, by the Selous Scouts, with air support by a K-Car, one G-Car, two Lynxes and a pair of Hunters. FAF 6 Chipinga was used by the Air Force for the close air support aircraft.

I had another reprieve from desk jockeying by being detached to FAF 1 - Wankie, in Lynx R 3048, on 9th December 1977. This was because of the need to release more operational pilots in the field. I had just got settled in my new, albeit familiar, surroundings when I was tasked to provide top cover over Victoria Falls. A break of three days followed because of a strained neck injury that made it extremely difficult for me to turn around to look in the small mirror on the port tail-boom. This twisting of the neck was necessary to verify rear engine propeller rotation during start up and in flight. The Wankie Colliery physiotherapist soon had me on the mend after connecting an interferential therapy machine (those machines that cause involuntary muscle spasms). The Nurse switched the machine on, turned a couple of knobs, and then left the therapy room. She had no sooner left than I started convulsing violently. The body twitching became progressively more pronounced, with me resembling a complete spastic. I didn't return for more torture.

Then on the 13th I carried out brief night flying circuits and NDB - non-directional beacon letdowns on the Wankie airstrip. Corporal Bezuidenhout came along for the ride.

On the 15th, Army Colonel Mike Shute requested an air reconnaissance of the minefields along the Zambezi. I got airborne with the Colonel and we landed at Sprayview airstrip at the Falls Township. I was briefed on the Bus Bleeper trials that were due to take place the next day. This was a Smersh (secret) operation that was planned to transport Rhodesian troops in a commandeered civilian bus. Then on the 16th, I flew a Mr Goodfellow from the Prime Minister's Department on the Bus Bleeper mission - all went according to plan and only minor fine-tuning adjustments were needed. I still don't know whether Goodfellow was the guy's genuine name, but suspected that this was used so as not to arouse undue suspicions.

I for one disliked, and even distrusted, a lot of the abuse that the Selous Scouts often subjected the Air Force to. However, in this case, SS Major Bert Sachse had been tasked to destroy the road bridges around Dombe. While Bert was doing his thing in the south-east, I was deployed in the opposite direction – in the north-west, doing my thing.

I duly got airborne in my trusty Lynx R 3048 on the 19th and carried out the two hour thirty minute top cover in the Panda-Ma-Tenga area as demanded from me. The mission was successfully completed without any undue risk or major dramas.

On landing, my job was complete, and so I loaded up my Lynx with Sergeant Wepener and LACs Sephton and Dormer and headed back to Thornhill. My No 4 Squadron Detachment to Wankie had lasted a mere ten days and I was thus able to chalk up another operation, successfully completed. Although it meant me returning to my desk job, I was well pleased by the fact that life in the Air Force permitted me to spend my R&R and the festive season with my family.

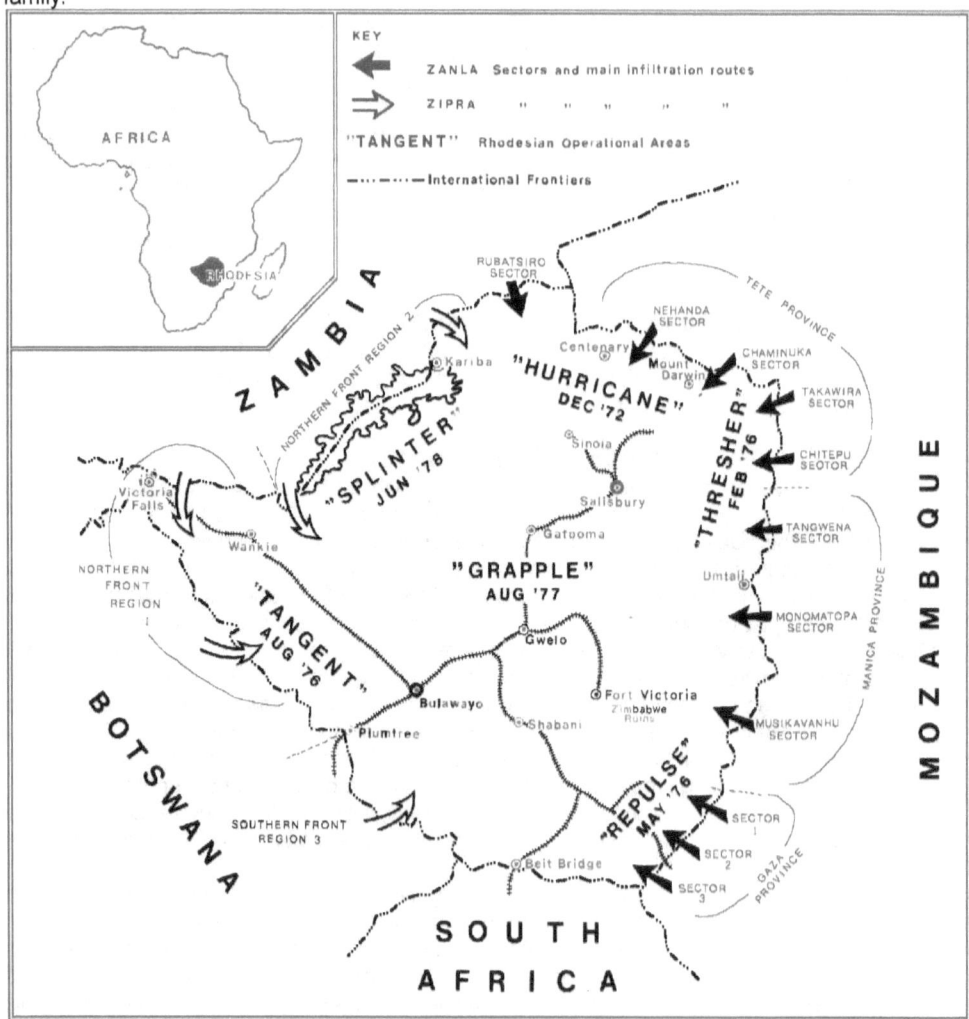

Air Strike Log: 08 to 10 February 1977 - Refer Nos 618 To 621
Aircrews:
- Ted Brent / Jim
- Al Bruce / Doug Pasea
- Greg Todd / Tony Merber
- Michael Borlace / John Jacobs
- Bill Sykes / Mark Jackson
- Mike Litson / Brian Crystal
- Ian Sheffield
- Bill Dawson / Carlos da Silveira

Target: VR067907, 10 n.m. north west of Mtoko
Result: Five Terrs killed, four African women killed, one African woman wounded.
Air Strike No 619 - 9 February 1977

Aircrew:
- Rich Brand
- Martin Lowrie

Target: Nyamzuwe, VR109901, 8 n.m. north of Mtoko
Air Strike No 620 - 9 February 1977
Aircrews:
- Mike Borlace / John Jacobs
- Bill Sykes / Mark Jackson
- Mike Litson / Brian Crystal
- Bill Dawson / Carlos da Silveira

Target: UR647365, 8 n.m. south west of Mrewa.
Result: Six terrs killed, four African local men killed, eight locals taken for questioning. (Suspect wrong grid ref – place called Hokodzi)

Mike recalls: "This (No 618) was a big punch-up along the side of some big bricks (hills) and the gooks were well holed up in rocks and caves, so the Cans (Canberras) came in and softened the whole area up with a couple of very good strikes. These were not easy to deliver on the side of the mountain."

"09/02/77 - One of the grid refs here is wrong, as the second contact was a return trip to the same place the next morning. I think the place was called Hokodzi."

FAF 8 – Grand Reef

Dick Gledhill, who was a PJI (Parachute Jump Instructor) in the Air Force, also served in One Commando of the Rhodesian Light Infantry. Dick committed some of his bush war experiences to paper and wrote a very interesting novel describing Fire Force tactics. Of particular significance is the historical fact that he was a Brownjob at Grand Reef when the FAF was attacked by some 200 gooks on 17th December 1977. His vivid description of the events preceding, during and after the incident, albeit fictionalised to some extent, does not detract from what goes through the minds of the Rhodesian airmen and soldiers who had witnessed the horrors of war.

FAF 8 was described thus: - "The airstrip at Grand Reef, not far from the town of Umtali, is quite a beautiful place with its rugged backdrop of the Vumba Mountains rising majestically to the south-east. The sealed runway, gently sloping with the contour of the land, gives the impression of following the curvature of the earth. In peacetime it would be a pleasant enough place to idle the time away waiting for a plane. War had transformed the place into a rough, stark fortress. On the western side of the runway, earth revetments surrounded the Fire Force base, dotted at intervals with bunkers and machinegun posts. At the northern end, high walls constructed from fuel drums filled with sand protected the aircraft from attack, with ceilings of wire netting to stop mortar bombs from landing. Inside the base were buildings and tents found in any camp to house the personnel required operating a military establishment. Surrounding the whole area was a minefield with a barbed wire fence."

Dick Gledhill, as a matter of interest, was born in Kenya, completed his schooling in the UK, joined the Australian army for three years, and in mid-1970s returned to Africa and enlisted as a trooper in 1 Commando, RLI. He saw action on Fire Force operations inside Rhodesia and on external raids during the bush war. He later transferred to the Rhodesian Air Force where, as a Sergeant at the Parachute Training School, he instructed Rhodesia's paratroops. He has more than 2000 parachute jumps to his credit. He left Zimbabwe after Independence in 1980 and returned to Australia.

Squadron Leader Derrick de Kock (elder brother to Harry Harwood de Kock, who was one of our fellow pilot trainees on 16 PTC – but who failed to make the grade), had this to say in his foreword to Dick's book: -

"While reading this book, memories of the hundreds of tough, dedicated young men, both black and white, who passed through the Parachute Training School, came flooding back. In 1961, five Royal Rhodesian Air Force volunteers, including myself, went to RAF Abbingdon in England and underwent training as Parachute Jump Instructors. Later that year, with the help of four Royal Air Force secondments, the Rhodesian Air Force Parachute Training School at New Sarum was in business. Initially we only trained 'C' (Rhodesia) Squadron of the British 22nd Special Air Service, with a limit of twenty men on each course.

"After Rhodesia's Unilateral Declaration of Independence from Great Britain in November, 1965, our RAF secondments went home and nothing much happened until 1970. At this time the Rhodesian SAS were operating outside our borders and it became evident that High Altitude Low Opening (HALO) Fee-fall training was required. It also became apparent that it was necessary to deploy more troops into the Fire Force contacts and the only way this could be achieved in Rhodesia was by parachute.

"The RAF had left us with a book of parachute rules but, by the early 1970s, with our bush war escalating on all fronts, these became obsolete and new methods had to be employed to gain the upper hand. The methods devised by us subsequently changed the way paratroops were deployed the world over. Our staff grew to five officers and over 75 PJI sergeants and dispatchers. The number of men trained in each course increased from 20 to 240 and three Fire Forces were permanently in the field (each with a PJI and two other dispatchers).

"Static line drop heights were reduced from 1000 feet to 500 feet, and, on many occasions, as low as 300 feet. HALO drops were increased to over 20,000 feet and often conducted at night with the navigation being done by a PJI with his head sticking out of the door during the final run-in, map reading the way to the target. Trees were deliberately used as drop zones as they provided cover on landing and open ground was avoided. Yet the injury rate remained below 0·7 %.

"During my last year as the Commanding Officer of the Rhodesian Air Force Parachute Training School, over 14,000 operational jumps were recorded and some troops of the RLI and the RAR recorded three operational jumps in one day. Most were done from DC3 Dakotas but on occasion troops, fuel and ammunition were dropped from a DC 7F.

"The staff of the Rhodesian Air Force Parachute Training School came from all corners of the globe including British, Welsh, Irish, Scottish, Australian and American. I was privileged to lead such a diverse, multicultural band of dedicated instructors, one of whom was Dick Gledhill." Derrick de Kock wrote this foreword to Dick's book in January 1997 – over 20 years after the attack on FAF 8.

Attack on Forward Airfield 8 – Grand Reef: 17 December 1977

On about 16th December 1977, Air Headquarters sent a warning signal to Officer Commanding FAF 8 – Grand Reef – Squadron Leader Rob MacGregor that the Forward Airfield was soon to be attacked. The message indicated that Security Forces had captured a detailed map of Grand Reef, presumed to have been made out by a casual worker on the camp. The contents were passed onto the Army Colonel, but he was sceptical that the large military complex would, or could be attacked.

The following night, the Brownjobs were all watching the TV "Bless 'em All Show", and thus no patrols were deployed. It seemed that a night summer storm was brewing, with thunder and lightning evident in the distance. At about ten o'clock that evening, Camp Commandant Robin Watson hit the sack. Robin was using one of the Department of Civil Aviation Authority – CAA – buildings, at the lower end of the camp, as his bedroom-cum-office. Then an hour before midnight, the Air Force Camp Commandant was awakened by what sounded like thunder, and with hailstones drumming on the roofs of buildings. When he peered outside, he discovered that the 'hailstones' were aglow, and that a steady stream of tracer was passing overhead. The 'thunder' turned out to be a tattoo of mortar bombs and rockets landing for the most part on the Army Camp. Shrapnel, or a bullet, pierced his windowpane.

Robin got dressed and reported to the Command bunker, and was joined by SWO Phil Clarke, who had a narrow escape when a rifle grenade exploded on the sandbag parapet outside his room. The explosion expedited his arrival at the Command bunker, absolutely starkers – and had to be reminded by the Camp Commandant to cover his nakedness, before volunteering for ammunition re-supplies duties. Meanwhile, Gun-pit No 1 was laying down sustained gunfire on the attacker's flank. The MAG gun operator, Air Force Territorial Force member Corporal Anstee, called the Command bunker on the radio for a resupply of ammunition.

SWO Phil Clarke, and another TF, volunteered to cross the open space of the aircraft parking area to go to the armoury from which to supply the gun-pit with enough 7·62 ammunition to continue repelling the attackers. This they did commendably, considering the hazards and that both remained at the gun-pit to assist the TF MAG gunner in re-loading and changing over-heated barrels. In addition, both AFVs (Air Force Regiment Armoured Fighting Vehicles) left the comparative safety of their revetments to join the battle, but were driven back precipitously by rockets aimed directly at them. They had both fired flares, but unfortunately without arming the fuses. In due course, all the firing ceased.

The Air Force escaped injury. The Brownjobs were not as lucky – a signals operator was killed by an air-burst, and two soldiers were severely wounded by mortar/rocket-fire. Squadron Leader Rob MacGregor casevaced the injured to Umtali General Hospital with the FAF spare Alouette helicopter, and in Robin Watson's words "had to play trains, because of the extremely low cloud base, by following the railway line through the mountains."

The Gooks also suffered losses. One was found dead, abandoned. His clothing was blown off and this was thought to have been caused by firing his last mortar bomb without the base plate, the bomb had landed very close to his own position. Blood spoor was also found during the retreat, so presumably there were other casualties as well.

Operation Acrobat (Russian Front): 12 February 1978

Operation *Acrobat* was carried out by South African troops disguised as Rhodesian Special Air Service soldiers, operating from Chiredzi and FAF 7 Buffalo Range, into the Gaza Province of Moçambique

In December 1977, fifty-five SADF 'A' Group 1-Reconnaissance Commando members assembled in Durban for a period of intensive training for a Smersh operation, destination unknown to the individuals. They expected to be deployed to SWA/Namibia, but when they boarded Dakotas instead of the expected C-130 Hercules aircraft at Louis Botha Air Force Base, they soon discovered that their destination was Rhodesia. Once on board, they changed into Rhodesian camouflaged uniforms and were given an in-flight briefing that they were headed for Funnyland – otherwise known as the 'Russian Front' or Moçambique. They received their orders from the SAS at Chiredzi – with tours of duty being about three months long. Rotations were made with 1-Recce's 'B' Group, with several soldiers doing up to four tours, for the whole of 1978.

Amongst the early deployments was Lieutenant Corrie Meerholz – with the SADF personnel forming 'D' Squadron of the Rhodesian Special Air Service. From FAF 7 Buffalo Range, the commando established its forward base at Mabalauta. Captain Hannes Venter commanded the unit, and spent most of his time on Telstar and control as a passenger in a Rhodesian Air Force Lynx. He spent a lot of time over-flying the Gaza Province, taking off from FAF 7 in the mornings, and using Mabalauta for refuelling stops during the day. They would locate patrols, establish radio contact and carry out supply drops. Airborne times would be up to eight hours a day – they would also patrol roads and carry out airstrikes on any vehicles seen – often being on the receiving end of heavy ground fire.

The Lynxes also acted as escorts for the Dakotas when they were deploying paratroopers, which inevitably attracted ground fire. The following quote from Peter Stiff's *The Silent War* warrants repeating: ".... To combat this (Lynx escorts for the Dakotas), they used the hair-raising tactic of diving down to fifty metres and strafing the guns with rockets and napalm to divert attention from the troopers. Pilots were rotated fortnightly, when the relief's arrived at Chiredzi fresh and eager to do battle. Hannes, who had spent almost three months on a diet of adrenaline, dodging FRELIMO ground fire with previous pilots on a day to day basis, developed a jaundiced view of their enthusiasm. This in no way detracted from the admiration he felt for them." Is that not a nice, worthy compliment for the Lynx pilots of No 4 Squadron?

The story of Lieutenant Douw Steyn's first deployment by No 3 Squadron Dakota into Moçambique is quite humorous, in that I got to know Douw well many years later, and had the opportunity to reminisce about the apprehension that was a part of life in those days. Douw recalled, and I quote verbatim:

"I remember it with vivid clarity. It was just after last light when we readied to jump by static line south of Mapai. We had ammunition and supplies for a three-week stint. We hooked up our static lines. My Boss, Lieutenant Kokkie du Toit, was first in the door, I was second and the other eight operators jostled behind me. The Dakota unexpectedly attracted 14,5-mm ground fire. I was scared stiff and watched fearfully as the glowing dotted lines of tracer seemed to reach up for the trundling old Dak. How they missed, I did not know. To my utter amazement Kokkie made no attempt to withdraw from the door. He merely stood there patiently waiting, as if it was a routine practice. As if it was just a firework display. The Rhodesian jumpmaster was also unconcerned.

" 'Surely he had the authority to call off this bullshit. What was the bloody fool up to? Sod this,' I thought, my heart pumping. 'They must be mad. Absolutely out of their minds. How can they drop us in shit like this?' The green light flashed and "I knew they were really insane". "Go!"

"I tumbled out of the door behind Kokkie. We landed uncomfortably in a sandalwood plantation. One operator was badly injured by a dry stick penetrating his arm and was casevaced the next day. FRELIMO knew we were around, but not exactly where. We remedied their lack of knowledge when the Rhodesian chopper came in for the casevac the next morning."

Authors note: The story did not end there. To quote from Peter Stiff, Douw did in fact do himself justice. The Recces began walking their planned route, intending to ambush the road and railway line, but things did not work out, because FRELIMO were hard on their tracks. They spent the day on the run and were lucky to survive an ambush. They had no vehicle mines because of weight limitations, but did have some South African *Rimi* anti-personnel mines. Douw Steyn, as the team's engineer, improvised a vehicle mine by combining P4 plastic explosive with one of their mechanisms. They knew that when FRELIMO vehicles struck mines, their tactic was to rapidly evacuate and disperse into the veld on both sides of the road. Douw buried his improvised vehicle mine in the road and camouflaged it, then imaginatively positioned ten anti-personnel mines on both sides of the road. Sure enough a vehicle appeared and detonated the landmine. True to form, the surviving FRELIMO soldiers leapt from the truck and dashed straight into Douw's devil's garden of anti-personnel mines. Twenty FRELIMO soldiers paid the ultimate price for their carelessness.

However, shortly thereafter, the Recces also mounted attacks in the Madulo Pan area, and during a contact on 11th February 1978, Lieutenant J H Kokkie du Toit (officially from 1RR) was killed in action. Because of bad guti at that time, a casevac couldn't reach them to evacuate the body. Douw had to carry his Boss around, continuously evading FRELIMO hunter groups, for two days, for the guti to lift. Eventually a helicopter arrived, with a No 4 Squadron Lynx, to casevac both Kokkie's body, and Douw, who had sustained a splinter injury to his foot. Douw was treated at the Triangle Hospital for his foot – plus a self inflicted injury to his buttocks and legs when a detonator he was working on exploded below his chair.

In another Operation O incident, Danny Svoboda was one of two Alouette helicopter pilots who flew over the Mapai area to extract a group of 'D' Squadron (SADF Recces) that had had two contacts with a FRELIMO mobile reaction unit known as X-ray forces. The Rhodesian pilots had to switch on the spotlight in the lead aircraft during their night casevac but also attracted a lot of ground fire. Danny was leading, and would switch off his lights whenever they needed to over-fly the rail sidings en route back to Rhodesia. Using exceptional flying skill combined with good luck and daring, they successfully evaded the ground fire without damage. Their final hurdle was the power line of the Cabora Bassa hydro-electric scheme, which ran north-to-south just within the Moçambique border – which they skipped over. Immediately afterwards one Alouette ran out of fuel, forcing them to land.

They were still uncertain if they were back in Rhodesia or still in Moçambique. Fortunately, as it turned out, they were just over the border. Danny Svoboda took off in the one with fuel remaining. Continuing the spotlight technique, he stayed just above treetop level and reached

Mtoko FAF 5: 1 to 7 February 1978

Sergeant Tweedy Reid-Daly was the K-Car Alouette III No 5719 gunner to Terence Murphy, deployed to Mtoko during the week 1st to 7th February. He recalls an interesting story whilst trooping with dummy drops during his stint in the bush.

"The Fire Force, K-Car together with the G-Cars, set out from Mtoko to carry out dummy drops across a river near the Moçambique border. As we neared the river the ground rose up to a hillock, on the other side of which ran the river. Flying over the hillock we noticed that, although there were huts and chickens, there was no sign of any inhabitants but down to and along the side of the river were well worn path and fishing / washing spots. We flew on and carried out our dummy drop exercise and on the return decided to fly back over the small compound we had seen.

"Directly overhead the compound, which still looked deserted, we suddenly encountered the familiar crackling of rifle fire and felt we had been hit. We flew on down the other side of the hill and checked temperatures, pressure and RPM's, - all okay except we were running rapidly out of tail rotor control and within seconds it had failed altogether. With one of the G-Cars as top cover we flew on to an old runway, on which the grass was about waist height, if not higher, and would have covered an ant-bear hole, but were pleased to see some Brownjobs parked on the left side of the runway. However, an old Bedford truck was parked too close to the centre of the runway and after frantic radio calls managed to get some action from the Brownjobs. To our horror, as we were descending and ready to put down the army driver turned the truck directly across our flight path instead of turning off the runway.

"It must have been a combination of good piloting and luck that Terence managed to coax the Alo over the truck, the cab of which disappeared by what seemed like inches below the nose of the helicopter. We managed to gain some more height and one of the G-Cars directed us – by now two very nervous and dry mouthed crew members – to another abandoned airfield on the other side of a range of hills, the Alo was fishtailing badly until we reduced speed. On approaching the now abandoned airstrip we had a quick briefing, it would be a good idea for me to hold onto the park brake and once down would be told to brake hard.

"Now to get to the park brake in a K-Car you had to unbuckle your seat harness and lean forward. All good and well, but once in position I noticed that a short distance in front of my face was the instrument panel and still remember thinking what I was going to look like if things went wrong. Finally we managed to put down without incident other than two dirty great skid marks (– on the ground!). We scrambled out with our weapons with Terence mumbling something about never wanting to see another helicopter in his life again. We found we had taken a bit of ground fire, the tail rotor cables had been severed, the tail boom, engine and I think the fuel tank had been hit and our brand new trusty "put-put" had been mortally wounded.

"We were flown back to Mtoko while the Brownjobs looked after our Alo while waiting for a repair crew to arrive.

"A day or two later we climbed into a PRAW aircraft to be flown out to retrieve our now serviceable Alo. We lined up at the end of the runway, the pilot running through his cockpit-checks, selecting flaps down as part of it, when we noticed that the pilots 'mitts' were nowhere near the flap selector and the flaps were by now doing their own thing by running back and forth – up and down. Terence nudged me, we were both sitting behind the two front seats, and whispered "Is this normal?" pointing to the flaps, I assured him that it wasn't and on consulting with our PRAW pilot on this matter was assured that it was okay and that it had been like this for a couple of weeks! (This is the same aircraft that Bruce Edward had also flown in).

"With two fidgeting and slightly apprehensive Bluejobs on board the throttle was opened and we rapidly gained speed. To our astonishment and some distance down the runway we noticed that the ASI needle was still firmly resting on the little pin where the zero indication mark was. The pilot realising that he had a problem shut the throttle and after fierce braking came to a halt at the end of the runway. The flaps were still doing their own thing.

"We clambered out of the PRAW aircraft and an irate Terence, using colourful phrases not exactly common to the good old Queens English, assured our most apologetic PRAW pilot that he would never fly in one of these things again and would fetch our aircraft on condition we were ferried by Air Force aircraft. He then promptly refused the PRAW pilots offer of a lift back to the top, and with bone dome and map case in hand stomped off towards the camp with yours truly trying to keep up.
"Our Alo was finally retrieved."

Air Strike No 777 - 6 to 9 February 1978
Aircrew:
- Mike Borlace / Beaver Shaw

Target: Contact C/s 14 and 42. Trooping C/s 43A
Result: Deploy dogs, top cover and casevac landmine victim. Op sorties 6th, 7th and 9th Feb.

Mike Borlace recalls: "This was a series of ops that started with an ambush of the Selous Scouts in which Basil Moss's son Keith was killed, and subsequently a white hitch-hiker was abducted and eventually taken to Moçambique - John Kenny (or Kenward perhaps?) - We just had the one helicopter but made contact with the group several times - this guy John subsequently wrote an account of the experience after the war - and we were apparently within yards of getting him several times."

Fire Force Charlie – Shabani: January 1978

Commanding the three or four Fire Forces placed an additional strain on available Air Force manpower resources. It came as no surprise to me that my turn would arrive sooner rather than later. Staff Officers were needed to perform Operational Commands as well.

I spent a short spell as Officer Commanding Fire Force Charlie. This entailed commanding a highly mobile tactical air support function with the Support Commando, 1 RLI - the crack, all white, Rhodesian Light Infantry unit. Aircraft allocation was four Alouette helicopters. One K-Car was fitted with Hispano 20-mm cannon and also carried the Army airborne commander, who would deploy his stopper groups using the remaining three G-Cars.

The Fire Forces invariably operated from the established FAFs – FAF 4 and 5 Mount Darwin and Mtoko for operations in the north and north-east, FAF 7 Buffalo Range for operations in the south-east, and FAF 8 Grand Reef near Umtali, for operations in the east. However, as the war progressed, the Fire Forces also deployed from numerous other locations like the JOC centres, Ruda in the Honda Valley, Fort Victoria (JOC *Repulse*), Mabalauta in the Lowveld, and from Shabani – as in the case of Fire Force Charlie. The tactical advantage of the Fireforce system was its flexibility – all that was needed was a reasonable airstrip.

The Fire Force principle required a high level of co-operation between the Air Force and the Army and this was maintained at all times. The Army provided the combat troops while the Air Force supplied the helicopters, fixed wing aircraft, pilots and its deadly firepower. The Commando OC directed ground operations from the K-Car from an orbit high enough above the contact area. The troop-carrying Alouette helicopters ferried troops to and from a contact zone, carried out casualty evacuations and re-supplying ground troops with arms and ammunition. The object was to deploy the required troops on the ground in a given area in as short a time as possible. Once the G-Cars/Z-Cars had disgorged the first wave of troops, they returned to base to collect the second or even third wave. Depending on distances, the second wave would sometimes proceed towards the contact area in vehicles loaded with drums of fuel for the helicopters, to reduce the turn-around time.

Acting in support of each Fire Force was a No 4 Squadron fixed wing aircraft – initially the Provost, then the Trojan, and latterly the Reims-Cessna F337 Lynx. Although ungainly with its pull-push power plants and twin tail booms, it made an excellent support weapons platform and could deliver its Sneb rockets, frantan (napalm) and twin Browning ·303 front gun fire with deadly accuracy. The Lynx usually initiated the attack while the 20mm Hispano cannon of the K-Car hammered away in support. Ground troops were put in as stop groups, to prevent the terrorists from escaping. After the initial airstrikes had gone in, the main sweep line moved forward toward the centre of the contact area, either killing the terrorists or driving them on to the guns of the stop groups. Any time during an operation, stick leaders could call on the K-Car and the Lynx for air support.

Fire Force Charlie – **at Shabani**

In order to maintain my flying currency, I commandeered Lynx R 3240 on 22nd January 1978 to carry out a rather too short thirty-minute general flying sortie in the vicinity of Shabani, with its many granite rocky outcrops.

The RLI was well known for achieving the highest enemy kill rates. Their high spirits would continue well into the night, more often than not resulting in high jinx. After one particular contact, their rowdy behaviour got the better of me. I got annoyed when the Commando Commander careered their staff car around the Air Force camp, ripping out our tent pegs, screeching with laughter as our tents collapsed, and generally just making a nuisance of himself. We conscientious airmen were trying to get some shut-eye, but there was no luck in store for us. As the most senior Bluejob on site, I lodged an objection in the strongest possible terms. Although one had learnt at an early stage that Officers should refrain from confronting drunken bums, the rowdiness left me with little option but to appeal to their better judgement - all to no avail. The RLI were hell-bent on letting off steam. The next morning I complained to the CO, but no apology was forthcoming from the Brownjobs.

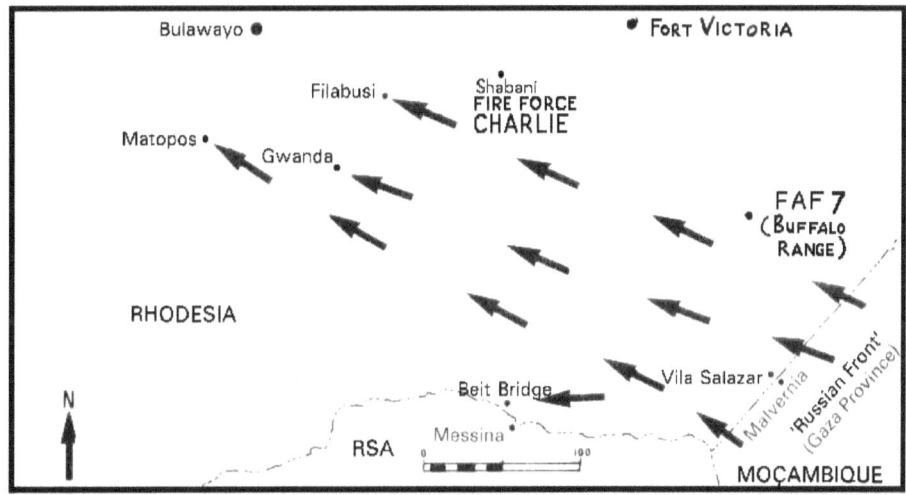

To confront ZANLA infiltration from the Russian Front into Southern Matabeleland
(See also the Air Strike Map, at the back of the book)

I was not prepared to let the matter ride. A couple of days later, the Fire Force was visited by high ranking General officers. I mentioned the unruly behaviour to the Air Force Chief of Staff, hoping that he would whisper in his counterpart's ear on the way to the main JOC at Fort Victoria. Whether he did so or not, I don't know. I also gave my Station Commander a feedback report. It appeared I was somewhat unpopular regarding my respect for military order and discipline.

On the positive side, Fire Forces achieved spectacular successes. It was an economical method of deploying highly mobile fighting units rapidly to scenes of unrest - without having to rely on the complex infrastructures required in the establishment of semi-permanent forward airfields - FAFs. In his book *One Commando*, ex-PJI Sergeant Dick Gledhill did an excellent job of describing several Fire Force actions. He mentions FAF 4 Mount Darwin, FAF 5 Mtoko, FAF 7 Buffalo Range, FAF 8 Grand Reef, and several assaults on terrorist camps in Moçambique. The tactics involved the use of the ground support Lynxes, with heliborne stop groups and K-Cars, plus airstrikes involving the Canberra bombers. Although his novel is fiction, it is very much based on fact. He was on the ground when FAF 8 was attacked by over 200 ZANLA terrorists on 17th December 1977, and later transferred to the Air Force serving as a PJI under Squadron Leader Derrick de Kock.

Chris Cocks, a stick leader in 3 Commando RLI, also does an excellent job of describing several Fire Force actions in his book, *Fireforce*.

Despite the very long hours, strain and tensions, I enjoyed my stint as Officer Commanding Fire Force Charlie. Shabani was not too bad. The PWD (public works department) guys had laid on running water and electricity for us, and the runway and small hardstanding had been tarred.

And so, after a while, it was back to Thornhill, to once again catch up with my uncontrollable OCAW in-tray. I maintained my flying currency by flying Air Sub-Lieutenant Brick Bryson to New Sarum on 2nd March 1978.

On 14th March, I flew the No 4 Squadron technical Warrant Officer, Jim Light to Air Headquarters for a meeting. I needed to brush up on some air weaponry and get in some instrument flying prior to another looming FAF 1 "retread stint". That same day I carried out an operational shoot, firing 400 rounds air-to-ground, 8 Bubs (break-up-bombs) and 8 x 37-mm Sneb rockets.

My choice of instrument flying was just as well. A week later an abnormal cold front bringing in the guti weather meant that actual instrument flying was carried out with some JPs as my safety pilots. ASL's Ray Haakonsen and John Kidson witnessed my NDB, VOR and radar controlled GCAs. I was now ready for my next FAF 1 deployment.

I had occasion to revisit Fire Force Charlie on 1st June 1978. It was not to be. My task was an Admin Staff Visit. My OC 'B' Squadron GSU Air Lieutenant 'Danger' Ncube, caterer Warrant Officer Danny van der Merwe, Security Officer Flight Sergeant Pete Horsborough and I took off from Thornhill in a Lynx to visit ADR - Air Detachment *Repulse,* FAF 7 Buffalo Range and FFC at Shabani. About forty-five minutes out we encountered a lot of low cloud, with 'guti' conditions moving in rapidly from the south-east. I decided to abort my journey to the Lowveld and I set course for Shabani. I found a gap in the clouds near Mashaba and spiralled to 'victor mike below' - VMC - visual meteorological conditions below cloud base. Then my problems started. The mountain range tops were sticking into the bottom of the cloud blanket. I managed to fly through a saddle but once on the other side I was faced with another range of hills in my path, running at right angles to my line of flight. The hilltops were in cloud. I turned round and headed back on my reciprocal track, but then discovered that my 'gap' through the saddle was no more. The cloud base had lowered, merging the mountain range with the cloud. I could not take a chance in view of the fact that missing the gap would mean crashing into the Mashaba Mountains. I then continued my low-level orbit and was barely some thirty feet above ground level. I couldn't find any other gaps and then did something very stupid. Instead of initiating a climbing spiral through the low cloud, I relied on my senses and previous Fire Force Charlie experience; I headed towards where I thought there was low ground in the range of hills between my position and Shabani airfield.

We were literally skimming the treetops. The ground was rising. All of a sudden I flew into a puff of cloud and lost sight of the ground. I thrust both throttles wide open, pulled the nose up and initiated the steep short take-off technique, with a touch of flap, hoping that I would clear any looming obstructions directly in front of my flight path. But I had four souls on board. With the extra weight, the response wasn't all that good. 'Danger' and Danny were mean heavyweights. That just added to my problems. Having committed myself to a climb straight ahead, I pulled the Lynx as close to the stall as I dared and hoped for the best. I could kick myself for not opting for the spiral climb when I had the opportunity. I expected to fly into the hillside. Fortunately, somebody up there was looking after me. My Guardian Angel tested my vertigo in the 8/8th cloud and I flew the next thirty minutes on instruments, landing back at Thornhill. I was lucky to record mission "aborted". My subordinates thought I was the greatest since bubble gum - they didn't seem to mind that our intended Staff Visit to ADR FAF 7 and FFC was a failure. It was, after all, a very narrow escape.

On 5th June 1978 Flight Lieutenant Ken Law - an old ex-OCU student of mine flew safety pilot for me during a formal instrument flying sortie, with NDB and radar controlled GCA letdowns. That night I flew my second sortie of the day, which included a quickie ground controlled approach. Tudor Thomas would be away and my role was three fold - take over as Acting OC FAF 1, No 4 Squadron relief pilot, and report for Operation *Elbow* air support for SAS Special Forces duties.

Operation Elbow: 1 January to 12 June 1978

Throughout January and February 1978 the Special Branch had been monitoring ZIPRA movements close to the Botswana/Rhodesia border. SB Mike Howie established that a ZIPRA transit camp about 15 km south of Kazungula and some six kilometres across the border inside Botswana was being used by terrorists along the Bulawayo/Plumtree railway line; robberies, landmine incidents, disciplinary killings and attacks on isolated farmers. The Special Air Services 'B' Troop was based up at the game rangers' houses on the banks of the Zambezi, a few kilometres from Victoria Falls. The SAS were monitoring ZIPRA movements, sending in a four-man reconnaissance team to select hot-pursuit ambush sites. The SAS was successful in ambushing a Botswana Defence Force/ZIPRA convoy, but this led to Botswana closing their Kazungula border with Rhodesia.

By March 1978 OC 'B' Troop SAS Captain Colin Willis had set up his tactical headquarters at Deka forward camp, a few kilometres from the Zambian border. They planned to attack the ZIPRA DK 1 and DK 2 terrorist camps, and to mine the road between Kabanga Mission and Simani Mine in Zambia. The Zambian Army Brigade headquarters was established at the mission. ZIPRA was known to be using Simani as a staging post for their DK camp incursions into the Lupane region of Matabeleland.

On 23rd March 1978 I was deployed to FAF 1 in Lynx R 3417 with my technician Sergeant Rautering. That night I took Senior Aircraftman Andrews up with me for a spot of night flying, in order to maintain my currency on type. One of the engines on Lynx R 3140 was surging and I took Sergeant Rautering up for a quick engine air test.

On March 25th I flew Captain Colin Willis and Special Branch D Birch, providing top cover for the Special Air Service 'B' Troop's recovery by helicopter to their Deka base. Several chopper lifts were required to pick up a lot of equipment, which the Special Branch was anxious to get their hands on. One SAS call-sign could not be located and it was decided that I should carry out a search the next day. Contact was established during the night and I got airborne again at first light the next morning with Army Medic Staff Sergeant Wiltshire to locate the lost call-sign. I landed at Binga to drop off the Medic.

On the 27th, I did convoy cover, landing at Cewali. Two days later, I was called to an ambush at Mananda Dam, for Telstar duties and I then routed to Woodvale for fuel, continued on to Brigade Headquarters at Kumalo, returning to Wankie after a decent three hours forty minute mission. On the last day of the month I carried out a reconnaissance sortie of all the Matetsi farm homesteads.

I flew a night flying sortie with NDB letdown on 2nd April and ended this short detachment spell the next morning by returning to base with Sergeants Pete Billet and Rautering. But I would return a month later. My Mahogany Bomber 'in-tray' needed attention – and besides, it was that time of the year to commence preparations for Ministry of Defence submissions on routine Major/Minor works.

My next detachment to FAF 1 lasted from 5th to 12th May 1978. Captain Fred Watts and his 1 Commando RLI had meanwhile also been deployed in support of Colin Willis and his SAS. I duly positioned Wankie in Lynx 3405, in order to take over my favourite, R 3048. The next morning I carried out a reconnaissance of Vic Falls airport - invariably to offer moral support for the South African tourist flights to the Victoria Falls.

On 7th May I was tasked to carry out a Telstar mission for the SAS, flying between Deka on the Zambezi River and along the Zambian road towards Simani Mine. The SAS had successfully blown up Alfred Nkita Mangena, the ZIPRA army commander (the number 2 i/c to Joshua Nkomo) - about 5 km south of Kabanga Mission. Colin Willis had scrambled a couple of helicopters with a small stick, hoping to recover the 'big fish' body, but they were beaten to it - the body had already been taken away by the time the helicopters got there.

On May 11th, I escorted a pair of 'Spiders' - helicopters, who hot-extracted one of Fred Watts' RLI chaps on a casevac from the Operation *Elbow* area. The following day my relief arrived from Thornhill. Lynx R 3034 was now overdue its routine second line servicing and I needed to return the aircraft to base. I accordingly flew Sergeant Nobby Clark and SAC Brooker back to No 4 Squadron. I resumed my desk job, just in time to submit my Estimates of Expenditure to the Secretary for Defence – obviously through the Station Commander – as well catch some well earned rest and recuperation.

My third on-the-trot deployment to FAF 1 lasted from 6th to 19th June 1978. I flew the courier Lynx to the FAF to relieve the 4 Squadron pilot for his return to base. I took over his Lynx R 3034.

My detachment got off to a good start. My first mission on the 7th was a lengthy top cover sortie over the Kariangwe area. Then immediately thereafter I was dispatched to Binga to uplift a Field Reserve volunteer Mr Boyd, and a CMED official Mr Stuart, plus urgent documents which were needed back at Wankie. I then had a couple of days of inactivity.

On 11th June 1978 my airtask was escorting, and providing top cover for the 'B' Troop SAS trans-border deployment by Spiders (code-word for helicopters). Trooping took two hours. It would appear that either the Zambians were aware of the activity, or that a punch-up had occurred. There was a call for a hot-extraction the next morning and I duly escorted the two helicopters back into Zambia. Operation *Elbow* had unfortunately claimed another SF victim and I sadly learned that Second Lieutenant Falzoi had been killed in action.

On 13th June I was requested to carry out a search and rescue mission for a lost police patrol. I agreed to take Section Officer Weinel along with me, which was just as well because we were able to locate the patrol at Lusulu. The reconnaissance had taken slightly over an hour. Later in the day I also carried out a meaningful top cover mission for 'B' troop SAS. They asked me to land at Deka and I duly uplifted Majors Pat Mincher and Peter Matkovitch for FAF 1. That night I carried out NF continuation training and also squeezed in a non-directional beacon letdown in slightly over half an hour. The 14th was a day of rest.

On 15th June 1978 there was a railway line explosion at Matetsi so I recce'd along the railway but found nothing. The perpetrators were long gone. Then later during the day it was back to provide top cover trooping for the SAS. The next day I was off to Wankie National Park airfield to uplift Squadron Leader Tudor Thomas for his return to the FAF to resume command. I had enjoyed standing in for him during his absence - it certainly made the days pass quickly, attending to all the matters that go into commanding a forward airfield. I had no sooner dropped Tudor off when I was off on a 'secret' mission with Special Branch (dispatching SAM-7s to Salisbury). My third sortie on the 16th was to drop Lieutenant Barthorpe and Ministry of Works official Hangartner at Wankie Main airfield, and I then continued to provide top cover for the Spiders who were re-supplying the SAS in Zambia. My fourth sortie of the day was top cover following a sighting of ZANLA terrorists at Dandanda.

Some decent flying was flown on the 17th. The ground forces assaulted targets in the Kariangwe area and I remained airborne for over three hours providing top cover. In the afternoon I was tasked to resupply the FFD - Field Force Detachment at Wankie National. Then early the next day I was tasked to carry out a dawn and dusk top cover for the helicopters.

My spell at Wankie was drawing to a close. I had enjoyed Acting as FAF Commander in Tudor's absence, conducted meaningful flying, and was ready to now enjoy my umpteenth honeymoon. I was probably approaching my limit to the good old Air Force saying "Absence makes the heart grow fonder". And so it came to pass that I returned to Thornhill, Gwelo, with Lynx R 3034, and my technicians Sergeant Logan and SAC McKillop.

Operation Turmoil: 26 February – 6 to 10 March 1978

Operation *Turmoil* was the airstrikes and attack on the Kavalamanja ZIPRA staging post (Mushika area, Zambia) by the Air Force Hunters and Canberras, together with various Army elements.

Information on the staging post first came to light in August 1976 when Special Branch heard that ZIPRA occupied a camp with Zambian soldiers and Chinese instructors. The camp was situated sixteen kilometres west of Feira, in Zambia (at the point where the Zambian, Moçambique and Rhodesia borders meet, on the Zambezi River). It was also known by various other names such as Geneva, Kanyemba as well as Feira Base. Canberras were tasked to target photo-reconnaissance but the interpreters found nothing suspicious. Then at the end of June, early July 1977, an SAS recce team was deployed; they also found no positive evidence of Rhodesian dissidents. However, a radio intercept in February 1978 indicated that 150 ZAPU terrorists were experiencing food shortages, and that their intended infiltration into Rhodesia had accordingly been delayed

A Territorial Force (TF) platoon established an OP and soon determined that there were definite signs of CT's (communist terrorists). When the CT's attempted to cross the Zambezi, the TFs sprang their ambush, which also alerted the main camp, which in turn duly retaliated with mortars and heavy machine guns.

This action prompted a call for air support and a pair of Hunters was quickly on the scene to neutralise the enemy fire. Then on 1st March 1978 No 7 Squadron helicopters dropped off a two-man recce group in the mountainous country to the west of Kavalamanja, to locate the anti-aircraft position armed with 14,5 and 12,7 millimetre guns and spy on the local movements. It was established that a Zambian Army camp was situated about ten kilometres from the ZIPRA complex and an assault was immediately launched – with units drawn from the SAS, RLI and RAR.

The attack took place on Sunday, 6th March 1978, at 10h00, with a Hunter strike followed by Canberras dropping Alpha bombs. Shortly behind the Canberras, Dakotas dropped paratroopers to the north-east of the target. In addition, an RLI Fire Force launched their assault from the west. Forty-two ZIPRA terrorists and five Zambian troops were killed, their large ammunition dump was destroyed and a number of vehicles demolished. Our casualties were one RLI trooper killed, six RLI and two Scouts wounded.

The ground troops were all recovered back to base the next day, and a helicopter was dispatched on 10th March to uplift the ground reconnaissance team.

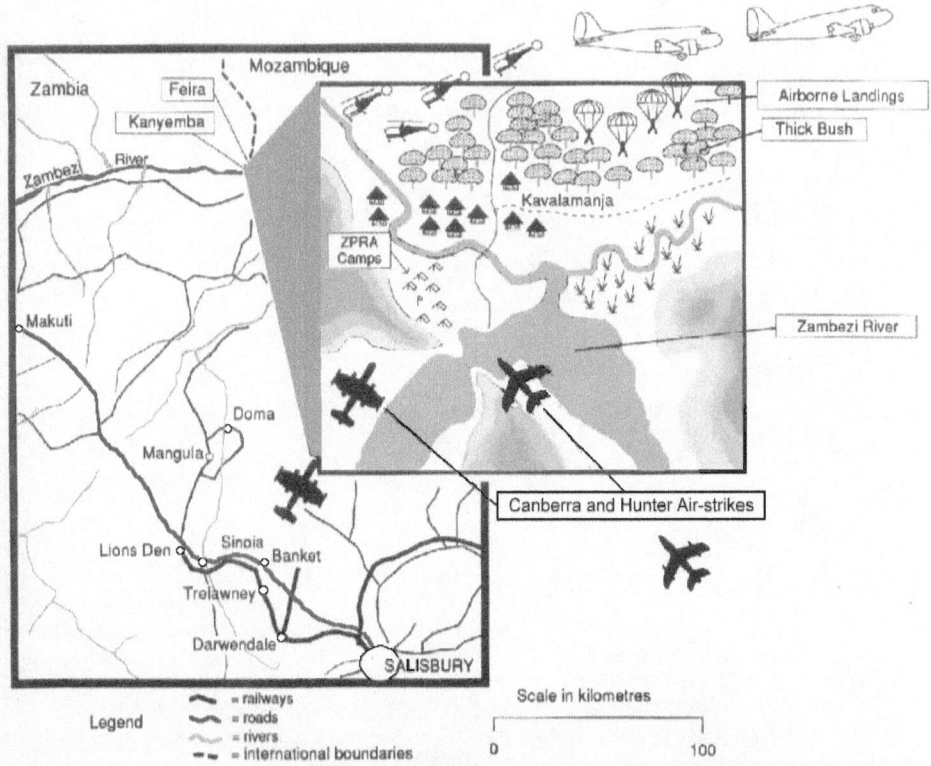

Operation Turmoil: the attack on Kavalamanja across the Zambezi River.

(Permission to use the original map by JRT Wood in *The War Diaries of André Dennison*, is gratefully acknowledged)

Air Strike Log No 790 – Operation Turmoil 6 March 1978

Aircrews:

- Vic Wightman (four sorties)
- Tony Oakley
- JR Blythe-Wood (six sorties)
- Glen Pretorius
- Dakota

Target: Kavalamanja terr complex, near Feira / Kanyemba, Mushika area Zambia
Result: Hunters destroyed 8 Zambian vehicles, killing 5 Zambian soldiers. 42 ZIPRA also killed. 2 Strela Sam 7 Ground to Air missiles and 51 landmines recovered. Refer JRT Wood, pages196-198

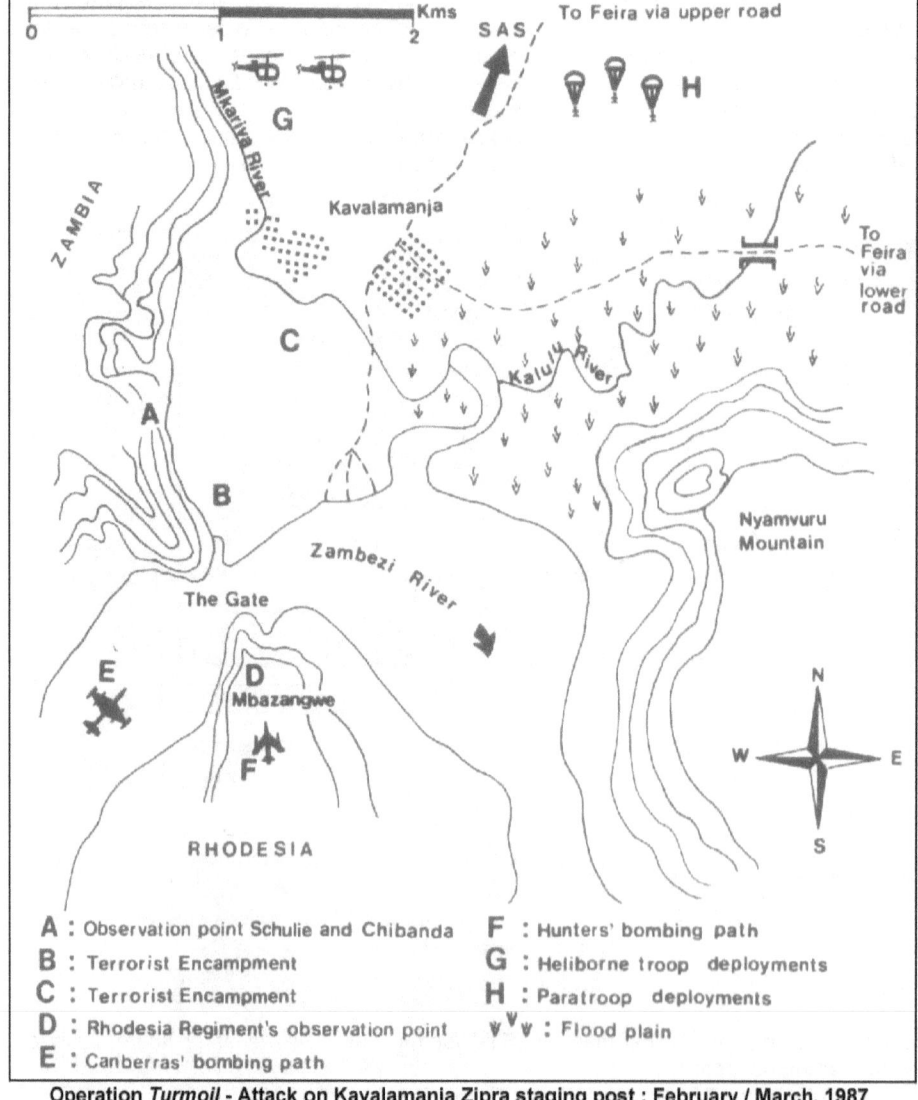

A : Observation point Schulie and Chibanda
B : Terrorist Encampment
C : Terrorist Encampment
D : Rhodesia Regiment's observation point
E : Canberras' bombing path
F : Hunters' bombing path
G : Heliborne troop deployments
H : Paratroop deployments
ᴠ ᴠ : Flood plain

Operation *Turmoil* - Attack on Kavalamanja Zipra staging post : February / March, 1987

Operation Pannier – 27 February 1978

Operation *Pannier* entailed the SAS recce's of ZIPRA terrorist camps in the Western Province of Zambia – such as Muchingwa, Forward Base Camp 1 & 2, Rama Farm, Katambora Camp Sinde / CH Plots, Lesumo and Pandamatenga.

Sam Sevens

The significant recovery of the SAM-7's warrants elaboration. On 16th June 1978 I flew Special Branch Superintendent Nicollys and Major Pat Mincher from Wankie to Victoria Falls airport. The purpose of our mission was to load two perfectly serviceable SAM-7 missiles into a twin-engined Cessna C 421 sent from Salisbury to collect these pristine condition heat seeking surface-to-air missiles which had been captured from ZIPRA terrorists. The ubiquitous missile is called Grail by NATO forces and Strela by the Russians. It weighs nine kilograms and is fired from a launcher held over the shoulder – the operator using a simple aperture sight. It is heat seeking and guided by sensors in its nose, firstly towards the light reflected from an aircraft and then to the infra red emissions from the hot metal of its engine exhausts.

We marvelled at the gyroscope within its glass dome, which controlled the tail fins. The SAM-7 is not very unlike the American Hawkeye missile used so effectively in Vietnam. It was designed as a lightweight infantryman's air defence weapon for ease of carrying and firing in the field. The trigger mechanism had a two-stage movement. The first stage would activate the battery power source, and the sight would glow red until target acquisition was achieved. Then as soon as there was a successful lock-on, and the target came within range, the sophisticated sight would glow green. It was then up to the infantryman to pull the trigger beyond the second stage in order to initiate rocket launch. There was a 'cold charge' to initiate the launch before ignition proper, so that there wasn't just a smouldering pair of 'vellies' left on the ground. The rocket then accelerated to well above the speed of sound on its way to the target.

The SAM-7 can reach a maximum height of five thousand feet, while the range is about three thousand five hundred metres. We soon found that among other limitations, it needed to be aimed and fired inside a cone of about six degrees of the line of sight of the aircraft, if it was to have any chance of locking on to the target. However, many pilots developed a healthy respect for the weapon – especially after a number of aircraft was hit.

The recovery of these deadly weapons certainly justified all the escorting of the SAA airliners that I had carried out in and around Victoria Falls airport. Tourists were still flocking to the Falls, but the Special Branch was careful to 'hide' the find from the civilian aviation authorities lest it adversely affected the lucrative tourist trade with its foreign capital injection into the Rhodesian economy. Unfortunately, the Viscount *Hunyani* disaster was destined to befall Air Rhodesia in September 1978. After safely loading the missiles onto the C 421, I returned my passengers to FAF 1. The SB impressed upon the pilot the need to treat his cargo - still in perfect compactors - with the utmost circumspection and to maintain secrecy as far as the mission was concerned.

It was perhaps ironic that about nine months later (March 1979), Nkomo's ZIPRA shot down two Zambian Air Force aircraft by mistake. I might add: "That certainly is sweet justice. It was music to my ears".

Operation Abduction: June/July 1978

Operation *Abduction* was a Selous Scouts scheme to make contact with terrorist groups in the Beit Bridge area in June 1978, and also in the Fort Victoria area in July 1978. The June exercise set up a white Scout, Sergeant Wally Insch, as an apparent Department of Wildlife ranger. Wally acted as a 'white capture' by terrorists, intent on an abduction to Moçambique. The plan called for the Selous Scout pseudo group to march Wally towards the border, and relying on the bush telegraph getting to the ears of the real terrorists that a white had been captured.

The 'march' started about ten kilometres west of the Bulawayo to Beit Bridge road, just south of Mazunga ranch, and then in an eastward route towards the Moçambique border. According to Special Branch, a large gook gang numbering about twenty was known to be operating in the Bubye area, and it was this gang that the pseudos were hoping to entice to take their "white capture" off their hands. When four real terrorists appeared, a Selous Scout suddenly fired his RPG-7 rocket launcher, struck one of the terrorists at point blank range – the rest scattered in all directions – upsetting the apple cart. After re-grouping, the pseudos crossed the Beit Bridge to Salisbury road and soon established contact with another terrorist detachment. The pseudos needed written permission from the local Sectoral commander to transit this sector. Whilst the two opposing sides were sussing each other out, a contact took place some five kilometres to their north-east, and the resultant gunfire caused such alarm and confusion that Wally Insch scooped up his weapon and shot two terrorists dead. This event compromised the objectives of the plan and thus put paid to any further local attempts to glean Special Branch intelligence for the Fire Force's attention.

Meanwhile, Flight Lieutenant Basil Moss was doing some sterling work for the Interim Transitional Government, operating in the Wedza area. Basil was tasked to control the Mangula-based former terrorists, who had turned in favour of the Muzorewa and Sithole faction. The Mangula gooks were deployed in the Wedza Tribal Trust Land, and the area was duly frozen – as per Selous Scouts normal *modus operandi*. This was thus another one of those *Top Secret* operations involving the Special Branch and Selous Scouts. On one Sunday, a PRAW pilot reported to Basil that he had seen about thirty ZANLA terrorists sprawled, apparently dead, by the roadside. The PRAW pilot landed at Wedza to uplift Basil, and he counted 41 corpses. It transpired that the Auxiliaries had made contact with real ZANLA gooks in the frozen area, were captured and then summarily executed. This led to a Fire Force deployment into the frozen area and 29 real gooks came short – being on the receiving end of the superior fire power that the Air Force provided from their K-Cars and G-Car helicopters, and Lynx close air support aircraft.

Operation *Abduction-2* was launched in the Fort Victoria area in July 1978. Sergeant Wally Insch was again set up as a white abductee from the Renco gold mine area. His mission was to make contact with a ZANLA commander, named Shelton, known to be operating in an area east of Fort Victoria that straddled the main road to Umtali. Shelton was a slippery and cunning fellow, but fancied himself as a competent medic. The Selous Scouts' plan called for Wally to be in need of medical treatment, as an abductee being marched to Moçambique. But the plan went wrong when Wally's pseudo group was led into a village where the locals started slowly feeding the 'white man' poisoned food. The locals demanded that the *"Mulungu"* be killed there and then – even before contact could be made with real gook Shelton. Wally's pseudo terrorists were able to bluff their way to a small hill from where radio contact was made with the *Repulse* JOC at Fort Victoria for Fire Force support. The JOC was not interested in acceding to the Selous Scouts' suggestion for a 'mock' Fire Force deployment, but did agree to have Wally and his call-sign extricated from their hilltop.

When the terrorists' *mujibas* witnessed Wally being airlifted by helicopter off the hill, the operation was compromised with the realisation that this had been the work of the *Skuz'apo* all along.

Operation Splinter: I May 1978

Operation *Splinter* was opened up in May 1978 to control the border along Lake Kariba. The South African Recces also sent their marine special forces to operate alongside our own Special Air Service - and contributed significantly to the Moçambique offensives on and along the Cabora Bassa project.

Operation Detonate: 1978

Chief Mola was abducted from the Sengwa Basin and taken across Lake Kariba to Zambia. Operation *Detonate* was launched when the SF assembled at the Bumi Hills Safari Lodge to conduct the BSAP follow-up. Air Force and PRAW flew to the Bumi Hills airstrip, together with SAAF helicopter crews. Bailiff David Lemon wrote in *Never Quite a Soldier* that the RLI were also involved, and that the gang of 23 terrorists that had captured Ignatius Sithole (and whose body has never been found) were believed to have rowed across the Lake. Rowing across the Lake was very unusual, as powered craft was considered the only safe means of crossing such an expanse of water.

A Roman (Nelson) Tragedy: 28 July 1978

Kevin Nelson's death and its aftermath are reminiscent of a classical Roman Tragedy. It will be recalled that I flew two sorties with Sergeant Kevin Nelson shortly after my hasty Lynx re-familiarisation a mere seven or eight months earlier. Kevin was my technician during our Operation *Tangent* deployment to FAF 1 in early November 1977. He also acted as my air observer during the Kazungula action when we accounted for one Zambian soldier killed.

Kevin's younger brother, Rob, had been killed in action the year before on 18th May 1977. He was Roger Watt's technician when their Alouette III was shot down. Roger was lucky to survive the helicopter crash although he sustained burns during the flaming descent. Rob was the air-gunner manning the twin Brownings of the G-Car, and as he was in the rear of the chopper the fire was more intense. He leapt out about four hundred feet above the ground to escape the flames and was killed. His death was a tragic blow to the family, especially for Rob's mother who had lost her 'baby'.

Kevin Nelson was also killed in action. Like his younger brother, he was the air-gunner. Another similarity was aircraft type. The only difference was that Kevin was in a Z-Car - an Alouette piloted by South African Flight Lieutenant (Captain) Francois du Toit, whom I knew well. Both pilot and technician were killed in Moçambique. This double death was just too much for the devastated mother. She took her own life. Her grief in losing both of her only two children was just too great to bear.

Mrs Nelson committed suicide shortly after the death of Kevin. It reminded me of a Roman tragedy worthy of comparison to classical Caesar, Othello or even Romeo and Juliet. As a tribute to the Nelsons, I saw fit to repeat Kevin's last moments as witnessed by the other Alouette pilot who documented the story to Bill Sykes (for *Pride of Eagles* inclusion – by Beryl Salt). The verbatim report reads as follows:

"Flight Lieutenant Francois du Toit and I were on hot extraction standby at Mount Darwin in support of Major Neil Kriel's Selous Scouts troops. My technician was Corporal Chris Saint and Francois had Sergeant Kevin Nelson. Both Francois and I had been awarded the MFC earlier that day. I am not sure what Francois got his for, but mine came as a big surprise as it was for the sort of operation everyone on 7 Squadron was doing regularly. Pride was mixed with embarrassment.

"Late in the day (28th July 1978), we were tasked for an uplift of someone else's troops north-east of Chioco in Moçambique. Neil Kriel was not pleased to see the two helicopters disappear. It was a long way and with only four soldiers, so we took lots of fuel and planned a pick-up of two soldiers each near last light. Our fuel load would preclude lifting the normal four in one helicopter. It was not supposed to be a 'hot extraction'. Little did I realise at that time what value the affect that the extra fuel would have some hours later.

"We planned our route carefully using all the latest intelligence on known enemy areas to avoid. This required lots of turning points. Flight Lieutenant Chris Abrams was airborne in the Lynx and we established comms with the call-sign without any problems. Francois was leading and I was in a wide echelon starboard. Running in about two minutes out, our routine became a nightmare; there was a ferocious eruption of ground fire, mostly to our left. Within seconds I saw Francois' G-Car (in fact South African Z-Car – author's note) descend rapidly into the trees. No fireball and no call on the radio. Chris Saint was blasting away and I was calling urgently to Chris Abrams in the Lynx. It transpired that we had over-flown an unmarked camp of over 300 terrorists. Whilst our helicopter had come under intense ground-fire, we must have been nearer the edge of the camp than Francois.

"With our own troops literally a few miles away, the obvious plan of action was to uplift two of them at a time and drop them as close as possible to the downed helicopter in an attempt to secure the area. Of course, at that time we had no idea how many we were up against but the almost constant firing was a clear indication that the opposition was huge. The light was not going to last but we had lots of fuel – still far too much for four troops. I called for two soldiers to prepare for uplift. Having heard all the firing and probably seen the tracers, they were understandably apprehensive as we prepared for the drop-off. I doubt that their fear was greater than mine was; for all of us, the anticipation was terrifying. Desperately hoping that the enemy would be just as frightened, I planned my approach from the position we had been when Francois and Kevin went down. It seemed logical to assume that the terrorists would not know how much opposition they had and were likely to be escaping to the east, away from the direction of most of the helicopter noise. By this time, Chris Abrams was giving us maximum support and I distinctly remember looking up and seeing his Lynx surrounded by 'flak'. I guess they were popping off every RPG-7 and SAM they had. I seem to recall that Chris had his technician with him – doubtless he would be regretting his predicament and wishing he was back at base sipping a cold lager and listening to the action on the HF.

"I don't remember much about the next bit except that we managed to over-fly Francois' helicopter at about 15 feet. It looked very flat – obviously a high rate of descent impact. The chance of survival seemed unlikely but we had to get the troops to confirm. The ground fire seemed to be continuous but I don't recall taking many hits; maybe they were firing blind, or aiming at the Lynx.

"We went back for the next two soldiers to get maximum support at the scene. Within a few minutes we were ready to make the second approach but, by then, the call-sign on the ground was screeching – pinned down by too much opposition, they felt they were being overwhelmed and could not advance to the crash site despite having been dropped about 50 yards away. Now we had a real problem on our hands – fading light, two troops needing to be extracted; two on board and way too much fuel to uplift within normal Alouette III limitations; plus we did not want to leave the downed crew. The troops on the ground were sounding more and more desperate. Chris Saint and I made a plan - we would lurk behind a ridge to the west and dump everything possible overboard. This would reduce our weight and allow maximum time for the situation to change. Maybe the troops would be able to get through. The thought of leaving our colleagues was horrendous and things were not looking too good.

"I told the call-sign to stand by with a white phosphorous grenade. On our run in, Chris would make a series of attacks in the Lynx. I would call for the white phos, over-fly their position and land at the next available clearing. This called for two prayers - one for a landing area before the main enemy concentration and one for a healthy engine and gearbox for the overweight take-off. As we flew up and down the ridge in relative security there was time to ponder. Pondering was not good – my legs were on the verge of uncontrollable shakes; my mouth was bone dry and speaking had become less natural. I felt pretty sure we would not make it. It's amazing how they seem so cool in the movies.

"After about ten minutes, with fading light and the situation on the ground not improving, we had to accept the inevitable. My memories of the uplift are a blur – running in with Chris attacking in the Lynx; desperate shouting on the radio; Chris Saint firing our Brownings; the white phos; a frantic search for a clearing; landing amongst the trees and in very long grass. Then the eternal wait for the desperate troops to find us. They scrambled on board and we hauled ourselves out from amongst the trees; guns firing, gearbox whining; away to the west and temporary safety. I hardly dared look at the collective gauge. It's a wonderful machine the Alouette.

"The trip home in the dark with not enough fuel for our original destination; re-planning for an alternate safe haven and having to leave the proven safe inbound track. After a long and tense sortie, we landed at Mary Mount Mission where I found the senior army officer was Rudd, a prefect from school when I was a junior. I remember having to clean his shoes and carry his books. It was good to see him. Having completed our 'Sitrep' to base, Rudd provided some welcome brandy. I needed plenty.

"The next day Chris and I were airborne before dawn. Our G-Car was fine – some holes but no serious damage. We were amazed to be tasked to Mount Darwin on 'hot extraction' duties for Major Kriel rather than on the rescue mission. Perhaps HQ thought our nerves would be shot. Maybe they were right.

"Flight Lieutenant du Toit and Sergeant Kevin Nelson were both found dead from gunshot wounds. For the past 22 years I have found it more comfortable to believe that these were inflicted before impact."

I was at FAF 7 when I heard the news that Kevin had caught the chop. It was a sad day. I was doing a spell of ground duty, and had not flown for over a month.
The next day, 29th July 1978, I commandeered Lynx R 3044 to carry out three circuits and landings at Buffalo Range. The sortie lasted a mere fifteen minutes, but it was sufficient for me to maintain my flying currency. I had previously flown on 19th June following my bush stint as

Acting Officer Commanding FAF 1 (Wankie). After FAF 7, it was back to Thornhill to do what I was being paid to do – fly OCAW's Mahogany bomber.

Operation Metric: 30 July 1978

Operation *Metric* target details are sketchy – but because Varky Varkevisser in a Vampire together with Vic Wightman and John Blythe-Wood flying Hunters out of New Sarum, the air-strike target was very likely northern Moçambique (or Zambia). The Air Strike Log shows that air strikes were carried out on 30th July 1978, the same day that Tembue II had been struck – see Operation *Mascot* below.

Operation Mascot: 10 July to 1 August 1978

Canberra aircraft on photographic reconnaissance had maintained a careful watch on the Tembue complex to the north of the Cabora Bassa Dam, ever since the raid by the Air Force, Special Air Service and Rhodesian Light Infantry, following their marked successes at Chimoio. In due course the Air Force photographic interpreters produced photographs showing a series of camps forming a new complex nearby the old one, which was named Tembue-2 (Maroro). The complex appeared to accommodate about five hundred and fifty terrorists.

A Dakota of No 3 Squadron, flown by Squadron Leader Dave Thorne and co-piloted by Flight Lieutenant George Sole dropped Selous Scout Captain Chris "Schulie" Schulenburg on the evening of 10th July 1978, from low level, and closer to the complex, than originally planned. The plan was to drop two 2-man sticks HALO (High altitude, low opening) and at a DZ (drop zone) west and north of the camp. Schulie convinced Officer Commanding No 3 Squadron Dave Thorne otherwise - he wanted to be dropped near the target. With George's exceptional navigational skills, the Dakota dropped the Scouts exactly where Schulie asked to be dropped and then waited with bated breath for Schulie's radio confirmation that they had landed safely. After a minute or so, the crews heard the whispered message "I think they've seen us but we're okay".

Group Captain Norman Walsh of Comops was not pleased that Schulie's request had been acceded to and had serious doubts about the outcome of this particular pre-operation assessment. Then on 19th July, the second Scout call-sign was compromised when they were shot at, and radioed for hot extraction. The operation was considered blown, but after two days Schulie reported that things had returned to normal. Although there were no properly organised camps.... mostly grass shelters with hides under trees and with campfires at night and smoke from early morning cooking fires. After some debate, Comops ordered an airstrike to be put in on the Sunday, 30th July, and that this would be followed by a ground assault immediately afterwards.

I take up Dave Thorne's story as follows: -

"No 3 Squadron's involvement was to drop 128 SAS and RLI paras around the base three minutes after the initial jet bombardment. This involved getting eight Dakotas, with 16 paras each, airborne early enough to be exactly five miles from the respective pre-selected DZ's (drop zones) at the moment of the jet strike. In order to do this, a number of Volunteer Reserve (VR) pilots had to be called up. These comprised all sorts: a department store manager, farmers, a photographic shop owner (who breeds Gaboon Vipers for a hobby), civilian pilots with no military experience (apart from these call-ups) and ex-Royal Air Force pilots. Most of our VRs had very little experience of flying in formation with two aircraft, let alone eight.

"The briefing had to be, therefore, much more detailed than normal. Included and stressed in the briefing was the fact that, from a timing point of view, we needed time in hand but, if we were too much ahead, we would have to do a 360-degree orbit in order to lose some time. If one stays abreast or beside the lead aircraft, any turn results in a requirement to change one's speed: being on the inside of the turn, requires a reduction of speed and being on the outside of a turn, requires an increase of speed. To cope with this, each aircraft simply has to move into a line-astern position, keeping its number within the formation, one behind the other. As every experienced Air Force pilot knows, the leader can do almost anything and following is a very simple and safe process, without the need for any great speed changes. I mentioned at the briefing that the orbit would probably be to the left.

"H-hour (the time for the jet-strike) was early in the day because, with an operation of this size, the whole day is required to ensure that: the objective is achieved; the wounded are casevaced; helicopter fuel is parachuted (by 3 Squadron) to a suitable, pre-designated DZ; helicopters are refuelled; parachutes are collected; the mop-up is thorough; soldiers re-positioned and, eventually, helicoptered to a suitable airfield where No 3 Squadron would be waiting to fly them back to base; etc. The list is endless. So, to meet H-hour plus three minutes, the eight Dakotas, each loaded with its quota of paras, lumbered into the air in the pre-dawn darkness at 30 second intervals and settled into a loose V formation, the leader in front with 3, 5, and 7 out to my left and 2, 4, 6 and 8 out to my right. Naturally, I had chosen my trusted colleague, George Sole, as my co-pilot once again.

"As dawn approached and ground features became discernible, George was able to pin-point our position (somewhat left of track) and relate it to the time that it would take us to reach H-hour plus three. It was immediately apparent that we were running, as planned, ahead of time and would need to lose about three minutes. An orbit was necessary.

"Also as planned, radio silence was an essential factor to the element of surprise, so not a word could be uttered to warn my followers that the briefed orbit was about to take place. No worries: my briefing had been thorough and detailed. Because we were left of track and because a gentle turn to the left would take us less than two minutes to do the 360 degrees, an orbit to the right was preferable. An orbit right would take a bit longer than two minutes to get to the new heading that was now required. Again, no worries: as every pilot familiar with formation flying knows, to follow an orbit, one simply has to slide into a line astern position.

"Imagine my horror when, after going about 30 degrees of turn, numbers six and eight (both VRs) appeared out to my right, abreast of me, trying desperately to slow down. They were getting dangerously close to the stall and had already selected flap to avoid this. I stopped turning and was forced to break radio silence:

"What are you doing?"

"We though you were going to orbit to the left."

Admittedly, at the briefing I had said the orbit would probably be to the left but this was no excuse for not getting into line astern. Instinctively, all the other pilots had slotted in behind me but numbers six and eight were now virtually ahead of the whole formation, having stayed on the inside of the turn so far.

"I growled: 'Move into line astern' and, after a few more minutes, we were able to continue our turn, regain track, make up a bit of lost time and, eventually, thanks to George, drop our paras on the planned DZs at the designated time: H-hour + 3. The attack went in at 08h00 on Sunday, 30th July. Schulie, meanwhile, had spotted about fifty terrorists from the camp below him who were escaping away to the west, and he couldn't make comms with either the Air Force or the ground troops to counter the gooks taking the gap.

"Operation *Mascot* turned out to be a bit of lemon in that only about 30 trainees were found in the camp and it was suspected by Comops that Schulie had indeed been spotted and then duped into believing that the camp was operating as normal."

Also, the compromise and hot extraction of the other Selous Scout call-sign did not help either. Meanwhile, the camp was being evacuated by the hardcore that left the 30 behind as bait. Lieutenant-Colonel Ron Reid-Daly subsequently claimed that the drop zones used were miles from the terrorist complex, and the terrorists easily made good their escape before the security forces had walked the long distance necessary to get there. The issue as to whether or not, the gooks had been there, when the attack was mounted, was hotly debated afterwards. The Air Force was puce with rage when they heard the Army was accusing them of ruining the attack, by dropping the paratroopers at the wrong place. Eventually, the Army and the Air Force found common ground and found sour grapes with the Selous Scouts.

The amusing sequel to this episode is that a very funny poem was circulated among the VR that depicted the erstwhile leader, of the eight Dakotas, to be the culprit of the orbit debacle (right versus left), causing the tail-end-Charlie to change his number from eight to one. Dave did not find the poem funny at all.

It is also noteworthy that in June 1978 Captain Chris Schulenburg' became the first holder of the Grand Cross of Valour, Rhodesia's highest bravery award.

During August 1978, Hansie Bezuidenhout was again involved in one of his many PATU call-outs. On or about 14th August, there was a contact with terrorists at Nunedon Mine in the Urungwe, which was well known to Hansie. His PATU stick was detailed to follow up on tracks, which they duly did. Having chosen an ideal spot, they set themselves up in ambush positions that only had a restricted killing ground – a large bush obstructed their view, just prior to the enemy being caught by complete surprise. Whilst lying in wait, the ambush's presence was compromised when the machine gunner's tripod slipped, and making enough noise to alert the gang as they approached the bush obstruction. Hansie had no option but to fire off the first shot – dropping one terrorist in his tracks. As soon as the first gunshot rang out, the terrorists bombshelled, scattering and merging with the surrounding bush with amazing speed. As a result of the compromise, and forced premature springing of the ambush, this action accounted only for the one terrorist shot by Hansie.

As a matter of interest, Hansie confided to the writer of the high regard in which the ground forces held the Air Force. He recalled one particularly long 'leap-frogging follow-up', with helicopter support – and paid tribute to pilot Nick Meikle who attended to PATU's every need.

Air Strike Log No 719 – 28 August 1978
Aircrews:
- Ted Lunt / Frank Robinson
- Geoff Oborne / Brian Booth
- Ray Bolton

Target: Terrorist camp located by PRAW 70km east of Bindura. (Or 120km west of Grand Reef?)
Result: Geoff Osborne shot down. Alouette damaged by ground fire – Cat 4

Geoff Oborne recalls the following: Chopper crash

"The Police Reserve Air Wing had one of their big camps where their many light aircraft were involved in looking for terrorist camps in the area east of Bindura. A mini Fire Force of one K-Car -Ted Lunt, two G-Cars - Ray Bolton and I and a Lynx were positioned at Bindura in support of the PRAW exercise. The army contingent was a few RAR sticks.

"On a clear day we were all milling around the Police Station waiting for a call to search the areas where the PRAW pilots thought there might be a terr camp. At around noon Ray Bolton was tasked to do a resupply mission, leaving just the one other G-Car. As fate would have it a call came in that a camp had been spotted and it looked like there were terrs present. Ted briefed us - the plan of attack being SOP - standard operating procedure - with the K-Car pulling up, etc. etc. The camp was about 70km east of Bindura on the side of a small hill next to a river. Our two choppers got airborne and routed via the airfield to wait for the Lynx to join us. The balance of the RAR troops boarded their trucks and made off down the road to a point south of the gook camp.

"The K-Car pulled up and I went into an orbit round the area. After about a minute Ted said that the K-Car had them visual and was opening fire. I could hear the 20mm cannon going wild in the background. On my second orbit Brian Booth my tech, said he had seen a gook running up the side of the hill in the open. We staggered over to the area (we were very heavy) and opened fire with our Brownings. The terr, realising he was caught in the open, just stood there and fired back at us. After what seemed an eternity and a lot of .303 rounds later he eventually dropped and lay face down in the grass.

"By now Ted wanted my troops to be put on the ground so he directed me to an LZ in amongst the trees. I landed and deployed the RAR stick. I then went to the road to pick up another stick. I returned to the contact area where I could see the Lynx putting in a Frantan strike. As we came into the orbit again we were shocked to see that the terr we thought we had killed had gone, a tactic we were to take note of for future contacts.

"Ted told me to drop my stick where the Frantan strike had gone in. I was quite happy as I thought if there were any terrorists around they would either be dead from the strike or wouldn't feel like fighting any more. I came into the hover and as I was about three feet from touchdown I saw two terrs stand up behind the bushes about 30 metres away in my two o'clock position (on the opposite side to the Brownings). They brought up their AKs and opened fire at the chopper. I pulled the collective lever up to the stop and we leapt into the air again. I pushed full right pedal to bring the guns to bear and also to place my armoured seat between the terrs and me. The clatter of gunfire was really loud and as we got to treetop level in a 30-degree bank the engine suddenly stopped. I shouted over the radio "I'm crashing" – there was no time for a formal 'Mayday' distress call. I managed to level the chopper as we hit the ground. The blades hit a tree off to the left and burnt grass and dust covered the chopper. Then it all went quiet. I looked behind to see if Brian and the troopies had survived the crash but they were nowhere to be seen. I un-strapped, jumped out and turned to grab my rifle. It was missing. I ran in the opposite direction from where I thought the gooks were and lay down behind a tree some 50 metres away. Above me the K-Car was orbiting my downed helicopter. I was wearing a green flying suit so I prayed that Ted and his gunner wouldn't mistake me for a terr. It also dawned on me that an immediate rescue was out of the question as the other G-Car was away.

"I looked around for friendly forces but all I saw was a dead body dressed in blue lying on the other side of the stream. After five minutes or so I noticed the RAR stick, with Brian in the middle, advancing towards the downed chopper. I whistled and they came over.

"I noticed that Brian had my AK 47 rifle which I promptly took back. He explained that he had grabbed the first weapon he could find as he fled. We all moved further away and into the riverbed where we used the banks as protection. I told Brian to wash his face in the river water as he was bleeding from a cut. When he had finished I decided to take a drink. Keeping an eye on the dead body across the river 20 metres away (in case it also suddenly came alive) I lowered my face to the cool water. As I was about to take a sip a huge explosion erupted next to my face. I flung myself back in fright only to see Brian killing himself with laughter. He had thrown a boulder into the water next to my face just to give me a scare. I nearly put a bullet into his leg!

"The RAR stick leader informed us we were to do a sweep of the gook camp. Cursing Ray Bolton for being away so long with the rescue chopper, we began to move through the camp looking for more terrs, not something for which we had been trained! As Blue Jobs we had to walk behind the sweep line, probably because we would have been a liability had there been a scene. We hadn't quite reached the camp area when we heard the sound of Ray's chopper.

"Three hours later we were in a PRAW aircraft on our way to New Sarum. There was nobody to meet us there so I went home and had a good sleep.

"The next day I phoned the squadron and was told there was a spare chopper available and that I was needed back at the sharp end. So off I went back to the bush.

"Oh! Well, that's war".

FAF 1 - Operation Tangent: 13 to 20 September 1978

On 13th September 1978 I again traded in my Mahogany Bomber for a Lynx. The powers that be required my "re-tread" services for another bush deployment in order to relieve the critical shortage of experienced pilots. My brief was to position Beit Bridge for a short two day Special Forces operation by the Selous Scouts in the Diti Tribal Trust Land. I was then to proceed to Wankie in support of the Special Air Service who were engaged on Smersh external operations. I was told "Don't worry; you can always catch up with your bumph when you return to the office - Thornhill will still be here when you return. Brian Byars will keep an eye on any urgent matters."

Having reported to No 4 Squadron the courier Lynx was already fuelled up and waiting for me. I flew due south and landed at Beit Bridge where I handed my Lynx over to a JP (junior pilot) for him to return to base for his R&R. My Lynx technician Corporal Fubbs assured me that Lynx R 3094 was in perfect shape - in fact 100% serviceable. I carried out a quick pre-flight inspection, verified my tech's findings, and hastened over to the Browns for their latest Sitrep (situation report). Captain Dale Collett briefed me to be at cockpit readiness because a punch up was brewing at Mtentengwe.

I was pleased to renew my friendship with Dale. He was not one to "bugger around". As a Second Lieutenant, Dale Collett was the first Rhodesian soldier to win the SCR Silver Cross of Rhodesia, the second highest award for gallantry in the Rhodesian Security Forces. I did not have long to wait (not that I was actually sitting in the cockpit).

Before I knew what hit me, Dale yelled "Get your butt into the air - I'll brief you once we're airborne." Dale directed me to the sighting in the Mtentengwe and requested that I put in an airstrike. I was only too glad to oblige, and selected rockets and front gun. I let loose with 1 x 37-mm Sneb for target marking purposes, followed by firing 100 x .303 from my twin Brownings. The airstrike was over in the blink of an eyelid. The bad news was we hadn't scored, but as a consolation we continued with our armed reconnaissance for a total of two hours flying, landing back at Beit Bridge. The rest of the first day was uneventful.

After a good night's rest, I was requested to conduct a top cover reconnaissance in the Diti TTL. This mission proved more fruitful, resulting in the killing of one ZANLA CT (Communist Terrorist). The Gooks had bomb-shelled and had gone to ground. The sortie lasted a mere eighty minutes. However, aircraft (and aircrews, I might add) were in short supply and pressure was on the Scouts to release me for urgent top cover for the SAS external into Zambia and Botswana. Later that afternoon, I packed my kit, uplifted my tech, Corporal Fubbs and flew to FAF 1. We arrived at Wankie on 14th September 1978.

I found myself jumping from the frying pan into the fire. The SAS had deployed their recce sticks in the Katombora area but were experiencing radio communications problems. My first night-stop at FAF 1 was disturbed. I was roused from my sweet dreams and asked to make contact with the SAS call-signs. I rose from the dead, noted cloud cover about but nevertheless got airborne well before sunrise. It was a rather short sortie of one hour ten minutes duration and I was able to make good use of twenty minutes flying in cloud - the enemy may well have heard me, but couldn't see me. I was able to carry out my Telstar duties satisfactorily and landed before the sun made its appearance. It was too late to hit the sack again, so I joined the caterers and helped myself to several cups of coffee plus a double breakfast of bacon and egg with plenty of toast.

On 15th September, I positioned my Lynx at Sprayview airstrip at Victoria Falls for standby duties. It was an uneventful day and I returned to FAF 1 by mid-afternoon. I had no sooner got back to Wankie than I was once again scrambled for SAS Telstar duties in Botswana and Katombora. The three-hour sortie meant a night landing, but this time I was in time for a late supper. I was in no mood to hit the pub and looked forward to an early night, because I knew that the morrow would entail helicopter deployment for the continuing external operations.

My first sortie on the 16th was top cover for the Spiders (helicopter) trooping 'C' Squadron SAS. We were monitoring the Zambian Army radio transmissions, and no doubt their intelligence blokes were doing likewise to all our transmissions. Radio silence and strict radio discipline was the order of the day. Trooping was completed within two and a half-hours. I had just landed to refuel when the first call came in of a contact. Major Pat Mincher jumped in my Lynx with me - in order to communicate with his troops on the ground. The contact resulted in two gooks killed. Pat Mincher and I really 'clicked' well together. Our teamwork was good. He and I had now flown together four times during Operation *Elbow*. He had got to know the capabilities of the Lynx pretty well.

We suffered one casualty of our own, which the helicopters were able to casevac to Sprayview. I was then tasked to uplift the casualty from Sprayview and fly the wounded man to Wankie where better medical facilities were available. The Colliery Hospital doctors were gaining valuable battle injury experience, and were often faced with amputations for landmine injuries.

The 17th September was a quiet day. By late afternoon I decided on a reconnaissance along the Botswana border and took VR Flight Lieutenant Harley Boxall along for the ride. Harley was from the Bulawayo squadron, performing FAF Camp Commandant duties. These volunteer guys certainly did a great job on the front line, relieving GD Pilots for the jobs they did best - flying. Anyway, to break the boredom, I dropped four Bubs bombs and fired 50 rounds .303 in the vicinity of Beacon 10 - just to let the gooks know we were around should they wish to spoil for a fight. I am sure Harley enjoyed the ride. Harley was a quiet, modest, ex-WW II pilot with many a hairy tale to tell.

On the 18th I was scrambled for a sighting from one of our O.P.s. These would be ground call-signs that would establish themselves on the top of 'gomos' (hilltops) overlooking suspected or known infiltration routes. Ten minutes after take-off I was recalled. It was a lemon. That was good about the SAS - they didn't waste air power unnecessarily. The sighting was some innocent locals that were mistaken for gooks. I didn't mind, it was the only flying I did that day. If it had been any unit other than the SAS, I would have muttered into my beer because some of the trigger-happy Browns, like the RLI, were accountable for more lemons that I would care to remember. A lemon leaves a sour after-taste for the action orientated pilots of the Air Force.

We hit a small jackpot on 19th September. We accounted for two CT's during a contact in the Wankie National Park. I was still airborne during my two-hour flight in the Lynx when I was asked to relay to the Special Branch chaps that the gook Sectoral Commander had been captured. The SB had their ways and means of making uncooperative terrorists squeal. My detachment was nearing its end and to account for such a big fish was like the cherry on the top of a very productive spell at the sharp end. Later in the day I provided top cover for the Spiders who were trooping the SAS. Lynx R 3094 had performed well on every day since my bush deployment. As fate would have it, the fifty five-minute top cover mission for the SAS and Alouette helicopters would in fact prove to be my last operational flying duty (as a retread pilot) for the remainder of the Rhodesian bush war.

Operation *Snoopy* commenced whilst I was doing my bit at FAF 1.

Operation Snoopy: 19 to 24 September 1978

Operation *Snoopy* was another major external operation mounted by the Air Force, Special Air Service and Rhodesian Light Infantry against 25 ZANLA camps within the Chimoio Circle (approximately 70km from the Rhodesian border). The present camps were to the north of the old Chimoio camp, which had been attacked by the Rhodesians the previous November. A newly qualified young Lynx pilot was carrying out a reconnaissance some 35 km to the south of where intelligence had estimated the presence of some 2,000 ZANLA. Troops were sent in to investigate and they came under fire from a different place. Reinforcements choppered in from the old abandoned camps also met with determined resistance - and pilots were reporting spotting tracks, trenches and small camps - and drawing heavy anti-aircraft fire.

The new target was ten times bigger than originally thought, being some thirty kilometres by forty kilometres and consisting of dozens of small camps. The ground forces were having contact after contact, resulting in the pilots having extreme difficulty pinpointing their targets. The haze that hung over the targets worsened once the camps began burning. There was a cacophony of aircraft milling around - Canberras were running in for their bombing runs, Hunters were attacking in another direction, Lynxes were keeping an extra good lookout, and the helicopters were dodging in and out. During the heat of the battle, a Golf bomb killed SAS Trooper Steve Donnelly (Steve was one of the Three Musketeers named by Johan Bezuidenhout. He died in *Small Bez* Johan's arms. The third Musketeer, Frans Nel, died when he was shot in the head during a paradrop. Small Bez had told the author that the Three Musketeers had made a name for themselves in the *Elite* SAS).

Hunters destroyed three Russian armoured personnel carriers that arrived in the camp. The battle raged on for three days, where-after the Security Forces withdrew back to Rhodesia. On Monday September 25, The Herald headline read "Border Raids: 25 Camps hit. Mission success: FRELIMO forces among dead". The headline photograph showed three dead FRELIMO soldiers outside their Russian-supplied armoured personnel carrier in a camp, which the terrorists called "Voetsek". The Combined Operations communiqué stated that the tasks of the security forces were the destruction of the bases, the collection of intelligence, the destruction of logistics and the elimination of terrorists. All these missions were successfully completed.

Operation Gatling: 19 October 1978

Operation *Gatling* was preceded with a diversionary attack on ZANLA encampments along the Pungwe River in Moçambique before mounting the attack on Westlands Farm near Lusaka, Zambia at 08h30 on 19th October 1978.

Westlands Farm, or Freedom Camp as it was called by its three thousand ZIPRA occupants, was situated just three miles north of the Zambian capital Lusaka. Being creatures of habit, the ZIPRA terrorists would be parading at 08h30 precisely, hence the timing of the attack by the strike force. The main strike force consisted of four Canberra B2 bombers of No 5

Squadron, called Green Section, and eight Hunter FGA 9s of No 1 Squadron, divided into four of Blue Section, two of Red Section and two of White Section. In addition, there were four Alouette III helicopter K-Cars, each fitted with twenty millimetre cannon, and the Command Dakota, a DC-3C of No 3 Squadron, call-sign Dolphin 3.

The Command Dak was fitted with numerous items of electronic equipment such as HF, VHF, UHF, and teleprinters capable of decrypting messages to and from Milton Buildings, the Rhodesian Air Force and Defence Headquarters in Salisbury. On board were the Air Force Director of Operations, Group Captain Norman Walsh, Commander Comops General Peter Walls and the Commander of the Special Air Service, Major Brian Robinson.

Briefings for the raid took place in the Parachute Training School hangar at New Sarum Air Force Base. The SAS Regiment and RLI Commandos also took part in this trans-border operation, and assembled two nights beforehand to be given their targets and battle orders. A huge scale model had been made, showing locations in minute detail. Everything was shown, including bunkers, trenches, and barrack blocks, lecture halls, messes, parade grounds and gun placements. There were three main targets in Zambia.

- Phase One of the operation would be the Air Force strike on the ZIPRA base at Westlands farm, just outside Lusaka.
- Phase Two was an attack by the entire SAS on the ZIPRA base at Mkushi 125-km north-east of Lusaka, simultaneous with the Westlands airstrike.
- Phase Three was the attack by the RLI on the CGT-2 (Communist Guerrilla Training Camp) ZIPRA base situated near the Great North Road, 15-km north of Lusaka.

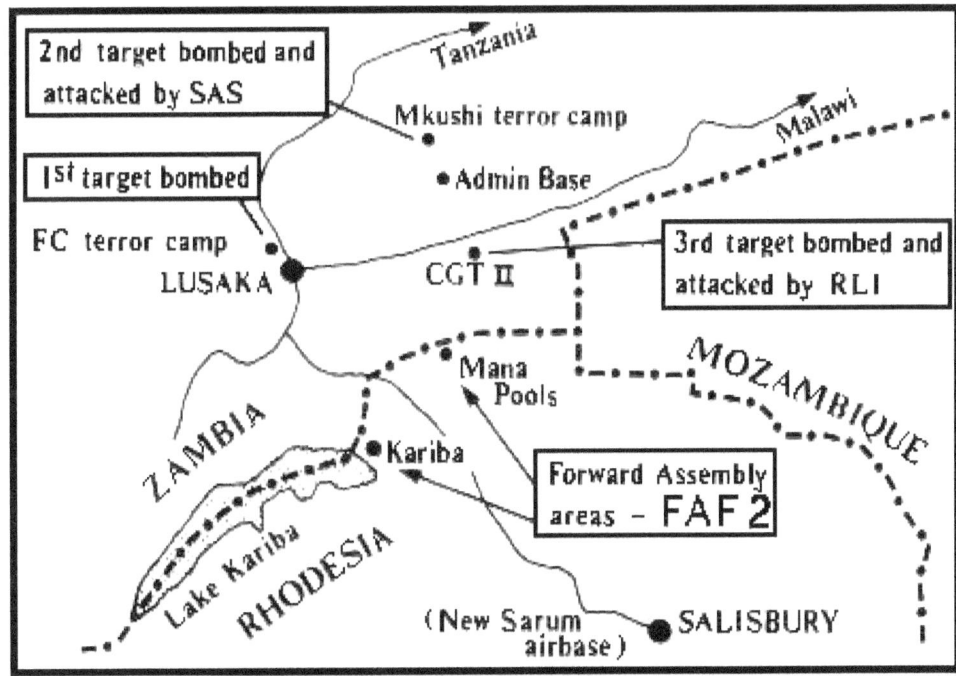

Operation Gatling – Chris Dixon and Green Leader fame

Each pilot had been allocated a specific duty or target. The helicopter K-Cars of No 7 Squadron took off first from Forward Airfield Kariba, heading into Zambia to their refuelling station at a small airstrip half way to Lusaka - occupied by troops of the Rhodesian Army. They were the third wave of attack, after the Canberras and Hunters had carried out their first run attacks. As with most air operations, precise flying and exact timings were required by all the aircraft.

The Canberras took off from New Sarum, to meet up with the Hunters. The Canberras were carrying a unique type of bomb unknown elsewhere in the world, code-named Alpha bombs. Each Canberra carried three hundred of this bright red, locally designed and manufactured lethal weapon.

The Hunters took off from Fylde near Hartley, the base of the Air Force Regiment, and headed for Makuti on the Zambezi escarpment. They flew at twenty thousand feet before descending on Mana Pools (giving the impression of a routine border patrol along the Zambezi) to join up with the four Canberras. The Hunters were armed with another locally developed Golf bomb, 68mm Matra rockets, 100-gallon Frantan (napalm) bombs and their normal weapon load of 4 x 30mm Aden cannons.

With the Canberras and Hunters having joined up, the formation flew at fifteen hundred feet above ground level to a point three hundred and twenty kilometres north-west into Zambia, then turned almost due west to Lusaka - on a course designed to avoid the Zambian Air Force base at Mumbwa. At a predetermined point, the four Hunters of Blue Section broke off, accelerated and climbed to fourteen thousand feet - and attacked the assembled parade, from the north, in steep dives, at twenty-second intervals. The Hunters were scheduled to perform four tasks. The four in Blue Section were the first into the attack, to stun the men on parade and mark the target for the low-level Canberras. The two in Red Section were tasked to orbit the main Zambian Air Force base at Mumbwa, near Lusaka, and to shoot down any military aircraft that took off to intercept the raiders. The remaining two, in White Section, were tasked to strike the encampment with frantan, after the K-Cars had begun the third wave of attack with their cannon. Finally, the four in Blue Section were to return and rake any remaining survivors with their Aden guns.

The ZIPRA forces were taken completely by surprise as the combination of the percussion Golf bombs and thousand pounders hit them on the parade ground. Forty-five seconds later, before those ZIPRA forces left standing had time to recover their senses, the four Canberras arrived, and flying in line abreast, with the navigators/bomb-aimers' lining up on the Hunter strikes. Then the familiar "Bomb doors open, Master on, left, steady, steady, right, steady, steady, bombs gone, bombs falling."

Then those magic words, which are music to any pilot's ears: "On Target."

The Hunters continued to discharge their deadly Frantans and 30-mm cannons. Then the four K-Car helicopter gunships, already in the area, joined the bun fight - their 20-mm cannon firing, with stoppages being expertly cleared by the highly trained and battle-experienced technicians / gunners.

Then came Operation *Gatling's* famous and widely publicised Green Leader's radio transmission to Lusaka Control Tower, effectively exercising complete control over Zambian air space - and in the process making a complete mockery of Zambia's ability to react to Rhodesian pursuits.

Chris Dixon   —   "Lusaka Tower, this is Green Leader"
Lusaka Tower —   "Green Leader – Lusaka Tower?"
Chris Dixon   —   "Lusaka Tower, this is Green Leader. This is a message for the Station Commander at Mumbwa, from the *Rhodesian Air Force*. We are attacking the terrorist base at Westlands Farm at this time. This attack is against Rhodesian dissidents and not against Zambia - Rhodesia has no quarrel, repeat no quarrel with Zambia or her Security Forces. We therefore ask you not to interfere or oppose our attack. However, we are orbiting your airfield at this time, and are under orders to shoot down any Zambian Air Force aircraft, which does not comply with this request, and attempts to take-off. Did you copy all that?"
Lusaka Tower -   "Copied"
Chris Dixon   -   "Roger. Thanks. Cheers."

John Edmond immortalised the airstrike in Zambia with his Ballad that reads as follows:
> Our wings are a fortress to our land.
> Today, a special mission's planned.
> Dear land, today I'll serve thee well.
> My motherland has gone through hell.
> No one in the world to heed her; tomorrow the world will know Green Leader.

Fight anywhere and everywhere.
Speed and Courage – and a prayer
Seek and Strike – Strike from above
Do it for the ones you love
And as our sections now deploy – a minute to run.
Seek and destroy
Swift to Support – men and machines
Aspire to achieve our dreams.
This is what God would have willed
Kill, or see the children killed
My little country cries for peace
No one would hear her case.
At last – no one in the world to heed her,
To-morrow the world will know Green Leader.
No one in the world to heed her, tomorrow the world will know Green Leader.

A little later the Zambian Air Controller requested permission from the Rhodesians for an international airline approaching from the north, to land. Permission was politely refused, with the instruction to make an orbit of the airfield, thereby delaying his landing.

Retorted the Kenya Airways airline transport pilot, "Who is in control - You or the Rhodesians?" "Well I think the Rhodesians do at this time." answered the Air Traffic Controller. After the airstrike, Norman Walsh came on the air with "Okay, you can carry on now" to the Controller, signing off the transmissions.

The attack by the Rhodesian Air Force was over. The raid was by no means the most significant attack made by the RhodAF, but it was one of the most publicised and it represented some of the earlier tactics employed, and the self-developed specialised weaponry.

The RLI attack could be mounted only after the Dakotas and Alouettes had finished delivering the SAS troops to Mkushi. They were flown to FAF 2 – Kariba, the night before, under cover of darkness, and went into battle by Dakota paradrop around midday.

Rhodesian intelligence conservatively estimated that one thousand five hundred terrorists were killed. But as proven time and time again, with the turmoil and resultant confusion, plus the wounded that crawled away to die elsewhere, there is no absolutely reliable method of assessing the casualties caused to the ZIPRA forces.

In addition to Operation *Gatling*, the Rhodesian Air Force took part in numerous combined operations during 1978. These included an attack in May on a barracks in the centre of the Moçambique town of Tete; the destruction of a ZIPRA base on the north side of Lake Kariba during July; an assault during September on New Chimoio (Chimoio Circle), in which the pilots of Canberras, Hunters and Lynxes operated almost blind through an intense heat haze; and an attack during December in which a single Hunter completely destroyed an ammunition dump in the north of Tete Province.

However, one fact is certain. The Viscount *"Hunyani"* and the peoples of Rhodesia were avenged.

Operation Bouncer: 11 October 1978

Operation *Bouncer* was planned to abduct ZANLA Commanders Rex Nhongo and Josiah Tongogara and although it failed in its mission it did demonstrate the excellent respect and co-operation between the Rhodesian Air Force and the Special Air Service. In addition, it further reinforced the technical ingenuity of our innovative and highly competent technical staff.

Operation *Bouncer* was mounted in the heart of Funnyland, otherwise known as the Russian Front, between Beira and Lourenço Marques (later Maputo). Rhodesian Intelligence had established that the ZANLA Commanders would travel from Chimoio, crossing the Sabi River at Vila-Franca do Save en route to the renamed Maputo. The briefing was for SAS to paradrop, capture prisoners and recover by Alouette helicopters.

The operation started going sour when the paradaks dropped the 12 SAS paratroopers into a populated "Freds" area - amongst the FRELIMO. Very soon OC FAF 7 was called out to dispatch four G-Cars to extract their compromised colleagues. However, the helicopters couldn't get there and back without refuelling and this necessitated additional fuel drops by Dakota. Then one of the two Lynxes providing top cover radioed FAF Commander Squadron Leader Peter Briscoe that one of the G-Cars couldn't get its rotors going again.

Without batting an eyelid, a stick of four SAS remained behind to guard the chopper, while Pete arranged for a new clutch from Salisbury, duly brought down to Chiredzi by Canberra. The clutch was uplifted by two helicopters and accompanied by a Lynx for top cover, set off for the stranded chopper in Funnyland. On arrival, the crews had already removed the burnt out clutch and the replacement was then installed in double quick time - of the order of three-quarters of an hour.

En route back, the weather deteriorated just as fast as dusk turned into night, forcing the three helicopters to night-stop in Fred territory, thus running the risk of the loss of nearly a complete Fire Force - something the Air Force could ill afford. Fortunately, all went well and a safe recovery was duly executed - which would not have been possible without the good co-operation which existed amongst AHQ, FAF, New Sarum, Canberras, Dakotas, Lynxes, Alouettes and last but not least, the trusty and dependable Special Air Service.

So much for Operation *Bouncer*.

Operation Jacket: 2 November 1978

Operation *Jacket* was an air raid on a ZIPRA terrorist camp on 2nd November 1978, in which ten to twenty men were killed, and fifty wounded. Zambia quickly asserted that it was a refugee camp but it soon became clear that it was a storage depot. As expected, the raid brought protests from all and sundry and even resulted in a violent reaction against whites living in Zambia. It also encouraged British weapons and monetary aid to rehabilitate the Benguela railway in Zambia / Angola.

However, there was very little world condemnation when ZIPRA terrorists from Zambia blew up our railway 34 kilometres south of the Victoria Falls – as it happened – on the same day that the air raids were launched.

Operation Vodka: December 1978

Operation *Vodka* was an attack on the ZIPRA camp at Mboroma in Zambia on 22nd December 1978. The camp was in a remote area one hundred and forty kilometres north of the Zambezi River. A Dakota paradropped the Selous Scout reconnaissance team into the area on 28th November. They were able to carry out their preparations from aerial photographs taken by Canberra. Intelligence revealed the presence of about one hundred and twenty prisoners of war, who were guarded by some 40 to 60 ZIPRA, additionally armed with 14,5 Russian anti-aircraft guns.

The attack commenced with a Hunter airstrike, followed by the Dakota paratroops. The ZIPRA resistance melted as the airstrike went in – no doubt due to the loss of some eighteen terrorists killed. About thirty prisoners were freed. Transport aircraft uplifted the assault force from a nearby airfield and the prisoners, together with the raiding party were uplifted to safety at a border base camp overlooking the Zambezi.

Quite a few Islander light transport aircraft from No 3 Squadron were used to fly out captured enemy documents and equipment. Dakotas were used for the paratroopers, and recovery of ZIPRA prisoners released from the Mboroma Detention camp.

Amongst those rescued was a former member of the police – BSAP – and a grandson of a Rhodesian Senator Chief. Both testified as to inhuman torture at the hands of the terrorists. The Sunday Mail summed up the operation in their Christmas Eve release thus: -

"Operation *Christmas Cracker* on Friday was unlike other Rhodesian raids which hit the enemy supply and training camps. This one, to rescue abducted Rhodesians held in appalling conditions, was a truly humanitarian action in the best spirit of Christmas. To the rescuers Rhodesians say: 'Well done, those men.'"

Operation Pygmy: November To 22 December 1978

Operation *Pygmy* was an airstrike by Canberras on the ZIPRA training base at Mulungushi, some one hundred kilometres north-east of Lusaka, on 22nd December 1978. The camp was located on the western shores of the Mulungushi Dam, and was used to school the enemy in conventional warfare. The timing of the Canberra airstrike coincided with the Hunter strike on the Mboroma camp (Operation *Vodka*).

An intercept of the Zambian Army radio-net revealed that thirty-three terrorists were killed in the airstrike, and many others wounded. At the time the camp had apparently contained a total of some two hundred and seventy conventionally trained ZIPRA terrorists.

Operation Shovel: 15 December 1978

Operation *Shovel* was mounted as a result of information gleaned from a high-ranking terrorist. The Special Branch established from the secretary of the ZANLA High Command for the Tete Province (whose immediate superior was the top operational commander Josiah Tongogara) that: -
- A certain hangar at Tete airfield contained a large amount of explosives and arms.
- Resupply for Tete was by rail, from Beira to Moatize, the station nearest to Tete.

Acting on this hot intelligence, Comops tasked No 5 Squadron to carry out the necessary photo surveillance. No 1 Squadron was tasked to carry out airstrikes on the explosives store (cache), and the Special Air Services, in conjunction with No 3 Squadron for support, to blow up the rail bridge (and hopefully, the re-supply train as well).

A pair of Hunters was duly scrambled. The leader's rockets fell short but the number two made no mistake, and his rockets scored a direct hit. It transpired that the massive arms dump (3,000 land mines) hoarded in the hangar blasted the hangar itself, plus the surrounding buildings off the face of the earth. So intense was the force of the explosion that the ammunition dump caused utter devastation over a wide radius.

A Dakota, meanwhile, took off from FAF 5 Mtoko to paradrop the SAS in the vicinity of the Mecito Bridge. The 1,000 kilograms of TNT charges was dropped by Dakota, but was unfortunately off target – and the poor old SAS troopies had to slog through the bush to locate the charges. Once on site with the charges, the SAS discovered that the bridge was a lot higher than the photo interpreters had revealed. Anyway "a Boer maak 'n plan", and so the charges were laid, and the ground forces awaited the arrival of a train to complete their demolition objective.

The demolition team did not have long to wait – on 15th December 1978 a steam train appeared – destined to end its journey at the bottom of the riverbed. The SAS group followed up, firing their RPDs and RPG-7s into the rear of the train and carriages. There was a token exchange of fire from the FRELIMO who were on board, but they quickly gave up the fight and fled into the Moçambican night.

At five o'clock in the morning on 20th December 1978, Small Bez (Johan Bezuidenhout) heard a rumble in the distance and called to an OP on a nearby hill to verify his suspicions of approaching vehicles. This was duly confirmed – a large convoy of about 20 assorted trucks appeared through the early morning rain half an hour later. The ambush was sprung when the SAS fired an RPG-7 rocket at a troop carrier, while the mission commander remotely detonated a landmine under a Land Rover. The explosions brought the assorted trucks following the convoy to an abrupt halt – they U-turned and sped off in the direction they had come. The convoy sought shelter in an orchard, but was spotted by an eagle eyed Lynx pilot. By 08h30 the low cloud cover had cleared sufficiently for the Lynx pilot to talk a pair of Hunters onto the target. Airstrikes accounted for the remaining vehicles, the cherry on the top being a ZANLA petrol bowser. Comops could, once again, chalk up another very successful airstrike, convoy and bridge demolition operation.

7 Operations 1979

Operation Inhibit: 17 December 1978 to 12 May 1979

A twenty-man SAS ambush team was parachuted by No 3 Squadron Dakota south-east of Malvernia tasked with the destruction of ZANLA and FRELIMO vehicles travelling to the Moçambican border town.

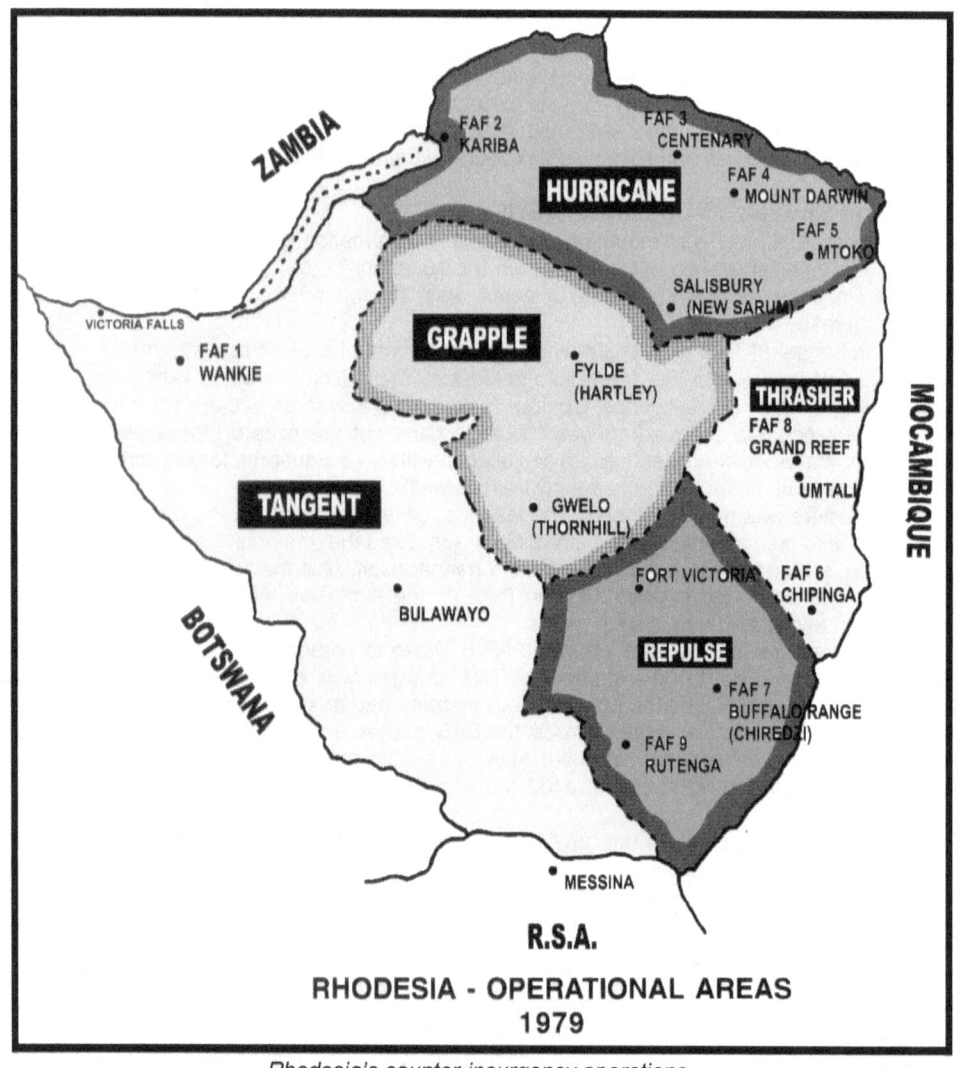

Rhodesia's counter-insurgency operations.

However, instead of vehicle movement, the ambush party was unexpectedly confronted by foot soldiers patrolling along the railway line. A first patrol numbering about forty ZANLA was permitted to pass through the killing ground. Not as lucky was a second patrol consisting of some eighty-plus the following day. Newly commissioned officer Lieutenant Rich Stannard sprang the ambush on this opportunist target and accounted for 17 terrorists killed in the ambush, with a further 28 terrorists dying later of wounds sustained (as revealed by subsequent radio intercepts).

Whilst the SAS guys were helping themselves to much needed drinking water, two FRELIMO soldiers appeared, strolling along the road. A fortunate sniper shot struck the rocket in the RPG-7 launcher, killing both FRELIMO.

The SAS lost Corporal Mo Taylor, for the 45 enemy they had accounted for. The kill rate on this operation proved to be one of the highest from a single SAS ambush. But the loss of one of their own took the edge off their victory. Operation *Inhibit II* followed simultaneously, from 8 February to 18 June 1979.

Operation Steeple: 9 to 20 January 1979

The first week of Operation *Steeple* was the Grove Road surveillance in Botswana by the SAS till the 13th, and the Livingstone Road and Simane Mine Road in Zambia up to 20th January, for any ZIPRA heavy convoy movements.

Operation Gaiter: 11 January – 22 March 1979

Operation *Gaiter* was a marginally successful external operation for the SAS. 10 ZANLA terrorists ambushed them near Hot Springs in Manicaland, killing Corporal C. Cripps and wounding two others. However, they avenged his death when the SAS in turn ambushed and command-detonated a landmine on the road to Muchanedze (Manica Province of Moçambique), destroying a vehicle and killing one terrorist. On 24th January the SAS destroyed another vehicle, and killed another terrorist in an ambush on 22nd March.

Helicopter Mid-Air Collision

As the war had intensified in the Midlands Operation *Grapple* area, the JOC there requested Fire Force cover. Operations in the Northwest were relatively quiet, and the Wankie Force was deployed to Thornhill. Just after mid-morning on 2nd January 1979, a number of CT's were seen moving in the Selukwe area. Three helicopters and a Lynx were scrambled and were soon overhead the reporting call-sign. In the K-Car were Air Lieutenant Ray Bolton, Sergeant Brian Cutmore and Army Captain Doug Havnar. Air Lieutenant Kerry Finn flew G-Car Yellow 1, and Air Lieutenant Colyn James was in Yellow 2.

The K-Car pulled up into its 700ft orbit and was trying to pick up the enemy whilst the G-Cars went into their usual low level circuit. Soon after dropping off his troops in a stop position, Kerry Fynn, with his renowned eyesight, saw the terrorists and engaged them with his Brownings. At the same time he attempted to talk the K-Car onto them. The bush was thick and this was no easy task. To make it easier to see, the K-Car descended. In order to get his guns to bear more effectively the G-Car climbed. All crewmen had their eyes fixed to the ground. Tragically, the two aircraft collided.

Air Lieutenant Kerry Fynn, Army Captain Doug Havnar, Sergeant Brian Cutmore and Sergeant Tony Turner were all killed. Miraculously Air Lieutenant Ray Bolton survived – possibly because the Alouette helicopter landed upside-down in a ditch – and his head, so to speak, was cushioned in the ditch.

Contact: 5 January 1979

Chris Cocks, a Corporal with 3 Commando RLI, gave a Brownjob description of a contact with a large group of ZANLA terrorists on 5th January 1979, which occurred fairly close to Grand Reef. His three years in the Rhodesian Army was drawing to an end. He recorded his experiences in an excellent book titled *Fireforce – One Man's War In The Rhodesian Light Infantry*. The "contact" was significant in that the action employed the Fire Force strategy of using paradrops by Dakota, calling for Canberra airstrikes, rounding up the cooks and bottle-washers as reserve forces, and more significantly, the loss of an abnormally large number of "houtie-slayers" (RLI slang for their own kind). His Sergeant at the time, Sergeant Hugh McCall wrote this report about the contact: -

"While deployed on a Fireforce operation on 5th January 1979, Stop 6 was put down by helicopter to act as a stop group, there being an as-yet undetermined but obviously large number of terrorists in the contact area. We moved into the thick bush area to await the arrival of Stop Seven from our rear.

"On arrival of Stop Seven at our position, due to the thickness of the bush they walked right on to our position before seeing us. I had to guide them in with a series of low whistles. Realising we were bunching up, the Stop Seven stick leader, Corporal Hughes, immediately told his men to move to the right and then came towards me to make a plan for our next move.

"Stop Seven then turned to move to our right, when without warning we were subjected to concentrated automatic weapons fire and grenades from close quarters to our right from an undetermined number of terrorists. Two members of Stop Seven, Troopers Pilbeam and Wilkens, were grievously wounded and incapacitated by the initial bursts of enemy fire.

(Pilbeam had taken a round through both eyes, and became totally blind. Wilkens was shot through the hip and his leg – and eventually recovered from his wounds). One of them fell on top of the other who had gone to ground and ended up in an ant bear hole where he was unable to move, being pinned down by the weight of his wounded comrade and his machinegun.

"The right hand man of Stop Six, Trooper Bob Smith, at once moved between the wounded and the enemy to protect them, with total disregard to his own safety. Smith then put down such rapid and accurate fire that he repulsed the flanking attack before the rest of Stop Six could swing around the wounded man to be in a position to help him. Once the remainder of the stick was in a position to help, Trooper Smith, being a trained medic, immediately began to administer first aid to his wounded comrades and prepare them for casevac, which had been called for. He gave the men swift and efficient first aid and assisted or carried them to the casevac helicopter at a LZ that was coming under enemy fire.

"Stop Six and the remnants of Stop Seven were then reinforced by Stop Eight and ordered to move forward in a sweep line into the bush to our front. After advancing about one hundred and fifty metres the right flank of the sweep line was subjected to automatic weapons fire, the first burst hitting Smith in the abdomen and exiting through his right buttock, knocking him back down with the force of it.

"Due to the thickness of the bush it was difficult to determine the exact position of the enemy. In spite of the severity of his wounds, Smith turned over and returned fire. The enemy fire was striking fiercely all around him, when Trooper Grace moved to Smith to pull him back to cover. He did this on his own initiative and with disregard for his own safety. Trooper Smith seemed to be annoyed that Trooper Grace was risking his life for him and obstinately continued firing. Trooper Grace was finally able to bring Smith back.

"No 3 Commando suffered five casualties in this contact. The others were Trooper Brad Little, killed in action and Trooper Hooley, who had been shot and bayoneted through the legs. During the course of this action twenty-seven terrorists were killed – including three high-ranking commissars. Then five months later, in June 1979, the Commando lost five men, including Sergeant Hugh McCall, who was killed on the last day of his final bush trip. Also, as mentioned earlier, the Commando CO, Major Bruce Snelgar was killed on 26th September 1979, in a helicopter crash (hit power lines near Umtali), just before a major cross-border operation in Moçambique."

Chris Cocks also wrote a sequel to his first *Fireforce* book, entitled *Survival Course*, published in 1999, and describes his experiences as a PATU stick leader while working for the Sabi-Limpopo Authority in the Lowveld. Although I found his typical RLI slang rather obnoxious, he does an excellent job of relaying the difficulties of young troopies coming to terms with the nightmares of their past, cold blooded killing, post-traumatic stress, alcoholism, broken marriage and drug abuse. Two Middle Sabi farmers, Peter Gunn and Peter Kenchinton were murdered by terrorists, and PATU units also successfully made regular contacts with ZANLA gooks. Cocks also recalled what was possibly one of the last follow-up actions of the bush war. An O.P. on Mutema Mountain spotted a small group of terrorists that failed to report to one of the pre-arranged Assembly Points and was thus successfully contacted on 16th April 1980, a matter of two days prior to the "election" of Robert Mugabe to power.

An event on 19th February 1979 warrants special mention. The bush war had taken a dangerous turn for fixed-wing pilots when an ADF Internal Affairs pilot, Byrne Gardener, was killed when his aircraft detonated a landmine on the runway at Mrewa. Contending with landmines on runways became an issue for the relevant JOCs to deal with, and special precautions were taken by aircrews and ground forces to ensure the relative safety of users.

Operation Grovel: 23 February 1979

Op *Grovel* was the Air Force airstrikes on terrorist bases in Zambia. Five days earlier Salisbury airport came under ineffectual terrorist attack, when fifteen mortar bombs landed well outside the perimeter – without causing any casualties. On 23rd February our Canberras bombed two ZIPRA camps west of Lusaka, killing eighteen and wounding one hundred and fourteen. Canberra pilot Glen Pretorius was reluctant to divulge to the writer who his navigator was (believed to be Paddy Morgan), or who the other crews were. Simple deduction would point to the late Ted Brent, with Jim Russell and / or Kevin Peinke with JJ Strydom. Vic Wightman told the writer that he flew two airstrike sorties on that day, but can't remember who his number two was. *Grovel* however, was overshadowed by the more daring raid deep inside Angola three days later – with SAAF Canberra support, on Operation *Vanity*.

Operation Vanity: 26 February 1979

On 26th February 1979, four Canberras of No 5 Squadron struck deep into Angola to destroy a ZIPRA base at Luso, 1,000 kilometres from the Rhodesian border, in a daring and highly successful raid.

This Israeli-type raid was in reprisal for Nkomo's ZIPRA shooting down the second Viscount *Umniati*, in which all 59 people on board were killed - Air Rhodesia Flight 827 from Kariba to Salisbury on the 12th February 1979. Bill Irvine, the co-Minister of Transport, had warned ZIPRA: "On the occasion of the last disaster I said that he who seeks to ride the wind will reap the whirlwind and it came to pass. I trust that before the Ides of March have come and gone Nkomo will once again be weeping tears of sorrow."

Flight Lieutenant Paddy Morgan, who was my navigator on Canberras, excelled himself. Squadron Leader Ted Brent led the Canberra formation. I felt proud, having been associated with both pilot and navigator, and particularly No 5 Squadron, for demonstrating its potent capability. As a matter of passing interest, Ted passed away in Pietersburg in 1994, and Paddy joined the SAAF, to become a Lieutenant Colonel by the late 2000s.

The target was a ZIPRA encampment at Vila da Luso in central Angola, close to the Benguela railway. It was believed to house three thousand hardcore terrorists, trained and equipped by East German and Cuban military advisors. Shortly before the attack, East Germany had flown five hundred more of these "advisors" to the frontline states, many of whom were destined for this camp. The terrorists were under the false impression that their base was considered outside of the range of the Rhodesian Air Force – and thus safe from air attack.

The Canberras positioned at Victoria Falls airport for a first light take off on 26th February. Chris Dixon's Canberra developed a radio snag, but managed to catch up with the rest of the formation over the Zambian town of Mongu, on the Zambezi, about three hundred and seventy kilometres en route to the target. They climbed to thirty nine thousand feet and soon found themselves flying between two layers of cirro-stratus cloud, complicating navigation. The Command Dakota, as well as Hunters from No 1 Squadron for top cover, followed the Canberras into Angola. The Canberras descended below cloud to their turning point west of the target, and on the Benguela railway, as planned. Then the fun and games started. Ted and Paddy noted to their horror that it was raining buckets, with visibility down to six hundred feet. They descended to treetop height and flew through the storm, which was directly on their track.

At five minutes to strike, the formation climbed to their bombing height of three hundred feet. With two minutes to run, they could just see Luso through the storm, and opened their bomb doors. Miraculously, the storm ended in a clean-cut edge, simultaneously with Paddy positively identifying the target. The rest of the Canberra formation was now in line abreast - all of them dropping their bomb loads on target (bar one thousand-pound hang-up). Once clear of the target, they dropped back to treetop height, heading south for five minutes. Then it was a climb up to forty one thousand feet and straight flight path for Vic Falls. This took the Canberras well into trail height – the height at which vapour trails form – but with plenty of cloud about the likelihood of being spotted from the ground diminished.

As soon as the top cover Hunters knew that all was well, they headed for home. The Canberras landed safely at Vic Falls, with only ten minutes low level flying left in the tanks. They were then faced with the drama of clearing the hang-up. The 1000lb bomb, already fused, was gingerly made safe and manhandled on to an enormous cushion made of BSAP mattresses and palliasses. Ted Brent was heard to say, "Fear I knew not. But terror – yes".

Due to brilliant intelligence work, the Rhodesian pilots had been able to ignore the British-manned defence installations in Zambia as well as the Soviet-run radar tracking system in Angola. The Soviet MiG-17s at the Russian and Cuban air base in Henrique de Calvalho did not have time to retaliate.

The result of this highly daring raid?

One hundred and sixty guerrillas were killed and 500 injured. In addition:
ZIPRA forces in Zambia shot down two Zambian Macchi aircraft.
Bill Irvine's prophecy was fulfilled.

It is opportune to recall the spoken word of Rhodesian Front MP Wing Commander Rob Gaunt when the first Viscount was downed. He said in Parliament "I believe we have done our utmost in this country to be reasonable and the time, I fear, is now upon us when Africa is going to see the first race of really angry White men."

Operation Neutron: 15 February To 18 March 1979

Operation *Neutron* was a classical FAC directed airstrike on the Moçambique terrorist camp known as the Vanduzi Circle, on 17th and 18th March 1979.

Within six months of the security forces' raid on ZANLA's Chimoio Circle, the area was again re-established as a terrorist base. They had re-sited their new base camp between two mountains, Monte Bossa and Monte Urueri, and named their new complex the Vanduzi Circle. This complex was situated some 15 kilometres from Chimoio town. ZANLA was wary of Rhodesian Air Force airstrikes and had thus dispersed their camp too widely for a conventional attack.

At the beginning of March 1979, Special Air Service commander, Martin Pearse, decided to deploy six soldiers by helicopter some 14 kilometres from the Vanduzi main camp. Their purpose was to establish a safe rendezvous point for two-man reconnaissance teams who would talk the Air Force strike aircraft onto appropriate targets. Rich Stannard crept up the Monte Bossa Mountain and observed the goings-on below. The airstrike commenced at first light on 17th March.

A pair of Hunters from No 1 Squadron was the first on target, firing their rockets and 30mm cannon amongst the thick trees covering ZANLA at their night base. According to the O.P., at their vantage point, there was only one terr up and about that morning .....and the gook stood mesmerised by the aircraft and their descending cargoes of death. Massive explosions tore the still sleeping camp apart, shredding branches off trees. Even John and Janet, the tame baboon early warning 'sentries', were caught napping - the surprise was absolute. Then, after the initial explosions, pandemonium ruled as the rudely awakened ZANLA ran amok.

Air Strike Nos 963 to 966: 17 to 20 March 1979. Vic Wightman, Glen Pretorius, Varky Varkevisser, Norman Maasdorp, Dave Shirley

The Canberras came in, then the G-Cars with K-Cars, followed by Lynxes from No 4 Squadron. Then trouble: as the helicopters came around a corner, the pilots were taken completely unawares as a 14,5 millimetre and two 12,7 millimetre heavy machineguns and small-arms fire opened up on them.

With ground fire now coming from areas they had been unaware of, it was becoming dangerously clear to the two SAS observers that they had been watching only a small portion of the camp. Instead of there being 300 or so ZANLA down there, there were probably more like one thousand terrorists, most blotted from view by the thick springy tree tops. Thus the two men on the mountain were totally surrounded by them. It was big odds, even for the SAS.

Then one of the fixed wing aircraft took a hit and had to turn back to Rhodesia. The two SAS men watched as the Air Force aircraft, their strikes over, returned to base in readiness for another visit to Vanduzi later that day. But the cloud base was too low over the camp and the plan had to be scrapped.

The next morning, the SAS men watched as FRELIMO cautiously approached the camp in an armoured personnel carrier followed by a Russian truck. They were armed with AKs on either side of the vehicles and were searching for landmines the Rhodesians might have left lying in wait for them. It was an opportunity not to be missed, and the O.P. once again called for the Hunters.

While the aircraft were on their long journey, thirty-wounded ZANLA were loaded onto the truck and ferried to a holding area. Eventually, a pair of Hunters swept in. They were talked onto the FRELIMO armoured personnel carrier and truck parked under cover of the trees. But the enemy had deployed a two-man Strela team to the top of a little rise that formed the lowest part of the mountain. As the lead Hunter completed its airstrike and was pulling out of its dive, a missile was fired. It homed in on the Hunter and rocketed through the air. The pilot in the mutually supporting second Hunter saw the tell-tale smoke pigtail in time to warn his leader to take evasive action. The lead Hunter headed into the sun and managed to avoid being hit by the deadly heat-seeking missile.

Then the two Hunters returned to give the Strela team a taste of their own medicine – and as the pilots struck, two of the enemy leapt from their hill and doubled away to the safety of the thick bush. The Hunters then eliminated the remainder of the personnel and some of the ground troops with their deadly 30mm cannon.

That night, a Rhodesian pilot sneaked over the mountain range to drop off a resupply of batteries and rations to the two men to enable them to maintain their vigil for a few more days. Due to pinpoint accuracy, the SAS provisions landed just a few metres from them. The O.P. had been living off their rations for two weeks and the resupply was badly needed. Shortly thereafter, the O.P. was radioed to vacate their position because an intercept revealed that FRELIMO had guessed that there were Rhodesian observers somewhere in the area, and troops were deployed to search for them.

Whilst making good their escape, the SAS were spotted. One of the men took a hit below the knee and a *hot extraction* was called for. A No 7 Squadron helicopter soon appeared, and lowered its sling bar for the SAS guys to clip their harnesses onto the ring. As the helicopter pilot changed from his hover to forward flight, the aircraft descended momentarily, dragging the poor guys right through the treetops – with some mishap. When they emerged on the other side all their kit had been ripped from them and their clothes were hanging in tatters. But they were alive, and as they flew home to safety, they marvelled at their good fortune.

Interestingly, subsequent intelligence revealed that Tongogara had been injured in the leg during the airstrike. It was the closest the Rhodesians were to come to eliminating him. Camp Vanduzi would be re-visited in the not too distant future – plus minus two months hence.

Operation Neutron Ii: 12 September 1979

According to the respected historian, Prof Richard Wood, Operation *Neutron II* was a recce and FAC by the SAS and Renamo of a ZANLA camp at Vanduzi, Manica, Moçambique on 12 September 1979.

Attack on Beira Fuel Depot: 23 March 1979

A combined force of Special Air Service and members of the MNR movement carried out a highly successful ground attack on the Beira fuel farm. This was an audacious operation far from home – with support from the Rhodesian Air Force. Aerial photographs, taken from Canberras, with their powerful cameras, provided the planners with the entire layout of the main target.

When the right moment arrived, the Command Dakota, specially fitted out for No 3 Squadron, took off with Rhodesian security force officers aboard, to monitor events on the ground as they unfolded. The tanks were successfully set ablaze – with FRELIMO letting rip with their 37 millimetre anti-aircraft guns – firing wildly into the air. Initially they thought that the depot had been bombed. High explosive shells were streaking across the night sky in every direction. Brilliant orange flashes from the flak were bursting over the city as FRELIMO proceeded to give the saboteurs, and the whole of Beira, an impressive fireworks display.

The Rhodesian security forces were able to make good their escape after their daring raid. The next morning, the citizens of Umtali (some 300 kilometres away) could see the pall of black smoke that hung over the burning fuel farm. Damage and losses was estimated at three million US dollars. The fires raged for 36 hours and FRELIMO was forced to call in South African expertise to extinguish the blaze.

Operation Petal: March/April 1979

Operation *Petal* was the ambushing and abduction of ZIPRA agents in Botswana by elements of the Selous Scouts, with Air Force support. Terrorist deployments into Rhodesia were once again in full swing.

Customs inspections at the border posts were reported as haphazard and perfunctory. Matabele Scouts had been deployed in the Kariba area, in the vicinity where ZIPRA had shot down the civilian Air Rhodesia Viscount – but it was decided to re-deploy them to the Botswana border – where the Matabele could more easily infiltrate, and be mistaken, for pseudo ZIPRA or even Botswana Defence Force soldiers. They were hurriedly picked up from the Kariba bush, bundled into an Air Force Dakota, and flown to Victoria Falls. The Matabele Scouts were then taken by Grey Scouts' vehicles to a drop off point in Rhodesia, from where they walked six kilometres into Botswana, and took up their ambush positions on the Grove Road.

Having set up ambush positions, the Scouts managed to land a really big fish. Although they had hoped to capture Dumisa Dabengwa, the ZIPRA commander, they caught Elliot Sibanda, who was the Senior Intelligence Officer for ZIPRA's' Southern Front. He surrendered gratefully after having been wounded in the stomach. A casevac was called for and the capture was uplifted and flown to Bulawayo. Sibanda was a very intelligent Matabele who had been extremely well trained. In spite of his high rank in ZIPRA, he displayed no basic difference in attitude to any of the other terrorists the Scouts had captured. Once he realised he would not be summarily executed, he told his Special Branch interrogators everything they wanted to know.

Then in April, a daring plan was put together to disguise Scouts in Botswana Defence Force uniforms, and vehicles, and they literally drove into the ZIPRA headquarters in Francistown, and arrested all seventeen occupants – including two trained female terrorists. They were handcuffed, documents seized, bundled into the pseudo Botswana Defence Force vehicles – and driven to Rhodesia. Except for a few minor officials, the entire ZIPRA command for the Southern Front was captured. The information obtained from the prisoner interrogation and gleaned from the documents, dealt the ZIPRA war effort in Matabeleland a severe blow.

As a direct result of this action a substantial arms cache was uplifted in the area of Manaka village south of Plumtree. A further arms cache, said to contain heavy weapons, was indicated as being sited a hundred and twenty kilometres within Botswana. A column was dispatched to capture the contents, but it was found dug up and already moved. On the return journey to Rhodesia, the column was ambushed one kilometre inside Botswana, and during the contact, one Selous Scout was killed and another seriously wounded. The wounded man died while being casevac'd to hospital.

Operation Instant: 7 April 1979

Operation *Instant* was an attack by the Reconnaissance Platoon of 1 Rhodesia Regiment on the ZANLA terrorist camp at Chintopo, in the Tete district of Moçambique, on 7th April 1979.

During the ground attack by this Territorial Force battalion, burning huts exploded and Rifleman G Mostert was killed. Operation *Instant* was but one of the many transborder offensives that were conducted during April 1979.

Operations Liquid and Racket: 10 To 14 April 1979

Operation *Liquid* was the bombing by Canberra of the ZIPRA Mulungushi camp in Zambia on 10th, 11th and 14th April 1979. Operation *Racket* was also Canberra bombing, on 11th and 12th April.

Air photography on a continuous basis, together with the intelligence picture gathered by Special Branch, indicated that Mulungushi camp had not been abandoned after the Canberra airstrikes on 22nd December 1978 during Operation *Pygmy*. The size of the camp had increased in leaps and bounds, and by April, it was estimated that some nine thousand ZIPRA were occupying the camp. Comops detailed the Selous Scouts to place some RAMS target marker flares down for a night bombing airstrike, and Captain Chris 'Schulie' Schulenburg with his side kick, Chibanda, spent a great deal of their time with No 5 Squadron, discussing and planning the best run-in and the best position for the flares.

The Air Force insisted that the raid should take place on the night of 10th April, because there would be ideal moonlight then. The time of the airstrike was also confirmed at 19h00. It was reckoned the relatively small number of casualties suffered by ZIPRA in the Operation

Pygmy raid, had been due to their taking cover in the extensive underground bunker system that was there. To stop this happening a second time, it was decided to put in the airstrike after dark, so that complete surprise could be achieved – and at 19h00 – according to known ZIPRA routine, they would be eating in the cookhouse areas. The darkness should stop the enemy sighting the bombers as they came in, and, the way the Canberras seem to run ahead of their sound, the bombs would be bursting on target before they would realise what was happening. Surprise was an important factor to the pilots too, as a large number of newly installed anti-aircraft weapons in bunkers had been pinpointed on aerial photographs taken of the camp and area. Alpha bombs, to be effective, have to be released at three hundred feet above ground level, which makes the Canberra a vulnerable target if sighted in good time.

Selous Scouts Schulie and Chibanda were deployed on the afternoon of 9th April, and by nightfall on D-Day, had counted no more than ten terrorists in the camp. He came on the air briefly, recommending that the airstrike be postponed until the next night. The request was relayed to Comops, but the Air Force was unhappy and said that because of the favourable moon condition, they were in favour of going ahead with the airstrike anyway. After weighing the pros and cons, Comops agreed and ordered the airstrike to go in as planned.

The Canberras, with Squadron Commander Chris Dixon and Jim Russell in the lead, took-off on time from New Sarum and headed for Zambia. The Scouts, meanwhile, oblivious that the raid was still on, were conducting a close in reconnaissance as the Air Force jets rapidly approached – and they had not set up the flares for the off-set bombing technique. Because Schulie had gone off the air, the Army had somehow not relayed the predicament to the Air Force that there would be no flare to aim at during the bombing-run. Chris Dixon was frantically calling the ground call-sign as they commenced their bombing run. When the flare failed to ignite as pre-arranged, the lead bomb-aimer activated the RAMS – but instead of an illuminated aiming point – the ground stayed dark. Then, the Canberra squadron swept on over the terrorist training camp.

The element of surprise had been lost. Chris decided they had come so far, so they would press home the attack – flare or no flare. While the pilots manoeuvred the bombers in a racetrack to re-position for a second bombing run, the navigators frantically re-set their bombsights. The formation executed a perfect synchronised turn, and although there was a premature greying of hair on least one of the aircrew's head, they all came through unscathed. After sorting themselves out, they lined up once more and homed in on the target – an area that was now well illuminated by a fireworks display of tracer being chucked up at them. They commenced their bombing runs – despite the report that 'there were only ten gooks seen in the camp.' However, with the element of surprise lost, there were few casualties – fortunately the Scouts also escaped being bombed.

The ZIPRA anti-aircraft gunners were soon thoroughly warmed to their job and continued to bombard the empty sky long after No 5 Squadron had departed for home – expending in the process a tremendous amount of ammunition.

There were harsh recriminations at Comops, with the heaviest "box-barrage" bracketing the Selous Scouts, especially for going off the air, and failing to set the ground flare in position, essential for the RAMS off-set bomb aiming technique which was crucial to night bombing. Anyway, Comops ordered the Canberras in again the next morning, hoping to catch ZIPRA off-guard, as, until then, camps had rarely been bombed two days in succession.

On 13th April, the Scouts reported heavy vehicle traffic on the road and also the presence of numerous ZIPRA foot patrols that were out scouring the area. In view of all the activity, the Air Force put in its third airstrike on the camp – this time on the afternoon of 14th April. On 18th April a convoy of nine vehicles was spotted on its way to the camp. But the Scouts on the ground were having ration shortages; they requested uplift and were flown back to Rhodesia. A plan to capture a ZIPRA terrorist to obtain feedback on the results of the airstrikes did not materialise.

Operation Aspect: 13 April 1979

Operation *Aspect* was a failed, in effect, Selous Scout attempt on the life of Joshua Nkomo. It involved ex-Air Force Flight Lieutenant Mike Borlace (or Mike Boardman – his

Zambian alias) who joined the Selous Scouts after the completion of his three-year Short Service contract engagement in July 1978. I remembered him for the number of Alouette helicopters that he had pranged. He was snatched up by Lieutenant-Colonel Ron Reid-Daly, sent through the School of Infantry course at Gwelo, followed by a Scouts course at Inkomo Barracks and dispatched to Lusaka via Botswana.

Mike's Land Rover broke down in Francistown and he then flew to Lusaka in a civilian aircraft. The Scouts weren't able to sort out the Land Rover, had it replaced by a Land Cruiser, and ran into complications at the Kazungula Ferry when a wide-awake Zambian Customs official couldn't get a satisfactory explanation for the extra fuel tank (containing concealed radio equipment). Mike, meanwhile, ran into financial difficulties at the Lusaka hotel he was staying at. This necessitated the Scouts doing some fancy footwork to resolve one hiccough after another. Despite frequent Alouette support sorties into Zambia, this operation became a classical 'coats on; greatcoats off' story.

The Operation was finally called off when ex-Flight Lieutenant (now Selous Scout Captain) Mike Borlace was arrested by the Zambians and chucked into gaol. This caused Comops to hand the operation to the Special Air Service instead – code-named Operation *Bastille*. The Scouts were even less charmed, when the SAS blew up the Kazungula ferry. Lieutenant-Colonel Ron Reid-Daly did not bury the hatchet (after the telephone-bugging saga) and saw fit to discredit the Army Commander at a subsequent cocktail party. This latter incident led to the untimely departure of Lieutenant-General John Hickman, and the Court Martial and conviction of Lieutenant-Colonel Ron Reid-Daly for insubordination. (Authors note; "You can fool some people some of the time, but not all the people all the time. Mike Borlace was called Martin, and sometimes Mike Boardman in Peter Stiff's story about the so-called 'Top Secret' story of the Selous Scouts, but the deception was corrected in Reid-Daly's *Pamwe Chete* published in 1999. I for one was not fooled).

Operation Bastille: 12 to 13 April 1979

While an intense airstrike programme was carried out against ZIPRA targets, including the conventional training camp at Mulungushi, 100 kilometres north-east of Lusaka, the Special Air Service mounted an attack on Joshua Nkomo's home in Lusaka.

The SAS assault in Lusaka was code-named Bastille and was timed to coincide with the Easter 1979 offensive. SAS Captain Martin Pearse and his men boarded the vessel Sea Lion on Lake Kariba on 12th April, five days before the elections were due to be held, and set sail for the Zambian shoreline at last light. Seven Sabre vehicles drove off the ferry and were soon on their way to attack Joshua Nkomo's home. As they approached the Kafue River Bridge, the command Dakota was already airborne in support. The Dakota was the Telstar relay to Comops in Salisbury, as well as the link to the standby helicopters. Also on board was the SAS commander, Lieutenant-Colonel Garth Barrett.

At 19h40, Siavonga police messages intercepted in Salisbury reported that the Sea Lion had been seen violating Zambian waters. They assumed that the Rhodesians were on their way to attack a nearby army camp. JOC Splinter was immediately called in to help and troops were sent across the lake to Chitepo harbour to harass and attack a fishing camp – a decoy tactic to mislead the Zambians. The diversion facilitated the SAS to continue their mission without further suspicion.

Martin Pearse and his "merry men" were able to achieve their objective with minimum resistance – but *The Fat Man* Joshua Nkomo apparently made good his escape by forcing his huge bulk through the toilet window. All they found of him was his general's uniform. By now, the command Dakota flying over Zambia picked up the first garbled and excited police reports of heavy firing. But the entire operation had been pulled off in 25 minutes, with the SAS soon on their way back to Lake Kariba. Three SAS men had been wounded and a casevac was called for.

The Rhodesian Air Force helicopters flew to a landing zone that had been hastily cut by the retreating assault force, and duly airlifted the three wounded soldiers from Zambian soil at about 10h00 the following morning. Some concern was expressed about a reaction from the Zambian MiGs, which did in fact occur. It subsequently transpired that a MiG was deployed to search for the escaping Rhodesians, but was heard to respond to an instruction that he was heading in the wrong direction thus: "No, no. It is not *my* job". By midday, the SAS had boarded the Sea Lion and were well on their way back to Rhodesia. They were met in the middle of the lake by one of the No 7 Squadron pilots who had the foresight to drop them a very welcome crate of beers.

On beaching, the SAS task force commander Major Graham Wilson was uplifted by helicopter, flown to Kariba Heights, and then from FAF 2 back to Salisbury, where he was able to personally report to Comops within two hours on the success of their mission.
Meanwhile, Rhodesian warplanes continued their Easter Offensive by blasting the ZIPRA conventional terror camp at Mulungushi, for the third time that week.

It was not a good time for the terrorist movements. The Afro-Asian People's Solidarity Organisation conference was meeting in Lusaka. Joshua Nkomo was humiliated. The Rhodesians had blatantly blown up his home, in the middle of Lusaka, and had attacked his training base willy-nilly.

Operation Dinky: 12 to13 April 1979

Operation *Dinky* entailed the destruction of the Kazungula ferry that plied the Zambezi between Zambia and Botswana. It was situated at the four-way border point shared with South West Africa and Rhodesia's most northwest corner. The area was well known to the SAS commander of the mission – Captain Colin Willis – OC 'B' Squadron. Colin and I had operated together a year earlier in the Deka area during Operation *Elbow*. Colin was also well versed in the capabilities of the Air Force, having acquired knowledge from all the sorties that the Special Air Service officers had shared, and their excellent relationship with the Bluejobs.

The controversy concerning the Kazungula ferry had raged within the corridors of power for over a year. The Army wanted the Ferry taken out because it was used to ferry gooks across the mighty Zambezi – whereas the Scouts and Special Branch was also using the ferry clandestinely, unbeknown to the other Security Forces! While Comops believed the job could most efficiently be carried out by the Air Force using a couple of rockets, the politicians considered that option as a somewhat *blatant* act, which would attract adverse world opinion. If it had to be done, they argued it had to be done *clandestinely*, so that no one could prove who did it. And so it came to pass that Colin Willis was tasked with the job.

Eventually, Friday 13th April was selected – to coincide with the Easter offensive. The decision had been taken to use a RAD – radio activated device – which had been developed from the highly successful RAMS that Squadron Leader Randy du Rand had helped to develop on No 5 Canberra Squadron (also used for offset bombing). Under cover of darkness the RAD was placed undetected on the ferry. Then at about 06h30 Colin Willis boarded a Lynx at Sprayview – from the Air Force at FAF 1 – and proceeded to a safe orbit north of the ferry in Zambian airspace. They were in for a long wait because the ferry only started its engines at 10h00 (two hours after the anticipated time – because of delays with vehicles lining up to be taken on board).

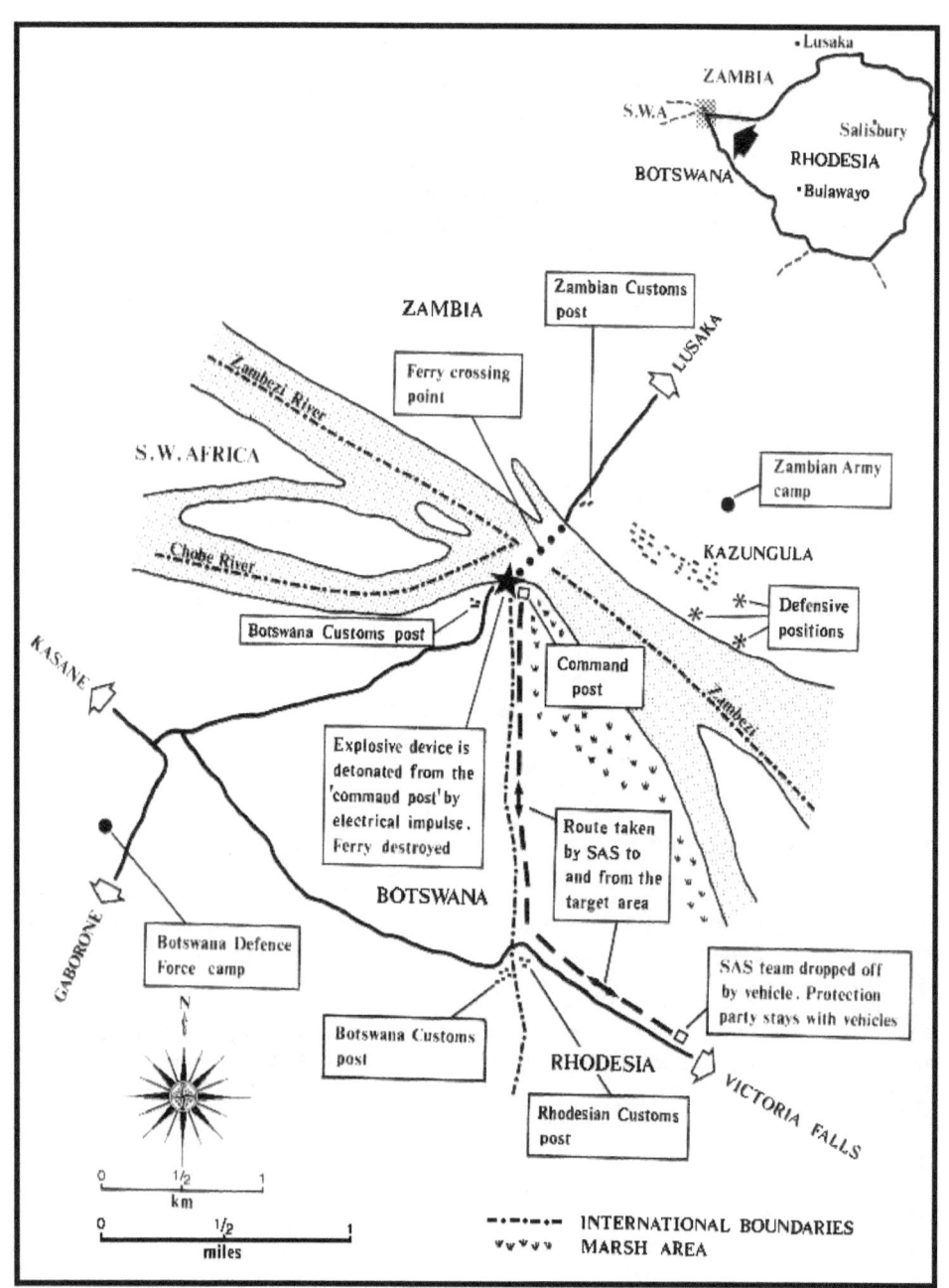

Operation Dinky

Then, just at the right moment, the radio activated device button was pressed and the well-placed explosion destroyed the ferry thus denying the enemy their cheeky method of sneaking men and materials across into Botswana for a trouble free journey into Rhodesia. The ferry had been sent on its final journey - downwards.

Extracts from Rhodesian Prime Minister Ian Douglas Smith's diary warrant quoting verbatim, "12.04.79 – For the past week I've been talking with Nat JOC about a few trans-border operations. From captured terrorists we have information that it is their intention to step up operations during our election in order to harass and embarrass us. ZIPRA has a base in Botswana, and they travel to and from Zambia using the Kazungula ferry. The ZIPRA HQ is in Lusaka, the nerve centre from which all their operations are planned. And they have a large base west of Lusaka from which operations in that area are conducted. One captive from that base tells us that they are planning a big operation to take over a landing strip in north-western Matabeleland, to which they will fly in aircraft from Angola. Our chaps on the ground are hoping that they will try, because they will all be eliminated and we would welcome a few extra aircraft to add to our fleet. But of course, they have neither the ability nor the nerve for such an operation.

"So we are going in tonight with a four-pronged attack, just to give them a reminder. The preparations have been meticulous, because at this kind of game the element of surprise is crucial and for that reason one seldom has a second chance. As always, there are great risks, especially with daring operations and one of these involves driving over the Kafue Bridge on the main trunk road, which is heavily guarded. But our SAS have a plan, and they are confident. These fantastic chaps have proved so many times in the past that they can do the almost impossible. I wished them well, and that night offered up a prayer for their safe return. Many a time I have heard visiting military specialists comment that our Army and Air Force must be, for its size, one of the finest in the world.

"13.04.79 – The operation was a success which exceeded our expectations, with everybody safely back – the most serious casualties were two cuts and a bruise. The snatch from the ZIPRA base in Botswana brought back 14 terrorists for interrogation, the Kazungula ferry was at the bottom of the Zambezi River, Nkomo's house, which is a stone's throw from State House in Lusaka, was demolished, and ZIPRA HQ and an arms cache nearby blown up. The base west of Lusaka was sent flying in all directions."

Quoting Mr Ian Smith's memoirs further – "Poor old Kaunda; I felt a certain sympathy for him, having to put up with all these humiliations. Our crack troops, SAS, Selous Scouts, RLI and Air Force went into Zambia whenever they wished, and the local army did the only sensible thing: they got out of the way. This particular occasion was especially embarrassing for Kaunda, as he was hosting an OAU summit in Lusaka attended by 300 delegates. Apart from having their sleep disturbed by the explosions and gunfire, however, they were in no danger. As all Zambians, Moçambicans and Botswanas knew, we were interested only in Rhodesian terrorists who had declared war on their constitutionally elected government, using women and children and innocent civilians as their principal targets. There was that occasion in 1978 when our Air Force put an aircraft over Lusaka airport (Green Leader – Canberra), giving instructions to the control tower to delay arrivals and departures, particularly those of the Zambian air force, while our aircraft bombed a nearby ZIPRA camp. The instructions – reinforced by a flight of Hunters circling the area – were all faithfully carried out until the operation was completed."

The Prime Minister went on to record in his personal diary,"14.04.79 – The news of yesterday's exploits has reverberated throughout the world – our friends are thrilled and our opponents mad. The fact that there were so many OAU leaders in Lusaka is the cause of considerable alarm – what if we had killed them? It would have been easy enough, but as I have said, that kind of action has never been part of Rhodesia's code of conduct. We despise terrorists and have never believed that their despicable acts give us licence to reciprocate. Our troops are meticulously disciplined, and although this might sound outdated in this dreadful world, there is great spiritual solace in knowing that one has been able to abide by those genuine standards of civilisation to which we have constantly paid lip service and claimed to support."

Ian Smith commented, "These successes were topped off by a general election. By Saturday 21st April, I could record: 'A very successful week with a 63 percent turnout of voters for the election, in spite of the fact that terrorists had attempted to intimidate people into abstaining'."

Abel Muzorewa was to take over power from the Transitional Government on 1st June 1979. In late April, Ian Smith called in the service chiefs, Lieutenant General Peter Walls, his deputy at Comops, Air Marshal Mick McLaren, and the commanders of the Air Force and Army, Air Marshal Frank Mussell and Lieutenant General Sandy McLean, with a plan for Muzorewa to approach Khama of Botswana and Kaunda of Zambia in search of reconciliation and promotion of trade. This necessitated a change in tactics. Rhodesia would desist from provocative attacks in and around Lusaka and deep penetration into Zambia – those acts, which were so humiliating to Kaunda. But, around our borders there would be no slackening of effort or lowering of our guard. Muzorewa agreed, but failed to deliver the goods.

Ian Douglas Smith spent his last day in office as Prime Minister on 31st May 1979. Bishop Abel Muzorewa took office of the new government of national unity the next day.

Operation Bondage Air Strike Log – Refer # 990 - 12 May 1979

Operation Paladin: 13 to 19 May 1979 & 10 to 11 October 1979

Operation *Paladin* was a recce by the SAS for an attack on a Tete Province Barracks. Then in October the SAS was supported by the Air Force in the demolition of three railway bridges near Moatize in the Tete Province, unleashing a swarm of bees – the so-called Front Line State politicians.

Operation Ecstasy: 17 May 1979

Operation *Ecstasy* was an ambush by the Special Air Service of enemy movement at Tembue, Tete, Moçambique after a SAS reconnaissance was compromised.

Operation Ingrid: 31 May 1979

Operation *Ingrid was* a combined SAS / Renamo sabotage and sinking of dredgers in Beira harbour. It coincided with Ian Smith's last day in office before handing over to Abel Muzorewa.

Operation Chamber: 4 June 1979

Operation *Chamber* was a Rhodesian Light Infantry attack on the ZANLA terrorist base camp at Chivinge in the Tete province of Moçambique on 4th June 1979. Corporal P O Rice and Lance Corporal E Nel were both killed in action.

Operation Mineral: 9 June 1979

Operation *Mineral* was a road ambush, by the SAS, at Inchope, Manica, Moçambique on 9th June 1979. 30 terrorists were killed and documents and weapons recovered.

Operation Mustard and Purple: 13 to 15 June 1979

These operations entailed mining in the Gaza Province, and a road in Tete south of Cabora Bassa. The last four operations, *Chamber, Mineral, Mustard* and *Purple*, followed one another. See also the Airstrike Map at page 280.

Operation Amnesty: 14 June 1979

Operation *Amnesty* was a dismal failure, by the Muzorewa Government, to convince the rank and file terrorists, to accept a general amnesty and hand themselves in. Muzorewa had convinced the powers that be that 'the boys in the bush' were tired of being thrashed by the Security Forces, and would be only too keen to lay down their arms.

The Air Force was tasked on leaflet dropping and sky-shouting missions. Although a very limited number of gooks took up the offer, many more hard-liners opted to continue with their 'armed struggle'. Ex-Premier Ian Smith was no longer in the driving seat, having handed over the reins of government at the end of May 1979. For his part, he now had fully kept to his side of the bargain thrashed out with Henry Kissinger – as per the capitulation of September 1976 – and within the three-year time frame agreed upon. Bishop Muzorewa had demanded an amnesty for all terrorists, including those that had been convicted of murder by the Rhodesian High Court, during the opening bout of the Victoria Falls Bridge Conference, back in August 1975. The elections that had brought the Bishop to power were claimed to be 'free and fair'. The six principles, which applied to the Anglo-Rhodesian negotiations, were now fully satisfied; and the Conservative government had to abide by its own manifesto. It had the duty to return Rhodesia to a state of legality, move to lift sanctions, and do its utmost to ensure that the new independent state of Zimbabwe-Rhodesia received international recognition. Now that the Bishop was in the driving seat, it was primarily up to him to make the current cease-fire campaign work – put his money where his mouth was, so to speak. Ian Smith speaks of his frustrations, in his autobiography, and one can hardly blame him for stating, "I told you so".

Meanwhile, the external terrorists were receiving all the help, material and financial, that they needed from Russia and Russia's allies (and China). To state that the Bishop had egg all over his face and had lost a lot of credibility would be an under-statement. For their part, the Security Forces weren't going to take matters lying down. External operations were stepped up a notch. In effect, the bush war raged on, costing more than 2,000 killed or wounded a month.

Operation Mulligan: 16 June 1979

According to Stick Leader Charlie Warren the RLI launched Operation *Mulligan* to the north-west of Salisbury in a bid to rescue Mrs Mulligan who had been kidnapped from a farm, by a gang of gooks. The RLI Fire Force was called out, with contact being initiated by the K-Car with an air strike at a kraal. In the ensuing fire fight, Troopers Bruce McKend and Canadian Eike Elsaesser were killed. The writer has no reason to doubt Charlie's account, because he was wounded in his hand by K-Car 20-mm cannon shrapnel. He lost all feeling, and in his own words "was busy shitting myself with the 20-mm HE rounds exploding around me - - - and bleeding like a slaughtered pig". Charlie was casevaced to the Andrew Fleming hospital for the removal of the shrapnel between his middle and third finger. Charlie mentions that Mrs Mulligan was not rescued that day, but the contact had indeed been with the group of terrorists who had intended abducting her to Moçambique.

Operation Carpet: 26 June 1979

Operation *Carpet* was a two-pronged external attack by the Hunters on ZIPRA's Mulungushi training camp, and the SAS assault on the ZIPRA intelligence headquarters – supported by the Bell 205 helicopters of No 8 Squadron.

Squadron Leader Ted Lunt commanded No 8 Squadron at the time. Barbara Cole's story adds authenticity to Ted's exploits during the Special Air Service's 26th June 1979 attack on ZIPRA's intelligence department in the heart of the Zambian capital, Lusaka. Joshua Nkomo's nerve centre was called the 'Department of National Security and Order' – NSO for short – and was modelled on the Russian intelligence service, the KGB, which had in fact trained all the NSO staff in Moscow – and the NSO was headed by Dumisa Dabengwa, who was second in command to Nkomo. The Assistant Director of Intelligence was Victor Mlambo. The cheeky plan by the SAS proposed that the Air Force's total of five Bell 205 helicopters be used to ferry the troops, putting them down right next to the security fence of the NSO – a mere two hour hop from the Rhodesian border to Lusaka. The far larger load capacity of the Bells would greatly assist external operations as they could carry almost four times the load of the Alouettes of No 7 Squadron.

Ted Lunt received a telephone call (before the operation was mounted), asking him to pop over to the SAS Barracks, Kabrit, to chat to SAS CO Garth Barrett. The SAS had a few questions they wanted to ask the helicopter pilot. They wanted to know whether it would be feasible to land troops with total surprise, at first light, in Roma suburb, Lusaka. Ted said that whilst it could be done, he very much doubted Comops, let alone the Commander of the Air Force, would sanction such a hazardous raid – as the chances of losing fifty percent of their air effort seemed pretty good. Ted's concerns were quickly put to rest – his task was to get 28 SAS to Lusaka, and return. It would be Martin Pearse's problem to sort out the ZIPRA intelligence headquarters.

Total secrecy was placed on the plan – because of a possible snitch in Comops, as was subsequently confirmed. It was Ted who had to plan the fuel requirements, which would be critical to the operation – because the maximum load of men and equipment was to be carried by each of the four 205s that would make the trip to Lusaka. The fifth Bell would be used as a reserve. The Squadron would need to get in below the Zambian radar, and avoid villages and terrorist camps that might raise the alarm. They would also need to fly as low as possible, in loose formation, at night, without the benefit of their navigational lights. A diversionary airstrike on the FC terrorist camp was part of the plan – to distract the Zambian army and air force.

High flying Canberras, for planning purposes took air photographs, and rehearsals by the SAS were conducted at an isolated area near Darwendale Dam. The pilots also practised the run-in to the NSO; the soldiers rehearsed deplaning as the helicopters came in to land, the allocation of call-signs, in fact every sequence so that everybody understood what to expect. There was to be no *cuffing*. No effort was spared to ensure that everybody had the right equipment for the task at hand. D-Day was set for 26th June 1979. The day before, the task force flew to Makuti, with the troops sleeping under the helicopters.

Everybody was up and about at four in the morning. Take-off, as planned, was an hour later. Air Commodore Norman Walsh and SAS Major Graham Wilson boarded the Command Dakota at New Sarum and set course for the target. At Thornhill Air Force base, four Hunters were readied for their diversionary airstrike on the Zambian FC camp. Two hunters were detailed to drop golf bombs, while the second pair was tasked to provide top cover. It was all systems go. It was going to be a significant raid in more ways than one. Not only was it going to strike at the nerve centre of ZIPRA's intelligence centre, but the air and ground forces were to launch their attack only hours before Bishop Abel Muzorewa's black-dominated coalition government of national unity took power.

It would take the Bell 205s about one hour 45 minutes to get to the target. The route was from Makuti, across the Zambezi, well east of Lusaka to a point about fifty kilometres north-east of Lusaka, and then westwards across the railway line towards the vicinity of the FC terrorist camp (just north of Lusaka), then on to their target. Approaching the outskirts of Lusaka, Ted would need to look out for a school from where he would set course for the NSO complex. It was pitch black when No 8 Squadron left Makuti. Time on target was planned for 06h15, when the occupants were expected to rise from their slumber. However, with the flight time taking longer, TOT was adjusted to 06h38.

Ted Lunt then asked Norman Walsh (on board the Command Dakota) to put in the airstrike on FC camp earlier. The Hunters were able to make up five minutes to oblige. After a quick conference with the Command Dakota, the twenty-minute delay to arrive at the NSO target, the thumbs-up was given for the mission to proceed. Ted duly located the school, which was his IP (initial point) and flew the requisite time and heading to reach his target area. The vacant plots by the side of the NSO complex could be seen. As they came down they could also see that the NSO had changed considerably since their aerial photographs had been taken. There were machineguns mounted outside the walls – not anticipated.

Fortunately, the gunners, although at their posts that morning, possibly thought that the helicopters belonged to the Zambian Air Force and as a result did not react. The armed guards, alerted by the racket from the Bell engines, began to spill into the courtyard. Others, who had been sleeping along the perimeter fence, took up their positions – and started firing. There were some 24 guards in all – three times more than expected. Ted was committed to landing the Bells among them; and was greeted by a tremendous hail of bullets. The Rhodesians also opened up. The helicopters were orientated at just the right angle to give our machine gunners full view of the building – with our chaps firing as the helicopters landed.

They had obviously succeeded with the surprise aspect of the mission. The enemy guards were being killed even before the Bells were on the ground. As the command helicopter landed, a round, from a lone terrorist who had run up an anthill on the outside of the building, smashed through the perspex bubble right next to the pilots head. Before the terrorist could do more damage, his weapon jammed. The pilot virtually landed on top of the terrorist, who nevertheless managed to flee down the hill. Garth Barrett leapt from the helicopter and quickly killed the terrorist. Ted and his team lifted off to their holding area, reporting to Norman Walsh that the situation on the ground was looking good. The helicopters flew the seven minutes to their holding area – and to take on vital fuel from the drums that they were carrying. Because of the shortage of fuel, the helicopter pilots shut down their rotors and the aircraft were throttled back to idle – ready to lift off at a moment's notice, if need be. Then the long wait, while the SAS went about their task of ransacking Nkomo's intelligence headquarters of every scrap of paper they could lay their hands on.

Bunker bombs were used to breach the perimeter walling and the buildings. It was just after Martin Pearse had thrown a bunker bomb into the guards' bedroom, and sought shelter round the side of the building, that things went horribly wrong. The blast of the bomb collapsed the sidewall as well, which then toppled onto Martin, causing fatal injuries (Martin Pearse had had a premonition of this incident and had related it to Major Brian Robinson a few days previously).

There was a Zambian Air Force reaction to consider as well. The eavesdroppers in the command Dakota orbiting Lusaka had already picked up the start of a reaction and called in the helicopters two minutes earlier than planned. As the helicopters touched down the troops ran out with bulging sacks of captured paperwork – plus one additional capture who claimed that he was the next door's gardener. Eventually, the daring raid lifted off at 07h30, staggering into the air and leaving a shambles behind. According to their original timings, they should have already been across the border. The two Hunters of No 1 Squadron were meanwhile orbiting above to provide top cover during the pullout phase.

Instead of diverting right around Lusaka, as planned, the helicopters opted for a more direct course over the city – because of low fuel holdings. As they flew home, thousands of leaflets were dropped over the city, calling for friendly relations with Zambia and stressing the raid had not been against the Zambian Government or her people, but against ZIPRA. Then the Command Dakota gave the alert that the Zambian MiGs had definitely been scrambled to search for them. The pilots made a beeline for the border, with some of them advising their soldiers on board to keep a sharp lookout for enemy aircraft. The helicopters flew low, constantly varying their route to take evasive action as well as to take advantage of the terrain for maximum protection. The spare Bell had brought fuel to a location just short of the Zambezi to refuel those in most need of it. Ted was able to get his whole squadron clear of Zambia without further incident.

Operation Carpet Air Strike Log No 1004 - 26 June 1979: Ted Lunt, Vic Wightman

After successfully carrying out their airstrike on the FC terrorist camp in the morning, the Hunters returned to Thornhill for a quick turn-round – in order to prepare for their next task – for a flag-waving mission, totally different in character from their earlier war-like efforts. They were needed for the ceremonial fly-past at the opening of the country's first black-dominated parliament.

True to his word, out-going Premier Ian Douglas Smith had now met all the conditions agreed with Henry Kissinger. And yet, the West still refused to acknowledge the Rhodesians' achievements. Meanwhile, back at Comops, the captured "canary" was singing music to the ears of Comops staff.

The "gardener" that had been captured turned out to be none other than Alexander Brisk Vusa, the Russian-trained deputy head of intelligence. It transpired that a spy ring existed at Comops, and the ZIPRA hierarchy had been forewarned of the attempts on the life of Joshua Nkomo – hence the trebling of the guard; and the additional machinegun positions. The documents captured from the NSO also provided incriminating evidence.

The raid made headline news. There was concern for the safety of Queen Elizabeth as she was due to address the Commonwealth Conference in Lusaka, at the Mulungushi Hall – a mere two kilometres from the scene of the raid. A *Sunday Mail* cartoon showed Rhodesian Air Force *Green Leader* (Chris Dixon), grinning from a Hawker Hunter and giving the Queen the thumbs up to land at Lusaka.

Operation Chicory: 1 July 1979

The captured Alexander Vusa soon squealed that Nkomo had a vast arsenal just south of the known JZ terror camp, about fifteen kilometres west of Lusaka. Apparently, Libyan aircraft had been making secret night time flights from Angola and landing at Lusaka, offloading their large supplies of weapons from Russia and East Germany under cover of darkness. The West's apparent lack of recognition of the Muzorewa government had encouraged the communist East to move in arms and men to train ZIPRA.

A Canberra was sent to over-fly the area on a photo reconnaissance mission. The resultant photographic interpretation indicated that there was indeed a vast amount of weaponry cached all over the bush. There were heavy vehicle tracks under practically every tree spread over a fifteen-acre area – and there were also bunkers and trenches. A lightning strike was decided on – before Nkomo could relocate his arsenal. The plan called for immediate airstrikes, with SAS, to destroy as much war material as possible. Killing terrorists and recovering any worthwhile documents and prisoners would be a bonus. Sunday, 1st July was decided as D-Day.

Because it was a Sunday, not many ZIPRA would be expected to be in the camp. The element of surprise was more crucial. At 12h45 the five Bell 205 helicopters of No 8 Squadron started their engines – with a ground force of 50 men drawn from all three SAS squadrons, and set off from Bumi Hills, across Lake Kariba. Almost an hour later, the Hunters and Canberras overtook the helicopters en route to their targets.

Operation Chicory Air Strike Log No 1006 – 1 July 1979: Vic Wightman, Varky Varkevisser & Glen Pretorius

The Canberra and Hunter airstrikes were spot-on target. Large clouds of black smoke and dust billowed up for the heliborne troops. The helicopters deployed their troops at designated areas – the munitions caches, and the political commissar's camp. As expected, there was only a small caretaker force on duty and resistance was light. Soon 100-metre high sheets of flame and debris were raining down all over the camp and 122 millimetre rockets were burning and zigzagging in every direction as the camp went up in smoke. At the nearby political commissar's camp, 500 tents full of belongings and weapons were destroyed.

Meanwhile, two Zambian Air Force MiGs were scrambled from Mumbwa, but were obviously very wary of the Rhodesian Hunters providing top cover for the helicopters. The Command Dakota was monitoring the situation and radioed the pilots to hold back and await any signs of Zambian aggression. Although the Hunter pilots sighted two silver MiGs, no aggression was evident. The Zambian radar-interception controller was furiously trying to direct the MiGs on to the Hunters, but their pilots were completely ignoring instructions. All they did was to fly from their bases to JZ Camp – then fly back home again. When a column of Zambian armoured vehicles approached, they wisely decided to keep well away from the Rhodesians.

As the helicopters lifted off with their troops on board, the odd enemy RPG-7 and Strela missile was fired indiscriminately – but none found their targets. The only damage sustained was a rotor blade that made friends with treetops.

SAS sources reported large quantities of arms and ammunition destroyed. What was once the biggest ammunition dump in Zambia was now a bombed and blackened reminder of the lightning Rhodesian raid.

Operation Fiddle: 6 to 7 July 1979

This was a Warning Order to the Air Force and SAS for ambush tactics at New Tembue, Tete, Moçambique. Then from 8 to 11 July 1979 Operation *Fiddle* extended to all south-eastern Provinces - and it combined with Operation *Bouncer*.

Operation Cucumber II: 6 to 9 July 1979

Operation *Cucumber II* was a South African coded operation, between 6th and 9th July, four SAAF Canberras accompanied Rhodesian Air Force Canberras on a low-level attack on a terrorist target south-east of Cabora Bassa dam.

Operation Inspan: 13 to 31 July 1979

Operation *Inspan* was an ambush on a road north of Tete, 13 to 15th June and again 23 to 31st July 1979. Results achieved are unknown.

Air Strike Log – Sf Auxilliary Operation: 21 to 22 July 1979

Al Thorogood recalls: "I flew top cover with Roelf Oeloffse. The army commander was from Op *Grapple*, Col Desfountain I believe. I'm afraid I can't remember the Op name or any other crews but there were about 10 or 11 Alos involved. It was trying to round up all the SFA (Security Force Auxiliaries) who scattered and then resisted - altogether not a very successful operation."

Operation Bulldog: 23 July to 22 August 1979

Operation *Bulldog* was a BSAP drive against cattle rustling, which had become endemic in the *Repulse* area. The Police were ably supported by Army and Air Force elements whenever joint forces were operating together or in close proximity to one another. CT's killed were added bonuses for us, but poor compensation for the ranchers – and an economic loss to the country. Particularly bad areas included the line of rail from Rutenga to Sarah, Snoop Farm, ranches along the Nuanetsi River and those bordering on the Matibi 1 tribal trust lands.

Operation Blanket Ii: 23 to 31 July 1979

Operation *Blanket II*, not to be confused with Canberra PR, was a SAS ambush mounted on the Inchope Road in the Manica province of Moçambique.

Operation Placid: 21 to 24 August 1979

Like *Cucumber*, this is a little-known SAAF assistance operation that took place sometime between 21st and 24th August 1979. SAAF Canberras accompanied RhodAF Canberras on four attacks on Mulungushi, one attack on Rufunsa and two attacks on Solwezi (also identified as Qumbo's Farm terrorist base) in Zambia. Winston Brent mentioned the latter two operations in *The Sanction Busters* (page 110).

Operation Boxer: 20 August to 19 September 1979

Operation *Boxer* was an SAS seaborne attack on the oil storage facility in Beira, Moçambique.

Operation Sponge: 22 August 1979
Operation Motel: 23 August 1979

Operation Uric: 2 to 8 September 1979

Between the beginning of April and the end of July 1979 alone, 3149 war deaths had been recorded within Rhodesian borders. Of those, 1808 were terrorists, 1161 were black civilians and 31 were white, while Security Force losses stood at 141. There were no figures for those killed outside the country's borders.

Intelligence confirmed that there were 10,800 ZANLA terrorists in Rhodesia. Some fifty percent were deployed through Gaza, with another 17,000 trainees in the pipeline – one-third was earmarked for deployment into Rhodesia through the so-called Russian Front. All had staged through Mapai; the FRELIMO 2 Brigade headquarters and controlling centre for ZANLA. Comops convinced the NATJOC – National JOC – that the FRELIMO and insurgent lines of communication had to be drastically disrupted. Long-range operations, supported by airstrikes, and aimed at disrupting supplies by paralysing vehicle movement took their toll of ZANLA arms and ammunition re-supplies, effectively putting a brake on aggression in the Operation *Repulse* area. In April, enemy incursions had taken on a new dimension. ZANLA/FRELIMO co-operation improved, grew stronger, and came to light when a FRELIMO soldier was captured as far inland as Kezi in Matabeleland. It was found that more than 200 FRELIMO were operating inside Rhodesia.

The time had come to kick the enemy off the doorstep, to take pressure off the *Repulse* and *Tangent* operational areas. Operation *Uric* was designed to smash Moçambique's road and rail communications. This would be achieved by the demolition of five tactical bridges – and a pre-emptive attack on the Mapai base. Pre-emptive airstrikes were to be made on Barragem, Mapai and Maxaila, and helicopter-borne troops would then be dropped off for the exploitation of that phase.

The operation would involve every available aircraft in the Air Force. These included eight Hunters, six Canberras, twelve Dakotas, six Lynx aircraft and twenty-eight helicopters, including the Bell 205s. Aircraft, and manpower, from South Africa, was also used – separately code named Operation *Bootlace*. 360 soldiers would be drawn from the SAS, RLI and the Engineers. D-Day was scheduled for 07h00 on Sunday, 2nd September 1979 – but the Guti at Chipinda Pools put paid to the helicopters taking off without top cover.

Then, on 5th September 1979, No 1 Squadron sent in four Hunters for their airstrike on Barragem, 320 kilometres inside Moçambique and 150 kilometres northwest of the capital Maputo. The Hunters swept down the Limpopo Valley to attack the enemy defensive positions on the road and rail irrigation canal bridge, the most important bridges in the south-east, feeding the irrigation for the entire area. All the aircraft encountered anti-aircraft fire, but the jets scored a number of direct hits on weapons, destroying two barrack blocks and all transport.

Exactly five minutes later the Helicopters arrived, with 48 SAS, and a Lynx aircraft as top cover. The helicopter-borne troops were dropped within one kilometre of the Barragem road and rail bridges, and lifted off immediately for their safe holding area. The SAS captured two enemy 23 millimetre anti-aircraft guns, and were able to use them in a ground role against enemy resistance, which came from both banks of the river. During this action, one SAS soldier was shot in the leg and a casevac was called for. As Flight Lieutenant Dick Paxton came in to uplift the casualty, he was shot down.

In the heat of the battle, the Bell flew over the main enemy position – and as Dick was descending into the LZ, an enemy RPG-7 rocket launcher was fired while the helicopter was still hovering. The rocket struck just below the blades, severing the main rotors. The Bell plummeted to earth and burst into flames. No 8 Squadron Technician Alexander Wesson was killed on impact. SAS Sergeant Flash Smythe pulled Dick Paxton from the flaming wreckage. Dick suffered a broken elbow and lacerations, but was lucky to be alive. The helicopter was burnt completely – a terrible waste of life and a vital aircraft (This was the second narrow escape for Dick Paxton – on 24th October 1973, Dick had been dropping troops around a terrorist base when he came under heavy ground fire. This action led to many terrorists being killed, the remainder fleeing and abandoning large quantities of clothing, equipment and documents of great value to the Security Forces).

It took the SAS five hours to prepare the five bridges for demolition, completing their tasks by 16h30. The troops sprayed thirty vehicles with machineguns, drained a fuel bowser and blew up two power sub-stations. By now, all the bridges, with the exception of Barragem, had been totally destroyed and the rail link severed. It transpired that the Barragem Bridge had been built stronger than the plans had indicated – and was thus still useable by light vehicles. By last light on D-Day, all the troops had been extracted and were back at their forward admin base – preparing for the assault on Mapai the next day.

Nos 1 and 5 Squadron continued their run of airstrikes on no less than eleven different targets. The Hunters and Canberras were striking targets at Barragem, Mabalane, Combomune, Mpuzi, Chicualacuala, and Malvernia - all along the line of rail, up to the Rhodesian border. Other pre-planned airstrike targets included Maxaila, Chigumane and Mabote that were well to the north-east of the railway line, as well as a terrorist base near Pafure, just south of the Limpopo River. Turn-round times were unfortunately about three hours, because of the need to return to Thornhill and New Sarum respectively, to re-arm and refuel.

Nos 3, 4, 7 and 8 Squadrons were operating out of forward airfields at FAF 7 (Buffalo Range), Mabalauta and the Chipinda Pools administrative base.

The Mapai base was struck on the morning of 6th September 1979. 500 and 1,000-pound bombs, as well as Golf bombs, were raining from the skies as the Rhodesian aircraft swept over their targets. The FRELIMO command element area and communications centre were demolished, and the Russian-occupied bunker collapsed from a direct hit. Lucky to be alive, the Russians quickly pulled out of Mapai. Scores of tents went up in smoke, a small armoury exploded, 22 FRELIMO were killed and 32 wounded. All the uninjured took up their defensive positions, and manned their anti-aircraft batteries.

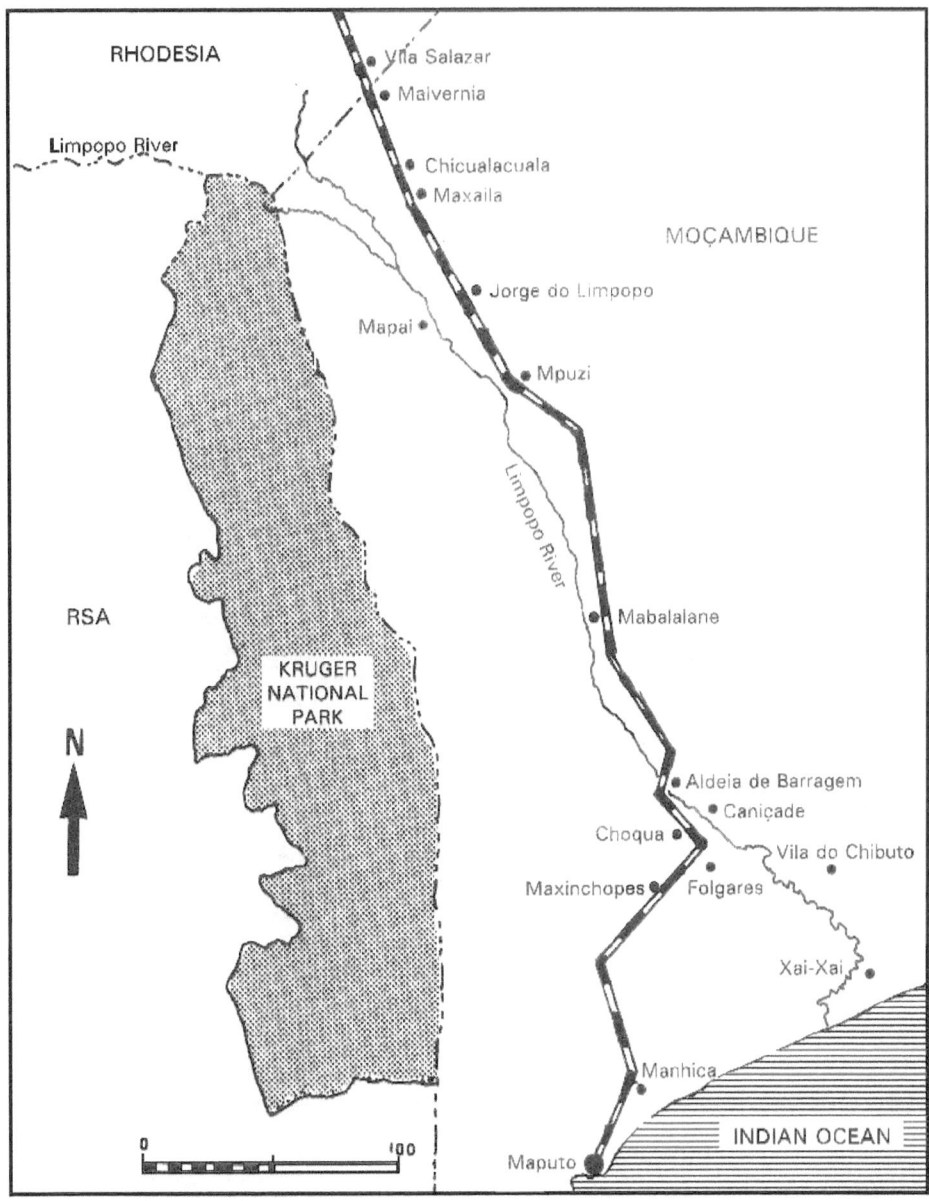

Operation Uric/Bootlace: Map showing general operational area of Moçambique involved in Rhodesian efforts to cut FRELIMO/ZANLA's road and rail logistical routes.

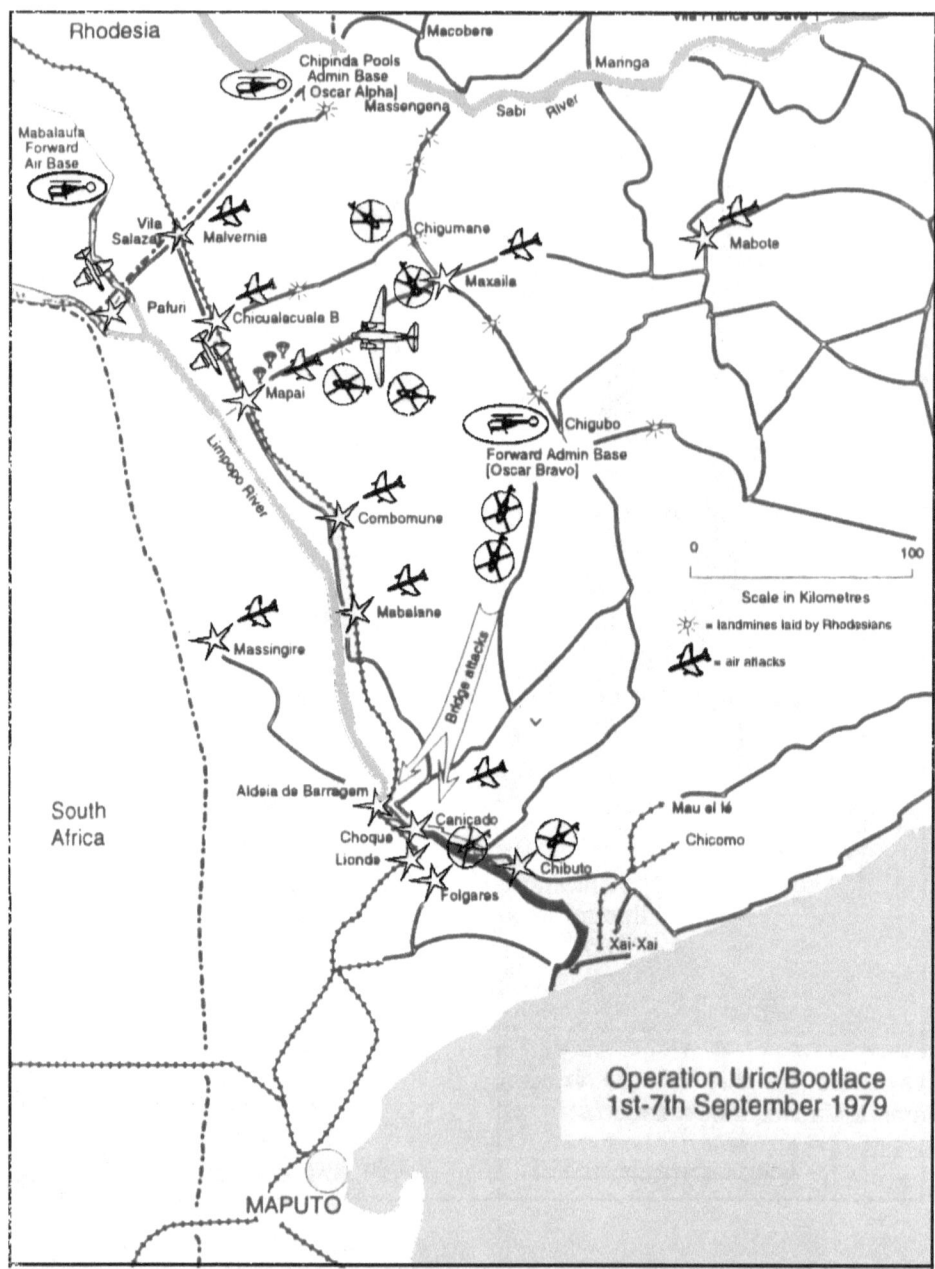

Operations Uric and Bootlace (SA) map – Rhodesian attacks on FRELIMO and ZANLA road and rail logistical routes in Moçambique

Half an hour later, the second wave of airstrikes commenced. The main radar station was knocked out, one anti-aircraft nest was destroyed and more people were wounded. The Hawker Hunters were subjected to severe ground fire, but miraculously escaped without casualties. The 192 helicopter-borne troops were meanwhile on their way to their pre-selected dropping zones, one kilometre from Mapai. Then tragedy struck.

A Smersh SA 330 Puma helicopter (from the South African Air Force) was hit by ground fire. As the pilot flew over a satellite camp, miles from their main target, the enemy opened fire. There were two distinctive bangs which were probably an RPG-7 rocket that struck the aircraft immediately behind the pilot. The Puma rolled to the right and crashed into the ground. They never stood a chance – it exploded in a ball of flame on impact, killing everyone on board. It was the worst single military disaster of the Bush War. Killed were the commander South African born Captain Joey du Plooy (27); Captain Charlie Small, the Operation *Uric* demolitions officer (29 – an exceptional Engineer, who I knew personally); 2nd Lieutenant Bruce F Burns (26); Sergeant Michael Jones (19 - British); Corporal LeRoy Duberley (27 - well-known national rugby star); Corporal Hugh Fry (20); Corporal Peter Fox (30); Trooper Jacobus Briel (20); Tpr JM Crow (19); Trooper Brian Enslin (20); Trooper Stephen King (27 - Australian) and Trooper David Prosser (26 – also Australian). The Puma crew were also killed - Captain Paul Velleman, co-pilot Nigel Osborne and Sergeant Dirk Retief.

An RLI call-sign went in to inspect the crash site and confirmed that everyone was dead; and that it was impossible to bring out the remains. The loss of our three airmen with their two helicopters, in two days, seriously affected the air support that the Air Force could now provide the Army. Besides, the loss of Charlie Small, the demolition expert, was a major blow to our covert capabilities. Bell R 6098 was irreplaceable, and the South Africans had to write off their SA 330 Puma helicopter. As a result of the helicopter casualties, a number of operational adjustments were made to the plan. It is of interest to note that the press release for the day made no mention of the Puma crash – the fact that the Bell had crashed the same day made a wonderful excuse to attribute all the deaths to just one helicopter accident – that of the Rhodesian Bell 205. The South Africans were not officially involved in the operation.

Meanwhile, the bulk of the SAS/RLI troops were dropped at their landing zones. It soon became evident that Operation *Uric* was not going to be a cakewalk. Jet strike after jet strike was called for from the ground troops, and other than during their absences on the long turn-round times, the Hunters and Canberras were able to satisfy most calls, in addition to carrying out their pre-planned airstrikes. The security forces on the ground were almost helpless during the period when all the aircraft were away for re-arming and refuelling. On their approach to Mapai, the SAS had discovered a series of early-warning stations built on platforms in trees, which were connected by landline to the FRELIMO central command post in Mapai. It was a fascinating find and explained how FRELIMO been able to monitor Rhodesian Air Force helicopter movements so accurately and for so long.

The SAS came up against a two-kilometre maze of typical Russian-designed interconnecting zigzag trench works. No sooner had they cleared one area than the enemy would pop up behind them. Meanwhile, the jets continued to put in strike after strike and the ground forces couldn't quite believe the amount of fire being directed at the aircraft. There were 37 millimetre and 23 millimetre guns, and there had to be about twenty of them spread over half a kilometre. The Canberras were forced to do a re-strike from 21,000 feet, as it was too risky to go any lower. And as they flew high over Mapai, every one of the twenty heavy weapons opened up on them.

Resistance remained fierce. General Peter Walls was airborne in the command Dakota and after a discussion with senior officers, he took the decision to curtail the assault on Mapai. A captured FRELIMO subsequently admitted that they had very little food and water, and were exceptionally tired. Had the security forces pressed home their attack on Mapai and remained for another two days, Mapai would have been taken. As it was, had the SAS lost many more men (and many more Air Force aircraft, for that matter), it would have had a dramatic effect on

The ground forces retreated to a safe distance and were uplifted by all the available helicopters. It became a race against time to get them all back to Rhodesia before dark. The long line of helicopters skimmed the treetops and made their way homewards through the dusk. The entire area appeared to be teeming with enemy and the Alouette and Bell helicopters were subjected to ground fire throughout their flight, coming under heavy fire as they over flew a FRELIMO Mobile column. It was a frightening experience for the troops and aircrews alike. The Rhodesians simply could not afford to lose another precious helicopter and more men. Eventually all the troops were returned to the Forward Admin Base area (refer above maps).

Fortunately, the air strike schedule had gone almost to plan. During the two-day period, airstrikes were put in on 14 enemy strongholds in Gaza. Much damage was caused including the destruction of the telecommunications and radar links at Malvernia. Barbara Cole paid a worthy tribute, in these words: "It was a truly magnificent effort by *The Blues*."

Operation Bootlace: 2 to 8 September 1979

The South Africans coded the Rhodesian Operation *Uric* as Operation *"Bootlace"*.

The abnormally large number of aircraft committed to the operations has already been mentioned. These were beyond Rhodesian resources, and the picture becomes more focused as soon as strategic thinkers put numbers together. South African Air Force assistance entailed providing three of the six Canberras used for bombing, six Dakota aircraft, Super Frelon, Puma and Alouette helicopters – in fact SAAF helicopters were in the majority of the twenty-eight used in the operations.

Winston Brent's research was censored, but he did establish that the Canberras flew no less than 26 operational sorties! These were three aircraft against Mapai on 5th September. The next day the three Canberras were used four times, all of them targeting Mapai. Then on the following day (7th September) three aircraft attacked Malvernia, followed by one Canberra to Mpuzi, one to Chicualacuala, then three to Ngala, and finally three Canberras on a night attack on Mapai (See *Rhodesian Air Force – The Sanction Busters,* published by Freeworld Publications, August 2001).

The Canberra bombers, from No 12 SAAF Squadron operated out of Fylde airfield (away from prying eyes), the Dakotas operated out of FAF 7 Buffalo Range, and all the helicopters operated out of a satellite FAF set-up at Chipinda Pools. In addition, the SAAF also placed a powerful force of Mirage and Buccaneer strike aircraft at cockpit readiness in South Africa – most likely at Hoedspruit, Pietersburg and Waterkloof Air Force Bases. They would intervene if MiGs of the Tanzanian Air Force threw their weight behind FRELIMO after the operation got underway, or if there were any other calamitous happenings.

As also mentioned, there were 350 ground troops drawn from the SAS, Rhodesian Engineers and RLI. What is not generally known is that the South African 1-Reconnaissance Commando disguised themselves as "D" Squadron of the Rhodesian Special Air Service. As a back up, the South Africans placed a battalion of paratroops, with Puma helicopter support, on standby at a base near the Moçambique border. The Recces flew into New Sarum in two Hercules C-130s on Wednesday evening, 29th August 1979. They were kitted out on the Thursday, and were flown to Buffalo Range on the Friday, in Jack Malloch's Air Trans-Africa DC8F. The South Africans were tasked to blow three bridges – the bridge over the Changane River at Vila do Chitbuto, the rail bridge at Maximchopes railway station (under the command of Major Bert Sachse), and a third bridge blown by Captain Dawie Fourie. The South African Recces were all deployed and airlifted by Puma helicopters.

Special mention needs to be made of the South African equivalent of the Rhodesian Command Dakota. Our Dakota was a humble C-47, code named *Warthog* equipped with the bare essentials – and flew a course skirting the Moçambique border between the Limpopo River and Phalaborwa in South Africa and back – transmitting intelligence for the ground forces and keeping well away from areas where they might be intercepted by the enemy. The South Africans had their own 'Warthog', a more sophisticated DC-4 they called *Spook*, which was simultaneously conducting a separate monitoring exercise. They had the capability of an advanced sensor system to locate and monitor the guidance systems of ground-to-air missile installations and identify surveillance radar systems. They could thus scramble the Mirage and Buccaneer aircraft that were standing by at cockpit readiness in South Africa.

The noteworthy Operation *Bootlace* tragedy for the South Africans, as well for the Rhodesians, was the loss of the Puma piloted by Captain Joey du Plooy, and Captain Charlie Small of the Rhodesian Engineers.

By Sunday 10th September 1979, the Recces had returned to the Durban Bluff.

Operation Norah: 12 September 1979

Operation *Norah* was an SAS/MNR sabotage mission of a tropospheric scatter station deep inside Moçambique, with air support from Nos 4 and 8 Squadrons of the Air Force. The highly sophisticated radio transmission and telecommunications centre was situated on top of Monte Xilvuo, Sofala, some 165 kilometres from the border, on the road to Beira. It took the two Bell helicopters from No 8 Squadron two lifts to get the heavily laden SAS/MNR group operators to their LZ deep inside Moçambique. Cutting the communications chain linking the major FRELIMO bases around the country would disrupt enemy communications, and force them to switch to a system that was easier for the Rhodesians to intercept and monitor.

During their escape, they ran into a roadblock and scattered in all directions. However, their getaway did not go too well because while fleeing, they split and three men got lost. One group made contact with base and requested air support. A No 4 Squadron Lynx was scrambled from the Grand Reef FAF, and soon made radio contact. The Telstar duty proved highly successful in that the call-sign that called the Lynx was able to make contact with, and locate the second group. A roll call established that three soldiers were still missing. The ground troops found themselves boxed in by pursuing FRELIMO, who were supported by tanks. Hunters were immediately placed on standby. The Army 'Sunray' on board the Lynx decided to call for a hot extraction, and requested a jet strike to keep the FRELIMO at bay.

The Hunters were quick to react and soon attacked, putting down their deadly payloads. When the jets' time overhead ran out, they returned to Thornhill. A pair of Bells arrived to extract the security forces, but could only take half the men on the ground to safety. Unfortunately, those left behind had to wait for the second lift, and the Lynx also needed to return to its FAF to refuel. Some anxious moments were spent by those remaining on the ground, anxiously listening out for the reassuring sound of their rescue aircraft.

After a worrying ninety minutes without air cover, the Lynx appeared overhead again. Shortly afterwards, the Bells arrived to take the rest of the troops home. Even before the helicopters had touched down, the operators had thrown in their kit. The Bells again struggled to lift off with such a heavy load – whereupon the Brownjobs obliged by throwing a couple of Bergens overboard – they did not fancy another long wait for a third round trip! The operators had quite a bit of adrenaline to replace that night and readily reverted to consuming large quantities of vodka. There was still no sign or word from the missing three guys – and the Blues did not begrudge their Brown counterparts' 'getting pissed'. After much speculation, the Air Force agreed to conduct a search for the missing Brownjobs. Early the next day, a Bell, with a Lynx as top cover, started an aerial search for the missing security force chaps. The operators on the ground, who had covered about twelve kilometres, heard but did not see, the helicopter. They threw green smoke grenades but failed to attract the pilots' attention. The trio felt only frustration as the chopper, which to them represented life itself, flew off, and the bush fell silent once again. The whirr of the rotors generally meant uplift and it was the most loved sound by any operational soldier. Their spirits sank.

Some time thereafter, the trio again heard a helicopter, and again failed to attract the pilot's attention. Then another put down 400 metres away from them to refuel from its inner fuel drums. But this helicopter lifted off before the missing Brownjobs could get near enough. The chaps then found an ideal spot and decided to lie low and wait for a search aircraft. Then at about 13h00, two Lynx aircraft came overhead, traversing the area for about twenty minutes – their square search bringing the aircraft quite close to their position. But the Lynxes were low on fuel, and disappeared from sight – much to the frustration of the guys on the ground. Two hours later, the Lynxes were back again. The Brownjobs realised this was their last chance - they lit fires and frantically used their heliograph. After about twenty frustrating minutes, a Lynx was observed waggling its wings. However, the pilot lost their position, and the guys on the ground thought they were now doomed to footslogging back to safety. Just then, in the aircraft Sergeant Karl Lutz,, who had volunteered to come along as an extra pair of eyes spotted his mates' ground fires and heliograph.

Barbara Cole, in "*The Elite*", records this event thus "...and the helicopter pilot came in with the usual Rhodesian Air Force precision. The LZ was only just big enough for the Bell to hover above them at six feet. The three men scrambled up into the chopper, and the chopper climbed out of the LZ and headed home."

Operation Enclosure: September 1979

Operation *Enclosure* involved the attempted abduction of a ZIPRA contact man staying at the Chobe River Lodge, who controlled the entire movement of terrorists from Zambia, through the Caprivi Strip, into Botswana. Special Branch intelligence had found that the contact man named Mkwananzi, was transporting terrorists from Kazungula to Panda-ma-tenga, Francistown, or Silibe Pikwe. There was a large ZIPRA terrorist camp at Silibe Pikwe, housing ZIPRA terrorists. Terrorists ex-filtrating from Rhodesia would get a message through to Kazungula for Mkwananzi to uplift them from the Grove Road for transportation to wherever they were destined for.

The Bulawayo Selous Scouts formulated a plan to send a pseudo group into Botswana with the objective of abducting the contact man, to disrupt terrorist incursions. The pseudo group duly positioned itself on the Grove Road, and roughed up a passing Coley Hall heavy transport driver, ordering him to relay a message to the Kazungula based contact man that they were a returning ZIPRA group waiting uplift. The pseudo group set up ambush positions and before long spotted the Ford pick-up coming down the road at high speed.

The pick-up had two terrorists in the back, and instead of stopping at the branch laid across the road, Mkwananzi drove straight over the obstruction – and out of the ambush killing ground. When the vehicle did not stop, as expected, the ambush team fired their RPG-7. The weapon misfired, and a pseudo dressed in ZIPRA uniform leapt out to spray the vehicle with his RPD light machinegun. The driver lost control of the vehicle, careered off the road and crashed. When the pseudos arrived at the vehicle, they found no sign of the driver, but the two terrorists that were on the back of the pick-up were dead.

An Air Force helicopter, carrying Captain Andy Samuels, was overhead almost immediately. He had been standing by across the border in case he was needed to uplift the prisoner. An aerial search was conducted, but neither the call-sign on the ground nor the helicopter found any trace of Mkwananzi. It was discovered later through radio intercepts that he had got away. He was hospitalised in Francistown – and had three bullets lodged in his body.

Then, on release from hospital, he rolled his private car while out driving, killing his wife and all his children – and putting himself back in hospital with a broken spine. So, although he had evaded the abduction attempt, and escaped the ambush killing ground, the notorious contact man was no longer able to continue his evil deeds.

Operation Bowler (SAAF): September 1979

Operation *Bowler* was essentially a South African Air Force operation in Matabeleland, based at Gwanda, and forming the core of Fire Force Zulu. A Lynx from No 4 Squadron supported the three "Jaguars" – Puma helicopters, as well as a Kiewiet (Cessna 182) employed in the sky-shouting role. South African parabats were deployed in SAAF Dakotas. Although they also operated from FAF 7 Buffalo Range, their main activities took place at Kezi, Matopos, Tuli Block, and Section 7 of Liebigs Ranch in the West Nicholson area.

The Fire Force Zulu Kiewiet had a bank of very powerful speakers mounted into the door for sky-shouting, and this was a great improvement over the original equipment used with the Dakotas. As opposed to the earlier version that used one or two massive speakers, the Kiewiet sky-shout used lots of smaller speakers and was much more powerful, yet much clearer, far easier to hear on the ground. The Kiewiets were also used in the role of spotting, tracking and reporting on the movement of terrorists and calling in the Fire Force when it looked like the gooks were going to stop long enough to bring in a successful attack.

Puma pilots Monster Wilkins and Crow Stannard are known to have taken part in this operation, and reported on one particularly successful contact in the Kezi area where eight gooks were accounted for.

Operation Bowler Air Strike Log No 1049 – September 1979: Monster Wilkins & Crow Stannard

Operation Miracle: 21 September to 6 October 1979

Operation *Miracle* consisted of attacks on five camps which formed the core of the Chimoio Circle - well defended by revetments, linked by trenches and spread over sixty-four square kilometres which could accommodate several thousand inhabitants. Chimoio Circle was Russian-planned and was dominated by a granite kopje dubbed Monte Cassino, complete with Russian 12,7mm and 37mm guns.

Prior to the start of Operation *Miracle*, but subsequent to the commencement of the Lancaster House talks, several intelligence-gathering sorties against the Chimoio Circle had been carried out with little success. Possibly the ZANLA High Command had learned their lesson after the complete destruction of the first Chimoio raid in 1976 and Operation *Dingo* in November 1977.

Firstly, air reconnaissance at high level failed to locate any new encampments. Then a Special Air Service force flown in by helicopter, had to be hastily hot-extracted by helicopter, with a Lynx as top cover and telstar. Next, a two man Selous Scouts call-sign also needed Rhodesian Air Force hot extraction when they ran into armed ZANLA women. The SAS readily admitted that if it had not been for the timely arrival of *The Blues*, the outcome may have been very different – such was the close call. They counted themselves lucky not to have taken casualties. A Canberra then flew another photographic mission over the area and the five camps were identified, facilitating the planning of Operation *Miracle* - which would commence with an airstrike made at first light.

However, a couple of days before the airstrikes were launched in this particular operation, tragedy befell the Air Force with the loss of a valuable gun-ship and its crew. Air Lieutenant Paddy Bate, flying the K-Car with Flight Sergeant Gary Carter, and with Major Bruce Snelgar (OC 3 Commando, RLI), were engaged in Fire Force operations in the Makoni and Mutasa Tribal Trust Lands. Their mission was to create deception with high-density operations within Rhodesia, and thereby distract attention from the external operation. Whilst on a Fire Force call-out, the K-Car flew into some power-lines, killing all aboard the Alouette gun-ship. But the show must go on, and Operation *Miracle* commenced with the Canberras' airstrike on the terrorist camp (Winston Brent mentions that two SAAF Canberras supported the Rhodesians – they were used on 27th September – see page 111 of his 'censored' *Sanctions Busting* book published August 2001).

Air Commodore Norman Walsh flying in the Command Dakota, together with SAS Colonel Brian Robinson controlled the operations by day. By night Lieutenant Colonel Ron Reid-Daly would take over. At 07h00 on 3rd October the Canberras went in to attack at low level with bouncing Alpha bombs, against Monte Cassino and the nearby gun emplacements. Visibility was poor, largely as a result of the smoke coming out of the bombed areas. Also, at this time of the year, haze was a problem for the aircrews.

The aircraft were subjected to intense anti-aircraft ground fire. It appears that Air Lieutenant Kevin Peinke made an attack with 50 Alpha bombs and went around for a re-strike. Kevin ran in from north to south, on his first attack, did the same in his second attack, and then appeared to be hit by ground fire. He turned to starboard, flew on for a short distance and then crashed about a kilometre short of the Rhodesian border, on the Girezi River, killing both Kevin and his navigator, Flight Lieutenant J J Strydom.

Unfortunately, the mobile ground forces column was still seven hours behind schedule and thus the ZANLA forces were able to evacuate their camp.

The next day, delayed by adverse weather conditions, the Hunters attacked their targets at 13h00 hours with Golf bombs. The Lynx pilot, flying through an incredibly dense curtain of flak, marked the target for the Hunters. The No 1 Squadron pilots also met extremely heavy anti-aircraft fire despite the dropping of sixteen 1000lb Golf bombs striking the defenders and devastating the area. The Hunters were called upon by the ground forces to blast each high point in turn until the high point ridge adjacent to Monte Cassino was taken by the Rhodesian troops. The performance of the aircrews was considered very brave by the Browns, and ".made a deep impression on the troops they were supporting." By now it was dusk. The troops dug in while ZANLA evacuated their strongholds as quickly as they could, leaving for some of the remaining strategic defences.

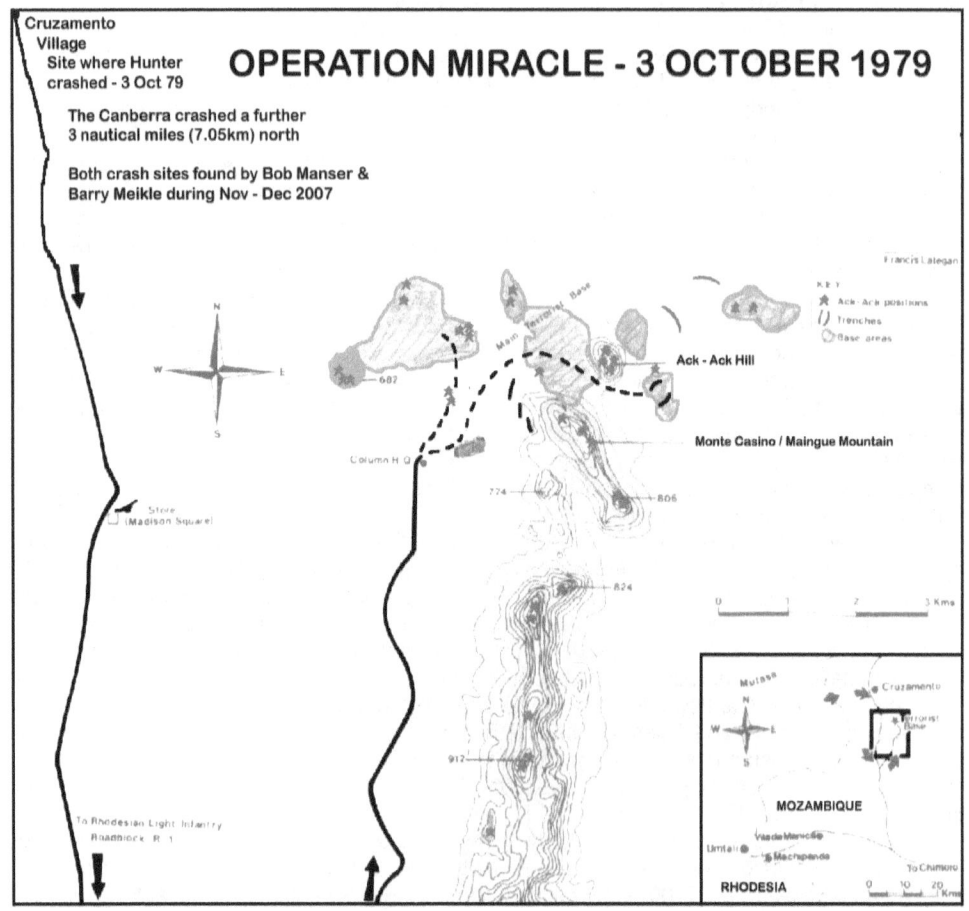

Operation *Miracle* Attack on ZANLA terrorist base in Chimoio circle September/October 1979

(Permission granted by Peter Stiff to use the above map is gratefully acknowledged)

The following morning the Selous Scouts resumed their attacks, with further help from the Hunters. Monte Cassino was reached at about 10h00 hours. The evacuation had been an orderly fighting retreat, and apart from bodies and abandoned equipment, each strongpoint had been held until the right moment. During the day, Air Lieutenant Brian Gordon in his Hunter FGA 9 was shot down and killed. This tragic event which, when added to our other losses, meant the Rhodesian Air Force had suffered its worst losses in any operation of the war.

The kill ratio was small in relation to the immense effort entailed. When Monte Cassino was eventually taken, a grand total of eleven enemy bodies were located. It was assumed the enemy had carried a lot of their dead and wounded away with them. Approximately two thousand out of a possible twelve thousand had defended Chimoio Circle. The protracted operation had permitted most of the enemy to take the gap in haste, and abandon huge quantities of military and logistic equipment such as the Russian 12,7mm and 37mm guns, food, medical supplies, and documents and records.

Also captured were John and Janet, the two tame air raid warning baboons, which became excited and noisy whenever an aircraft approached even at a distance.

During the night FRELIMO mounted an attack using six Soviet T-34 tanks and infantry. But they quickly withdrew after sustaining a direct hit from a Rhodesian Artillery twenty-five pounder shell. The next morning No 4 Squadron Lynxes spotted the tanks but before an airstrike could be mounted the tanks had vanished.

The camp was an incredible 64 square kilometres, far larger than expected. There were so many gooks there that they had burned fully-grown trees, not merely logs, for their cooking fires. Shoes and clothes lay in heaps as the wearers ran out of them in their haste to escape. Plates of sadza porridge lay scattered in the trenches. When the bomb run had been put in on the camp, the elusive Rex Nhongo and his driver had jumped into Nhongo's green Land Cruiser and bolted. The driver panicked and crashed into a tree, whereupon the occupants leapt out and ran away. ZANLA commander Josiah Tungamirai, seen hiding in his vehicle under the trees, also managed to get away with his life.

The next day, the Rhodesians withdrew their forces nineteen kilometres back across the border.

Operation Miracle Airstrikes – refer Nos 1046, 1051, 1052, 1054 & 1055 - 27 September to 3 October 1979
Date: 27 and 28 September 1979
Aircrews:
- Vic Wightman
- JR Blythe-Wood
- John Annan
- Ziggy Seegmuller

Target: Monte Cassino, New Chimoio, Hill 761, Moçambique
Result: Trooper Gert O'Neill killed
Date: 3 October 1979
Aircrews:
- Brian Gordon
- Ziggy Seegmuller
- Tony Oakley
- Varky Varkevisser
- John Annan
- Kevin Peinke / JJ Strydom

Result: Brian Gordon killed. See also PB's *Winds of Destruction*, page 556. Canberra aircrews killed – shot down by FRELIMO

At the going down of the sun, and in the morning, we will remember gallant Brian Gordon, Kevin Peinke, J J Strydom, Paddy Bate and Garry Carter.

Manser / Peinke Connection

The reason for Bob Manser's interest is that he is trying to locate Kevin Pienke's Canberra crash site. Bob is a radio fitter off No 16 Course, who fondly remembers Kevin choppering him as a TF ex-Regular on Cashel Valley assignments. They got to know each other when Bob was on TF call up and found Kev a very cheerful chap, full of fun and bounce and always had time for a chat. Bob runs a history/environmental society which included organising an over-land trip to Senna on the Zambezi, the site of Mary Livingstone, nee Moffat's grave.

Bob had heard from farmers in the area that some of the locals vaguely remember the air crash, but after 30 years, memories are fading rapidly. Any metal is a valuable commodity. It is thus not surprising that not much, if any, would have remained after the Canberra crashed. Bob commented: "If I do locate the place, I do not expect to find much in the way of wreckage as all metal here is like gold and chopped up and sold to the metal collectors who scavenge the country-side buying up anything, all sent back to China". Most of the locals in Manica Chimoio area speak Shona (rather than Portuguese), and this may aid Bob in locating the exact site.

Local Manica town historian of note, James "Tackie" Bannerman, kindly supplied the Mozambique maps, which helped to establish where the Canberra and Hunter crash sites occurred, in order to assist Bob Manser in his search. Take note that what the Rhodesians called Monte Cassino is in fact called Maingue by Mozambique.

The riddle was further solved when ex-Selous Scout Willie van der Riet e-mailed the writer and had this to say: "I was on an OP to the north west of Monte Cassino, observing the Frelimo convoy being attacked by the Air Force. Peter Curley was with me. I can confirm that the Hunter went down at the junction of the two roads – marked Mavonde Aldeira. The FREDS had stopped firing and possibly a minute or so had gone by before I heard the Canberra going down to the north of my position". See annotated map below.

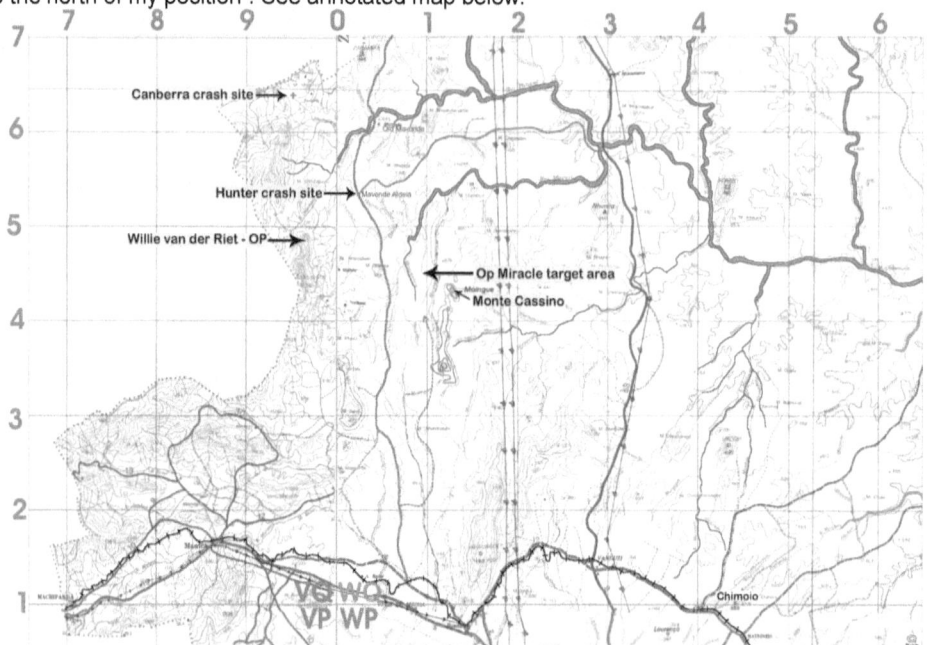

Operation Miracle Map – kindly supplied by Manica historian James "Tackie" Bannerman

Peter Petter-Bowyer, who was serving in Comops at the time, was of immense value in re-constructing the events leading up to, and actions taken, with the loss of the two strike aircraft. Comops concluded that the Frelimo columns were headed for a retaliatory assault against the Ruda Base in the Honde Valley – which is why Comops has reacted to Willie's OP observations.

Immediately prior to going to print, I received the following e-mail from Bob: "My mate Barry Meikle went to a braai yesterday and mentioned our quest for the missing planes to our friend here, Porky Christie-Smith. Porky works for Mozambique Leaf Tobacco (Universal Tobacco) and is in charge of thousands of small scale farmers in Manica. He told Barry that his men have often told him that there is still the tail plane of an Ndege in Manica. Porky has not seen it himself but knows the spot. I am sure if we find one, through Porky's vast African farmer network we will find them both". The mystery of this 'ndege tail plane', at the time of going to press, remained unresolved. However, I am confident that Bob's tenacity will solve this riddle before long.

Monte Cassino – Maingue

This photograph of Maingue, dubbed Monte Cassino, was taken by Bob Manser in September 2007, while flying with Kevin Tidy in the latter's Cessna 182. Bob is quite at home in the air, having flown Microlights for the past 10 years. Bob and Kevin Tidy were in for a particularly bumpy flight because of several bush-fires, heavy haze, poor visibility and a blustering wind blowing. Inserting the photograph here is to give the reader a clearer picture of the terrain that needed neutralisation in order for Comops to achieve their objective of destroying the well defended Russian assisted Zanla terrorist base.

Maingue – Monte Cassino

Tony Oakley recollects: "The operations around this area were conducted in appalling visibility. My recollection is something more of a ridge line than a gomo away to the right when attacking from south to north. Couldn't help but notice it as it lit up like a firework display any time you came close to it!" The writer was not able to contact Ziggy Seegmuller for his input, who was flying with Brian Gordon, on that fateful day.

PB wrote this conclusion in his *Winds of Destruction*: "Op *Miracle* had been successful but the cost to Rhodesia was unacceptably high. Two airmen and an RLI officer had been lost, together with an Alouette, in the high-density operation performed in direct support of Op *Miracle*. One Selous Scout was killed while clearing trenches on Day-One. Another was killed and three seriously injured on Day-Three when a captured weapon exploded as it was being made safe. Then on Day-Five the Air Force suffered the loss of three officers, a Canberra and a Hunter.

Operation Cheese: 3 to 12 October 1979

The Tanzam Railway and its political, military, social and economic implications had been the subject of my Officers Promotion examinations. Not only had I known it well, but I also had had the privilege of flying its entire length up to the Tanzanian border on Canberra photographic reconnaissance (targeting PR) sorties. It was a communist foothold across Africa when the Chinese built the Tanzam railway connecting the Zambian rail system with the port of Dar es Salaam in Tanzania. The building of the railway was beset with disputes between the peoples of the three countries concerned, and it was just as inefficient and vulnerable.

One of the more vulnerable bridges on the Tanzam railway was the Chambeshi road and Rail Bridge. Rhodesian intelligence was fully aware of this fact, as this railway was the weakest link in the Zambian economy. And so, in October 1979, it was decided to blow up the

Chambeshi Bridge which lay five hundred and forty kilometres from Lusaka, and the same distance from the Rhodesian border.

No 3 Squadron's Cessna 421 carried out extensive reconnaissance followed by Jack Malloch flying his sanctions-busting DC-7. The SAS, having completed their rehearsals for the mission which was to include a paradrop, were deployed to a secret staging area, at Fylde. Fylde was an unpublicised military airfield (funded by the South Africans, if my memory serves me correctly) between Gatooma and Hartley – about 150 kilometres from Salisbury. Fylde, by the way, later became the home of the Air Force Regiment, commanded by Wing Commander Bruce Harrison. On Jack Malloch's first high level reconnaissance sortie on 12th September a suitable SAS dropping zone was selected, about forty kilometres downstream from the target. Unfortunately there was heavy haze over the Chambeshi that night and the SAS free-fallers' mission was postponed. They then had to wait for the next moon phase, and were successful with their second attempt in October.

On 3rd October Jack dropped a four man SAS Pathfinder reconnaissance team from thirteen thousand feet above ground level, followed on 8th October by twelve more SAS parachuting from one thousand feet. The SAS men collected their equipment, including one ton of explosives, assembled their canoes and paddled upstream. Soon after reaching the target they completely destroyed both the railway-bridge and road bridge. They hijacked a truck and drove it three hundred kilometres to a point sufficiently close to the Rhodesian border for the Cheetah helicopters to uplift them on 13th October.

This was one of the most brilliant and successful operations of the war. Ten thousand tons of copper was stranded inside Zambia, unable to be exported and causing the loss of much needed foreign currency. Also, eighteen thousand tons of imports, including perishable foodstuffs, were sitting on the docks at Dar es Salaam, clogging the work of the port.

With the lifeline cut, the effects of Operation *Cheese* on Zambia were shattering.

Operation Manacle: 11 October 1979

Whereas recent external operations had been directed against ZIPRA logistical routes and the Zambian economy, it was now decided to direct a major thrust against Moçambique's shaky economy and ZANLA in particular.

Accordingly, Comops planned ambitious Operation *Manacle* so as to blow up the remaining key road and rail bridges throughout the Moçambique provinces of Tete, Manica and Sofala.

On 11th October 1979, two Paradaks airlifted teams of Special Air Service men and flew along the air corridor used by commercial airlines between Salisbury and Blantyre in Malawi. They were not detected and the SAS were successfully dropped to destroy a new road bridge over the Zambezi at Tete in the Central Province, as well as the long railway bridge built in the 1920s over the Zambezi at Sena, plus a third railway bridge. The SAS blew all three bridges and were later airlifted to base by Air Force Cheetah helicopters, from a rendezvous inside Moçambique.

However, because of ZIPRA crossings from Zambia, and due to limited Rhodesian resources, Comops decided to shelve Operation *Manacle* against ZANLA on 8th November and concentrate efforts against ZIPRA (Operation *Dice*). SAS units with Air Force support were standing by at Chipinda Pools when the cancellation order was received with much disappointment. For the interim, support for the Moçambique resistance movement MNR was maintained, with the objective of harassing both ZANLA and the Moçambicans (Operation *Bumper*).

Chopper Down - Middelton 17 October 1979

Air Lieutenant Allistair Middelton told his story of what really happened to Alouette III R 5723 on 17th October 1979, as follows: -

"I was flying out of Grand Reef with my tech Jack Dent. We were tasked, along with 'Split Pin' McCall in the K-Car and Pat Richards in the other G-Car to fly to Gorongoza Mountain. Basically this was a changeover of SAS personnel (working with Renamo), and a casevac. We flew via Ruda for fuel and then straight to Gorongoza Mountain. Due to the distance involved we did not have much scope to change the route in from the route out by much. Therefore a Lynx flown by Jerry Skeeles was tasked to fly up and down the main road north from Chimoio to make sure that the road was safe for our crossing. The anti-aircraft convoy that had shot down Kevin Peinke and J J Strydom in the Canberra on 2nd October and Brian Gordon in the Hunter two days later, was still around, and was a threat.

"We crossed inbound uneventfully, did our bit and were now on our way back. I had the Renamo casevac and one SAS medic on board. We got clearance to cross the road from Jerry in the Lynx. As we were about to cross we came under very intense fire, with tracer. Split Pin, in the K-Car called us to 'break right, break right' - which we did still under fire. We then crossed the road further down. At this time the Lynx was on the radio to someone, calling that a chopper was down on the road. I could see both other Alos, still flying, and called that we were all okay, to which came the answer that one of us was on fire. The other two weren't. So Jack Dent looked out the back and confirmed that we were trailing smoke - then the warning lights (not that there were many on the Alo panel) started to flicker on… Now I know there is some debate as to whether one is shot down or forced down, but which ever this was, there was no doubt that we were not going to make it back to Rhodesia in this helicopter. We landed in a convenient vlei line straight ahead and shut down. There was no fire; the smoke was obviously caused by oil leaking onto the exhaust. I asked Jack to remove one of the Dayglo panels, changed the radio frequency, took my maps, and with the casevac we gapped it and jumped into Pat Richards helo - Pat had landed right behind us - and we were out of there.

"We flew back to Ruda. Another Alo III, flown by Biffo Mike Gardner, met up with us and we all flew back to Grand Reef.

"We were debriefed by Rex Taylor. That night I spoke to Hugh Slatter and it was decided that although R 5723 was intact, it was not recoverable because of where it was. Ginger (Baldy) Baldwin and I think Guy Dixon was tasked to destroy it the next day. Much to his disgust, Baldy's weapons jammed and it was left to Guy Dixon to do the job. Later through intelligence it was confirmed that this was the same convoy that had shot down the Canberra and the Hunter earlier in the month."

Operation Tepid: 18 to 20 October 1979

Operation *Tepid* was a major airstrike on a ZIPRA camp in Zambia, situated approximately half way between Kariba and Lusaka. Nos 1, 3, 4, 5, 7 and 8 Squadron aircraft were involved. Early events leading up to launching the operation included helicopters being fired on during a hot extraction about sixty kilometres south-west of Chirundu. A Canberra from No 5 Squadron flew a subsequent photographic reconnaissance mission, but the photo interpreters found nothing significant. The area under scrutiny was around Lusuto, 21 kilometres northwest of Siavonga on the Zambian side of Lake Kariba, and 70 kilometres from Kariba Township.

By a stroke of luck the photo interpreters identified what appeared to be well-camouflaged trenches and signs that the enemy, at battalion-strength, was cleverly ensconced.

Operation Tepid Air Strike Log – refer Nos 1058 to 1061: 18 to 21 October 1979 - Varky Varkevisser, Ziggy Seegmuller, Ted Lunt, Trevor Jew, Vic Wightman, Cocky Benecke / Bruce Jameson, Colyn James, Martin Hatfield

On the 18th October 1979, Hunters from Thornhill and Canberras from New Sarum led the paratroopers in. The SAS had positioned at FAF 2 – Kariba – and followed the jet airstrikes into the target area. The troops were dropped in two groups, one on either side of the ridge bisecting the target area. After the airstrikes a Dakota from No 3 Squadron, circled the area, then flew up one ridge and down another, dropping incendiaries. The incendiaries were dropped out of the door, from 200 feet, in the hope of burning the place out – thus making any ZIPRA there more vulnerable. Although the Dakota Pilot reported seeing the trenches, he could see no occupants.

The two SAS fighting patrols could see no reaction either – not a single shot was fired at the jets or the Dakota. Because of nil reaction, a third Hunter airstrike was called off. The top cover Lynx, piloted by Trevor Jew, with Army Captain Bob McKenna on board, evaluated a lemon, believing that the camp had already been vacated or abandoned by ZIPRA. The troops on the ground were instructed to remain overnight and await helicopter uplift the next day.

However, later that day, a twenty-man enemy sweep line was observed advancing towards the main killer ambush group, and in the resultant firefight, one ZIPRA was killed and the remainder took flight. Then during the night, as one of the groups inched their way up to the crest of the larger hill, they came under fire and Lance Corporal John McLauren was severely wounded in the stomach.

A night casevac was requested for the wounded troopie, but it was too dark for a helicopter to come to his assistance, and poor John McLauren died of his gunshot wound five hours later. The next morning the casevac helicopter arrived to uplift the body, and a second troopie suffering from heat fatigue.

Whilst sweeping the crest line of the ridge, the ground forces again ran into an ambush, with Lieutenant Phil Brooke stopping a bullet in his buttocks, and his corporal being shot in the arm. Brooke came under fire from rifles, recoilless rifles, mortars, 12,7 and 14,5 millimetre heavy weapons – and he and his men were thoroughly pinned down. With that sort of enemy aggression, Hunters were requested. The FAF 2 Commander wasted no time calling Thornhill, and scrambled Trevor Jew by Lynx with Bob McKenna aboard to act as top cover and FAC when the Hunters arrived. When the Brownjobs reported opposition by about 20 enemy, Trevor turned in for a frantan and 37mm Sneb rocket attack; then suddenly, all hell broke loose. Instead of twenty enemy, there were closer to one hundred gunners directing all their fire onto the Lynx.

Trevor wisely aborted his airstrike. As he turned for safety, the Lynx was hit by anti-aircraft fire. An armour-piercing incendiary tracer from a 14,5 millimetre weapon smashed into the control panel between Trevor and McKenna the SAS man. The round then glanced off the instrument panel and came to rest in the front engine. Shrapnel went into the pilot's legs and other bits pinged into the aircraft. The cockpit filled with smoke and it got so bad that neither man could see the other – despite being seated side-by-side. A flash of flame burned the hair on the soldier's legs. Their immediate concern was the possibility of a fuel or armaments mid-air explosion. Trevor jettisoned his weapon load, called "Mayday, Mayday", and instructed his SAS passenger to stand by to bale out. "No ways," shouted Bob McKenna, "I'm staying" (Now that is the sort of paratrooper I like).

Trevor Jew managed to coax the stricken Lynx back to Rhodesia. His hydraulics had been shot away – and had no flaps or undercarriage for his forced landing. Kariba airport had monitored his Mayday call, and had all their emergency rescue teams at the ready. Whilst trying out his hydraulics, hot fluid sprayed all over the cockpit, so they quickly gave that up as a bad job. Fortunately, none of the control surfaces were affected, but the front engine gave out as they were crossing the northern shore of Lake Kariba. As they approached FAF 2, Trevor again asked the paratrooper whether he wished to parachute to safety before crash landing. Bob elected to stay with the pilot.

Trevor orbited the airfield, commenced his approach, shut down his rear engine, and glided down for a belly landing on the tar runway. It was a real greaser, albeit sparks flying all over the place as the belly made contact with the tar. As soon as the aircraft came to a stop, the men abandoned ship – in case of fuel catching alight and a possible explosion. The crash crews were quickly on the scene and sprayed foam all over the aircraft as a precautionary measure.

Meanwhile, the Hunters arrived overhead the target area and were directed onto the well-defended gun emplacements. The noise as their airstrikes went in was music to the ears of the Rhodesian security forces. As assessments indicated a disciplined enemy force numbering about two hundred, a counter attack of at least 150 soldiers would be needed. We did not have the luxury of what was needed to neutralise the enemy. It was decided to pull out the ground troops by helicopter. Brooke's groups pulled back about ten kilometres where they found a good landing zone, and were flown out by the Air Force helicopters.

The other group, led by Lieutenant Rich Stannard, spotted three men sitting under a rocky outcrop near their selected LZ. They shot two and captured the third – who turned out to be the camp logistics officer – and were immediately casevac'd back to Rhodesia – and into the arms of eagerly-awaiting Special Branch officers.

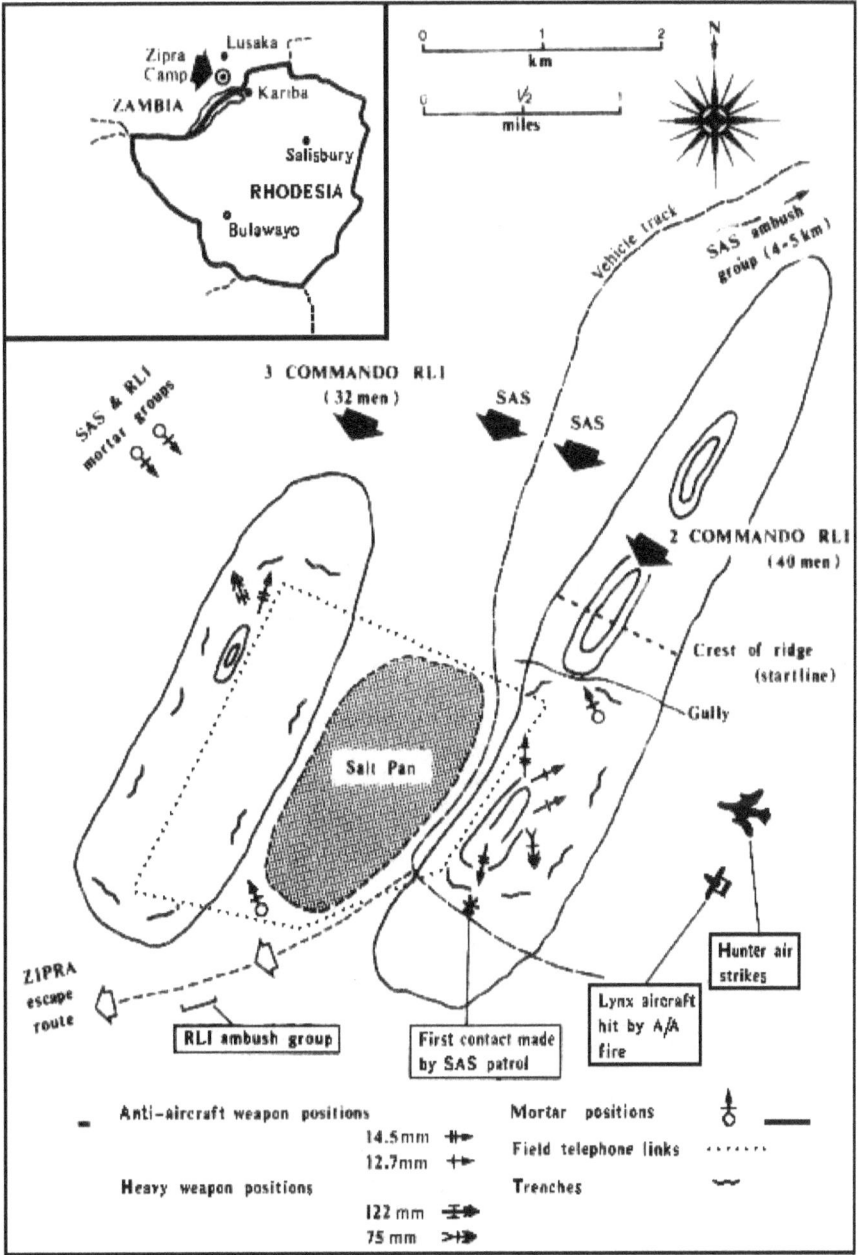

Further interrogation revealed that the capture was part of the First Battalion of ZIPRA's First Brigade and that they had moved into that particular piece of Zambian territory five weeks earlier from Mulungushi. It was to serve as their forward base until such time as the word came to cross the border in force into Rhodesia. They did not have a full complement of men yet and the man advised that at the time of his capture there had been 244 there. Another 100 men were expected as reinforcements soon. They had followed orders to the letter during the initial airstrikes and had held their fire, hoping the Rhodesians would conclude that the place had been abandoned. They had been schooled in conventional warfare according to Russian doctrine, and trained to hold their position. An elaborate command and control organisation existed, with radio communications to their regional commander based in nearby Lusuto, and he in turn had direct contact with Lusaka.

Armed with this hot intelligence, Comops decided to launch a full-scale assault with the two RLI Commandos in support of the Special Air Service. The Commandos were flown to FAF 2, while the Hunters and Canberras were being bombed up. Because the RLI outnumbered the SAS, Lieutenant-Colonel Ian Bate was placed in overall command, with Lieutenant-Colonel Garth Barrett of the SAS providing the alternative command function. Both were to use the airborne method of command from a No 4 Squadron Lynx aircraft. Two Hunters from No 1 Squadron were allocated in direct support of the ground troops for the duration of the operation. Canberras from No 5 Squadron were used on specific bombing missions, and Squadron Leader Ted Lunt and his five Bell helicopters were used for trooping and casevac roles. What is little known is that in fact three SAAF Canberras from No 12 Squadron also participated in the attack on the complex – on 18th October – operating and flying out of Fylde.

On Saturday, 19th October 1979, 'C' Squadron SAS was pre-positioned by air, and despite rain delayed timings, the five Bells ferried the remaining troops across Lake Kariba early the next morning. A total of nine waves or lifts was required to get the 72 men across, and to drop them about three kilometres from their assault targets. Then at 10h00 two Canberras carried out their bombing runs – to soften up and demoralise the well-entrenched ZIPRA. However, the enemy was dug in so well that the airstrike was essentially ineffective. The airstrike was followed at 11h00 by the helicopters that flew in to drop off the RLI and SAS mortar teams. Their sighting was not ideal and ZIPRA was able to put down very accurate and effective RPG-7, 75 millimetre and mortar bombardment amongst our troops.

With all our troops in position to commence their advance, they once again met with fierce resistance – with 14,5 millimetre anti-aircraft fire being accurately directed at the advancing troops. They were stopped in their tracks and had to call for more airstrikes. When it became obvious that the RLI mortars would be of no help, Major Pete Hean called in the Hunters as well. The Hunters' targets were the two 14,5 millimetre gun positions, but their airstrikes were ineffective in neutralising both the anti-aircraft gun and enemy mortar positions. As soon as Pete Hean advanced, his men again came under effective ground fire. The Hunters were recalled to neutralise the enemy. The camouflage in the trenches was so good that the extremely vulnerable pilots could not positively identify the gunners – and most of the airstrikes were off-target.

Pete Hean then tried a flanking manoeuvre along the little gully where the ZIPRA light mortars were positioned. But all he got for his efforts was some eight of his own men being pulled back with flesh wounds. A casevac helicopter reacted, bringing in a 14,5 millimetre gun from Kariba – so that our own lightly armed ground troops could return the 'medicine'.

As the troop commander talked in Squadron Leader Ted Lunt, the commander mistook Ted's helicopter for another Bell – and ended up talking the Officer Commanding No 8 Squadron straight over the enemy positions. ZIPRA stared in amazement as the lone helicopter flew low level above their major support weapons positions. They soon recovered their senses and gave poor old Ted a full go as he pulled away. A trail of angry tracer followed Ted as he made for the safety of the ridge. Fortunately, Ted reached the casevac LZ unscathed. (Ted Lunt survived the war, to pass away in Port Elizabeth on 28th July 2000).

While the injured troopies were being loaded on board, another pair of Hunters arrived to try and eliminate the 14,5 position for the final time that day. The sun was just starting to go down, and Pete Hean was talking to the leader, trying to indicate the exact position of the heavy weapon. He dropped mortar smoke down on the position, and then gave FAC corrections to bring the pilot onto the right spot.

"Hang on," said Red Lead, "I'll send Red Two in first; watch for the tracer coming up and follow him in. Red Two will strike where we think it is: I'll see exactly where the fire is coming from and strike on it." As number two turned in – and before he was halfway down his attack, the 14,5s on both ridges opened on the Hunter. Red Lead delayed his dive, holding back about 15 seconds, and came in at a different angle. "Okay. I've got the bugger," he said, referring to the heavy weapon gunner on the main ridge. The enemy gunners were giving both Hunter pilots stick, as they in turn let rip with their 30mm Aden cannons. It was a pinpoint airstrike and as the dust and stones flew everywhere and the weapons pit erupted, the weapon was momentarily silenced. Then the cheeky bugger of a gunner shook his head, grabbed hold of the 14,5 and swung it around again, firing up at the Hunter as it pulled out of its dive. The red tracer followed the Hunter as it flew off into the sunset. The ZIPRA gunner had been so well protected that short of getting it between the eyes, he was safe.

It was clear that the Rhodesians were not going to take the position that day, and the RLI men on both ridges pulled back for the night – day one, round one, to the gooks, for a sterling resistance.

Operation Murex: 2 November 1979

Little known Operation *Murex* – 2 November 1979 involved the Selous Scouts, and Trooper William Robert Wixley was killed in action.

Operation Dice: 16 to 20 November 1979

This four-day operation was planned to disrupt the Zambian economy and eliminate the routes by which Joshua Nkomo's ZIPRA forces could send motorised columns into Rhodesia. The modus operandi had become Paradak or Cheetah deployment of the ground forces followed by vertical helicopter uplift, often with Hunters as top cover, Hunters and Canberras for softening up and Lynx as AOPs - command air observation posts.

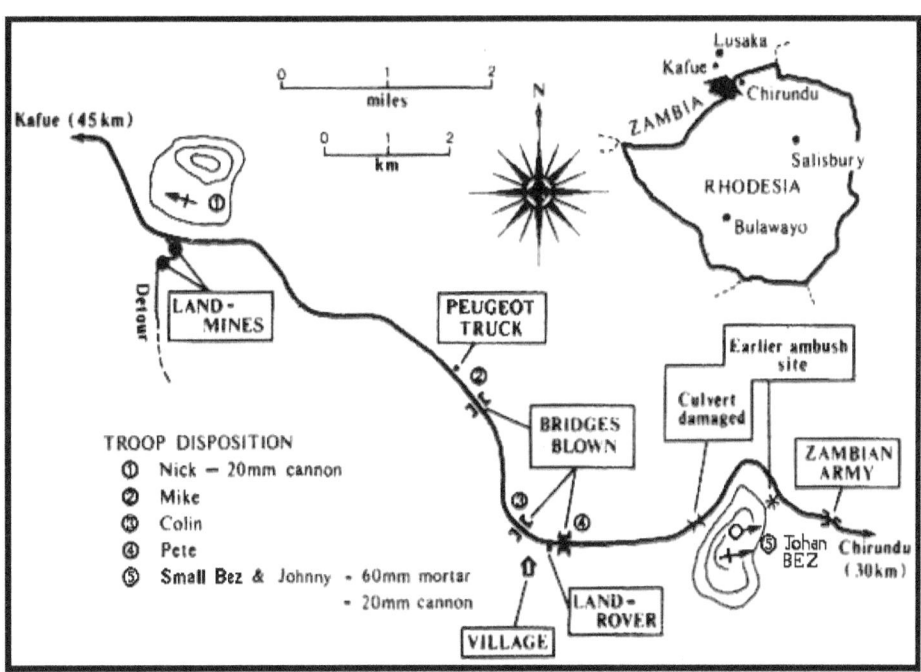

Nine bridges, all surrounding the Zambian capital of Lusaka, were blown up or destroyed mainly by Special Air Service demolition teams. These included the road and rail links from Zambia to Tanzania some three hundred kilometres from Lusaka; three bridges on the road to Lilongwe in Malawi, and Beira in Moçambique; the Keyla Bridge some hundred and seventy five kilometres from Lusaka on the road to Livingstone and Kazungula, and four bridges linking Lusaka and the Rhodesian border at Chirundu.

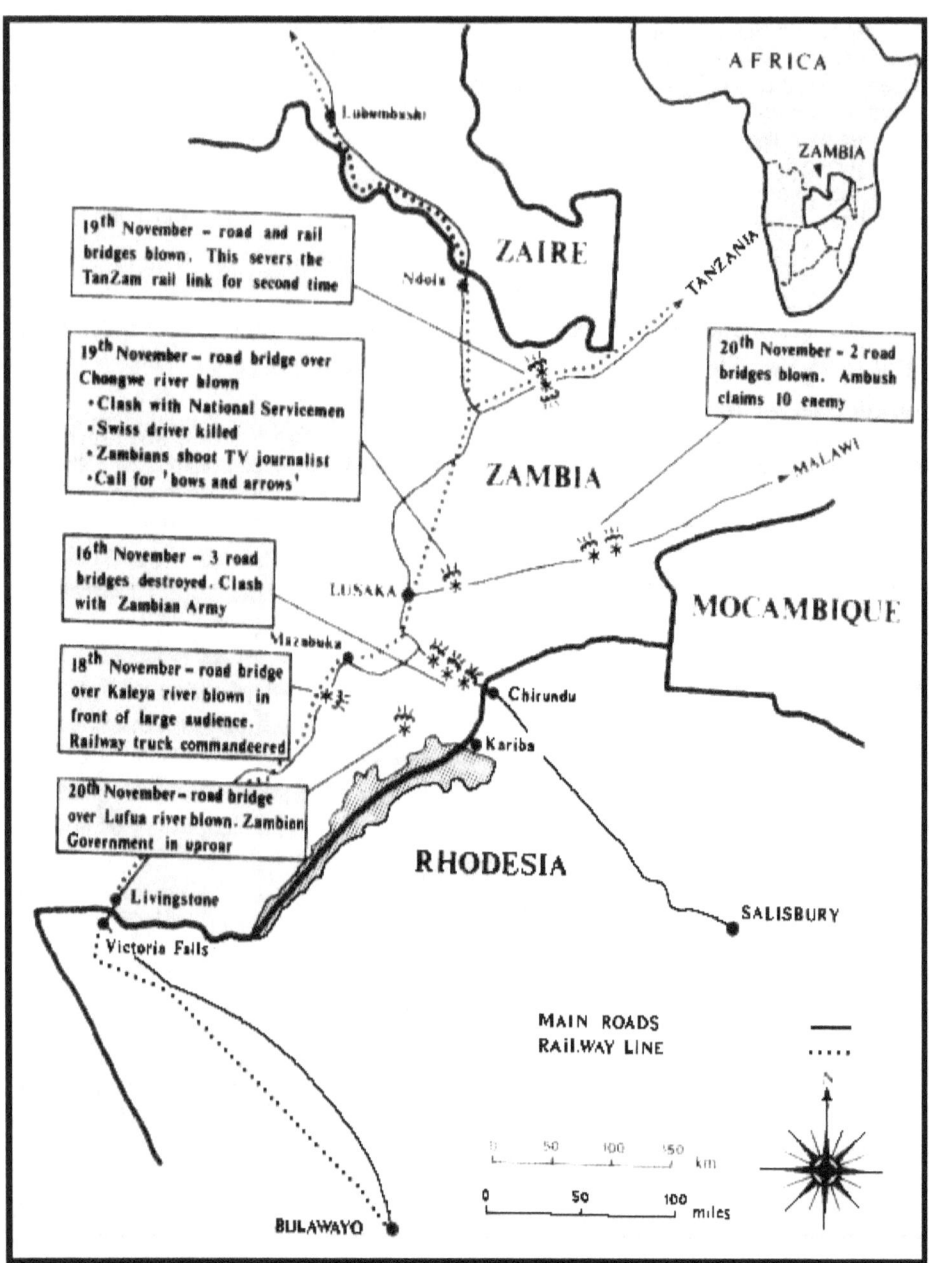

Operation Dice – Halting ZIPRA motorised columns in their tracks

ZIPRA were crossing the Zambezi in ever increasing numbers and it seemed that these incursions might be a prelude to an invasion on more conventional lines. ZIPRA, well equipped with Russian weapons, were entrenched in ten positions along the banks of the Zambezi and the shores of Lake Kariba. Comops knew there were between 18,000 and 25,000 ZIPRA massing in Zambia, most of them trained in conventional warfare. Joshua Nkomo had been training his motorised infantry battalions at Mulungushi camp north of Kabwe and was ferrying troops down to an assembly point known to us as CGT-2 some fifty kilometres to the north-east of Lusaka on the Great North Road.

The next day, the 16th, when Operation *Dice* clearance was given to blow the bridges, a 20-millimetre gun crew, which had been flown in by four Bell 205s of No 8 Squadron, joined Johan "Small Bez" Bezuidenhout – for positioning on an excellent O.P. The reinforcements had been helicoptered in from FAF 2. The Bells returned to uplift all the troops to FAF 2 and on landing found that the tail rotor cable of one of the helicopters was about to snap. The Bell was immediately grounded to effect emergency repairs – had the cable snapped whilst trooping, it is most likely that everybody on board would have perished.

Then on 18th November, with only three Bells serviceable, the SAS were flown in to blow the Kaleya River Bridge outside Mazabuka, on the road to Livingstone. The troops commandeered a railway truck, drove it for sixty kilometres and dumped it into a small dam – to await their uplift back to FAF 2 by helicopter. As they landed at the FAF, the bearings on the main rotor of another Bell failed – but this did not detract from the exhilarating run of successes, which the Rhodesians were enjoying.

On 19th November 1979, two further strikes were carried out. The first was the daring blowing of the Chongwe River road bridge, east of Lusaka on the road to Malawi. Hunters supported this strike, and although a pair of Zambian Air Force MiGs cruised high over the bridge, they were in no mood to take on the Rhodesians. The second demolition mission on 19th November entailed dropping the road and rail bridges south-east of Ndola, which severed the Tanzam rail link - for the second time.

Operation Dice – Blowing up of Zambian Bridges

Whilst the SAS got on with their bridge demolitions, the Air Force also provided helicopter and Hunter top cover support to elements of the Selous Scouts who were engaged on ambushing sections of the arterial road between Lusaka and Livingstone. The Scouts selected targets in and around the airfield at Livingstone, and ambushed the road between Lusaka and Mazabuka. The Reconnaissance Troop operated in the airfield vicinity, and whilst en route to the Sindi plots, about five kilometres from the airfield, they stopped a ZIPRA Land Rover with Bob Dongo on board. He was the Deputy Commander for ZIPRA's Northern Front-2. In the skirmish that followed, Bob Dongo was wounded, and the driver – Sam Wright, plus two other ZIPRA were captured. Selous Scout operator Lieutenant Edward Piringondo called for air support, and they and their prisoners were extricated by helicopter to Victoria Falls. Dongo died of his wounds before he could get to a hospital for treatment. In another action, a Lynx aircraft carried out an aerial reconnaissance of a section of road east of Mazabuka and west of Munali Pass. This was prior to the deployment of 16 Scouts by two Bell 205 helicopters. The Scouts duly ambushed a ZIPRA Southern Front GAZ resupply truck loaded with ammunition.

Only five days later did Zambian police arrive on the scene; they surveyed the carnage, lifted all the anti-personnel mines that had been planted by the Scouts, and left the scene. Some days thereafter, the Scout ambush party got caught between four Zambian Army trucks loaded with soldiers, and a handful of ZIPRA terrorists. Before long, the jittery enemy forces started to exchange fire between themselves. Whilst the battle was raging, air support was summoned and a section of Hawker Hunters soon neutralised the Army convoy with accurate rocket airstrikes. This enabled the Brownjobs on the ground to make good their escape, for uplift by helicopters.

On 20th November two road bridges were blown further east of Lusaka (on the road to Malawi). An ambush claimed 10 enemy killed. Another bridge, over the Lufua River west of Chirundu and Kariba, was blown. The Zambians were furious – and its government in uproar. Whilst the bridges were demolished by the SAS, the Air Force attacked in their well-established pattern - Hunters, then Canberras followed by ground troop paradrops or Fire Forces and then recovery by Cheetahs.

Operation Damper: 12 September to 26 December 1979

Operation *Damper* ran concurrently with Op *Dice*, and involved the SAS and Scouts on bridge demolition and various tasks in Moçambique. 2RAR elements moved to Mrewa in support; as did FAF 5 Mtoko.

Operation Bumper: 1977 to December 1979

Operation *Bumper* was the brainchild of Ken Flower of the Central Intelligence Organisation. The Special Air Services Regiment was tasked with the formation of the Moçambique MNR Renamo and the Rhodesian Air Force was required to provide air support in the form of logistic resupply and SAS air transport.

The SAS had moulded Renamo into an extremely effective organisation, establishing its main base on the Gorongoza Mountain inside Moçambique, half way between the Eastern Highlands town of Umtali and the port of Beira. Gorongoza Mountain is in fact a plateau measuring eighteen by ten kilometres, some one thousand metres high and thus ideal for Dakota dropping zones.

In addition to military equipment and other stores, there was also a continuous movement of SAS advisors and instructors, usually transported by Cheetah helicopters. As a result, the Rhodesians were richly rewarded for their help since the Renamo guerrillas caused havoc in the central province of Moçambique. André Matsangaίssa, ably led Renamo. By the end of the late 1970s FRELIMO had a serious insurgency on its hands, trained and deployed by the Rhodesian army. It was the price that the new president Samora Machel was obliged to pay for providing bases to Robert Mugabe's Zimbabwean terrorists. Often accompanied in the field by white Rhodesian officers, the anti-FRELIMO insurgents became steadily more effective.

I recall, while standing in for Group Captain Tol Janeke on the main Operation *Repulse* Joint Operational Command (JOC) at Fort Victoria, being awoken one midnight by large transport aircraft over-flying the FV non-directional navigation aid beacon. I went outside and noticed that the aircraft were flying without their navigation lights on – and they sounded like C130 and C160 Hercules and Transall transport aircraft. Only Steve Kesby confided in me that the South Africans were supporting the Renamo movement.

~~~OOO~~~

The Rhodesians were enjoying tremendous success in Zambia with their bridge demolition escapades - and Samora Machel of Moçambique was dreading similar treatment, expecting quite rightly that the Rhodesians were ready to dish out like treatment to him.

Matsangaίssa was killed in 1979 near Gorongoza. He had served with FRELIMO but had fallen out with his colleagues, and was accused of car theft. After his escape from a re-education camp the Rhodesians had selected him to lead the MNR. The circumstances of his death are obscure - it is said that FRELIMO invited him to negotiations and killed him as he was arriving - in another story, local witch doctors, or *curandeiros*, misled him about FRELIMO's dispositions in Gorongoza. Matsangaίssa decided on an attack but met with a far bigger force than he expected. The MNR deputy, Afonso Dhlakama succeeded André Matsangaίssa. The populist movement became more widely known as Renamo.

On 22nd November 1979, the SF (Security Forces) was ordered to scale down Renamo support, but some operations carried into December. Meanwhile, Machel was exerting pressure on Mugabe and Nkomo at Lancaster House, and with their change of heart this was followed by Rhodesian orders a month later to halt external actions.

In 1980 the South Africans took over where the Rhodesians had left off. Renamo was by now a fighting force of one thousand, and under the aegis of South Africa this number began to increase. So did Renamo's area of operations, for units could now move with impunity across the common border with South Africa, opening fronts in the south. Malawi too began to serve as a rear base and made FRELIMO's rule untenable in much of the country. Before long Renamo was operating in most of the country - especially the drought-prone Central Provinces - and FRELIMO was unable to meet the challenge. In 1984, four years after Pretoria "inherited" Renamo (from the Rhodesians), Machel and the South African president, P.W. Botha, signed a non-aggression pact. There would be no ANC bases in Moçambique; in return, South Africa would cease supporting Renamo - but not even the Nkomati Accord could dampen the Renamo/MNR spirit.

Eighteen months later, when Renamo's centre at Gorongoza was overrun, captured documents implicated Pretoria in continued support. The deeper Moçambique slid into ruin, the smaller the incentive to run a destabilisation programme in the country. Samora Machel was killed in a Russian plane crash in 1986 - further evidence, to some, of South African subterfuge - and when Joaquim Chissano took his place, Pretoria's ambitions in Moçambique were all but realised. FRELIMO had ceased to pose either an ideological or a logistical threat to South Africa. As a government, FRELIMO was ineffectual; it sheltered only a handful of anti-apartheid elements, its Marxism-Leninism was a thing of the past, its army was in pitiful shape, its people were desperate and it was begging for help.

"Funnyland" Moçambique became a tangle of foreign credit lines - the Rhodesian origins and objectives, militarily and politically, had been achieved. Moçambique's woes were perpetuated when the South Africans took over where the Rhodesians had left off – refer to Operations *Altar* and *Mila*.

……….But the die had been cast good and solid.

Note: Many years later, it was recalled that the MNR skeleton came out of the cupboard to haunt the President Nelson Mandela regime – with the 'new SA' becoming 'bedfellows' with Moçambique (Samora Machel had been killed in an aircraft 'accident' in 1986; and Joshua Nkomo died twenty years later in July 1999).

Operation Capsule: 8 To 12 December 1979

Operation *Capsule* was another South African 'sanctions busting' contribution. Between 8th and 12th December four SAAF Canberras accompanied Rhodesian Canberras on airstrikes in Zambia and Moçambique. Two attacks were carried out on Camp CGT 2 and another on Nkume Camp in Zambia, and New Mavonde in Moçambique. On 5th November, three SAAF Canberras accompanied RhodAF Canberras on an attack on a target in the south-west of Zambia – unfortunately the operation code of this one is not known (possibly Op *Murex* but more likely Operation *Dice*).

As mentioned earlier, the Lancaster House Conference was drawing to a close and on 22nd December the Rhodesian Security Forces were instructed to halt all external offensive action. The Rhodesian SAS had formed the spearhead of the drive against the economies of Zambia and Moçambique, although the Rhodesian Air Force was an integral part of the combined operations.

AFZ - Air Force Of Zimbabwe

Fire Force operations, airstrikes and external raids continued for a time until the Lancaster House agreement between the warring parties led to a cease-fire.

The Lancaster House cease-fire agreement allocated the Rhodesian forces 47 operational bases, and the Patriotic Front 14 Assembly Points. The greatest fear that Mugabe had, was that the Assembly Points were vulnerable to being bombed by the Rhodesian Air Force. The peace agreement was signed in the great hall of Lancaster House on 21st December 1979.

Josiah Tongogara was killed in very mysterious circumstances. His Mercedes had crashed into the back of a truck while it was trying to overtake a lorry on a road near the town of Palmeira about 100 miles north of Maputo. It was pitch dark at the time of the accident and the truck did not have its lights on (unlikely, being pitch dark and in the process of over taking). Tongogara, who was sitting in the front passenger seat, was decapitated as he was hurled through the windscreen on impact. His driver was injured. Mugabe's attempts to get the body back to Maputo quickly turned into a fiasco that served only to fuel the suspicion and rumours that Tongogara had been murdered. A member of one of the local Salisbury funeral parlours was tasked to get to Maputo to inspect the body – he came back with dubious evidence that there were no bullet wounds.

The monitoring force comprising many nations arrived in the country to oversee the new elections. Vast Assembly areas were set up to accommodate the estimated 50,000 guerrillas expected to flood into the country from Moçambique and Zambia. In terms of the Lancaster House Agreement, both the ZANLA and ZIPRA forces, for the time being united under the Patriotic Front banner, were supposed to be confined to these points until after the elections on March 3, 1980. The British Government believed it had the perfect plan to establish a stable coalition government in an internationally recognised Zimbabwe. And the Plan didn't include the ultimate winner – Robert Mugabe.

The Rhodesians (and British, for that matter) believed that Joshua Nkomo's ZAPU faction would win enough seats in the new 100-seat parliament to warrant the senior position in a coalition which would also contain 20 constitutionally-entrenched white seats and several dozen for Bishop Abel Muzorewa's UANC party.

The cease-fire was very fragile indeed. Notable breaches included:
On February 11th, a bomb exploded underneath the motorcade taking Mugabe to the Fort Victoria airfield. Five guards in the car behind him were injured.
Mugabe falsely accused the Rhodesian Air Force of bombing two villages in the north-east on the Moçambique border. Lord Soames ignored it.

Neither the British nor, ironically, the Rhodesians for all their knowledge of Africa, had grasped the basic concept of African rule. While the Rhodesian authorities complained bitterly, they were unable to convince the newly installed temporary British governor, Lord Soames, that wholesale intimidation was being conducted by Mugabe's gooks in the rural areas where eighty percent of the voters lived ("*unable to convince*" is putting it mildly – Ian Douglas Smith did not mince his words – he aptly titled his book *The Great Betrayal*).

This intimidation was brutal, widespread and very, very effective. It was later estimated, and corroborated by several ZANLA officers, that up to sixty percent of all guerrillas in the Assembly Points were, in fact, *mujibas* – local youths armed with rusting, unworkable weapons. This gave the impression that PF forces were abiding by the rules, while in reality the hardened men of the terrorist ranks were in the field doing what they knew best – coercing simple peasants into voting "the right way". By permitting the intimidation to continue, the British lost control of events. When the results were announced, Mugabe had swept the board with 57 of the available 80 unreserved seats.

As one German observer put it: "If that was a fair and free election, I am a Chinaman".
On the stroke of midnight on 17th April 1980, Zimbabwe-Rhodesia became Zimbabwe. The violence that followed included: -
At Assembly Point X-ray, near the town of Mtoko, the guerrillas took the law into their own hands, seizing control of the main roads around the town and arbitrarily ambushing civilian and military vehicles. Police and farmers in the town were killed.
At Chitungwiza, 25 km from the centre of Salisbury, Nkomo's men were fighting Mugabe's units.

Open warfare broke out on the streets of Bulawayo in November 1980 – the Battle of Entumbane, when at least 55 people died and more than 200 were wounded in street battles between the two rival armies for control.

Chaos reined, a flood of emigration followed; and both General Peter Walls, for the economically active whites, and Edgar Tekere were victims of the New Zimbabwe. In Tekere's case, he was tried for murder, having personally led an attack on a farmhouse whilst being a cabinet minister in Mugabe's regime. Walls fell from favour when Mugabe learnt that he had written to Margaret Thatcher about the election irregularities.

The people who really lost out were not the whites, but the Africans themselves. At no time were they ever given a real say in what they wanted; rather, they were told what they would get. True, they were given the right to vote, but that one vote put them under a much harsher yoke than the white men ever did. "One man, one vote is what the people want," the slogan went. One man, one vote is all the majority of the population has really received since that day in March 1980. In the 20 years since Zimbabwe was born, the country has been nothing but a *de facto* One Party state; and with its President listed as the 11th richest man in the world. This, in a country whose economy has collapsed – with the highest inflation rate in the world!

I carried out a brief survey of those Rhodesians who were killed or died between 11th November 1965 and 30th March 1980. A total of 1 873 Security Force personnel paid the supreme sacrifice. This figure of 1873 was made up of 55 Air Force, 933 Army, 506 Internal Affairs and 379 BSAP members.

Operation Agila: 20 to 27 December 1979

Operation *Agila* commenced the day before the Lancaster House agreement signing ceremony, and entailed the Royal Air Force and USAF uplifting the CMF - Commonwealth Monitoring Force to Rhodesia.

Major-General John Ackland commanded the CMF consisting of 1500 soldiers from Britain, Australia, New Zealand, Kenya and Fiji. Their task was to monitor the so-called guerrillas in the Assembly Points, as well as the Rhodesian Joint Operational Centres distributed around the country, provide logistic support for the assembly points and defuse tensions between the Rhodesians and terrorists - who had little reason to trust each other.

Hostilities were meant to cease on 28th December and all the gooks should have been in the rendezvous points by 4th January 1980 for transportation to sixteen Assembly Points. In the week between the agreement being signed at Lancaster House on 21st December and the cease-fire becoming effective on 28th December over 100 people had been killed. By 4 January, 9,000 terrorists had assembled. By the next day, the number had swollen to 17,000, with more coming in - mainly of low calibre such as Mujibas.

Ackland described Operation *Agila* as one of the most successful in British military history. That may have been the case for British consumption; but certainly not the case as far as Rhodesians were concerned.

Operation Midford: 20 December 1979 To 16 March 1980

Operation Midford was the New Zealand Army Truce Monitoring Contingent – NZATMC for short – in support of Operation Agila. The New Zealand contingent departed from RNZAF Base Whenuapai on the 20th December 1979, arriving at New Sarum two days later. After initial security briefings, and being kitted out, they set up their base HQ at Morgan High School under Colonel DWS Moloney. The New Zealanders were deployed to Assembly Points Lima and Mike.

Operation Hectic: 1 March 1980

Operation *Hectic* was a highly secret plan of action against selected personnel. The plan called for a two-phase operation, the second code-named Operation *Quartz* – the elimination of major targets in Salisbury as well as others dotted around the countryside. Robert Mugabe had to be assassinated for the military plan to succeed. An attempt on his life during an election rally at Fort Victoria failed when the radio activated explosive device missed his vehicle. He also escaped with his life when a Selous Scout, hidden in an ambulance, failed in his task to kill Mugabe as he arrived at Bulawayo airport. A back-up plan by the SAS was in place to take him out on his way to a city stadium – but the plots were all foiled – Mugabe's trip was called off as he was about to board the aircraft – as if he had been tipped off.

An extra-special briefing held in Comops, attended by the commanders of the Special Forces – Lieutenant-Colonels Garth Barrett of the Special Air Service, Charlie Aust of the Rhodesian Light Infantry and Pat Armstrong of the Selous Scouts. Plans were made to initiate Operations *Hectic* and *Quartz*, with the "Go" to follow immediately a secret code-word was given. Until now, all military personnel had been led to believe that Mugabe did not stand a "snowball's chance" of winning the elections.

By many accounts, Nkomo appeared to enjoy more popular support amongst the locals than Mugabe. Appearances, they say, can deceive.

Operation Milk Float

Operation *Milk Float*, according to Harry McCallion (author of *Killing Zone – A life in the paras, the Recces, the SAS and RUC* – Bloomsbury, London 1995), was a plot by the SAS, with assistance by South Africa's 4-Recce Commando, to assassinate Mugabe at his Maputo villa.

A captured ZANLA terrorist, facing the death sentence for the murder of a white farmer and his family, had revealed specific information on the routine movements of ZANU leader Robert Mugabe, who was apparently spending a lot of time at his Maputo villa, in an effort to evade the gallows. Utilising this information, the SAS intended to insert an eight-man assault team, commanded by Major Graham Wilson, into Maputo to assassinate him. 4-Recce was tasked to assist the SAS towards the end of 1978. The South Africans would not be involved in the actual assassination bid, which was a task for the Rhodesians. I, for one, could understand why the South Africans would give the Operation a different code name.

The plan called for the SAS to be shipped to a launch point off Maputo by the South African Navy, and boated ashore by the 4-Recces. The Recces would lie offshore until the attack was over, then return with the team to the mother ship. Planning began immediately, with 4-Recce putting into practice theory they had long been developing. Theory does not always work in practice, however, and it also failed this time.

The SAS raiding party moved to Langebaan in late January 1979 for rehearsals. Their first launch from the deck of a submarine in heavy seas was a near disaster – the floor of the single Zodiac buckled under the weight of the troops and equipment. The casing of the submarine was too cramped for such launches. After a re-think someone came up with the idea of using a strike craft, and the craft was duly deployed to Langebaan. The size of the SAS team was increased to eight operators, using three Zodiacs. When it was found that the Zodiacs couldn't be launched within strict time constraints, the South Africans promptly laid on a second strike craft. With rehearsals complete, the flotilla set sail from Langebaan in mid February 1979 – having received news that the target was in residence at his villa. The SAS team was duly boated ashore by the South Africans, and reached the villa without difficulty. But Mugabe was absent. Graham Wilson waited in ambush, hoping that Mugabe would return, but time restrictions forced them to leave.

On their way back to the strike craft, the deck of one of the Zodiacs buckled by a wave, and it had to be scuttled. The two remaining Zodiacs made it back to the strike craft without further event, and the assassination party returned to South Africa. My purpose in documenting this operation is to record South African co-operation during the bush war – and to mention the tactics employed.

Operation Quartz: 1 March 1980

Operation *Quartz* was planned for the bombing and elimination of all the assembly points. Special Force personnel, positioned on suitable OPs, would assist directing the jets onto targets. The SASs mission involved the assassination of Robert Mugabe at his home in Quorn Avenue, Mount Pleasant, Simon Muzenda at his home in Enterprise Road, Highlands; plus ZANLA commander Rex Nhongo and ZIPRA's Dumiso Dabengwa and Lookout Masuku.

The price of peace had indeed been grievously high. White Rhodesian casualties have been calculated as being proportionately ten times more than those suffered by the Americans in Vietnam and half of Britain's losses during the Second World War. The red soil of Africa had been stained a deeper hue with the blood of more than 27,500 black and white Rhodesian lives (insurgents, servicemen and civilians). Some 275,000 had been wounded and injured, with 1,5 million refugees, homeless and displaced people.

For thousands of others – the orphaned, widowed and bereaved on both sides – the mark of war would never be erased. That perhaps explains why, I felt a need to tell this story, and get it off my chest.

Operation Seed: November 1980

Operation *Seed* – short for Soldiers Employed in Economic Development, was modelled on the Red-Chinese idea of employing soldiers in agricultural and related ventures so they could earn their keep in times of peace. ZANLA was sent to the Middle Sabi and ZIPRA cadres were put at the Silalabuhwa Dam irrigation scheme on the Mzingwane River, south-west of Filabusi. However, this was Africa and not Red-China, and it did not take long for the two groups to have a go at each another. This conflict became more likely when elements were moved in to high density low cost housing areas at Entumbane Township in Bulawayo, and Chitungwiza Township near Harare.

Operation Winter: February 1980

Operation *Winter* was the recruiting of the Rhodesian military for the South African Defence Force, by Major Mike Curtain, who was seconded to the South African Diplomatic Mission. The SADF liaison officer in Salisbury was Commandant André Bestbier. A substantial amount of sensitive equipment was flown out from New Sarum, Thornhill and Fylde Air base by SAAF C-130 Hercules and C-160 Transall transport aircraft. This was necessary in view of the unexpected outcome of the Mugabe election. South African embarrassment needed to be minimised at all cost. In July 1980, the Zimbabwe Government announced it was downgrading the South African Diplomatic Mission in Harare to the status of trade mission. The reason given was that the South African diplomats had been recruiting spies and mercenaries.

Project Barnacle

Project Barnacle had its origins in D40, and prior to that, in the *Section of Pseudo Operations* of the South African Special Forces. The Commanding General Special Forces, Fritz Loots, was interested in recruiting a team of professional clandestine operators from the Rhodesian Security Forces. The South African Special Forces obtained Renosterspruit Farm, south of Hartbeespoort Dam and north of Johannesburg, as a base from which D40 operated. Rhodesian recruits started arriving there in June and July 1980 – including one particularly notorious ex BSAP Special Branch operator known only presently as "Brian" – and referred to as *Major Brian* in Peter Stiff's *Cry Zimbabwe.* However, Major Brian's identity was revealed in *Umkhonto we Sizwe,* written by Thula Bopela and Luthuli. Brian's true identity is none other than ex-BSAP Gray Branfield (who Thula Bopela described as a particularly *deadly operator*).

Gray Branfield, alias Major Brian had been stationed in Bulawayo, with the rank of Detective Inspector, and had commanded a Special Branch pseudo team of regular detectives, both black and white, as well as captured terrorists who had been converted to the Rhodesian cause. These were the "turned" or "tame" terrs of Security Forces' parlance. They were used mainly on external operations to pinpoint terrorist camps and establish infiltration routes. Branfield's area of expertise lay in Rhodesia, Botswana and Zambia.

CSI – Chief of Staff (Intelligence), was headed by a Major Pete (*nom de guerre*) and specialised in operational intelligence. Major 'P' was also an expert on cross-border activities into Zimbabwe. CSI also absorbed intelligence officers not involved in Project Barnacle. This tended to create a rift and some jealousies between the former Special Branch (BSAP) officers doing their own thing with the Rhodesians of Project Barnacle and those absorbed by the greater SADF. The Barnacle posts were considered plum jobs. (My own tastes differ. I also held an Int. Officer appointment while flying Hunters. I preferred flying to trying to interpret intelligence.).

The single black operators were accommodated at Renosterspruit and in Hillbrow, and the whites were dispersed to the Fourways area in northern Johannesburg. Their pay cheques came from Armscor. A pseudo/front company, NKTF Properties, was established, and later changed to President Security Consultants (Pty) Ltd – with a head office listed in Verwoerdburg. The Managing Director was Colonel Rautenbach of Special Forces. President Security was funded entirely by the SADF. Renosterspruit was expanded with the construction of office blocks, mechanical workshops and armouries. Much money was spent.

Project Barnacle operatives were involved with, and implicated in, several closely guarded events in Zimbabwe. These included the sabotage of, and discovery of explosive devices found in Zimbabwe Armoured Regiment vehicles at KGVI Barracks in December 1980; a car bomb blast at Second Street and Central Avenue, Salisbury on Old Years Eve 1980; the elimination of Joe Gqabi on 31st July 1981; Operation *Gericke* in November 1981; support for and armament supplies to ZIPRA dissidents and with covert activities associated with CSI. Project Barnacle ultimately became the BSB – Burgerlike Samewerking Bureau – whose activities were partially made public during the Doctor Wouter Basson testimonies in South Africa's Truth and Reconciliation Commission (TRC) hearings. Ex-Recce operator Douw Steyn assured the writer many years later, that we "have heard nothing yet." It will be interesting what unfolds in the future – but that is presently outside the scope of this story.

Last, but by no means least of Project Barnacle's covert activities, was the sabotage of Hawk and Hunter aircraft at the Air Force base at Thornhill.

A certain Project Barnacle *'Team Oscar'* operator, responsible for gathering intelligence in the Midlands, passed on vital information about the Air Force whilst on leave in South Africa. The report on the current strengths of Hunter, Canberra and Lynx aircraft was passed on to Gray Branfield (Major Brian) – as well as the imminent arrival of the British Aerospace Hawk Mk 60 fighter/strike aircraft. The plan, formulated by Gray Branfield, which included the use of an Air Force contact and an ex-Selous Scout operator, was approved by SADF Major-General Kat Liebenberg. The firm EMLC (Electrical, Magnetic, Logistical Component Technical Consult (Pty) Ltd) of Speskop assembled the custom-made explosive demolition devices to sabotage the Rhodesian aircraft. These each consisted of a wooden box packed with TNT slabs taken from a Soviet anti-tank mine and used in combination with an ex-Rhodesian white phosphorous grenade.

But more about this intriguing story, concerning the sabotage of the Thornhill aircraft (see "*Sabotage – Thornhill*", later).

-o-0-o-

Operation Mixer: 31 July 1981

Operation *Mixer* was the planned South African Special Forces' assassination of Joe Nzingo Gqabi, the ANC's chief representative and MK operational chief in Zimbabwe.

Joe Gqabi had held the same position with the ANC in Botswana but the South Africans instigated his deportation in 1979. He then moved to Zambia and relocated to Zimbabwe after the ZANU PF government was installed. The first attempt to assassinate him on 24th February 1981 failed when the detonator in a matchbox placed behind the front wheel of his car failed to initiate the seven kilograms of TNT attached. The explosive device was similar to the one used to kill ZANU PFs Herbert Chitepo in Lusaka during the Rhodesian War. The task of assassinating Joe Gqabi was then given to Project Barnacle – specifically to ex-BSAP Gray Branfield, of SADF Special Forces. Four teams were selected, varying in numbers from one to three people, and included CSI (Chief of Staff Intelligence – SADF) operatives as well as contacts within Zimbabwe, ex-Special Branch officials who were in positions to conduct surveillance and monitoring observations.

Project Barnacle established their base at Renosterspruit Farm, south of Hartbeespoort Dam and north of Johannesburg. A safe forward base was sited at Messina, from where teams were flown to Induna airfield (between Cement Siding and Ntabazinduna, outside Bulawayo). A chartered aircraft flew Gray Branfield from Induna to Charles Prince airport at Mount Hampden on Sunday 18th July 1981. A safe house was set up in the Salisbury suburb of Greendale and the various teams were able to monitor and track the movements of their quarry. Joe Gqabi was seen with high profile ANC officials, including the MK chief Joe Modise.

Operation Gericke: 15 November 1981

Captain Patrick Gericke was responsible for blowing up the ZNA Army weapons arsenal at Inkomo Military Barracks on 16 to 17th August 1981. Gericke, a SADF Recce operator serving with Zimbabwe's Engineer Corps, was arrested, interned at the Central Police Station by the CIO, and rescued from prison in a bold operation executed by notorious Gray Branfield under orders from Project Barnacle – on 15th November 1981. SADF General Fritz Loots, who commanded the Special Forces, ordered the rescue to be given the highest priority.

The Inkomo barracks was the former home base of the by-now disbanded Selous Scouts and was used as the main national armoury. It included underground bunkered stocks of Air Force 455kg and 900kg bombs – with a total value estimated at Z$36 million or about US$12 million. The Defence Ministry officially attributed the initial cause to exploding gas cylinders. A Board of Enquiry was convened, including explosive experts from Britain and Yugoslavia, who correctly concluded that the blast was due to deliberate enemy action against Zimbabwe. Gray Branfield, quickly hatched a plan to use a fellow by the name of Varkevisser in the rescue bid to extricate Gericke to South Africa. Two Project Barnacle Piper Seneca's arrived at Hartley (now Chegutu) airstrip to fly the South African escapees, and the abducted Varkevisser, back to South Africa.

Note the name "Major Brian", now known to be deceased Gray Branfield, featured prominently in other Project Barnacle operations as well as the Hawk/Hunter sabotage saga.

Operation Anvil: 25 November 1981

Operation *Anvil* was the failed coup attempt on the Seychelles by "Mad" Mike Hoare and his mercenaries – and which included former Rhodesian Air Force pilots Chas Goatley and Vernon Prinsloo – plus Nick Wilson, pilot trainee with the Air Force of Zimbabwe. Chas was one of our mates, and reference to the Air Strike Log section will reveal that he participated in no less than 21 air strikes. His last action in the Air Force was on 12th August 1979. The inclusion of Operation *Anvil* in this record is self-explanatory, albeit a story in itself. Suffice it to say, his task in the coup attempt was to take over the Mahé airport control tower, which he achieved.

Chas was later awarded the SAAF Air Force Cross for saving lives at sea during the sinking of the *Oceanos* off the Transkei coast in 1991.

Operation Octopus: July To October 1982

Operation *Octopus* was mounted to locate and seize weapons following the upsurge of ZIPRA activities in Matabeleland. Skyshouts were carried out over Bulawayo by Air Force helicopters and light aircraft. The message was that people should surrender all their weapons or face the consequences.

Operation Mute: 1982

Operation *Mute* was SADF assistance to Zimbabwe's ZIPRA in 1982 – and the forerunner to the SADF's Project Barnacle raid on the Air Force of Zimbabwe Thornhill Air Base in July of the same year.

Peter Stiff, in his book *Cry Zimbabwe*, concluded that, "There was a widespread fear of the Air Force of Zimbabwe. Not only could it mount air strikes, but it was the key factor in the deployment of Fireforces against their groups (i.e. ZIPRA forces). The Air Force's capabilities remained virtually undiminished since the days of the Bush War and posed the main threat to ZIPRA's activities." Further on, on page 106 of *Cry Zimbabwe*, Stiff adds, "unbeknown to Jan Brytenbach and Dunning who had no 'need to know', Barnacle and Special Forces were even then engaged in planning a major strike against the Air Force of Zimbabwe". However, allow me first to recap on the events immediately prior to and leading up to Operation *Mute*.

Operation *Mute* ended early in 1984. South African support for ZIPRA dwindled following the murder of numerous white farmers in the Kezi district, and the slaughter of other innocent white civilians.

When the Rhodesian Special Forces were forced to disband, the South Africans built complete replacement barracks to accommodate them – lock, stock and barrel. And, they were not slow to recruit the cream of the crop.

Sabotage – Thornhill: 25 July 1982

The date of my official retirement from the Air Force of Zimbabwe was 15th June 1982 – after 20 years and 93 days' service. I had left the country in December 1981, on "six-months leave, pending retirement" and started to work for board manufacturer Masonite, in Estcourt, Natal. I reported to Air Force Headquarters in the third week of July 1982 to carry out final clearances. Group Captain Pete Nicholls, the current Officer Commanding New Sarum Air Force base, met me in the corridor at Air HQ and mentioned that I had just missed the arrival of the Hawk aircraft the previous Wednesday at New Sarum after their ferry flight from Britain. The Hawk is a two-seat lightweight fighter and advanced weapons system training aircraft with enhanced ground attack capability. As Station Commander, he had arranged that Prime Minister Robert Mugabe meet Air Marshal Norman Walsh who accompanied the Hawks to Zimbabwe.

By the time I retired, the Air Force of Zimbabwe could field only 53 aircraft, and had just 43 pilots left serving on five squadrons. No 1 Squadron = 6 aircraft + 7 pilots; No 2 Squadron = 2 aircraft + 2 pilots; No 3 Squadron = 6 Dakotas + 6 pilots; No 6 Squadron 20 Genets + 8 pilots; No 7 Squadron = 8 Alouette and 5 Bell 205s + 14 pilots.

I had no sooner crossed the border into South Africa than the press headlines screamed "Air Force Crippled – Sabotage". Realisation hit me immediately. The South African Secret Service had paid me a very unexpected visit soon after I had arrived in Estcourt – six months prior to the Thornhill sabotage. I had brushed them off at that time, but it haunted me that the Secret Service was on my trail so soon after arriving in South Africa. Also, more sinister – I had no doubt that I would be considered a prime suspect by the Zimbabweans – having left Air HQ and returned to South Africa a mere 24 hours before the sabotage occurred. A 'spy' to check out the security arrangements? Perhaps it was too much to expect that my brief visit to Zimbabwe was pure co-incidence. I dared not go back in a hurry – horrifying stories were splashed all over the media as events in the once highly respected Rhodesian Air Force unfolded.

Thornhill Sabotage Photographs – 25 July 1982

Lynx remains

Hawk No 602 Destroyed

Remains of a valuable Hunter.

Below, top photo – Hangar roof caved in

Left: The crumpled remains of a once-proud Hunter. Below: The roof of the Hunter hangar - and Air Force morale - caved in the night the saboteurs paid a visit to Thornhill

Above: All that remained of the standby Hunter outside the Ops Room.

Hawk No. 603 which had a bomb placed in its starboard air intake. The canopy which was open at the time, was damaged.

Top left- The crumbled remains of a Hunter
Top Right – Caved in roof of the aircraft hangar
Third from top – Remains of the Stand-by Hunter outside the Operations Room
Bottom – Damaged Hawk No 603, had a bomb placed in its starboard air intake

Sunday 25th July 1982 will be remembered as the day when seven Hawker Hunter FGA 9, one British Aerospace Hawk Mk 60 and a Lynx were totally destroyed at Thornhill Air Force base. The loss was assessed at Z$ 7,2 million, equivalent to R10,9 million Rand, 9,6 million US dollars and 5.5 million British pounds. An eighth Hunter and three other Hawks were damaged, as were Nos 1 and 2 Squadron aircraft hangars. The Board of Inquiry determined that a small team of saboteurs had been dropped by vehicle next to the airfield perimeter fence along the Mvuma (Umvuma) road. They had trampled down the fence, crossed a storm drain, and then cut holes in the security fencing, thus gaining access to the air-base' hardstanding area. The saboteurs had then crossed the dispersal area to the far western side and gained access to No 1 Squadron, thence into the aircraft hangar where six Hunters were parked. Each aircraft had a tailor-made bomb placed in the air-intake, comprising plastic explosive wired to a white phosphorus grenade, with Revue watch fuses and Duracell battery power packs. Bombs were also placed in the cockpit of one Hunter as well as in a gunpack in the corner of the hangar.

Entry was then gained into No 2 Squadron building (with the use of pre-arranged duplicate keys), which housed the four Hawks that had arrived from Britain just ten days earlier. Bombs were placed in the engines of the four aircraft. A Lynx that was outside on the hardstanding was booby-trapped, as were another two Hunters. All told, sixteen timing devices were placed – 9 were deposited in eight Hunters, one each in the four Hawks and the Lynx, one in a Hunter 30-mm Aden gunpack and the last in a crate.

The Air Force Board of Inquiry consisted of four senior officers headed by Director of Operations Air Commodore Phil Pile. The other members were Wing Commander Peter Briscoe – Staff Officer Training, Wing Commander Eddie Hobbs – Technical member, and Air Lieutenant Nigel Lewis-Walker – Thornhill Defence Commander.

Arrests that followed in quick succession were: - Monday, 25th July (the day after the sabotage) – Air Lieutenant Neville Weir – No 2 Squadron pilot, ex SAS, was taken into custody. After torture, a confession was extracted, and he was released on Saturday 31st July 1982. He was re-arrested on Monday, 16th August. Tuesday, 27th July – Air Lieutenant Nigel Lewis-Walker. Wednesday, 28th July – Air Lieutenant Barry Lloyd – beaten up, tortured, and made to write a confession, implicating former Chief of Staff, Air Vice-Marshal Len Pink, Air Commodore Phil Pile, Wing Commanders Pete Briscoe and Wing Commander John Cox, and also claiming that three former SAS operatives had carried out the sabotage. Lloyd attempted to commit suicide. Friday, 6th August – Squadron Leader Johnson *Danger* Ncube, Officer Commanding 202 General Service Unit, arrested, beaten up and released. He became a nervous wreck (being a Matabele), turned State witness and was discredited during the High Court trial. Tuesday, 17th August – Wing Commander John Cox arrested Tuesday, 17th August – Group Captain David 'Dag' Jones – released a week later on Tuesday 24th August. Tuesday, 24th August – Wing Commander Pete Briscoe – the second Board member to be arrested. Tuesday, 31st August – Air Commodore Phil Pile (Board Chairman), together with Air Vice-Marshal Hugh Slatter.

Barry Lloyd was arrested on Monday 16th August, taken to Umvuma, then moved to Harare on the following Thursday, tortured at Selukwe on Saturday 21st August and forced to make a false written confession the next day.

In Lloyd's confession, he claimed that, "A committee had existed in the Air Force for eighteen months, the aim of which was to destroy the Force and bring about the downfall of Prime Minister Robert Mugabe, who would be replaced by an extreme radical. This would cause a mass exodus of whites, which would seriously damage the financial position of Zimbabwe. Such attitudes appeared to have been engendered on racial lines and ill feeling about financial restrictions and the impending Africanisation of the Force. "Known members" (of the so-called Committee) were former Chief of Staff, Air Vice-Marshal Len Pink, Air Commodore Phil Pile, and Wing Commander Pete Briscoe. Wing Commander John Cox was to be the manager and paymaster, and the committee had decided that the 'incident required' was a sabotage at Thornhill. Cox recruited three former SAS men from Johannesburg, named Verwoerd, Jones and Swanepoel, who were briefed to collect incendiary devices at the Fylde Air Force Depot at Chegutu (formerly Hartley)."

"Cox briefed Lloyd about the arrangements, and Lloyd went to the Depot to tell the three men about security at Thornhill. John Connolly, the Officer Commanding the Fylde Depot, showed him a completed incendiary device. It consisted of plastic explosive and phosphorus enclosed in a plastic bag, with two watches attached. Security at Thornhill had started to be undermined following directives by Cox. The saboteurs were to be driven to Thornhill by Connolly. Swanepoel would be given a false name at the Guardroom and say he had an appointment with Neville Weir, who would take the saboteurs to see the new aircraft. The saboteurs would be locked in the hangar washrooms. Air Lieutenant Nigel Lewis-Walker was to cut a hole in the security fence, the saboteurs would place the devices in the hangars, then sabotage any planes outside on the hardstanding. The devices had a three-hour delay and "during the chaos occasioned by the fires. . . "they were to make their way out to meet Weir who would drive them to Bulawayo to catch the first flight to Johannesburg."

The confession was a complete fabrication – but the die was cast and it led to the rapid arrest of Air Force personnel – most of whom were tortured to make collaborating confessions.

By Friday, 20th August, the Board of Inquiry had determined that a South African Air Force Canberra had flown over Thornhill on 10th June. Several witnesses also testified that they heard a helicopter, believed to be a SAAF Puma helicopter, fly over the Guinea Fowl radio mast shortly after the first explosions had gone off at Thornhill. The evidence pointed to South African involvement.

Neville Weir, the first airman to be arrested on the Monday 26th July, was removed from prison on Wednesday 25th August, interrogated and beaten. Beatings followed the next day as well. He was threatened with death, was assaulted on the Friday and eventually broke and made a false confession on Saturday, 28th

Air Vice-Marshal Hugh Slatter was arrested on Tuesday 31st August 1982. He was interned at Mkoba (Gwelo), moved to Umvuma on 9th September, then taken to Mtoko on Sunday 12th September and tortured. He had a heavy blue-coloured cloth bag pulled over his head, and handcuffed – minus shoes, socks, belt and jacket. He was then taken to a remote area and tortured with electric shocks – needle electrodes were inserted into the top of his back and the base of his spine. His body was racked by spasms as the current was increased – his back arched violently and he gasped involuntarily. He felt as though hundreds of burning fishhooks were tearing his muscles in every direction. So excruciating and frightening was the pain that all his efforts were directed at staying conscious. He was then subjected to intense interrogation, still hooded and handcuffed. Any denials of complicity resulted in further electric shock treatment. In spite of the late night chill, he felt damp with perspiration and was having difficulty breathing. He felt he was suffocating. The interrogation was hostile in the extreme, calling the Air Vice-Marshal "you white bastard", "all lies and bullshit", with many other expletives and abusive language. Slatter was then subjected to a second torture session - and he realised how the confessions had been extracted from the other airmen. Phil Pile was also tortured and a false statement extracted from him.

Air Marshal Norman Walsh

Meanwhile, retired Air Vice-Marshal Len Pink had written (from South Africa) to the Prime Minister Mugabe, expressing his dismay at the arrest of Slatter and Pile. "From this distance, I can only assume the detention of these two officers will have done irreparable harm to the Air Force. If your trust cannot be placed in two men of such high integrity then I suggest there is little hope of building a truly multiracial and harmonious Air Force, let alone a country. Once again, I urge you to reconsider your decision and to examine not only the possible motives of the officers concerned but the source and reliability of the information or misinformation that may have been passed to you." Len Pink's letter had no effect whatsoever – and the airmen remained in prison. It soon dawned that the dictatorial black government was gambling on a plan to rid the Air Force of its white leadership. No black airman had the ability or capacity to replace the arrested white Air Force hierarchy. World pressure mounted against Zimbabwe for a fair, open trial. American Vice President George Bush extracted a promise from deputy premier Simon Muzenda that the trial would be in open court. A year after the arrests, the trial opened on Monday, 23rd May 1983 – and lasted until mid June. The court was adjourned for six weeks, with judgement being given on Wednesday, 31st August 1983.

Respect for the rule of law deteriorated rapidly amongst the Force's rank and file. More and more Air Force people were emigrating. Even the Thornhill CO, Dag Jones, "took the gap". To fill the gap, Pakistanis arrived on contract in the wake of the white exodus.

The trial took 44 days; Judge Enoch Dumbutshena, Zimbabwe's first black judge and later Chief Justice, presiding. He castigated the State for withholding legal counsel from the accused airmen, found that their confessions had been obtained under extreme duress (torture), and bravely acquitted them. As the Air Force Officers walked from the court as free men, they were re-arrested for indefinite detention, and taken back into custody on the same charges of which they had just been acquitted. An immediate hue and cry followed from civilised society – and within days Air Vice-Marshal Hugh Slatter and Air Commodore Phil Pile were placed on an Air Zimbabwe flight and "deported" to London on 9th September 1983. The Air Zimbabwe Captain welcomed them aboard over the intercom and was soundly castigated afterwards by government. Nigel Lewis-Walker had been set free earlier, on 16th November 1983. Peter Briscoe, John Cox, Barry Lloyd and Neville Weir were released just before Christmas.

Air Marshal Norman Walsh retired on 22 May 1983. Boss Norman was replaced by Pakistani Daudpota, who duly handed over the reins to Josiah Tungamirai. The latter had no air experience – not even a pilot training crash course (pun intended).

Culprits Still At Large

The culprits of the Thornhill sabotage were South African Defence Force Project *Barnacle* Special Forces operatives. The Air Force Board of Inquiry had already established that South African Air Force aircraft were identified before the senseless arrests of Air Vice-Marshal Hugh Slatter and Air Commodore Phil Pile. A Canberra had carried out a photo-reconnaissance directly over Thornhill, and a large Puma type helicopter was seen in the vicinity of Guinea Fowl shortly after the Hunters and Hawks blew up. At an early stage, the Air Force had concluded that a South African based organisation was responsible for the Thornhill sabotage.

One of the reasons for the lengthy detention of those mistakenly involved would be that Mugabe did not wish them to make any revelations to the South African Truth and Reconciliation Commission and thus cause him embarrassment. It is also understood that even though Mugabe knew that South African operatives were involved in the Thornhill sabotage, further embarrassment resulted in this being kept reasonably quiet – because Mugabe had openly but somewhat prematurely stated that the Rhodesians were the guilty parties.

Interestingly, Peter Stiff named an insider as "Team Oscar's guide" – who also made and hid the duplicate Nos 1 and 2 Squadron crew-room keys in order for the saboteurs to gain access to the Hunter and Hawk aircraft hangars. Gray Branfield, the so-called 'Major Brian' had ordered that Team Oscar's three operators and the 'friendly airman' jointly conduct the operation. Two operators would do the actual job while the third (ex-Scout – now deceased) would drive the getaway car. The airman was responsible for conducting the detailed reconnaissance, since it was a simple task for him because he had free access to Thornhill. Stiff also claims that the so-called 'guide' (who liaised with Major Brian/Gray Branfield), was also interrogated, routinely beaten up, but not detained – unlike others like Flight Sergeant James Lochran who was detained for 53 days. Stiff also claims that the insider's promised SAAF appointment never materialised.

The discovery of the Revue timing device watches, and particularly the use of Duracell batteries (unobtainable in Zimbabwe), was a dead give away – in fact a stupid oversight by EMLC – the organisation responsible for making, adapting or acquiring special equipment for SADF Special Forces.

Relevant extracts from Peter Stiff's *Cry Zimbabwe* read, "The strike against the Thornhill Air Base was the most closely guarded secret of all the covert operations investigated by the author" and, "The first coy admission of responsibility for the Thornhill attack came only on 3 August 1997, when the erstwhile commander of the Special Forces Brigade, Brigadier Cornelius 'Boris' Borrnman conceded to the *Sunday Independent* that South Africans had been involved in assisting ex-Rhodesians who wanted to settle old scores. To correct the record for the sake of history, the operation was approved by the then Commanding General Special Forces, the late Major-General Kat Liebenberg, and almost certainly given the nod by the Chief SADF and the State Security Council. It was not an exercise by ex-Rhodesian mavericks out 'to settle old scores', but by Project Barnacle operatives from the SADF's Special Forces acting under orders. That they might have been ex-Rhodesians was irrelevant. The purpose of the raid was to destabilise Zimbabwe and lend assistance to ZIPRA by reducing the Air Force of Zimbabwe's fireforce capabilities". Peter Stiff wrote me in July 2007: "I believe beyond all doubt that the Thornhill sabotage information is correct as portrayed in Cry Zimbabwe. The information was given to me by Gray Branfield (ex-Detective Inspector) who was put in the book under the nom de guerre of Major Brian because of the sensitivity of the ops he undertook. His real name can now be revealed because he was killed in Iraq a couple of years back. There is no doubt in my mind that the operation was motivated by Branfield's report on page 140 of *Cry Zimbabwe* which was the only original document I could lay my hands on. The decision to 'go' was made by Major-General Fritz Loots who I have interviewed but not about Thornhill because I knew nothing about it at the time. Unfortunately although still alive, he is suffering from advanced Alzheimer's so that cannot be taken further. I honestly don't believe Woods (Kevin) knows much about Thornhill from a first hand point of view. He was only given orders but I can say for certain that he did not take part in the Thornhill raid."

The CIO, CID and the ZANU PF government - inherited the Air Force of Ruins.

Air Force of Ruins

Major-General Mike Shute, the last white General army officer, was so upset by the arrest and detentions that he retired when refused an audience with Mugabe. Air Marshal Norman Walsh retired as soon as the last detained airman was released. Air Marshal Daudpota, from the Pakistani Air Force was contracted as a stopgap commander to take over from Norman Walsh. Daudpota's brief was simple: turn the Air Force black. Daudpota left and was put in charge of PAL, Pakistan Air Lines, where within two years he was ignominiously thrown out for corruption, nepotism and general inefficiency.

Major-General Josiah Tungamirai, by then a senior staff officer with the National Army, was transferred to the Air Force as Chief of Staff to understudy Daudpota. He took over as Air Force Commander with the rank of Air Marshal on 1 January 1986.

The by-then Commander of the Air Force, Air Marshal Perence Shiri (who was more used to slaughtering innocent Matabele civilians in his old post as commander of the infamous Fifth Brigade) excused his errant pilots and suggested they lost their way due to 'human' (pilot) error. The *Sunday Independent* more pertinently asked: "How can the air force defend the country effectively against foreign intrusion when its pilots can't even find Bulawayo?" In *Cry Zimbabwe*, Peter Stiff aptly describes Air Marshal Perence Shiri as the Butcher of Bhalagwe as well as the Beast of Bhalagwe, for the role he played in the War of Gukurahundi. It came as no surprise when Robert Mugabe chose him to lead the troops and airmen to support Laurent Kabila in the Congo. Shiri was also instrumental in seconding 700 soldiers and 500 airmen, together with the necessary rations, tents, sleeping bags, transport and logistics to facilitate the farm invasions. Shiri plotted the farm invasions with Mugabe in March 2000 as a pre-election ploy after which ZANU PF was nearly beaten by the MDC.

Operation Altar: 1982 - 1984

Operation *Altar* was the SADF assistance to Renamo, or MNR, after the Selous Scouts and Special Air Service had been disbanded in Rhodesia/Zimbabwe. This included Recce raids made on FRELIMO installations. There was a series of sabotage attacks on the oil pipeline that ran from Beira to Mutare, and the associated road and rail routes. Typical examples of these operations occurred in mid October 1981.

SADF headquarters in Pretoria announced that Lieutenant Alan Gingles had been killed "in action against terrorists on 15th October in the operational area". At the same time, FRELIMO in Maputo announced that four unidentified 'Boer' soldiers had been killed by an FPLM patrol while attempting to sabotage an unspecified target on the route between Mutare and Beira. They had, it was claimed, been blown up with their own explosives that detonated during the contact. Pretoria dismissed the claim as lies and propaganda. Research conducted by Peter Stiff (The Silent War) concluded that Gingles, from Ireland, had attested into the Rhodesian Army, and moved to Phalaborwa with what was left of the Selous Scouts to join what ultimately became 5-Recce Commando. Stiff also found out that the others killed in the incident were two 5-Recce black operators (Riflemen B Michael and F Tombo) and a Renamo guerrilla. When Stiff broached the question with the deputy commander Special Forces in 1987, he classified the subject as too sensitive to discuss. The Truth and Reconciliation Commission in the late 1990s subsequently confirmed his death.

The Beira to Mutare railway line was blasted in three places on 16th December 1981. Moçambique's National Highway One, a pot-holed road (a highway in name only), had been built for the use of the Portuguese military. The road runs north/south from Beira to Maputo and was also targeted by Renamo.

In February 1982 a fifteen-man team from 5-Reconnaissance Regiment's 2-Commando took over from a team already at Renamo's Savi base in the Inhambane Province. They flew by SAAF C-130 Hercules from Hoedspruit Air Base to Durban. Then they flew out at night, headed out to sea, turned north, proceeded along the coast, turned west and dropped the Recces 50 kilometres south of the Save River. Renamo President Afonso Dhlakama, who had travelled especially from his Gorongoza base, met the Recces.

The *SAS Tafelberg* and *SAS Protea* were used to supply Renamo with huge quantities of supplies and war material. Renamo also established another base 30 kilometres west of Maborte. During 1983, 300 Renamo guerrillas were sent to Impala Ranch, Phalaborwa, for further training. They were taken out by sea, while others flew out by SAAF Dakotas, from bush airstrips. The discerning reader may query what Operation *Altar* had in common with the Rhodesian Bush War. The answer lies in the fact that the MNR/Renamo was the brainchild of Rhodesian Intelligence, and illustrates the covert skills that South Africa inherited with the support and training of ex-Selous Scouts and Special Force operators. Another consequence of Operation *Altar* was the commitment of army units by Zimbabwe to guard the Beira to Mutare route, to free FRELIMO units for offensive actions.

Covert operations did not cease with Operation *Altar*. "Dirty tricks" continued under the guise of other code-words.

Operation Mila and Operation Bristol: 1983

Operation *Mila*, and Operation *Bristol*, took over where Operation *Altar* ended. It concerned South African assistance to Renamo – to Nkomati and beyond. On 25th May 1983, four C-130s para-dropped five Renamo leaders, with sixty palettes containing massive amounts of supplies and munitions. Renamo succeeded in destroying ninety-three locomotives, 250 rail cars and killing 150 rail workers. A Recce team had sabotaged the strategic bridge across the Zambezi River, at Sena, the longest railway bridge in Africa. The Limpopo Valley railway, effectively destroyed by the Rhodesians in the last stages of the Bush War, had remained closed, despite attempts to reopen it.

It is ironic that Colonel Dudley Coventry, the highly respected ex-commander of the SAS, afterwards controlled the reconnaissance of the base and the successful assault. He had originally established the base for Renamo in the old Rhodesian days, so he knew it well. Samora Machel presented Coventry with a Swiss Army knife in gratitude for capturing the base. Like most successful ZNA assaults, it was conducted as a Fire Force attack in the dashing style of the old Rhodesian Army / Air Force (Dudley was murdered by intruders at his home in Harare in the mid-90s). The two volumes of the 'Gorongoza Papers' provided incontrovertible evidence of the SADF's continued co-operation with Renamo in contravention of the Nkomati Accord.

Aircraft Types (Alphabetically) and Squadrons
Alouette (K-Car, G-Car and Z-Car), No 7 Sqn: 8 shot down + 11 losses
Bell Helicopter, No 8 Sqn: 1 shot down + 2 losses
Canberra, No 5 Sqn: 2 shot down + 1 loss
Dakota, No 3 Sqn: 1 shot down + 2 losses
Genet, No 6 Sqn: 1 loss
Hawker Hunter: No 1 Sqn: 2 shot down
Lynx, No 4 Sqn: 3 shot down + 1 loss
Trojan, No 4 Sqn: 2 shot down + 1 loss
Vampire, No 2 Sqn: 1 shot down
Total shot down 20 + 19 losses.

Rhodesian Air Force Aircraft Shot Down or Crashed

(Due to enemy action; k = killed; ASR = Air Strike Report Log number; n/c = No crash)
Trojan R3244; 14 Apr 74; Flt Lt Chris Weinmann (k) / SAC Pat Durrett (k); ASR 133
Trojan R3427; 20 Apr 74; Air Sub Lt Willy Wilson (k)/ FS Rob Andrews (k); ASR 139
Canberra R2156; 04 Apr74; Air Lt Keith Goddard (k)/ASLt Rich Airey (k); ASR 127
Alouette SAAF 111; 14 Aug 74; Lt Hobart Houghton / Sgt Ray H Wernich (SAP) / Maj E Addams (k); ASR 191
Alouette R7524; 27 Mar 76; Flt Lt Michael Borlace / Sgt Mike Upton; ASR 318
Hunter R1280; 10 Jun 76; Flt Lt Tudor Thomas; ASR 370
Alouette R5076 n/c; 18 Jul 76; Flt Lt Michael Borlace / Sgt J Pat Graham (k); ASR 404
Alouette R7524 n/c; 01 Sep 76; Flt Lt Ian M Harvey / Sgt HF 'Beef' Belstead (k); ASR 460
Lynx R3413; 02 Sep 76; Flt Lt HWH 'Starry' Stevens (k); ASR 461
Alouette R7524; 22 Dec 76; Flt Lt Vic Cook / Sgt Mike Upton; ASR 567
Canberra R2514; 12 Jan 77; Flt Lt Ian Donaldson (k)/ ASLt Dave Hawkes (k); ASR 587
Lynx R4306; 04 May 77; ASLt Rob H Griffiths / AC CWD Brown (k); ASR 685
Alouette R5725; 18 May 77; Flt Lt Roger J Watt / SAC Rob G Nelson (k); ASR 693
Dakota R3702; 31 May 77; Flt Lt Bruce Collocott (k) / Flt Lt Jerry Lynch; ASR 703
Alouette R5713; 23 Aug 77; Flt Lt Geoff A Oborne / Sgt Frank Robinson; ASR 719
Lynx R3042; 02 Sep 77; Air Lt DL du Plessis (k) / Sgt John Underwood (k); ASR 722
Vampire R1386; 23 Nov 77; Air Lt Phil W Haigh (k); ASR 753
Alouette R5757 n/c; 12 Jan 78; Flt Lt Norman Maasdorp / F.Sgt HAJ Jarvie (k); ASR 768
Alouette R5701 n/c; 12 Jan 78; Flt Lt Chas Goatley / F.Sgt 'Flamo' Flemming (k); ASR 768
Alouette R5177; 28 Jul 78; Air Lt GH Francois du Toit (k), Sgt Kevin P Nelson (k); ASR 844
Alouette R5773/SAAF106; 22 Aug 78; Flt Lt Geoff A Oborne / Sgt Brian Booth; ASR 855
Alouette R5731; 20 Oct 78; ASLt Mark Dawson / Sgt Roelf P Oeloffse; ASR 889
Alouette R5372; 16 Jun 79; Air Lt Ian Henderson / Sgt Joubert
Agusta Bell 205A-1 Helicopter R6098; 03 Sep 79; Flt Lt Dick R Paxton / AC Alex JC Wesson (k); ASR 1035
Hunter R1821; 03 Oct 79; Air Lt Brian K Gordon (k); ASR 1054
Canberra R5203; 03 Oct 79; Flt Lt Kevin L Peinke (k) / Flt Lt JJ Strydom (k); ASR 1055
Alouette SAAF 111; 14 Aug 74; Lt Hobart Houghton / Sgt Ray H Wernich (SAP) / Maj E Addams (k); ASR 191
Alouette R7524; 27 Mar 76; Flt Lt Michael Borlace / Sgt Mike Upton; ASR 318
Alouette R5076 (no crash); 18 Jul 76; Flt Lt Michael Borlace / Sgt J Pat Graham (k); ASR 404
Alouette R7524 (no crash); 01 Sep 76; Flt Lt Ian M Harvey / Sgt HF 'Beef' Belstead (k); ASR 460
Alouette R7524; 22 Dec 76; Flt Lt Vic Cook / Sgt Mike Upton; ASR 567
Alouette R5725; 18 May 77; Flt Lt Roger J Watt / SAC Rob G Nelson (k); ASR 693
Alouette R5713; 23 Aug 77; Flt Lt Geoff A Oborne / Sgt Frank Robinson; ASR 719
Alouette R5757 (no crash); 12 Jan 78; Flt Lt Norman Maasdorp / F.Sgt HAJ Jarvie (k); ASR 768
Alouette R5701 (no crash); 12 Jan 78; Flt Lt Chas Goatley / F.Sgt Al 'Flamo' Flemming (k); ASR 768

Alouette R5177; 28 Jul 78; Air Lt GH Francois du Toit (k), Sgt Kevin P Nelson (k); ASR 844
Alouette R5773 SAAF 106; 22 Aug 78; Flt Lt Geoff A Oborne / Sgt Brian Booth; ASR 855
Alouette R5731; 20 Oct 78; ASLt Mark Dawson / Sgt Roelf P Oeloffse; ASR 889
Bell Helicopter R6098; 03 Sep 79; Flt Lt Dick R Paxton / AC Alex JC Wesson (k); ASR 1035
Canberra R2514; 12 Jan 77; Flt Lt Ian H Donaldson (k) / ASLt David Hawkes (k); ASR 587
Canberra R5203; 03 Oct 79; Flt Lt Kevin L Peinke (k) / Flt Lt JJ Strydom (k); ASR 1055
Dakota R3702; 31 May 77; Flt Lt Bruce Collocott (k) / Flt Lt Jerry Lynch; ASR 703
Hunter R1280; 10 Jun 76; Flt Lt Tudor Thomas; ASR 370
Hunter R1821; 03 Oct 79; Air Lt Brian K Gordon (k); ASR 1054
Lynx R3413; 02 Sep 76; Flt Lt HWH 'Starry' Stevens (k); ASR 461
Lynx R4306; 04 May 77; ASLt Rob H Griffiths / AC CWD Brown (k); ASR 685
Lynx R3042; 02 Sep 77; Air Lt DL du Plessis (k) / Sgt JS John Underwood (k); ASR 722
Trojan R3244; 14 Apr 74; Flt Lt Chris Weinmann (k) / SAC Pat R Durrett (k); ASR 133
Trojan R3427; 20 Apr 74; Air Sub Lt RJ Willy Wilson (k) / FS Rob S Andrews (k); ASR 139
Vampire R1386; 23 Nov 77; Air Lt Phil W Haigh (k); ASR 753

Aircraft Lost On Operations (During air support of Rhodesian Security Forces)

Alouette R7500; 15 Feb 73; Air Lt John Smart (k) / Sgt Tinker Smithdorff (k)
Alouette R5087; 19 Nov 73; Sqn Ldr Eddy Wilkinson / F.Sgt D Woods / Sgt W Huck
Alouette R5697–SAAF 37; 23 Dec 75; Lt JJ van Rensburg / Sgt P van Rensburg (k)
Alouette R5076; 25 Jul 76; Flt Lt Mike Borlace / Sgt Butch Graydon
Alouette R5172; 17 Mar 77; Flt Lt Mike Mulligan / Cpl Fletcher
Alouette R5701; 04 Jan 79; Flt Lt Ray Bolton / Cpl Brian N Cutmore (k); ASR 923
Alouette R5170; 04 Jan 79; Flt Lt Kerry J Fynn (k)/Cpl AHW Tony Turner (k)/ Capt D Havnar(k); ASR 923
Alouette R5705; 26 Sep 79; Flt Lt Paddy M Bate (k) / Sgt Garry R Carter (k) / Maj Bruce Snelgar (Army)(k); ASR 1045
Alouette R5876-SAAF 36; 25 Dec 79; Flt Lt AJ Senekal SAAF (k); ASR 278
Bell Helicopter R6807; 09 Feb 79; Air Lt Bud Cockcroft
Bell Helicopter R6084, 17 Jan 80; Flt Lt Mark Vernon
Canberra R2156; 04 Apr 74; Air Lt Keith Goddard (k)/ Air Sub Lt Rich Airey (k); ASR 127
Dakota R3034; 06 Jan 77; Sqn Ldr Peter Barnett (k) / Flt Lt Dave Mallet (k)
Dakota R7307; 21 Feb 75; Flt Lt Ed Paintin / Flt Lt Frank Wingrove
Genet R6330; 23 Dec 79; Air Sub Lt S Tickle
Islander R3718; 15 Feb 78; Flt Lt B van Huysteen; ASR 781
Lynx R4312; 14 Mar 77; Air Lt John Kidson / Lt Col Brian Robinson (SAS)
Trojan R4326; 17 Dec 74; Air Lt Brian Murdoch (k) / Cpl TM Parker (k) / Cpl RJ Povey (k)

The 38 Air Force Fatalities during the Rhodesian War 1973 to 1979
17 x Pilots killed + 3 x Navigators killed + 16 x Technicians killed + 2 x Airmen / ground staff killed.

Total Operational Losses – by Aircraft Type; Squadron; Shot Down; Losses
Alouette No 7 Sqn 9 Shot down + 11 Losses = 20 total Alouette helicopters

Agusta Bell 205A-1 helicopter No 8 Sqn 1 Shot down + 2 Losses = 3 total Agusta Bell 205A-1 helicopters

Canberra No 5 Sqn 2 Shot down + 1 Losses = 3 total Canberras

Dakota No 3 Sqn   1 Shot down 2 Losses = 3 total Dakotas

Genet No 6 Sqn   0 Shot down 1 Loss = 1 total Genet

Hunter No 1 Sqn 2 Shot down 1 Loss = 3 total Hunters

Islander No 3 Sqn 1 total loss

Lynx No 4 Sqn 3 Shot down 1 Loss = 4 total Lynxs

Trojan No 4 Sqn 2 shot down 1 Loss = 3 Trojans

Provost No 4 Sqn - Nil losses

Vampire No 2 Sqn 1 Shot down 0 Loss = 1 total

21 Shot Down + 20 Losses = Total 41 Aircraft shot down or lost on Operations

Zimbabwe Aftermath

As this manuscript was being prepared for the printers (April 2007) I could not help but reflect that the somewhat trite sayings of the last few years have actually come to pass:
The "Jewel of Africa" has gone to the dogs. The jewel referred to by Nyerere is no longer. The "breadbasket of Africa has become the basket case of Africa".

Zimbabwe has been on the skids ever since Britain coined the phrase NIBMAR (No Independence Before Majority Rule). The much-coveted "Majority Rule" has had a poor record over the past twenty-seven years since ZANU PF came to power. Despite the lifting of sanctions and billion-dollar injections that came with world recognition of Zimbabwe, the decline in standards has accelerated into free-fall. All engineered by Mugabe and his henchmen in the party, driven by greed, without a care for the consequences of land-grabs, 'war veterans', gagging of the press, prostitution of the national assets to the East, legalised destruction of human rights, purging of whites, massacre of the Matabele people and violence by the state against any opponent of the Mugabe mobs. Those consequences are real – and they extend across the full spectrum of the suffering of Zimbabwe's people, from economic to human.

We could say of the Rhodesian War. "It was worth it. We did the correct things. We did them correctly, realistically, idealistically, bravely. Lives were laid down through pride and passion for the protection of our rights. The putting off of the evil day was worth all those lives lost."

If only the world had taken the middle road – a growth path towards full enfranchisement, a tolerant attitude, accepting that civilisation comes only after Man has a full belly, an education and a roof over his head, and working towards that ideal. Civilisation will never come from communism, lawlessness, greed, or empty political promises. Those things are killers, not builders of a country.

Zimbabwe is a tragedy. Perhaps Rhodesia was all in vain . . . . But I don't think so.

~~~OOO~~~

Air Marshal Frank Mussell presenting the Exemplary Service Medal award

EPILOGUE
RINA

Dedicated to Rina, my inspirational ever-loving wife.

I dedicate this book to the mother of my children, who has been a shining example to everyone that she has come into contact with. I have been blessed to witness how she has touched the lives of many people. I have seen how men and women, girls and boys have admired her for her courage, the example she has set, her ability to overcome trials and tribulations, her inspiration, and above all, her love for her fellow being.

Many years ago, in fact many more than I care to admit, I started on this project for my children. As time went on, I realised that Renene and Pey had outgrown my desire to superficially impress them, and that I should instead write this life story for the benefit of our very dear grandchildren. But in the end – as I am now drawing to a close, I have come to the conclusion that I need to not only honour my offspring, but also to acknowledge that the person who shared my life and my love for so long was indeed Rina. To Courtney, Brendan, Matthew, Lucy, Mia and the very special memory of Jake Pey, I trust you will come to really know that Oumie is indeed somebody very special. I trust that you will harvest the many blessings that Rina has knowingly, as well as un-knowingly, sown into the soul of your lives.

To my soul mate Rina, I say simply, "Gogga, I love you."

When Oumie's time is up, the Good Lord will marshal Rina in with "Enter, my good and faithful servant".

To my family and friends, I praise the Lord for making this all possible. A quote from my favourite Scripture (Ecc 3.1) reads: – "There is a **right** time for everything" (the quote from the wisest man that ever lived, in the past and in the future – Solomon).

> There is a right time for everything;
> A time to be born, a time to die;
> A time to plant;
> A time to harvest;
> A time to kill;
> A time to heal;
> A time to destroy;
> A time to rebuild;
> A time to cry;
> A time to laugh;
> A time to grieve;
> A time to dance;
> A time for scattering stones;
> A time for gathering stones;
> A time to hug;
> A time not to hug;
> A time to find;
> A time to lose;
> A time for keeping;
> A time for throwing away;
> A time to tear;
> A time to repair;
> A time to be quiet;
> A time to speak up;
> A time for loving;
> A time for hating;
> A time for war;
> A time for peace.

(Ecclesiastes 3, 1-8.)

Rhodesian Air Force
Air Strike Log

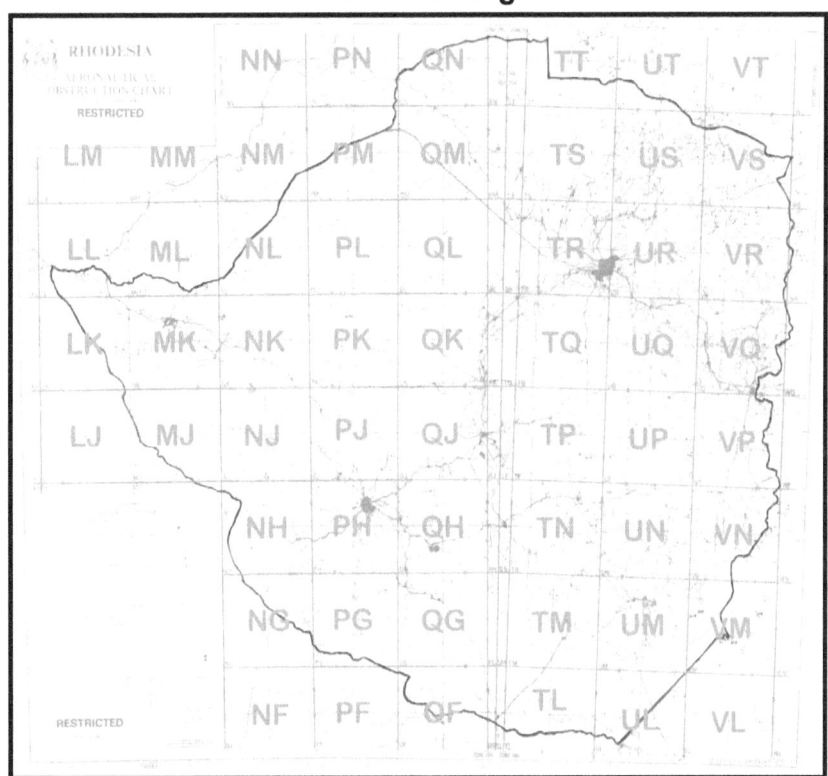

Epub Books Do Not Support Or Allow Tables, Charts Or Text Boxes.
This means that it is not possible to tabulate the AIR STRIKE LOG as per the hardcopy of Rhodesian Air Force Operations with Air Strike Log. Because of this limitation, I have elected to summarise only some of the more dramatic airstrikes. Those readers who wish to see the whole log should e-mail me at oupey@editek.co.nz and I will send appropriate Air Strike Log extracts to readers who request them.

Or alternately, get the Barnes and Noble e-pub copy of the book.

Air Strike Log Summary

Air Strike Report No 03; Date 14/08/1967 Operation Nickel
Aircrews:
- Prop Geldenhuys with Richard Beaver
- Murray Hofmeyer

Target: MK 650505 Inyantue Ridge, Wankie area; Aircraft Provost 309 and Alouette III
Weapons: 230x.303 Browning
Result: Two BT killed, possibly from the battle the night before.

Air Strike No 05: Date 18/03/1968 Operation Cauldron
Aircrews:
- Bill Jelley
- Prop Geldenhuys / Barry Roberts
- Mark McLean / Butch Graydon
- John Rodgers
- Norman Walsh / Brian Warren
- John Barnes / Monty Maughan

Target: RM 115587 Angwa River contact by ground forces with eleven ters. RLI. Aircraft 2 x Vampires, Canberra, 3 x Alouette helicopters 3 x 60lb Squashhead, 151 x 20mm cannon, 96 Frags
Results: Vampires on target. Excellent smoke marking by Alouette. See also Peter Petter-Bowyer's "*Winds of Destruction*" - page 177.

Air Strike No 07; Date 18/07/1968
Aircrews:
- Norman Walsh with Tinker Smithdorff
- Mick Grier with Butch Graydon
- Bill Jelley
- Keith Corrans
- Prop Geldenhuys
- Rich Brand

Target: Contact with 30Terrs, Zambezi – Kariba; Aircraft 2 x Alouette + 4 x Vampire
Result: Insufficient safety distance between FLOT – forward line of own troops – and the target, to permit jet strikes. First pair of Vampires diverted to New Sarum.

Air Strike No 09 20/07/68 Operation Mansion
Aircrews:
- Prop Geldenhuys
- Keith Corrans
- Wally Galloway
- Graham Cronshaw
- Peter Cooke
- Terry Jones / Willy Armitage
- Peter Woolcock / John Digby

Target: Zambezi Valley Devils Gorge, South Bank - approx ML870110
Results: Trojan hit five times by ground fire. See also Peter Petter-Bowyer's "*Winds of Destruction*" - page 192

Air Strike No 18 25/11/1970 Operation Oxtail
Aircrews: Prop Geldenhuys

Target: Nyamasoto, Demo Shamva. Hunter air strike.
Results: 60 x 30mm cannon and 2 x 60lb RP

Air Strike No 24 05/03/1973 Operation Hurricane
Aircrews:
- Prop Geldenhuys / Doug Pasea
- Rob Gaunt
- Rick Culpan
- Dag Jones
- Ginger Baldwin

Target: Airstrike on 12.7mm Anti-aircraft post and porters camp.
Results: 96 x 20lb Frag bomb box. See also Peter Petter-Bowyer's *"Winds of Destruction"* - page 469, Camps deserted

Air Strike No 28 29/04/73 Op Hurricane (External)
Aircrews:
Target:
Results:

Air Strike No
Aircrews:

Target:
Results:

No 246 Op Newton 24/06/75.
Fire Force
Result: 6 terrs killed and I captured in 3 Fire Force contacts - as per Selous Scouts *Top Secret War*, pages 150-151.

No 247 - 25/06/75 Op Hurricane
Aircrew:
- Dave Thorn / Tony Merber
- Slade Healey (SAAF)

Target: Six terrs sighted at US410720, 16nm north of Mt Darwin
Result: Five terrs killed, one wounded and captured. Suspected that one terr escaped.
Comment: good effort by Thorn. Four terrs killed by K-Car. Good airborne control. The Army was advised to implement the day-glo panels.

No 249 - 19/07/75 Op Hurricane
Aircrew:
- Ken Newman / Dave Boyce
- Dave Lowe / Pete Retief
- Solo van Rooyen / Bill Riley

Target: Target in open ground with sparse trees amid riverbed with thick vegetation, at VS009664, near new Rushinga airfield
Result: Two terrs believed to have been wounded. Air Lieutenant Dave Lowe hit by a bullet. One dead terr found by the sweep. The comment was that it was good effort by the crews. The terrs chose the 'field'. The more effective Frantan could not be used due to Rhodesian forces casualties in close proximity to the cave. The stoppage rate of 1 in 300 rounds (MAG) was felt not be too bad.

No 262 11/08/75 Op Hurricane
Aircrews:

- Peter Petter-Bowyer
- Cocky Benecke

Target: 15 terrs, Nyadiri River, north of Mtoko
Results: 15 terrs killed – Refer PB's book *Winds of Destruction*, page 359 - 360

No 263 15/08/75 Op Hurricane
- Aircrew: Danny Svoboda; Cocky Benecke; Pete Simmonds / Steve Stead; Mike Litson; Dave Lowe; Chris Milbank; Peter Petter-Bowyer

Target: Seven terrs in a camp at US428701 (14nm north of Mt Darwin) in the Kandeya Tribal Trust Land, found by Cocky Benecke
Results: 4 terrs killed, 3 wounded and captured. The Camp accounted for. Comment: Commander: Good show by all concerned. Classic Air Force operation - well planned and co-ordinated. Special mention of Benecke, Simmonds and Stead. Refer also P-B's *Winds of Destruction* – page 360.

No 266 31/08/75 Op Hurricane
Aircrews:
- Solo van Rooyen / Bill Riley
- Chinky Pretorius / Org Kriel
- Dave Lowe / Frik Fourie
- Neil Liddell / Sewes Smit
- Greg Todd / Fynn Cunningham
- Mike Litson / Mike Upton
- Bill Sykes / Bob Thompson
- John Blythe-Wood / Philip Tubbs
- Chris Milbank / Grant Williams
- Joe Syslo / Mac McCormick

Target: Approximately 15 terrs at US808165 in the Umfurudzi Wild Life Area, 30nm north west of Mtoko (and 26nm south east of Mt Darwin)
Results: The terrs were moving north for the first sighting point. First contact made at US811178. Four terrs killed (two from air action), three wounded and captured (2 from air action). Terrs returned fire and killed one RAR in a G-Car.
Comment: Smoke grenades are being actioned. The teething troubles associated with this incident were inevitable with the recent induction of direct entry crews.

No 269 09/09/75 Op Hurricane
Aircrews:
- John Blythe-Wood / Ginger Morris
- 3 SAAF Z-cars;
- Cocky Benecke

Target: Ters in river gully at US501867, 15nm south of Mukumbura, and 23nm north of Mt Darwin
Results: Seven terrs killed, four wounded and captured. No return fire from terrs. One hang-up on Provost's Frantan. Comment: Commander - Recorded 'A Good Show by all concerned'. Excellent effort resulting in a most successful engagement. Refer also Peter Petter-Bouwer's "*Winds of Destruction*" – page 362 – Nehanda caretaker Terr group.

No 274 20/10/75 Op Hurricane
Aircrew:
- Dave Rowe / Peter McCabe

Target: Ters on east bank of the river at US412606, 9nm north north-west of Mt Darwin and 5nm south west of Dodito
Result: Two terrs killed. Two weapons and kit recovered. One Security Force wounded but not seriously, Comment: The Commander recorded 'A first class effort by David M. Rowe and Peter

McCabe. The terrs probably bombshelled due to aircraft activity. Considering the contact took place two hours after the Fire Force had arrived at the scene. Crew alertness resulted in two terrs killed out of six.

No 278 26/12/75 Op Hurricane
Aircrew:
- Andre Senekal (SAAF)

Result: Killed – flying accident. Snared barbed wire of protective fencing

No 01/02/76 Op Hurricane
Aircrew:
- Trevor Troup / Boertjie Becker
- Pete Simmonds / Doug Sinclair
- Karl Volker / Maplot Pretorius

Target: Ten terrs at VS740333, 7nm northeast Kotwa – and west of Nyamapanda. (Choppers based Kotwa)
Results: The terrs opened fire on the helicopters. Six terrs killed, two wounded and captured. Simmonds slightly wounded (after relay change Nyamapanda – Police hit landmine). 10 RR pax also hit and wounded by ground fire. Aircraft moved from Kotwa to Mudzi on 8 February 1976.

No 286 06/02/76 Op Hurricane
Aircrews:
- Rob MacGregor / Tony Merber
- Joe Syslo / Henry Jarvie
- Gavie Venter / Loubsher (SAAF)
- George Sole (PB's book – p 381)
- Hamie Dax – PRAW Copper 08

Target: 22 terrs at US029823, 6nm north west of Albert's Mission – Mavuradonha Mountains
Results: Five terrs killed. Further eleven by ground forces. Heavy fire, Provost N4 called.
Comment: 'Good Show' 17 out of 22 terrs accounted for in a combined Army-Air Force operation.

No 306 28/02/76 Op Hurricane
Aircrews:
- Pete Simmonds / Hansi Steyn
- Ray Fitzpatrick / Thomas
- Malcolm Baldwin / Frank Robinson
- George Sole / Pat Graham
- Mike Litson / John Britton
- Martin Hutchings / Eddie Strever
- Gavie Venter / Stapelberg
- Alan Reynolds / Jakes Jacobs (SAAF)

Target: US673678, 17nm north east of Mt Darwin
Results: 17 killed and one wounded captured. Comment: An extremely good show and team work superb. See also write-up of this contact – written by Pete Simmonds

No 317 25/03/76 Op Hurricane
Aircrews:
- Bill Stevens
- Dick Paxton / Brian Warren
- Trevor Troup / Boertjie Becker

Target: VS534739, 12nm north east of Marymount – on Moçambique border
Results: Two terrs killed, five wounded and captured. First Lynx strike – as reported by "PB", in his book, page 384.

No 318 31/03/76 Op Hurricane
Aircrews:
- Cocky Benecke
- Mark McLean / Bert Keightley
- Perry Childs / Duppie du Preez
- Michael Borlace / Mike Upton
- Allan Hutchings / Eddie Strever
- Slade Healey / Kriel (SAAF)
- Daryl Squance

Target: VS534739, 12nm north east of Marymount – on Moçambique border
Results: Several signals received. Major Ainslie killed by ground fire. Perry Childs wounded by flying shrapnel. Mike Borlace / Mike Upton shot down, rescued by Dick Paxton. (See P-B's book, page 384).

No 346 14/05/76
Aircrews:
- Michael Borlace / Dave Boyce
- Perry Childs / Chris Hoebel
- Dave Atkinson / Tiro Voster
- Cecil van Vuuren / Wayne Ferreira
- Cocky Benecke
- John Bennie

Target: US379692, 15nm north west of Mt Darwin
Results: Six terrs killed, one captured. G-Car 5773 was hit twice by ground fire. Provost 3163 was also hit. Captain Len Pitch wounded, but died subsequent to his casevac.

No 356 24/05/76
Aircrews:
- Martin Hutchings / Chris Rademan
- Kevin Peinke / Bert Keightley
- Neil Ellis / Ray Wernich SA
- Trevor Troup / Pete Retief

Target: VS362202, 8nm north west of Mudzi
Results: Six terrs killed and one captured wounded.

No 358 27/05/76 Op Repulse
Aircrews:
- Ian Armstrong
- Tudor Thomas
- Doug Reitz
- Joe Syslo / Pete McCabe
- Phil Haigh

Target: TM525778, 17nm north north-west of Rutenga. Sighting of 13 terrs
Results: 5 terrs killed, one wounded and one captured. Lynx from FAF 7, K-Car from FAF 6 Chipinga and G-Car from FAF 9 Rutenga. See also *Pride of Eagles*.

No 360 28/05/76 Op Thrasher
Aircrews:
- Joe Syslo / Pete McCabe
- Ian Sheffield

Target: VN940823, 6nm east of Lusitu Mission. VN930830, 4nm east (Chimanimani)
Results: Eleven terrs seen to fall and not to get up.

No 361 29/05/76 Op Hurricane
Aircrews:
- Trevor Troup / Willie Beaurain
- Kevin Peinke / Bert Keightley
- Neil Ellis / Ray Wernich SA
- Frikkie Rheeder / Pete Retief SAAF

Target: VS353207, 8nm north west of Mudzi. See also Air Strike 354, 355 and 356.
Results: The K-Car killed five and three were captured. The K-Car was hit in the radio compartment. G-Car 7578 suffered slight damage to the tail boom and rotor tip during avoiding action. Comment: Air Lieutenant Troup was praised for his recognition of the terrs despite their attempt at bluffing him. Sgt Retief was praised for his influence.

No 363 01/06/76 Op Thrasher
Aircrews:
- Michael Borlace / Henry Jarvie
- Chris Dickinson / Philip Tubbs
- Dave Atkinson / Griffon
- Ray Bolton

Target: VP506534, Odzi river, 15nm north of Hot Springs and 28nm south of Grand Reef.
VP502542 – slightly further south of above
Results: 13 terrs killed. Griffon shot in both feet. Refer also to Peter Petter-Bowyer's *"Winds of Destruction"*, page 394 to 396.

No 364 02/06/76 Op Hurricane
Aircrews:
- Ray Fitzpatrick / Wayne Ferreira
- Ed Potterton
- Ray Bolton
- Danny Svoboda / Rick Singleton

Target: US618540, 10nm north east of Mt Darwin, on the Ruya river, 6nm west of Karanda Mission. A/T 1315
Results: 13 terrs killed and one captured. Seven were killed by airstrike and six by ground forces.

No 368 10/06/76 Op Thrasher
Aircrews:
- Russell Broadbent
- Tudor Thomas
- Martin Lowrie

Target: Gun emplacement at VN760383, 4nm south of Mount Selinda
Results: On target, 11 terrs killed. Heavy ground fire neutralised by Lynx

No 370 10/06/76 Op Thrasher (External)
Aircrews:
- Tudor Thomas
- Martin Lowrie
- Russell Broadbent

Target: International boundary VN760383, 1nm south east of Espungabera, Moçambique
Results: Hawker Hunter 1280 Hydraulic failure and ejected (near Thornhill).

No 372 11/06/76 Op Hurricane
Aircrews:
Ray Fitzpatrick / Funqueil

- Ken Newman / Paul Braun
- Danny Svoboda / Rick Singleton
- Nick Meikle / Hansi Steyn
- Dag Jones / Peter Petter-Bowyer
- John Bennie
- Bill Stevens

Target: Terr camp at US548729, 6nm north east of Dodito and 17nm north of Mt Darwin. Air Tasks 1390 & 1394.
Results: Eleven terrs killed and one captured wounded. See also PB's "*Winds of Destruction*" – Page 390

No 374 13/06/76 Op Hurricane
Aircrews:
- Solo van Rooyen / Willie Beaurain
- Frikkie Rheeder / Maplot Pretorius
- Terence Murphy / Steve Russell
- Dave Johnston / Johan Lewis

Target: 15 terrs sighted at VR443757, 14nm east of Mtoko
Results: Six killed and four wounded by the K-Car.

No 380 19/06/76
Aircrews:
- Cocky Benecke
- Bill Stevens
- Ray Fitzpatrick / Org Kriel
- Mike Litson / Pete McCabe

Target: Terr camp at US358719, 16nm north north-west of Mt Darwin
Results: Six terrs killed and one wounded and captured.

No 388 25/06/76
Aircrews:
- Dave Atkinson / Org Kriel
- Ken Newman / Flamo Flemming
- Cocky Benecke

Target: Terr camp found by Air Recce at US621618, 13nm north east of Mt Darwin
Results: Seven terrs killed and one wounded and captured. TOT 13h30

No 405 20/07/76 Op Hurricane
Aircrews:
- Mike Saunders
- Phil Haigh
- Chris Milbank / Willie Beaurain
- Trevor Troup / Boertjie Becker Barry Roberts / Johan Lewis
- Danny Svoboda / Pat Graham

Target: Koppie VS6352, 16nm north of Kotwa
Results: Three terrs killed, one captured, and ten civilians killed. Sgt John Patrick Graham killed by ground fire, air strike could have been 18 July, not the 20th?

No 422 02/08/76 Op Repulse
Aircrew:
- Cocky Benecke

Target: Ters living in bush at UM536376, 14 n.m. south of Hippo Valley
Results: Three terrs and five local females killed. See also P-B's book, page 397.

No 431 Op Eland
Aircrews:
- Chris Abrams
- Martin Lowrie

Target: Support of Selous Scouts at WQ085770, 14 n.m. east of Inyangani Mountain, on Moz border
Results: 12.7mm machine-gun silenced – vicinity of Tatandica, north of Nyadzonia/Pungwe base in Moçambique

No 433 10/08/76
Aircrews:
- Bill Michie
- Don Northcroft
- John Blythe-Wood / Ginger Morris
- Tony Snyders / Ray Wernich (SAAF)
- John Annan / Flamo Flemming
- Piet Claasens / Pete Haley / Halsy? (SAAF)
- Barry Roberts / Mike Smith

Target: Ters being fed at VR413958, 18 n.m. north east of Mtoko
Results: Ten local males, four local females killed and eleven captured.

No 447 18/08/76
Aircrews:
- Rob MacGregor / Paul Braun
- Mark McLean / Tony Jordan
- John Blythe-Wood / Doug Sinclair

Target: Eleven terrs at VQ497333, 18 n.m. north of Grand Reef.
Results: Eleven terrs killed: eight by the K-Car, two by the Army and one by the police.

No 454 27/08/76 Op Repulse
Aircrews:
- Malcolm Baldwin / Garry Whittal
- Dick Paxton / Mike Upton
- Mark Knight / George Bushney
- Ted Lunt / Alan Shields
- Norman Maasdorp

Target: 30 terrs and recruits at UL870990 in the Gona-re-Zhu, 25 n.m. north east of Malvernia.
Results: 18 terrs-recruits killed. (Tol Janeke reports 40 killed and 13 captured wounded, FAF 7 & 9 Fire Forces – as per Peter Petter-Bowyer's *"Winds of Destruction"* – page 400).

No 459 08/76 Op Prawn External
Aircrews:
- John Blythe-Wood
- Lynx / Rob Warracker

Target: Yellow Submarine - Selous Scouts tasks: Chicualacuala - Moz
Results: Op Prawn – Moz railway and train demolition – Barragem to Malvernia.

No 460 01/09/76 Op Repulse
Aircrews:
- Murray Hofmeyr / Bob St. Quentin
- John Annan / Beef Belstead KIA
- Dick Paxton / Nick Tselentis
- Chris Dixon / George Bushney

Target: UM650375 Matibi 2, Lundi River, 15 n.m. south east of Hippo Valley.

Results: Beef Belstead killed by ground fire. Pilot Ian Harvey? See "*Winds of Destruction*", page 414.

No 461 02/09/76 Op Thrasher
Aircrews:
- Bill Stevens KIA

Target: Hot pursuit – north east border, Moçambique
Results: Bill Stevens killed – aircraft shot down

No 473 21/09/76 Op Hurricane
Aircrews:
Ken Law / Tony Jordan
Ed Potterton
Target: US786745, 24 n.m. north east of Mt Darwin
Results: Ten terrs killed, two killed by the K-Car and two by the Lynx.

No 475 22/09/76 Op Thrasher
Aircrews:
- Mike Litson / Rick Singleton
- Richard Dives
- Ian Harvey / Bob Thompson
- Mark Aitchison / Steve Russell
- Michael Borlace / Mike Upton

Target: Ters in bush at VP110388, 28 n.m. north west of Birchenough Bridge, 35 n.m. north of Chipinga (Nyanyadzi)
Results: Six terrs killed and one wounded and captured by a combined air-ground effort.

No 479 22/09/76
Aircrews: K-Car with SAS Brian Robinson; Dakota with 18 paratroopers
Target: Refer P-B's *Winds of Destruction*, page 418
Results: First use of Dakotas in support of Fire Force.

No 480 23/09/76 Op Repulse
Aircrews:
- Pete Simmonds / Brian Warren
- Danny Svoboda / Hansi Steyn
- Bill Sykes / Garry Whittal
- Mark Dawson / Pete McCabe
- Mick Delport

Target: Terr resting place at VM059933, 8 n.m. south west of Chisumbanje
Results: Seven killed and one captured.

No 483 30/09/76 Op Repulse
Aircrews:
- Pete Simmonds / Pete McCabe
- Terence Murphy / Flamo Flemming
- Danny Svoboda / Hansi Steyn Mark Dawson / Brian Daykin
- Bill Sykes / Garry Whittal
- Vic Cook / Rory Perhat
- Peter Cooke / Finch Bellringer;
- Cocky Benecke
- Mick Delport

Target: 20 terrs at UM814062, 45 n.m. south east of Buffalo Range.

Results: Twenty-eight terrs killed, five wounded, and three captured. Lynx 3042 hit six times in fuel tank, wing and boom. See also write-up in *Pride of Eagles*, page 548 and 549

No 492 10/10/76 Op Repulse
Aircrews:
- Ken Law / Tony Merber
- Joe Syslo / Brian Daykin
- Kevin Peinke / Norman
- Nick Meikle / Brian Crystal
- Cocky Benecke
- Bruce Smith / Wally Galloway

Target: UM273147, 10 n.m. north west of Boli
Results: Ten killed and two captured. (P-B reports Brian Robinson in K-Car with Ken Law, and together with Cocky, accounted for 14 CT's – see page 418 of P-B's book)

No 493 11/10/76 Op Thrasher
Aircrews:
- Giles Porter / Henry Jarvie
- George Sole / Bert Keightley
- Chris Dixon / Keith Rayne
- Greg Todd / Brian Booth

Target: Seven-eight terrs at VN501857
Tanganda, 12 n.m. north west of Chipinga
Results: Eight terrs killed, two by the K-Car and six by ground forces after being wounded by the K-Car.

No 498 19/10/76 Op Hurricane
Aircrews:
- Rob MacGregor / Philip Tubbs
- John Blythe-Wood / Wally Wallace
- Trev Baynham / Nick Tselentis
- Bill McQuade / Frank Robinson
- Dag Jones

Target: US5459, 7 n.m. north east of Mt Darwin
Results: Seven terrs killed.

No 503 28/10/76
Aircrews:
- Rob MacGregor / Mike Upton
- Bill McQuade / Keith Rayne
- Ken Newman / Jenkie Jenkins
- Mike Borlace / George Bushney
- Alf Wild

Target: Seven terrs at US435120 18 n.m. south of Mt Darwin
Results: Seven killed and one captured

No 512 07/11/76 Op Thrasher
Aircrews:
- Mark Knight / Terry Warner
- Chris Wentworth / Tony Merber
- Chris Dickinson / Wally Wallace

Target: Three terrs feeding at VN370860, 6 n.m. south east of Birchenough Bridge. Sighting by RAR OP

Results: Seven terrs killed. Army follow up arrived late, but got a few stragglers. K-Car sustained hits necessitating blade change back at Grand Reef.

No 513 09/11/76 Op Hurricane
Aircrews:
- Ken Newman / Norman Farrell
- Bill McQuade / Keith Rayne
- Bill Sykes / Bert Keightley
- Alf Wild

Target: US449944, 10 n.m. south west of Mukumbura, in Zambezi Valley, below Mavuradonha mountains
Results:

No 518 12/11/76 Op Repulse (External)
Aircrews:
- Chris Abrams
- Martin Lowrie
- Mark Knight / Ginger Morris
- Michael Borlace / Steve Russell
- Chris Dickinson / Wally Wallace
- Mick Delport
- Clive Ward
- Graham Cronshaw / Bob Fletcher
- Greg Todd / Tony Jordan
- Mark Aitchison / Frank Robinson
- Dick Paxton / Brian Daykin

Target: VM510386, 8 n.m. south east of Mavue, Save River. And VM459405, 6 n.m. east of Mavue – in Moçambique
Results: 18 terrs killed and one captured. Mick Delport and Clive Ward destroyed two heavy machine guns.

No 524 15/11/76 Op Hurricane
Aircrews:
- Baldy Baldwin / Rick Singleton
- John Barnes / Finch Bellringer
- Vic Cook / Rory Perhat
- Russell Broadbent

Target: VR4346, 23 n.m. south east of Mtoko
Results: Eight terrs killed.

No 527 15/11/76 Op Thrasher
Aircrews:
- Chris Wentworth / Tony Merber
- Tudor Thomas / Brian Warren
- Trev Baynham / Ted Holland

Target: VQ7443, 30 n.m. north east of Grand Reef
Results: 31 terrs killed and one captured. See also P-B's book *Winds of Destruction*, page 414.

No 539 24/11/76
Aircrews:
- Ted Brent / Jim Russell
- Ed Paintin / David Hawkes
- Rich Brand

- Mark Vernon
- Phil Haigh
- John Barnes / Mike Upton
- Kevin Peinke / Brian Crystal

Target: VR7169, 33 n.m. east of Mtoko
Results: 13 terrs and two African local men killed. Two captured.

No 545 28/11/76 Op Hurricane
Aircrews:
- John Barnes / Mike Upton
- Vic Cook / Rory Perhat
- Bill McQuade / Finch Bellringer
- Clive Ward

Target: VR5253, 24 n.m. south east of Mtoko
Results: Five terrs killed by K-Car, five terrs wounded and then killed by K-Car and Lynx, three terrs wounded and captured (one mortally wounded), three terrs killed by ground forces. Total 14 killed and two captured.

No 549 09/12/76 Op Repulse
Aircrews:
- Prop Geldenhuys

Target: TN873410, 7 n.m. south east of Morgenster Mission and south of Zimbabwe Ruins. Nyajena TTL
Results: Lynx 3154. Two 15-gallon Frantan, five 37 mm SNEB rockets

No 554 11/12/76 Op Hurricane
Aircrews:
- Al Bruce / Jim Russell
- Randy du Rand / Mike Ronne
- Mark Aitchison / Gary Whittal
- Harold Griffiths / Jenkie Jenkins

Target: UT522402, 3 n.m. west of Mukumbura
Results: Nine terrs killed.

No 555 14/12/76 Op Thrasher
Aircrews:
- Mark McLean / Tony Jordan

Target: VQ045108, 22 n.m. west of Grand Reef
Results: Nine local males and one female killed.

No 560 16/12/76 Op Mardon / Repulse (External)
Aircrews:
- Prop Geldenhuys / Capt. Irvine
- Al Bruce / Jim Russell
- John Blythe-Wood / Doug Sinclair
- Baldy Baldwin / Alan Shields
- Mark Knight / John Chamberlain
- Chris Dickinson / M. Summersgill

Target: UL921754 Moçambique – Chefu River, Chitanga terr base, north east of Malvernia
Results: Four terrs killed - one by K-Car 5178, three by ground forces. Chitanga terr camp in Moçambique – Op *Mardon* – with 'A' Coy 2 RAR and 1 Indep Coy

No 561 17/12/76 Op Repulse
Aircrews:

- Prop Geldenhuys
- John Blythe-Wood / Doug Sinclair
- Baldy Baldwin / Alan Shields
- Mark Knight / John Chamberlain
- Chris Dickinson / M. Summersgill

Target: UL915854, UL938845 Moçambique, north of Chefu river, 22 n.m. north east of Malvernia and 38 n.m. south of Chipinda Pools
Results: Two terrs and one local male killed and one local male casevaced

No 564 19/12/76 Op Repulse
Aircrews:
Prop Geldenhuys
Target: TL540468 Approx. 5 n.m. north of Limpopo and 35 n.m. east of Beitbridge
Result: 1x37mm smoke SNEB rocket - Tshiturapadzi – Matsai contact, casevaced one AMJ. Flew with SAS G. Wilson

No 565 19/12/76 Op Repulse
Aircrews:
- Prop Geldenhuys / Capt. Wilson
- Baldy Baldwin / Alan Shields
- Mark Knight / Beaver Shaw
- Chris Dickinson / Rob Nelson
- Rick Culpan

Target: Four juveniles at UN 8738, 4 n.m. east of Matsai and 40 n.m. north east of Buffalo Range
Result: 1x37mm SNEB; 73x20mm cannon shells

No 567 22/12/76 Op Repulse
Aircrews:
- Vic Cook / Mike Upton

Target: Malapati
Result: G-Car 7524. Shot down – Cat 5

No 568 22/12/76 Op Repulse
Aircrews:
- Prop Geldenhuys / Brigadier Barnard / Captain Wilson
- John Blythe-Wood / Doug Sinclair
- Baldy Baldwin / Alan Shields
- Mark Knight / Beaver Shaw
- Nick Meikle / Mario Venutti

Target: Ten-twelve terrs at UN015235, 10 n.m. north-west of Bangala Dam, Lowveld
Result: Five terrs killed and one captured. SAS Boet Nel and Gerry Seymour killed. Torty King shot and badly wounded. Lynx hit by ground fire.

No 570 27/12/76 Op Thrasher
Aircrews:
- Ian Harvey / Rory Perhat
- Greg Todd / Hansi Steyn
- Kevin Peinke / Pete Caborn
- George Sole / Mark Jackson
- Mark McLean / Chris Joubert
- John Carhart

Target: VP3670, 18 n.m. south of Grand Reef
Result: Six terrs killed and one captured, 21 African local men killed and ten wounded

No 571 28/11/76 Op Thrasher (External)
Aircrews:
- Michael Borlace / Brian Booth
- Murray Hofmeyr / Lionel Davel
- Jan Mienie / Billy Watt
- Ken Newman / Chris Joubert
- Randy du Rand / Mike Ronne
- Al Bruce / Doug Pasea
- Chris Abrams
- John Annan
- Rich Beaver
- Rich Brand
- Martin Lowrie
- Ed Potterton
- Mark McLean / Rory Perhat
- Greg Todd / Hansi Steyn
- Kevin Peinke / Pete Caborn
- George Sole / Mark Jackson
- John Carhart
- George Alexander / Dave Barbour / Johnny Green

Target: WR0355, 15 n.m. east of Elim Mission, in Moçambique
Result: 200 Mk2 Alpha bombs, 200 Mk2 Alpha bombs, 850x30mm Aden cannon, 43x68mm Matra, 3x37mm smoke SNEB rockets, nine 37mm boosted SNEB rockets, 28x20mm cannon shells, 218x7.62mm MAG.

No 572 28/12/76 Op Thrasher
Aircrews:
- Prop Geldenhuys
- Baldy Baldwin / Bert Keightley
- Nick Meikle / Mario Venutti
- Chris Wentworth / Beaver Shaw
- Mark Knight / Alan Shields

Target: UN6419, 6 n.m. east of Lake MacDougall and 25 n.m. north northeast of Buffalo Range
Result: 18x37mm SNEB rockets, 2x15-gall Fran, 65x20mm cannon 40x7.62mm. One terr killed by Crusader elements - Matsai

No 573 29/12/76 Op Hurricane
Aircrews:
- Ray Bolton
- Bill McQuade / Bob Fletcher

Target: VR3296, 14 n.m. north east of Mtoko
Result: 16 terrs killed and some 48 wounded.

No 579 06/1/77 Op Thrasher
Aircrews:
- Harold Griffiths / Rory Perhat
- Chris Wentworth / Ettora Crivellari
- Rex Taylor / Jeff Dartnall
- Ken Newman / M. Summersgill
- Greg Todd / Hansi Steyn

Target: Eight terrs at UN8021, 11 n.m. north of Mkwasine

Result: Seven terrs and one AM killed. Six local females and two local males killed. One male captured. One terr killed by ground forces later.

No 587 12/01/77 Op Manyatela (External)
Aircrews:
- Randy du Rand / Mike Ronne
- Al Bruce / Doug Pasea
- Ted Brent / Jim Russell
- Ian Donaldson / David Hawkes KIA
- Rich Brand
- Dave Bourhill
- Chris Abrams
- Ken Law

Target: Terr camp at UL932005, 38 n.m. south east of Malvernia – in Moçambique
Result: Canberra shot down over Malvernia. Ian Donaldson, David Hawkes, and their Selous Scouts passenger Rob Warracker were killed. Alpha bombs on target. 10 ZANLA killed and 101 wounded. Refer also P-B's *Winds of Destruction*, page 427.

No 591 16/01/77 Op Repulse (External)
Aircrews:
- Prop Geldenhuys
- Michael Borlace / John Britton
- Tudor Thomas / Bob Thompson
- Mark Aitchison / Ralph Harding
- Bill McQuade / Doug Sinclair

Target: VN8250, 6 n.m. north east of Espungabera, in Moçambique
Result: 200x.303 Browning Mk2, 20x20mm cannon shells; One terr killed, one captured.

No 592 16/01/77
Aircrews:
- Prop Geldenhuys
- Michael Borlace / John Britton
- Tol Janeke

Target: VN3927, 18 n.m. north east of Chisumbanje and 15 n.m. south east of Sabi Exp Stn
Result: 18x20mm cannon shells

No 594 19/01/76
Aircrews:
- Michael Borlace / John Britton
- Mark Aitchison / Mario Venutti
- Bill McQuade / Doug Sinclair
- Dick Paxton / Ronny Scott
- Daryl Squance

Target: UM8505, 26 n.m. south of Chipinda Pools and 7 n.m. north west of Chalanda (on Moçambique border)
Result: 19 terrs and recruits killed, 16 terrs and recruits captured. Good shooting by John Britton.

No 600 24/01/77 Op Thrasher
Aircrews:
- Ian Harvey / Philip Tubbs
- Rex Taylor / Keith Hicken
- Mark Dawson / Bert Keightley

- Ian Armstrong

Target: VP550419, 12 n.m. west of Cashel
Result: Six terrs killed – three by the K-Car and three by the ground forces.

No 603 26/01/77 Op Thrasher
Aircrews:
- Ian Harvey / Philip Tubbs
- Rex Taylor / Keith Hicken
- Mark Dawson / Bert Keightley
- Baldy Baldwin / Tony Jordan
- Ian Armstrong

Target: VR645317, 15 n.m. west of Regina Coeli Mission
Result: Ten terrs killed and two wounded by the K-Car.

No 620 09/02/77 Op Hurricane
Aircrews:
- Mike Borlace / John Jacobs
- Bill Sykes / Mark Jackson
- Mike Litson / Brian Crystal
- Bill Dawson / Carlos da Silveira

Target: UR647365, 8 n.m. south west of Mrewa. (Suspect wrong grid ref – place called Hokodzi)
Result: Six terrs killed, four African local men killed, eight locals captured.

No 627 17/02/77 Op Thasher
Aircrews:
- Mark Aitchison / Rory Perhat
- Greg Todd / Hansi Steyn
- Graham Cronshaw / Bob Thompson
- Dick Paxton / Frank Tyrrell
- Bill McQuade / Flamo Flemming
- Phil Haigh
- Ed Paintin / Jim Russell

Target: UP925500
Chiwaka River, approx. 22 n.m. west of Birchenough Bridge
Result: Six-eight terrs killed by K-Cars.

No 641 06/03/77 Op Thrasher
Aircrews:
- Harold Griffiths / Philip Tubbs
- Greg Todd / Flamo Flemming
- Norman Maasdorp / Jenkie Jenkins
- Bill Michie / Finch Bellringer
- Ian Peacocke / Bob Thompson
- Stig Ohlsson / McCormack
- Ian Sheffield

Target: VR841688, 8 n.m. north east of Elim Mission
Result: Seven terrs, four recruits and one African woman killed.

No 642 07/03/77 Op Hurricane
Aircrews:
- John Blythe-Wood / Alan Aird
- Mike Mulligan / Tony Merber
- Steve Murray / Ettora Crivellari

- Keith Spence / Keith Rayne
- Bruce Smith / Rich Truman

Target: VR323215, 32 n.m. south south-east of Mtoko
Result: Nine terrs killed. One terr captured wounded. Ten recruits captured.

No 644 09/03/77 Op Thrasher
Aircrews:
- Harold Griffiths / Philip Tubbs
- Norman Maasdorp / Jenkie Jenkins
- Ian Peacocke / Mac McCormick
- Bill Michie / Finch Bellringer

Target: VR673054, 12 n.m. north west of Inyanga
Result: Nine terrs killed by air and ground forces.

No 647 11/03/77 Op Hurricane
Aircrews:
- John Blythe-Wood / Tony Merber
- Mike Mulligan / Bob Fletcher
- Steve Murray / Ettora Crivellari
- Keith Spence / Keith Rayne
- Bruce Smith / Rich Truman
- Ian Sheffield
- Don Northcroft
- Al Bruce / Doug Pasea
- Ed Paintin / Terry Bennett

Target: VR428118. North east of Headlands, between St Benedict Mission and Inyanga. TOT 11h15
Result: Eight terrs killed and one captured. Five African women killed and one captured.

No 653 21/03/77 Op Hurricane
Aircrews:
- John Blythe-Wood / Tony Merber
- Keith Spence / Keith Rayne
- Vic Cook / Rory Perhat
- Danny Svoboda / George Bushney
- Don Northcroft

Target: US597533. Ruya river 8 n.m. north east of Mt Darwin
Result: Six terrs killed.

No 654 22/03/77 Op Hurricane
Aircrews:
- Ken Newman / Philip Tubbs
- Bill Sykes / Mac McCormick
- Norman Maasdorp / Jenkie Jenkins
- Bill Michie / Finch Bellringer
- Ian Peacocke / Ronny Scott
- Ed Potterton
- Cocky Benecke

Target: VR058120, 2 n.m. north of St Benedict Mission, 28 n.m. south east of Mrewa
Result: 15 terrs killed and two captured by air and ground forces.

No 655 22/03/77
Aircrews:

- Mike Litson + FAF 8 Fire Force
- Peter Petter-Bowyer

Target: Terr camp for 38 terrs, Marandellas area, located by air recce
Result: 16 terrs killed, one captured, as per *Winds of Destruction*, page 436

No 656 23/03/77 Op Thrasher
Aircrews:
- Al Bruce / Doug Pasea
- John Blythe-Wood / Tony Merber
- Danny Svoboda / George Bushney
- Vic Cook / Rory Perhat
- Keith Spence / Keith Rayne
- Don Northcroft
- Leon du Plessis
- Chris Spalding / Ian Armstrong

Target: VR609018, Approx. 20 n.m. north west of Inyanga
Result: Nine terrs killed.

No 659 26/03/77 Op Repulse
Aircrews:
- Michael Borlace / Lionel Davel
- Chris Wentworth / Brian Crystal
- Brian Meikle / Frank Tyrrell
- Kevin Peinke / Nick Tselentis
- Mark Dawson / Keith Hicken
- Daryl Squance
- Mike Russell / Cyril Hirst

Target: TM2853, 8 n.m. west of Maranda and 22 n.m. west of Rutenga
Result: Three terrs killed. One SF killed. (Corporal J.W. Smith, 1 Independent Company, Rhodesia Regiment)

No 661 27/03/77 Op Hurricane
Aircrews:
- Danny Svoboda / Mike Upton
- Vic Cook / Rory Perhat
- Keith Spence / George Bushney
- Geoff Oborne / Coen van Staden
- Leon du Plessis
- Steve Murray / Mark Jackson
- Al Bruce / Doug Pasea
- Don Northcroft
- Carlos da Silveira / Tom Tarr

Target: US482522, 4 n.m. north of Mt Darwin. East of the road and south of Ruya river.
Result: Six terrs killed and one captured. Two African women killed.

No 662 27/03/77 Op Hurricane
Aircrews:
- Danny Svoboda / Mike Upton
- Vic Cook / Rory Perhat
- Geoff Oborne / Coen van Staden
- Mike Litson / Tony Jordan
- Cocky Benecke
- Ed Potterton

- Carlos da Silveira / Tom Tarr

Target: US482522, 4 n.m. north of Mt Darwin
Result: Four terrs killed and one captured. Four African local men killed and one captured.
Ed Potterton posted to 7 Sqn 16/06/77.

No 668 09/04/77 Op Thrasher
Aircrews:
- Chris Wentworth / Bert Keightley
- Nick Meikle / Rob Nelson
- Mark Knight / John Jacobs
- Pete le Roux / Beaver Shaw
- Chas Goatley / Pete Caborn
- Harold Griffiths
- Chris Dixon / Mike Ronne

Target: VR750298, near Regina Coeli Mission, west of Nyamaropa airstrip, north of Troutbeck.
Canberra Air Task 298
Result: Six terrs killed and one captured. Seven African women killed.

No 669 10/04/77 Op Thrasher
Aircrews:
- Chris Wentworth / Bert Keightley
- Nick Meikle / Rob Nelson
- Mark Knight / John Jacobs
- Pete le Roux / Beaver Shaw
- Chas Goatley / Pete Caborn
- Harold Griffiths

Target: VQ041115, 22 n.m. west of Grand Reef – 12 n.m. south of Inyazura
Result: Nine terrs killed.

No 672 13/04/77 Op Repulse
Aircrews:
- Mark Knight / Henry Jarvie
- Chris Wentworth / Bert Keightley
- Nick Meikle / Philip Tubbs
- Pete le Roux / Mark Jackson
- Chas Goatley / Finch Bellringer
- Roger Bowers

Target: UP946434, Marabada Hills, 36 n.m. south east of Buhera
Result: Five terrs killed. 17 African women killed.

No 673 15/04/77 Op Hurricane
Aircrews:
- Vic Cook / Alan Shields
- Geoff Oborne / Brian Booth
- Norman Maasdorp / Ettora Crivellari
- Ray Bolton / Chris Tucker
- John Hood / Tony Thomas

Target: VR120936, 10 n.m. north north-west of Mtoko
Result: Nine terrs killed

No 674 18/04/77 Op Repulse
Aircrews:
- Chris Wentworth / Bert Keightley

- Chas Goatley / Mark Jackson
- Pete le Roux / Finch Bellringer
- Nick Meikle / Philip Tubbs
- Mark Knight / Henry Jarvie
- Roger Bowers

Target: UP971487, Marabada Hills 29 n.m. south east of Dorowa
Result: Four terrs killed. Three African youths killed. Eleven African youths wounded. One African local man wounded. One African woman killed.

No 676 24/04/77 Op Hurricane
Aircrews:
- Michael Borlace / Keith Rayne
- Geoff Oborne / Brian Booth
- Norman Maasdorp / Ettora Crivellari
- Greg Todd / Alan Shields
- Chris Tucker
- Vic Culpan / Tony Thomas

Target: VR334908, 12 n.m. north east of Mtoko
Result: 10 terrs killed. 5 escaped. Subsequent contact, with group of 30 terrs resulted in a further 4 terrs killed. During sweeps, 5 more were killed and 9 terrorist recruit trainees captured.

No 677 24/04/77 Op Repulse
Aircrews:
- Baldy Baldwin / Tony Merber
- Steve Murray / Nick Tselentis
- Keith Spence / Ronny Scott
- Ken Newman / Keith Hicken
- Mick Delport
- Alan Bradnick / Hugh Travers

Target: QG926976, 35 n.m. south west of Shabani, 12 n.m. south west of Belingwe Peak
Result: Four terrs killed. Three local African men killed. One African man wounded.

No 679 27/04/77 Op Thrasher
Aircrews:
- Mark Knight / Philip Tubbs
- Dick Paxton / Henry Jarvie
- Danny Svoboda / Steve Russell
- Bill Michie / Mark Jackson
- Ted Lunt / Finch Bellringer
- Harold Griffiths

Target: VP420505, 28 n.m. south of Grand Reef
Result: Eight terrs killed. Two terrs captured. Three African women and one African local man killed.

No 685 04/05/77 Op Thrasher
Aircrews:
- Rob Griffiths / David Brown

Target: 20 miles south of Umtali
Result: David Brown, killed as a passenger

No 686 11/05/77 Op Thrasher
Aircrews:
- Danny Svoboda / Mike Smith

- Mark McLean / Doug Sinclair
- Chas Goatley / Steve Russell
- Bill Michie / Garry Carter
- Dick Paxton / Adrian Rosenberg
- Martin Hatfield

Target: VQ721416 In vicinity Honde valley, between Juliasdale and Penhalonga. Approx. 23 n.m. north of Umtali
Result: Eleven terrs killed.

No 688 11/05/77
Aircrews:
- Danny Svoboda / Mike Smith
- Chas Goatley / Steve Russell
- Bill Michie / Garry Carter
- Dick Paxton / Adrian Rosenberg
- Mark McLean / Doug Sinclair
- Martin Hatfield

Target: VQ012276 In vicinity 8 n.m. west of Inyazura
Result: Five terrs killed. Three local African men and two African women killed

No 692 15/05/77 Op Hurricane
Aircrews:
- Chris Dixon / Doug Pasea
- Nick Meikle / Bert Keightley
- Mark Knight / Jenkie Jenkins
- Ken Newman / Jim Cocking
- Mark Dawson / Peter Platt
- Roger Bowers
- Mike Russell / Pat Forbes

Target: VR318817. Near Rogogo airfield, halfway between Mrewa and Inyanga
Result: Eight terrs killed.

No 693 18/05/77 Operation Grapple
Aircrews:
- Roger Watt / Rob Nelson
- Rob MacGregor

Target: PK4478 Sengwa Gorge, between Gokwe and Lusuku
Result: Aircraft caught fire after shot. Gunner Rob Nelson jumped from 300 feet to his death.

No 702 30/03/77 Operation Aztec (External)
Aircrews:
- JR Blythe-Wood
- Hunter
- Chris Dixon / Doug Pasea

Target: Mapai / Jorge do Limpopo Ops
Result: Attacked mortar and rocket positions – Mapai and Jorge de Limpopo outskirts.

No 703 31/03/77 Op Azrec (External)
Aircrews:
- Jan Mienie
- Jerry Lynch / Bruce Collocott
- Ed Paintin / Doug Pasea

Target: Madulo Pan, Mapai airfield in Moçambique

Result: Bruce Collocott killed, aircraft hit on take-off by RPG 7 and ground fire, and Dakota destroyed.

No 710 17/07/77 Op Thrasher
Aircrews:
- Ian Harvey / Philip Tubbs
- Chris Wentworth/Ettora Crivellari
- Rex Taylor / M. Summersgill
- Ginger Baldwin / Tony Jordan

Target: VQ395572, 18 n.m. east of Rusape
Result: Seven terrs killed and two captured.

No 719 28/08/77 Op Hurricane
Aircrews:
Ted Lunt
Geoff Oborne / Frank Robinson
Ray Bolton
Lynx
Target: VP4545 – Manyika TTL – PATU report of 30 terrs near St Killians Mission
Result: Geoff Oborne shot down. Alouette damaged by ground fire – Cat 4

No 722 02/09/77 Op Thrasher
Aircrews:
- Leon du Plessis / John Underwood
- JR Blythe-Wood

Target: Cross border raid, 20 miles south of Umtali
Result: Pilot and technician killed during front gun pull out.
Hunter A/T 897

No 725 08/09/77 Op Hurricane
Aircrews:
- Fire Force – Mtoko
- Willie Knight / Rick Singleton

Target: VR540222 – Tande TTL – Sighting of 10 terrs, east of Mrewa.
Result: 8 terrs, 11 AFA/AFJ's running with terrs killed and 7 AFJ's wounded

No 728 12/09/77 Op Hurricane
Aircrews:
- Fire Force – RAR

Target: VR055602 – Mtoko TTL – Fire Force deployed to area where helicopters were fired upon
Result: 8 terrs and 12 recruits killed. 31 male / female recruits captured. 5 locals injured

No 736 12/10/77 Op Terminate + Op Melon
Aircrews:
- JR Blythe-Wood
- Hunter

Target: Convoy of three trucks in the Russian Front: Mague-Mukumbura Rd
Result: Mercedes, Toyota and Isuzu trucks destroyed. 3+ FRELIMO killed, 14 wounded and 3 missing. On 15/10/77 JR another airstrike on Op Melon 3 vehicles destroyed. 2SAS wounded (JRT Wood)

No 738 18/10/77 Op Tangent
Aircrews:

- Rich Beaver
- Rich Brand
- Spook Geraty

Target: Zambezi Gorge crossing
Result: Boat with terrs sunk. FAC for jet strike across river

No 744 30/10/77 Op Repulse
Aircrews:
- John Blythe-Wood
- Martin Lowrie
- Canberra – A5
- Canberra – C5
- Jan Mienie – E4
- Martin Hatfield – H4
- Dakota – F3
- Ken Newman / André Dennison
- Mike Litson / Brian Robinson

Alouette
Alistair Davies – Copper 95
Target: UL123380 -UL134353 Sengwe TTL, 4 n.m. north of the Limpopo river, 27 n.m. south west of Mabalahauta. Sighting of 100 terrs entering the country.
Result: 28 terrs killed. See page 161 JRT Wood "*War Diaries of André Dennison*". K-Car hit several times by ground fire. Refer also Ken Newman's ASR as per page 451 in Peter Petter-Bowyer's "*Winds of Destruction*".

No 746 01/11/77 Op Melon (External)
Aircrews:
- Giles Porter
- Hunter x 2

Target: Moçambique – ZANLA convoy Mapai / Maputo road
Result: Airstrike on FRELIMO 4th Brigade HQ (Mobile) – 21 vehicles destroyed

No 750 13/11/77 Op Melon (External)
Aircrews:
- Vic Wightman + Hunter No 2

Target: Convoy Mapai – Mabalane Rd, Gaza
Result: 17 vehicles destroyed. Tank spares, ammo and Russian dictionary found

No 753 23/11/77 Operation Dingo (External)
Aircrews:
- Rich Brand
- Vic Wightman
- Steve Kesby
- JR Blythe-Wood
- Randy du Rand
- Glen Pretorius / Paddy Morgan
- Tol Janeke
- Varky Varkevisser
- Ken Law
- Phil Haigh
- Vic Cook / Jeff Dartnall
- Harold Griffiths
- Keith Spence / Rick Singleton

- Ian Peacocke / Frank Tyrrell
- Bill Sykes + whole of 7 Sqn (see next column)
- Mark McLean
- Chris Tucker
- Bob d'Hotman
- Norman Walsh
- Jack Malloch /George Alexander

Target: Chimoio – Vanduzi Camp WQ030525 Manica and Tembue Camp, VU815525, Tete Province north of Cabora Bassa
Result: Phil Haigh killed, during forced landing in Vampire. Vampire targets were the northern part of the Chimoio training element, anti-aircraft weapon sites and barrack blocks. JRT Wood tabulates 800 terrorists killed, 750 wounded. In addition to Haigh, Trooper G.J. Nel killed and 6 RLI wounded. Camp and all equipment destroyed. Paddy Morgan confirms two airstrikes carried out – Air Task 1285. See also P-B's *Winds of Destruction*, pages 457 to 465
(Other participants are: Finch Bellringer, Paul Braun, Pete Caborn, Ernie Crivellari, Brian Crystal, Flamer Fleming, Mike Homan, Hoss Hossack, Mark Jackson, Henry Jarvie, Dave Jenkins, Bert Keightly, Hugh McCormick, Tony Merber, Barry Ord, Frank Robinson, Dave Rowley, Keith Rayne, Tweedy Reid-Daly, Dave Rowley, Hansi Steyn , Wally Tolmay, Phil Tubbs)

No 754 24/11/77 Op Dingo (External)
Aircrews:
- Vic Wightman
- JR Blythe-Wood
- Glen Pretorius
- Varky Varkevisser (top cover)
- Keith Spence / Rick Singleton

Target: Tembue base – VU 815525
Result: (JRT Wood logs 400 terrorists killed at Tembue, VU 815525 on 26.11.77)

No 755 26/11/77 Op Virile (External)
Aircrews:
- Chris Tucker
- Vic Wightman
- JR Blythe-Wood
- Rich Brand
- Spook Geraty
- Tol Janeke
- Varky Varkevisser
- Glen Pretorius / Paddy Morgan

Target: FRELIMO – ZANLA convoy Espungabera / Dombe road, Moçambique
Result: Support of Scout column, against enemy convoy and targets – over 1000 Terrs strong. (JR – 3 sorties, Tol – 2 sorties). See P-B's book *Winds of Destruction*, page 470.

No 768 12/01/78 Op Hurricane
Aircrews:
- Chas Goatley / Flamo Flemming
- Norman Maasdorp / Henry Jarvie
- Al Thorogood
- John Mussell

Target: Near Mtoko
Result: Tech gunners killed in action, hit by ground fire. See also P-B's book *Winds of Destruction* page 471.

No 786 27/02/78 Op Repulse
Aircrews:
Fire Force Bravo + Dakota crews
Target: UP897952 – Sighting of 14 terrs east of Renco gold mine
Result: 7 terrs, 3 AMA's killed, 2 AFA wounded. Notebook revealed terrs as Chiduku Det

No 790 06/03/78 Op Turmoil
Aircrews:
- Vic Wightman (4 sorties)
- Tony Oakley (4 sorties)
- JR Blythe-Wood (6 sorties)
- Glen Pretorius / Paddy Morgan
- Canberra / Jim Russell
- Dakota x 4
- Alouette crews x 10

Target: Kavalamanja terr complex, near Feira / Kanyemba, Mushika area Zambia – Grid Ref approx TT2375. Air Task 297
Result: Hunters destroyed 8 Zambian vehicles, killing 5 Zambian soldiers. 42 ZIPRA also killed. 2 Strela G to A missiles and 51 landmines recovered. RLI soldier killed, 6 wounded. Refer JRT Wood, pages 196-198. Paddy Morgan sustained schrapnel wounds to chest

No 807 20/04/78 Op Thrasher
Aircrews:
- Lynx
- K-Car / Keith Rayne
- Nigel Lamb / Beaver Shaw
- Ian Peacocke / Ray Wernich (SAAF)
- Dakota

Target: Camp south of Weya TTL. Contact made at VR121002 Headlands farming area. 13 n.m. north east of Headlands
Result: FFA control. Lord Richard Cecil, only foreign journalist in the war, killed. Lynx put in two airstrikes. One terr, two locals killed. 8 wounded. JRT Wood page 220 & 222

No 812 26/04/78
Aircrews:
- Ian Peacocke / Beaver Shaw

Target: Contact – Top cover
Result: 15 terrs and 8 locals killed (Ian says 25 or 27 April!)

No 815 01/05/78 Op Hurricane
Aircrews:
- Ian Peacocke / Beaver Shaw
- Vic Wightman
- Tony Oakley

Target: Enterprise top cover
Result: 10 terrs and 6 aiding civilians killed

No 816 02/05/78 Op Hurricane
Aircrews:
- Ian Peacocke / Beaver Shaw

Target: Shamva farming area
Result: 6 terrs killed

No 830 10/06/78 Op Hurricane

Airstrike:
Target: Dombashawa – north of Salisbury
Result: 22 locals killed in cross-fire – JRT Wood page 249

No 833 20/06/78
Aircrews:
- Cocky Benecke
- Ian Peacocke / Phil Archenoul

Target: *Winds of Destruction* – page 473
Result: 7 terrs killed (Possibly two separate sorties)

No 835 23/06/78
Aircrews:
- Peter Petter-Bowyer
- Ted Lunt / Bob Thompson
- Hamie Dax / McCay

Target: Katoog use south-east of Mtoko – Terr camp US400294
Result: 6 terrs killed. Refer also Ted's ASR as per *Winds of Destruction*, page 482

No 838 27/06/78 Op Repulse
Target: Sighting and contact with 10 terrs at UN778759 – Bikita TTL
Result: 5 terrs, 1 Mujiba and 3 local females killed. Bruce Thompson SCR and RAR Leonard Mpofu killed.

No 843 21/07/78
Aircrews:
- Lynx pilot
- Vic Wightman
- Tony Oakley

Target: Gp of terrs exiting the country
Result: 37 terrs killed

No 844 21-28/07/78 Op Hurricane (External)
Aircrews:
- Chris Abrams
- Francois du Toit / Kevin Nelson KIA
- Nigel Lamb / Chris Saint
- Tony Oakley

Target: Mt Darwin hot-extraction of Selous Scouts from Chioco – Moz approx VS8285 - AT 975
Result: Du Toit and Nelson killed, shot down by RPG7 rocket. Glen Pretorius Canberra 2055 on Search & Rescue next day 29/07/78.

No 851 10/08/78
Target: 2RAR Contact, 2nd Lt Graeme Tass
Result: 13 terrs killed, by 2RAR. Lt G Tass awarded SCR

No 855 28/08/78 Op Hurricane
Aircrews:
- Ted Lunt
- Ray Bolton
- Geoff Oborne / Brian Booth
- Lynx Pilot

Target: PRAW sighting of terr camp 50 kilometres east of Bindura

Result: Geoff Oborne / Brian Booth crashed, hit by ground fire (R5773 = SAAF 106)

No 866 14/09/78 Op Repulse
Target: TN772478 Victoria TTL – Police Sighting of 40 CT's
Result: 3 terrs, 5 AMA recruits killed and 8 wounded / captured.

No 867 19/09/78 Op Repulse
Aircrews:
- Ian Peacocke / Brian Cutmore
- Fire Force Charlie + Lynx

Target: UM307396 BJB Ranch – Contact with 9Terrs
Result: 6 terrs and 1 AFA running with terrs killed. Mini Golf malfunctioned. Fran on tgt.

No 868 20/09/78 Op Snoopy (External)
Aircrews:
- Vic Wightman
- Alf Wild
- JR Blythe-Wood
- Tony Oakley
- Dave Bourhill
- Brian Gordon
- Ted Brent / Paddy Morgan
- Glen Pretorius / Paul Perioli
- Varky Varkevisser

Target: Suppress AA – A/T 1343. Attack 25 camps, spread over 33km² - Chimoio Circle, approx. 70km from Rhodesian border.
Result: SAS trooper Steve Donnelly accidentally killed by Golf Bomb. Dave and Glen both hit by Strela – Dave below starboard aileron, and Canberra port engine. *Winds of Destruction* - page 497.

No 872 25/09/78 Op Repulse
Aircrews:
- Fire Force Charlie + Lynx
- Ian Peacocke / John Chamberlain

Target: UN722790 Bikita TTL – Sighting of 10Terrs
Result: 8 terrs, 1 AFA and 1 AMA killed. JRT Wood page 270.

No 874 27/09/78 Op Repulse
Aircrews:
- Mark Vernon / Beaver Shaw

Target: Mtetengwe TTL – north of Beit Bridge
Result: 18 CT's and 2 civilians killed in Fire Force ops

No 881 08/10/78 Op Repulse / Op Tangent
Aircrews:
- Jan Mienie
- Canberra + Fire Force Charlie and Delta + Dakota x 2

Target: Terr camp QG866775 in Belingwe TTL, believed to house 100 gooks
Result: 4 terrs and 7 AMAs killed, - one collaborator wounded, casevaced to West Nicholson

No 882 09/10/78 Op Repulse
Aircrews:
- Jan Mienie
- Tony Oakley

- Hunter
- Terry McCormick / A. Dennison
- Ken Blain / Beaver Shaw
- Dakota

Target: Sighting of 10 terrs in Matibi 1 at TM724844, Lundi River, and 7 n.m. south of Ngundu Halt.
Result: 16 terrs killed 1 captured, 40 AMAs killed. FFC 2 RAR Maj André Dennison wounded in left knee. See also "*Only my friends call me Krouks*" – Dennis Croukamp

No 883 10/10/78 Op Hurricane
Aircrews:
- Ian Peacocke / Mike Smith
- Ken Blain / Beaver Shaw

Target: Bindura Fire Force / Nottingham
Result: 6 terrs killed (suspect 2 separate contacts)

No 887 19/10/78 Op Gatling
Aircrews:
- Chris Dixon / Mike Ronne
- Ted Brent / Paddy Morgan
- Greg Todd / Doug Pasea
- Glen Pretorius / Jim Russell / Paul Perioli
- Tony Oakley
- JR Blythe-Wood
- Dave Bourhill
- Alf Wild
- Jim Stagman
- Graham Cronshaw / Sgt Ferreira
- Mark Dawson / Roelf Oeloffse
- Chas Goatley / Mike Smith
- Nigel Lamb / Finch Bellringer
- Ian Peacocke / Beaver Shaw
- Cocky Benecke
- Tol Janeke
- Varky Varkevisser
- Vic Culpan / John Fairey
- Command Dak (Norman Walsh)

Target: ZIPRA Chikumbi camp at Westlands Farm (Green Leader fame)
A/T 1521
Result: Green Leader fame. *Winds of Destruction* – p 499 *Pride of Eagles* – page 626. Beaver Shaw recalls at least 200 terrs killed in his logbook. 226 killed, 629 wounded (See P-B, p 501). JR and Varky x 2 sorties Glen Pretorius and Paul Perioli x 3 sorties. Vamps ex Fylde

No 888 19/10/78 Op Gatling
Aircrews:
- Chris Dixon / Mike Ronne
- Ted Brent / Paddy Morgan
- Glen Pretorius / Paul Perioli
- Rick Culpan
- Ginger Baldwin
- JR Blythe-Wood
- Tony Oakley
- Tol Janeke

- Varky Varkevisser
- G-Cars
- Dakota
- Vic Culpan / John Fairey

Target: Airstrike on Mkushi. A/T 1521
Result: One SAS Jeff Collett killed. 47 enemy killed & ZIPRA Logistics Officer Mountain Gutu captured – See P-B's *Winds of Destruction*, page 502. Ted Brent / Paddy Morgan flew a third sortie, in 5203. Paddy recalls second strike (with 1000lb) was female camp further north.

No 889 19/10/78 Op Gatling - Zambia
Aircrews:
- Varky Varkevisser
- Vampire
- Cocky Benecke
- Mark Dawson / Roelf Oeloffse
- Nigel Lamb / Finch Bellringer
- Chas Goatley / Mike Smith
- Ian Peacocke / Beaver Shaw
- JR Blythe-Wood
- Dakota

Target: CGT-2 camp 100km SE of Lusaka
Result: Alouette hit by cannon fire in Zambia – Cat 5
Vamp ex Fylde Mark Dawson wounded in leg; K-Car crashed and was destroyed by SAS. Roelf sustained back injuries. Total casualties for the 3 ops were 396 killed, 719 wounded and 192 missing (P-B, *Winds of Destruction* page 503)

No 892 02/11/78 Op Jacket (External - Zambia)
Aircrews:
- Vic Wightman
- Tony Oakley
- Ted Brent / Paul Perioli

Target: Air raid on ZIPRA storage depot in Zambia
Result: 10 to 20 men killed and 50 wounded

No 904 29/11/78 Op Shovel (External)
Aircrews:
- Vic Wightman – three sorties
- Tony Oakley – 2 sorties Op Shovel

Target: Main munitions hangar at Tete
Result: Single rocket caused colossal explosion. SAS destroyed nearby railway bridge.

No 907 07/12/78
Aircrews:
- Nigel Lamb / Beaver Shaw

Target: Karoi area contact
Result: 8 terrs killed

No 911 22/12/78 Operation Inhibit and Op Vodka (External)
Aircrews:
- Vic Wightman
- Ted Brent / Paddy Morgan
- Glen Pretorius / Paul Perioli
- Varky Varkevisser

- Steve Kesby?
- Ian Armstrong / John Fairey

Target: Mboroma – ZIPRA Terr camp 140km north of Zambian border
Result: Rescue of 100 prisoners – *Pride of Eagles*, page 643. 18 enemy killed (Armstrong and Fairey in Command Dakota).

No 912 22/12/78 Operation Pygmy (External)
Aircrews:
- Ted Brent / Paddy Morgan
- Glen Pretorius / Paul Perioli

Target: Mulungushi, ZIPRA base 100km from Lusaka
Result: 33 killed, many wounded

No 914 26/12/78 Op Repulse
Aircrews: Fire Force Charlie + Dakota
Target: Sighting of eleven terrs in Matibi 1 TTL at TM498683 – 12 n.m. north west of Rutenga
Result: 12 terrs and 15 locals killed – terr group known as 'Demolition Team Charlie Beitbridge to Rutenga'.

No 921 31/12/78 Op Repulse
Aircrews: Fire Force Charlie
Target: TM 421248 Sighting of 18 terrs
Result: 8 terrs killed (three by K-Car)

No 923 02/01/79 Op Grapple
Aircrews:
- Ray Boulter / Brian Cutmore
- Kerry Fynn / Tony Turner / Capt Doug Havnar

Target: Contact, near Selukwe
Result: Mid-air collision - Kerry Fynn, Brian Cutmore, Tony Turner and Captain Havnar killed

No 926 06/01/79 Op Repulse
Aircrews: Lynx + Fire Force Charlie + Dakota
Target: UM380395 Matibi 2 TTL – report of feeding in progress
Result: 7 terrs killed

No 937 02/02/79 Op Repulse
Aircrews:
- Keith Spence / Beaver Shaw
- Fire Force Delta (Shabani)

Target: Sighting of 8 terrs TM 529764 Matibi 1 TTL, 15 n.m. north west of Rutenga
Result: Four terrs killed (3 by Beaver Shaw), two captured, two AFAs and one AMJ killed. Wood – page 300

No 940 04/02/79 Op Repulse
Aircrews:
- Keith Spence / Beaver Shaw
- Fire Force Charlie
- Dave Barbour / John Fairey

Target: Sighting of eight terrs at TM487845 Matibi 1 TTL 23 n.m. north west of Rutenga
Result: Three terrs killed (one by Shaw) and one captured. One mujiba and two AFAs also killed. FFC control.

No 942 05/02/79 Op Repulse

Aircrews:
- Keith Spence / Beaver Shaw
- Fire Force Charlie
- Dave Barbour / John Fairey

Target: Sighting of 15 terrs – difficulty experienced in pin-pointing area
Result: 4 Mujibas killed. During the sweep, FFC called to another scene just two minutes flying time away.

No 944 06/02/79 Op Dabchick (External)
Aircrews:
- Vic Wightman
- Tony Oakley

Target: Muchanedze WN122578, Manica, Moçambique
Air Task 219
Result: 24 terrorists killed. Weapons and documents recovered but the main man (Nhongo) missed completely

No 952 22/02/79 Op Repulse
Aircrews: Fire Force Delta
Target: Contact 12 ZANLA UL 128518 Sengwe TTL
Result: 9 ZANLA killed, 2 captured and one escaped

No 953 23/02/79 Op Grovel
Aircrews:
- Glen Pretorius / Paul Perioli
- Chris Dixon
- Vic Wightman (two sorties)
- Glen Pretorius / Paul Perioli

Target: Two ZIPRA camps, west of Lusaka, Zambia
Result: Eighteen killed and one hundred and fourteen wounded. See Wood, and *Pride of Eagles* page 646

No 954 26/02/79 Op Vanity (External - Angola)
Aircrews:

- Ted Brent / Jim Russell
- Chris Dixon / Mike Ronne
- Kevin Peinke / Paul Perioli / JJ Strydom?
- Glen Pretorius / Paddy Morgan
- Rudi Kritsinger - SAAF 12 Sqn
- Roley Jones – SAAF 12 Sqn
- Willie Meyer - SAAF 12 Sqn
- 1 Sqn Hunters

Target: ZIPRA training camp at Vila de Boma, south of Luso, in Angola
Result: Six hundred inmates killed and a thousand wounded
(Hunter top-cover)
See also P-B's *Winds of Destruction*, page 513. 174 ZIPRA killed, 533 wounded.

No 956 01/03/79 Mozambique (External)
Aircrews:
- Vic Wightman

Target: ZANLA buildings at Mutarara in the Tete province of Moz – approx GR YR5070
Result: JRT Wood page 324. Zambians claimed on 3 March that the air raid killed five women and injured two.

No 958? 06/03/78 Mozambique (External)
Aircrews:
- Vic Wightman

Target: Five ZANLA camps Mtetengwe TTL north of Beit Bridge – SL 978892,TL 016872
Result: 4 ZANLA + 8 Civilians killed
Canberra aborted due to communications problems. JRT Wood Counter-Strike page 206-207

No 959 12/03/79 Mozambique (External)
Aircrews:
- Vic Wightman

Target: Arms depot at Chokwe and a ZANLA HQ and barracks at Barragem in the Gaza province of Moçambique
Result: Sixteen ZANLA killed and seven injured

No 963 17/03/79 Op Neutron (External)
Aircrews:
- Vic Wightman
- Tony Oakley
- Kevin Peinke / Paddy Morgan
- Glen Pretorius / Paul Perioli
- Fire Force

Target: Vanduzi, 15km from Chimoio town, Moçambique Manica Province
Air Task 459
Result: JRT Wood – and *Pride of Eagles* page 650. SAS and 1RLI. Petter-Bowyer – *Winds of Destruction* page 518

No 974 11/04/79 Op Racket (External)
Aircrews:
- Chris Dixon / Jim Russell
- Ted Brent / Paddy Morgan
- Glen Pretorius / Paul Perioli
- Vic Wightman
- Tony Oakley

Target: Op Racket – ZIPRA Shilende training camp
Result: 134 killed, over 200 wounded. Hunters Ex Vic Falls

No 986 27/04/79 Op Repulse
Aircrews:
- Chas Goatley / Beaver Shaw

Target: Fort Victoria top cover
Result: 6 terrs killed and 4 captured

No 988 07/05/79 Op Thrasher
Aircrews:
- Vic Wightman
- Ginger Baldwin

Target: OP sighting – Burma valley VP7070? (P-B, page 531)
Result: 26 killed – *Winds of Destruction* – page 532

No 995 / 1132 25/05/79
Aircrews: Fire Force Grand Reef
Target: Sighting of 40 terrs approx 30mins flying time north-west of FAF 8

Result: 33 terrs killed. RLI Mike MacDonald wounded. Charlie Warren awarded BCR. See *Stick Leader* p141

No 1001 09/06/79 Nyajena Op Repulse
Aircrews:
- Bill Michie / Beaver Shaw

Target: Nyajena contact
Result: 1 terr killed and 18 civilians killed in cross fire

No 1002 11/06/79 Op Repulse
Aircrews:
- Bill Michie / Beaver Shaw

Target: Fire Force top cover - Repulse
Result: 9 terrs killed

No 1002 16/06/79 Op Mulligan
Aircrews: RLI Fire Force
Target: Contact at a kraal north of Salisbury. (Mrs Mulligan kidnapped)
Result: RLI Tpr B. McKend and E.Elsaesser killed. Sgt C. Warren wounded. See "Stick Leader" – page 114.

No 1004 26/06/79 Op Carpet (External)
Aircrews:
- Ted Lunt
- Vic Wightman
- Tony Oakley

Target: Airstrike on ZIPRA camp at Chikumbi, north of Lusaka
Air Task 1398
Result: Twenty to fifty people killed. Martin Pearse killed. R Wood page 350 / P-B page 534

No 1006 01/07/79 Op Chicory (External)
Aircrews:
- Vic Wightman
- Varky Varkevisser
- Tony Oakley
- Glen Pretorius / Paul Perioli
- Ted Lunt
- Cheetah crews x 5 total

Target: Air and ground attack on munitions and supply depot 30-35km west of Lusaka. Air Task 1452
Result: 100 tons of weapons, ammunition and equipment destroyed. Tony Oakley 2 sorties. See also *Winds of Destruction*, page 539

No 1008 07/07/79 Op Fiddle
Aircrews:
- Vic Wightman
- Varky Varkevisser
- Tony Oakley
- Kevin Peinke / Paddy Morgan
- Glen Pretorius / Paul Perioli
- Colyn James / Beaver Shaw

Target: Operation Fiddle. Fire Force – Zimbabwe Ruins. Air Task 1474. Paul records Tembue as the target
Result: 10 terrs killed

No 1010 16/07/79 Op Repulse
Aircrews:
- Fire Force – Buffalo Range
- John Fairey / Keith Fincham

Target: Contact – 10 minutes out from FAF 7.
Result: RLI Sgt Hugh McCall and Tpr Steve Dwyer killed. See Charlie Warren's *Stick Leader*, page 147.

No 1012 21-22/07/79 Op SFA
Aircrews: Fire Force Air support
Target: Securit Force Auxiliary Mutiny
Result: 183 Auxiliaries killed. (Fire Force).

No 1018 Botswana (External)
Aircrews:
- Chas Goatley / Beaver Shaw
- Pete Mason / Rod Parson

Target: Francistown ZIPRA camp, Botswana
Result: K-Car forced down BDF Botswana Islander aircraft, while G-Car uplifted Scouts

No 1020 11/08/79
Aircrews:
- Chas Goatley / Beaver Shaw

Target: Top cover
Result: 6 terrs killed

No 1023 16/08/79
Aircrews:
- Norman Maasdorp / Beaver Shaw

Target: Ters on hill. Fire Force Chiguwi, near Birchenough Bridge – VN 2288?
Result: Shaw spotted terrs on side of hill and opened fire. Graham Turkington 3CDO killed by rifle grenade shrapnel

No 1026 22/08/79 Op Placid (External)
Aircrews:
- Vic Wightman
- Tony Oakley
- Glen Pretorius / Paul Perioli

Target: ZIPRA installations at Mulungushi, Rufunsa and Solwezi. Six targets, known as Moscow, in Zambia
Result: Interception by two MiG 19s

No 1034 05.09/79 Operation Uric (External)
Aircrews:
- Vic Wightman
- Varky Varkevisser
- Tony Oakley
- Ziggy Seegmuller
- Glen Pretorius
- Kevin Peinke / Paul Perioli
- Dick Paxton / Alex Wesson
- Breytie Breytenbach / Jakes Jacobs SAAF
- Rob Dean

- Monster Wilkins / Phil Meredith
- Ronnie Jonsson / Tony Johnson
- Doc Hawker
- Paula Kruger
- Vic Swanepoel / Bertus Roos

Target: Moçambique bridges, Conbomune, Mabalane, Barragem
Air Tasks 1827, 1835 to 1838
Result: Bell aircraft shot down by RPG 7 at Barragem Alex Wesson killed. SAAF helicopters based at Chipinda Pools, and Helicopter Admin area established 100 kilometres inside Moçambique

No 1037 06/09/79 Operation Uric / Operation Bootlace (SAAF)
Aircrews:
- Vic Wightman
- Varky Varkevisser
- Tony Oakley
- Ziggy Seegmuller
- Glen Pretorius
- Kevin Peinke / Paul Perioli
- Breytie Breytenbach / Jakes Jacobs SAAF
- Rob Dean
- Monster Wilkins / Phil Meredith
- Paul Velleman / Nigel Osborne – Dick Retief (SAAF)

Target: Mapai, Mozambique
Result: Assault on Mapai curtailed after fatal SAAF Puma shot down by RPG 7 with the loss of SAAF crew and RSF casualties Johannes du Plooy, Charlie Small, Frazer Burns, Michael Jones, LeRoy Duberley, Hugh Fry, Peter Fox, Jacobus Briel, Jeremy Crow, Brian Enslin, Stephen King, Adrian Coleman, Colin Neasham and David Prosser

No 1045 26/09/79 Op Thrasher
Aircrews:
- Paddy Bate / Gary Carter

Target: Makoni TTL – VQ4553?, east of Rusape
Result: Maj. Bruce Snelgar killed, as well as both aircrews – aircraft hit power lines.

No 1049 09/1979 Op Bowler - SAAF
Aircrews:
- Lynx pilot 4 Squadron
- Monster Wilkins
- Two other Puma pilots
- Kiewiet Skyshout

Target: Fire Force Zulu ops Gwanda, Kezi, West Nicholson (Liebigs), Guyu and Tuli Block
Result: 8 terrs killed Kezi

No 1051 28/9/79 Op Miracle
Aircrews:
- Kevin Peinke / Paul Perioli
- Canberra + Lynx + G-Car
- Vic Wightman
- Ziggy Seegmuller
- Hunter

Target: Monte Cassino, New Chimoio Hill 761

Result: Kevin / Paul x two sorties. Trooper Gert O'Neill killed

No 1054 03/10/79 Op Miracle
Aircrews:
- Brian Gordon
- Ziggy Seegmuller
- Tony Oakley
- Varky Varkevisser
- No1055 03/10/79 Op Miracle

Target: Chimoio – convoy of vehicles close to Monte Cassino
Air Task 2046
Result: Brian Gordon killed. See also PB's *Winds of Destruction*, page 556.

Aircrews:
- Dave Rowe / Paul Perioli
- Kevin Peinke / JJ Strydom
- John Annan
- Ziggy Seegmuller

Target: Chimoio – neutralise road convoy at Cruzamento village
Result: Canberra aircrews killed – shot down by FRELIMO 23mm Anti-Aircraft battery

No 1061 21/10/79 Op Tangent
Aircrews:
- Cocky Benecke / Bruce Jameson
- Colyn James
- Tony Oakley
- Martin Hatfield
- Vic Wightman

Target: Contact – Kalisosa Vlei, 3km west of Vic Falls, Air Task 2162
Result: 30 terrs killed. Lynx hit five times by ground fire. Lynx hit by ground fire – rear engine shut down. Grey Scouts. Cocky SCR

No 1068 01/12/79 Op Huricane
Aircrew:
Nick Meikle / Beaver Shaw
Target: Mtoko top cover
Result: 15 plus 4 killed. One direct hit

No 1073 28/12/79 Operation Thrasher;
Target: Ruombwe – St Anne's Mission, south west   of Inyazura
Result: 15 terrs killed. RLI

CEASE FIRE – MIDNIGHT 28 DECEMBER 1979
Prop Geldenhuys
July 2008

The Kevin Tidy constructed Memorial (commemorates Operation DINGO) – Photo Bob Manser

8 Air Strike maps
Operation Hurricane Airstrikes

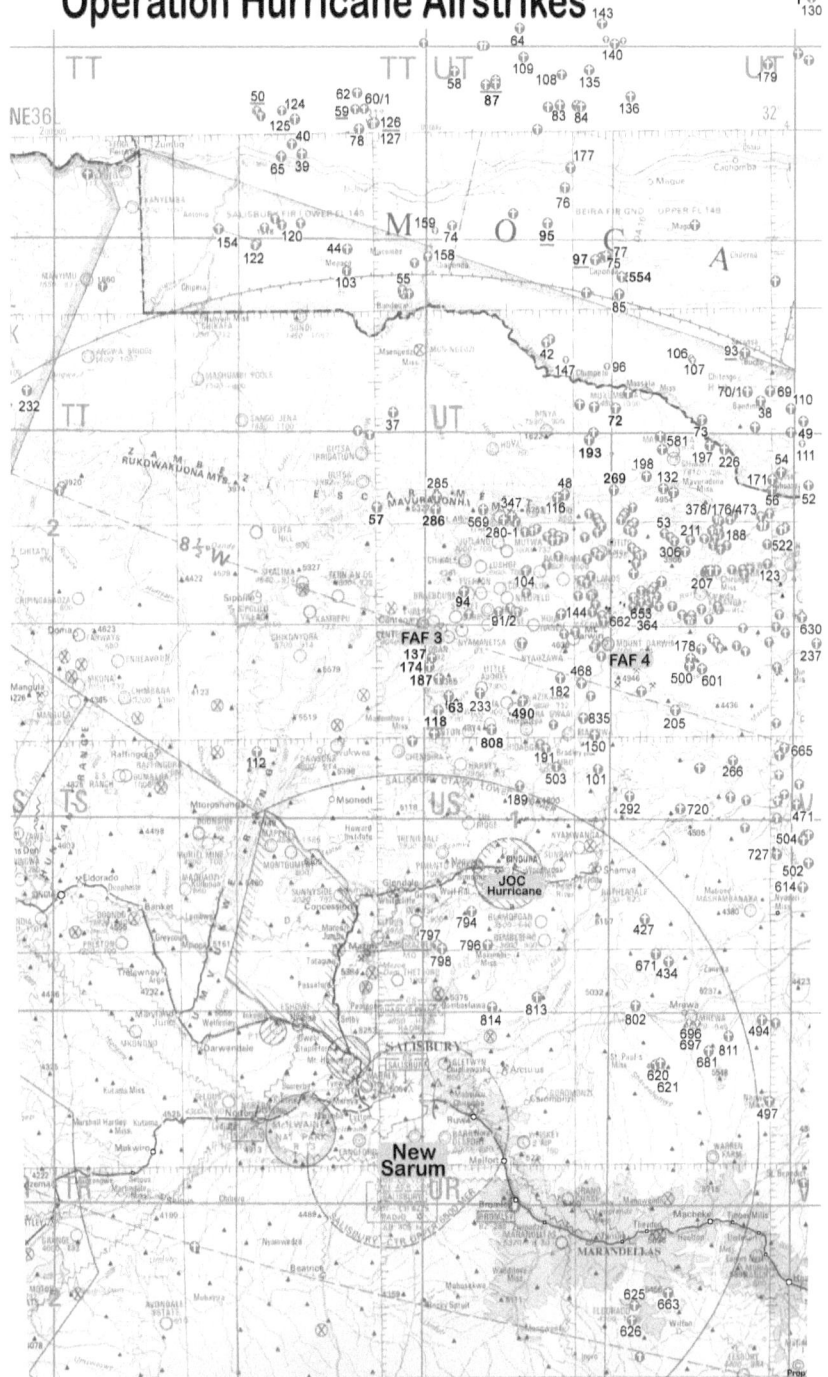

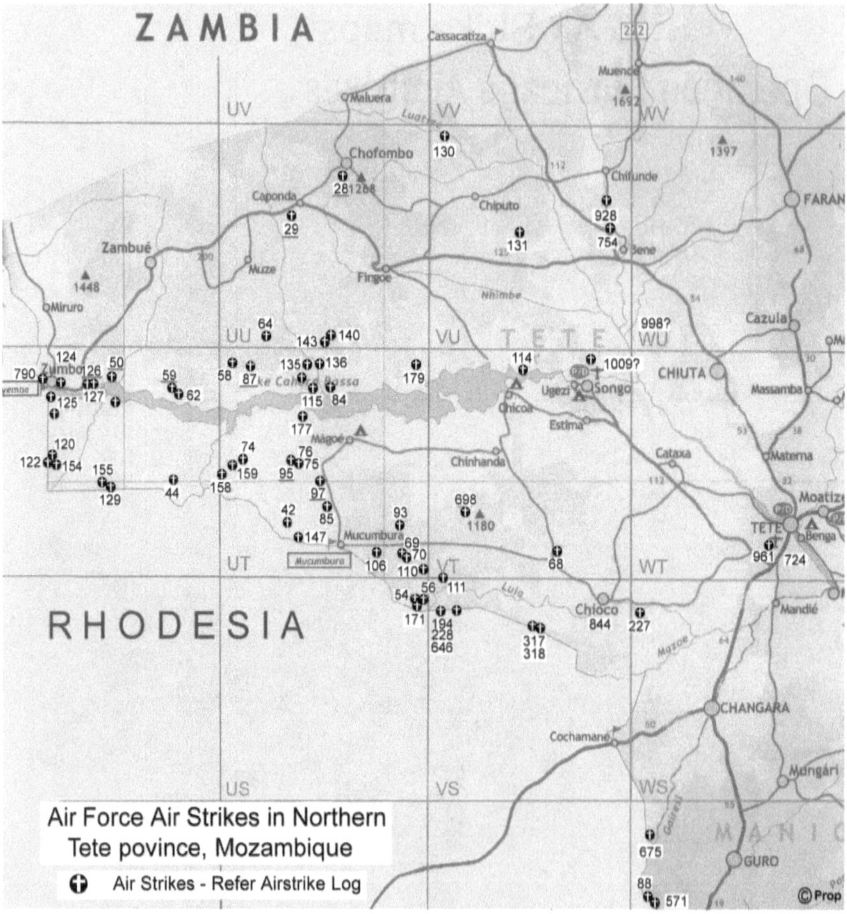

ZAMBIA
RHODESIA
Air Force Air Strikes in Northern
Tete povince, Mozambique
Air Strikes - Refer Airstrike Log
Cassacatiza
Maluera
Chofombo
Caponda
Zambué
Miruro
Zumbo
Muze
Fíngoè
Chiputo
Chifunde
Muende
Bene
Nhimbe
Cazula
CHIUTA
Massamba
Songo
Ugezi
Chicoa
Estima
Cataxa
Chinhanda
Màgoè
Mucumbura
Materna
Moatize
TETE
Benga
Chioco
Mandié
CHANGARA
Cochamano
Mùngári
GURO
UV
VV
WV
UU
VU
WU
UT
VT
WT
US
VS
WS
©Prop

Mozambique Airstrikes
TT
UT
NE36
Zumbo
KANYEMBA
SALISBURY FIR LOWER FL 145
BEIRA FIR GND UPPER FL 145
Mague
Cachomba
Chikafa
Mushumbi Pools
Sango Jena
Rukowakuona Mts.
Msengedzi Miss
Muzarabani
Mukumbura
Bandera
M
O
C
A

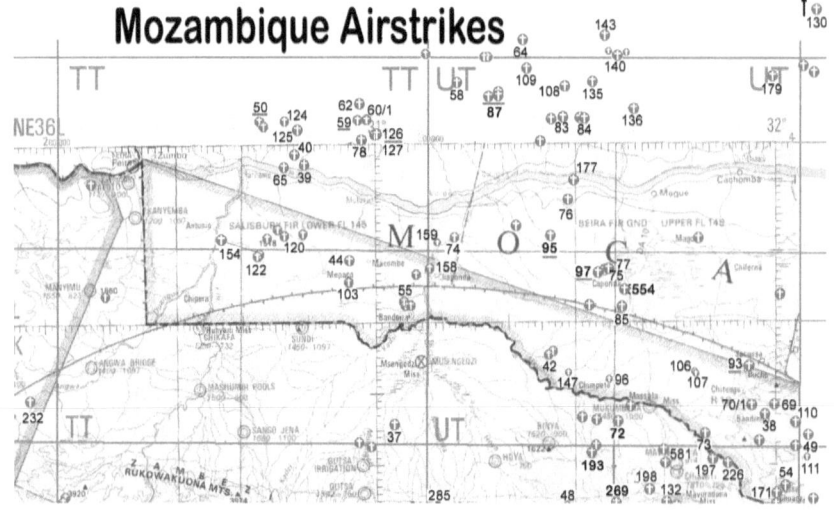

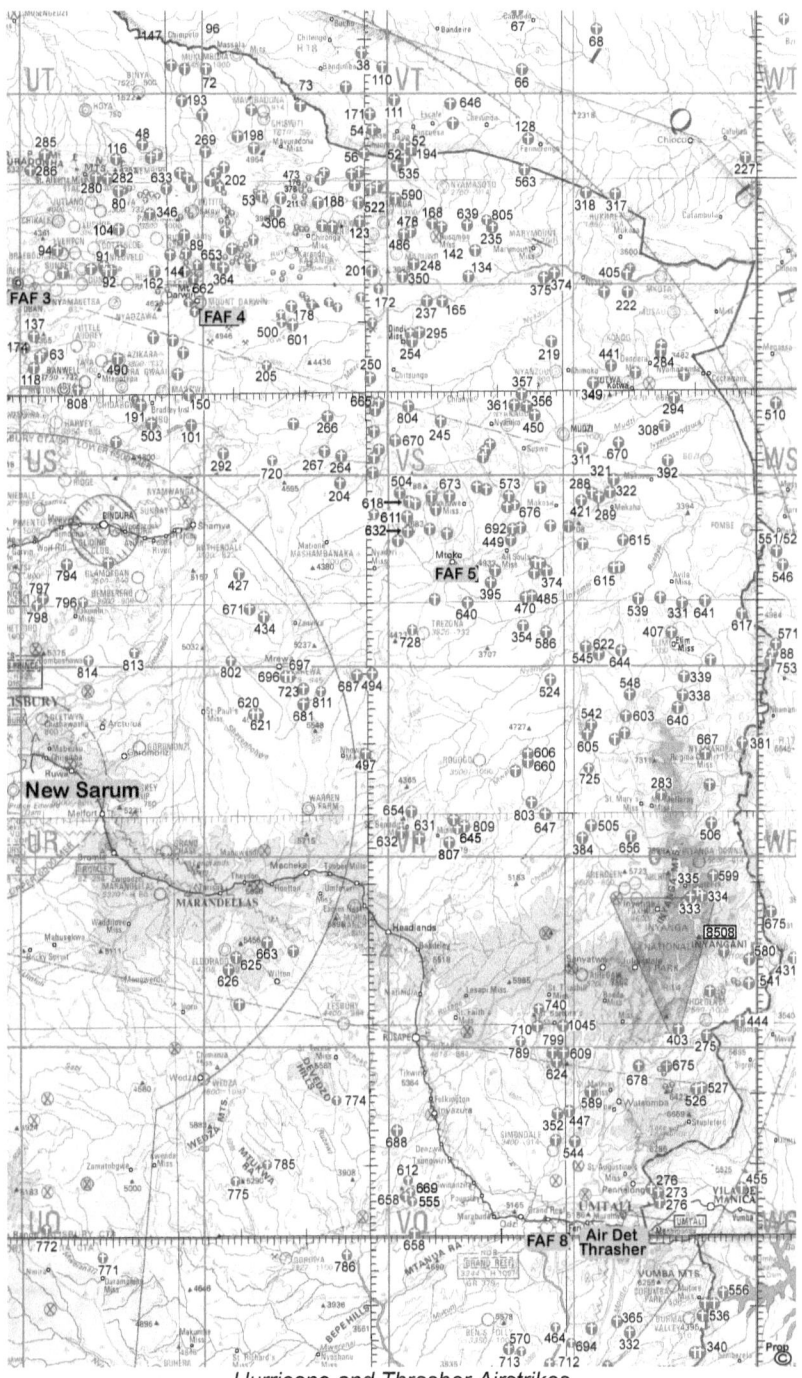

Hurricane and Thrasher Airstrikes

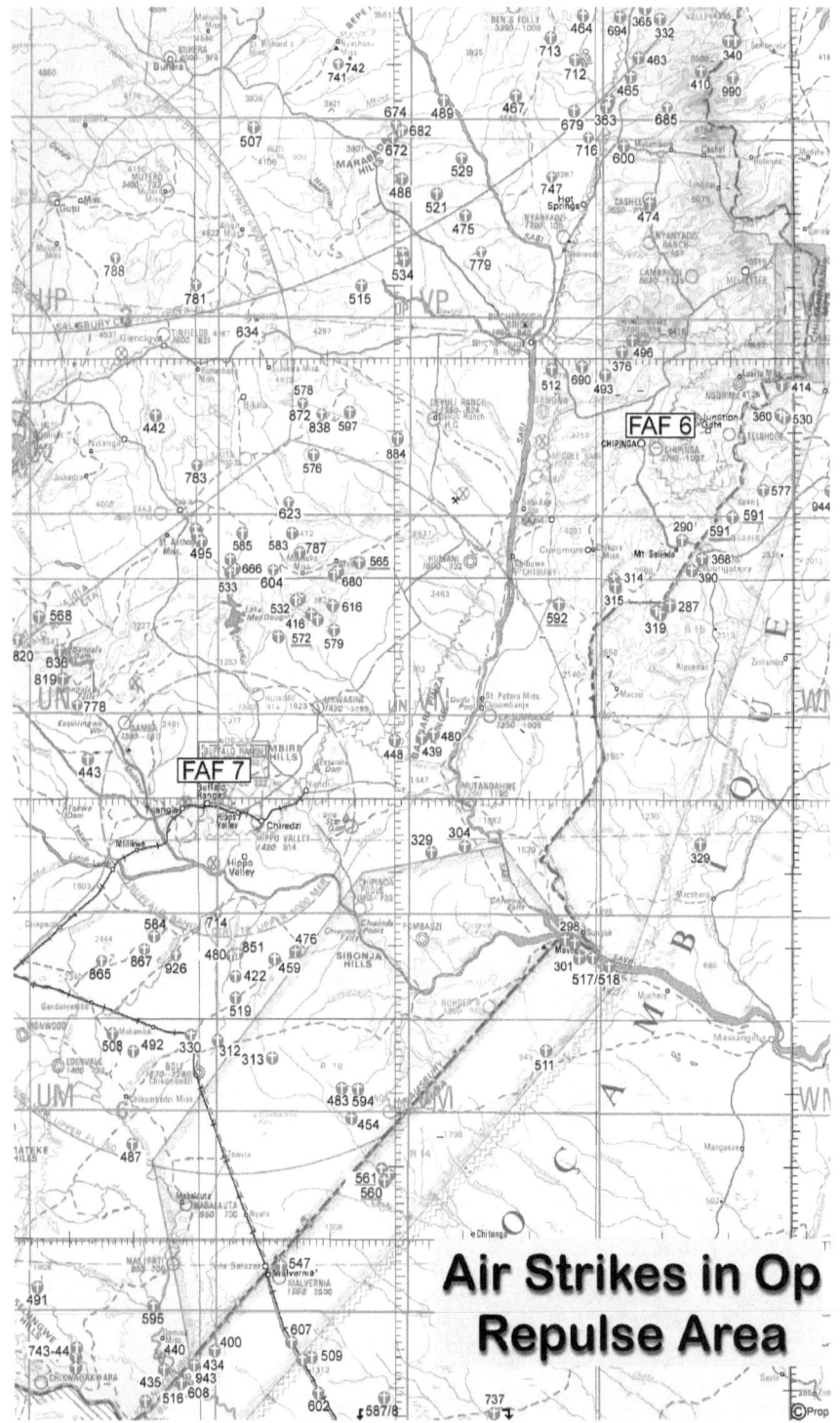

OPERATION REPULSE AIRSTRIKES

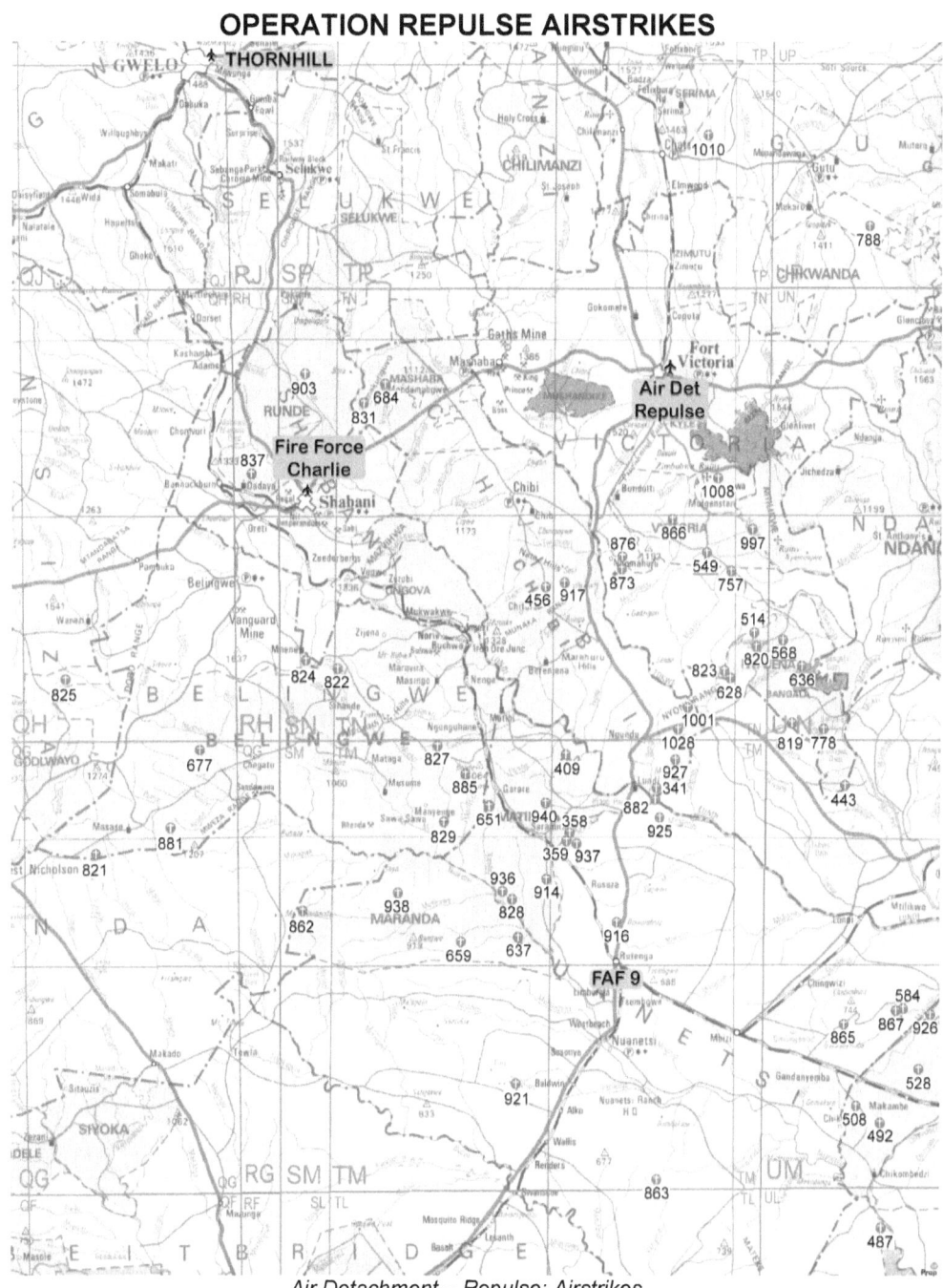

Air Detachment – Repulse: Airstrikes

Fire Force CHARLIE - Shabani : Air Strikes

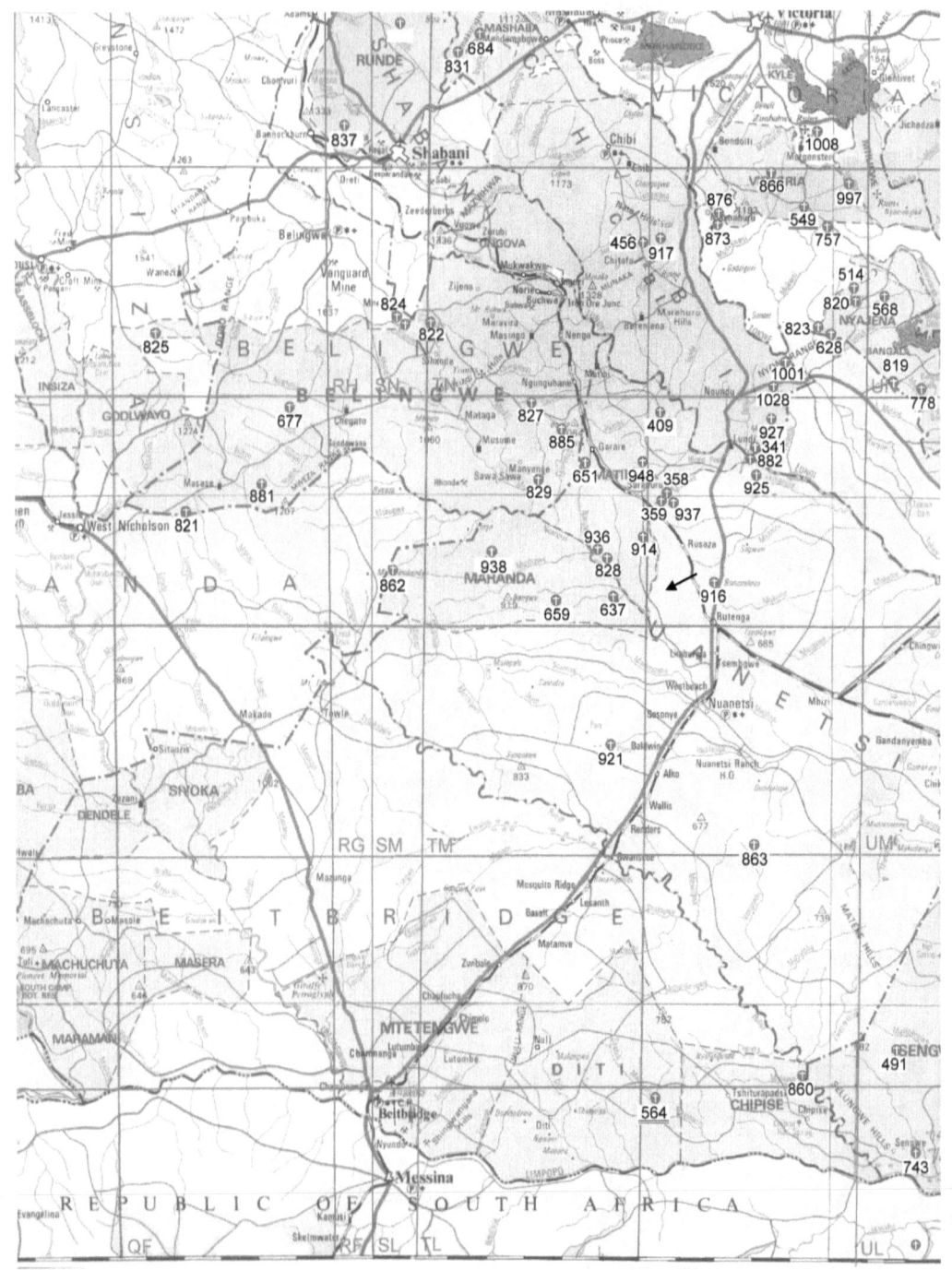

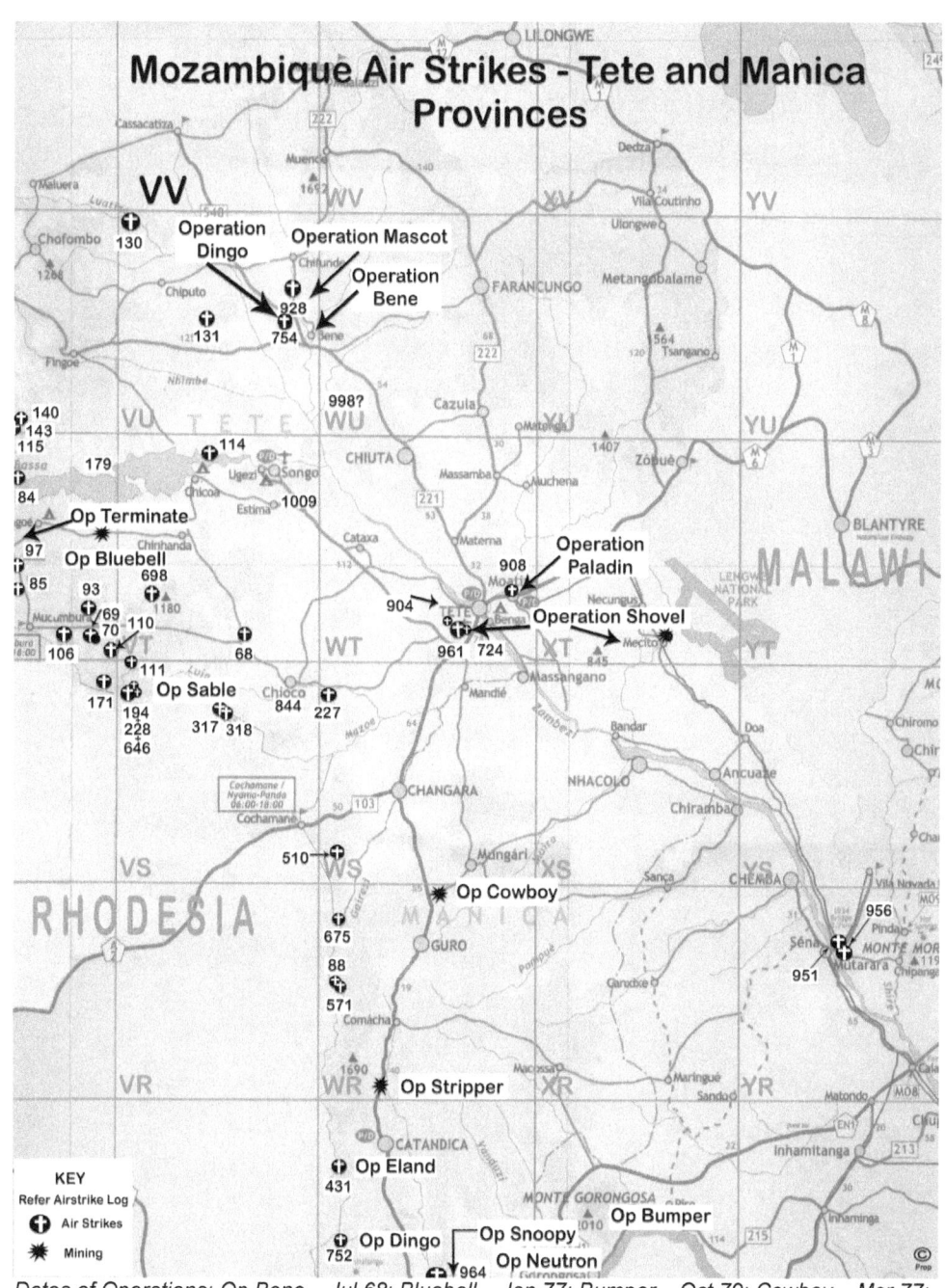

Dates of Operations: Op Bene – Jul 68; Bluebell – Jan 77; Bumper – Oct 79; Cowboy – Mar 77; Dingo – Nov 77; Eland – Aug 76; Lobster – Sep 71; Mascot – Jul 78; Neutron – Mar 79; Paladin – May 79; Sable – May 72; Shovel – Dec 78; Snoopy – Sep 77; Stripper – Mar 77; Terminate – Sep 77

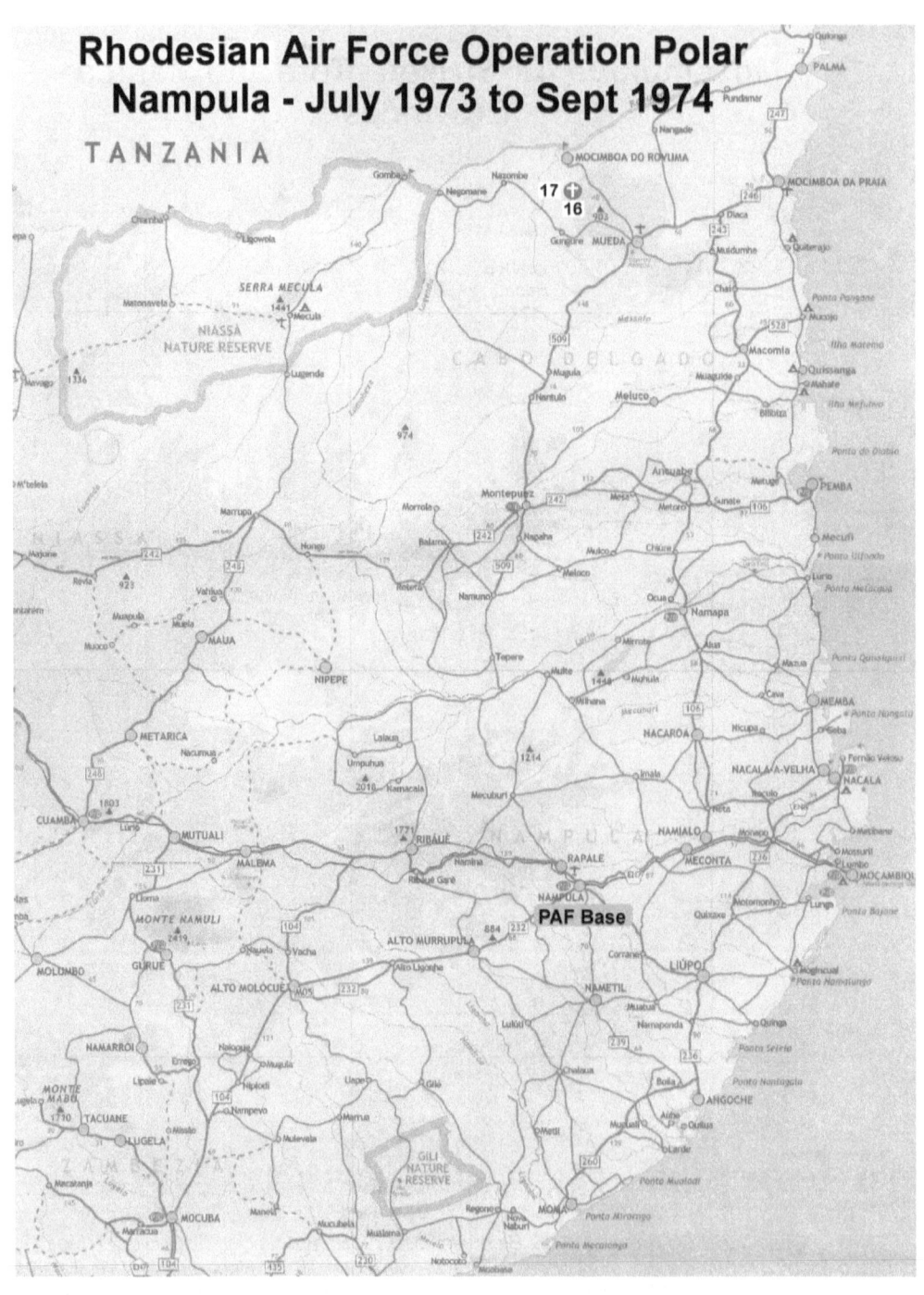

Rhodesian Air Force Operation Polar
Nampula - July 1973 to Sept 1974

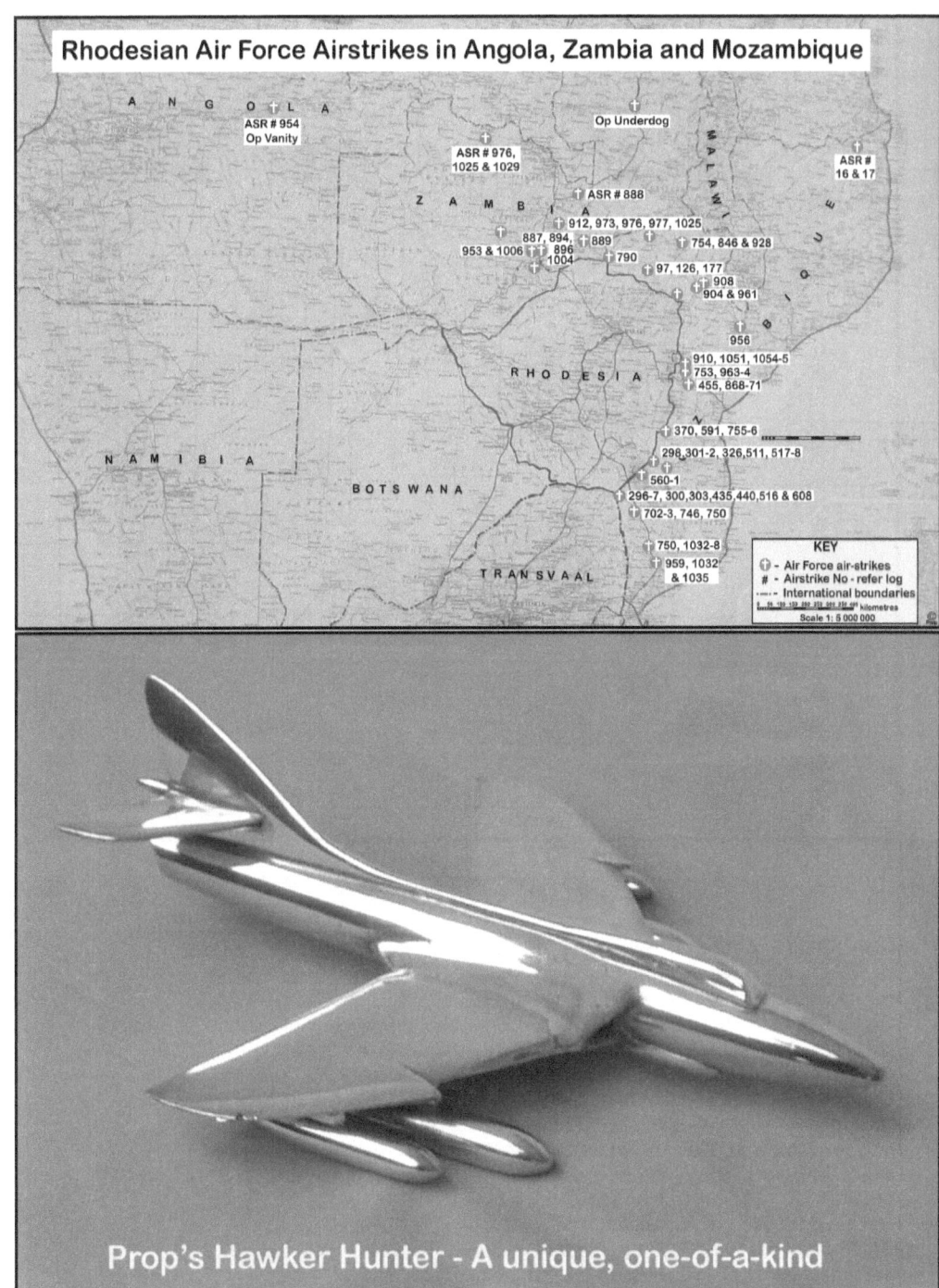

MAP OF RHODESIA – Showing the Grid Squares

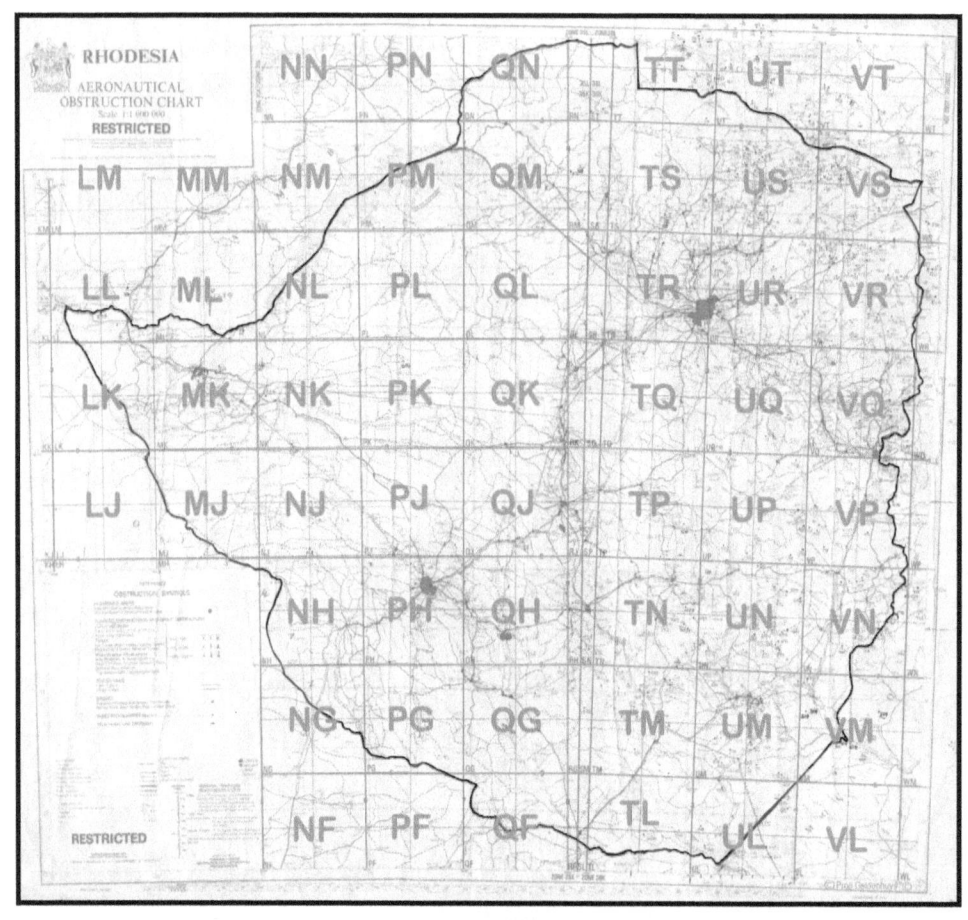

Roll Of Honour

(KIA - Killed in Action: KOAS – Killed on active service: AC - Aircraft Accident)
Air Force personnel
KIA Air Sub-Lt Richard WR AIREY Canberra B2, with Keith Goddard - 4 Apr 74
KIA Flt Sergeant Roger S ANDREWS Trojan, shot down with Willy Wilson - 20 Apr 74
Flt Lt Don ANNANDALE, - Aircraft accident - Kiewiet C185 Kutanga/QQ - 7 Jan 69
Sqn Ldr Peter A BARNETT, KOAS Dakota, with Dave Mallet - 7 Jan 77
KIA Air Lt Paddy M BATE , Alouette K-Car, with Gary Carter - Sep 1979
KIA Sergeant 'Beef' HF BELSTEAD Alouette - contact - 1 Sep 76
Air Sub-Lt Ray J BOULTER - Aircraft accident - Provost (Gwelo) - 19 Jun 75
Air Sub Lt David D BROWN - Aircraft accident - Vampire T11 (Gwelo)   - 4 Aug 72
AC CWD BROWN - Aircraft accident - Lynx (see Griffiths) - 4 May 77
Flg Off Eric CAREY   - Aircraft accident - Vampire FB9 - 9 Feb 61
KIA Flt Sergeant Gary R Carter, Alouette K-Car, with Paddy Bate - Sep 1979
Flt Sergeant John CHILDS   Heart attack 19 Oct 97
Flt Lt Dave CLEMENTS Hilton, Natal Nov 1998
KIA Flt Lt Bruce Collocott Dakota, Moçambique 31 May77*
Lt RV CORRUTHERS - Aircraft accident - Auster J/5 14 Dec 52
Sqn Ldr Rick CULPAN - Aircraft accident - SA 20 Mar 98

Sergeant Brian N CUTMORE - Aircraft accident - Alouette, with Kerry Fynn 2 Jan 79
Off Cdt Barry M DELPORT - Aircraft accident - Vampire T11: Gwelo 3 Jun 75
KIA Flt Lt Ian H DONALDSON Canberra B2, with David Hawkes 12 Jan 77
KIA Air Lt Andre 'Doop ' DU PLESSIS - Lynx 2 Sep 77
KIA SAC Pat R DURRETT Trojan, with Chris Weinmann - 14 Apr 74
KIA Flt Lt GH Francois DU TOIT Alouette Z-Car ex SAAF - 28 Jul 78
Flg Off Henry ELLIOT - Aircraft accident - Vampire FB9 - 20 Dec 64
KIA Flt Sergeant Ian 'Flamer' FLEMMING Alouette K-Car (Air gunner) - 12 Jan 78
Flt Lt Kerry J FYNN - Aircraft accident - Alouette, with Brian Cutmore - 2 Jan 79
Flt Sergeant Pete J GARDEN - Aircraft accident - Alouette, with Munton-Jackson - 17 Jan 72
Pilot Off R GARRETT - Aircraft accident - Vampire FB9 - 21 Aug 56
KIA Air Sub-Lt Keith W GODDARD Canberra B2, with Rich Airey - 4 Apr 74
KIA Air Lt Brian K GORDON Hunter FGA 9 - 3 Oct 79
KIA Sergeant J Pat GRAHAM Alouette K-Car (Air gunner) Inyanga - 18 Jul 76
Sqn Ldr Colin GRAVES - Aircraft accident - Vampire FB9   - 6 May 59
Air Lt Phil W HAIGH KOAS Vampire T52 - 22 Nov 77
KIA Air Sub-Lt David HAWKES Canberra B2, with Ian Donaldson - 12 Jan 77
Flt Lt Mike R HILL - Aircraft accident - Alouette, with Gordon Nettleton   - 1 Jul 70
Flt Lt Roy R HULLEY - Aircraft accident - Vampire T11 at Kutanga Range - 21 Oct 76
KIA Flt Sergeant 'Haj' Henry JARVIE Alouette K-Car - 12 Jan 78
Flt Sergeant Solly JOUBERT KOAS Training - Aircraft accident -C: fell down mountain - 11 Dec 71
Flt Lt Dave E MALLET KOAS Dakota, with Peter Barnett - 7 Jan 77
Lt R MARITZ - Aircraft accident - Spitfire Mk22 - 4 Dec 53
Pilot Off Barry MATTHEWS - Aircraft accident - Provost, with Sandy Trenoweth - 24 Mar 65
Flg Off Bruce McKERRON - Aircraft accident - Vampire FB9 - 22 Jun 6
Air Lt Guy MUNTON-JACKSON - Aircraft accident - Alouette, with Pete Garden - 17 Jan 72
Air Lt Brian MURDOCH KOAS Trojan, night Casevac - 17 Dec 74
Off Cdt RJ NAHKE - Aircraft accident - Provost - 6 Jul 56
KIA Sergeant Kevin P NELSON Alouette Z-Car Moz. with du Toit - 28 Jul 78
KIA SAC Rob G NELSON Alouette. Shot down with Roger Watt - 18 May 77
Sqn Ldr Gordon E NETTLETON - Aircraft accident - Alouette, with Mike Hill - 1 Jul 70
KIA Cpl NYAKAZA KOAS Landmine - 19 Nov 73
Sergeant O LOVE - Aircraft accident - Spitfire Mk22, over France - 16 Dec 52
KIA Air Lt Kevin L PEINKE Canberra B2, with JJ Strydom - 3 Oct 79
Pilot Off J ROBERTS - Aircraft accident - Vampire FB9: Belingwe Peak   - 1 Jul 60
Air Lt Guy N ROBERTSON - Aircraft accident - Canberra B2, with A. Roughead - 16 Nov 71
Flt Lt Alec G ROUGHEAD - Aircraft accident - Canberra B2, with G. Robertson - 16 Nov 71
Sqn Ldr Rusty GA ROUTLEDGE - Aircraft accident - Kiewiet at Grand Reef - 16 Feb 76
Pilot Off Terry RYAN - Aircraft accident - Provost - 4 Feb 63
Flt Lt Andre J SENEKAL - Aircraft accident - Alouette, FAF 4, Mt Darwin - 25 Dec 79
Air Lt John E SMART KOAS Alouette with T. Smithdorff - 21 Feb 73
Sergeant Tinker K SMITHDORFF KOAS Alouette with John Smart - 21 Feb 73
KIA Flt Lt 'Starry' Bill HWH STEVENS Lynx (Prop's "star" Nav) - 2 Sep 76
KIA Flt Lt JJ STRYDOM Canberra B2, with Kevin Peinke - 3 Oct 79
Ch Tech Sandy TRENOWETH - Aircraft accident - Provost, with Barry Matthews - 24 Mar 65
Sergeant Tony AHW TURNER - Aircraft accident - Alouette, with Kerry Fynn & Cutmore - 2 Jan 79
KIA   Sergeant John S UNDERWOOD Lynx with 'Doop' du Plessis   2 Sep 77
Lt JJ VAN RENSBURG SAAF Z-Car with General John Shaw - 23 Dec 75
Sergeant P VAN RENSBURG Alouette with JJ van Rensburg & Shaw - 23 Dec 75
KIA Flt Lt Chris BC WEINMANN Trojan, with Pat Durrett - 14 Apr 74
KIA Aircraftsman Alex JC WESSON Bell 205 shot down with Dick Paxton - 3 Sep 79
Cyril WHITE peacefully, in his sleep - Jun 1992
KIA Air Sub-Lt Willy RJ WILSON Trojan shot down with Roger Andrews - 20 Apr 74

Sergeant Andy HD YOUNG KOAS Bomb dump explosion - 26 Mar 71
======= ALSO =======
ADF Pilot B GARDNER - Air Accident - Feb 79
PRAW Pilot AD LAWTON - KOAS Air Accident - 6 May 67
AFVR Pilot Jack MALLOCH - Aircraft accident - Spitfire Mk22 ex New Sarum - 26 Mar 82
PRAW Pilot Bill SPRINGER - KOAS Air Accident - 19 Jul 69

and the most senior officer killed: Major General John SHAW Chief of Staff Army, KOAS Air Accident Z-Car 23 Dec 75 (SAAF Alouette)

At The Going Down of The Sun, and in the Morning, We Will Remember Them

Rhodesians owe a debt to these (especially those killed in action), for they paid the supreme sacrifice for the survival of the country and the Rhodesian nation.

Index

2

24 September 1976 - Capitulation 157

A

Abrams, Chris 219, 220, 299, 302, 305, 306, 317
Ackland, Major-General John 273
Addams, Maj E 286
Ainslie, Maj 141, 296
Aird, Alan 307
Airey, Rich - Air Force 286
Airey, Richard 75, 82, 89, 91, 93, 95, 97, 98, 104, 107, 108, 177, 179, 180, 287, 338, 339
Aitchison, Mark 125, 172, 300, 302, 303, 306, 307
Alexander, George 16, 192, 305, 315
Amin, Idi 79
Anderson, Dennis 87
Anderson, Jock 19
Anderson, Sheila 157
Andrews, Rob - Air Force 286
Andrews, Roger 71, 287, 338, 339
Andrews, SAC 213
Andrews, Sgt 73
Annan, John 123, 259, 299, 305, 327
Annandale, Don 338
Archenoul, Phil 317
Armitage, Willy 292
Armstrong, Ian ... 158, 296, 307, 309, 321
Armstrong, Pat 97, 273
Atkinson, Dave ... 145, 153, 296, 297, 298
Atkinson, Geoff 18, 20, 159
Aust, Charlie 273

B

Baldwin, Baldy 139, 163, 164, 166, 293, 302, 303, 304, 305, 307, 311, 313, 323
Baldwin, Ginger 138, 147, 162, 164, 263, 313, 319
Baldwin, Jeremy 142
Baldwin, Malcolm 295, 299
Baldwin, Steve 17, 72
Banda, Hastings 79
Bannerman, James "Tackie" 259
Bannerman, James 'Tackie' 260
Barber, Jock 14
Barbour, Dave 305, 321, 322
Barfoot, Commissioner 19
Barker, James 50
Barnard, Brigadier Bertie 143, 156, 160, 164, 165, 166, 304
Barnard, Burie SAP 43
Barnard, Ted 185
Barnes, John .. 17, 69, 292, 302, 303
Barnett, Peter 16, 287, 338, 339
Barrett, Garth 90, 113, 240, 245, 246, 266, 273
Barthorpe, Lt 214

Bate, Ian 110, 266
Bate, Paddy ... 125, 257, 259, 287, 326, 338
Battle of Bangala 164, 165, 169
Battle of Inyantue 28
Baverstock, George 104
Bax, Tim 136, 146
Baynham, Trevor ... 58, 117, 169, 301, 302
Beaurain, Willie SAAF 297, 298
Beaver, Rich ... 28, 29, 30, 32, 34, 35, 36, 37, 38, 55, 56, 75, 78, 81, 82, 91, 92, 93, 187, 188, 305, 314
Beaver, Richard 30, 292
Becker, Boertjie 295
Becker, Boertjie SAAF ... 137, 295, 298
Bellringer, Finch ... 300, 302, 303, 307, 308, 310, 311, 315, 319, 320
Belstead, Beef ... 286, 299, 300, 338
Belstead, 'Beef' - Air Force 286
Benecke, Cocky ... 140, 143, 145, 148, 169, 263, 294, 296, 298, 300, 301, 308, 309, 317, 319, 320, 327
Bennett, Terry 308
Bennie, John ... 17, 22, 23, 75, 91, 93, 94, 104, 107, 110, 145, 158, 177, 179, 296, 298
Bentley, AM Raf 14, 19
Bestbier, André 275
Bezuidenhout, Cpl 203
Bezuidenhout, Hansie 223
Bezuidenhout, Johan "Small Bez" 226, 231, 269
Billet, Pete 213
Birch, D Special Branch 213
Blain, Ken 319
Blair, Robbie 15
Bland, Bob 90
Blumeris, Reg 71
Blythe-Wood, John ... 16, 58, 156, 162, 163, 164, 165, 166, 187, 188, 192, 193, 202, 216, 221, 259, 294, 299, 301, 303, 304, 307, 308, 309, 312, 313, 314, 315, 316, 318, 319, 320
Boardman, Mike ... 240, *See* Mike Borlace
Bolton, Ray ... 153, 223, 224, 233, 287, 297, 305, 310, 313, 317
Bomford, Hugh 158
Bone, Eric 164
Booth, Brian ... 169, 286, 287, 301, 305, 310, 317, 318
Booth, Peter 114, 223, 311
Booth, Trevor 26, 27
Bopela, Thula 39, 275
Borlace, Mike ... 129, 138, 141, 145, 153, 169, 172, 173, 175, 204, 205, 210, 239, 240, 286, 287, 296, 297, 300, 301, 302, 305, 306, 307, 309, 311
Bornman, Cornelius 'Boris' 284
Bosman, Herman 52
Bouch, Bob 24
Boulter, Ray 74, 321, 338
Bourhill, Dave 140, 306, 318, 319
Bowers, Roger 310, 311, 312
Boxall, Harley 225
Boyce, Dave 145, 293, 296
Boyd, Field Reservist 214

Boyd, Jimmy 70
Boyd-Sutherland, Lt. 24
Bradnick, Alan 311
Bradshaw, Dickie 15, 16, 17, 107
Brand, Rich ... 15, 16, 51, 52, 56, 58, 64, 75, 91, 92, 187, 188, 192, 205, 292, 302, 305, 306, 314, 315
Branfield, Gray ... 275, 276, 277, 283, 284
Braun, Paul 298, 299, 315
Breedt, Capt SAAF 50
Brent, Ted ... 15, 16, 17, 204, 235, 302, 306, 318, 319, 320, 321, 322, 323
Brent, Winston 12, 44, 249, 254, 257
Breytenbach, Breytie SAAF ... 325, 326
Briel, Jacobus 253, 326
Brink, R Rct 49
Briscoe, Pete 230, 281, 283
Brislin, AC 24
Britton, John ... 140, 172, 173, 295, 306
Broadbent, Russell 297, 302
Brodryk, Rodney 52
Brooke, Phil 264
Brooker, SAC 213
Brown, 'Alistair' 173
Brown, Charlie WD 287, 338
Brown, CWD - Air Force 286
Brown, David 311, 338
Brown, John 'Wedge' 75, 78, 85, 89, 91, 93, 95, 99, 100, 110
Brown, Sgt 78
Brown, Sid 71
Brown, Tony 79, 80, 83, 89, 106
Bruce, 2nd Lt. 253
Bruce, Al 66, 71, 77, 162, 163, 204, 303, 305, 306, 308, 309
Bryson, Brick 212
Brytenbach, Jan 277
BSAP ... 4, 148, 156, 157, 171, 218, 230, 235, 249, 273, 275, 276, 350
Buckle, Bill 22, 23, 24, 55, 56
Burford, Peter 159
Burmeister, Ken 56, 82, 88
Burns, F 253, 326
Bush, George 283
Bushney, George ... 299, 301, 308, 309
Butcher of Bhalagwe ... See Perence Shiri
Byars, Bryan 186, 224

C

Caborn, Pete 304, 305, 310
Caborn, Peter 315
Caetano, Dr. 68, 95
Cahill, Mick 24
Canter, Dr Paul 158, 159
Carhart, John ... 69, 70, 71, 304, 305
Carey, Eric 338
Carter, Garry 287
Carter, Gary ... 257, 259, 260, 312, 338
Cecil, Lord Richard 316
Chait, Andy 165, 166, 168
Chamberlain, John ... 163, 303, 304, 318
Chamunorwa, Chifombo camp commander 89
Chauke, Justin 64, 85
Chibanda 238, 239

Chidyamuyu - Spirit Medium 86
Chikafu, Simon..............................29
Childs, John........................185, 338
Childs, Perry SAAF140, 141, 145, 296
Chimoio Memorial......................195
Chipfeni - Spirit Medium 86
Chitepo, Herbert23, 24, 120, 121, 195, 276
Chona, Mark.................................97
Christie-Smith, Porky 260
Claasens, Piet SAAF 299
Clark, Nobby..............................213
Clarke, Phil........................206, 207
Clegg, Bob.................86, 87, 88
Clements, Dave..................123, 338
Cloete, Dirk..................................14
Cockcroft, Bud...........................287
Cocking, Jim..............................312
Cocks, Chris...............212, 233, 234
Coetzee, Capt. 27
Coetzee, Gerry SAAF 81
Cole, Barbara........245, 254, 255
Coleman, Adrian........................326
Coleman, Harry............................16
Collett, Dale 150, 159, 224
Collett, Jeff................................320
Collins, Nelson.............................71
Collocott, Bruce56, 82, 88, 176, 177, 182, 287, 312, 313, 338
Collocott, Bruce I - Air Force 286
Commanders of The Air Force 14
Conn, Maj.....................................20
Connolly, John...........................281
Conway - SAS / SB 27
Cook, Vic55, 56, 192, 286, 300, 302, 303, 304, 308, 309, 310, 314
Cooke, Peter16, 40, 56, 102, 158, 292, 300
Cookson, Cpl............................140
Corbishley, Peter...............141, 142
Corrans, Keith15, 16, 51, 52, 55, 125, 136, 292
Corruthers, Lt V........................338
Cous, Theo SAP 124
Coventry - SAS / SB 27
Coventry, Dudley.......................285
Cowan, Peter.............................185
Cowderoy, Dudley...............67, 195
Cox, John 185, 281, 283
Cripps, C....................................233
Crivellari, Ernie..........................315
Crivellari, Ettora305, 307, 308, 310, 311, 313
Cronshaw, Graham17, 62, 292, 302, 307, 319
Crous, Jas SAP 43
Crow, JM....................253, 326
Crystal, Brian204, 205, 301, 303, 307, 309, 315
Culpan, Rick36, 64, 66, 96, 100, 125, 164, 293, 304, 319, 338
Culpan, Vic...............311, 319, 320
Cunningham, Fynn 294
Cunnison, Dad 15, 16
Curley, Peter..............................260
Currie, Al...................................158
Curtain, Mike.............................275
Curwen, Sgt...............................190
Cutmore, Brian233, 287, 318, 321, 339
Cyprus Detachments 74

D

d'Hotman, Bob............99, 192, 315
da Silveira, Carlos204, 205, 307, 309, 310
Dabengwa, Dumisa ...238, 245, 274
Dakyns, Father 75, 76, 77, 91, 92
Dalgleish, Archie.........................88
Dams, Chris.........15, 16, 17, 44, 58
Dartnall, Jeff............192, 305, 314
Daudpota 14, 283, 284
Davel, Lionel............175, 305, 309
Davies, Alistair..................142, 314
Davis, Vonda.............................148
Davison, Cpl................................29
Dawson, Bill 16, 204, 205, 307
Dawson, Mark169, 286, 287, 300, 306, 307, 309, 312, 319, 320
Dax, Hamie......................295, 317
Daykin, Brian 300, 301, 302
Dayton, Rob..........................58, 66
de Arriaga, Kaulza..........67, 68, 106
de Beer, Chris..............................97
de Borchgrave, Mark 88, 89
de Kock, Derrick 205, 206, 211
de Kock, Harwood 205
de Spinola, Antonio.....................95
de Waal, Titch 142
Deall, Johnny...............................14
Dean, Rob 325, 326
Delport, Barry............................339
Delport, Mick92, 93, 100, 104, 107, 108, 110, 118, 148, 177, 179, 189, 300, 302, 311
Dennison, Andre143, 162, 164, 314, 319
Dent, Jack........................262, 263
Desfontein, Trevor.......................27
Desfountain 248
Devine, Sgt Maj. 22
Deysel, Dux...................142, 186
Deysel, Ernie.............................142
Dhlakama, Afonso............270, 285
d'Hotman, Bob..........................175
Dickinson, Chris153, 162, 163, 164, 297, 301, 302, 303, 304
Dietricks, Tpr 140
Digby, John 141, 292
Dillon, Pat....................................40
Dives, Richard...........................300
Dixon, Chris16, 17, 36, 68, 69, 70, 71, 100, 101, 158, 161, 227, 228, 235, 239, 247, 299, 301, 310, 312, 319, 322, 323
Dixon, Guy................................263
Dixon, Ian....................................40
Dodson, Dave alias Graham Wilson
....160
Domoney, Grant...............172, 185
Donaldson, Ian17, 90, 92, 93, 100, 102, 104, 107, 110, 170, 171, 177, 185, 287, 306, 339
Donaldson, Ian H - Air Force 286
Dongo, Bob...............................269
Donnelly, Steve 226, 318
Dormer, LAC.............................203
Douglas-Home, Sir Alec 19, 78
Dowden, Bill................................17
Driver, George.................31, 33, 34
du Plessis, Andre 339
du Plessis, 'Doop' DL - Air Force286
du Plessis, Leon........287, 309, 313
du Plessis, Sgt Doop 26

du Plooy, Capt. Joey .253, 254, 326
du Preez..................................140
du Preez, Duppie SAAF 296
du Preez, SAAF Tech...............140
du Rand, Randy15, 16, 17, 61, 83, 86, 95, 96, 98, 100, 104, 107, 110, 116, 154, 170, 177, 178, 179, 181, 192, 241, 303, 305, 306, 314
du Toit, Danie SAP 51, 52
du Toit, Francois219, 220, 287, 317, 339
du Toit, GHF 'Frans' - Air Force.286
du Toit, Kokkie.........................208
du Toit, Ryno SAP 43
Dube, John...........................31, 39
Duberley, LeRoy...............253, 326
Dumbutshena, Chief Justice Enoch
....283
Duncan, Butch 146
Dunning, Special Forces 277
Durrett, Pat......................287, 339
Durrett, Pat R - Air Force..........286
Duvanage, Steve 142
Dwyer, Steve............................325

E

Edmond, John 228
Edward, Bruce..........................209
Edwards, Ken KAS15, 16, 22, 23, 61, 98, 123, 130
Elliot, Henry..............................339
Ellis, Capt. 18
Ellis, Neall........................296, 297
Elsaesser, Eike.................245, 324
Emmerson, Emmo......................71
Enslin, Brian 253, 326
Erasmus, Rfn 169
Erasmus, Willie 113
Exercise
 Army FAC................................18
 Longdrag.................................20
 Panther...................................20
EXERCISE
 Armchair......................7, 22, 24
 Army FAC.........................7, 159
 Aurora..............................7, 23
 Birds Nest........................7, 71
 Black Jack.......7, 79, 80, 93, 119
 Brass Ring 7
 Broken Arrow............................7
 Brown Water.............................7
 Cauliflower....................7, 102
 Chessman.........................8, 80
 Cobra................................8, 25
 Crocodile Fever...............8, 26
 Evaluation..................................8
 Fabric.....................8, 26, 27
 Irish Stew 9, 58
 King..73
 King Kabanga..................9, 72
 Liberator...........................9, 26
 Longdrag...................................9
 Luanda................................106
 Luanda, Angola9, 106, 119, 121, 123
 Mannix 9, 61
 Oxtail.....................10, 66, 79
 Panther..................................10
 Pea Soup 10
 Police Reserve Air Wing..........69

PRAW 10, 223
Promptforce 10, 26
Treble Chance 11
Vanguard 11, 112
VR-Preston 11

F

Fairey, John 319, 320, 321, 322, 325
Fairlie, John 142
Falzoi, 2nd Lt - KIA 214
Farrell, Norman 71, 302
Fenn, Geoff 71
Fennell, Robin 128
Fenton-Wells, Steve ..141, 142, 152
Ferreira, Sgt. 319
Ferreira, Wayne SAAF 296, 297
Few, Blake 59
Finn, Kerry 233
Fire Force Charlie 210, 211, 212, 318, 321, 322, 350
Fitzpatrick, Ray SAAF 139, 140, 295, 297, 298
Flemming, Al 'Flamer' - Air Force 286
Flemming, Ian 'Flamo' 286, 298, 299, 300, 307, 315, 339
Fletcher 287
Fletcher, Bob 302, 305, 308
Flower, Ken 19, 31, 40, 68, 106, 270
Forbes, Pat 312
Ford, Gerald 157
Forsyth, Malcolm 148
Fourie, Dawie 254
Fourie, Frik SAAF 294
Fox, Peter 253, 326
Franklin, Alan 'Stretch' 97
Freeland, Rfn. 171
Fry, Hugh 253, 326
Fubbs, Corporal 224, 225
Funqueil, SAAF Tech 297
Fylde 228, 254, 262, 266, 275, 281, 320
Fynn, Kerry 233, 287, 321, 339

G

Galloway, Wally 292, 301
Garden, Pete 339
Gardener, Byrne 234
Gardner, B 340
Gardner, Mike 263
Garrett, R 339
Gaunt, Rob ...16, 100, 135, 236, 293
Gedye, Mike 16, 136
Geldenhuys, A C F Preller 57, 81
Geldenhuys, Jake Pey 290
Geldenhuys, Lucy and Mia 290
Geldenhuys, Matthew 290
Geldenhuys, Pey 290
Geldenhuys, Prop 2, 3, 5, 22, 30, 51, 55, 56, 58, 64, 66, 70, 75, 91, 93, 94, 100, 104, 107, 110, 128, 163, 164, 165, 166, 168, 172, 177, 178, 179, 292, 293, 303, 304, 305, 306, 327
Geldenhuys, Renene 290
Geldenhuys, Rina 2, 290
Geldenhuys, Tony SAAF 43, 125
Geraty, Spook 58, 70, 72, 125, 187, 188, 192, 314, 315
Gericke, Patrick 276

Gillespie, Athol 152, 159, 170
Gingles, Alan 285
Gledhill, Dick 205, 206, 211
Goatley, Chas 277, 286, 310, 311, 312, 315, 319, 320, 323, 325
Goddard, Keith 93, 104, 107, 108, 177, 179, 180, 287, 338, 339
Goddard, Keith W - Air Force 286
Gomes, Costa 68
Goodfellow 203
Goodwin, Brian 181
Gordon, Brian 258, 259, 261, 263, 287, 318, 327, 339
Gordon, Brian K - Air Force 286
Goss, Terry 142
Gqabi, Joe Nzingo 275, 276
Graaff, BG 60
Grace, Anthony 28
Grace, Tpr 234
Graham, JP - Air Force 286
Graham, Pat 138, 139, 286, 295, 298, 339
Graves, Colin 15, 16, 339
Graydon, Butch 51, 52, 61, 287, 292
Green, Johnny 305
Grey Scouts 143, 148, 156, 162, 173, 238, 327
Grier, Mick 17, 29, 38, 51, 52, 292
Griffiths, Harold 15, 16, 17, 22, 38, 192, 303, 305, 307, 308, 310, 311, 314
Griffiths, Rob 287, 311, 338
Griffiths, Rob – Air Force 286
Griffon, G-Car Tech 153, 297
Grinaker, Olla SAAF 130
Guevara, Che 122
Gumbo, Rugare 195
Gunn, Peter 234
Guy, Mike 102, 103, 171

H

Haakonsen, Ray 212
Haigh, Dot 193
Haigh, Phil 139, 170, 191, 192, 193, 195, 287, 296, 298, 303, 307, 314, 315, 339
Haigh, Phil W - Air Force 286
Hale, Dr. 171
Haley, Pete SAAF 299
Hall, Rfn 171
Halsy, SAAF Tech 299
Hamadziripi, Henry 121, 195
Hamence, Mike 75
Hammarskjold, Dag - United Nations Secretary General 18
Hammond, Terry 40
Hangartner, Ministry of Works 214
Hani, Chris 39
Hani, David 87
Harding, Alo Tech 172
Harding, Ralph 306
Harrison, Bruce 262
Harrison, Eric 142
Harrison, Maj 185
Harvey, Ian 175, 286, 300, 304, 306, 307, 313
Hatfield, Martin ..263, 312, 314, 327
Havnar, Doug Capt 233, 287, 321
Hawker, Doc SAAF 326
Hawkes, David 170, 171, 185, 287, 302, 306, 339

Hawkes, David - Air Force 286
Hawkins, Harold 14, 19, 31, 112
Hawksworth, Gerald 90
Healey, Slade SAAF ..141, 293, 296
Hean, Pete 266
Heard, Barry 69, 71, 72
Heindriks, Wally 123
Henderson, Ian 286
Henning, N J Capt SAP 52
Heron, George 104, 177, 178
Hicken, Keith 306, 307, 309, 311
Hickman, John 98, 99, 185, 240
Hill, Mike 65, 339
Hill, Pat 110, 164, 165
Hingeston, Brigadier 142
Hingeston, Peter 142
Hinricks, Wally 15
Hoare, Mike 277
Hobbs, Eddie 281
Hobbs, Pilot Officer 19
Hoebel, Chris SAAF 296
Hofmeyer, Murray 30, 292
Hofmeyr, Murray 28, 29, 31, 81, 82, 141, 299, 305
Holland, Ted 302
Hollingworth, Don 78, 79
Homan, Mike 315
Hood, John 310
Hooley, Tpr 234
Hopedzichirira 89
Hore, Sebastian alias Matsikachando 85
Horsborough, Pete 212
Hosking, Peter 18, 30, 110, 159, 169
Hossack, Hoss 315
Houghton, Hobart SAAF 286
Houston, Mo 56, 95
Howard, Matthew Dylan 290
Howden, Maj. 22
Howie, Mike 213
Howman, Jack 53, 55, 66
Huck, W. 287
Hughes, Cpl. 233
Hulbert, Marty 169
Hulley, Roy 58, 74, 339
Hunzvi, Chenjerai 188
Hutchings, Allan 139, 140, 296
Hutchings, Martin 295, 296
Hutchings, SAAF pilot 141

I

Ignatius, Father 133, 134
Insch, Wally 217, 218
Inyantue, Battle of 28, 29, 30, 33, 39, 110
Irvine, Bill 235, 236
Irvine, Capt 162, 163, 169, 303

J

Jacklin, Ted 14
Jackson, Mark 204, 205, 304, 305, 307, 309, 310, 311, 315
Jackson, Peter 196
Jacobs, Jakes SAAF 140, 295, 325, 326
Jacobs, John 204, 205, 307, 310
Jairos 89
Jakachaka 97
James, Colyn 233, 263, 324, 327
James, Snr Tech. 27

Jameson, Bruce................263, 327
Janeke, Tol3, 4, 15, 16, 17, 56, 58, 59, 68, 69, 70, 73, 74, 75, 78, 80, 82, 91, 93, 94, 95, 99, 110, 140, 141, 157, 160, 170, 171, 172, 185, 186, 192, 270, 299, 306, 314, 315, 319, 350
Jarvie, HAJ - Air Force 286
Jarvie, Henry153, 286, 295, 297, 301, 310, 311, 315, 339
Jefferies, Wally 185
Jelley, Bill15, 16, 22, 44, 45, 46, 51, 52, 54, 55, 58, 68, 72, 73, 81, 84, 91, 292
Jelley, Brendan............................290
Jelley, Courtney..........................290
Jenkins, Dave 315
Jenkins, Jenkie301, 303, 307, 308, 312
Jew, Trevor.....................263, 264
Johnson, Maj. 18
Johnson, Phyllis..............................88
Johnson, Rfn...............................169
Johnson, Tony SAAF................326
Johnston, Dave SAAF 138, 298
Jones, Dag15, 16, 64, 66, 170, 188, 189, 281, 283, 293, 298, 301
Jones, Michael..................253, 326
Jones, Roley SAAF 322
Jones, Terry 27, 292
Jonsson, Ronnie SAAF 326
Jordan, Tony129, 130, 299, 300, 302, 303, 307, 309, 313
Joubert...286
Joubert, Chris 304, 305
Joubert, Johan JJ Joubs............169
Joubert, Solly 339

K

Kabila, Laurent 284
Kangai, Kumbirai........................121
Karoni, Pte. 29
Kaunda, Kenneth46, 64, 97, 104, 121, 125, 130, 153, 243, 244
Keightley, Bert140, 296, 297, 301, 302, 305, 306, 307, 310, 312
Keightly, Bert..............................315
Kemsley, Keith 15, 16, 17, 73
Kenchinton, Peter.....................234
Kenny, Rfn Garry.......................158
Kesby, Steve16, 23, 192, 270, 314, 321
Keyter, Leon 150
Khama, Seretse 104, 153, 244
Kidson, John......174, 175, 212, 287
King, Pat 168
King, Stephen 12, 253, 326
King, Torty SAS .165, 166, 168, 304
Kissinger, Henry 125, 157, 244, 247
Knight, Mark162, 163, 164, 166, 167, 168, 299, 301, 302, 303, 304, 305, 310, 311, 312
Knight, Willie..............................313
Knobel, Peter 16, 17, 193
Korb, Sgt Maj. Aubry 30, 40
Kreil, SAAF Tech 141
Kriel...296
Kriel, Neil......................219, 220
Kriel, Org SAAF 294, 298
Kritsinger, Rudi SAAF..................322
Kruger, Paula SAAF 326

L

Labuschagne, SAAF Lt.................18
Lafferty, Cpl 26
Lamb, Nigel 316, 317, 319, 320
Lardner-Burke, Desmond 53, 55
Law, Ken27, 51, 192, 212, 300, 301, 306, 314
Lawton, AD 340
le Roux, Bill..................................71
le Roux, Pete 310, 311
Lemon, David 218
Lewis, Johan SAAF 298
Lewis-Walker, Nigel...........281, 283
Liddell, Neil SAAF......................294
Liebenberg, Major-General Kat - SADF..................................276, 284
Light, Jim.....................................212
Lindner, Alan 123
Litson, Mike72, 73, 138, 140, 204, 205, 294, 295, 298, 300, 307, 309, 314
Little, Tpr Brad KIA 234
Lloyd, Barry 281, 283
Lochran, James 283
Lockley, Lt...................................159
Logan, Sgt. 214
Loots, General Fritz SADF275, 276, 284
Lotringer, E Tpr 162
Lotter, Chas................................193
Loubsher....................................295
Love, Owen 339
Lowe, Dave SAAF 293, 294
Lowrie, Martin205, 297, 299, 302, 305, 314
Lunt, Ted17, 55, 59, 223, 245, 246, 247, 263, 266, 299, 311, 313, 317, 324
Luthuli, Daluxolo.........................39
Lutz, Karl 255
Lynch, Jerry 286, 287, 312

M

M'nangagwa, Emmerson..........126
Maasdorp, Norman124, 236, 286, 299, 307, 308, 310, 311, 315, 325
Mabunu, Kenneth (Peter?) 123
MacDonald, Mike......................324
MacGregor, Rob206, 207, 295, 299, 301, 312
Machel, Samora95, 104, 131, 136, 153, 154, 270, 271, 285
MacLaughlin, Porky ...15, 17, 58, 73
MacMaster, Sgt Maj....................24
Major Brian, alias Gray Branfield275
Major Pete 275
Makoni, Andrew...........................97
Makuwa, James.........................148
Malan, Phil 104
Mallet, Dave...........287, 338, 339
Malloch, Jack136, 192, 200, 254, 262, 315, 340
Mandela, Nelson 34, 39, 271
Mangena, Alfred Nkita...............213
Manser, Bob 195, 259, 260
Marita, Ndau 86
Maritz, R......................................339
Márquez, Gabriel Garcia 122
Marshall, Benjamin......................50
Martin, David 88

Mashangara, Kefas 96
Mashiko, Graham........................39
Masimini, James 31
Mason, Clive 174
Mason, Pete....................125, 325
Masuku, Lookout 274
Matkovich, Roy..........................147
Matkovitch, Peter 140, 159, 214
Matsangaíssa, André..................270
Matsikachando, alias Sebastian Hore...85
Matthews, Barry............19, 20, 339
Maughan, Monty 21, 292
McCabe, Pete...............295, 296, 300
McCall, Hugh 233, 234, 325
McCall, 'Split Pin'.........................262
McCallion, Harry 273
McCay 317
McClurg, Peter 16
McConnell, Capt. 20
McCormack, SAAF....................307
McCormick, Mac...............294, 308
McCormick, Terry 319
McGregor, Rob 17, 64, 147
McIlwaine, Herbert......................26
McKend, Bruce 245, 324
McKenna, Bob ...113, 200, 263, 264
McKenzie, John 'Kutanga' Mac73, 77
McKerron, Bruce 339
McKersie, Max 174, 175
McKillop, SAC 214
McLaren, Mick MJ14, 15, 16, 17, 93, 135, 136, 150, 243
McLauren, John.........................264
McLean, Mark22, 23, 44, 61, 69, 140, 192, 296, 299, 303, 304, 305, 312, 315
McLean, Sandy..................143, 243
McQuade, Bill172, 301, 302, 303, 305, 306, 307
Mdlulu, Rfn.................................171
Meddows-Taylor, Pat............22, 23
Meerholz, Corrie SADF 207
Meikle, Barry..............................260
Meikle, Brian..............................309
Meikle, Nick164, 166, 169, 223, 298, 301, 304, 305, 310, 311, 312, 327
Merber, Tony204, 293, 295, 301, 302, 307, 308, 309, 311
Meredith, Charles........................14
Meredith, Phil SAAF 326
Meyer, Lt.....................................159
Meyer, Willie SAAF 12 Sqn 322
Michael, Rifleman B - SADF.....285
Michie, Bill299, 307, 308, 311, 312, 324
Middelton, Allistair 262
Mienie, Jan 305, 312, 314, 318
Milbank, Chris 294, 298
Mincher, Pat........159, 214, 217, 225
Mlambo, Victor...........................245
M'nangagwa, Emmerson............19
Modise, Joe..........................34, 276
Modise, Tim 34
Mola, Chief - Sengwa Basin 218
Moore, Norman............................89
Morgan, Paddy56, 75, 82, 83, 89, 91, 93, 95, 96, 104, 107, 110, 113, 114, 116, 118, 119, 120, 160, 177, 234, 235, 314, 315, 316, 318, 319, 320, 321, 322, 323, 324

Morgan-Davies, Capt 153
Morris, Ginger 294, 299, 302
Morris, Roy 16, 60, 64, 66, 110
Moss, Basil20, 97, 117, 150, 185, 210, 218
Moss, John 14
Mostert, G Rfn 238
Mpofu 64
Mpofu, Leonard 317
Mudzi, Mukudzei 121
Mugabe, Robert19, 23, 53, 88, 98, 104, 121, 126, 153, 154, 160, 188, 190, 193, 195, 234, 270, 271, 272, 273, 274, 277, 281, 282, 283, 284, 289
Muller, Hilgard 124, 157
Mulligan, Mike58, 60, 68, 287, 307, 308
Mulligan, Mrs See Operation Mulligan
Mullin, M Tpr 49
Munton-Jackson, Guy 339
Murdoch, Brian58, 69, 70, 71, 74, 118, 287, 339
Murphy, John 173
Murphy, Terence 209, 298, 300
Murray, Steve72, 307, 308, 309, 311
Murrupa, Dr Miguel 106
Mussell, Frank14, 15, 17, 189, 243, 289
Mussell, John15, 16, 76, 77, 189, 315
Mutch, Sandy 15, 19
Mutizwa, Soloman88, See Rex Nhongo
Mutsati, Livisoni 155
Muzenda, Simon 274, 283
Muzorewa, Abel78, 104, 218, 243, 244, 246, 247, 272
Mxwaku, Mjojo 39

N

Nahke, RJ 339
Ncube, 'Danger' 185, 212, 281
Neasham, Colin 326
Nederlof, Sos 38
Nehanda, Mbuya 86
Nel, Boet 165, 166, 167, 168
Nel, Boet SAS KIA 166, 304
Nel, Frans 226
Nel, GJ Tpr 192, 315
Nel, Jannie 150, 151
Nelson, Kevin189, 219, 220, 287, 317, 339
Nelson, Kevin - Air Force 286
Nelson, Mrs 219
Nelson, Rob164, 286, 304, 310, 312, 317, 339
Nelson, Rob - Air Force 286
Nesbit, Roy 67, 195
Neto, Agostinho 122, 123
Nettleton, Gordon 17, 65, 339
New Sarum157, 158, 185, 189, 190, 206, 212, 221, 224, 227, 228, 230, 239, 246, 250, 254, 263, 275, 277, 340
Newman, Ken138, 293, 298, 301, 302, 305, 308, 311, 312, 314
Nhari Rebellion 121
Nhari, Thomas 89, 121

Nhongo, Rex88, 89, 136, 153, 195, 229, 259, 274, 322
Nicholls, Pete 52, 277
Nickel Cross 12, 38, 40, 65
Nicollys, Supt. 217
Niesawand, Peter 105
Nightingale, Nobby 22, 36, 64, 66
Nkala, Enos 98
Nkomo, Joshua18, 19, 31, 104, 153, 169, 213, 217, 235, 239, 240, 241, 243, 245, 246, 247, 248, 267, 268, 270, 271, 272, 273
Nkosi, Leonard 31, 39
Noakes, Dave 114, 116
Norris, Eddy 148, 183
Northcroft, Don ..100, 299, 308, 309
Nyagumbo, Maurice 53, 98
Nyakaza, Cpl 339
Nyerere, Julius 104, 153, 288
Nyika, Pte 40
Nzo, Alfred 39

O

O'Neill, Gert 259, 327
Oakley, Tony72, 189, 216, 259, 261, 316, 317, 318, 319, 320, 322, 323, 324, 325, 326, 327
Obasi, Cpl 187
Oberholtzer, Petrus 19, 24
Oborne, Geoff223, 286, 287, 309, 310, 311, 313, 317, 318
OCFW – NS 15
Oeloffse, Roelf 286
Oeloffse, Roelf P 287
Oeloffse, Roelf SAAF138, 248, 319, 320
Ohlsson, Stig 307
Operation
  Broken Arrow 20
  Coondog 18
  Hedgehog 18
  Phoenix 19
  Reptile 20
  Sabre 18
  Slipshod 20
  Spider 18
  Sunrise 18
OPERATION
  Abduction 7, 217, 218
  Acrobat 7, 207
  Agila 7, 273
  Alcora 7, 81, 95, 101, 102, 119
  Altar 7, 271, 284, 285
  Amnesty 7, 244
  Anvil 7, 277
  Apollo 7, 67
  Armchair 7
  Askoek 7
  Aspect 7, 239
  Aztec 7, 176, 177
  Bastille 7, 240
  Bene - Tete 7, 335
  Big Bang 7, 67, 112, 113, 139
  Big Push 7, 65
  Birch 7, 62, 153
  Biscuit 7, 117
  Blanket 7, 111, 114, 116, 119
  Blanket II 7, 249
  Bluebell 7, 173, 335
  Bluebolt 7, 124
  Bondage 7

Bonfire 7, 44
Bootlace 7, 249, 252, 254
Bouncer 7, 229, 230, 248
Bowler 7, 256
Boxer 7, 249
Breampool 7, 20
Breeze 7
Brisket 7, 186
Bristol 7, 285
Bulldog 7, 249
Bumper 7, 262, 270, 335
Cantata 7
Capsule 7, 271
Cardigan 7, 50
Carlota 7, 122
Carpet 7, 245
Cauldron7, 44, 46, 47, 49, 50, 88, 96, 144
Chamber 7, 244
Cheese 7, 262
Chestnut 8, 62, 63
Chicory 8
Chinaman 8, 43, 44, 272
Christmas Cracker 8, 230
Condor 8, 74
Coolith 8
Coondog 8
Cosmic 8
Cowboy 8, 174, 335
Crater 8
Crusader 8, 12
Cucumber 8, 248, 249
Dabchick 8
Daffodil 8, 44
Damper 8, 270
Detachment 8, 142, 146, 147
Detonate 8, 218
Dice 8, 262, 268, 269, 270, 271
Dingo8, 190, 192, 194, 195, 200, 257, 328, 335
Dinky 8, 241
Dirk 8, 124, 125
Disco Scene 8
Dragon 8, 188
Driver 8, 175
Ecstasy 8, 244
Eland 8, 154, 155, 195, 335
Elbow ..8, 212, 213, 214, 225, 241
Enclosure 8, 256
Ermine 8, 44
Excess 8, 27, 53
Exodus 8, 13
Fiddle 8, 248, 324
Flock 8
Flotilla 8
Free-fall Jump 8
Gaiter 8, 233
Gatling 8, 226, 227, 228, 229
Gericke 8, 275, 276
Glamour 8
Glove 8
Gordion Knot 8, 67
Grampus 8
Granite 8, 61
Grapple8, 85, 186, 187, 190, 233, 248
Gravel 8
Greenhills 8
Greentrees 8, 21
Griffin 8, 50, 51, 52
Grinder 8, 188
Grovel 8, 234, 235
Hectic 9, 273

Hedgehog 9
Hemp 9
Heup 9, 96
Hooper 9, 188
Hottentot 9, 56, 57, 58, 59, 69, 70, 71, 125
Hurricane 9, 64, 83, 85, 88, 89, 90, 92, 93, 95, 107, 108, 123, 126, 137, 139, 179
Husk 9, 27
Hustler 9, 174
Hydra 9, 12
Ignition 9, 160
Ingrid 9, 244
Inhibit 9
Inhibit II 9, 232
Inspan 9, 248
Instant 9, 238
Irish Stew 60, 61
Isotope 9, 25, 26, 27, 39, 53
Isotope II 9, 27
Jacaranda 9, 67
Jacket 9, 230
Jezebel 9, 44
Junction 9, 56, 80, 81
Knuckle 9, 10, 54
Kodak 9, 173, 174
Lion Cub 9
Liquid 9, 238
Lobster 9, 73, 335
Long John 9, 150, 151
Luso, Angola 9, 235, 322
Mackerel 9
Manacle 9, 262
Mansion 9, 50, 52
Manyatela 9, 160, 161, 169, 170, 171, 184
Marble . 9, 107, 108, 110, 119, 180
Mardon 9, 161, 162, 163, 164, 168, 181, 303
Market Garden 9, 117
Mascot 9, 222, 335
Mayibuye 9, 18
Melon 9, 188, 200, 202
Meltone 9, 44
Metric 9, 221
Mica 9, 117
Mila 9, 271, 285
Milk Float 9, 273
Mineral 9, 244
Miracle 9, 257, 261
Mixer 10, 276
Modular 10, 188
Mulligan 10, 245
Murex 10, 267
Mustard 10, 244
Mute 10, 277
Natal 10, 11
Natal (Tripper) 61
Neutron 10, 236, 335
Neutron II 10, 237
Newton 10, 123
Nickel 10, 18, 27, 28, 30, 31, 33, 35, 38, 39, 40, 41, 43, 45, 50, 52, 56, 65, 69, 74, 82, 86, 88, 110, 125, 143, 144, 189
Nimbus 10, 77
Noah 10, 22
Norah 10, 255
Octopus 10, 277
Onyx 10, 95, 102, 125
Oppress 10
Overload 10, 96, 101

Overtone 10, 44
Packer 10, 188
Pagoda 10, 24, 187
Paladin 10, 244, 335
Panga 10, 71
Pannier 10, 217
Pantechnicon 10, 27
Parker 10, 151, 152
Partisan 10, 203
Peptic 10, 186
Petal 10, 237
Peyboy 10
Phoenix 10
Placid 10
Pluto 10, 64
Polar 10, 95, 104, 111, 112, 114, 119
Polo 10, 124, 125, 173
Prawn 10, 155, 171, 299
Purple 10, 244
Pygmy 10, 230, 238, 239
Pyramid 10, 44
Quartz 10, 273, 274
Racket 10, 238, 323
Ranger 10, 189, 190
Reindeer 10, 121
Reptile 10
Repulse 10, 85, 87, 137, 141, 152, 157, 160, 164, 249
Rhino 10
Robinson 11
Robust 11, 44
Sable 11, 82, 335
Sabre 11, 18
Salops 11, 190
Sand 11, 125, 126, 188
Sculpture 11, 24, 25
Sea Sheikh 11
Seed 11, 274
Shovel 11, 231, 335
Show Plane 11
Sinoia 11, 23, 24, 31, 53
Slipshod 11
Small Bang 11, 138, 139
Snoopy 11, 226, 335
Spider 11, 18
Spiderweb 11
Splinter .. 11, 85, 130, 218, 240
Starjump 11, 174
Steeple 11, 233
Stripper 11, 174, 335
Sunrise 11
Swordstick I 81
Swordstick I 11
Swordstick II 11
Tangent 11, 157, 186, 189, 249
Tarpaulin 11
Teak 11, 62
Tempest 64, 83, 85, 86, 87, 88, 89, 90, 127
Tempest I 85
Tempest I 11
Tempest I and II 85
Tempest II 11, 85
Tepid 11, 263
Terminate 11, 187, 335
Terminate II 11, 187
Thrasher 11, 85, 136, 153, 154, 157
Tombola 11, 13
Traveller 11, 144
Tripper 11
Turkey 11, 128, 129

Turmoil 11, 186, 214
Underdog 11, 136
Uric 11, 249, 252, 253, 254
Vanguard 112
Vanity 11
Vermin 11, 24, 25
Virgo 11, 173
Virile 11, 193, 203
Vodka 11, 230, 231
Winter 11, 274, 275
Wizard 11, 21, 60, 89
Wrestler 11, 174
Yodel 11, 24, 25
Oppenheimer, Harry 78
ORAFs 148
Orchard, Cpl Roy 158
Osborne, Nigel 253
Osborne, Nigel SAAF 326
Owen, David 195

P

Paine, Lt HT SAP 124
Paintin, Ed 63, 287, 302, 307, 308, 312
Parker, Dave 132
Parker, Jim 152
Parker, Maj 159
Parker, TM 287
Parson, Rod 325
Pasea, Doug 75, 90, 91, 92, 93, 95, 96, 98, 100, 101, 102, 104, 106, 107, 110, 113, 116, 118, 119, 120, 177, 178, 179, 181, 204, 293, 305, 306, 308, 309, 312, 319
Passaportis, Dennis 148
Patton, Brian 25, 26
PATU 187, 223, 234, 313
Paxton, Charles .15, 16, 17, 74, 136
Paxton, Dick 58, 69, 70, 71, 138, 141, 172, 250, 286, 287, 295, 296, 299, 302, 306, 307, 311, 312, 325, 339
Peacocke, Ian 307, 308, 315, 316, 317, 318, 319, 320
Peake, Mike 181
Pearce Commission 78
Pearce, Dumpie 44, 96
Pearse, Martin 159, 160, 236, 240, 245, 247, 324
Peinke, Kevin 138, 235, 257, 259, 263, 287, 296, 297, 301, 303, 304, 305, 309, 322, 323, 324, 327, 339
Peinke, Kevin L - Air Force 286
Penton, Brian 28, 33, 34, 37
Penton, Ozzie 12, 15, 16, 17, 67, 98
Perhat, Rory 300, 302, 303, 304, 305, 307, 308, 309
Perioli, Paul 318, 319, 320, 321, 322, 323, 324, 325, 326, 327
Petter-Bowyer, Peter 16, 19, 23, 61, 98, 102, 171, 192, 260, 292, 293, 294, 295, 296, 297, 298, 299, 300, 301, 302, 306, 309, 314, 315, 317, 319, 320, 322, 323, 324, 351
Phillips, Buff 120
Phillips, Fred 28, 29, 30, 33, 40
Pienke, Kevin 259
Pierson, Ken 35, 36, 37, 40
Piggot, Peter 21

Pilbeam, Tpr 233, 234
Pile, Phil......................281, 282, 283
Pink, Len.................15, 126, 281, 282
Piringondo, Edward 269
Pitch, Capt Len..........................296
Pitch, Len...................................145
Platt, Peter.................................312
Pletts, Roland 28
Plumsteel Douglas,...................148
Police3, 137, 142, 148, 187, 223, 249, 272, 276, 295, 318
Police Reserve Air Wing3, 37, 69, 142, 223
Porter, Giles.........58, 200, 301, 314
Postance, Polly....21, 36, 60, 89, 95
Potgieter, Fred SAP...............43, 44
Potterton, Ed17, 64, 66, 71, 76, 297, 305, 308, 309, 310
Povey, Lance Cpl.......................118
Povey, Lance Cpl RJ..........118, 287
PRAW142, 157, 187, 209, 210, 218, 223, 224, 295, 317, 340
Preller, Bob 81
Preston, Tom 141
Pretorius, Chinky 294
Pretorius, Glen186, 192, 216, 234, 236, 314, 315, 316, 317, 318, 319, 320, 322, 323, 324, 325, 326
Pretorius, Hennie 185
Pretorius, Maplot 137, 295, 298
Price, Nicky 156
Price, Sgt 162
Pride of Eagles12, 32, 40, 80, 112, 117, 219, 296, 301, 319, 321, 323
Prinsloo, Vernon 277
Project Barnacle7, 275, 276, 277, 283, 284
Prosser, David 253, 326
Pullar, Ian 159
Purnell, Derrick 23
Putterill, Maj. Gen. 19

Q

Queen Elizabeth 247

R

Rabie, Andre 96
Rademan, Chris........................296
Rainey, Derrick 26, 37
RAR139, 143, 148, 159, 160, 162, 163, 165, 193, 206, 215, 223, 224, 294, 301, 303, 317, 319
Rautenbach, Col - Special Forces 275
Rautering, Sgt 213
Rayne, Keith301, 302, 308, 309, 311, 315, 316
Readings, Alan 131
Reid-Daly, Ron97, 98, 100, 152, 176, 222, 240, 257
Reid-Daly, Tweedy 209, 315
Reitz, Doug 125, 296
Renamo237, 244, 262, 263, 270, 271, 284, 285
Retief, Dirk 253
Retief, Pete 296, 297
Retief, Pete SAAF 293
Reynolds, Alan 295
Rheeder, Frikkie SAAF 297, 298
Rich, Capt. 21

Richards, Pat 262, 263
Ridge, Eric - nephew of E. Trollip .45
Riley, Bill............................117, 293
Riley, Bill SAAF 294
Ritchie, Jim 34
RLI140, 143, 144, 145, 147, 155, 161, 162, 172, 176, 190, 192, 195, 205, 206, 210, 211, 212, 213, 215, 221, 226, 227, 229, 233, 234, 243, 244, 245, 249, 253, 254, 257, 261, 266, 267, 273, 315, 316, 323, 324, 325
Roberto, Holden 122
Roberts, Barry 292, 298, 299
Roberts, Jack 339
Roberts, Ken......................168, 169
Robertson, Guy 60, 75, 339
Robinson, Brian12, 18, 20, 24, 25, 68, 133, 134, 174, 175, 227, 247, 257, 287, 300, 301, 314
Robinson, Frank138, 139, 223, 286, 295, 301, 302, 313, 315
Rodgers, John 292
Rogers, John......................15, 17
Rogers, Mrs. Traude..................196
Ronne, Mike56, 76, 77, 78, 79, 80, 81, 82, 83, 89, 90, 91, 116, 117, 120, 181, 303, 305, 306, 319, 322
Roos, Bertus 326
Rosenberg, Adrian.....................312
Roughead, Alec 75, 339
Routledge, Rusty 339
Rowe, Dave 97, 294
Rowley, Dave 315
Ruby, VR Officer..........................19
Rudd, Army officer.....................220
Russell, Jim93, 104, 110, 162, 163, 177, 204, 235, 239, 302, 303, 306, 307, 309, 312, 316, 319, 322, 326
Russell, Mike 309, 312
Russell, Steve138, 298, 300, 302, 311, 312
Ryan, Terry 339

S

Sachse, Bert152, 155, 159, 160, 171, 176, 184, 203, 254
Saint, Chris 219, 220, 317
Salt, Beryl 32, 40, 219
Samuels, Andy 256
Sanderson 90
Sanderson, Dennis......................90
SAS139, 143, 144, 154, 155, 159, 160, 162, 164, 165, 166, 169, 172, 173, 174, 175, 176, 186, 187, 188, 200, 202, 206, 207, 212, 213, 214, 215, 217, 221, 225, 226, 227, 229, 230, 231, 232, 233, 236, 237, 240, 241, 243, 244, 245, 246, 248, 249, 250, 253, 254, 255, 257, 262, 263, 264, 266, 269, 270, 271, 273, 274, 281, 285, 300, 304, 318, 320, 323
Saunders, Mike 15, 298
Savimbi, Jonas Malheiro 122
Scales, Peter 36, 37
Schooling, Phil76, 82, 85, 89, 91, 92, 120
Schrag, Lt...................................164

Schulenburg, Chris 'Schulie'113, 160, 221, 222, 238, 239
Schulenburg, Chris 'Schulie' 90
Scott, Alec 71
Scott, David...............................156
Scott, Ronny 172, 306, 308, 311
Seegmuller, Ziggy259, 261, 263, 325, 326, 327
Selous Scout 261
Selous Scouts139, 142, 143, 146, 150, 151, 152, 155, 159, 160, 162, 165, 169, 170, 172, 174, 176, 193, 203, 210, 217, 218, 219, 222, 224, 237, 238, 239, 240, 243, 256, 257, 258, 267, 269, 273, 276, 284, 285, 293, 299, 306, 317
Senekal, Andre SAAF287, 295, 339
Sephton, LAC............................203
Seymour, Gary 165, 166, 168
Seymour, Gerry SAS KIA ..166, 304
Shaw, Beaver164, 165, 166, 304, 305, 310, 316, 319, 320, 321, 322, 324, 325
Shaw, General John 339
Shaw, John Major General, Chief of Staff Army..............98, 339, 340
Sheffield, Ian......204, 296, 307, 308
Shelton, Zanla 218
Shields, Alan163, 164, 166, 299, 303, 304, 305, 310, 311
Shiri, Perence......................14, 284
Shumba......................................64
Shungu, Herbert........................125
Shute, Mike...............123, 203, 284
Sibanda, Elliot...........................238
Simmonds, Pete72, 102, 131, 137, 139, 140, 294, 295, 300
Simpson, Colin 154
Sinclair, Dave 142
Sinclair, Doug137, 138, 163, 164, 165, 166, 169, 172, 295, 299, 303, 304, 306, 312
Singleton, Rick297, 298, 300, 302, 313, 314, 315
Sithole, Ignatius 218
Sithole, Ndabamaningi53, 98, 104, 218
Skeeles, Jerry 263
Slatter, Hugh15, 16, 17, 22, 126, 263, 281, 282, 283
Slovo, Joe 35
Small, Capt Charlie....253, 254, 326
Smart, John 90, 287, 339
Smit, Sewes SAAF 294
Smit, Tony 51
Smith, Bill 16, 57
Smith, Bob 234
Smith, Bruce55, 56, 58, 60, 118, 301, 308
Smith, Cpl JW............................309
Smith, David 23, 193
Smith, David 154
Smith, Mike299, 311, 312, 319, 320
Smith, Nic.............................36, 40
Smith, Premier Ian Douglas12, 19, 21, 25, 26, 36, 37, 39, 40, 53, 55, 56, 68, 78, 81, 97, 104, 121, 124, 125, 136, 157, 195, 242, 243, 244, 245, 247, 272
Smith, Tracker 139, 140
Smithdorff, Mark 90

Smithdorff, Tinker 51, 52, 61, 90, 287, 292, 339
Smythe, Flash 250
Snelgar, Bruce 134, 135, 234, 257, 287, 326
Snyders, Tony SAAF 299
Soames, Lord 272
Sole, George 139, 221, 222, 295, 301, 304, 305
Spalding, Chris 309
Special Air Service 159, 206, 207, 213, 218, 221, 224, 226, 227, 229, 230, 236, 237, 240, 241, 244, 245, 254, 257, 262, 266, 267, 273, 284
Special Branch 138, 142, 145, 152, 153, 170, 174, 213, 214, 217, 218, 226, 231, 238, 241, 256, 264, 275, 276
Speight, Spotty 181
Spence, Keith 308, 309, 311, 314, 315, 321, 322
Spiret, Conex Officer. 23
Spoor, Ken 24, 25
Springer, Bill 340
Squadron Commanders 15
Squance, Daryl 141, 170, 173, 296, 306, 309
St. Quentin, Bob 61, 299
Stagman, Jim 60, 71, 73, 95, 125, 319
Stannard, Crow 256
Stannard, Crow SAAF 256
Stannard, Rich 232, 236, 264
Stanton, Pete 86
Stapelberg, SAAF Tech 140, 295
Station Commanders – Thornhill ..14
Stead, Steve 132, 133, 138, 294
Stein, Ian 142, 173
Stephens, Dave 98, 160
Stevens, Bill 'Starry' 75, 78, 81, 83, 90, 91, 92, 93, 95, 100, 104, 107, 177, 179, 287, 295, 298, 300, 339
Stevens, Bill 'Starry' 298, 300
Stevens, HWH 'Starry' - Air Force 286
Stevenson, Ted 17
Stewart, Roy 117
Steyn, Douw 207, 208, 275
Steyn, Hansi 138, 139, 295, 298, 300, 304, 305, 307, 315
Stiff, Peter 40, 106, 117, 207, 208, 240, 258, 275, 277, 283, 284, 285
Stokes, Capt. 20
Storie, Cpl. 133, 134
Strever, Eddie 140, 141, 295, 296
Strong, Jerry 50, 51
Strydom, JJ 235, 257, 259, 263, 287, 322, 327, 339
Strydom, JJ - Air Force 286
Stuart, CMED official 214
Stuart, Sgt. 80
Styles, Rod and Clive 142
Summersgill, M 163, 303, 304, 305, 313
Svoboda, Danny 69, 70, 71, 124, 208, 294, 297, 298, 300, 308, 309, 311, 312
Swanepoel, Vic SAAF 326
Swarts, Maryna 47
Sykes, Bill 56, 59, 71, 99, 130, 192, 204, 205, 219, 294, 300, 302, 307, 308, 315

Syslo, Joe 134, 158, 294, 295, 296, 301

T

Takawira 53
Tambo, Oliver 34
Tarr, Tom 309, 310
Tasker, Rob 22, 23, 74
Tass, Graeme 317
Tatton, Sgt. 22
Taute, Keith 14
Taylor, Mo 232
Taylor, Rex 104, 263, 305, 306, 307, 313
Team Oscar 276, 283
Tekere, Anne 193, 195
Tekere, Edgar 98, 193, 195, 272
Templar, John "Fluff" 87, 88, 156
Terrorist Camps 111
  Bembe - Angola 45
  Binda 111
  Cangudzi 187
  Caponda 102, 144, 145, 173
  CGT-2 .... 227, 269, 271, 320
  Chamba 111
  Chamboko 111
  Chicoa 67, 86, 102
  Chifombo 86, 89, 102, 111, 120, 121
  Chigamane 162
  Chikumbi 319, 324
  Chimoio 155, 190, 191, 192, 193, 195, 221, 226, 229, 236, 257, 315
  Chintopo 186, 238
  Chitanga .162, 163, 165, 168, 303
  Chivinge 244
  Doeroi 196
  Forward Base Camp 1 & 2 217
  Freedom Camp 226, 246, 247
  Horteiro 97, 111
  Itumbi 19, 111
  Jorge do Limpopo 162
  JZ 247, 248
  Kafwambila 188
  Kaswende 89
  Katambora 217
  Kingolwiro 101
  Lesumo 217
  Lindi 111
  Lukwila 111
  Madulo Pan 208, 312
  Massangena 162
  Maxaila 162
  Mboroma 101, 230, 231, 321
  Mgagao 73, 101, 111
  Mkushi 101, 227, 229, 320
  Mtwara 105, 111
  Muchingwa 217
  Mulungushi 230, 238, 240, 241, 245, 247, 249, 265, 268, 321, 325
  Mzarabani 111
  Nanchingwea 101, 111
  Newela 105, 111
  Nkume 271
  Nyadzonia 102, 154, 299
  Nyamuomba 188
  Pea 101, 114, 139
  Pondoland 112, 113, 114
  Qumbo's Farm 249

  Rama Farm 217
  Rufunsa 249, 325
  Sinde / CH Plots 217
  Solwezi 249, 325
  Songea 111
  Sundi 111
  Tembue 102, 192, 221, 244, 248, 315
  Tunduru 111
  Vanduzi Circle 236
Thatcher, Margaret 272
Theron, Danie 150
Thomas, S Patrol Officer 37
Thomas, SAAF Tech 139, 295
Thomas, Tony 310, 311
Thomas, Tudor 16, 26, 27, 61, 158, 172, 212, 214, 286, 287, 296, 297, 302, 306
Thompson, Alec 135
Thompson, Bob 172, 294, 300, 306, 307, 317
Thompson, Bruce SCR killed 317
Thompson, Professor - BSAP 49
Thomson, George 53
Thorn, Dave 293
Thorne, Dave 17, 221
Thorne, Lt. 159
Thornhill 141, 150, 158, 159, 161, 170, 172, 184, 185, 186, 189, 190, 191, 203, 212, 213, 214, 221, 224, 233, 246, 247, 250, 255, 263, 264, 275, 276, 277, 278, 280, 281, 283, 284
Thornley, M Tpr. 49
Thorogood, Al 248, 315
Tickle, S 287
Tidy, Kevin 195, 196, 260, 328
Tiffin, Barry 28, 29, 33
Timitiya, Warrant Officer ...36, 37, 40
Todd, Greg 72, 204, 294, 301, 302, 304, 305, 307, 311, 319
Tolmay, Wally 315
Tombo, Rifleman F - SADF 285
Tongogara, Josiah 88, 89, 120, 121, 193, 195, 229, 231, 237, 271
Travers, Hugh 311
Trenoweth, Sandy 20, 339
Trollip, E - Secretary for Defence..45
Troup, Trevor SAAF 137, 138, 295, 296, 297, 298
Truman, Rich 308
Tselentis, Nick ... 299, 301, 309, 311
Tubbs, Phil 315
Tubbs, Philip 153, 294, 297, 301, 306, 307, 308, 310, 311, 313
Tucker, Chris 192, 310, 311, 315
Tungamirai, Josiah 14, 259, 283, 284
Turkington, Graham 325
Turner, Ken 168, 170
Turner, Tony 233, 287, 321, 339
Tyrrell, Frank 307, 309, 315

U

Ullyett, AC 90
Umkhonto we Sizwe 18, 28, 39, 275
Underwood, John 287, 313, 339
Underwood, John S - Air Force .286
Upton, Mike 141, 286, 294, 296, 299, 300, 301, 303, 304, 309
Urimbo 64, 86
Utton, Derrick 27

V

Valerie, Scottie 71
van den Berg, TJ 61
van den Bergh, Gen. 40
van der Byl, P K Pieter (Minister of Information)......................46, 131
van der Merwe, Cpl 26
van der Merwe, Danny 212
van der Riet, Willie 260
van Greunen, Const SAP 52
van Heerden, Karel SAP 43
van Heyningen, Kon SAAF..43, 125
van Huysteen, B 287
van Rensburg, JJ................287, 339
van Rensburg, P 287, 339
van Rooyen, Sgt 158
van Rooyen, Solo SAAF117, 293, 294, 298
van Schalkwyk, Rfn 171
van Staden, Coen 309
van Vuuren, Cecil SAAF 296
van Vuuren, SAAF pilot 145
van Zyl, FC 68
Varkevisser...................................276
Varkevisser, Varky16, 22, 23, 31, 68, 70, 71, 192, 221, 236, 248, 259, 263, 314, 315, 318, 319, 320, 324, 325, 326, 327
Vaughan, Bernie36, 56, 77, 79, 80, 81, 82, 89, 91, 92, 93, 95, 97, 98, 100, 102, 104, 107, 110, 116, 119, 120, 177, 178, 179
Velleman, Paul 253
Velleman, Paul SAAF 326
Venter, Gavie......................140, 295
Venter, Hannes SADF 207
Venuitti, Mario 165
Venutti, Mario164, 166, 172, 304, 305, 306
Vernon, Mark 287, 303, 318
Verster, Tony 131
Verwoerd, Jones and Swanepoel 281
Viljoen, Johannes and Barbara24, 90, 187
Vine, Trevor 71
Visser, Nick - SADF 68
Volker, Karl SAAF......137, 138, 295
Vorster, John35, 40, 97, 98, 104, 117, 121, 124, 125, 157
Vorster, SAAF Tech 145
Voster, David 159

Voster, J H Lt SAP.......................52
Voster, Tiro SAAF.......................296
Vusa, Alexander 247

W

Waddell, Gordon...........................78
Wall, Rick....................................181
Wallace, Wally....................301, 302
Walls, Lieutenant General Peter143, 153, 157, 227, 243, 253, 272
Walsh, Norman14, 15, 17, 50, 51, 61, 192, 221, 227, 229, 246, 257, 277, 282, 283, 284, 292, 315, 319
Ward, Clive 302, 303
Wardle, Ian.....................33, 40, 52
Warner, Terence........................301
Warracker, Rob99, 113, 152, 156, 170, 171, 299, 306
Warren, Brian 292, 295, 300, 302
Warren, Charlie 245, 324, 325
Wars Rhodesian......................287
Watson, Robin 206, 207
Watt, Billy 169, 305
Watt, Roger58, 117, 219, 286, 312, 339
Watts, Fred 213
Weinel, Section Officer...............214
Weinmann, B Chris - Air Force..286
Weinmann, Chris20, 22, 23, 28, 29, 30, 36, 68, 69, 70, 110, 287, 339
Weir, Neville 281, 282, 283
Wentworth, Chris55, 62, 68, 69, 70, 71, 168, 301, 302, 305, 309, 310, 313
Wepener, Sgt 203
Wernich, Ray SAAF286, 296, 297, 299, 316
Wessels, C Tpr.............................49
Wesson, AJC - Air Force 286
Wesson, Alex250, 287, 325, 326, 339
White, Cyril..............16, 72, 124, 339
White, Keith................................108
White, Pete (Bronzi) 140
Whitehead Government................18
Whittal, Gary......117, 299, 300, 303
Whyte, Bob...................................29
Whyte, Doug 15, 16, 54
Wickenden, John 24
Wightman, Vic15, 16, 100, 192, 193, 202, 216, 221, 235, 236, 247,

248, 259, 263, 314, 315, 316, 317, 318, 320, 322, 323, 324, 325, 326, 327
Wilcox, Pete................................103
Wild, Alf68, 69, 70, 71, 103, 125, 294, 301, 302, 318, 319
Wilkens, Tpr.......................233, 234
Wilkins, Monster 256, 326
Wilkinson, Eddy15, 17, 58, 72, 131, 132, 135, 287
Williams, Colin............................158
Williams, Grant...........................294
Willis, Colin159, 160, 200, 201, 213, 241
Wilmot, Frank 90
Wilson, AOG Archie 14, 66
Wilson, Graham159, 160, 164, 165, 166, 241, 246, 274, 304
Wilson, Harold 19, 21, 25
Wilson, Mike 102, 103
Wilson, Nick...............................277
Wilson, R....................................110
Wilson, Willy 71, 287, 338, 339
Wilson, Willy RJ – Air Force 286
Wiltshire, Staff Sgt.....................213
Winds of Destruction 261
Wing Commanders – OCFW........15
Wingrove, Frank 287
Wixley, Robert 267
Wood, Professor Richard52, 186, 187, 188, 192, 202, 216, 237, 313, 314, 315, 316, 317, 318, 321, 322, 323, 324
Woods, D....................................287
Woods, Kevin 284
Woodward, Bob 15, 16
Woolcock, Pete...................90, 120
Woolcock, Peter 292
Wright, George 24
Wright, Sam 269
Wrigley, George 17

Y

Young, Andrew..........................195
Young, Andy 340

Z

Zichirira, Hope............................101
Zindoga, Amon 64, 85
Zvamutsana, Kennedy.................97

The Author:

Served for 20 years in the Rhodesian Air Force, retiring in he rank of Wing Commander. He was a Flight Commander on the Canberra and Hunter squadrons, and commanded Forward Airfields Kariba (FAF 2) and Buffalo Range (FAF 7); and also Fire Force Charlie (based Shabani).

Readers are invited to e-mail the author at oupey@editek.co.nz with their comment, criticism, input, or any other relevent matter to this and any other publications

REVIEWS

This book records the operations of the Rhodesian Air Force. It includes a log of over 1100 airstrikes carried out as well as maps where most of these strikes have been meticously plotted. The maps are printed in full colour. There are numerous black and white photographs that illustrate the text.
John Dovey – Just Done Productions

~~~oOOOo~~~

To those historians and collectors of militaria, this book is one that fills in much detail. It shows how operations in Rhodesia started slowly and built up to a situation where virtually the entire country became involved. The mass of little numbered dots on the maps shows the position of widespread strikes in all the operational areas. To the very end the Air Force kept up its valiant task of securing the airspace for our troops, the BSAP, the farmers and industry. This in addition to the direct support for those missions across the borders.
Tol Janeke – the author's Commanding Officer on No 2 Squadron (Vampires), No 5 Squadron (Canberras), Air Detachment JOC Repulse and Air Force Station Thornhill.

~~~oOOOo~~~

This book is a follow-up on Nickel Cross and is again a very personal account of the author's participation in the anti-terrorist war. A short introduction to the Rhodesian Air Force is followed by a detailed account of operations in which the author was involved, or of which he has received first hand accounts. The period covered is from the early start of counter-insurgency operations in 1964 up to the sabotage of aircraft at Thornhill in 1982 and the South African support to Renamo until 1983. The writer's feelings and reminiscences run through the narrative, making it exclusively "Prop's" war.
Following the narrative comes an exhaustive chronological list of 1145 airstrike reports, each one with all the available information included. Equally important are the meticulously researched maps of operations and air strikes, illustrating fully the extent of air operations during the "Bush War". The book is well illustrated with black and white photographs and line drawings depicting people, operations and aircraft. These latter are particularly useful to non Air

Force members. Finally there is a Rhodesian Air Force Roll of Honour, and a comprehensive index is included.

All in all this is a highly readable, extremely detailed account of the Rhodesian Air Force's part in the war against terrorism.

Mike Russell – Flame Lily Foundation - Review of "Props" War, for the Rhosarian publication

~~~oOOOo~~~

Considering the political turmoil that brought about hurried separation and destruction of Air Force records in March 1980, Prop's attempt to save whatever could be recovered for this work is highly commendable. Certainly there are errors and omissions that arise from late searches and faded memories. Nonetheless these records will prove most useful to historical researchers.

Peter Petter-Bowyer – author of *Winds of Destruction*

~~~oOOOo~~~

Geldenhuys has produced a comprehensive account of the Rhodesian Air Force role in the war in Rhodesia. The work includes one of the most detailed summaries of Rhodesian military operations to have been published, and in this respect serves as an excellent work of reference. However, the book is much more than this, as the author's personal experience leaps from every page, producing a fascinating combination of memoir and historical account.

Dr Timothy Lovering - Research Fellow at the University of the West of England

~~~oOOOo~~~

Rhodesian Air Force Operations

978-0-9941154-1-6

Peysoft Publications

ISBN: 978-0-9941154-0-9

www.ingramcontent.com/pod-product-compliance
Lightning Source LLC
Chambersburg PA
CBHW021831220426
43663CB00005B/204